SOMETHING
IN THE
BLOOD

OTHER BOOKS BY DAVID J. SKAL

NONFICTION

*Hollywood Gothic: The Tangled Web of Dracula
from Novel to Stage to Screen*

The Monster Show: A Cultural History of Horror

Screams of Reason: Mad Science and Modern Culture

Dark Carnival: The Secret World of Tod Browning
(with Elias Savada)

V is For Vampire: The A to Z Guide to Everything Undead

Death Makes a Holiday: A Cultural History of Halloween

Claude Rains: An Actor's Voice
(with Jessica Rains)

Romancing the Vampire

FICTION

Scavengers

Antibodies

When We Were Good

EDITOR

Dracula: A Norton Critical Edition
(with Nina Auerbach)

*Dracula: The Ultimate, Illustrated Edition of the
World-Famous Vampire Play*

SOMETHING IN THE BLOOD

The Untold Story of Bram Stoker,
the Man Who Wrote Dracula

DAVID J. SKAL

LIVERIGHT

LIVERIGHT PUBLISHING CORPORATION
A DIVISION OF W. W. NORTON & COMPANY
INDEPENDENT PUBLISHERS SINCE 1923
New York • London

For information about permission to reproduce selections from this book,
write to Permissions, Liveright Publishing Corporation,
a division of W. W. Norton & Company, Inc.,
500 Fifth Avenue, New York, NY 10110

For information about special discounts for bulk purchases, please contact
W. W. Norton Special Sales at specialsales@wwnorton.com or 800-233-4830

Manufacturing by Berryville Graphics
Book design by Faceout Studio
Production manager: Julia Druskin

ISBN 978-1-63149-010-1

Liveright Publishing Corporation
500 Fifth Avenue, New York, N.Y. 10110
www.wwnorton.com

W. W. Norton & Company Ltd.
15 Carlisle Street, London W1D 3BS

1 2 3 4 5 6 7 8 9 0

for

PETER GÖLZ

CONTENTS

"Let's root out Brimstoker and
give him the thrall of our lives."
JAMES JOYCE, *Finnegans Wake*

INTRODUCTION

BRAM STOKER: THE FINAL CURTAIN?

WHAT MANNER OF MAN IS THIS?
—Bram Stoker, *Dracula*

There are no photographs of Bram Stoker smiling.

The real Bram Stoker—at least the human being verifiably documented, dozens of times, by a succession of curious cameras over a period of six decades, from the mid-nineteenth century to the early twentieth—is serious, studious, at times stuffy, and very often startled-looking. He doesn't enjoy being scrutinized. The image is completely at odds with a lifetime of people describing a warm and genial man brimming with Irish good humor. In his working notes for *Dracula*, he imagines that his vampire king also has an image problem, namely that photography has the power to penetrate his flesh, starkly revealing his skeletal core. Painters can't see the skeleton, or capture Dracula's likeness at all. The finished canvas always looks like someone else.

Stoker's earliest photographic portrait, and the only one that survives his childhood, shows an uncomfortable-looking boy of eight in a suit of "breeching" clothes staring directly at the camera, as if wondering what is expected of him. It is a characteristically haunted expression, one that

The only known photograph of Bram Stoker writing.

would be repeated many times in his life, whenever a camera closed in. "Haunted" is a particularly good word for a youngster whose memories prior to the age of eight revolved around disease and hovering death, and whose legacy would center on a fantastic revenant impervious to both.

A previous biographer complained that "Stoker dispersed memories as selfishly as an old crone ladling soup." And it's true. He left behind no real accounting of his life, almost no candid or personal writings. As a result, much of what has been written about Stoker has focused on the amply documented minutiae of his long employment as business manager for the great Victorian actor-manager Sir Henry Irving, which only deflects attention from the question that has always interested readers most: What, exactly, was going on inside the head of the man who wrote *Dracula*?

Stoker's prodigious capacity for work (for instance, writing as many as fifty letters a day for Irving's signature) and the extra reserves of energy that fueled the furious production of potboiler novels in his supposed "spare" time have mostly been treated with awestruck admiration. The modern concept of workaholism was unnamed and unacknowledged in Stoker's time, but he was the very Victorian model of overcompensation and insecurity. The Protestant work ethic has always had a problematic dark side, and it was a realm Stoker inhabited with a frightening force.

Stoker chronicles have also suffered from a dismaying echo-chamber effect, as certain assumptions and factoids have been repeated so frequently they are accepted as gospel. For instance, to what degree did Stoker take inspiration from the legend of the Wallachian warlord Vlad the Impaler, aside from borrowing his historical sobriquet "Dracula"? The answer is really not much—even if the idea has given birth to self-sustaining cottage industries of commentary, criticism, and filmmaking. And what about the widely accepted notion that Irving himself was the direct model for Dracula? Here, the truth is more nuanced. Certainly, Irving's celebrated impersonation of Mephistopheles in *Faust* bears a family resemblance to the master vampire, or at least to the sardonic, charming Draculas that evolved in the twentieth century, owing very little to Bram Stoker's character. *Dracula* indeed has theatrical origins, but the Count's essential roots are better traced to the demon kings of the Christmas pantomimes that first ignited Stoker's imagination as a boy. His rapturous and only recently rediscovered writings on these traditional theatrical wonder tales are revelations, and you can read them in this book for the first time since he put them to paper. Just as *Dracula* would become a frightening fairy tale for adults, Irving's *Faust*, with more than a little help from Stoker, found success as a kind of grown-up pantomime from hell.

Of course, everything about *Dracula* leads us inexorably to sex. Did he have a sexless marriage? Did syphilis contribute to his death? Was he gay or bisexual? There were no such categories for most of his lifetime, no concept of sexual orientation as a fixed condition, and it is doubtful Stoker would have even understood such labels. But a number of his closest friends—novelist Hall Caine, actress Genevieve Ward, and playwright W. G. Wills—had fascinatingly veiled personal lives that were hardly scrutinized in an age that revered "romantic friendships" between men and men or women and women. Stoker thrived in a male-dominated world in which a pervasive homosociability allowed more intimate male connections to hide in plain sight—at least until the scandal and downfall of Oscar Wilde, when (to paraphrase cultural critic Mark Dery) the perimeters of male sexuality became culturally electrified. In the late Victorian era, the perimeters were both electrically charged *and* quietly gaslit.

Both Dubliners, Wilde and Stoker were familiar if not completely friendly acquaintances from the 1870s until Oscar's trial and imprisonment in 1895. As I wrote nearly a quarter century ago, "Wilde and Stoker present a fascinating set of Victorian bookends, shadow-mirrors in uneasy reciprocal orbits." Intervening decades of research and study have only reinforced my observation. Both were deeply influenced by intelligent and assertive mothers (of diametrically opposed temperaments); both attended Trinity College; both were drawn to the theatre, were fascinated by folklore and fairy tales, admired Walt Whitman and Henry Irving, and gravitated romantically to a beautiful Dublin girl, Florence Balcombe. Oscar, perhaps, courted his "Florrie" out of an aesthetic ardor; Stoker actually married her, though their marriage would be called passionless. Both men wrote masterpieces of macabre fiction about Victorian monsters that drain and destroy. And both expressed an enduring fascination with the conundrums of sex and gender—Bram in his writings, and Oscar, far more messily, in his life. It is also fascinating that Stoker was drawn to Wilde's parents as flamboyant surrogates to his own conventional, straitlaced family. While one of *Dracula*'s most famous lines—"Children of the night—what music they make!"—immediately brings to mind the vocal stylings of Bela Lugosi, it was the flamboyantly theatrical mother of Oscar Wilde who provided the original inspiration. Lady Wilde's son, like a character from a classic Gothic novel, was a hovering doppelgänger throughout Stoker's life, both creatively and psychosexually—in the same way *The Picture of Dorian Gray* shadows and illuminates *Dracula*. It is no coincidence that Wilde was persecuted as a sexual threat to Victorian London at the same cultural moment Stoker created the greatest sex monster of all time.

This book addresses questions about sexual identity and anxiety in the larger context of existential nineteenth-century upheavals over science, religion, and personhood. Stoker's passionate youthful correspondence with Walt Whitman and his declaration of same-sex camaraderie are presented here in unprecedented detail (the full texts of their letters have never been included in any book on Stoker), as are his hitherto unknown authorial hand in an embattled 1875 Dublin production of *Sappho*, his newly discovered, sexually ambiguous poetry, and, finally, a fragment of a never-finished and subtly homoerotic novel, *The Russian Professor*, only recently unearthed.

Stoker's reflexive instinct for privacy—his automatic reluctance to reveal too much, about himself or about Henry Irving—served both men well. Irving and his leading lady Ellen Terry were revered as the benevolent wizard king and fairy godmother of the British stage, but their private lives were checkered, and it's doubtful Irving ever would have been so lionized, or even knighted, had the public known that he had impulsively abandoned his wife and two sons, or that Terry had a pair of children born out of wedlock. Stoker's duties included discreetly managing their travel arrangements and accommodations, and generally deflecting attention from an adulterous relationship carried on in plain sight. It is supremely ironic that Irving and Terry extraordinarily elevated the reputation of the theatre, since they could have been so easily charged with the stereotypical traits of moral turpitude that had dogged actors since Shakespeare's time. Due to Stoker's vigilant discretion in public relations, this never happened.

Stoker's managerial acumen, brilliantly deployed by Irving, radically transformed the Victorian stage. But Stoker, working for himself, transformed the future of popular culture by creating the most mediagenic superstar of all time, a creature born in the oral traditions of folklore, gestated in the written word, and made immortal in the age of the moving image. Despite his talent, Irving simply didn't have the range, or the reach. Dracula did.

The working title of this book was *Bram Stoker: The Final Curtain*, the "curtain" intended to rise and fall on three levels. First, it is an apt reference to a master of macabre literature who was also a consummate man of the theatre. Second, while this will certainly not be the last book written on Stoker (the volume of published material, for both academic and popular audiences, continues to grow exponentially), the discovery of new documents shedding light on Stoker the man is most unlikely. On a third and far more personal level, the original title described what will be my own final book-length excursion into the land of Bram Stoker and the enduring fascination of *Dracula*.

But in the end I realized that there is nothing final about Dracula at all, nor can there be. Dracula never ends. Not in my life, or in yours. His immortality and cultural omnipresence have everything to do with the magic of blood, the oldest and deepest and most paradoxical human symbol. As shapeshifting as Dracula himself, with the uncanny power to assume endless metaphorical forms, blood is the all-enveloping essence and measure of everything: life and death, sickness and health, anger, passion, and lust—all are blood driven and blood conceptualized. Blood ties bind us to our families. Bloodlines provide a link to our atavistic past, while serving as our primary connection to the future. The sight of blood terrifies some, is eroticized by others, and never fails to draw attention. We are thinking about blood all the time, whether or not we think we are.

Stoker understood all these dimensions and meanings of blood, or at least intuited them powerfully, especially as they pertained to questions of sex, masculinity, and gnawing Victorian fears about blood corruption, contagion, and the strange blood-borne doctrine of evolutionary "degeneration." He wrestled with them all in *Dracula* just as he wrestled with them in his life. In the end, Stoker seems to tell us, ultimate meanings inevitably revolve around something in the blood. Secrets in the blood. Revelations in the blood. Mysteries in the blood.

To borrow the words of avowed *Dracula* admirer Sir Winston Churchill on the mystifying nature of Russia (historically and coincidentally a great source of undead lore), Bram Stoker himself amounts to "a riddle wrapped in a mystery inside an enigma; but perhaps there is a key."

I hope that *Something in the Blood* finally provides a missing set of keys to Stoker's inner vampire castle, or at least unprecedented entry to some of its previously inaccessible rooms.

DAVID J. SKAL
Los Angeles, 2016

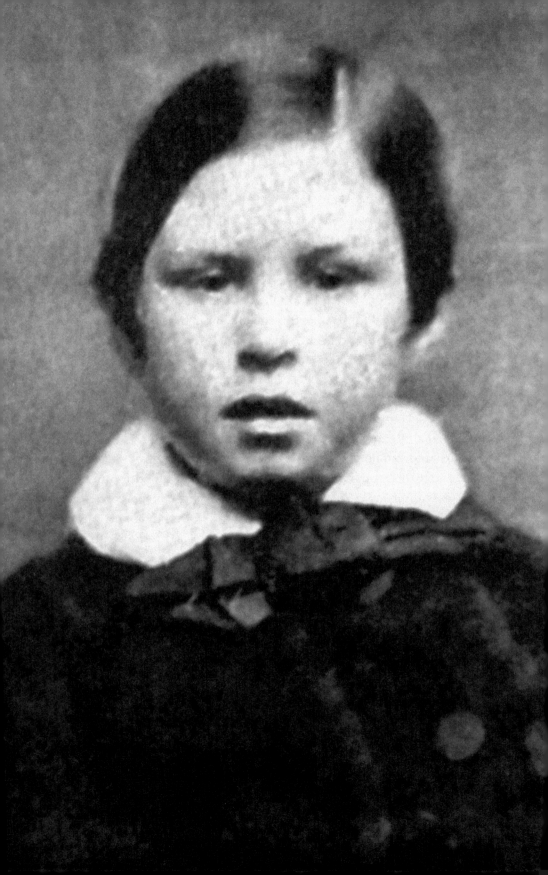

CHAPTER ONE

THE CHILD THAT WENT WITH THE FAIRIES

MONSTER! GIVE ME MY CHILD!
—*Dracula*

"In my babyhood," Bram Stoker wrote of his early years in Victorian Dublin, "I never knew what it was to stand upright." Mysteriously bedridden "until nearly the age of seven," he would eventually grow into a robust giant of a man, a prizewinning athlete bigger and taller than his father or brothers, looming over his entire family from a height of six foot two, at a time when the average height of men in Britain at the age of twenty-one was only five foot five. Stoker directly attributed the uncanny growth spurt to "long illnesses, as a child," according to his son, writing on the one hundredth anniversary of his birth in 1947. But this only adds another mystery, since medical statisticians correlate adult height as much with early childhood health as with genetics.

Stoker's story, therefore, defies medical science, just as it defies common sense. Nonetheless, both he and his family insisted it was true. However, as Stoker's late-life friend Sir Arthur Conan Doyle opined on more than one occasion through the fictional mouthpiece of Sherlock Holmes, "When

Bram Stoker as a child, circa 1854. Photographer unknown.

you have excluded the impossible, whatever remains, however improbable, must be the truth."

Or, at least, there might begin an understanding.

The history of ancient Ireland is inextricably bound to its folklore. The earliest Irish settlers arrived sometime around 7000 BC, by sea or, as many historians speculate, via a land bridge to Scotland lost to rising waters at the end of the Ice Age. Neolithic Irish tombs predating the Pyramids of Giza by five hundred years and Stonehenge by a thousand offer enduring testimony of a primitive society that left no written accounts of its beliefs, only a rich archaeological repository recording an agrarian culture as keenly attuned to the presence of death and the supernatural as it was to the circles of the seasons and the transit of the stars. Funeral rites had a central prominence. Located northwest of Dublin near Kells is Newgrange, Ireland's oldest structure and most monumental tomb. A mound of earth and stone three hundred feet wide, Newgrange was ingeniously designed by ancient astronomers to have its interior illuminated by the rising sun every winter solstice, marking the beginning of a new cycle of life and its harvest. Newgrange's intricate Stone Age carvings of circles, spirals, and undulating waveforms are today universally recognized as "Celtic" design motifs, even though the Celts did not arrive on Irish shores until much later, during the Iron Age. Ireland had never been invaded by the Roman Empire, whose people called the island Hibernia—the land of winter—and considered it wild, barbaric, and impervious to civilizing. The farthest western outpost of Europe was, for all practical purposes, the end of the world.

When the Roman Empire crumbled, the Celts moved into Britannia and Hibernia from central Europe, bringing with them a hierarchal society with no small amount of its own barbarity. Classical writers, including Julius Caesar, described harvest rituals of human sacrifice performed by Celts and supervised by their priestly class, the Druids. The whole Celtic world, according to Caesar, was "to a great degree devoted to superstitious rites." He took particular note of the Celtic belief "that souls are not annihilated, but pass after death from one body to another, and they hold that by this teaching men are much encouraged to valor, through disregarding the fear of death."

The most important Celtic crop festival was Samhain, or November

Eve, at which time the worlds of the living and dead were permitted to mingle. At harvest time, sacrifices to pagan gods were made to assure passage through the winter. With the coming of Christianity to Ireland by way of St. Patrick and other missionaries beginning in the fifth century AD, pagan holidays began to blur with Christian, and in the ninth century, the better to encourage conversion, Pope Gregory's calendar realigned church holidays to coincide with the old pagan festivals. Christmas was moved from the spring to coincide with the Roman festival of Saturnalia, and the Feast of All Saints now fell on November 1, encouraging an alternate kind of communion with the dead to compete with Samhain, which was never completely suppressed, and survives to the present day as Halloween.

Irish folklore was not at all diminished by Christian teaching, from which it often drew a good deal of inspiration. Old pagan gods were transmogrified into a delirious variety of fairy folk, while the Christian God and the devil not infrequently made sideline appearances. The Catholic Church made no real effort to discourage Irish folk beliefs, and the populace evidenced no inability to balance two supernatural belief systems. The resulting oral tradition became one of the most richly textured in the world.

Catholic monasteries in Ireland introduced the Roman alphabet and kept alive literacy and scholarship throughout the Dark Ages—some have gone as far as saying they saved civilization—and their transcription and preservation of Irish sagas and legends, as well as the production of extraordinary illuminated Latin gospels like the *Book of Kells* (circa 800) speaks to a profound love of language often regarded as the wellspring of a bottomless Irish capacity for storytelling. No other country of Ireland's size has made such an enormous contribution to world literature, and no other can boast of four Nobel Prize–winning writers, all in the twentieth century: W. B. Yeats, George Bernard Shaw, Samuel Beckett, and Seamus Heaney. The achievement of the medieval scribes is all the more impressive in that it overlapped with more than a hundred years of Viking raids beginning in the early ninth century, in which monasteries were regularly sacked. Before they were absorbed into Irish society, the Vikings built settlements that would evolve into major cities, especially Dublin, Wexford, Limerick, and Cork.

The Irish language, like Scottish and Manx, is Celtic/Gaelic, descending from the same Indo-European roots. Middle English was introduced to Ireland in the twelfth century, but no form of English predominated in Ireland until the nineteenth century, and then only after centuries of

English/Irish political and religious strife. Seven centuries of Norman and English rule began in 1169, when mercenaries invaded the island. The English Reformation set off a brutal period of Catholic suppression, including the confiscation of land and wholesale massacres. By the end of the eighteenth century, 95 percent of Irish land was owned by Protestants.

By the nineteenth century, Dublin, Ireland, was one of Britain's largest cities and centers of trade, sometimes called the Second City of the British Empire. Its intractable problems with overcrowding, squalor, and disease were equally oversized and, in fact, among the worst in Europe. Death was a living presence, even if that grim vitality was expressed indirectly, through the sullen exertion of gravediggers, the unceasing procession of mourners, and the incessant writhing of worms.

On October 8, 1847, a letter from the local cleric Richard Ardille was published in the *Dublin Evening Mail*, addressing a perceived central issue: "The evil to be remedied, which I think demands the serious attention of the government, and of every person, is the practice that now prevails of having burial in church yards within the city, surrounded as they are by neighborhoods densely populated, the inhabitants of which are constantly inhaling an atmosphere noxious in its character and effect." Ardille continued with some direct observations:

> I have attended funerals where the remains of seven bodies were exhumed to make room for an eighth about to be interred; and I would ask any rational man if he could expect that a city could be healthy where such scenes were of frequent recurrence? In no country, save in Great Britain and Ireland, do interments take place within the walls of cities or towns. . . . On the continent of Europe such an offence against propriety is unheard of. Amongst barbarous natives, as they are termed, the dead are either consumed by fire, or interred at a distance from their dwellings; but in refined and civilized England the pernicious system is yet tolerated.

There was no proven connection between putrefaction in Dublin cemeteries and any outbreak of disease. But crowded cemeteries did produce noxious smells, which much occupied the minds of early nineteenth-century promulgators of "miasma theory," ever anxious to find environmental—even meteorological—reasons for confounding health problems in congested urban centers. Disease, in the miasmic worldview, was, in essence, understood as the mysterious action of wafting phantoms. In the case of cemeteries, the ghostly analogy is particularly apt, for just beneath the pseudoscientific surface of miasma theory percolated ancient, stubborn superstitions about the fearful powers of the dead to reach out from their graves and weaken the living.

In point of fact, it was not uncommon for dead bodies in Victorian Dublin to leave their graves. When Bram Stoker was born, only fifteen years had passed since Britain's Anatomy Act was made law, allowing corpses to be donated for medical dissection. Previously, surgeons were dependent on "resurrection men"—that is, grave robbers—to provide cadavers for study and instruction. Dublin's Glasnevin Cemetery, Ireland's largest, was a natural target. Two stone watchtowers had been built into its walls for night-time surveillance, and they stand to the present day, their purpose already enshrined in Irish memory when Stoker was a boy. The Anatomy Act had been fiercely debated for years before its passage. The bodies ultimately liberated to laboratories were overwhelmingly procured from hospitals, jails, and workhouses, as they were all throughout Britain (Robert Louis Stevenson's 1884 story "The Body Snatcher," based on the notorious crimes of Burke and Hare in the 1820s, was set in Scotland). Much opposition to the anatomy law fell along class divides. The noted journalist and pamphleteer William Cobbett questioned whether the act was really necessary for the purposes of medical science. "Science? Why, who is science for? Not for poor people. Then if it be necessary for the purposes of science, let them have the bodies of the rich, for whose benefit science is cultivated." Needless to say, Cobbett's modest proposal was never considered, much less adopted. Fear and anxiety about nineteenth-century science would persist as an essential ingredient of the Gothic literary energies that would eventually catapult the name Bram Stoker to worldwide fame.

It is often said that death is a normal part of life, and this was especially true in Victorian Ireland. People mostly died as they were born—at home, amid familiar persons and surroundings. The processes of death were not clinically sequestered; in fact, a definite social stigma was attached to the very idea of dying "in hospital." Not without cause, medical institutions were often seen, and feared, as de facto death houses, shelters of desperate and truly final resort. Life expectancy in midcentury Dublin was miserably short; to live much past what we now consider middle age could be a pleasant surprise in even middle-class households, and among the artisan

Top: Mount Jerome Cemetery, Dublin, Stoker family burial site.
Bottom: Cenotaph with Celtic serpent, Mount Jerome Cemetery. (Photographs by the author)

classes and the poor an impossible dream. Grimmer still were the infant mortality rates. Nearly a quarter of all children born died before the age of five, and among the poorest of the poor, the death rates could approach half. Although infant fatality served to skew downward all life expectancy statistics, the overall numbers were dismal in any case. Many working-class children in Great Britain were routinely enrolled in so-called burial clubs at birth, to guard families against ruinous funeral expenses, or the shame of a pauper's grave.

At the age of twenty-nine, Charlotte Matilda Blake Stoker (née Thornley) was an intelligent, educated, forward-minded woman from a military family in the northwest of Ireland. She married Abraham Stoker, a Dublin civil servant eighteen years her senior, in 1844; by 1847 the couple already had two children, William Thornley (born in 1845 and known as Thornley) and Charlotte Matilda (born in 1846, known as Matilda). Their third, Abraham Jr., familiarly and later famously called Bram, followed on November 8, 1847, at 15 the Crescent (now Marino Crescent), Clontarf, a seaside parish in north Dublin. Four more children would follow: Thomas (1849), Richard (1851), Margaret (1853), and George (1854).

The Stokers identified strongly with the Protestant Ascendancy, though just how far they ascended themselves during the children's formative years is another matter entirely. Abraham was a product of the commercial artisan classes (his father manufactured corset stays) and the first in his family to achieve a foothold in the Dublin middle class, or at least step up to its lower and more precarious rungs in the civil service. His progress was hampered, however, perhaps due to a certain lack of personal and professional assertiveness, but also because of the escalating presence of Roman Catholics in the commercial and public spheres.

Bram Stoker came into the world midway through a century of scientific and technological change more rapid and destabilizing than human beings had previously experienced. The tension between religious and scientific worldviews was especially pronounced, and Stoker's own intellectual development and literary output would amount to a lifelong juggling act of materialism versus faith, and reason against superstition. In the sciences, 1847 witnessed the births of Thomas Alva Edison and Alexander Graham Bell, the first use of chloroform as a surgical anesthetic, and the first sighting by telescope of a comet invisible to the naked eye.

In 1847, the world of arts and letters welcomed the premiere of Verdi's

Left: Undated portrait of Bram's mother, Charlotte Stoker. Photographer unknown.
Right: Abraham Stoker, Bram's father (1865). Photographer unknown.

opera *Macbeth* and saw the publication of Emily Brontë's *Jane Eyre* and Charlotte Brontë's *Wuthering Heights*,[1] two novels highly pertinent to Stoker studies for depicting the Gothic grip of childhood traumas. Interestingly enough, both books make references to vampires. In *Jane Eyre*, the title character, is kept apart from the man she loves, Edward Rochester, by his wife, Bertha, a raving madwoman locked in an attic and from there ruining everything. She reminds Jane of "the foul German spectre—the Vampyre" and is duly described like the fluid-fattened undead of folklore, with "a discoloured face," "lips swelled and dark," and "bloodshot eyes." Vampires in the folk tradition were ruddy peasants; only in literature would they eventually achieve a deathly aristocratic pallor. Bertha growls and bites like an animal and, like many a vampire of legend, is ultimately destroyed by fire. In *Wuthering Heights*, the über-Byronic antihero Heathcliff, after having every other demonic epithet imaginable flung at him, finally prompts

---

[1] First published under the pseudonyms Currer Bell and Ellis Bell, respectively.

Nelly Dean, the narrator, to wonder (just about the time he is digging up the grave of his lost love), "Is he a ghoul, or a vampire?"

The same year, thirsty nocturnal creatures were the subject of the book publication of the rambling penny-dreadful serial *Varney the Vampyre; or, The Feast of Blood* by the anonymous and prolifically prolix writer James Malcolm Rymer. The absurdly attenuated narrative, luridly illustrated, occupied popular attention in much the same way as would television's *Dark Shadows*—a similarly endless Gothic soap opera of the late 1960s, with a vampire named Barnabas Collins more or less standing in for Lord Francis Varney, in new installments five days a week. At some point many years later, Stoker would encounter a no doubt well-thumbed copy of *Varney* and closely adapt material for key scenes in *Dracula*.

Charlotte may easily have read *Jane Eyre* and *Wuthering Heights* but almost certainly did not read *Varney*. Then again, she might not have had time to read any of them, for Charlotte's pregnancy with Bram would have been anxious indeed. William Thornley had been born in the first year of an ominous potato crop failure, and Matilda during the second, worsening year. It was the beginning of a nightmarish national tragedy no one could have anticipated and would never forget. On Christmas Eve 1846, when Matilda was barely six months old, an alarmed official report was published in the House of Commons Sessional Papers, detailing miserable Irish scenes "such as no tongue or pen could convey" but nonetheless going on to describe a family of "six famished and ghastly skeletons, to all appearances dead" who were "huddled in a corner with some filthy straw."

The disturbing firsthand account continued, with descriptive details that evoked the language of Gothic romances but were based on fact: "I approached with horror, and found by a low moaning that they were still alive—they were in fever, four children, and what once had been a man. It is impossible to go through the detail. Suffice it to say, that in a few minutes I was surrounded by at least 200 such phantoms, such frightful spectres as no words can describe, either from famine or from fever. Their demoniac yells are still ringing in my ears, and their horrible images are fixed upon my brain."

By the time Charlotte was pregnant with Bram, the effects of the potato famine were being fully felt throughout Ireland; starving and evicted tenant farmers flooded into the city slums and workhouses, and with them dysentery, famine fever, and typhus. Terrifying accounts reached Dublin from

County Mayo, where workhouses had begun the inexorable transition into death houses. About the time of Bram's conception, the *Mayo Constitution* reported the grim effects of fever: "In Ballinrobe the workhouse is in the most deplorable state, pestilence having attacked paupers, officers, and all. In fact, this building is one horrible charnel house. . . . The master has become the victim of this dread disease; the clerk, a young man whose energies were devoted to the well-being of the union, has been added to the victims; the matron, too, is dead; and the respected and esteemed physician has fallen before the ravages of pestilence, in his constant attendance on the diseased inmates."

The Stokers endured the appalling health crisis within the bulwark of

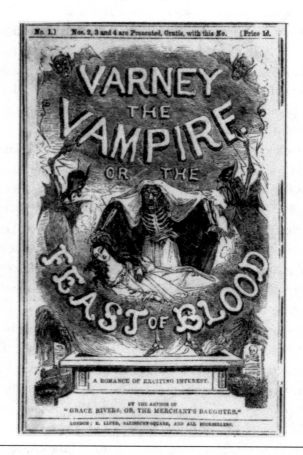

James Malcolm Rymer's penny-dreadful serial **Varney the Vampyre,** *published in 1847, the year of Bram Stoker's birth.*

their Clontarf row house. Still standing, it has a deceptively simple façade, but its three stories are filled with handsome decorative moldings, marble fireplaces, and a distinctive bowed back wall not typical of Georgian construction; its rear windows give onto a long, sunken backyard accessible through the basement kitchen. Infant food prepared in this heavy-beamed room would have consisted mainly of gruels and porridges made of grain and water, and sometimes sugar. Commercial baby foods were still decades away, as was pasteurization. Milk, despite its nutritive benefits, was still a risky business. The basics of child nutrition weren't even comprehended—fruits and vegetables, for instance, were widely considered unhealthy for the very young. Given this ignorance, the scourge of infant mortality and early childhood disease becomes much less surprising.

Ironically enough, the very kitchen that provided less-than-sumptuous sustenance to the three Stoker children would, in the early twentieth century, serve as the closely guarded hiding place for an unparalleled visual feast: the Russian crown jewels, acquired as collateral for a $25,000 loan by the Irish Republic to the Bolsheviks, who had no practical use for such an extravagant reminder of the Romanovs. In 1920, Catherine Boland, mother of Irish patriot Harry Boland (who helped broker the loan), was called upon to secrete the hoard at 15 Marino Crescent, which she had recently purchased. It was not an ostentatious house and would not draw attention. The jewels included the legendary crown created for Catherine the Great in 1762, adorned with five thousand Indian diamonds, pearls, and the second-largest spinel in the world. The precious stash remained hidden at Bram Stoker's birthplace until 1950, its location revealed to no one until after the Soviet Union repaid the original loan. This outlandish but true story was not unlike an incident in one of the adventure novels Stoker loved as a boy and would eventually write.

Above the kitchen, the first floor boasts a long entry hall leading to a reception parlor flanked by a formal sitting room and dining room. The upper two floors contain several bedrooms, though no one has ever determined exactly which were occupied by which of the three Stoker children. Bram might have shared a room with his brother, or might well have had his own dedicated sickroom-nursery. It has been imagined that Bram's room might have faced the street, overlooking the handsome iron-gated park opposite, with a glimpse of the Irish Sea beyond, fueling his dreamy imagination, the park itself being the spot to which he remembered being carried to lie "amid cushions on the grass if the weather was fine."

However idyllic, this is also unlikely. Episodic memories before the age of two (the approximate time the family moved from the Crescent) are universally irretrievable, subject to the well-studied phenomenon of infantile amnesia, a normal part of childhood development. Bram's memories of cushions and grass had their origins later and elsewhere. Also, the Clontarf waterfront, which previously attracted swimmers and sunbathers, was now becoming an odiferous slobland at a time when "vapors" and "miasmas" were blamed for all manner of disease; in later years, owing to concerns about sewage dumping, the sea frontage would be completely landfilled. Despite its close proximity, the mouth of the Liffey was hardly the place a concerned parent would take a sickly child.

The precise onset of Bram Stoker's debilitating illness is not recorded, but his baptism was delayed nearly seven weeks, until December 30, and then conducted at the Protestant Church of St. John the Baptist, which still half-stands in Clontarf as a picturesque ruin. The site is appropriately suggestive of the Gothic masterpiece Stoker would publish fifty years later. *Dracula* is the overwhelming reason for most people's interest in Bram Stoker today, and since Stoker chose to leave us no full accounting of his own life, only his fictions, it is not surprising that biographers, critics, and essayists have long employed imaginative (and often overreaching) speculation to link the king of vampires to a sickness and symptoms initially as baffling to onlookers as those endured by Dracula's victims.

Vampirism involves bloodletting, which, in the mid-nineteenth century, was an ancient medical practice still widely used. Henry Clutterbuck, MD, whose "Lectures on Blood-Letting" appeared in the *London Medical Gazette* in 1838, told his readers that "blood-letting is a remedy which, when judiciously employed, it is hardly possible to estimate too highly. There are, indeed, few diseases on which, at some periods, and under some circumstances, it may not be used with advantage, either as a palliative or curative means." The most cursory look at the medical literature of the day confirms the universality of the prescription, even for conditions like childhood asthma and adolescent acne. Clutterbuck especially advocated "prompt and vigorous application of the remedy" to "inflammatory affections of the brain that are so common in early life." The concept of "brain fever" in the 1800s was remarkably elastic and seems to have comprised

Bram Stoker's Clontarf birthplace. (Photograph by the author)

everything from meningitis to simple moodiness. A child so afflicted "loses his appetite, complains of thirst, is languid and spiritless, his sleep is scanty and disturbed," Clutterbuck observed.

A languid boy like Bram Stoker, showing signs of chronic motor weakness, would have been a prime candidate for phlebotomy. Bloodletting physicians no longer invoked the principle of balancing "humors," an idea dating from antiquity, but the similarly ancient idea of "plethora," or excess blood, as a cause of illness was still very much in vogue. If Bram was treated by doctors, it would have been at home. Hospitals, especially during the time of famine fever, were resorted to cautiously, if at all. Bloodletting was performed by three means: by lancet, by "cupping" with a heated glass that created a siphoning vacuum, and by medicinal leeches. Great Britain at the time imported nearly forty million medicinal leeches annually from France. Since Dracula himself is described by Stoker as "a filthy leech, exhausted in his repletion," one wonders about his personal experience or observation of the bloodsucking worm, or how a helpless boy might process or reconcile the ritual threat of having of his flesh being penetrated and bled by an imposing male figure wielding a lancet. When Stoker's alter ego Jonathan Harker wanders into a forbidden room at Castle Dracula and meets the Count's undead wives, he experiences a powerful erotic thrill as he anticipates imminent penetration by bladelike teeth:

> The skin of my throat began to tingle as one's flesh does when the hand that is to tickle it approaches nearer—nearer. I could feel the soft, shivering touch of the lips on the supersensitive skin of my throat, and then the hard dents of two sharp teeth, just touching and pausing there. I closed my eyes in a languorous ecstasy and waited—waited with beating heart.

There is an old adage, "When the blood flows, the danger is past," which goes a long way to explain ancient practices of human and animal sacrifice, and the relief of sexual tension through blood fetishism. As a young man, Stoker would be powerfully attracted to the poetry of Walt Whitman, who wrote almost ecstatically about bleeding in *Leaves of Grass*: "Trickle drops! My blue veins leaving / Oh, drops of me! Trickle, slow drops . . ."

Bloodletting, with its inevitable relationship to vampires, is not only a possibility in Bram Stoker's early life but a probability. For all the nineteenth-century advances in anatomical studies (considerably abetted by grave robbing) and surgery, when it came to healing the sick, early nineteenth-century doctors had an extremely limited bag of tricks. A well-regarded doctor's reputation typically required a comforting bedside manner, a judicious dose of bluster and professional mystification, and a certain generosity with opium, not to mention a surfeit of sustained good luck.

And leeches.

Befitting a boy whose childhood was destined to be shaped by fairy tales, his father, Abraham Stoker Sr., actually worked in a castle—Dublin Castle, the seat of government administration, where he was a career civil servant. The vestiges of an impressive Norman fortification no doubt carried strong legendary associations for his son; the castle's medieval Record Tower (the oldest surviving part of the much-renovated complex, dating to 1204) once displayed the freshly impaled heads of Irish traitors on its battlements. Still vigorous in middle age, the elder Stoker is said to have walked to work each day, a brisk daily journey of an hour and a quarter from Clontarf, down the North Strand Road and into the commercial hurly-burly of Talbot Street, then down Sackville Street and over the Carlisle Bridge (today O'Connell

Street and the O'Connell Bridge) into the city center on the south bank. Family accounts of Abraham's daily perambulations may well be exaggerated, or refer to a later time when the family lived in the city center. The nearly three-mile walk would be almost impossible as a daily matter in winter, and Clontarf was one of the first Dublin suburbs to be serviced by horse-drawn omnibuses and trams, as well as trains. But the story does illustrate the Stoker family's characteristic emphasis on discipline, thrift, and self-reliance.

Charlotte Stoker was a practical, no-nonsense woman who nonetheless had a countervailing and lifelong weakness for things irrational, fantastic, and macabre. County Sligo, where she was raised, is one of Ireland's richest repositories of Celtic folklore, and Charlotte partook of a vibrant oral

Dublin Castle in the nineteenth century.

tradition—the same legacy that would powerfully inspire Ireland's greatest poet and folklorist, William Butler Yeats, who spent much of his childhood in Sligo and claimed it as his muse and spiritual home. Northwest Ireland can boast of the country's most romantic and soul-stirring landscapes, including the purported Neolithic rock-pile tomb (or cairn) of Queen Mebh or Maeve, her name meaning "she who intoxicates." Mebh is the warrior monarch of Celtic mythology commemorated in English literature as the fairy Queen Mab evoked by Edmund Spenser, William Shakespeare, and Percy Shelley. Legend has it that Mebh is buried upright, alert and ready to take on enemies, even after death.

Charlotte claimed to have personally heard the wail of the *Bean-sídhe*, or banshee, the ghostly Irish harbinger of mortality, heralding her own mother's death. Some modern observers have linked the rise of banshee legends in the eighteenth century to the collective grieving of traditional Irish culture under an increasingly heavy Protestant heel. According to Yeats, "An omen that sometimes accompanies the banshee is the *coach-a-bower* (*cóiste-bodhar*)—an immense black coach, mounted by a coffin, and drawn by headless horses driven by a *Dullahan* [headless coachman]. It will go rumbling to your door, and if you open it . . . a basin of blood will be thrown in your face." Haunted coach rides are a common motif in horror fiction, perhaps archetypally so in *Dracula*, as a living-dead figure associated with blood and with an affinity for coffins drives a mysterious coach with four black horses through wildest Transylvania.

When young Charlotte Thornley wasn't hearing banshees, she might have occupied her time like the voraciously literate heroine of Jane Austen's *Northanger Abbey* (1818), when coming-of-age popular reading for young women included the Gothic novels of Ann Radcliffe (*The Mysteries of Udolpho*, 1794, and *The Italian*, 1797), Matthew Lewis (who had barely come of age himself when he published *The Monk* at the age of nineteen in 1796), and the Irish cleric Charles Robert Maturin (*Melmoth the Wanderer*, 1820). For Irish Protestant readers, these books distilled the complicated sentiments of long sectarian strife. The Gothic novels portrayed Catholicism with a lurid—and alluring—savagery. The cruel debaucheries of villains like Ambrosio, the lustful Capuchin in *The Monk* (some of whose description and demeanor would be appropriated almost verbatim in Stoker's delineation of Count Dracula), were sensationally attractive to readers like Charlotte, and later her son, exuding all the dependable fascination of the forbidden, a dynamic the Irish historian R. F. Foster describes as "a mingled repulsion and envy" for "Catholic magic."

Charlotte also read the works of Edgar Allan Poe, and near the end of her life would compare her son superlatively to the world-famous author of *Tales of Mystery and Imagination*. "Poe," she would write in 1897, upon the publication of *Dracula*, "is nowhere." That is saying much, since the terrors of both "The Masque of the Red Death" and "The Premature Burial" were very nearly eclipsed by the events of Charlotte's own childhood. As a thirteen-year-old girl in Sligo, she had personally witnessed the horrors of the 1832 cholera epidemic that claimed more than twenty-five thousand lives. At Bram's request, she put the story to paper in 1873.

> In the days of my early youth so long ago . . . our world was shaken with the dread of the new and terrible plague which was desolating all lands as it passed through them. And so regular was its march that men could tell where it next would appear and almost the day when it might be expected. It was the *Cholera*, which for the first time appeared in Western Europe. And its utter strangeness and man's want of experience or knowledge of its nature, or how best to resist its attack, added if anything to its horrors.

British landlords and Roman Catholics provided vampire metaphors
for Irish political cartoonists in Victorian Ireland.

Charlotte knew how to tell a tale, and the written version of the chilling oral account she gave to her children included the italicized inflections she must have given it vocally, building suspense and gooseflesh with equal calculation: "But gradually the terror grew on us, as time by time we heard of it nearer and nearer. It was in France, it was in Germany, it was in *England,* and (with wild affright) we began to hear a whisper pass[:] '*It was in Ireland.*'"

Sligo was one of the worst-afflicted areas. Charlotte's later reading of Poe's ruminations on live burial would no doubt have triggered memories of a specific victim: "One I vividly remember, a poor traveler was taken ill on the roadside, some miles from the town, and how did those Samaratines tend him[?]" she asked. "They dug a pit and with long poles pushed him living into it and covered him up alive. But God's hand is not to be thus stayed and severely like Sodom did our city pay for such crimes." In total, five-eighths of Sligo's citizens would perish.

Premature burial, or its threat, especially haunted her. She recollected two instances of souls who narrowly escaped the fate. One was a woman whose husband recognized her red neckerchief; she had already been piled over with corpses awaiting a mass grave. Another was a man who awoke from a deathlike stupor only when undertakers attempted to break his legs to fit an undersized coffin.

"One house would be attacked and the next spared," she wrote. "There was no telling who would go next, and when one said 'good-bye' to a friend, he said it as if forever." This was vividly demonstrated when a family the Thornleys visited one night were dead—and buried—the following morning. She remembered throwing a jug of water on a persistent coffin maker who would not stop banging at the door.

Cholera brings on a hideous death, beginning with fever and cramping, blue and puckered lips, then uncontrollable and fatal diarrhea. The disease was all the more frightening because the exact means of transmission—contaminated drinking water—was then unknown, and would remain unknown until the 1850s. In 1832, censers of burning tar and other substances were employed, much as they were during medieval plagues, in a desperate attempt to purify the air. Plates of salt moistened with vitriolic acid were laid outside windows and doors.

All the Thornleys, including Charlotte, took a daily morning dose of ginger-thickened whiskey, and she believed the nostrum was largely

Famine in nineteenth-century Ireland, personified as malignant invading phantom.

responsible for her family's survival. Without this desperate, home-mixed concoction, "no one moved a yard." The Jesuit priest Theobald Mathew of Cork, later one of the great figures of the nineteenth-century temperance movement, had nothing to offer the sick and dying but Irish whiskey. Elsewhere, opium was liberally used. Those tending to the sick inexorably sickened themselves. "The nurses died one after another," Charlotte wrote, "and none could be found to fill their places but women of the worst description, who were always more than half drunk." The constant sound of bells attached to the cots of the dying and the carts conveying the dead would never leave Charlotte's memory.

At the height of the epidemic the entire Thornley family fled Sligo and narrowly escaped death, not from the disease but from the wrath of a mob outside of Donegal who dragged them from their carriage, determined to "*burn the cholera people*" in a fiery exorcism atop their own luggage.

In 1971, Tom Stoker's great-grandson Daniel Farson, a colorful London journalist and television personality, consulted with Hammer Films, the British studio that had already produced seven *Dracula*-inspired movies and was now interested in developing a biographical drama based on Stoker's life. Farson shared some additional family lore regarding Charlotte's cholera ordeal, omitted from her written account but vividly recalled by

Farson's own grandmother—that "on one of the last, desperate days" of the epidemic, the Thornley family was under siege by a zombie-like horde of cholera victims, and Charlotte was forced to take extreme measures. Hammer screenwriter Don Houghton wrote a treatment involving young Bram directly in the trauma by moving the action to a fictional cholera epidemic of the 1850s when Charlotte is already a mother, fiercely protecting her son. The climactic scene strikingly anticipated the house-under-siege motif of countless modern horror films:

> A man, his face yellow, drawn and ghastly . . . his teeth bared in fury, appears at the window, forced forward by the mob behind him. In terrible detail the child sees the horror of what happens next. The MAN thrusts his arm through the glass to tear at the boards barring the window. The arm, white with disease, gropes into the room, like an ugly tentacle, wavering like a monstrous worm.
>
> On the table in front of CHARLOTTE there is a knife. In a fit of angry panic, she takes hold of it. The child screams as she hacks at the arm. Blood spatters over her. The fingers tear at her fingers as she continues to slash at it.

In what Houghton calls "the final, terrible picture," Bram backs away screaming from the squirming, severed arm that has fallen to the floor, and his mother rushes to comfort him. But it does no good, for "her clothes are red with gore. . . . She is like a spectre of death."

Farson's grandmother put an ax in Charlotte's hand in place of a knife, and it's a bit surprising that Houghton chose to pull the extra visual punch. It would have been a perfect Hammer moment. But for all of its melodramatic excess, the never-filmed scene underscores a certain psychological truth. Young children can be acutely attuned to parental anxiety, with lasting emotional effect. And, in a fact previously overlooked by Stoker biographers, Bram's early bonding with his mother did take place during a cholera epidemic, one even more deadly than the 1832 plague, reaching Dublin during the winter of 1847–48. Only days before Bram's birth, Charlotte could have read an ominous account in the *Dublin Evening Mail* headlined CHOLERA MORBUS. The correspondent in Malta described the spread of "this scourge of mankind" from the Black Sea and warned that "experience has proved the utter inutility of resorting to quarantine." More than thirty-five thousand Irish would perish, a death toll exacerbated in a population already weakened by hunger and fever.

It is also surely significant that Stoker's seven-year illness coincided almost exactly with the worst years and immediate aftermath of the Great Famine, Ireland's towering trauma in a notoriously tumultuous history. His birth year became known as "Black '47," with the total failure of the potato crop. By the mid-nineteenth century, Ireland's predominantly Catholic population of rural tenant farmers had become almost totally dependent on the potato for subsistence. Many earned no money at all, working as indentured sharecroppers in exchange for primitive housing and meager patches of land on which they could cultivate potatoes.

Scientific plant breeding was then unknown, and the tubers had no immunity against a virulent fungus, *Phytophthora infestans*, that had crossed the ocean from North America on steamships. For all that was understood about fungal life in 1847, the organism might as well have been supernatural in origin. It was believed that funguses were—impossibly—a living by-product of organic decomposition, a concept with roots in medieval alchemy (the idea, for instance, that flies were directly generated by rotting meat). The mechanism of fungal parasitism amounted to a kind of vegetable vampirism: telltale surface marks, easily overlooked, yielded quickly to a fatal corruption.

By modern consensus, a million Irish perished, most not from hunger but from diseases attacking the weakened and malnourished. "The actual starving people lived upon the carcasses of diseased animals, upon dogs," the House of Commons Sessional Papers recorded, "and even in some place[s] dead bodies were found with grass in their mouths." Over and over, those who were spared starvation would hear harrowing stories of death, and living death. In the countryside, shallow mass graves were rifled by scavenging animals. In Dublin, a few months before Stoker's birth, Cork Street Hospital was forced to close its doors against new fever victims. A local journal reported that "among the close pestilential atmosphere of crowded lanes and alleys," victims would "writhe and perish . . . dragging all who come in contact with them to share their untimely graves."

The tragedy was compounded by continued large shipments of Irish grain to England, despite the need for food at home. The perception that official British policy was deliberately worsening the famine stirred resentment and outrage, and still fuels historical debate. In early 1847, with especially chilly bureaucratic sangfroid, a medical officer reported to the Poor Law commissioners that "it is a well-known fact that many dying persons are sent for admission [to hospitals and workhouses] merely that coffins may be obtained for them at the expense of the Union."

Lady Jane Francesca Wilde, the mother of Oscar, was a fiery nationalist polemicist and poet who published under the pen name Speranza. In 1848, she wrote "The Famine Year," protesting unionist inaction:

> Fainting forms, hunger-stricken, what see you in the
>   offing?
> Stately ships to bear our food away, amid the stranger's
>   scoffing.
> There's a proud array of soldiers—what do they round
>   your door?
> They guard our master's granaries from the thin hands of
>   the poor.

The years of Bram Stoker's childhood were filled with oral accounts of horrors attending the famine. Most poignant and tragic were the now-legendary tales of the "coffin ships," which carried typhus and cholera along with desperate immigrants headed for North America. Many never arrived alive; as many as a hundred thousand refugees were interred in one mass grave at a St. Lawrence River quarantine station in Quebec. Bram undoubtedly heard these stories, told and embellished like folktales, and later could have read published first-person accounts of doomed passengers like Gerald Keegan and his new bride, Aileen, written in 1847:

> [30 April] The fever spreads and to the other horrors of the steerage is added cries of those in delirium. While coming from the galley this afternoon, with a pan of stirabout for some sick children, a man suddenly sprang upward from the hatchway, rushed to the bulwark, his white hair streaming in the wind, and without a moment's hesitation, leaped into the seething waters. He disappeared beneath them at once.
>
> [13 May] . . . I saw a shapeless heap move past our ship on the outgoing tide. Presently there was another and another. Craning my head over the bulwark I watched. Another came, it caught in one cable, and before the swish of the current washed it clear, I had caught a glimpse of a white face.

I understood it all. The ship ahead of us had emigrants and they were throwing overboard their dead.

Aileen lasted only a few days in quarantine, Gerald only six weeks. His heartbreaking journal, preserved by his uncle, was finally published in 1895 as "The Summer of Sorrow." Stoker may or may not have read it, but in any event would have known the basic story by heart from childhood. Not long after, he would incorporate the log of a doomed ship into *Dracula*, in which a literal "coffin ship" would return to British shores, doomed not by famine or plague but by a spectral figure embodying both terrible hunger and pestilential dread.

Outright starvation did not impact the city the way it did the country-side, but concurrent epidemics knew no geographic boundaries. A concern about unwholesome waterfront air and row-house crowding may have been the reason Charlotte and Abraham chose to move farther inland, although simple financial pressure or the need for larger quarters may also have played a role. As renters, rather than leaseholders, their continued tenancy could have been subject to rising rents or landlord whim. In any event,

The interior of a peasant's hut during the Great Famine.

around the time of Thomas Stoker's birth in 1849, the family relocated about a mile and a half northeast to Killester, and after the birth of Richard Stoker in 1851, to Artane Lodge in nearby Donneycarry.

Virtually nothing is known of the Killester address, save for its entry on baptismal records, but Artane Lodge was a residential villa—in the sense of a freestanding house, not because of any grandeur—set on an open parkland that is now the Clontarf Golf Club. If nothing else, the location met Victorian standards for healthy air at a time when miasma theory was still taken on faith. Abraham's father had roots in the area, and family connections may well have facilitated the move. Whether the change was for Bram's immediate benefit or not, his childhood incapacitation apparently persisted in three separate homes.

Bram never contracted cholera, or famine fever, or any other disease or condition (such as a spinal injury) that might medically account for his inability to walk. Rheumatic fever weakens the heart, making his later exemplary health and athleticism problematic at best. Asthma creates breathing problems, not immobility. Psychological or psychosomatic conditions understandably provide more fertile ground for sleuthing. Since vampires circle endlessly around any attempt to uncover Stoker secrets, the phenomenon of paralyzing night terrors, long posited as a source of incubus and vampire legends, immediately springs to mind. Night terrors primarily trouble children, are believed to have their roots in developmental biology, and usually disappear as the child matures. Autohypnosis and forms of deep meditation can also freeze the mind and body, but where does a Victorian toddler pick up the techniques? Nonetheless, we know (maddeningly) that Stoker had a lifelong interest in mesmerism and hypnosis, but little else. And somewhere in the vast spectrum of twilight consciousness called hypnagogia, there might well be the key to understanding strange states of suspended animation, but the esoteric subject is nearly as slippery and daunting as the comprehension of consciousness itself.

Sigmund Freud famously cured patients of what used to be known as hysterical paralysis, a condition formally called conversion disorder, in which neurological symptoms such as motor weakness, muscle spasms, aphasia, or even blindness manifest, all in the absence of physical disease. With Josef Breuer, Freud published *Studies on Hysteria* in 1895; the book introduced the concept of the unconscious as a distinct substratum of the mind and posited the "talking cure" to relieve such symptoms by bringing buried conflict or trauma to conscious examination. Although Freud's hysteria studies focused almost exclusively on women, conversion disorders are now recognized in men, but very uncommonly in young children of either sex. They are believed to occur most often in response to strict family or institutional structures in which normal emotional expression is repressed, or dysfunctional interactions denied.

That Bram Stoker's paralysis might have been the result of childhood sexual abuse or incest has been summoned up by a number of commentators, often achieving a near-parody of armchair psychologizing. Certainly, the argument goes, a forced or furtive glimpse of his mother menstruating would have triggered the archetypal image of the *vagina dentata*—and neatly explain his later literary evocation of the engulfing/penetrating vampire's mouth, oozing with blood. Alternately/concurrently, could paralysis be a defense reaction to murderous Oedipal rage directed at his brothers or his father?

The statement "The Irish are impervious to psychoanalysis" (or that the Irish constitute "one race of people for whom psychoanalysis is of no use") is often attributed to Freud, along with the equally provocative assertion that he split the world into two categories: the Irish and the non-Irish. In reality, there is no proof that he wrote or said any such thing, but the legend lingers, and especially colors the often frustrating challenge of illuminating the inner life of Bram Stoker. The attraction of Freudian theories for Stoker psychobiographers is understandable; many of the twentieth-century stage and film adaptations of *Dracula* were quite consciously molded around Freud's ideas, but the approach can be anachronistic and off target if one's goal is to understand the Victorian world as it understood itself. Ideas about menstrual exhibitionism in Victorian homes aside, much of Freud's work rests on universal truths. For instance, it is simple fact, not psychosexual theory, that a child first experiences his mother as food and is vulnerable to adult harm, or that for centuries children have been cruelly exploited and abused, and initiated into the dangerous adult world through frightening stories of infanticide and cannibalism. A child's first smile, it should be remembered, is an automatic reflex, a survival mechanism to reinforce parental care and feeding.

Parenthood in the best of circumstances is stressful, and young children can be preternaturally attuned to parental anxiety. In the case of Bram Stoker and his mother, their early bonding was clearly fraught with fearful emotions, the potential of devastating disease, and the common reality of infant mortality. Charlotte was almost constantly pregnant from 1845 to 1854, with all the attendant dangers to herself and her children. Statistically, she should have expected to lose at least two children to still-birth, complications of birth, or early childhood sickness. Each surviving child only increased fears for the next. If her pregnancy with Bram had been especially difficult, or his birth an ordeal, extra or even excessive vigilance on Charlotte's part would be a completely natural response.

Overprotection of Victorian children took some fascinating if surprisingly underexamined forms. A universal childhood custom in Ireland and throughout Western Europe was the practice of dressing both girls and boys in female attire until approximately the age of seven. The practice continued far beyond any practical utility—in toilet training, for instance. Maintaining boys in a sexually undifferentiated or aggressively feminized state until "breeching" into shorts or trousers was a curious, long-lived, and still remarkably underexplored historical custom. Laurence Sterne, in *The Life and Opinions of Tristram Shandy, Gentleman* (1759–67) treated the subject humorously, as a kind of tug-of-war between husband and wife, each rationalizing his or her own reticence in finally dealing realistically with their child's sex. "We defer it, my dear," Tristram quotes his father, "shamefully." They both try to convince themselves that the boy looks just fine dressed as he is. And might not male clothing be "aukward"? "When he gets these breeches made," the father frets, "he'll look like a beast in 'em."

Nonetheless, the breeching ritual marked the transference of a child from the mother's ethereal, domestic realm to the father's beastly, worldly domain. Some mothers took proactive steps to delay this fall from grace. Not a few Victorian boyhood photographs depict shoulder-length ringlet curls and petticoats under the skirts. Whatever her conscious motivation, many a Victorian mother succeeded admirably in tricking out her darling son like date bait for Lewis Carroll. Oscar Wilde is a case in point. A tinted daguerreotype of Wilde at the age of two shows him dressed in an ornate, off-the-shoulder royal-blue frock, his cascading hair artificially curled. One acquaintance, especially catty, published a memoir after the death of both mother and son maintaining that Lady Wilde, desperate for a daughter, kept Oscar in female dress until the age of ten, transforming him for all practical purposes into "a neurotic woman."

One Wilde family chronicler found a justification for cross-dressing in

Oscar Wilde as a child.

Irish folklore: he reported that in parts of rural Ireland boys were tradition-ally disguised as girls to protect them from being spirited off by the fairies, "for of course, the fairies are only interested in little boys."[2] It is intrigu-ing that the first recorded use of the word "fairy" as a homosexual slur occurred in 1895, the same year as Wilde's notorious trial for "gross inde-cency with male persons." In the two short decades following Wilde's down-fall, hundreds of years of tradition were overthrown as parents became acutely vigilant for any sign of effeminacy in their sons. The practice of dressing young boys in skirts all but ended around World War I, except for the yet-enduring custom of christening gowns.

What does a boy think about, immobilized for years as a kind of frag-ile female doll? "I was naturally thoughtful and the leisure of long illness

[2]A local superstition, certainly, since Irish legends teem with accounts of fairies abducting attractive children of both sexes, as well as adults.

gave opportunity for many thoughts which were fruitful according to their kind," Stoker tells us, which isn't much. A healthy child would be expected to engage in normal play, but in Stoker's case he would have been a help-lessly passive observer of normally abled children and adults, all of them costumed as female except his father. Among the imaginative fruits of Bram Stoker's peculiar early years may have been a lifelong fascination with gender instability and ambiguity. Indeed, near the end of his life he would devote a large section of *Famous Impostors* (1910) to the theory that the "virgin" Queen Elizabeth could have been a man, deliberately raised all her life as a girl in an elaborate plot to secure the throne—an extraordi-nary gambit, even by the conspiracy standards of the Tudors.

Modern critical studies of *Dracula* have been dominated by psycho-sexual investigations into the book's multiplicity of gender transgressions that all bubble over into horror: "new women," mannishly assertive, send the male characters into stereotypically "female" hysterics, while the title character, supernaturally frozen in an erotic limbo, absorbs and mingles transfused male fluids sucked from female veins. In his fourth-to-last novel, *The Man* (1905), a man obsessed with having a son tells his dying wife that the daughter she has just delivered is a boy, whom they name Stephen. The father thereafter experiences "a certain resentment of her sex," though "he never, not then nor afterwards, quite lost the old belief that Stephen was indeed a son. . . . This belief tinged all his after-life and moulded his policy with regard to his girl's upbringing. If she was to be indeed his son as well as his daughter, she must from the first be accustomed to boyish as well as to girlish ways. This, in that she was an only child, was not a difficult matter to accomplish."

Charlotte's forceful personality also raises questions about her own influence on Bram's early perception of sex roles and about who actually wore the trousers in the Stoker household. Although the word "mannish" is not used in any family reference, it is clear that Charlotte was not a typ-ical Victorian mother, was outspoken on public issues in a manner more typical of men, and had a dominating influence in her family. Nearly two decades younger and more vigorous than her spouse, Charlotte is described by Stoker editor and critic Clive Leatherdale as "a handsome, strong minded woman who, if she could see no ambition in her husband, was determined to invest it in her sons." Abraham Stoker would be warmly remembered by family members, but not for a forceful personality or rising career achievements. The first of his family to break above the artisan class, Abraham settled into decades of career complacency as a junior clerk at Dublin Castle between 1815 and 1837, when he finally became an assistant clerk, and only applied for the position of senior clerk in 1853, twelve years before his retirement. This final advancement came amid the pressures of a growing family and the births of their final three children. Certainly, Charlotte would have shared in her husband's decision, if not demanded it. According to Daniel Farson, his grandmother Enid (married to Thomas Stoker in 1891) "was not a fanciful woman and told me that the family were in awe of Charlotte if not actually afraid of her. When one of the boys failed to come in first in an examination, Charlotte did not conceal her resentment, even though he came second out of a thousand." Charlotte's identification with male striving is further evidenced by the opinion of her grandniece Ann Dobbs that she "didn't care a tuppence" about her own daughters' schooling and by her own published opinion that, to be honest, female education was mostly a practical matter of "matrimonial speculation."

Above all, Charlotte believed passionately in the power and importance of language and literacy. A man's mind without language, she wrote, "is a perfect blank; he recognizes no will but his own natural impulses; he is alone in the midst of his fellow-men; an outcast from society and its pleasures; a man in outward appearance, in reality reduced to the level of brute creation." Words, to Charlotte, were an essential component of Christian salvation. Take, for instance, deaf mutes (their education became one of her favorite causes), who, through their affliction, could have "no idea of a God."

Fully half of Ireland was illiterate in the mid-nineteenth century. The famine spurred a huge interest in the teaching of reading, which, increasingly, was understood as a necessity for nonagrarian employment and emigration. Outside the cities, children often learned to read under the charitable auspices of church-run "hedge schools," so called because many classes were conducted outdoors, or in barns. In urban areas, paid tutors found themselves in high demand. A parent like Charlotte, with a keen interest in education, might well have taken on the responsibility herself.

There are few activities better suited to engaging the attention of an invalid child than reading, and it is safe to assume that Bram Stoker's early years were occupied by storytelling to a greater degree than those of his normally active siblings. Abraham Stoker proudly collected books, and all manner of reading material would have been at the disposal of Charlotte or the nurse. The Bible, of course, was the central book in a Protestant home (where the Stokers, typical of their class, offered daily prayer), though its vocabulary and diction would present difficulties for children of three and four; Bram was not presented with a personal copy until the age of ten.

However, illustrated chapbooks of all descriptions supplemented the standard textbooks and the Bible, in school and out. According to Yeats, it was a rare Irish household that lacked chapbooks of fairy tales: "They are to be found brown with turf smoke on cottage shelves and are, or were, sold on every hand by the pedlars, but cannot be found in any library." Among the most popular titles were *The Royal Fairy Tales*, *The Hibernian Tales*, and *The Legends of the Fairies*. By the time of Stoker's birth, most of the classic German and French fairy tales were readily available in English. Charles Perrault's *Tales of Mother Goose*, including "Little Red Riding Hood," "The Sleeping Beauty," "Puss in Boots," "Cinderella," and "Bluebeard," had been in translation since 1697. "Beauty and the Beast" by Jeanne-Marie Leprince de Beaumont appeared in English almost immediately after its French publication in 1756. Edgar Taylor had first translated the Brothers Grimm as *German Popular Stories* in 1823; Edwin Lane brought *The Arabian Nights* to English-speaking shores in 1840; Mary Smith translated Hans Christian Andersen's *Wonderful Stories for Children* in 1846.

The Famine years were a mordantly appropriate time for fairy tales, since so many of them are about families and children struggling with hunger. The parents of Hansel and Gretel cannot provide food for their children, and so abandon them in the woods, where they meet an even hungrier nemesis, a cannibal witch. "The Juniper Tree," sometimes called "My Mother Slew Me; My Father Ate Me," is one of the most disturbing tales in the Grimm canon. A wicked stepmother kills the boy she hates, then serves him up as a stew to his clueless father. The more he eats the boy's flesh, the more ravenous he becomes. In the opening lines of "The Children in the Time of the Famine," a mother gets to the point without artifice or indirection: "There once lived a woman who fell into such deep poverty with her two daughters that they didn't even have a crust of bread to put in their mouths. Finally they were so famished that the mother was beside herself with despair and said to the older child: 'I will have to kill you so that I'll have something to eat.'"

Such tales would later inform Stoker's depiction of a supremely menacing father-figure driven by blood famine from his native land. Echoing a theme of many fairy tales, the threatened characters of *Dracula* are predominantly orphans.

Endangered children are less often emphasized in traditional Irish stories than are childlike adults. In the view of Lady Wilde, this is only appropriate, since the "mythopoetic faculty" exists "naturally and instinctively, in children, poets, and the childlike races, like the Irish—simple, joyous, reverent, and unlettered, and who have remained unchanged for centuries, walled round by their language from the rest of Europe, through which separating veil science, culture, and the cold mockery of the skeptic have never yet penetrated." Naïve, wonder-filled adults appeared in the first major collection of Irish lore, T. Croften Croker's *Irish Fairy Legends and Traditions of the South of Ireland*, published in three volumes between 1825 and 1828 and later as a single work.

Given Stoker's early baptism in gender-bending, it would be revealing to know what he thought of Croker's opening woodblock illustration, showing an androgynous, even hermaphroditic fairy deity, lifted and adored in an unmistakably Christlike pose. If nothing else, it is a striking example of the fusion of Christian and pre-Christian iconography, strikingly seen in the Celtic cross, which juxtaposes the Christian cruciform and the pagan circle. Christianity figures far more prominently in Irish fairy tales than in those of continental Europe, often featuring priests, the devil, and various tests of faith. The unseen world comprised not only heaven and hell but an abundance of other supernatural dimensions as well.

In German and French compilations, the word "fairy" was used very broadly, including narratives that didn't feature fairies at all. But in Ireland and Great Britain generally, wonder tales wove an intricate taxonomical skein of fairy-folk, a full spectrum of magical beings including pixies, pookas (possessed animals), leprechauns, banshees, devils, ogres, giants, and witches. For those delving deeply into magical belief systems, Ireland was (and is) an incomparable source for study.

A strong current in contemporary fairy tale criticism argues that oral versions of the classic stories were imbued with a rebellious proletariat spirit that was essentially hijacked and subverted by the bourgeoisie, the published versions repurposed to indoctrinate middle-class children with a materialistic work ethic and respect for established authority. The former

Illustration of an androgynous Christ-fairy from T. Crofton-Croker's **Irish Fairy Legends** *(1825).*

may or may not be true, but the latter certainly would be in keeping with Charlotte Stoker's family values. The Irish folktales she shared with her children were less purposefully crafted but often conveyed messages about miscreants and moral retribution.

Irish tales don't feature vampires in the sense that Bram Stoker would later depict them, but they are replete with accounts of the returning dead (often walking corpses encountered on churchyard roads) and the succubus-like *Leanan-sídhe*, whose draining charms prove fatal to poets who embrace her as a muse. A story from Ballinrobe, "The Hags of the Long Teeth," features shapeshifting crones with gruesomely exaggerated overbites. Victorian folklorist Douglas Hyde notes that "long teeth are a favourite adjunct to horrible personalities" in Irish tales. Toothed or not, one well-documented and definitely blood-drinking demon of Irish folklore is the *Dearg-dul*. Another sanguinary spectre, repeatedly cited in modern sources but with no historical proof, is the *Dreach-fhola* (supposedly meaning "bad blood," and pronounced "Drok-ola"), which more than one observer has found to be a suggestive (if not an overly obvious and even invented) homophone for "Dracula."[3] Less problematic vampires could be found by young Bram in Perrault's "Hop o' My Thumb and the Seven-League Boots" with its evocative description of an ogre's brood: "They were yet young, and were of a fair and pleasing complexion, though they devoured human flesh like their father; but they had little round grey eyes, flat noses, and long sharp teeth set wide from each other. They promised already what they would some day grow to be; for at this early age they would bite little children on purpose to suck their blood."

It would be indeed surprising if Stoker did not encounter Heinrich Hoffmann's *Slovenly Peter* (also known as *Shockheaded Peter*) sometime during his childhood. First published as *Struwwelpeter* in Leipzig in 1845, and translated anonymously into English roughly at the time of Bram Stoker's birth, the book was one of the best-selling children's titles of the late nineteenth century; by the 1870s, the German edition alone had no less than a hundred printings. Hoffmann's illustrated stories, written in rollicking verse, imparted moral instruction by dramatizing the disastrous consequences of even the smallest misbehaviors. In "The Dreadful Story of Pauline and the Matches," a girl's fascination with flame leads almost instantly to industrial-strength incineration. "Fidgety Philip" cannot sit still at the dinner table and ends his existence in an avalanche of sharp cutlery and broken china. The copious tears of "The Cry-Baby" loosen her eyeballs, which fall from their sockets, the optic nerves stretched like strings of taffy to the ground. One of the most famous tales, "The Story of Little Suck-a-Thumb," scares up a spectral tailor to perform a corrective mutilation with giant scissors. Animals and animalism are everywhere, and especially apropos to a discussion of Stoker are the characters of Idle Fritz, whose escape from responsibility leads to his being devoured by a wolf, and Oswald, "the Night Wanderer," whose repeated nocturnal ramblings transform him, permanently, into a bat: "Oh! yes, my dears it was too true; / An ugly bat away he flew; / His parents' tears streamed down like rain; / They never saw their child again."

The titular Slovenly Peter was a feral-looking child with wild, matted hair and curling fingernails. He had no real story of his own; Hoffman

---

[3] Having consulted several nineteenth-century Irish/English lexicons, this author remains unconvinced. Furthermore, there is no evidence that Stoker or anyone in his family could read or speak Irish. In the years following the Famine especially, the old language was vigorously discouraged by the Protestant establishment.

The English edition of Struwwelpeter *by Dr. Heinrich Hoffmann,*
a frightening best seller for Victorian-era children.

presented him as mostly an image and object lesson, an unforgettable distillation of the book's cautionary crusade. Victorians were already obsessed with the idea of progress as both a religious and secular ideal, and Hoffmann's supreme wild child emblemized the frightening flipside of progress: social, moral, and physical backsliding. The publication of Charles Darwin's *On the Origin of Species* in 1859, and the monumental controversies that followed, would fuel an ever-growing preoccupation with atavism and what would come to be known as "degeneration," a pseudoscientific catchall term that wormed its way into every nook and cranny of late Victorian social, political, and economic discourse and is one of the most frequently discussed themes of *Dracula* today. Darwin himself made no case whatsoever for evolution-in-reverse, but no matter—the public's assimilation of evolutionary theory was a process of freewheeling osmosis, fueled by the pervasive rhythms of repeated cultural metaphor, a dynamic closer

Oh! yes, my dears, it was too true;
An ugly bat away he flew;
His parents' tears streamed down like rain;
They never saw their child again.

Stoker's first exposure to the idea of human-into-bat transformation may well have been the story of Oswald, "the Night Wanderer," in Struwwelpeter.

to the mechanics of folklore than to the workings of science. To a large segment of the public, Darwin's theories had the fearful, fantastical appeal of fairy tales, complete with anthropomorphic animals and magical transformations. Like Freud, Darwin shares many of the traits of a good Gothic novelist—both men alarmed the public with compelling narratives about the past's strange ability to extend a controlling hand into the present.

To a child in Victorian Britain, reading fairy tales was only a prelude to a much more exciting experience: the annual Christmas-season pantomime, a theatrical spectacular enjoyed by young and old alike but intended for the child in everyone. The Christmas "panto" was in no way a religious event, and didn't utilize even secular Christmas themes, but it did coincide with the holiday calendar and usually ran well into January. Producers typically found the event to be their most profitable attraction of the year. Bram's father was a stage aficionado and would have taken pleasure in introducing his children to the yearly extravaganza at Dublin's Theatre Royal, an impressive venue with technical capabilities matching those of any stage in London.

Pantomimes had many antecedents in the theatre, most notably medieval morality plays and the commedia dell'arte. From the morality plays came characters and stories depicting clear conflicts between Good and

Evil. Malign characters—often including a Demon King—entered from the sinister stage left, and personifications of goodness from the right. A production often credited as the first recognizable English pantomime was *Harlequin Dr. Faustus*, produced at Sadler's Wells in 1723. In place of Bible stories were plots borrowed (sometimes very loosely) from classic fairy tales and *The Arabian Nights*. From 1855 to 1864, the years between Bram's first steps and his enrollment at Trinity College, the pantomime offerings at the Theatre Royal on Harcourt Street included *Bluebeard* (with its Draculean themes of female bloodletting, forbidden rooms, and castle imprisonment), *Little Bopeep, Babes in the Woods, Sleeping Beauty, King of the Castle, Jack the Giant Killer, Aladdin, Cinderella, Puss in Boots,* and *The House That Jack Built.*

One aspect of the panto that may have especially resonated for a boy who had just spent years languishing helplessly in female clothing was the centrality of cross-dressing to the whole event. The tradition is usually attributed to the great London clown Joseph Grimaldi, who around 1800 introduced the travesty "dame" character in holiday shows at Sadler's Wells and Drury Lane. To these rotund, farcical matrons he gave names like Queen Rondabelly and Dame Cecily Suet. One of the most enduring was (and remains) the Widow Twanky, a working-class laundress with a healthy disrespect for authority. The dames provided (and still provide) slapstick fun as the mothers of young male heroes—Jack the Giant Killer, Dick Whittington, or Aladdin—said heroes played by actresses whose tights displayed more leg than would ever have been tolerated in a straight female role. These theatrical precursors of Peter Pan (not portrayed onstage until 1904, but thereafter almost always by a woman) provided dependable and provocative eye candy for adult men attending, be they seasoned theatre devotees like Abraham Stoker or merely seasonal chaperones.

"Going to its first pantomime is the greatest event in the life of a child," Stoker wrote. "It is to it a great awakening from a long dream. All the rest of life must have been nothing but one continued sleeping vision, and this is the real world in which the dawning imagination has sought and found a home to suit itself."

Stoker's initiation into the world of the theatre was liberating and life altering, coinciding with his transgender metamorphosis from a sleeping fairy princess to a real live boy. Appropriately, the highlight of each pantomime was the "transformation scene," in which the main characters

Demon kings and travesty dames were central features
of the Christmas pantomimes that captivated Stoker as a child.

would shed their identities and assume the personae of a traditional harlequinade, accompanied by spectacular stage effects, and in time the figures Harlequin and Columbine gave way to other displays of character morphing. The "real" world Stoker discovered in the theatre was an imaginative realm of illusion; concealed, revealed, and transformed identities; strange creatures and humanized animals; a dreamy, gaslit refuge from grim realities of midcentury Dublin, and an escape from his strange affliction.

Stoker's childhood was filled with images from the other-land of fairy tales and pantomimes, but he never described the precise content of his reveries. However, one of his later Trinity College classmates, Alfred Perceval Graves (the father of the poet Robert Graves), gave his own striking account of the fantastic interior life of a Dublin boy in the 1850s. Graves had been introduced to Spenser's *The Faerie Queen* at a very early age and recounted its "strange effects upon my imagination. Night after night I would see the most vivid processions of knights and ladies, giants and dwarfs moving afoot or on horseback from left to right across the darkened walls of my nursery." The visions were often far from pleasant. "Often the light on the point of a spear or the jewel on a queen's crown would suddenly expand into a hideous face" or, even worse, "a phantasmagoria of evil faces bursting out of the darkness." Other fears were engendered by adults, in the daylight. "I was an imaginative and no doubt a troublesome child," Graves wrote, recalling that "when I was naughty the servants threatened to hand me over to the coal man, who would carry me away in his empty sack. This was a real terror that seemed always impending, for the great, grimy fellow bending under his weight of coal often came staggering up the staircase to pitch his load with a thundering crash into the wooden bin outside the nursery door." The idea of a fearful creature dragging a sack who whisks children away to a terrible fate is such a deeply ingrained legend in cultures throughout the world that it might well be considered an archetypal fixture of childhood nightmares. Examples are to be found in Germany, Austria, Spain, and India, as well as Central and South America and Asia. In Ireland it is mostly subsumed by a large body of lore concerning the child-stealing tricks of the fairy-folk. It is a resilient narrative, and modern, unembellished variants can still be found. As recently as 2008, in Lance Daly's coming-of-age film *Kisses*, a pair of runaway Dublin preteens worry explicitly about a lurking "sack man" who, once the children are bagged, kills them by smashing the sack against a brick wall.

Whether originally related by Stoker's parents, his nurse, or siblings, some version of the universal sack-man tale eventually inspired the following passage in *Dracula*—one of the most chilling scenes in all of horror fiction—in which the Count drives back his hungry wives as they prepare to make a buffet of his half-conscious guest, Jonathan Harker:

> "Are we to have nothing to-night?" said one of them, with a low laugh, as she pointed to the bag which he had thrown upon the floor, and which moved as though there were some living thing within it. For answer he nodded his head. One of the women jumped forward and opened it. If my ears did not deceive me there was a gasp and a low wail, as of a half-smothered child. The women closed round, whilst I was aghast with horror, but as I looked they disappeared, and with them the dreadful bag.

It's understandable how a Freudian folklorist might interpret the bag as a symbolic uterus, and the whole constellation of sack-man tales as a collective return-to-the-womb nightmare—a child's frightened response to overwhelming separation anxiety and the terrors of individuation. As a near-paralytic, Stoker was bound to his mother in a deeper way than other children. It's difficult to return to a womb one hasn't really left. A distinctly "uterine" view of the Irish mind and imagination was put forth by Freud's disciple Ernest Jones in his 1923 book *Essays in Applied Psycho-Analysis*. Jones described the Irish mind as a problematic case, owing to the island country's unique "geographic insularity" unconsciously associated with the idea of uterine confinement. According to Jones, "All aspects of the idea of an island Paradise are intimately connected with womb phantasies," a sentiment indirectly—if endlessly—echoed in countless literary and popular descriptions of the Irish as childlike and escapist, whether by means of poetry, storytelling, and fairy legends or the alternate, liquid womb of alcohol. In another book, especially interesting apropos of Stoker's sickly dependence on his mother, Jones maintained that the incest complex fueled Eastern European vampire lore.[4]

Charlotte Stoker would have had the same difficulty understanding her son's illness as modern readers have deciphering his psychology. With no other remedies at hand, many mothers like Charlotte turned to readily available drugs. The possibility that Bram's paralysis was induced by a drug like opium is not as outlandish as it might at first sound. Charlotte's true-believer experience with whiskey-based nostrums during the cholera plague would have predisposed her for stronger medicine during the far more cataclysmic famine. By the mid-nineteenth century, the administration of laudanum—a mixture of alcohol and opium—to children, even infants, as a cure-all and prevent-all, was frighteningly common. The homespun concoctions of the Thornley family in 1832 had by the 1840s been replaced by wildly popular commercial laudanum preparations such as "Godfrey's Cordial," "Infant's Preservative," and "Mrs. Wilkinson's

---

[4]Whereas the aristocratic vampires of literature and film characteristically feed Marx-like upon their socioeconomic inferiors, vampirism in European folklore is largely a family affair among the peasantry. In his 1931 book *On the Nightmare*, Jones attributes vampire belief to unresolved incestuous longing for dead children by their parents, and for dead parents by their children.

Soothing Syrup." Some advertisements even carried reassuring endorsements from Queen Victoria.

For parents, laudanum was the Ritalin of Victorian times. Today, the squirming behavior of Fidgety Philip would be immediately diagnosed as attention deficit hyperactivity disorder, and be summarily subdued with drugs. As the novels of Charles Dickens amply dramatize, many Victorian adults had little tolerance for the raucous—or even mildly elevated— energy of childhood. That children needed to waste time growing at all, much less move, play, or have any developmental needs, was an idea greeted with impatience, contempt, and resentment. Is it any wonder that opium preparations were intentionally abused by unscrupulous nurses and nannies, rewarded for their uncanny skill in keeping children manageable and quiet? Or that laudanum might be effectively employed by tacitly infanticidal "baby farms," from which illegitimate or unwanted children were unlikely to ever again emerge? High levels of infant mortality often provided an acceptable cover for all manner of malfeasance. In a perverse way, a bedridden boy like Bram Stoker was an ideal Victorian child, shielded from interaction with a corrupted and corrupting world. Sick or dead children were the only real angels. Funerary photographs of the period, showing children formally posed after death and surrounded by their families, convey the eerie sense of grace attending the merciful avoidance of earthly struggle.

How many nineteenth-century writers, especially writers of horror and fantasy, had their early imaginings or mature productions colored and intensified by childhood perceptions of death and the experience of opium? Early death was everywhere, and laudanum use was so accepted and widespread that it may not have registered as a particularly remarkable reminiscence. But it is almost impossible to imagine Poe's claustrophobic tales not being informed by his famous abuse of alcohol, or not to link Dr. Jekyll's nightmarish personality transformations (reliably triggered by a liquid potion) to Robert Louis Stevenson's own lifelong struggle with binge drinking. The use of opium as a creative stimulant by the Romantic poets is well known, and that Percy Shelley administered quantities of opium to the teenaged Mary Wollstonecraft Godwin is hardly controversial. Shelley personally took laudanum to quell horrifying "waking dreams" that plagued him as a young man, but only succeeded in intensifying them. Can it be a coincidence that Mary Shelley would attribute the inspiration for *Frankenstein* to her own waking dream, experienced "with a vividness far beyond the usual bounds of reverie"? In popular imagining, the famous literary house party on Lake Geneva at which Mary, Percy, Lord Byron, and John Polidori engaged in a writing contest that inspired not only *Frankenstein* but Polidori's "The Vampyre"—an acknowledged precursor to *Dracula*—was notoriously drug fueled.

Thomas De Quincey, in *Confessions of an English Opium-Eater* (1821), notably described his own drugged visions, which seem almost drawn from the grandiose terrors in a wild and exotic adventure novel for boys, the sort of thing Bram Stoker himself would eventually practice: "I was stared at, hooted at, grinned at, chattered at, by monkeys, by paroquets, by cockatoos. I ran into pagodas, and was fixed for centuries at the summit, or in secret rooms; I was the idol; I was the priest; I was worshipped; I was sacrificed." With opium came dreams of immortality. "Thousands of years I lived and was buried in stone coffins, with mummies and sphinxes, in narrow chambers at the heart of eternal pyramids. I was kissed, with cancerous kisses, by crocodiles, and was laid, confounded with all unutterable abortions, amongst reeds and Nilotic mud."

Withdrawal from opium was in itself debilitating, encouraging continued use. Infants wasting away from "poppy tea" and other opium preparations "shrank up into little old men" or became "wizened like little monkeys," descriptions that could be taken almost verbatim from Irish folktale descriptions of changelings, the replacement children left by the fairies, and typically described as ancient, withered things—or sometimes just gnarled wooden effigies. More often than not, changeling tales end sadly, as in the master Irish fantastist J. Sheridan Le Fanu's wistful story "The Child That Went with the Fairies" (1870). But occasionally the missing child is returned, through the cleverness of mortals or simply by the whim of the fairies. Stripped of mythopoetics, changeling stories provide a filtered but still disturbing record of the plight and fate of sick and disabled children, and the age-old pressures thrust upon parents faced with incomprehensible childhood maladies.

However much Stoker sought escape into the exuberant, shapeshifting freedom of pantomime and fairy tale characters, the special case of the abject changeling may shed improved light—or at least some illuminating dream-logic—on the confounding and irrational nature of his illness, in a land particularly susceptible to making end-runs around pure reason.

Harry Clarke's 1922 llustration "The Last Hour of the Night" evoked the perennial shadow side of Dublin that shaped Stoker's youthful imagination.

According to Lady Wilde, "Ireland is a land of mist and mystic shadows; of cloud-wraiths on the purple mountains; of weird silences in the lonely hills, and fitful skies of deepest gloom alternating with gorgeous sunset splendours. All this fantastic caprice of an ever-varying atmosphere stirs the imagination, and makes the Irish people strangely sensitive to spiritual influences." The Irish "see visions and dream dreams, and are haunted at all times by an ever-present sense of the supernatural. . . . The people are enthusiasts, religious, fanatical; with the instincts of poetry, music, oratory and superstition far stronger in them than the logical and reasoning faculties."

Given the elusive, perplexing nature of Stoker's seven-year affliction, we might be far better served to take Lady Wilde's observations as a guide, and seek explanations in a realm beyond the rational. The number seven has age-old associations with luck, magic, and the uncanny. The seventh son of a seventh son was believed to have occult powers. Seven-league boots were similarly enchanted. A false oath made on a holy relic would curse a family unto the seventh generation. Stoker himself would use the numeral in the title of an early short story, "How the 7 Went Mad," and in a late supernatural novel, *The Jewel of Seven Stars* (1903).

Perhaps, in their strange wisdom, the fairies simply removed the sickly Stoker changeling from his mother's frightened charge, and replaced him after seven magical years with the fine strapping boy who would grow up to write *Dracula*.

CHAPTER TWO

MESMERIC INFLUENCES

HE WANTED TO MEET IN THE REAL WORLD
THE UNSUBSTANTIAL IMAGE WHICH HIS SOUL
SO CONSTANTLY BEHELD.

—James Joyce, *A Portrait of the Artist as a Young Man*

Despite Stoker's early imaginative leanings, his parents had more practical plans, and his early adolescence was devoted to intense preparation for the daunting entrance examination at Trinity College, Dublin. Trinity was, and remains, the sole constituent college of the University of Dublin, the youngest of the seven Ancient Universities of Britain (the oldest being Oxford and Cambridge).[1] The revered institution was founded in 1591 by Queen Elizabeth as "the College of the Holy and Undivided Trinity, near Dublin." Trinity was a bastion of the Protestant Ascendancy, and Stoker's parents—especially his mother—were determined that their sons rise in the world.

Admission to Trinity in 1864 required passing a competitive entrance

---

[1] The Ancient Universities comprise Oxford (founded 1096), Cambridge (1209), St. Andrews (1413), Glasgow (1451), Aberdeen (1495), Edinburgh (1582), and Dublin (1591).

"Hypnotism" by Sascha Schneider (1904). During his student years at Trinity College, Stoker was drawn to pseudoscientific theories of mind, body, and eros.

Trinity College Dublin entrance examination room as it appeared in the late nineteenth century.

examination for which almost no sixteen-year-old today would be even remotely prepared. According to the *Dublin University Calendar,* "At the Entrance Examination, Candidates will be examined in Latin and English Composition; Arithmetic; Algebra (the first four rules, and Fractions); English History; Modern Geography, and any two Greek and two Latin books, of their own selection" from a list including, in Greek, such works as the Gospels of St. Luke and St. John, Homer's *Iliad,* Euripides's *Orestes,* Sophocles's *Antigone,* Plato's *Apologia Socratis,* Xenophon's *Anabasis,* and, in Latin, Virgil's *Aeneid,* as well as the *Odes, Satires, and Epistles* of Horace. Stoker's selections are not known, but given his already strong interest in theatre and wonder tales, it would be surprising if he hadn't favored the epics and dramas.

He identified his only teacher prior to Trinity College as the Reverend Dr. William Woods, who ran a day school on Rutland Square (now Parnell Square) and was associated with the Bective House College. Originally the Bective House Seminary for Young Gentlemen, the preparatory academy was long favored by families with an eye on Trinity College for their sons.

Woods himself would later buy the school, but in the mid-1850s he took students privately. Rutland Square itself was ideally located for the Stokers; the family had moved yet again, to 17 Buckingham Street, Summerhill, only blocks away. Thornley had previously been sent to Wymondham Grammar, a well-regarded boarding school in England; that expense may well have necessitated a less costly option for Bram, and an independent tutor was far less expensive than the faculty and resources of a full school. One special feature of Rutland Square, on the site presently occupied by the Garden of Remembrance (commemorating the 1916 Easter Rising), was a large playing field, easily accessible to the students. Here they eagerly sharpened their skills at rugby football, a game then rapidly gaining popularity in Britain, especially among students and enlisted men. Stoker would later be an enthusiastic player at Trinity.

What did Reverend Woods make of the odd boy presented to him around the age of eleven? Stoker had possessed normal motor skills for only about three years. Yet, since he had already been presented with his own inscribed Bible, his basic reading skills were presumably in place, giving credence to Charlotte's possible role as homeschooler. And by the age of twelve his verbal gifts, mathematical aptitude, and generally prodigious capacity for assimilating and organizing information would have been more than evident.

But on a purely developmental level he was unusual indeed. Illness had robbed him of many basic formative experiences and socialization, and now, with only thirty-six months of anything approaching normal volition and mobility, he was about to become a prototypical "little adult," faced with daunting responsibilities. It was the beginning of a life pattern of punishing overwork and an obsessive drive to overachievement.

At the cusp of adolescence, Stoker was lucky to be a member of the middle class, however tentative and precarious. His counterparts in the artisan and working classes faced brutal conditions in an age that placed almost no regulations on child labor. The mills and factories exploited children as a grueling matter of course. Perhaps the most horrible occupations for young children were those of "apprentice" chimney sweeps, who began work as early as the age of three, whose skills were useless after they had grown too big, and who were often permanently incapacitated by skeletal deformities and respiratory ailments brought on by their toil.

What Stoker had in common with these unfortunate youngsters was a harsh Protestant work ethic (for poor Catholics, less a value than a cruelly imposed condition of political and economic life). Everyone had to work and strive. Survival of the family often depended upon all members pulling their own weight, and more. In the case of the Stokers, the education of their sons was more about long-range stability than immediate survival, although in the end even several successfully educated sons would never provide true economic security for their aging parents.

Bram passed the Trinity entrance examination but placed only fortieth in a class of fifty-one. Ranking just under the twentieth percentile—less than half the average score—did not bode well, at least under Charlotte's exacting standards. One might have expected an imaginative boy who was "already a bit of a scribbler" to pursue a moderatorship (an honors degree) in literature at college, but in his distracted dreaminess he may not have had any particular goals except those his parents, who were paying the bills, dictated. For the Michaelmas term in the autumn of 1864 he was enrolled in the no-nonsense, dry-as-dust Ordinary Course of Studies, emphasizing Greek, Latin, mathematics, and physics. Not until the third year, as Junior Sophisters, were students scheduled to have cursory exposure to classical Roman drama, and even then nothing beyond Euripides's *Medea* and Terence's *Adelphi*. Nowhere in his assigned reading could Stoker expect to encounter such stirring and essential classics as Euripides's *The Oresteia* or Sophocles's *Oedipus Rex*, the comedies of Aristophanes, the basic dramatic and literary concepts of Aristotle's *Poetics*, nor anything whatsoever of Shakespeare or English literature. The young man who later spent much of his career immersed in the Shakespearean *Sturm und Dräng* of Sir Henry Irving would discover the Bard of Avon on his own.

Tuition, exclusive of room and board, was charged by social and economic rank. Noblemen paid £60 upon entrance and another £33 at half year; Fellow Commoners £30/£16; Pensioners £15/£8; and Sizars £5/£0. The Stoker family qualified as Pensioners. Bram lived at home during his studies and avoided the costs of boarding.

Religious observance was a strict daily requirement ("Roman Catholics[2]

---

[2] Following British religious emancipation in 1829, Catholics could no longer be banned from Trinity altogether, but they were relegated to second-class status and could never become fellows or professors. Catholics who nonetheless desired admission required the express permission of their bishop, a restriction that did not end until the 1970s.

and Dissidents excluded"), with students expected to attend morning and evening prayer services. According to the *Dublin University Calendar* for 1865, "On Sundays and holidays, and also at Evening Prayer on Saturdays, and the eves of such holidays as have vigils, all students must wear surplices, with the hoods belonging to their degrees, if they be Graduates. But on Ash-Wednesday and Good Friday gowns are worn." The rules were ritualistically enforced, as the *Calendar* made clear: "*Correction.*—at half-past eight o'clock on Saturday evenings the junior Dean attends in the hall, and reads out the names of all students who have been punished for neglect of duties or other offenses during the week. It is in the interest of those who can excuse themselves to be present, and if the excuses are extended to the Dean, the fines are taken off."

Since Stoker had been raised in an observant Protestant home, including daily prayers and a mother who maintained a formal list of the "Rules for Domestic Happiness" according to Christian principles, religious obligations wouldn't have been particularly burdensome. It is interesting, however, that his later first-person, nonfiction writings contain no mention of his personal religious convictions or practices. But repeated references to God, prayers, and praying would erupt in nearly all the twenty-seven chapters of *Dracula*.

"Every day let your eyes be fixed on God through the Lord Jesus Christ," Charlotte's first rule reads, "that by the influence of his Holy Spirit you may receive your mercies as coming from him, and that you may use them to his glory." Although it is not clear whether she wrote these commandments herself or, far more likely, transcribed them from another source, "domestic" in Charlotte's usage means "marital," and the rules all speak to the relations between husband and wife. They outline an approach to life that is strikingly at odds with family descriptions of Charlotte's willful, dominating personality. "Whenever you perceive a languor in your affections, suspect yourself," "Always conciliate," and "Forbearance is the trial and grace of this life" are not sentiments that comport well with the legend of a woman who relished cracking the whip. For all her supposed disappointment at Abraham's lack of career drive, she reminded herself on paper, at least, "Forget not that one of you must die first; one of you must feel the pang and charm of separation. A thousand little errors may then wound the survivor's heart." An element of humility and even contrition runs through Charlotte's "Rules," although nowhere in her papers is there evidence of any regret for the ax murder she committed in Sligo at the age of twelve. Surely the name-less cholera victim whose hand she severed bled out and died. A doomed, disease-maddened mob breaking into the family's house would hardly have carried tourniquets, much less the necessary tools to cauterize a spurting stump. Is it possible that her fervent rules, with the self-exhortation to "Pray constantly, you need much prayer, prayer will engage God on your behalf," helped her address conflicts outside her marriage as well?

Like most young people in their inaugural college terms, Stoker was exposed to a more expansive number of ideas, religious and otherwise, than at any time in his sixteen years on earth. For nearly half his natural life before freshman matriculation, his universe had been constricted to a sickroom and his mother's hovering apprehension. At Trinity there were Dissenters and Catholics, politics both worldly and academic, and gener-ally more things in heaven and on earth than his family's domesticated, Protestant, nose-to-the-grindstone virtues had ever made room for. With clockwork regularity, he had moved with his always-struggling clan every few years, never developing a strong sense of place or permanence, but now he was part of a university and traditions that had held their own for 175 years.

His assigned tutor was Dr. George Ferdinand Shaw. In the first year, reading for Junior Freshmen included, in Greek, the three Olynthiac Orations of Demosthenes and, in Latin, Cicero's *Milo*. Euclid's mathemat-ics, including arithmetic, algebra, and trigonometry, filled out a somewhat dreary curriculum. His second year, from November 1865 through the spring of 1866, offered considerably more mental stimulation, with the requisite courses in logic (via John Locke), Plato's *Socratic Dialogues*, more Cicero, and revisitation of Virgil and Homer (the *Aeneid*, as well as the *Iliad* and the *Odyssey*), the latter two authors almost certainly having been part of Reverend Woods's curriculum.

But the most interesting second-year text for Stoker was Victor Cousin's *Elements of Psychology*, a work not much referenced today but seminal in its time. Its lasting impact on Stoker is evidenced by the mention of Cousin more than four decades later in the introduction to his penultimate book, *Famous Impostors*. Cousin was a French philosopher and educator who offered a strong rebuke to creeping materialism, arguing for the concur-rent existence of an immaterial, immortal soul and an innate "natural intelligence" independent of the body and sensations.

Cousin's philosophical eclecticism bridged many of the divisions between science and religion that would intensify throughout the nineteenth century, especially after the publication of Darwin's *The Descent of Man* in 1871. Cousin's view of God was expansive: "He is one and several, eternity and time, space and number, essence and life, individuality and totality, beginning, middle, and end; at the top of the ladder of existence and at the humblest round; infinite and finite both together; a trinity, in fine, being at once God, nature, and humanity." Cousin's scriptural cadences were rhetorically compelling, but some detractors accused him of promulgating pantheism rather than Christianity. The idea of a God who didn't sit remotely on a celestial throne but instead permeated everything made Cousin attractive to the American transcendentalists, especially Ralph Waldo Emerson.

In the lengthy introduction to *Elements of Psychology* by its English translator, Caleb S. Henry, Stoker became acquainted with the concept

Stoker's second-year reading at Trinity College included the French intellectual and educator Victor Cousin, whose philosophical psychology attempted to bridge a widening gap between materialism and spirituality.

of "sensualism," also known as "sensationism" or "sensationalism." In his critique of eighteenth-century thought, Cousin rebuked as dehumanizing the notion of all reality and meaning being reduced to sensory stimulation: "Sensualism was the reigning doctrine," wrote Henry. "All knowledge and truth were held to be derived from Experience; and the domain of Experience was limited exclusively to Sensation. The influence of this doctrine spread to every development of intellectual activity—art, morals, politics, and religion, no less than the physical and economical sciences." This "new faith" managed to supersede "the forgotten or ill-taught doctrines of Christianity. It was in all books, in all conversations; and, as a decisive proof of its conquest and credit, passed into instruction." The resulting degeneration of intellectual and educational standards, Cousin suggested, had led directly to the chaos of the French Revolution.

Although Cousin considered the reign of philosophical sensualism/ sensationism at an end, the descended, secondhand idea of literary sensationalism was by the early 1860s coloring the reception of wildly popular novels like Wilkie Collins's *The Woman in White* (1859–60) and Mary Elizabeth Braddon's *Lady Audley's Secret* (1861–62). Stoker knew both books well, and each dealt with female insanity, asylums, and sociopathic crime. Sensation novels had successfully appropriated the popular-reading niche formerly occupied by writers like Ann Radcliffe and Matthew Lewis. Unlike the Gothic novel, sensation fiction took place in the very modern present, the past figuratively represented by atavistic criminality instead of ancient, moldering castles. A psychological primitivism replaced histrionic history. *Dracula*, of course, would draw upon both traditions, pitting modern characters against medieval menace in a single, compulsively readable narrative.

Critics of sensation novels worried that mere descriptions of extreme emotions and actions could be as mentally overstimulating as the actual experiences themselves, with potentially dehumanizing effects. In a nutshell, the perceived harm of such entertainment was the fear of literally becoming what you consumed or beheld—a very primitive response, but one endlessly echoed even today by censors of all stripes. It was a rather crude reduction of the concerns of Cousin—who at least believed in the power of God-given moral knowledge—but Victorians who felt religion slipping away were inclined to distrust encroaching materiality as a simple matter of caution.

Critiques and condemnations of sensationalism constituted a kind of

pseudoscience closely aligned to the nineteenth-century cults of mesmerism, phrenology, and spiritualism. All made grandiose claims about the
connections between the material world and the besieged citadel of the
self or soul, increasingly and alarmingly viewed by conventional science as
a mere by-product of the brain. Phrenology (the purported revelation of
personality through cranial analysis) amounted to a kind of physical mind
reading or divination. The theatrical rituals and protocols of séances and
mesmerism employed faux-methodologies that seemed to offer a vernac-
ular competition to the scientific method and access to ethereal realms.
Pseudoscience reassured the anxious that there was still an unseen yet
accessible transcendent reality, that the afterlife *did* exist, that the human
mind was something greater than the physical brain. Pseudoscientific and
supernatural inquiry intrigued Stoker all his life. And, of course, crises of
religious faith and existential riddles of the "who am I, what am I" variety, and the seeking of alternatives to conventional religion, are common
among college students and young adults, especially those who have lived
sheltered lives.

As a child, Stoker practically inhabited a cocoon. But as a college student, he had privileged access to one of the great repositories of knowledge
in Great Britain—the Trinity College Library—and it must have been a revelation akin to his sudden ability to walk. Only four years before his matriculation, the ceiling of the library's stately, nearly two-hundred-foot Long
Room had been raised to its present, barrel-vaulted height, the first level
lined with white marble busts of the greatest thinkers and writers in history.
The Long Room today is one of the most iconic and atmospheric scholarly spaces in the world. The library was one of the designated copyright
depositories for books published throughout Great Britain; however, it was
exempted from accepting acquisitions automatically and chose very selec-
tively. While the institution's long-standing refusal to catalog the complete
poems of Walt Whitman (a writer soon to put a mesmeric spell upon Stoker)
was clearly censorious, it also more generally reflected a bibliographic
blind spot for whole swaths of nineteenth-century writing, even titles now
considered canonical. The library's printed catalog for 1872 reveals that
Stoker would have looked elsewhere to discover Mary Shelley's *Frankenstein*,
for instance (though her travel writings and edited volumes of her husband's writings had made the grade), or anything of Poe except his poetry.
John Polidori's "The Vampyre" (1818) was there, and Gothic classics like

Horace Walpole's seminal *The Castle of Otranto* were likewise present, while Ann Radcliffe and Matthew "Monk" Lewis were completely ignored. Emily Brontë's *Wuthering Heights* was also conspicuous by its absence. Sensation novels were available in a wafer-thin sampling including *Lady Audley's Secret* and *The Woman in White.*

In poetry, Baudelaire's notorious *Les fleurs de mal* (1857) with its "Metamorphoses of the Vampire" seems to have been repellant enough to be repelled itself, though Henry Thomas Liddell's "The Vampire Bride" (1833) had accepted its invitation to cross the Trinity threshold:

> He lay like a corse 'neath the Demon's force,
> And she wrapp'd him in a shround;
> And she fixed her teeth his heart beneath,
> And she drank of the warm life-blood!

Several of the nonfiction books Stoker consulted for *Dracula* were available to him as a Trinity undergraduate, though it is an open question whether his fascination for the paranormal, already keen, would have led

The Long Room at Trinity College Dublin Library as it appeared in the 1860s.

to curious perusal. Augustin Calmet's *The Phantom World* (1850), including an important historical treatise on vampires, was there, along with Sabine Baring-Gould's *The Book of Were-wolves* (1865) and *Curious Myths of the Middle Ages* (1866). Two other books on the occult, Joseph Taylor's *Apparitions* (1815) and *Fiends, Ghosts and Sprites* by John Netten Radcliffe (1854; author no relation to Ann Radcliffe), also escaped embargo by Trinity's gatekeepers.

Elsewhere in the library were back numbers of the *Dublin University Magazine*, in which Stoker could have found solemnly credulous essays on mesmerism as a bridge between life and death, as well as the ghostly short stories and serialized novels of J. (for Joseph) Sheridan Le Fanu, one of Dublin's literary luminaries, if not its most prominent contemporary star. Great-nephew of the Restoration playwright Richard Brinsley Sheridan, and Trinity educated himself, Le Fanu had purchased the *Dublin University Magazine* in 1861, the better to showcase his own work. An Irishman of Huguenot extraction, Le Fanu was greatly influenced by the eighteenth-century mystic Emanuel Swedenborg, whose philosophy embraced extradimensional angels, demons, and even extraterrestrial entities.

Stoker entered Trinity College just as the *Dublin University Magazine* finished its serialization of Le Fanu's sinister novel *Uncle Silas*, which was then immediately published in book form. Le Fanu added a defensive introductory note, arguing that his novel—a story of an orphan's peril at the hands of her cadaverous guardian and her equally unpleasant governess—did not deserve the label of "sensation" fiction, despite its being exactly that. Whether Stoker read *Uncle Silas* immediately or later, it had a strong effect on him. A few decades later, he would specifically recommend the book to his son—the only literary endorsement ever reported by his family. The book was a teeming storehouse of macabre metaphor and description, which he would add to the wealth of otherworldly words and images he began mentally amassing in childhood.

In particular, Le Fanu's description of Silas Ruthyn would eventually merge seamlessly in Stoker's mind with that of Ambrosio, and the licentious Capuchin of *The Monk* (a hawkish profile, conjoined eyebrows, and a flamelike, penetrating gaze) with Silas's own unearthly presence: "a face like marble, with a fearful monumental look," "dazzlingly pale" and "bloodless," like a "ghost" with "hollow, fiery, awful eyes!" Silas's voice is "preternaturally soft," his aspect "spectral," and he dresses in "necromantic black."

Although Le Fanu stopped short of identifying Silas as one of the walking dead (the novel was a chilling thriller, but not one of his ghost stories), the vampiric evocations were made complete in his villain's surname, Ruthyn — a barely altered version of Ruthven, the eponymous character of Polidori's "The Vampyre." Polidori's story was the first, and most imitated, vampire narrative in English, having inspired several popular stage adaptations in England and France, as well as a German opera. Later, Le Fanu, and Stoker especially, would give Polidori a memorable run for his blood money.

In his memoir *Seventy Years of Irish Life*, Le Fanu's brother, William, gives an illuminating anecdote about Joseph's youthful imagination: "At an early age my brother gave promise of the powers which he afterwards attained. When between five and six years old a favourite amusement of his was to draw little pictures, and under each he would print some moral which the drawing was meant to illustrate." One William recalled especially and regarded as "a masterpiece of art, conveying a solemn warning. A balloon was high in the air; the two aeronauts had fallen from the boat, and were tumbling headlong to the ground; underneath was printed in fine bold Roman letters, 'See the effects of trying to go to heaven.'"

Elsewhere in his book, William gives an interesting account of his own experiments in the "electro-biology" of hypnotism. "I have made a lady, who had the greatest horror of rats, imagine that my pocket-handkerchief, which I had rolled up in my hand, was one, and when she rushed away terrified, I made her think she was a cat, and she at once began to mew, seized the pocket-handkerchief in her teeth, and shook it," he boasted. "I have made people believe they were hens, judges, legs of mutton, generals, frogs, and famous men; and this in rapid succession. Indeed so complete was their obedience, that I have again and again refused, when asked, to suggest to them that they were dead."

Having a keen interest in mesmerism, the younger Le Fanu could not have been unaware of Edgar Allan Poe's "Facts in the Case of M. Valdemar" (1845), a sensational cautionary tale about the dangers of mixing death and hypnosis, in which prolonged suspended animation reduces the title character, upon waking, to an alarming condition. Poe's breathless narrator recounts, "As I rapidly made the mesmeric passes, amid ejaculations of 'Dead! dead!' absolutely *bursting* from the tongue and not the lips of the sufferer, his whole frame at once—within the space of a single minute or even less, shrunk—crumbled—absolutely *rotted* away beneath my hands. Upon the bed, before that whole company, there lay a nearly liquid mass of loathsome—of detestable putridity."

The story was published in England in pamphlet form the following year as "'In Articulo Mortis.' An Astounding and Horrifying Narrative Shewing the Extraordinary Power of Mesmerism in Arresting the Progress of Death." Since "Mr. Edgar A. Poe, Esq., of New York" was a known working journalist, and the piece was not labeled as one of his fictions, many took the story as fact. Poe's creepy spin on the dangers of mesmerism was additionally startling because it threw cold water on the pseudoscientific claims about trance communication with the dead, a major feature of the spiritualism movement rapidly growing in both America and Europe. Death was death, M. Valdemar's story seemed to say, and in the end we all went to dust—or its loathsome liquid equivalent.

A growing interest in extracurricular esoterica may have caused a precipitous drop in Stoker's grades toward the end of his second year. His interest in the fantastic and occult certainly took him to a cabinet of curiosities just across the street from the Trinity campus that advertised regularly in the *Dublin Evening Mail*.

MAGIC PHANTASMAGORIA AND
DISSOLVING VISION LANTERNS

A large collection of Dioramic Effects, Astonishing
Mechanical Contrivances and Illusions, including Ghosts,
Acrobats, Magic Visions, and other novelties.

Mr. E. Solomons, Optician, Mathematical
and Philosophical Instrument Maker
(Established in Dublin 50 years)
19 Nassau Street

But it was Stoker's college career that was becoming a real "dissolving vision." Thirty years later, he would claim that he "graduated with honours in pure mathematics." This wasn't a small distortion of the truth— it was simply a lie, completely unsubstantiated by the records. The claim was all the worse in light of criticism that, in poor comparison to other

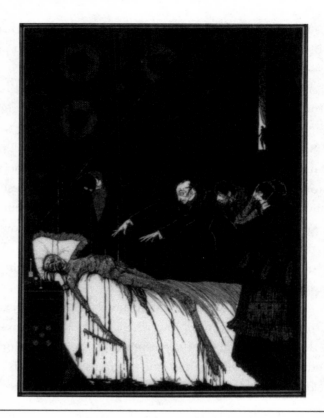

Irish illustrator Harry Clarke's nightmarish rendering of Edgar Allan Poe's
"The Facts in the Case of M. Valdemar."

British universities, Trinity's "average number of mathematical honourees has been a fraction over three. And this in a mathematical university!" In Stoker's year of graduation, only two such honors were bestowed.

Even in today's world, such a misrepresentation of one's college record might have serious professional repercussions. Perhaps making the claim so late in his life (1906, six years before his death) did not seem to him a substantial risk. It is also possible that decades of theatrical press-agenting made routine puffery such a second-nature reflex that he came to believe his own publicity. Granted, he had some reason, if not an excuse, to fudge the record. Stoker didn't merely fail to graduate cum laude. He was an uninspired and mediocre student; his low entrance exam scores had been prescient. One can only imagine his mother's disappointment. Stoker fell painfully short of Charlotte's expectations, coming nowhere near the "second out of a thousand" status she would have disdained anyway. As the narrator of one of his later novels, *The Mystery of the Sea* (1902), would explain, "At school I was, though secretly ambitious, dull as to results." In college he seems to have been positively bored.

He achieved only middling examination grades for two years, after which his attendance became erratic and finally nonexistent. The academic archives themselves are intact; it is only Stoker's records that are missing. No doubt with his family's encouragement—or outright insistence—and through his father's connections, he applied for and received a civil service post at Dublin Castle in 1866. It was a full-time, six-day-a-week position, so it's not surprising that his academic status was "downgraded" in 1867. At this point, his academic career appears to crash completely.

But after a year's absence, he would return—as an utterly changed person who would complete his education in a thoroughly unorthodox way.

First and foremost, all vestiges of the sickly child who couldn't control his limbs were gone. Growth spurts in very late adolescence are not unknown, and in Stoker's case might well explain the sudden, keen interest in athletics two years into his college career. There is no indication whatsoever that he participated, or had any interest, in sports before 1866, when his involvement in physical culture became both time-consuming and obsessive for the next four years. As he would observe of himself fictionally in *The Mystery of the Sea*, at college "my big body and athletic powers gave me a certain position in which I had to overcome my natural shyness."

With no prior challenges or visibility, he suddenly scored a victory in the Dublin University Foot Races of 1866. For the university's general sports competition on May 22 and 23, 1867, Stoker won the champion cup, an engraved silver tankard, one of many still proudly owned by his descendants. The next year saw him win the seven-mile walking race. He demonstrated impressive expertise on the trapeze, in vaulting, and in rowing. In rugby, he played on both the Trinity and the Civil Service teams.

While academic records of his last four years are nil, there is ample documentation of ambitious extracurricular activities that extended far beyond sports. He was the only Trinity man to have served as both auditor of the College Historical Society and president of the Philosophical Society, the top positions attainable. The Hist and the Phil (as they were informally known) were Trinity's extracurricular organizations dedicated to discussion and debate. In addition to undergraduates, both groups included as members prominent and influential figures such as Sir William

As both an undergraduate and graduate, Stoker excelled athletically at Trinity College Dublin competitions, depicted here in the **Illustrated London News,** *1874.*

Wilde (father of Oscar, and a distinguished eye surgeon, statistician, and ethnographer), John Pentland Mahaffy, Trinity's leading classicist and later its provost, and Edward Dowden, an academic wunderkind who would become the college's first professor of English Literature and a special mentor to Stoker. Given his interests, it is not surprising that Stoker chose "Sensationalism; in Fiction and Society" for the title of a paper he delivered at the Phil in the spring of 1868. Among the literary topics debated at the Hist was the proposal "That the Novels of the Nineteenth Century are more Immoral in their Tendency than those of the Eighteenth." Stoker opposed the motion. Intriguing as these and many other topics are, Stoker's paper on sensationalism has not survived, and the substance of the debate argument was not recorded.

Both societies were excellent places for Stoker to network and curry favor with some of the most powerful men in Dublin. He may have needed to. With all his time devoted to his job at Dublin Castle, athletics, and the Hist and the Phil, he completely neglected formal academic study. Yet, on Shrove Tuesday in April 1870, he was—somehow—conferred his baccalaureate.

How on earth was it possible for Stoker to circumvent a normal course of lectures and examinations and nonetheless receive a degree? The *Dublin University Calendar* makes no mention of the possibility of such an unusual arrangement. All histories of Trinity College in the nineteenth century emphasize the central importance of examinations. But at Trinity, a certain amount of self-tutelage could lead to advancement. For example, J. P. Mahaffy contemptuously called Edward Dowden "an autodidaktos" who "never worked under a Master." According to Max Cullinan, an especially harsh critic of the institution in the *Fortnightly Review*, "A most distinguished Dublin 'grinder' [an academic coach] recently told this writer that his pupils frequently ask him whether they ought to attend lectures. His answer is, that, if they have plenty of time to spare, lectures can't do them any harm."

Stoker's interpersonal skills and personal magnetism certainly had

Bram Stoker, age twenty-five, serving as auditor of the Trinity College Historical Society for 1872–73.

something to do with his receiving what was essentially an honorary degree based on his extracurricular activities and personal popularity. The role of his tutor, Dr. Shaw, is unknown, though they stayed on friendly terms long after Stoker's graduation. But he certainly knew how to deploy personal charm, and he must have deployed it strategically and could easily have played the role of teacher's pet if necessary. He was unusually bright, tall, athletic, and while not extraordinarily handsome was more than passably good-looking and, by 1870, quite accustomed to impressing people with both his brain and his body. He would later write, "I represented in my own person something of that aim of university education *mens sana in corpore sans* [from Juvenal: a sound mind in a sound body]." As one female acquaintance in Dublin remembered him, "He was an excellent 'party' young man, and of course, always had heaps of invitations." She described his confident, imposing physicality: "When he stood up to dance, [he] had a way of making a charge, which effectively cleared a passage through the most thronged ball-rooms. Everyone made way for Stoker—his coming was like a charge of cavalry, or a rush of fixed bayonets—nobody dreamed of not giving way before him, and so he and his partner had it all their own way. How my heart used to jump in my dancing days when Bram Stoker asked me for a waltz! I knew that it meant triumph, twirling, ecstasy, elysium, ices, and flirtation!"

He would have been attractive to men as well, on any number of levels, and in ways that were not overtly homosexual. However Stoker understood or found advantage in the homosocial dynamics of Trinity College, he knew how to work the all-male environment effectively enough to achieve an all-important objective: the validation of a college degree. By whatever means he used, he succeeded.

Because everyone made way for Bram Stoker.

Nonetheless, he would soon turn the trajectory of his own life over to the spell of a man far more charismatic and persuasive than himself, a legendary exercise in male bonding that would control and dominate his life for the next three decades.

Stoker's interest in the theatre had continued straight through his Trinity years. He attended and greatly admired *Ali Baba and the Forty Thieves*, the Theatre Royal's pantomime for 1867. His love for wonder tales brought to life onstage had never left him. The other holiday offerings at the Theatre

Royal during his college career included *The House That Jack Built* (1864), *Beauty and the Beast* (1865), *Sinbad the Sailor* (1866), *Little Red Riding Hood* (1868), *Robinson Crusoe* (1869), and *The White Cat* (1870).

At the end of August 1867, Stoker attended a production of Sheridan's comedy classic *The Rivals*, performed by a London company at the Theatre Royal. It is a bit surprising Stoker had not chosen another of the company's offerings—an adaptation of *Lady Audley's Secret*, which had proven just as much of a sensation on the stage as on the page. But had he chosen the frightening charms of Lady Lucy Audley over the verbal manhandling of Mrs. Malaprop, he would have missed a performance destined to change his life.

In the leading role of Captain Absolute, who woos the beautiful Lydia Languish under the assumed identity of a lowly ensign, was an actor whom Stoker found absolutely riveting. His stage name was Henry Irving. Born John Henry Brodribb (who had considered—and wisely rejected—"Henry Baringtone" as a professional moniker), Irving was a self-trained performer from the provinces who, like Stoker, had become infatuated with the theatre as a young boy. Unlike Stoker, who had fallen under the spell of the pantomime, Irving had a stage epiphany at a production of *Hamlet*.

Watching Irving act, Stoker had an epiphany of his own, one that exceeded even his discovery of the Christmas pantos, where his life had become real. Pantomime had introduced him to the theatre as a spectator, and now he was beholding the transformative figure who would invite him to step across the threshold. He was stunned, though hardly rendered speechless, by the impressively tall, angularly handsome thespian. "What I saw, to my amazement and delight, was a patrician figure as real as the persons of one's dreams, and endowed with the same poetic grace . . . handsome, distinguished, self-dependent; compact of grace and slumbrous energy. A man of quality who stood out from his surroundings on the stage as a being of another social world. A figure full of dash and fine irony, and whose ridicule seemed to *bite*; buoyant with the joy of life; self-conscious; an inoffensive egoist even in his love-making; of supreme and unsurpassable insolence, veiled and shrouded in his fine quality of manner."

To Stoker, Irving was a supreme, swashbuckling presence that "could only be possible in an age when the answer to insolence was a sword-thrust; when only those dare to be insolent who could depend to the last on the heart and brain and arm behind the blade."

MR. HENRY IRVING.
ELLIOTT & FRY   55, BAKER STREET, W.
                 AND AT 7, GLOUCESTER TERRACE, S.W.
                        COPYRIGHT

Souvenir postcard of Henry Irving as a rising actor in the 1870s.

Today, Stoker's first-sight, swept-away infatuation with Irving might well be described by discreet circumlocutions of "man crush" or "bromance," but they don't do justice to a fixation that would eventually swell into an all-consuming, lifelong preoccupation. Stoker's later, intimate friend Hall Caine commented on the Irving connection, "I say without any hesitation that I have never seen, no do I expect to see, such absorption of one man's life in the life another," and called Stoker's devotion to the actor "the strongest love that man may feel for man." The homoerotic implications were not openly commented upon during Stoker's lifetime, but it is significant that the words "love" and "loving," in Stoker's personal writing and in his correspondence, are used almost exclusively to describe relationships with men. Though women could be greatly admired, closely befriended, or even married, depictions and discussions of heterosexual romance would remain within the constructs of Stoker's fiction.

The Irving epiphany roughly coincided with the crumbling of Stoker's academic work, and a general distraction with activities unconnected to formal study can easily be inferred. It would be nearly five years before Irving returned to Dublin—five years in which Stoker would throw himself into as much extracurricular distraction as his day job at Dublin Castle would allow, and that amounted to quite a bit. His modest salary still allowed him pit seats at the Theatre Royal. The surfeit of theatrical interests, athletic achievements, and go-for-broke commitments to the Hist and the Phil (with all the nighttime reading and preparation they demanded) raises the question: When, exactly, did "Abraham Stoker, Jnr." ever sleep?

He didn't directly witness Irving's spectacular rise during this period, but the actor's growing fame was steadily noted in the press. Irving reached a major professional plateau in 1871 with *The Bells*, a melodrama about an innkeeper, Mathias, whose carefully concealed murder of a Polish Jew is involuntarily revealed by court-ordered hypnotism and a truly show-stopping confession. The overwhelmingly positive reception of *The Bells* reflected not only Irving's increasingly dazzling artistry but also the degree to which the general public enthusiastically responded to the claims made for mesmerism and pseudoscience in general.

What Stoker didn't know about Irving included the tumultuous details of his hero's domestic life. Irving had been married to the former Florence O'Callaghan since 1869. She had pursued him in the face of her father's disapproval, only to be disappointed by the realities of the theatrical life, particularly the long hours and Irving's garrulous actor friends, whom she found unbearable. After having their first child, the couple separated, then reconciled. Pregnant again, Florence was tired, resentful, and venomous. On the very night of his London triumph in *The Bells*, she snapped at him on the carriage ride home: "Are you going to keep making a fool of yourself like this for the rest of your life?"

Irving responded by abruptly quitting the carriage at the very corner of Hyde Park where he had proposed to her. He never forgave Florence, and never lived with or even spoke to her again. When his second son was born, he refused to attend the christening. The Irvings would remain married in name only.

Stoker, who would ultimately prove more unconditionally supportive of Irving than any wife, keenly anticipated the actor's return to the Theatre Royal in late spring 1871, not with *The Bells* but with a meticulously studied character turn in James Albery's comedy *Two Roses*. Once more, the local press couldn't have cared less. According to Stoker, "There was not a word in any of the papers about the acting of any of the accomplished players who took part in it; not even their names."

In Stoker's telling it was a personal last straw, the culmination of "my growing discontent with the attention accorded to the stage in the local newspapers," in whose pages he could find no reflection of his own keen appreciation of the theatre, and most particularly his feelings about Henry Irving. While Stoker would have us believe that the public was being deprived of his hero, Irving himself had a very different account of the Dublin engagement. "*Two Roses* has created in Dublin a theatrical excitement unknown for many years," he wrote. "The dress circle (there are no stalls) which is the largest in any theatre out of London, holds 300 persons (and during our engagement the price has been raised from 4s. to 5s.) and on Saturday night it was crowded and on Friday too, with the elite and fashion of the city. This is here unprecedented. The dress circle, I am told, and sometimes with the most popular stars, is generally empty—comparatively and excepting Italian opera, which is here a great institution, such audiences as we have had are never drawn to the theatre."

Stoker overestimated the power of the local press. And it was probably not the goal of motivating audiences as much as an ego-driven hunger to be published and read and recognized and, above all, become part of a world where giants like Henry Irving strode that led him to become a drama critic. He had begun keeping a journal of colorful local sketches and story ideas, and by this time had a drawer full of fictional juvenilia—the "scribblings" later described by his son. His burning desire to express himself on the printed page couldn't have been less intense than his quest for athletic prizes, an activity that was now coming to an end.

Some might have considered his opinions (both of the theatre and of himself) prematurely lofty for a twenty-three-year-old, but at some time between May and November of 1871 Stoker took his grievances and ambitions directly to Dr. Henry Maunsell, co-proprietor of the *Dublin Evening Mail*.

The fact that it took him nearly half a year to approach the *Mail* suggests that he tried other publications without success. Since Maunsell's ownership partner was J. Sheridan Le Fanu, it has often been suggested that the celebrated author of *Uncle Silas*, which Stoker greatly admired, somehow took a personal interest in the younger writer and facilitated his employment. But Le Fanu (who, a decade earlier, had also purchased the *Dublin University Magazine*) had grown increasingly reclusive after the death of his wife, who succumbed in 1859 after a losing struggle with an emotional disorder that included terrifying religious visions. Le Fanu thereafter became known as "Dublin's Invisible Prince," rarely venturing out of his Merrion Square residence, where he continued to write in solitude. In 1871, he was nearing his own death while preparing for publication a final collection of stories, *In a Glass Darkly*, containing the provocative vampire tale *Carmilla*, a major influence on *Dracula*. Since he had no hand in the day-to-day running of the *Mail*, speculation about his acquaintance with Stoker is mostly conjecture to force an interpersonal connection to *Carmilla*. Given Stoker's lifelong weakness for name-dropping, had he had even the slightest relationship with Dublin's leading literary lion, he would surely have been the first to tell.

In Dublin, plays opened on Monday evenings, but due to the time required to typeset and print the paper—the contents had to be "put to bed" around midnight—the timeliest reviews didn't appear before Wednesday. The aspiring critic pointed out to Maunsell, quite rightly, that such an institutionalized delay was unfair to both the presenting theatre and the touring artists, who were often in Dublin for only a week. Stoker was a speedy writer and offered to quickly prepare first-night reviews for publication the next day, to be followed by more leisurely appraisals later in the week. Maunsell couldn't have required much arm-twisting. After all, Dublin's theatres were the paper's most prominent advertisers, their bills posted each day on page one, top left, just under the masthead—the most advantageous and expensive placement possible. Anything that helped sell tickets helped the *Mail* as well, especially when snippets of its own reviews were recycled and paid for by the typeset line.

Maunsell told him that there was no money for the work, which was usually assigned to staffers. Stoker accepted nonetheless, later justifying his financial sacrifice as a kind of moral cause: "When the floodgates of Comment are opened, there comes with the rush of clean water all the scum and rubbish which has accumulated." And, although he would have us believe his high-minded goal was to increase the quantity of clean critical water, another motivation is immediately discernible. Regular theatregoing was expensive on a civil servant's salary, and about to become more so with the highly anticipated opening of another Dublin playhouse, the Gaiety, which would virtually double the local stage offerings—as well as the cost of attendance for a theatre-smitten young writer. Complimentary reviewer's tickets were the keys to a kingdom he had long dreamed of entering.

He was also given unusual editorial latitude. "From my beginning the work," Stoker recalled, "I had an absolutely free hand."

Two weeks after his twenty-fourth birthday, on Monday, November 21, 1871, Stoker took his first night's seat as a critic at the Theatre Royal, and his review appeared on Tuesday, a respectful evaluation of *Amy Robsart*, Andrew Halliday's adaptation of the Sir Walter Scott novel *Kenilworth*. The title character was the wife of Robert Dudley, the first Earl of Leicester; the plot involved her clandestine and long-endured rivalry with Queen Elizabeth for his affections, and her ambiguous death, dramatized as murder in both the novel and the play. It is interesting to note, in this inaugural review, that Stoker tipped his hat toward the specific kind of production that first drew him to the stage. "In a spectacular sense it is simply excellent," he wrote. "The one scene representing the grand pageant at Kenilworth [Castle] will suffer nothing by comparison with the finest scenes in our best pantomimes."

All of Stoker's reviews were published anonymously, but his identity was no secret, his authorial voice easily recognizable behind the royal-sounding editorial "we" affected by the twenty-four-year-old, self-appointed cultural arbiter of Dublin.

From the beginning, Stoker's pieces reflected a keen eye for, and interest in, visual stagecraft—scene painting, costumes ("the dresses," as they were called, for both male and female performers), and mechanical effects—all the most emphasized features of the pantomimes. "The story may be engaging, the libretto clever, and the acting good," he wrote, "but still if the scenery and appointments are not in sufficient taste and splendor, the play will be, at best, a negative success—an escape from failure." His further thoughts reflect an ongoing interest in the senses and sensationalism. "For of all the organs of sense the eye is the quickest and most correct in its working: the untrained ear may allow a discord to pass unnoticed, or the world-hardened body may be touched unknowingly, but the eye is never-failing in its receptive power; it is ever keen to judge of beauty or deformity. . . . The eye will infallibly judge of those minor details, from whose accumulated force the general effect arises."

Not at all surprising, an emphasis on vivid scene-setting would later characterize his fiction; *Dracula*'s "general effect" is achieved through a pantomime-like procession of unforgettable imagery. It is difficult to overstate the impact of theatrical pantomime on Stoker. He began his work as a critic shortly before the holidays, and when the panto arrived at the Theatre Royal at the end of December, his newspaper appraisal went beyond normal reviewing into a series of effusive essays on the art and appeal of the beloved Christmas ritual, with the most interesting appreciation saved for a completely offstage aspect: the audience itself.

"To look at the legions of sparkling eyes, the parterres of flushed cheeks and pearly teeth that rise away from the footlights to the gloom beyond the galleries—to note the innumerable types of minds and bodies of those children who are the germs of men and women of the future—is, indeed, a pleasure," he wrote, finding it "a curious study to observe the component elements of a juvenile audience," including "numerous copies of young gentlemen [each of whom] considers himself quite a man of the world, and who secretly borrows his sister's scissors to shave with, in the vain hope that he can force on his moustache by such artificial means." He then describes the theatregoing youth, who—like the precocious and opinionated theatre critic—has quite an opinion of himself. "This individual appears in very tight gloves and a very large collar. He is at first quite at his ease—very much so, indeed—and gives fierce directions as to the observance of certain of the proprieties to his younger brothers and sisters, *sotto voce*. Gradually, however, the stiffness wears off as the good fairy who has her home in the Bowers of Orange-peel and Sawdust[3] begins to assert her sway. Our young friend then takes more interest in his brothers and his sisters and less in himself, and, in the expansion of heart, the change comes over him which came to the Ancient Mariner when he saw the water snakes playing around the becalmed vessel, and 'blessed them unawares.'"

---

[3] The pelting of performers with rotten tomatoes is not noted until the late Victorian age, but the abusive implementation of orange peels dates to Shakespeare's time. An 1864 article in Charles Dickens's weekly journal *All the Year Round* describes the scent of a theatre performing a pantomime as "the old delicious inexplicable fragrance of commingled gas, damp sawdust, and squeezed orange-peel." Responding to an Edinburgh clergyman's charge in 1909 that "there are three things that stick to the theatre—they are orange peel, sawdust, and vice," Sir Herbert Beerbohm Tree responded, "If there is any orange peel in this theatre, the management will, I am sure, at once see that it is removed. I am assured sawdust is not employed in this theatre. I believe it is largely used in circuses."

Completing the Coleridge comparison, Stoker watches approvingly as his young alter ego "finds his reward, and the albatross slips from his neck," when he discards "boyish snobbishness" and takes "the first step into real manhood."

Real men are exemplified by the fathers in attendance and described collectively as "papa." They are conventional middle-class males "who, we think, in our heart of hearts, [do] not care much for ogres, or dwarfs, or fairies. We know quite well that papa could beat any ogre, if he chose. However, papa is with us now, and seems to be enjoying himself. How he laughs at the shadow scene!"

Another less domesticated and less inhibited brand of masculinity was more to Stoker's liking. Dublin was a major port city, and sailors on leave apparently took their pleasures beyond the local pubs and brothels. Stoker noticed this type with evident appreciation. "Everyone has observed the sailor in the pit, who chooses a juvenile night to go to the pantomime in preference to any other. He seems to take more enjoyment out of the play than anyone else, even the juveniles—for their enjoyment has occasional lapses into awe and fear, but his has not; indeed the giants and murderers are the most mirth-provoking to him. He does not even try to contain himself; he goes into the theatre to laugh, and is not ashamed. . . . He 'glories in the act.' He screams, roars, nay, he even chokes and gurgles with laughter, till he infects all around him with his own mirth." The other audience members "hold rather aloof from him: they are affected with some of the morbid vanity that weights so heavily on the young man with the collar and the gloves, but gradually they join his mirth." The sailor, wrote Stoker, "enjoys the pelting of the carrots, and the assault and battery of old women and policemen, as much as the wildest schoolboy in the theatre; and when [the actor] throws the policeman's helmet into the pit, he seizes it wildly and flings it back again."

Stoker also gives us a discursive theatrical aside on female family dynamics, presumably drawn from his own experience. He repeatedly refers to a boy as a sexually undifferentiated "it" acknowledged as male only in passing, an interesting echo of his own androgynous infancy. "The small child looks up with great veneration to its mother, and has a sort of well-bred affection for its older sister, who is its occasional playmate and the originator of most of its amusements; but it is chiefly to his aunt that it looks for that sympathetic appreciation of and participation in enjoyment which is so pleasant for the young and old." The mother, perhaps, "is too high above its level, its sister is too near it, but the aunt who calls mamma by her Christian name, and who knows all the little secrets of both boys and girls, she is the real friend and chosen companion of the child." The evidence? "Look how it clings to her and holds her hand when the roaring of the giants is heard. See how it turns its eyes to her for information when there is anything which it doesn't misunderstand. Mark how it looks round in the height of its enjoyment, to see if aunty likes it too, and to gather a new joy from sympathy with her. Surely," Stoker concludes, "there is no such sympathetic relative for a child, in its pleasures, at all events, as an aunt. We don't count uncles."

Since so many of Stoker's observations on pantomimes and children are obviously self-referential, a question immediately arises: Was Stoker himself ever accompanied to the theatre by an aunt, or perhaps an older female cousin? His mother definitely had no sisters. Abraham was the youngest of six children who survived childhood;[4] he had an older sister named Frances who married in 1816, but it is his unmarried sister Marian, born in 1778 (one year older than Abraham), who was likely to still be alive during Bram's childhood.

The possibility of an extended Stoker family, including a stage-struck aunt, is intriguing. It is statistically unlikely that Bram's grandfather William Stoker was an only child, and any brothers would have had sons, and the sons would have had wives. One of these might easily have been Eliza Sarah Stoker, an otherwise obscure family member represented by a single 1882 letter in the family papers. In the letter, addressed to an otherwise unidentified Mrs. Billington, Eliza describes herself as a former actress, forced into retirement and difficult circumstances after having broken her leg. Theatrical records reveal that an actress (or actresses) identified alternately as "Miss" and "Mrs." Stoker was (or were) active at London's Adelphi Theatre between 1850 and 1871. Or is it possible Eliza

---

[4] According to modern research by the Stoker family, no birthdates can be determined for any of Abraham's older siblings other than Marian, but some of their marriage dates are recorded. Peter Stoker was the oldest and married Elizabeth (maiden name unknown) around 1804; the next oldest was Frances Stoker, who married Walter Dyas, an apothecary, in 1816; Richard Stoker was the next born, marrying Olivia (maiden name unknown; died in 1853); last before Abraham was William Stoker, physician, who died in 1848, three years before his wife Frances's death in 1851.

is the "Miss Eliza Pitt (Mrs. Stoker)," born in 1801 and died in 1885, who worked at the Adelphi under her maiden name from 1821 to 1823? Stoker biographer Paul Murray has suggested that Eliza Sarah Stoker's difficult life may have been a reason Abraham cautioned his son against a life in the theatre. Another clue to Bram's knowledge of or acquaintance with Eliza is that he used the name "Billington" for the fictional solicitor who facilitates the shipment of Dracula's earth-boxes to England. It has been well established that Stoker was fond of using the names of real people in his stories.

Beyond his discussion of aunts (and dismissal of uncles), Bram closed his notice with a most intriguing statement. "Old maids are great at pantomimes," he wrote, "but we have no time to do them justice now." Here, the spinster Marian Stoker might fit the bill. Unfortunately, he never found the time to do the complete subject justice, but it would be fascinating to know Stoker's thoughts about sexual frustration and the wanton allure of the stage.

A final observation on Stoker's pantomime review is the inclusion of aunts, siblings, fathers, sailors, a curt dismissal of uncles—but no mention whatsoever of mothers as part of the cherished childhood excursion. Did Charlotte, perhaps, regard the theatre as frivolous, or of questionable morality? Such a prejudice was not at all uncommon among observant Protestants. It was the Catholics who went for pomp and theatre. Only five years later Charlotte would explicitly express her dismissive opinion of her son's idol Henry Irving as "a strolling player."

Disapproval at home might account for a condescending and slightly pompous tone that creeps into some of his reviews. Unwilling to criticize his parents directly, he can easily criticize Dublin and Dubliners generally. Some of his notices read like lecture notes that are as much demonstrations of his superior taste and theatrical knowledge as they are appraisals of performance. At times his impatience with Dublin and its audiences—already implicit in the know-it-all reviews—boils over into public scolding, as in his review of a particularly unpleasant night at the opera. "One sad drawback, we are sorry to say, is the behavior of the persons in the upper gallery," he wrote of a Theatre Royal performance of Gounod's *Faust*.

> It is simply an abominable nuisance to all the rest of the house, and ought to be at once put an end to. We cannot speak of it as anything else than a sort of revival of Donnybrook Fair. The foolish and unmanly persons

who create such a horrible din between the acts by their brawling wholly forget that the rest of the occupants of the house would much prefer perfect silence so that the past portions of the opera might dwell in their memories, and assist their pleasurable anticipation of what is to come. But instead of that they are night after night compelled to listen to vulgar attempts at singing, the coarse vanity displayed in which is the most offensive feature of the whole thing. . . . It is high time that there should be an end of what would not be tolerated in any other civilized city.

Stoker may have been especially irked because the disruptions occurred during *Faust,* an opera that particularly fascinated him and would influence the writing of *Dracula.* He attended several productions of the Gounod opera in Dublin and eventually witnessed Henry Irving play Mephistopheles in his own dramatic version more than eight hundred times, in London and on tour. Mephistopheles was a character drawn from morality plays and pantomimes and in many ways embodied the magical essence of theatre for Stoker during his formative years.

Another work that left its stamp on Stoker's imagination was J. Sheridan Le Fanu's *Carmilla,* about a vampire who cheats death for nearly two centuries. (A supernaturally extended life is also a key ingredient in *Faust.*) Published when Le Fanu was less than a year away from his own last breath, *Carmilla* would become his most famous, provocative, and influential piece of fiction—not least of all in the shadow it left upon *Dracula.* The story drew surprisingly little critical attention when it appeared, and no reviews at all in Dublin. It is set in Styria, a region of Austria, and concerns a mysterious visitor named Carmilla Karnstein, seemingly a young woman, and her passionately malignant fixation on the first-person narrator, Laura. "Sometimes after an hour of apathy, my strange and beautiful companion would take my hand and hold it with a fond pressure, renewed again and again; blushing softly, gazing in my face with languid and burning eyes, and breathing so fast that her dress rose and fell with the tumultuous respiration," reads one of its more provocative passages. To Laura, Carmilla's hungry attention "was like the ardour of a lover; it embarrassed me; it was hateful and yet overpowering; and with gloating eyes she drew me to her, and her hot lips travelled along my cheek in kisses; and she would whisper, almost in sobs, "You are mine, you *shall* be mine, and you and I are one for ever."

Due to the appalling neglect of Le Fanu's immediate heirs in preserving

Death mask of J. Sheridan Le Fanu, author of Carmilla.
(Copyright © Anna and Francis Dunlap, all rights reserved)

his papers, neither the manuscript nor any working notes for *Carmilla* have survived, so it is not possible to ascertain his precise inspiration for so obviously a lesbian vampire. A fashion for morbid Sapphism had, however, taken root in the poetry of Coleridge, Baudelaire, and others, and Le Fanu may have simply decided to appropriate the exotic conceit in prose. Today, no discussion of *Carmilla* omits the lesbian theme, but the topic was never raised critically until the twentieth century. A contemporary review by the *Saturday Review* found the whole idea of vampires unwholesome enough. The anonymous appraiser felt that readers "may be thankful to be spared an account of the most foolish and offensive of all his tales—that, namely, of the Vampire. When an author has the grave opened of a person who had been buried one hundred and fifty years, and describes how 'the leaden coffin floated with blood, in which, to a depth of seven inches, the body lay immersed,' we are, we think, more than justified in declining to analyse his silly and miserable story. We should hope that this time he will find he has miscalculated the taste of the subscribers to seaside lending libraries, for whom he probably writes."

Given *Carmilla*'s bloody footprints all throughout the text of *Dracula*, there can be no doubt that Stoker was thoroughly familiar with the story, even if his personal relationship with the reclusive Le Fanu remains conjectural. As an admirer of Le Fanu's fiction, he would have eagerly anticipated *In a Glass Darkly*, the 1872 collection in which it appeared, if he had not already read its 1871–72 serialization in the magazine *The Dark Blue*. One suggestive piece of evidence that he read the story near the time of its original publication is a curious contemporaneous entry in his journal—the description of a coverlet made of cat skins. In *Carmilla*, the vampire comes to Laura's bed, covering her in the form of a cat.

But another previously presumed influence on *Dracula*, that of Dion Boucicault's melodrama *The Vampire: A Phantasm* (1852), may be nonexistent. The Dublin-born Boucicault was a playwright, actor, and manager-producer, and one of the nineteenth century's leading theatrical personalities in the English-speaking world. Stoker first met and talked with him in Dublin in 1872, during a long repertory engagement at the Theatre Royal. Boucicault is best known today for still-revived plays like *London Assurance* (1841) and *The Shaughraun* (1874). *The Vampire* was written for the acclaimed actor Charles Kean, who rejected it, leaving the acting chores to Boucicault himself.

The reception was mixed—Queen Victoria herself attended the production at London's Princess Theatre twice, and, while initially impressed with Boucicault's performance as the bloodsucking revenant Sir Alan Raby ("I can never forget his livid face and fixed look. . . . It still haunts me," she wrote in her journal), she had second thoughts about the play itself upon a repeat viewing. "It does not bear seeing a second time," Victoria concluded, "and is, in fact, very trashy." That didn't, however, deter the Queen from commissioning a watercolor portrait of Boucicault in costume. "Mr. Boucicault . . . is very handsome," she admitted, adding that he "has a fine voice" and "acted very impressively."

Boucicault shortened and revived the play as *The Phantom* at Wallack's Theatre in New York in 1856, after which he completely dropped it from his repertory, despite reports of excellent American box office. Neither version ever played Dublin, and if Stoker later read the published script, he would have found little inspiration for his own vampire. For instance, Boucicault's was brought back from death by moonlight and was dispatched with a gunshot. Stoker would eventually standardize the governing rules of literary vampirism through other, largely folkloric sources. His first and quite possibly his solitary exposure to a vampire onstage, only very recently documented, occurred just after Christmas 1872, when he reviewed a Boxing Day performance of *The Vampire*, a comic dance piece set to Offenbach, at the Gaiety, calling it "a ballet of great cleverness and novelty." *The Vampire*, Stoker wrote, "is a good deal after the manner of a harlequinade in a pantomime, but, at the same time, has perfectly original characteristics." But the morning performance Stoker witnessed was more than a little slapdash in execution. "Nobody expects a first performance of such an entertainment to in any way approach perfection; but when one finds that stage appurtenances won't work, or, in plainer terms, are not worked, somebody is surely accountable." His heart went out to the "Mr. Collier" who invented and performed the piece, for being placed in "an awkward and embarrassing position. These remarks apply mainly to the morning performance of *The Vampire*; in the evening the improvement was most notable." Whether he returned for the second show out of concern for Mr. Collier or the simple fascination of the subject matter, we will never know for sure, but we are free to hazard a guess.

Among the stage devices prone to dysfunction were any of the various trapdoors that were a standard feature of pantomimes. The pentagonal star trap was the most spectacular. Actors playing sprites or demons were gymnastically launched from below the boards by a system of counterweights, up through the air above the stage, the jaws of the five-pointed trap snapping shut just in time to catch their landing. The mechanism required dexterity on both the part of stagehands and performers, and casualties were not unknown. Stoker would twice make melodramatic use of star trap mishaps in his fiction. An alternate device, the vampire trap, introduced in (and named after) James Robinson Planché's *The Vampire; or, The Bride of the Isles* (1820), was a less tricky affair, employing painted rubber flaps permitting a performer to suddenly enter or exit through an apparently solid wall or floor. When it was combined with strategic lighting, fog, or flash bombs, ghostly appearances and disappearances were startlingly impressive.

One of Stoker's new acquaintances, and one who especially adored dramatic entrances, was Lady Jane Francesca Wilde, flamboyant wife of Sir William and mother of two sons: Willie, who attended Trinity at the same time as Bram, and Oscar, who matriculated a bit later. By the early 1870s Stoker had become a regular at her salons. Writing as "Speranza," Jane was a fiery poetess of Irish nationalism, revolutionary by temperament and outlandish in demeanor, a Catholic-leaning avatar of bohemianism with a quick and acerbic wit, who seems to have been as much drawn to Stoker as he to her.

It is sometimes suggested that Stoker first made the acquaintance of the Wildes through his mother, eager to advance her son in Dublin society. This speculation is based on Charlotte's reading of her 1864 pamphlet essay "On Female Emigration from Workhouses" at the Statistical and Social Inquiry Society of Ireland. Sir William Wilde was among the society's founding members (one of roughly sixty), but it is not known whether he actually attended Charlotte's January 20, 1864, presentation, or whether he was even aware of her. No doubt, she addressed the society for the simple reason that it was one of the few institutions in Dublin that would permit the equal participation of women.

Charlotte would have known Sir William far better from a messy Dublin scandal in 1864 in which a young woman, Mary Travers, accused him of rape after having been anesthetized by chloroform in his surgery. She stalked the Wildes and distributed defamatory pamphlets in which Sir William was barely disguised as the rapacious "Dr. Quilp." When Jane publicly denounced her, it was she who was sued for libel. The resulting trial might have taken place in a sensation novel. Travers won the suit, but the court expressed its contempt by awarding her a mere farthing in damages.

Sir William was indeed a notorious philanderer. One of his critics speculated that he "had a family in every farmhouse in Ireland." He supported one illegitimate son in Dublin and paid for his training as an eye doctor. Two out-of-wedlock daughters had been moved discreetly to County Monaghan and drew little attention, but in November 1871 they died horribly after their dresses were set ablaze at a ball. They were both rolled down the outside steps into the snow, to no avail. In the absence of any effective treatment for serious burns and infection, they lingered miserably for two weeks. The tragedy was quietly kept out of the Dublin newspapers, but that hardly stopped the gossip.

Oscar Wilde as a young dandy.

The personal hygiene of Sir William and his sons was also a regular target of ridicule. A nasty joke circulated among Trinity men: "Why are Sir William's fingernails black?" The answer: "Because he scratched himself."

Could Charlotte Stoker's reaction to Jane Wilde and her family, and her son's association with them, have been anything but revulsion? Bram had chosen to keep company with a surrogate mother of dubious moral character—her son Oscar flippantly described her salon as "a society for the suppression of Virtue"—and whose every social, cultural, and religious value was the diametric opposite of her own. It was a slap in the face. Bram had been robbed of a normal early life but had found a way to act out adolescent rebellion in young adulthood, establishing his own identity clearly separate from that of his family.

"Portraits of her husband, sons, and dead daughter [Isola Wilde, who died in 1867 at age nine] depended brooch-like from parts of her person," wrote Wilde family chronicler Joan Schenkar, describing Jane moving among her guests, "dispensing outrageous comments far more liberally than her tea." The resurrection of Isola as a postmortem fashion accessory led a guest to describe the child's mother as "a walking family mausoleum." (It is possible Stoker had his first glimpse of Oscar in one of these pendulous brooches. There are very few photographs of Oscar in his youth; his brooch may well have displayed the three-year-old boy in his dress, next to the real daughter in hers.) Moon-faced and moon-driven, she entered a room as if by tidal propulsion. "She must have had two crinolines on," one guest observed, "for as she advanced there was a curious, swaying, swelling motion like that of a vessel at sea. Over the crimson silk were flounces of Limerick lace, and round where there had been a waist was an Oriental scarf. In her hands, always gloved in white, she carried a bottle of scent, a lace handkerchief and a fan."

A fantastical species of feminine female impersonator, Lady Wilde was not far removed from the outlandish dames of the Christmas pantomimes who had captured Bram's imagination in childhood. And therein may have lain another, potent aspect of her appeal.

If ridiculing her manner of dress didn't satisfy, critics could, and did, focus mercilessly on her face and body. She wore heavy makeup, "too thick for any ordinary light," compounded the offense of vanity by covering candles with pink shades, and even in daytime pulled the curtains, the better to "hide the decline of her beauty and the shabbiness of her furniture." In a further avoidance of bright light, she rarely had guests before five in the afternoon. It is only appropriate that this sun-repelled woman of the shadows provided Bram Stoker one of his most memorable descriptive phrases in *Dracula*: "children of the night," the vampire's evocative description of gathering wolves, was originally her own description, in *Ancient Legends, Mystic Charms, and Superstitions of Ireland* (1887), of the Berserker-like, wolf-skinned warrior tribes of ancient Ireland.

Oscar Wilde's friend and biographer Robert Sherard missed any *Dracula* connection, but definitely saw in Lady Wilde forewarnings of *The Picture of Dorian Gray*. "Her clinging to youth, her efforts to mask the advance of age, her horror for the stigmata of physical decay," Sherard wrote, "were all characteristics which she transmitted to her son." Wilde's writings, Sherard notes, "are full of rhapsodic eulogies of youth; he never tires of satirising maturity and old age." *Dorian Gray* would roundly satirize Victorian vanities, all the while emphasizing stigmata and horror.

Lady Jane Wilde, idealized and in travesty. Right: Watercolor portrait by Bernard Mulrenin (1864). Left: A particularly vicious caricature by **Punch** *cartoonist Harry Furniss.*

Attacks on Lady Wilde were more than skin deep, and were extended with relish to her general person, if not her genetics. George Bernard Shaw, a Dubliner who later came to know the Wildes in London, offered a peculiar biological theory, an odd exercise in full-body phrenology: "You know there is a disease called gigantism, caused by 'a certain morbid process in the sphenoid bone of the skull—viz., an excessive development of the anterior lobe of the pituitary body' (this from the nearest encyclopedia). 'When this condition does not become active until after the age of twenty-five, by which time the long bones are consolidated, the result is acromegaly, which chiefly manifests itself in an enlargement of the hands and feet.'" Shaw admitted to never having seen Lady Wilde's feet, "but her hands were enormous, and never went straight to anything, but minced about, feeling for it. And the gigantic splaying of her palm was reproduced in her lumbar region."

Given such appraisals, one might well imagine Lady Wilde as a kind of oversized Irish piñata, endlessly bludgeoned with shillelaghs. *Punch* cartoonist Harry Furniss depicted her and her husband as ridiculous zoo specimens. Seen from behind, her callipygian figure is expanded to elephantine proportions, and Sir William shrunken and shriveled into a kind of clinging monkey. The adjective "simian" was regularly deployed by his detractors; in a letter attributed to Trinity don and classicist Robert Tyrrell, the similar ape-slur "pithecoid" was used.

The year 1871 marked the publication of Darwin's *The Descent of Man*, and its explicit linkage of humankind to lower animals had much to do with the ensuing Victorian penchant for atavistic discourse, which would reach an apex (or nadir) at the time of Oscar Wilde's downfall, when Speranza's son would be described as something almost literally subhuman. But the cultural preoccupation with animalism was a pump already primed by the dominant view of physical, mental, and spiritual progress as enduring Christian virtues. Mind-body-soul backsliding had long been the stuff of cultural metaphors, even without Darwin.

Lady Jane and Sir William Wilde, caricatured by Henry Furniss.

Oscar Wilde's preparatory education, at the Portora School in the north of Ireland, coincided almost exactly with Stoker's academic career at Trinity. The two young men could have met at one of Lady Wilde's salons when Oscar was on holiday from Portora, but it is more probable that their first encounter occurred after Oscar's graduation, when he came home to matriculate at Trinity in late 1871. His leave-taking from boarding school had been accompanied by a distinct personal revelation, and the first glimpse of the unconventional life journey that awaited him.

A surprisingly insistent schoolmate had insisted on accompanying him to the train station for his departure to Dublin. As Oscar remembered, "he did not say 'goodbye' and go, and leave me to my dreams, but brought me papers and things and hung about." The friend made it clear he intended on staying on board the train until the sound of the station guard's whistle. When the signal came and the train began to move, the boy suddenly exclaimed, "Oh, Oscar," and "before I knew what he was doing he had caught my face in his hot hands and kissed me on the lips. . . . I became aware of cold, sticky drops trickling down my face—his tears." Oscar wiped his face and experienced an epiphany:

"This is love: this is what he meant—love."

Disoriented, Oscar trembled, "all shaken with wonder and remorse."

Whenever Bram and Oscar actually met, their similarities and dissimilarities would have been immediately apparent. They were both blue-eyed, tall, and physically imposing. They were both precocious, ambitious, intellectually gifted young Dubliners with a passion for literature and the arts, but were polar opposites in their response to Trinity's emphasis on physical culture—in all senses of the term. Oscar had little use for Trinity men, whom he dismissed as "barbarian" and "worse than the boys at Portora. . . . They thought of nothing but cricket and football, running and jumping; and they varied these intellectual exercises with bouts of fighting and drinking. If they had any souls they diverted them with coarse *amours* among barmaids and the women of the streets; they were simply awful. Sexual vice is even coarser and more loathsome in Ireland than it is in England."

Wilde may have had a low opinion of Trinity men, but there were those at the college who found him equally odd. His friend Vincent O'Sullivan recalled talking to an army officer who was Oscar's classmate at Trinity, who maintained he was mad. "I'll prove it to you," he told O'Sullivan. "One night we heard a frightful row in his room. Myself and another man rushed to his door. He was half undressed and jumping about the floor. 'What on earth is the matter?' we asked. 'There's a huge fly in my room,' replied Oscar, 'a great buzzing fly.'" Nothing could calm his hysteria over the insect. The conversation took place in 1895, after Wilde's fall and imprisonment. "It's ridiculous to put him in prison," the man said. "What he needs is a nursing home." Since the incident was fresh in the officer's mind more than twenty years after the fact, one might assume it was talked about around the university at the time it happened and might well have come to Stoker's attention, since Stoker was nothing if not attentive. In his Dublin journal, he had already made note of another peculiar insect fixation: "I once knew a little boy who put so many flies into a bottle that they had not room to die!" Eventually these kinds of impressions would be strongly echoed in his portrait of the hungry, fly-obsessed madman Renfield in *Dracula*.

Oscar Wilde would remain a hovering background presence in Bram Stoker's life until his downfall, exile, and death. And though they were destined to be romantic rivals in Dublin, accomplished men of the theatre in London, and the authors of masterwork novels whose title characters remain supernaturally young by destroying Victorian innocents, Stoker would never publicly put Wilde's name to paper—not even once, in all the thirty-odd years they knew each other. It was as if Oscar represented a part of his own life and psyche Stoker simply chose not to recognize or validate, or at least not to share with the world.

Except, perhaps, with Walt Whitman.

CHAPTER THREE

SONGS OF CALAMUS, SONGS OF SAPPHO

LET SHADOWS BE FURNISHED WITH GENITALS!
—Walt Whitman, *Leaves of Grass*

Gypsy-like as ever, the Stoker family continued their series of Dublin reloca-tions during Bram's college years. By the age of twenty-four he had known seven family homes, moving an average of once every three years and four months, and always, presumably, because of money. The household had pulled up stakes again in the mid-1860s, taking a new address at 5 Orwell Park, Rathgar, on Dublin's south side, and by the beginning of the 1870s they were back in the city center at 43 Harcourt Street, an address that would be retained by Thornley until his successful medical practice earned him an exceptionally handsome house at one of Dublin's best addresses on St. Stephen's Green.

The rest of the family would never be quite so comfortable. Abraham retired from the civil service in 1865 on a modest pension. He remained heavily in debt after putting four sons through college—three through medical school—and having borrowed against a life insurance policy. The

---

Walt Whitman's poetry electrified Bram Stoker's generation.
Frontispiece engraving for **Leaves of Grass** *(1854).*

family's special attention to finances is reflected in Charlotte's meticulous ledger of expenditures, in which the rising monthly cost of meat is clearly recorded. Her monthly payments to the Rathgar Road butcher Edward Flynn rose sharply in a five-year period, from £29 in early 1867 to £70 at the beginning of 1872, and even more as the year wore on. The inflationary pressure must have been horrendous, and a prime reason for the family's constant relocations over two and a half decades.

Among the most prominent themes in Irish history are emigration and expatriation. By 1872 Charlotte had determined that the cost of Abraham, Matilda, Margaret and herself living abroad in Italy, France, and Switzerland, in *pensiones*, would be more advantageous than remaining in Dublin. While the move might be glamorized (or rationalized) as some grand and well-earned retirement tour of the Continent, it appears to have been a move dictated primarily by money, not wanderlust, and they put off saying their farewells repeatedly. Charlotte must have chafed at the ugly irony of personally facing the kind of economic exile she had once fervently advocated for the most destitute Irish women. Now she confronted a genteel version of their banishment herself. Abraham and the Stoker women finally said good-bye to Bram and his brothers in the summer of 1872. For Abraham, the leave-taking would be permanent.

The family departure also marked a year in which Stoker would have yet another of his life-changing epiphanies, this time the momentous discovery of an American poet. In 1868, William Michael Rossetti had published *Selected Poems of Walt Whitman*, the British debut of selections from *Leaves of Grass* (1855, but revised and expanded for the rest of the poet's life). To Whitman's chagrin, the volume was heavily edited, but even a bowdlerized Whitman shook the literary world with lyrical blank verse that embodied the voice of the American everyman. "Embodied" is the operative word, for the Whitman cosmos, as unforgettably proclaimed in "I Sing the Body Electric," revolved around a physical self that transcended all dualities of mind and spirit: "And if the body does not do fully as much as the soul? / And if the body were not the soul, what is the soul?"

Evoking transcendentalism, pantheism, and the all-pervasive "electricity" of mesmerism, Whitman tackled the nineteenth century's struggle to reconcile the spiritual with the material. In an age when communication with the ethereal dead was all the rage, and "materialization" provided the big bang at séances, Whitman's poetry effectively coaxed together proto-plasm and ectoplasm. These were also interests of Stoker's, prompted by his first-year college readings of the philosophical writings of Victor Cousin, which urged him not to forget that the soul was bodiless and immortal, whatever science might say. Such ideas dovetailed with a growing fascina-tion with pseudoscientific belief systems, especially mesmerism and phre-nology/physiognomy. Whitman was an avid phrenologist, believing that human personality traits had physical locations within the cranium. It helped that his own phrenological readings indicated a superior character.

Stoker heard a great deal about *Leaves of Grass* before he ever read it. He first read of Whitman three years earlier, in the October 1869 issue of the London magazine *Temple Bar*, which featured an anonymous essay titled "The Poetry of the Future." The piece began as a seemingly evenhanded evaluation of the American poet but quickly took sides. Some of Whitman's partisans had rapturously embraced the poet as the second coming of Homer, and the critic was determined to provide a corrective. Whitman's style had "nothing in common with either the Bible, Shakspeare, or Plato."[1]

Stoker related, "For days we all talked of Walt Whitman and his new poetry with scorn—especially those of us who had not seen the book." But when he met a man on campus actually carrying a copy, he asked to see it. "Take the damned thing!" was the man's reply. "I've had enough of it!" Stoker took the book to College Park, the site of most of his athletic events, "and in the shade of an elm tree began to read it. Very shortly after my own opinion began to form; it was diametrically opposed to that which I had been hearing. From that hour I became a lover of Walt Whitman."

Whitman's disregard for traditional poetic conventions and struc-ture offended many, but what really disturbed certain readers from 1855 onward was his frank discussion of sex, and not just ordinary male-female sex, but seemingly endless references to affectionate male-male camara-derie and "manly love," including men kissing and embracing, and per-haps even more, given all the blunt talk about "man-balls" and "man-root" along the way. The rigid stalks of calamus grass, evoked in the particularly

---

[1] "Shakspeare" was a common Victorian spelling, along with "Shaksper" and "Shakespear." "Shakespeare" was not uniformly adopted until the twentieth century. Holdouts included George Bernard Shaw, who insisted on "Shakspeare."

controversial section of poems entitled "Calamus," were quickly understood by many to be phallic symbols, while other readers were much slower on the erotic uptake.

To modern sensibilities, Whitman is tame indeed, but in the mid-1800s his language was unprecedentedly shocking to general readers, and unprecedentedly liberating to a specially intended audience. Whitman's verses often referred to women, but they were evoked in a muscular, ambiguously earthy language. It was Whitman's manner of winking at male readers in the know.

"The bitter-minded critics of the time absolutely flew at the Poet and his work as watch-dogs do at a ragged beggar," Stoker wrote. "In my own university the book was received with Homeric laughter, and more than a few of the students sent over to Trübner's[2] for copies of the complete *Leaves of Grass*—that being the only place where they could then be had. Needless to say that amongst young men the objectionable passages were searched for and more obnoxious ones expected."

However, as he had to admit, "unfortunately, there were passages in the *Leaves of Grass* which allowed of attacks."

The initial, most vociferous barrage had come in America, from Rufus Griswold in the pages of the *Criterion*. Griswold had been the dubious, self-appointed literary executor of Edgar Allan Poe and was largely responsible for the sordid, slanted accounts of Poe's alcoholic death, which a good number of scholars now question. Griswold had even less regard for Whitman's character. He called *Leaves of Grass* "a mass of stupid filth" that "serves to show the energy which natural imbecility is occasionally capable of under strong excitement." He accused the poet of promulgating the "degrading, beastly sensuality, that is fast rotting the healthy core of all the social virtues." In simply describing the book, Griswold "found it impossible to convey any, even the most faint idea of its style and contents, and of our disgust and detestation of them, without employing language that cannot be pleasing to ears polite; but it does seem that some one should, under circumstances like these, undertake a most disagreeable, yet stern duty. The records of crime show that many monsters have gone on in impunity,

---

[2] A music publisher in London from whom scores, librettos, and—according to Stoker—imported volumes of poetry could be obtained.

because the exposure of their vileness was attended with too great indelicacy. "*Peccatum illud horribile, inter Christianos non nominandum.*"

Griswold couldn't bring himself to describe homosexuality—"*That horrible sin not to be mentioned among Christians*"—but he clearly interpreted passages as doing so. He wouldn't be alone. The following lines from "Song of Myself" in particular have long been interpreted as a paean to oral sex between men:

> I mind how once we lay such a transparent summer
>   morning,
> How you settled your head athwart my hips and gently
>   turn'd over upon me,
> And parted the shirt from my bosom-bone, and plunged
>   your tongue to my bare-stript heart,
> And reach'd till you felt my beard, and reach'd till you
>   held my feet.

As Stoker recalled, "From these excerpts it would seem that the book was as offensive to morals as to taste." His Trinity friends "did not scruple to give the *ipsissima verba* [exact words] of the most repugnant passages."

Stoker never divulged his own favorite sections, or commented in any way on the content or meaning of *Leaves of Grass*. But it means something that his Whitman epiphany coincided with the height of his athletic obsession with his own body and the bodies of other competitive young men. Whitman spoke in a private poetic code to a wide audience of male readers discovering, or grappling with, troublesome emotions. In "Two Vaults," he wrote: "These yearnings why are they? These thoughts in the darkness why are they? / I hear secret convulsive sobs from young men at anguish with themselves."

Other lines, more open about secret yearnings, may have spoken directly to Stoker the sportsman: "For an athlete is enamored of me—and I of him, / But toward him there is something fierce and terrible in me, eligible to burst forth, / I dare not tell it in words."

Although universally recognized today as an icon of gay history, Whitman never openly acknowledged his affairs with men. Indeed, the language barely existed to do so. In the 1870s, the word "gay" described heterosexual promiscuity in general, and female prostitution in particular. Same-sex attraction and behavior between men was almost universally condemned as aberrant and immoral, but was also considered a moral failing that could potentially entrap anyone. In this sense the Victorians, usually considered narrow-minded, were actually rather expansive in their understanding of the sexual spectrum, even if they disapproved of one end. The word "homosexual" was coined in Germany by Karl Maria Kertbeny in an 1869 pamphlet advocating the repeal of Prussian sodomy laws and didn't appear in English until the 1891 translation of Krafft-Ebing's *Psychopathia Sexualis*, where it was used as a clinical adjective; it was never used as a noun designating a person or class of persons with an innate orientation during the lifetime of either Whitman or Stoker. The term and concept of "heterosexuality" were similarly confined to obscure medical usage until the 1920s, when it first appeared officially in the Merriam-Webster dictionary and popularly in the *New York Times Book Review* (as "hetero-sexuality.")

In the many public controversies it generated, Walt Whitman's poetry received no overt support for its homoeroticism, but it accrued more palatable accolades for the proxy values of freedom, progressiveness, comradeship, and red-blooded manliness. At Trinity College, Whitman received a spirited defense from growing ranks of students, including Stoker. "Little by little we got recruits among the abler young men till at last a little cult was established," he wrote in his reminiscences. "We Walt Whitmanites had in the main more satisfaction than our opponents. Edward Dowden was one of the few who in those days took the large and liberal view of the *Leaves of Grass,* and as he was Professor of English Literature at the University his opinion carried much weight."

Only four years older than Stoker, Dowden today would be considered an academic rock star. He blazed across the Trinity firmament, being elected professor of oratory and English at the age of twenty-four. He was personally attractive as well as intellectually formidable. One of his students wrote that his appearance "recalls the features which Vandyke so loves to paint. He has a handsome, dreamy face, with pointed beard and a soft, somewhat melancholy voice. He is surrounded by a coterie of literary and would-be literary people. . . . By his admirers, he is regarded with an almost idolatrous affection."

At a meeting of the Phil on May 4, 1871, Dowden brought the topic of Whitman's poetry to an audience Stoker called "the more cultured of the

Edward Dowden, academic wunderkind of Trinity College Dublin, and Stoker's mentor.

students" with his paper "Walt Whitman and the Poetry of Democracy." Stoker was given the honor of opening the debate that followed.

Dowden couldn't avoid talking about Whitman and sex, but a truly honest discussion of the kind of sex the poet was writing about—much less a defense of it—would have been a public impossibility. And we honestly don't know what Dowden privately thought or felt on the subject of male-male sex, only that in public he adopted the roundabout, ultimately disingenuous approach that would color Whitman studies for decades to come. "If there be any class of subjects which it is more truly natural, more truly human *not* to speak of . . . then Whitman has been guilty of invading that sphere of silence," Dowden said in his paper.

> He deliberately appropriates a portion of his writings to the subject of the feelings of sex, as he appropriates another, "Calamus," to that of love of man for man, "adhesiveness" as contrasted to "amativeness," in the nomenclature of Whitman, comradeship apart from all feelings of sex.

That article of the poet's creed, which declares that man is very good, that there is nothing about him which is naturally vile or dishonourable, prepares him for absolute familiarity, glad, unabashed familiarity with every part and act of the body.

"Adhesiveness" and "amativeness" were concepts drawn from phrenology, which located love for men (adhesiveness) and love for women (amativeness) at specific places in the brain, readable in the shape and bumps and ridges of the skull. However odd it seems today, phrenology had an enormous following and deep cultural penetration in the nineteenth century,[3] and it seems to have been useful for people who wanted to parse their personalities and categorize, analyze, and control troubling drives and passions.

In the year that followed Dowden's lecture, Stoker had ample time to examine his mind, body, and soul in light of Whitman's revelatory worldview. He learned from Edward Dowden that Whitman was planning a visit to England to meet Alfred, Lord Tennyson, and Dowden had asked him to extend his trip with a stay in Dublin—and share the visit with Dowden and himself. "Dowden was a married man with a house of his own. I was a bachelor, living in the top rooms of a house, which I had furnished myself. We knew that Walt Whitman led a peculiarly isolated life, and the opportunity which either one or other of us could afford him would fairly suit his taste." Offering a bed to Walt Whitman? Could it actually happen? Time passed and there was no confirmation of Whitman's trip. Finally, when Stoker could no longer contain his feelings, he spilled them all into a letter to the poet himself.

DUBLIN, IRELAND, FEB 18, 1872

If you are the man I take you to be you will like to
get this letter. If you are not I don't care whether you
like it or not and only ask that you put it into the fire

---

[3] The belief system was so widespread that it would be difficult for nineteenth-century audiences not to think of phrenology during the graveyard scene in Hamlet, when the prince examines the skull of Yorick and enumerates details of the dead man's character. Stoker reviewed five productions of *Hamlet* while in Dublin, and may have seen many others in his student years and before joining the *Evening Mail*.

without reading any farther. But I believe you will like
it. I don't think there is a man living, even you who
are above the prejudices of the class of small-minded
men, who wouldn't like to get a letter from a younger
man, a stranger, across the world—a man living in
an atmosphere prejudiced to the truths you sing and
your manner of singing them. The idea that arises in
my mind is whether there is a man living who would
have the pluck to burn a letter in which he felt the
smallest atom of interest without reading it. I believe
you would and that you believe you would yourself.
You can burn this now and test yourself, and all I will
ask for my trouble of writing this letter, which for
all I can tell you may light your pipe with or apply to
some more ignoble purpose—is that you will in some
manner let me know that my words have tested your
impatience.

What an opening. Stoker repeatedly challenges Whitman to destroy
his letter, with four incendiary references: to "put it in the fire," "have the
pluck to burn a letter," "You can burn this now," and "You may light your
pipe with [it]." That last suggestion, to use the paper "for some more ignoble purpose," went beyond self-effacement, essentially reducing himself to
toilet paper. Perhaps he is trying to appeal to Whitman's earthiness. But in
one sense he is talking to himself as much as to Whitman, both messages
implying "Stop me before I write more."

Put it in the fire if you like—but if you do you will
miss the pleasure of the next sentence which ought
to be that you have conquered an unworthy impulse.
A man who is certain of his own strength might try
to encourage himself by a piece of bravo, but a man
who can write, as you have written, the most candid
words that ever fell from the lips of a mortal man—a
man to whose candor Rousseau's Confessions is
reticence—can have no fear for his own strength. If
you have gone this far you may read the letter and I

feel in writing now that I am talking to you. If I were
before your face I would like to shake hands with
you, for I feel that I would like you. I would like to
call YOU Comrade and to talk to you as men who are
not poets do not often talk. I think that at first a man
would be ashamed, for a man cannot in a moment
break the habit of comparative reticence that has
become second nature to him; but I know I would not
long be ashamed to be natural before you. You are a
true man, and I would like to be one myself, and so
I would be towards you as a brother and as a pupil
to his master. In this age no man becomes worthy of
the name without an effort. You have shaken off the
shackles and your wings are free. I have the shackles
on my shoulders still—but I have no wings. If you are
going to read this letter any further I should tell you
that I am not prepared to "give up all else" so far as
words go. The only thing I am prepared to give up
is prejudice, and before I knew you I had begun to
throw overboard my cargo, but it is not all gone yet.

More mysteries. Almost as if he is teasing his idol to guess, or intuit,
exactly what he isn't ready to "give up."

I do not know how you will take this letter. I have not
addressed you in any form as I hear that you dislike
to a certain degree the conventional forms in letters.
I am writing to you because you are different from
other men. If you were the same as the mass I would
not write at all. As it is I must either call you Walt
Whitman or not call you at all—and I have chosen
the latter course. I do not know whether it is usual for
you to get letters from utter strangers who have not
even the claim of literary brotherhood to write you.
If it is you must be frightfully tormented with letters
and I am sorry to have written this. I have, however,
the claim of liking you—for your words are your own

soul and even if you do not read my letter it is no less
a pleasure to me to write it. Shelley wrote to William
Godwin and they became friends. I am not Shelley
and you are not Godwin and so I will only hope that
sometime I may meet you face to face and perhaps
shake hands with you. If I ever do it will be one of the
greatest pleasures of my life.

After an extraordinary preamble—a former athlete's warming up,
perhaps—Stoker finally introduces himself properly.

If you care to know who it is who writes this, my name
is Abraham Stoker (Junior). My friends call me Bram.
I live at 43 Harcourt Street, Dublin. I am a clerk in the
service of the Crown on a small salary. I am twenty-
four years old. Have been champion at our athletic
sports (Trinity College, Dublin) and have won about a
dozen cups. I have also been President of the College
Philosophical Society and an art and theatrical critic
of a daily paper. I am six feet two inches high and
twelve stone weight naked and used to be forty-one
or forty-two inches around the chest. I am ugly but
strong and determined and have a large bump over
my eyebrows. I have a heavy jaw and a big mouth and
thick lips—sensitive nostrils—a snubnose and straight
hair. I am equal in temper and cool in disposition and
have a large amount of self control and am naturally
secretive to the world. I take a delight in letting
people I don't like—people of mean or cruel or
sneaking or cowardly disposition—see the worst side
of me. I have a large number of acquaintances and
some five or six friends—all of which latter body care
much for me. Now I have told you all I know about
myself.

All he knew about himself? Perhaps he believed Whitman would immediately glean what he needed through his knowledge of phrenology. If

Whitman spoke in code, than so could Stoker. The disclosure of a bump on his forehead is intriguing, since it was a trait that did not bode well under phrenological scrutiny. Some practitioners would have said it indicated a tendency toward murder. The details about his jaw, nose, and mouth might also have been associated with "degenerate" behavior of various kinds by criminal physiognomists. Stoker might well have been signaling his own anxiety over the possibility of hidden negative tendencies. He also seems to have a peculiarly distorted self-image: no photograph of him reveals lips that are particularly thick (they actually look rather thin), the small protuberances above his eyes look completely normal, and by no stretch of the imagination does any Dublin portrait support his self-description of being "ugly." And as for that "worst side of me"—what on earth were those unpleasant people shown, and surprised to see?

> I know you from your works and photograph,
> and if I know anything about you I think you
> would like to know of the personal appearance
> of your correspondents. You are I know a keen
> physiognomist. I am a believer of the science myself
> and am in a humble way a practicer of it. I was not
> disappointed when I saw your photograph—your late
> one especially.

It is not clear which photos Stoker references, or how "late" the more recent one was. The famous daguerreotype of a rugged, behatted young Whitman from the original 1855 *Leaves of Grass* was reproduced in Rossetti's *Selected Poems of Walt jWhitman*. Photos early in the Civil War show a ruggedly handsome Whitman strongly resembling Ernest Hemingway; from the end of the war onward he assumes the more familiar persona of a long-bearded, Gandalf-like sage.

> The way I came to like you was this. A notice of your
> poems appeared some two years ago or more in the
> Temple Bar magazine. I glanced at it and took its
> dictum as final, and laughed at you among friends.
> *I say it to my own shame but not to regret for it has taught*
> *me a lesson to last my life out—without ever having seen*

your poems. More than a year after I heard two men
in College talking of you. One of them had your
book (Rossetti's edition) and was reading aloud some
passages at which both laughed. They chose only
those passages which are most foreign to British ears
and made fun of them. Something struck me that I
had judged you hastily. I took home the volume and
read it far into the night. Since then I have to thank
you for many happy hours, for I have read your poems
with my door locked late at night and I have read
them on the seashore where I could look all round me
and see no more sign of human life than the ships out
at sea: and here I often found myself waking up from
a reverie with the book lying open before me. I love
all poetry, and high generous thoughts make the tears
rush to my eyes, but sometimes a word or a phrase of
yours takes me away from the world around me and
places me in an ideal land surrounded by realities
more than any poem I ever read. Last year I was
sitting on the beach on a summer's day reading your
preface to the Leaves of Grass as printed in Rossetti's
edition (for Rossetti is all I have got till I get the
complete set of your works which I have ordered from
America). One thought struck me and I pondered
over it for several hours—"the weather-beaten vessels
entering new ports," you who wrote the words know
them better than I do: and to you who sing of your
land of progress the words have a meaning that I can
only imagine. But be assured of this, Walt Whitman—
that a man of less than half your own age, reared a
conservative in a conservative country, and who has
always heard your name cried down by the great mass
of people who mention it, here felt his heart leap
towards you across the Atlantic and his soul swelling
at the words or rather the thoughts. It is vain for me
to quote any instances of what thoughts of yours I like
best—for I like them all and you must feel you are

reading the true words of one who feels with you. You
see, I have called you by your name. I have been more
candid with you—have said more about myself to you
than I have ever said to anyone before.

If the last statement is true, Stoker was truly secretive. Despite its emotionality, the letter actually says very little about him, but much about his
unwillingness to reveal anything more than brief biographical detail, a
physical description, and a passionate admiration for Whitman's poetry.

You will not be angry with me if you have read so far.
You will not laugh at me for writing this to you. It was
with no small effort that I began to write and I feel
reluctant to stop, but I must not tire you any more. If
you would ever care to have more you can imagine,
for you have a great heart, how much pleasure it
would be to me to write more to you. How sweet a
thing it is for a strong healthy man with a woman's
eyes and a child's wishes to feel that he can speak to a
man who can be if he wishes father, and brother and
wife to his soul.

The last sentence is the one most often cited by Stoker commentators.
It wasn't the first time he had expressed almost the identical sentiment, if
only in his private journal the year before. On August 1, 1871, he made the
entry "Will men ever believe that a strong man can have a woman's heart
& the wishes of a lonely child?" In another, undated entry he writes, "I felt
as tho' I were my own child—I feel an infinite pity for myself—Poor, poor
little lonely child." His letter to Whitman is shot through with a sense of
loneliness, even if he never uses the word. He is reaching out for a different
kind of friend than those he knows in Dublin.

I don't think you will laugh, Walt Whitman, nor
despise me, but at all events I thank you for all the
love and sympathy you have given me in common
with my kind.

BRAM STOKER

Although he managed to finish the letter—and we have no idea how many false starts may have been involved—he could not bring himself to mail it. At least not then. He kept it hidden—in a drawer, or perhaps folded in a book—for the next four years. The letter remains the most personal and passionate document Stoker ever wrote (or, at least, that has survived), but until now it has never been quoted in full for any biography or Stoker critical study. This may well be because it raises as many questions as it seems to answer.

On first reading, the letter does seem to support the notion that Stoker is making a bold psychosexual disclosure—especially given everything we know about Whitman today. But Stoker's description of himself as having "a woman's eyes" is curious; since we already know he considers himself unattractive, he's surely not talking about prettiness. Rather, it suggests a strongly transgender perspective ("eyes" here intended as "viewpoint") that is not necessarily homosexual. Perhaps it was not Whitman's barely disguised descriptions of male-male lust that attracted Stoker to *Leaves of Grass* as much as the poetry's all-pervasive androgyny. On the other hand, one of the common "explanations" of homosexual desire at the time, first advanced by pioneering German activists of the 1860s in a plea for tolerance, was that a female soul had somehow become trapped in a male body. For anxious men of Stoker's generation, with no other real model for understanding contrarian sexual feeling, the idea of "inversion" sounded plausible and became deeply ingrained.

A major difficulty in making modern sense of sexual identities from the horse-and-buggy age is the tendency to wear twentieth- and twenty-first-century horse blinders. Today's popular understanding of sexual orientation is an either/or, gay/straight template, seemingly drawn from the off/on binary switching of digital information. Computers are actually terrible models for understanding the human mind and body, much less the subjectivity of emotional attractions, but the idea is stubborn and pervasive. And, although the acronym LGBT (lesbian, gay, bisexual, and transgender) is used ubiquitously today, suggesting some monolithic homogenization, there is often a contentious and suspicious relationship between the comprised groups. Despite recent clinical studies finally affirming the existence of bisexuality, and decades of research indicating that human sexuality falls on a wide and often ambivalent spectrum many gays and straights still reject the idea that true bisexuality even exists.

Understanding Bram Stoker's mind and imagination may require a willing suspension of this kind of psychological straitjacketing. (In the final analysis, after honestly considering the vastness and variety of human attraction and the infinite shadings of desire, it may be a fair conclusion that we are all sexual minorities of one.) Stoker lived in a time when the lines between same-sex friendship and same-sex sex often blurred, and people didn't necessarily worry about it. As historian Jonathan Ned Katz notes in *Love Stories: Sex Between Men Before Homosexuality*, "The universe of intimate friendship was, ostensibly, a world of spiritual feeling. The radical Christian distinction between mind and body located the spiritual and the carnal in different spheres. . . . And yet, from our present standpoint, we can see that these intimate friendships often left evidence of extremely intense, complex desires, including, sometimes, what we today recognize as erotic." Katz cites evidence of "a surprising variety of physical and sometimes sensual modes of relating among male friends in the nineteenth century."

Stoker's circle of friends and acquaintances in the worlds of theatre and literature would include a significant number who could be easily described with such Victorian euphemisms as "bohemian," "confirmed bachelor," "female bachelor," "artistic," "intensely private," "hero worshipper," and many other circumlocutions for persons with unconventional affectional preferences, many of whom would not fit easily into our present-day system of sexual pigeonholing.

Or, to alter only slightly one of the most famous lines from *Hamlet*, one of Stoker's favorite plays, "There are more things in Heaven and Earth, Horatio, than are dreamed of in your sexology."

By the end of 1872, Stoker had two publications appear under his byline, "Abraham Stoker." His first known short story, "The Crystal Cup," was published in the September number of *London Society* magazine. An unnamed first-person narrator is held against his will in a castle, anguished over the fate of his beloved, Aurora. He channels all his life energy—literally—into the creation of a beautiful crystal vase, which absorbs his soul upon its completion. The vase is displayed at a royal event, the Festival of Beauty, where the narrator (or his ghost) sees the heartbroken Aurora, now the dejected consort to a morose King. The exquisite beauty of the crystal moves Aurora to sing.

Sad and plaintive is the song; full of feeling and tender love, but love over-shadowed by grief and despair. As it goes on the voice of the singer grows sweeter and more thrilling, more real; and the cup, my crystal time-home, vibrates more and more. . . . The monarch looks like one entranced, and no movement is within the hall. . . .The song dies away in a wild wail that seems to tear the heart of the singer in twain; and the cup vibrates still more as it gives back the echo. As the note, long-swelling, reaches its highest, the cup, the Crystal cup, my wondrous home, the gift of the All-Father, shivers into millions of atoms.

A metaphysical maelstrom engulfs the narrator. "Ere I am lost in the great vortex," he concludes, "I see the singer throw up her arms and fall, freed at last, and the King sitting, glory-faced, but pallid with the hue of death."

A striking example of Stoker's juvenilia, the story owes a strong debt to Poe, indicating a youthful familiarity with the American master of the macabre. The story takes place in a kingdom by the sea, where two lovers have been separated and one imprisoned, an homage to "Annabel Lee;" the words "never more" appear repeatedly, clear echoes of "The Raven;" and the device of a soul transmigrating into a work of art provides the cli-max of Poe's story "The Oval Portrait" ("And then the brush was given, and then the tint was placed; and, for one moment, the painter stood entranced before the work which he had wrought; but in the next, while he yet gazed, he grew tremulous and very pallid, and aghast, and crying with a loud voice, 'This is indeed *Life* itself!' turned suddenly to regard his beloved:—*She was dead!*") The overwrought atmosphere of storm and struggle in "The Crystal Cup" also points to a familiarity with Goethe's *The Sorrows of Young Werther,* and German Romanticism in general.

The second publication was the text of his November 13 Hist address, "The Necessity for Political Honesty." Although it included an explicit allusion to one of his favorite pieces of dark literature, *Macbeth*, "The Necessity" couldn't have been a more different piece of writing than "The Crystal Cup." The lecture was a rhetorical tour de force, and a bit of a humorous jab. The Hist's bylaws prohibited outright political debate, but Stoker cleverly contrived to talk about politics without bringing up a single political argument (although he almost crossed a line with some thoughts on Ireland that effectively declared his nationalism). The society's proscription on politics was outdated and counterproductive, Stoker argued.

> Oratory is not in itself a sufficient object for a body like ours. It is an art as well as a science—it needs practice as well as theory; and the aspiring speaker must have some materials with which to work. We can no more practice oratory, as an art by itself, than we can chisel a statue from the air, or work an engine without fuel. Not the mere articulation of syllables, but the expression of ideas makes an orator, and, without ideas to express, his words are as
>
>   —a tale
>   "Told by an idiot, full of sound and fury,
>   Signifying nothing."

The address then turned to Irish identity. "The Celtic race is waking up from its long lethargy, and another half century will see a wondrous change in the position which it occupies amongst the nations of the world," he wrote, echoing the sentiments of Lady Wilde without explicitly calling for home rule. Instead, he predicted that a Celtic revival would be most fully realized in the United States. The Irish people, "this leavening race of future America—this race which we young men may each of us directly and indirectly influence for good or ill, may become in time the leading element of Western civilization." Stoker's romantic fascination with the American experiment, fueled by his fascination with Walt Whitman, would only continue to grow. After the address, he received a certificate for oratory, and his tutor George Ferdinand Shaw made the successful motion to have the address printed at the Hist's expense.

The following year brought sad news. Walt Whitman had suffered a debilitating stroke at his home in Camden, New Jersey, and was now partially paralyzed. "He could at best move, but a very little; the joys of travel and visiting distant friends were not to be for him." Stoker already considered Whitman a friend, even though he had never mailed his letter of introduction.

Even without Whitman on hand, the general subject of blurred gender was not too difficult to find in Dublin in 1873. Stoker reviewed, with apparent pleasure, an "Operatic Boufferie" at the Gaiety called *Kissi-Kissi*, a topsy-turvy confection about transvestism. The Persian princess Kissi-Kissi "has evinced a strong partiality to strong sports and exercises, greatly to her father's horror." The father doesn't know his daughter is actually a son, his sex concealed from birth by his mother, fearful of her boy being conscripted. Kissi-Kissi, who also believes she is a girl, has a "timid lover" named Kikki-Wikki. But Kissi-Kissi's masculine side "makes up for her lover's shyness, and they vow eternal devotion to each other. Alas for the course of true love!"

A less amusing treatment of impossible love took shape the following year in Stoker's unpublished poem "Too Easily Won," entered in his private journal. Sexually ambiguous, it is addressed to a male object of adoration who rejects the poet's declaration of love:

> So ends my dream. My life must be
> One long regret and misery
> Loved not, though loving, what care I
> How soon I die.
> For whilst I live my wail must ever run
> Too lightly won! Too lightly won.
>
> His heart when he was sad & lone
> Beat like an echo to mine own
> But when he knew I loved him well
> His ardour fell.
> Love ceased for him whene'er the strife was done
> And I was won. Too lightly won.
>
> Had I been fickle, false or cold
> His love perchance I might still hold
> Alas! To grieve for spoken truth
> For blighted hope—for ruined youth
> Oh life of woe and anguish soon begun
> Alas! For love too lightly won—too lightly won.

Whether the poem is read as a man's heartbreak over another man, or as Stoker experimentally writing from a woman's point of view, normative gender boundaries are provocatively blurred.

As if he didn't have enough to occupy himself, in late 1873 Stoker accepted the position of editor for a new four-page daily, the *Irish Echo*. The paper mixed general news and commentary with digested pieces from other papers and telegraph services, colorful local vignettes, and, not surprisingly, drama criticism, or at least the space to expand on his shorter pieces in the *Evening Mail*. Correspondence with his family indicates that the work was remunerative, if undependably so, unlike his ongoing work for the *Mail*, and it supplemented his civil service income until the spring of 1874, when the overall demands on his time and energy may well have reached a breaking point and he resigned.

At this juncture one might ask: Exactly what constituted a breaking point for Stoker? The *Echo* job was an editorial one-man show, the original writing being all his. It is impossible to imagine a daily schedule entailing a full-time civil service job and work for two daily papers that required him to attend two of Dublin's major theatres several nights a week—including frequent return visits to let readers know about improved performances and technical problems overcome; the endless, enthusiastic follow-up reports on his beloved pantomimes especially suggest an almost literal camping-out at the Theatre Royal and the Gaiety night after night after night. He was also writing fiction, more than he actually published; his first encounter with Walt Whitman occurred serendipitously in the pages of the *Temple Bar* magazine, which he initially read for its light fiction, and to which he would soon, albeit unsuccessfully, submit his own fledgling stories.

How could any human being accomplish this much work? By some fantastic ability to complete work in a special dimension outside the constraints of time? Via some supernatural skill at being in more than one place at the same time, through astral projection? Through an unknown form of permanent, high-functioning insomnia? By helpful intervention of the fairies? In the real world, only one thing makes sense—that Stoker simply stole the time for journalism, criticism, and fiction writing during his day job at Dublin Castle. It would not be difficult for a man with prodigious mental organizational skills and almost effortless capacity for quick written expression to run rings around the typical bureaucrat, a species notorious for stretching all work to the maximum time allotted. He completed his daily assignments in record time, discreetly maintained his personal notebooks, and simply didn't let anyone be the wiser. Why should he?

While the *Echo* job lasted, Stoker infused the paper freely and anonymously with his own personality; beyond the stage reviews, the paper was peppered with humorous filler and anecdotes that often read suspiciously like many of his own droll journal entries. On November 25, 1873, he entertained readers with a secondhand account of another sea monster first reported by the *San Diego Union*, in which a certain Captain Charlesworth and his crew, hunting curlew along the coast, instead encountered in a cove

> a frightful monster, fully thirty feet in length, shaped like a snake, with three sets of fins, a tail like an eel, and a head like an alligator's. The head was a little wider than the neck, but very thick at the base, and had small eyes, which appeared to be covered with a dark skin, which assumed a yellowish cast on the belly. The three pairs of fins were shaped like those of a sea lion, were each between three and four feet in length, the forward pair being much the heaviest, and situated about two feet back of the neck. . . . [Charlesworth] said the terrible looking thing had drawn itself nearly out of the water, and was lying motionless on the sand when he first saw it. At his approach the serpent fish raised its head and swung it directly towards him, and as he was not more than a couple of rods off, his only thought was to increase that distance.

The crew fired at the thing, but since their guns were loaded with birdshot, the result was predictable. Stoker's taking notice of a monstrous snake story may have been prompted by the simple novelty of the report, but the material also resonated with him on an imaginative level. Every child in Ireland grows up with snakes, or at least images of them. The serpent is extraordinarily prevalent in Irish folklore, even if the reptile is not native to the island. As a symbol of paganism imported by the Celts, serpents were supposedly banished by St. Patrick, but they have never left Irish art and iconography. The familiar, decorative Celtic knot is a stylized snake symbol, and it slithers all over the form of many a Celtic cross. Decorative serpents abound in the illuminated pages of the *Book of Kells*. Snake imagery had already begun to appear in a cycle of fairy tales Stoker was writing, even though he wouldn't publish them for another decade. His novel *The Snake's Pass* would evoke Ireland's legendary past, and his final book, *The Lair of the White Worm* (1911), would use the snake as an image of overwhelming, nightmarish horror. But in the case of the San Diego monster of 1872, his attitude is skeptically humorous.

Another tongue-in-cheek report in the *Echo* recounts an EXCITING SCENE IN ST. JAMES CHURCH, in which a London vicar "worked up one of those sensational sermons now too often delivered in churches. The subject was 'Death.' Gradually, and undoubtedly fluently, he had nearly disposed of every member of different families, when a lady, who appeared to be a widow, about sixty or seventy years of age, went into hysterics." She fainted and was removed to the vestry. The sermon continued, resulting in two more women collapsing and being carried out, "after which the service was obliged to be closed, otherwise there is no doubt there would have been some danger of an accident occurring, as the people had risen from their seats and were getting very excited." Had Stoker lived to review the West End stage adaptation of *Dracula*, produced fifteen years after his death, he would have been similarly amused by the fainting/collapsing stooges attending his own strange sermon on mortality.

Stoker ran another mordantly funny item, PINCHING AN ACTRESS. It told of an actor in Plymouth who, unhappy with the capability of an actress playing the Marquise de Pompadour to convincingly die in his arms, gave her a sharp pinch to induce the appropriate convulsion. "We have heard that 'the gallows is the only thing to put life into an Irishman and make him quicken his paces,' although this was the first occasion on record in which a pinch in the side has been found necessary to make a lady die properly. The magistrates dismissed the case, as well they might. It would never do just at Christmas time to make an assault on the stage a punishable offense, and even in our most quiet seasons Macbeth must not indict Macduff for a murderous attack." Stoker concluded that "if it is a part of a woman's business to die on stage before a provincial audience," she should "show at least as much physical distress in the region of the heart as a pinch in the side will help her to do."

But the most significant personal contribution Stoker made to the *Echo* was a hitherto unknown short story, "Saved by a Ghost," which appeared on December 26, 1873. Boxing Day was also the usual debut date for the annual pantomimes, which were hardly the only fantastical tradition associated with an English Christmas. The telling of ghost stories on or around Christmas was a venerable British ritual, a persisting vestige of pagan times, when the winter solstice, the longest, darkest night of the year, was believed to be especially attuned to the supernatural.

Stoker published "Saved by a Ghost" anonymously, like everything else he wrote for the *Echo*, but it has many of the features of his later fiction, including a fascination with seafaring, supernatural or otherwise, and male comradeship. The story begins with an unidentified speaker asking simply, "Do any of you believe in ghosts?" The person addressing us is Captain Charles Merwin, "standing with his back to the fire in the coffee room of the Royal Hotel, Liverpool," who has clearly secured his audience's attention, as well as the reader's. "The reason I ask," he continues, "is because a ghost was a principal cause of a sudden reformation, which has been the making of me."

Then, in an unbroken monologue, he recounts an incident from seventeen years past. At the age of eighteen, the captain tells us, he was already "a thorough sailor and a thorough drunkard." Homeward bound from the East Indies, with "an unusually hard crew, all of them, except myself, being taken out of gaol and put on board the ship in irons," he suspects foul play when the third mate, Billy McLellan, goes into convulsions while Charles writes a letter for him, and dies in his arms. Charles himself is named as the dead man's replacement while a plot is hatched among the discontented crew to poison the officers with arsenic and force a landing for replacement officers. Then, one night, Billy returns.

> It did not frighten me, but I was considerably astonished. There he sat, natural as in life, with his night dress on, and the right sleeve of his shirt rolled up above the elbow. His eyes were cast down, and he was occupied with his pocket-knife cutting a notch on the top of my chest. I was so astonished that I was not sure whether I was asleep or awake, but after pinching myself several times, I concluded I was in full and perfect possession of my senses. I then tried to speak, and asked, "Is that you, Billy?" As soon as I had spoken the apparition looked up and full at me with a smiling face. This gave me more courage, and after a moment I asked, "What do you want, Billy?" At this question the smile on the face turned to a scowl, such as I had often seen in life when something displeased him.

Billy thereafter becomes a protective spirit, repeatedly alerting Charles to fights brewing on the ship, which, to all observers, he has an uncanny ability to anticipate and stop. But he doesn't foresee the difficulties that follow his captain's request that Charles personally hold twenty-seven thousand rupees in freight fees. A bank failure in Bombay prevented him from depositing the money. "He did not dare to leave it on shore, or change it into notes and keep it on his person, for fear of robbery; and the banks were all slinkey, and on the verge of breaking; bills of exchange were worthless." Actually, he sees the chance to steal the rupees by blaming their loss on Charles, whom he knows to be a drunkard, previously dismissed from more than one seafaring position. Charles came to this ship sober after Mary Tracey, the daughter of an Irish hotelier in Bombay, promised to marry him if only he could prove himself reformed. The money scheme is a Faustian bargain, almost literally, since the captain is being advised by a mysterious man from Bombay: "The stranger was introduced to me as the ship's agent. I had seen the man's face before, but could not tell where. It was an intelligent but evil-looking countenance, made more sinister by the carefully-waxed and jet-black Mephistophelian moustache which decorated his face. Liquors were put on the table, the doors closed."

For the moment, Charles abstains, but the pact includes a key to the captain's cabin, where he is encouraged to help himself to a drink anytime he likes.

> Left to myself, I became very lonesome, very blue, and very beat, and in a moment of weakness I thought that a bottle of "Bass's Pale Ale" would be good company and act as an antidote to the blues, and cool me off. I only thought twice of it before I got a bottle and drank it. It acted like a charm. My loneliness and the blues disappeared in company, and I didn't mind the boat a bit. In about ten or fifteen minutes I drank another pint, and a dim recollection entered my mind that there was a decanter of brandy somewhere on board.

The captain returns, and this time insists on sharing the brandy. After an uncounted number of additional drinks, Charles goes back to his bunk to pass out atop the chest containing the freight money. Hours later, the sound of breaking wood startles him, but even more disquieting is the sight of Billy's ghost standing next to his bunk, pointing at the captain and his henchman—the same sailor who had poisoned Billy—who has begun to break open the chest with a hatchet. In the ensuing struggle, the hatchet man is killed—Charles seizes the weapon and axes him several times in the head—while the captain begins to stab Charles. He hears a gunshot as he slips into unconsciousness.

Weeks later he awakens in the Traceys' hotel and finally understands what happened. After giving Charles drugged brandy, the captain and the ominous agent had met onshore at the same hotel and were overheard by Mary discussing the details of their plot, including the fact that Charles had been drugged. She takes her father's revolver and follows them back to the ship in a dinghy. Coming upon the captain raising his knife over Charles for a final, fatal thrust, she shoots him. We learn that he lives to stand trial and be sentenced for life to a chain gang in Pulo Penang. The owners of the ship make Charles captain, and a year later he and Miss Tracey marry.

"Not until I fully established my reputation for sobriety did I tell my wife I had drank liquor on that day," says Charles, "and as she had learned to trust me, it did not cause her much trouble then." He assures his listeners that he never took another drink, and that Billy McLellan never again appeared to him. "Now, gentlemen," he finishes, "my story's told; you know how I was saved from the gutter, got command of a ship, and gained a wife—all through a ghost."

"Saved by a Ghost," only his second published piece of fiction, already evidenced Stoker's keen interest in the fictional possibilities of the returning dead, as well as a fascination with the Faust legend, which would only grow. As a holiday tale of supernatural redemption, Stoker's story observed the template of Charles Dickens's *A Christmas Carol* (1843). Dickens continued to entertain readers with spooky Yuletide offerings in his popular newspapers *Household Words* and *All the Year Round.* Although Marley's ghost is the best-remembered vestige of the tradition, it had its roots in the early juxtaposition of Christmas with the winter solstice, which, like November Eve, had great supernatural significance to pagan cultures. In *The Winter's Tale* (circa 1611), Shakespeare tells us, "A sad tale's best for winter: I have one. Of sprites and goblins." Christopher Marlowe, in *The Jew of Malta* (1589), writes of the seasonal tales of old women "that speak of spirits and ghosts that glide by night." In the late Victorian era, best-selling writer Jerome K. Jerome's *Told after Supper* (1891) assured readers that "whenever five or six English-speaking people meet before a fire on Christmas Eve, they start telling ghost stories. Nothing satisfies us on Christmas Eve but to hear each other tell authentic anecdotes about spectres." As he noted,

"There must be something ghostly in the air of Christmas—something about the close, muggy atmosphere that draws up the ghosts, like the dampness of the summer rains brings out the frogs and snails." The tradition enjoyed an Edwardian revival at Cambridge after World War I, when the King's College provost, M. R. James, supplemented his prodigious scholarship with legendary, exclusive-invitation Christmas Eve gatherings at which he would read aloud the ghost stories he wrote for his own pleasure, and which became classics of the genre. First collected and published in 1931, they have never been out of print.[4]

Aside from ghost stories—a plentiful British commodity in the 1870s—Stoker had frequent exposure to uncanny themes in the operas he reviewed for the *Evening Mail*. Bellini's *La Sonnambula* was presented twice at the Theatre Royal during Stoker's tenure as critic. Like mesmerism, sleepwalking would be a significant plot element of *Dracula*; in his review of the 1875 Hawkins Street production, Stoker took special notice of the character Amina, a Swiss ingénue whose uncontrollable night-wandering takes her smack into the bedroom of a mysterious, recently arrived count. Evaluating one Mlle. Albani, in her Dublin debut in the title role, Stoker found her singing "little short of perfection, and if we selected items for special notice we should be tempted to praise everything. She is fascinating in style, and she acts gracefully and intelligently." If it isn't already obvious, the name Amina is extraordinarily close in spelling and sound to Mina, the embattled heroine of *Dracula*, who deals with her own and others' problems of sleepwalking, mesmerism, and the attentions of a certain elusive count.[5]

Dracula suggests that vampirism results from dealings with the devil, and so may have been somewhat influenced by Stoker's familiarity with the opera *Robert le diable* (1831), which combined Mephistophelian machinations with a central spectacle of the dead resurrected. Little produced

---

[4] Far more recently, there is Andy Williams's still-durable Christmas song from the 1960s, "The Most Wonderful Time of the Year," with the lines "There'll be scary ghost stories / And tales of the glories / Of Christmases long, long ago."

[5] Another speculative source for the name is the character Minna in *The String of Pearls*, a gruesome penny dreadful that galvanized the Sweeney Todd legend. Published anonymously as a serial in 1846–47, it is believed to be an authorial collaboration of Thomas Peckett (or Preskett) Prest and James Malcolm Rymer—also author of *Varney the Vampyre*, which began its own serial run less than a year before *String*. Whenever Stoker later read *Varney*, he evidently devoured the tale. Is it likely he could have resisted Sweeney?

since the nineteenth century, *Robert* was extraordinarily popular and much imitated in its time. Composer Giacomo Meyerbeer and librettists Eugène Scribe and Germain Delavigne loosely adapted a medieval legend about a young man sired by Satan and stalked by one of his emissaries into a sumptuous production that stabilized the standard conventions of grand opera as we enjoy them today.

First produced at the Paris Opéra, *Robert* proved a dependable, money-spinning repertory favorite throughout Europe and the Americas. Stoker thought highly enough of Meyerbeer to rank him alongside Bellini, Donizetti, and Verdi, and presumably researched the Theatre Royal archives to make note of two previous Dublin productions, one five years earlier (which he may well have seen as a student) and one dating to his bedridden years as a child.[6] *Robert* borrowed elements from Goethe's *Faust* nearly twenty years before Gounod's opera and recounted the story of the title character, shadowed by a sinister companion, Bertram. The latter knows of Robert's half-diabolical heritage and is eager to have him sign over his soul for purposes of eternal damnation. In the end, it is Bertram who faces a fiery recall to regions below.

The opera is more or less bisected by a show-stopping ballet in which white-shrouded nuns rise from their tombs for a haunting *danse macabre*—one of the first examples of *ballet blanc*, the now-familiar convention of costuming ballerinas completely in white. Degas famously commemorated the original scene, and its audience. White skirts and tutus would become a standard fixture of ballet, especially in supernaturally themed works like *Les sylphides*, *Giselle*, and *Swan Lake*.

Stoker called *Robert le diable* (performed in Italian as *Roberto il diavolo*) "mystic yet picturesque," with a "crowded and attentive" first-night house. "The plot of the incidental ballet, which was a prominent feature in last night's performance," Stoker wrote, "is in no way inconsistent with the supernatural nature of the plot, [and] although slightly incongruous, is at least novel and ingenious." The devilish Bertram's entrance "was greeted with hearty plaudits. His make up in sable and flame coloured habiliments was sufficiently suggestive of the weird mentor."

---

[6] Having ready access to the Theatre Royal's collection of programs and press clippings would explain Stoker's seemingly encyclopedic command of theatrical information as he dashed off his columns.

Back from the dead: Edgar Degas's 1871 impression of the haunting
danse macabre *from the Meyerbeer opera* Robert le diable.

Coinciding with the beginning of his work for the *Echo*, Stoker made the acquaintance of an actress who required absolutely no assistance registering pain or passion—or, indeed, histrionic states of any kind—and who would become a lifelong friend and confidante. In his *Personal Reminiscences* Stoker describes his first exposure to the work of the American actress Genevieve Ward as having occurred at her performance of Ernest Legouvé and Eugène Scribe's *Adrienne Lecouvreur* at the Theatre Royal. In reality, he had already seen her twice during her twelve-night engagement, first in Victor Hugo's *Lucrezia Borgia*, then in W. G. Wills's English adaptation of Legouvé's *Medea* (advertised as *Medea in Corinth*).

It was a rainy night in late November 1873 when Stoker took his favorite reviewer's seat at the back of the house at the Theatre Royal—"the end seat O.P." (meaning "opposite prompt," referring to the prompter's traditional position in the stage-right wings). The attendants kept the preferred seat open for him whenever possible. That night it wasn't even necessary;

attendance was disappointing, and "the few hundreds scattered about were like the plums in a foc'sle duff."[7]

Stoker described Ward's first-night audience for *Lucrezia* as only "cordial and appreciative," a reception he attributed to the role itself. "The character she chose for what may be designated her *debut* is not one to evoke much sympathy. Of all the wicked women who in every age have wrought evil, none has been represented as exceeding the enormities attributed to Lucrezia Borgia." And, certainly, using the sleepwalking scene from *Macbeth* as a curtain raiser for the play did little to make her warm and accessible. But Stoker himself had quite a different response than the other first-nighters. Ward "interested me at once," he wrote, likening her to "a triton amongst minnows. She was very handsome; of a rich dark beauty, with clear cut classical features, black hair, and great eyes that flashed with fire. I sat in growing admiration of her powers. Though there was a trace here and there of something which I thought amateurish she was so masterful, so dominating in other ways that I could not understand it."

He wrote in his diary, "(Mem. will be a great actress)."

Ward's twelve nights at the Theatre Royal were heavy with female ferocity, which Stoker seemed to relish as much as her acting. After Lady Macbeth and Lucrezia Borgia came Medea. In his *Echo* review (like his separate notice in the *Mail*, it ran the following day), Stoker wrote: "It is a daring thing for a young actress to make her debut, as *Medea*, in a Theatre where Ristori has lately performed the same part. . . . A poor performance would appear horribly mean by contrast; and Miss Ward may well consider last night's applause an omen of high histrionic renown." Adelaide Ristori was a legendary Italian tragedienne, with whom Ward had trained.

From first to last runs a series of scenes of wild ungovernable passion— love like the love of Swinburne, that bites and strains, hate such as consumes no other woman of fact or fiction; this love, this hate, with rage, despair, fury, revenge, jealousy, all blaze both by turns as though the heart of the woman were but one smoldering fire which needed but a breath to fan into flame.

---

[7] A boiled pudding sprinkled with dried bits of plums or raisins; a favorite of ship's cooks, hence the name "foc'sle," from the nautical "forecastle," or upper deck.

After the performance of *Adrienne Lecouvreur*, he was introduced to Ward backstage, and four nights later arranged for a more formal social introduction through the American consulate. "And then there began a close friendship that has never faltered, which has been one of the delights of my life and which will I trust remain as warm as it is now till the death of either shall cut it short."

Many writers on Stoker have suggested a romance with Ward, perhaps because she is the only female acquaintance in Dublin, other than his mother, Lady Wilde, and the woman he would marry, for which there is any documentation. But this surmise overlooks the fact that platonic friendships between men and women have always been common in the theatre. It also brushes aside obvious general conclusions about Stoker's sexual interests that might be drawn from his Whitman correspondence. The theatrical world has always been full of young men who idolize and fetishize older, actressy actresses, especially the divas who specialize in "strong" parts: Lady Macbeth, Lucrezia Borgia, and Medea are classic examples. At the age of thirty-six, Ward was twelve years older than Stoker, closer to his mother's generation than his own, especially given that the age of sexual consent in Victorian Britain was twelve.

And then there is Ward herself, whose own peculiar adventures in heterosexuality, or its contrived simulacrum, paint a picture of a woman with little use for men.

Ward was the American granddaughter of a New York City mayor, Gideon Lee, and the daughter of wealthy, globetrotting parents, Col. Samuel Ward and Lucy Leigh Ward. The family maintained residences in New York, London, Paris, and Rome.

By 1873, when she met Bram, Ward's life, on and off the stage, already had the makings of a sensation novel, or at least a feverish chamber opera. Years earlier she was, in fact, an opera singer of some note. Her mother had also been a gifted singer, with a four-octave ranged deemed "not human" by one amazed teacher, but she didn't pursue a professional career, channeling her ambitions instead into her musically talented daughter. Genevieve's international career was given a huge public relations boost by the tabloidesque melodrama of a star-crossed marriage at the age of nineteen to a Russian aristocrat, Count Constantine de Guerbel of Nicolaeiff, a dashing and magnetic young man said to bear a striking resemblance to Czar Nicholas I, whom he served as aide-de-camp.

Genevieve Ward as Lady Macbeth (left) and as Margaret D'Anjou in **Richard III.**

What the Wards didn't know about de Guerbel was that, according to his commanding officer in the Russian army, he "had all the vices of a full grown man, and seemed to know as much." As an adult, he displayed the makings of a Gothic novel villain. Ward's biographer Zadel Barnes Gustafson noted that de Guerbel's "personal power with both men and women was something inexplicably great. He was able to embarrass and lethargize the reasoning faculties, while intensifying the emotional."

Mesmerizing young women came easily to the count, who made an impulsive proposal of marriage in Nice, to the delight of Ward's ambitious parents. There is no evidence of an actual romantic bond—as Jane Austen, that astute chronicler of nineteenth-century matchmaking observed, real connubial happiness "is entirely a matter of chance."

Luck was not on Ward's side, emotionally or practically. The couple was married in a civil ceremony, which, under Russian law, was only a formality of engagement until the union could be consecrated in a Russian church. That never happened, and the count went on to other conquests. A jilted woman in Victorian times was considered to be damaged goods, and the scandalized Wards appealed through an intermediary to the Russian emperor himself to enforce de Guerbel's promise. Nicholas had neither the power to validate or dissolve the marriage, but he did order de Guerbel to Warsaw to complete the Russian end of the bargain and marry in a church. Ward's furious father carried a pistol to the "gruesome" service, at which the bridegroom was reported to tremble visibly, and at which the bride wore black. When an attendant questioned Mrs. Ward about the appropriateness of her daughter's wedding gown, she replied icily, "I consider it a funeral."

Ward didn't care; she had what she (or at least her mother) wanted—an aristocratic title to adorn her rising operatic career—and thereafter toured the world as "Madame de Guerbel," the juicy backstory of her marriage being an essential part of her press kit. Afterward she affected a studied indifference to men. She claimed, for instance, to have received eleven proposals of marriage in the wake of the de Guerbel affair, and sadistically toyed with insistent suitors, assigning them numbers, in the manner of a butcher shop, which they were expected to recite when or if they returned for additional humiliation.

When de Guerbel finally died a miserable death, being widely known as the widow of a syphilitic rake hardly made for good box office. Ward's stage name was modified to "Madame Guerrabella," which her mother claimed in interviews was Italian for "beautiful war," though it was her own coinage. Nonetheless, she meant it as a poignant reference to Genevieve's battle for her marital honor, a saga that now somehow involved an unnamed recreant husband and the Greek Orthodox Church. Fact-checking in Victorian entertainment journalism was decidedly relaxed, even by today's slippery standards.

The next improbable (but this time true) melodramatic juncture in Madame de Guerbel/Guerrabella's singing career was its abrupt conclusion through a fateful bout with diphtheria contracted during an engagement in Cuba in late 1872. Her singing voice was ruined. Not to be undone, she immediately took acting lessons from Adelaide Ristori and re-rechristened herself Genevieve Ward. She had been acting under her own name, to somewhat spotty audiences but increasing critical notice, for less than a year when she met Stoker.

In his review of Ward's *Medea*, Stoker had written, "None but genius of the highest class can touch or attempt 'Medea' without failing. The play is a touchstone; and the hush of silence, the shudder of sympathetic fear, and silence, the enthusiastic bursts of applause, that matched the progress of the piece, leave no doubt of the fact that not here alone, Miss Ward's reputation as the first tragedienne, the successor of Miss Cushman, is made."

"Miss Cushman" was Charlotte Cushman (1816–76), the leading American actress of her day. "She was a grand woman in every way—a fine, intellectual, big-hearted creature, a great tragic actress—and America may be proud of her," wrote Ward. "She had not much regular teaching—her genius was innate. She was generous to her fellow actresses, and to me especially; in fact she told a very dear friend of mine that her mantle had fallen on my shoulders. It was the highest and most stimulating praise I ever received."

Ward's biographer Richard Whiteing noted the "strange similarity, not so much, if at all, in the genius of the two players as in the mere circumstances of their lives. Both began as singers, both came to grief by trying to do too much with their voices, with the result of incurable overstrain." Cushman's musical career was derailed not by illness, like Ward's, but by bad notices. For both women, losing one's singing voice to artistic overdedication was a more palatable public relations story. They shared a taste for rarified sensibilities and bohemian personalities far beyond American shores.

"Both felt the tremendous allurement of Europe," wrote Whiteing. "There was a certain identity in their taste for pieces." Each actress had interpreted Lady Macbeth to acclaim, Cushman's especially fearsome portrayal declaimed opposite several prominent actors. (One can only wonder at the shudders later provoked in those who remembered her playing the role opposite John Wilkes Booth as the bloody thane. Two years later Booth followed the dagger of his own mind, straight into Ford's Theatre.) According to Whiteing, both Cushman and Ward "won their way quite as much by character as by genius—that is, by the determination to succeed. Both had the same passion for the stage even in later life. These sympathies naturally brought them together as friends, and the older woman always spoke with generous confidence of the younger's career."

Cushman was also a surprisingly open lesbian, who, much like Walt Whitman, successfully walked a tricky same-sex tightrope throughout her career. Whitman, in fact, was a great admirer; as a newspaperman he declared that "Charlotte Cushman is probably the greatest performer on

Charlotte Cushman as Romeo.

the stage in any hemisphere." Audiences were especially fascinated by her highly convincing "breeches" roles, including Romeo, Hamlet, and Orlando in *As You Like It* (an all-female production), and chose to largely ignore the in-your-face implications of the lifelong lack of a Mr. Cushman and the omnipresence of close female friends. Even when these relationships became publicly tempestuous, the public chalked things up to artistic temperament.

Like Le Fanu's Carmilla—never explcitly identified as lesbian—Cushman maneuvered out in the open and under the radar. Unlike sex between men, lesbian relations had never been criminalized, or even acknowledged as "real" sex. How could they be, with no male member involved? Or, to rephrase Stoker's vampire hunter Abraham Van Helsing, the strength of the nineteenth-century lesbian was that people would not believe in her.

Although she lived until 1922, Ward never made a film or recording. The "bottled orations" of the phonograph, she wrote, seemed "to come from the bowels of the earth, as from gnomes in torture." But her legacy and technique lived on and can still be observed in the recorded work of younger actresses she encouraged and mentored, like Martita Hunt, another "strong" actress never married or linked romantically to men, and a specialist in eccentric roles like Miss Havisham in David Lean's *Great Expectations* (1946), and—of special interest to Stoker connoisseurs—the baroness turned into a vampire by her son in the Freudian-flavored camp-fest *The Brides of Dracula* (1960).

Ward socialized in Dublin with the likes of Jane Wilde and Edward Dowden and, when away from the Irish capital, carried on a friendly correspondence with Stoker, but the fact that she began her letters "Dear Mr. Stoker" is more evidence their relationship was not what some would like it to have been. In the summer of 1874 Stoker visited Ward and her mother in Paris, planning to meet his parents in Switzerland afterward, but the City of Light proved to be of much greater interest, and he snubbed them. Charlotte wrote to him afterward, in Dublin, expressing regret that he didn't visit. But the City of Light had much that might delay his departure,

Genevieve Ward's protegée Martita Hunt was memorable
as the vampire baroness in **The Brides of Dracula** *(1960).*

and theatrical Paris must have been a revelation. The Comédie-Française was, once more, the professional home of Sarah Bernhardt, and in 1874 she played Racine's *Phèdre*. The Comédie's director was Émile Perrin, lately of the Paris Opera, who had introduced subscription tickets to attract well-heeled and well-behaved Parisian audiences. There were no Dublin-style donnybrooks in the aisles.

Stoker returned to France in 1875 and 1876 and was impressed by aspects of Paris far apart from its stages. During these trips he took notes for one of his most memorable short stories, "The Burial of the Rats" (published in serial installments in 1896, and only posthumously as an intact text, in 1914). In a vast dust heap at the city's periphery, a first-person protagonist is stalked by a predatory band of rag pickers. The title is creepily misdirecting: it is not rats that are buried, we learn, but rather the human corpses they strip to the bone that are figuratively interred—in their digestive tracts. As one of the dust-heap denizens explains, "He died last night. You won't find much of him. The burial of the rats is quick!"

The story includes a particularly unsettling sustained metaphor of invertebrate feeding that must have come from Stoker's study of Parisian maps and plans of the city's radiating streets, rails, and sewers. In the highly centralized city, he saw "many long arms with innumerable tentaculae, and in the center rises a gigantic head with a comprehensive brain and keen eyes to look on every side and ears sensitive to hear—and a voracious mouth to swallow." The hunger of this metropolis was highly irregular:

> Other cities resemble all the birds and beasts and fishes whose appetites and digestions are normal. Paris alone is the analogical apotheosis of the octopus. Product of centralisation carried to an *ad absurdum*, it fairly represents the devil fish,[8] and in no respects is the resemblance more curious than in the similarity of the digestive apparatus.

Stoker had hopes of becoming a playwright, and Ward encouraged him in the writing of a play based on the life of Madame Roland, a leading figure in the French Revolution. Stoker wrote to his father that he was writing

---

[8] A term usually used to describe the horned manta ray's "devilish" appearance, but sometimes also in general reference to the octopus—frightening in the popular imagination even without horns.

the play for a "Miss Henry," who has never been further identified. Some have speculated (or hoped for) a romance, but it is far more reasonable to assume that Miss Henry was simply a protégée of Miss Ward.[9] Nothing came of Stoker's Madame Roland play—no script or notes have ever been discovered—but the possibility of writing for the stage stuck with him. In his journal he jotted a note that Poe's "The Fall of the House of Usher" might be a good basis for an opera, and his instinct was astute. Stoker never developed it himself, but Claude Debussy would partially finish a libretto and score for *La chute de la maison Usher* between 1908 and 1917; Philip Glass would complete his own version in 1987.

Work for the stage was collaborative and contingent upon many variables and vagaries. For Stoker, fiction was a much more manageable creative outlet, and he had been working steadily at the craft since the publication of his first two short stories. In early 1875, *The Primrose Path*, a novella by "A. Stoker, Esq.," was serialized in five issues of the Dublin magazine *The Shamrock*. The successive and cumulative improvement in Stoker's narrative skills from "The Crystal Cup" to "Saved by a Ghost" to *The Primrose Path* suggests a sudden eruption of honed craftsmanship that is probably misleading. We don't know how closely one composition followed upon the other. "The Crystal Cup" may well have been a very early piece of juvenilia. "Saved by a Ghost" appeared only after he had more than a year of grueling journalism under his belt, an experience sure to improve any kind of writing. Clive Leatherdale, Stoker's most prolific modern editor, notes that young Bram may have been "hardened to rejection," submitting an untold number of stories to Dublin and London periodicals in the early 1870s. "It is a safe bet," Leatherdale writes, "that many of Stoker's early works languished in drawers, never to be published." In structure, dialogue, and

---

[9] Rupert Hart-Davis, editor of Max Beerbohm's *Letters to Reggie Turner*, provides some interesting information on the parentage of Wilde's best friend and Oxford classmate, born in 1869, which may also shed some speculative light on the identity of Miss Henry: "The general belief was that Reggie's mother was a French actress or singer called (probably only on the stage) Miss L. Henrie." In London, for the opening of the Gaiety Theatre on December 21, 1868, Henrie essayed the male role of Ferdinando in W. S. Gilbert's *Robert the Devil* (after Meyerbeer). Over the next few years she made four more appearances in plays and opera/opera bouffe—two more of them "trousers" parts, à la Charlotte Cushman—"after which Miss L. Henrie disappears from theatrical and all other history." Could this possibly have been the "Miss Henry" (the name Anglicized by Stoker), considering a comeback at Ward's encouragement, in Stoker's never-finished play?

characterization, *The Primrose Path* resembles stage melodrama, to which Stoker had regular exposure during his years as a critic.

It also reflects an extraordinary ambivalence *about* the theatre, which could only have come from Stoker's own struggle to balance practicality and stability with the powerful pull of his heart's desire. The protagonist, Jerry O'Sullivan, is a Dublin carpenter struggling to support his wife, Katey, and their baby daughter. He receives an offer of employment from a theatre in London, which revives "a strange longing to share in the unknown life of the dramatic world," a realm as alluring and esoteric as "the mysteries of Isis to a Neophyte."

> Moth-like he had buzzed around the footlights as a boy, and had never lost the slight romantic feeling which such buzzing ever inspires. Once or twice his professional work had brought him within the magic precincts where the stage-manager is king, and there the weirdness of the place, with its myriad cords and chains, and traps, and scenes, and flies, had more than ever enchanted him.

Jerry's wife is heartbroken when he leaves for London, even though he explains that it's all for the good of the family, and he will soon be able to send for her and their daughter. But not long after he arrives at his new place of employment, a costumed actor playing the role of Mephistopheles in a dramatic version of *Faust* ("the dresses were the same as those used in Gounod's opera") invites him to a tavern across the street during a break in the dress rehearsal for a beer. Just as in "Saved by a Ghost," a Mephistophelian character is present at a crucial moment of alcoholic temptation. The make-believe devil introduces Jerry to a genuinely frightening and diabolical figure: "When the bar-keeper turned round Jerry met the most repulsive face he had ever seen—a face so drawn and twisted, with nose and lips so eaten away with some strange canker, that it resembled more the front of a skull than the face of a living man."

The barkeep's name is Grinnell (Stoker's less-than-subtle way to evoke the rictus grin of a death's head), and he quickly entices Jerry into daily drinking, then daily drunkenness. When Katey and the baby finally arrive, he is unemployable and beyond salvation. In a bestial frenzy, he kills Katey with a hammer, then cuts his throat with a carpenter's chisel.

The term "primrose path" was coined by Shakespeare in *Hamlet*,

First publication of Stoker's **The Primrose Path** *(1875).*

meaning the best or most assured means of self-destruction, and in *Macbeth* the Bard employs a colorful variant: "the primrose way to the everlasting bonfire." Stoker had seen the great tragedian Barry Sullivan barnstorm Dublin in both plays and remembered both vividly. Thirty years later he would quote or reference both works in *Dracula*. *The Primrose Path,* in fact, strongly foreshadows *Dracula*: a young man makes a voyage by sea and land and comes under the controlling influence of a ghastly, corpselike man who later sets his malignant designs on the man's wife when she comes to London to rescue him. *Faust* is evoked; the Mephistophelian villain's power resides in the inculcation of an uncontrollable thirst that dehumanizes its victims, who devolve into bestial transgressors themselves. In both stories, an atavistic evil runs riot in modern London. Count Dracula wields power from within a wooden box, while Grinnell metaphorically projects his evil from the inside of an oaken whiskey barrel.

Why Stoker chose to write successive stories in the form of temperance tracts is an interesting puzzle. There are no reports of him overindulging as an adult; the one time recorded that he refused a glass of wine was on account of gout. The fact that his mother was thoroughly convinced that her family was spared cholera through the daily prophylactic use of alcohol might yield a clue. The Thornleys were otherwise healthy, but what larger dose might be "needed" by a sick child? Is it possible Bram's father drank to excess? After all, it was a classic activity, if not *the* classic activity, for henpecked husbands. Might Abraham have been a functional alcoholic—the kind whose drinking didn't land him in the gutter but interfered with career ambition and advancement? Drinking problems run in families, but we know nothing about the habits of his brothers. It's also interesting that Charlotte, while she was a social reformer, had never taken up the temperance cause that swept Ireland in the 1840s. Bram, though, frequently took note of sloppy drinkers. In his journal, he wrote several humorous impressions of thoroughly drunken Dubliners. One in particular was both funny and disgusting: an account of an inebriated celebrant at a dance using vomit to lubricate his slides across the floor.

A verified alcoholic whom Stoker did know very well at the time of *The Primrose Path* was his Trinity friend and sometime theatre companion Willie Wilde, Oscar's brother. Willie was an enthusiastic college carouser whose drinking career progressed rapidly after graduation and effectively sabotaged any real career he would pursue. His 1875 "call to the bar" took on more than one meaning in the shape of a debauched celebration at 1 Merrion Square on the occasion of receiving his law degree. Like everyone else who knew the Wildes, Stoker would have noticed Willie's doppelgängerish similarity to Oscar—"a veritable tragedy of family resemblance," Max Beerbohm would observe. Wilde family chronicler Joan Schenkar described him in his later London days: "Outsized (perhaps six foot four inches) like Oscar and with a high laugh like Oscar's, ungainly and slow-moving like his mother, unkempt like his dead father, Willie Wilde's large features, sensuous, mobile lips, brilliant blue eyes, and long, graceful hands were enough like Oscar's to invite invidious comparison."

It was said that Willie finally grew a beard (or was paid by Oscar to wear one; accounts vary) to avoid being mistaken for his brother, but his own behavior assured that he would draw unfavorable opinion, a matter much exacerbated during his brother's ultimate humiliation and fall. His first marriage, to the American socialite and publisher Mrs. Frank Leslie, ended disastrously (and didn't begin well, with Willie telling the press, "America needs a leisure class, and I'm going to see that they get one!"). Willie's second marriage produced a daughter, Dorothy, better known as Dolly, who would take the Wilde name to an early grave, mixing her father's propensity for drink with her own weakness for drugs. She bore a startling physical resemblance to her father, uncle, and grandmother and was especially fond of trompe l'oeil impersonations of Oscar for the camera and for friends. Imitative of her uncle in reckless disregard for propriety, and aggressively open in lesbianism (which she pursued with élan and abandon in Parisian artistic circles), Dolly Wilde would succumb to her addictions in 1941 at the age of forty-seven.

Willie Wilde wasn't the only possible inspiration for a cautionary tale about alcohol. Given Stoker's lifelong fascination with fairy tales, he could easily have come across George Cruikshank's *Fairy Library* (1853–54), much later republished and better known as *The Cruikshank Fairy-Book* (1897). The celebrated illustrator of Dickens had become a devoted follower of temperance after renouncing his own soggy history, and chose to revise several classic tales along soberly moralistic lines. The cruel adult behavior displayed in so many of the original versions, Cruikshank maintained, could only be explained by drunkenness. The idea that a parent might willfully abandon a child in the woods was "not only disgusting, but *against nature*" (Cruikshank's italics, of which he was rather fond), "and consequently unfit for the pure and parent-loving minds of children." And, certainly, "any father acting in such a manner either must be mad, or under the influence of intoxicating liquor, which is much the same thing; and therefore, wishing to avoid any illusion to such an awful affliction as insanity, I accounted for the father's unnatural conduct by attributing it to *that cause* which *marks its progress daily and hourly by acts of unnatural brutality*."

Cruikshank was especially offended by the ogre's blood-sucking children in traditional versions of "Hop-o'-my-Thumb" that Stoker had doubtless read as a boy, and the general moral collapse indicated in story after story (like "Puss in Boots") with "happy" plot resolutions turning on imposture, deceit, and thievery. But he saved his most extensive and preachy revisionism for "Cinderella": interceding with both italics *and* capital letters

when the King orders that fountains of wine be run in the streets to celebrate the nuptials of Cinderella and her Prince, the fairy godmother (a
Munchkinish dwarf in this version) rushes forth to plead her case like a
fantasyland incarnation of Carrie Nation. Even if it disappoints his subjects, the King must abandon the established custom, for "the use of strong
drink . . . is marked on every page by *excess, which follows, as a matter of course,
from the very nature of its composition*, and is always accompanied by ill-health,
misery and crime," including "brutal fights, and violent deaths." When the
King inquires if drink is not intended by Providence for human use, the
sobriety tirade continues in full for more than one unbroken page:

> "With all deference to your Majesty," said the dwarf in reply, "most assur-
> edly not; for such is the power of the CREATOR that, if it had been neces-
> sary for man to take stimulating drinks, the ALMIGHTY could have given
> them to him free from all intoxicating qualities, as He has done with all
> solids and liquids necessary and fit for the support of man's life. . . . And as
> to *moderation*, Pardon me, your Majesty, but so long as your Majesty contin-
> ues to take even half a glass of wine a-day, so long will the drinking custom
> of society be considered respectable, and thus it follows, as a necessary
> consequence, that thousands of your Majesty's subjects will be constantly
> falling by excess into vice, wretchedness, and crime; and as to people not
> being able to do without stimulating drinks, I beg your Majesty to look at
> Cinderella, who has never taken any in all her life, and who never will."

For a child exposed simultaneously to fairy tales and a combination of
alcohol and opium, as Stoker may have been, Cruikshank's bizarre stories
might well trigger an ambivalent reaction, to be wrestled with in fiction.
Or perhaps *The Primrose Path* was not really about alcoholism, which could
have served the euphemistic function known in psychology as a screen anxiety. Rowdy behavior among audiences and the occasional tipsy thespian
aside, drinking has never been a stereotypical vice ascribed to the theatre.
Female prostitution and male homosexuality, however, were always perceived as hovering dangers, and alcohol was frequently invoked as both a
cause and an excuse for a man's transgressions with other men. More than
one acquaintance of Oscar Wilde would blame drink for his ultimate fall.

The previous year, while visiting Genevieve Ward in Paris, Stoker was introduced by the actress to a writer from whom she had commissioned a classical drama about the Lesbian poetess Sappho, to be premiered in Dublin the following spring. It was a particularly provocative choice, as the Greek icon was increasingly depicted in nineteenth-century poetry and art as a lowercase lesbian as well. It was a role even Charlotte Cushman had never ventured to essay.

William Gorman Wills was a Dublin-born playwright, poet, and painter (the latter only "of sorts," in the qualified estimation of Ward, despite a few royal commissions) who attracted and exasperated friends and collaborators in equal measure all through his life. He was also a cousin of Oscar Wilde, whose full name was Oscar Fingal O'Flahertie Wills Wilde. A lifelong bohemian bachelor, he maintained a residence in London and, later, an atelier in Paris. According to Ward's biographer Richard Whiteing, when Wills summered at Étretat on the Normandy coast to work on a play, he "was immediately surrounded, as he always was, by a bevy of charming and refined women, drawn to him by their sheer sense of his want of mothering, rather than wifing."

Indeed, the only intimate relationship Wills maintained was with his own mother. His voluminous correspondence with her was, in fact, his only writing of a personal nature, and upon his own death, and at his orders, all the letters were destroyed. This made his brother's posthumous biography rather difficult, but he reported that Wills was so shaken by her death he couldn't bear to attend the funeral, and afterward quite literally lost the will to live.

Nonetheless, in his more vital years Wills repeatedly entered into facetious courtships with the women who showed him kindness and looked after his life. "He had proposed to each of his ministrant angels in turn, and then 'taken it back' in sheer terror of the prospect of an ordered life," Whiteing wrote. Eventually, understanding that Wills was not really interested in or constitutionally oriented for marriage, the spurned women of Étretat staged a "specially convened" tea-party intervention and "asked him not to make a fool of himself again."

Of Wills, Stoker wrote, "His nature was a most affectionate one. I suppose that in the whole multitude of his friends and acquaintances—and they were many—there was not one who did not love him." Stoker described an extended visit with Wills in Normandy:

Sappho *playwright and Stoker friend W. G. Wills.*

It was on this holiday, where we spent the days idly together, that I saw most of poor Wills; and it was then that I learned to see the true sweetness and depth of his character through that veil of weakness which was all his own. He had an indecision which became a positive quality. Many a morning, when we had started for a ramble together, he would change his mind twenty times as to what form our excursion would take, or whither it would tend, whilst we were crossing the terrace of the Casino. But there was always one end which suited us both, and when in doubt I would play this trump.

The seaside was their frequent destination:

Then a short while would find us swimming out in the blue waters of the little bay, he wearing a battered old straw hat which seemed to have a special charm for him. He would stay for a long time in the water, lazily floating whilst he enjoyed the picturesque outlines of the flanking cliffs and the views of the distant headlands caught through the bold caverns and the storm-pierced rocks. He was a man full of bright and sweet imaginings, and on some of our Étretat days, as we strolled through the leafy woods or along the summits of the cliffs, he would reveal perfect glimpses of a fairyland of a mind full of tender thoughts and delicate fancy.

Wills worked on his plays in creative isolation, and his final scripts weren't always exactly what his clients expected. But he had already proved his power at the box office, with hit plays like *Charles I* for Henry Irving, and his clients gave him a wide berth. Like Lady Wilde, he preferred to write in bed, *en dishabille*. And frequently, he would rather just not write at all.

The Sappho project came to him with unusual creative freedom, since real historical documentation of the character was essentially nil. Aside from the small fragments of poetry that had survived from antiquity, the Sappho of drama and art was a creature who took shape from centuries of imaginative projection. The historical Sappho, the lyric poet of Lesbos whom Plato extolled as "the tenth muse," lived approximately 620–570 BC. Increasingly sexualized portrayals of Sappho had recently provided nineteenth-century "decadent" writers a backdoor way of raising the general topic of homosexuality, simply by evoking its more acceptable female incarnation. In his notorious poem "Anactoria" (1866), Algernon Charles Swinburne had already presented Sappho as not only lesbian but lesbian-vampire-cannibal. Sappho tells her lover Anactoria of her desire to "drink thy veins as wine and eat / Thy breasts as honey!" and the wish that "Thy body were absorbed and consumed, / and in my flesh thy very flesh entombed." It is possible that J. Sheridan Le Fanu took some inspiration from "Anactoria" for Carmilla's protestations of love to her victim. Lines like "You are mine, you shall be mine, and you and I are one forever," Carmilla's sobbing declaration over lesbian kisses, neatly distill the merging of identity and blood in "Anactoria."

Swinburne himself may or may not have had sex with men—opinion is mixed—but he did nothing to dispel the notion. Oscar Wilde dismissed him as "a braggart in matters of vice," who never actually practiced what he preached. The transgressive and unrestrained emotionality of his poetry,

Sappho as imagined by painter Charles August Mengin (1877).

however, was well known to Stoker, evidenced by the reference in his review of Ward's *Medea.*

Wills's script has not survived, but from what can be gleaned from Stoker's reviews and his engrossing account of the production deleted from the published version of *Personal Reminiscences*, Wills freely adapted the story of Sappho and her unfaithful lover Phaon from Ovid's *Heroides.* Phaon's infidelity drives Sappho to seek female company on the island of Lesbos. In Wills's telling, Sappho has a sister, Myrrha, who has betrayed her with Phaon. The pent-up, same-sex energy of the Lesbos maenads erupts, leading directly to the destruction of the Temple of Hymen. Sappho is condemned, and Myrrha pleads to die in her place, but Sappho stoically accepts her fate and hurls herself into the sea.

Unfortunately, trouble was gathering. Stoker, fascinated as ever by Ward and her work, followed the production's progress carefully, especially because it was all coming together on the familiar stage of the Gaiety Theatre. He recalled that Wills, working from London, delivered the acts "fitfully," and following the penultimate, Saturday rehearsal, Sappho's fatal leap was still unscripted.

According to Ward, "We were in full rehearsal before I could get a sight of the final scene. When it came at last, it ended only in a few lines penciled round the edge of a torn letter, and in Greek, if you please, to bring down the curtain."

"That'll fetch 'em," Wills had written. "One of her finest fragments." And it was the last Wills ever had to say on the subject of *Sappho*.

Ward was "in great distress" at Wills's failure to finish the commission, according to Stoker. One can only imagine her offstage histrionics. The only reliable, deadline-oriented writer to whom she could turn on short notice was Stoker himself. He knew Greek, after all. And even though *Madame Roland* had never come to fruition, Ward knew better than anyone else his secret aspirations as a playwright.

"It was a large order to finish another man's play at a moment's notice," Stoker wrote. He agreed to the assignment, despite already having a potentially conflicting commitment the following evening, when the play was to premiere. Would he even be able to see his own work? "The story was completed as far as the point where [Sappho] announces her willing sacrifice," he recalled. The fragments of poetry offered little inspiration, since Sappho herself never wrote about anyone's suicide. Her leap into the sea was a later dramatic invention, but the Trinity library would not be available on a Sunday for Stoker to peruse Menander, Ovid, or any of the many incarnations of the legend.

Like the fictionalized Sappho, Stoker would have to take a leap himself.

The snippets of his own dialogue Stoker recorded are prosaic, though serviceable. "Live, Sappho! Live! Live!" the chorus of citizens exhorts the doomed poetess. "Live!" Sappho responds. "I shall live in all the days to come. The soul of Sappho does not thus [pass] away! Whilst hearts can break and lips be false to love, Sappho shall live."

During Sunday night's final rehearsal, Stoker was lecturing on "Art in Ireland" at the Fortnightly Club,[10] and it was, no doubt, a distracted presentation. Rushing several blocks to the Gaiety afterward, he arrived just in time for the last scene, and was "elated on hearing my own lines spoken with exquisite force and pathos."

Stoker's decision to review *Sappho* without revealing his own part in it was a tad unseemly, although it rose nowhere near the audacity of Walt Whitman's anonymous self-reviewing of *Leaves of Grass*. But the conflict of self-interest was compounded by his spreading the coverage over three days—he was acting less as a critic than as a covert personal press agent. On Monday, his advance piece advised readers that "the play is one of great force, and, as it affords many opportunities for histrionic display is especially suited to Miss Ward. We have every confidence that Miss Ward will equal the expectation which we formed of her on her first appearance—that of being the first [e.g., foremost or leading] tragic actress on the British stage." To Stoker,

> the soul of Sappho is no empty name, but a living thing. It is hard to realize in our tame century the wondrous fire and passion of the Lesbian poetess who could stir to madness the hearts of Greece; and we scarcely believe in the reality of her presence until we have seen her life and passion— the wondrous depth of her love—the struggles and tortures of her soul, although but on the mimic stage. With Miss Ward we can go back at one bound, and stand amidst the Grecian peoples and priests, with the temples of the gods rising around us, and see everywhere the traces of passionate hearts and natures of keenness unknown in our colder world.

In Stoker's completely misleading assessment, "The production of *Sappho* was effective, and marred by not a single one of those hitches which are almost inseparable from the production of a new play." Had he forgotten the matter of the play being unfinished? His recollection is much better when he simply describes the action. "When she joins the Maenads, it is

---

[10] This lecture, along with the fact that Stoker described himself as an "arts critic," rather than merely a drama critic, for the *Dublin Evening Mail*, raises the question of how much of the paper's unsigned coverage of cultural events beyond the stage also may have been written by Stoker.

the woman who speaks and not the poetess. She drops the lyre to wield the thyrsus." The thyrsus was, and is, a fairly blatant phallus surrogate, in the same league as calamus grass, and symbolic of the fearsome energy that could be wielded by an empowered woman. In ancient times, a decorated thyrsus might have its shaft encircled by veinlike vines, and, if that imagery wasn't sufficiently evocative, topped off by a large pine cone dripping with honey. Even in classical times, the connection between such devices and lesbianism was clearly understood. In the dialogue *Amores (Affairs of the Heart)*, attributed to Lucian, we find the following:

> If males find intercourse with males acceptable, henceforth let women too love each other. Come now, epoch of the future, legislator of strange pleasures, devise fresh paths for male lusts, but bestow the same privilege on women, and let them have intercourse with each other just as men do. Let them strap to themselves cunningly contrived instruments of lechery, those mysterious monstrosities devoid of seed, and let woman lie with woman as does a man.

There are no surviving drawings, photographs, or other record of *Sappho*'s production's design, so exactly how far it pushed phallic symbolism is anyone's guess. But it should be noted that plays in Dublin, unlike those in London and the English provinces, were not subject to prior censorship by the Lord Chamberlain (most likely because of geographical logistics) and were therefore much freer to push the boundaries of propriety for artistic effect. Twenty-two years later, in London, Stoker would fully understand the unseemly symbolism of a wooden shaft when he chose to delete the description of his vampire Lucy Westenra being gruesomely stake-pierced in his staged copyright reading of *Dracula*, which required the Lord Chamberlain's full approval. What on earth the censors thought happened in the truncated scene is anyone's guess, but Stoker did get his license.

One of Stoker's more prominent fellow members at the Philosophical Society was John Pentland Mahaffy, the distinguished Trinity professor of classical literature, who published a "special discussion" of Greek homosexuality, platonic and otherwise, in the first edition of his *Social Life in*

Greece: From Homer to Menander (1874). The topic was groundbreaking in a publication intended for general readers, and Mahaffy approached it gingerly—one might even say as if with a pair of tweezers. In describing "the peculiar delight and excitement felt by the Greeks in the society of handsome youths," he admitted that older males experienced "the same sort of agreeable zest which the young men of our own time feel in the company of young ladies." He asked his readers to "imagine a modern Irishman transplanted to an old Greek symposium, and there observing that in spite of the romantic feelings existing between the men present, nothing was done, or even hinted at, inconsistent with the strictest taste and propriety." While allowing that "this sentiment in the Greek mind did ally itself with passion, and lead to strange and odious consequences," Mahaffy took pains to reassure his modern audience that the Attic Greeks almost always sublimated baser impulses. "The Darwinians say that these feelings are all based on a purely physical want, and have written (especially Häckel)[11] things justly offensive to modern taste on the subject." Even if the Darwinians were right, "their argument does not the least affect the present case, so long as these physical springs are not *consciously felt*. Every English gentleman, who has not gone in search of low philosophy to palliate bad morals, will testify that though there is a distinct difference in his sentiment as regards friends of the opposite sex, yet to him, consciously at least, any physical cause is not only rare, but abhorrent."

The esteemed don may well have strained the credulity of less sanctimonious, more observant Victorian readers with his assertion that "a great proportion of the passing attachments among our young people have no conscious physical source, nor does such a notion present itself to the purer minds among us." One wonders what he would have made of the well-known if not widely acknowledged fact that Dublin men interested in Whitmanesque encounters in the 1870s needed to look no further than the public urinals on College Green under the statue of Thomas Moore, steps from the Trinity gates. Additionally, a discreet male brothel flourished on a street behind Dublin Castle.

Mahaffy himself was married but maintained his own residence in

---

[11] Ernst Haeckel (1834–1919), German biologist and philosopher, curiously influenced by both Darwin and the Romantic movement. Among his numerous achievements, Haeckel coined many familiar scientific terms, including "stem cell" and "ecology."

Dublin, ostensibly because his wife had an intractable aversion to socializing. He lived his life in town like a bachelor. The historian Brian Lacey, in *Terrible Queer Creatures: Homosexuality in Irish History*, suggests that Mahaffy had "a whiff of the 'musical'" about him—"musical" being a common insider's sexual euphemism of the time, like "psychological." Although Mahaffy was a clergyman, he had eccentric religious ideas. For instance, his observations about pagan influences on Christianity prompted quiet charges of heresy. He eschewed the modern clerical collar for the traditional white tie of the early 1800s, and when asked by a confused stranger if he was actually a man of the cloth reputedly answered, "Yes, but not in any offensive sense." His flippant reply, when queried by evangelicals on the matter of whether or not he was saved, ran along the lines of "Yes, but so narrowly that I don't boast about it." When he asked a new student to state his religion and received the answer "Christian," Mahaffy is supposed to have said, "Oh, no, we don't have that here at all—you must answer Catholic or Protestant." He was also known for his quips and witticisms; for example, his answer to the question "What is the difference between a man and a woman?" was "I can't conceive."

Mahaffy's former Trinity student Oscar Wilde, then at Oxford, assisted in the preparation of *Social Life in Greece* while in Dublin and apparently had a hand in writing some of the trickier arguments. Anticipating the tone of Wilde's later and more devilish epigrams, one passage read, "As to the epithet *unnatural*, the Greeks would answer probably, that all civilisation was unnatural, that its very existence presupposed the creation of new instincts, the suppression of old, and that many of the best features in all gentle life were best because they were unnatural." It has been suggested that what Wilde didn't borrow from his mother in creating his public persona, he found in the person of Mahaffy. Indeed, many photographs and even cartoons of Mahaffy could, at a quick glance, easily be mistaken for Wilde.

For all its intended euphemism and delicacy, the "special discussion" in *Social Life in Greece* caused enough embarrassment for Mahaffy that he deleted it from all subsequent editions, along with his acknowledgment to Oscar. This was not the result of excoriating reviews or public denunciations. Actually, the book was politely, even enthusiastically received. What pressure was placed on Mahaffy came from within the academy. Mahaffy had spoken about homoeroticism in a homosocial community, and was bound to offend or threaten someone. Although he removed some pages, he never retracted his opinions. As his biographers W. B. Stanford and R. B. McDowell note, "In place of the offending pages he had adroitly substituted an appreciation of 'female beauty' in ancient Greece and a discussion of other matters of wholesome feminine interest."

Wilde and his Trinity mentor had a strange, off-and-on relationship for many years after. Mahaffy discouraged Wilde from visiting Catholic Rome and instead took him to Greece "to make a proper pagan" of him. Wilde would frequently acknowledge his academic debt to Mahaffy but eventually published an anonymous, truly vicious review of one of his later books. In the end, after the catastrophic scandal, Mahaffy would only say, "We no longer speak of Mr. Oscar Wilde," and dismiss him as "the one blot on my scholarship."

The year following *Sappho,* and while Mahaffy's book was still causing embarrassment behind closed doors, Stoker once more had the chance to publicly come to the defense of Walt Whitman, whose "Children of Adam" poems in *Leaves of Grass* had come under "a violent, incisive attack" at a meeting of the Fortnightly Club. He followed Edward Dowden at the lectern and afterward wrote in his diary, "Spoke—I think well."

But that was only the beginning of his night's writing. He retrieved the hidden letter he had written but had never sent to Walt Whitman almost exactly four years earlier, and stayed up until three in the morning, writing a new one to accompany it, and this time he mailed them both.

DUBLIN, FEB. 14, 1876.

My dear Mr. Whitman.
I hope you will not consider this letter from an utter stranger a liberty. Indeed, I hardly feel a stranger to you, nor is this the first letter that I have written to you. My friend Edward Dowden has told me often that you like new acquaintances or I should rather say friends. And as an old friend I send you an enclosure which may interest you. Four years ago I wrote the enclosed draft of a letter which I intended to copy out and send to you—it has lain in my desk since then—when I heard that you were addressed

as Mr. Whitman. It speaks for itself and needs no comment. It is as truly what I wanted to say as that light is light. The four years which have elapsed have made me love your work fourfold, and I can truly say that I have ever spoken as your friend. You know what hostile criticism your work sometimes evokes here, and I wage a perpetual war with many friends on your behalf. But I am glad to say that I have been the means of making your work known to many who were scoffers at first. The years which have passed have not been uneventful to me, and I have felt and thought and suffered much in them, and I can truly say that from you I have had much pleasure and much consolation—and I do believe that your open earnest speech has not been thrown away on me or that my life and thought fail to be marked with its impress. I write this openly because I feel that with you one must be open. We have just had tonight a hot debate on your genius at the Fortnightly Club in which I had the privilege of putting forward my views—I think with success. Do not think me cheeky for writing this. I only hope we may sometime meet and I shall be able perhaps to say what I cannot write. Dowden promised to get me a copy of your new edition and I hope that for any other work which you may have you will let me always be an early subscriber. I am sorry that you're not strong. Many of us are hoping to see you in Ireland. We had arranged to have a meeting for you. I do not know if you like getting letters. If you do I shall only be too happy to send you news of how thought goes among the men I know. With truest wishes for your health and happiness believe me

BRAM STOKER

In *Personal Reminiscences of Henry Irving*, Stoker significantly altered the facts surrounding his correspondence, without revealing the content of either letter. He suggested he had sent more than one piece of fan mail in the past, though "my letters were only of the usual pattern and did not call for an answer" (especially if never mailed). He merged both the 1872 and 1876 missives into one, misleadingly characterizing the new letter as the "one in which I poured out my heart. I had long wished to do so but was, somehow, ashamed or diffident—the qualities are much alike. That night I spoke out; the stress of the evening had given me courage."

Had he known both letters were destined to be read, pondered, and debated by the public more than a century after his death, he might never have been so brave. But whatever small embarrassment he may have felt the dead of that cold February night was supplanted by emotions of a completely different kind at what arrived in his mail several weeks later.

41 STEVENS ST. CAMDEN,
N. JERSEY, COR. WEST.
U.S. AMERICA,

March 6, '76

BRAM STOKER,—My dear young man,—Your letters have been most welcome to me—welcome to me as a Person and then as Author—I don't know which most. You did so well to write to me so unconventionally, so fresh, so manly, and affectionately too. I, too, hope (though it is not probable) that we will some day personally meet each other. Meantime, I send my friendship and thanks.

Edward Dowden's letter containing among others your subscription for a copy of my new edition has just been recd. I shall send the book very soon by express in a package to his address. I have just written to E.D.

My physique is entirely shatter'd—doubtless permanently—from paralysis and other ailments. But I am up and dress'd, and get out every day a little, live

here quite lonesome, but hearty, and good spirits.—
Write to me again.

WALT WHITMAN

The letter, of course, stunned him—as it would stun any young acolyte to receive such a personal, open, and generous response from an idol.
And though neither he nor Whitman could imagine it then, they would
eventually meet. In the meantime, the next few years of Stoker's life would
turn on as yet unknown events and his own momentous decisions. Could
he possibly make a living as a professional writer? In the theatre? Would he
remain in Dublin? Was there a way to achieve middle-class marriage and
domesticity while fulfilling his deep yearning for an ecstatic connection to
another man?

These were not easy questions. But in the manner of courtship, he
would soon follow the example of Oscar Wilde.

CHAPTER FOUR

ENGAGEMENTS AND COMMITMENTS

WOMEN ARE PICTURES. MEN ARE PROBLEMS.

—Oscar Wilde, *A Woman of No Importance*

In *Oscar Wilde: A Certain Genius*, biographer Barbara Belford observes that "Wilde noticed women's faces, but seldom describes their bodies."

Much the same can be said of Bram Stoker.

In his first published works of fiction, "The Crystal Cup" and *The Primrose Path*, women have no physical presence whatsoever, even though they are central to the plots. The princess Aurora in "The Crystal Cup" is as ethereal and weightless as her name, an elusive ghost unattainable by the male narrator. In *The Primrose Path*, the main female character is described in the opening line as a "pretty little wife" and then is seen no more, at least not in visual specifics. Her behavior is virtuous, her person incorporeal. Men are routinely described in detail in Stoker's stories and novels, with a typical emphasis on facial detail and clothing. But he has no interest in applied physiognomy when it comes to women, and he doesn't even care what they wear.

Florence Balcombe, later Florence Stoker,
as sketched by her unsuccessful suitor Oscar Wilde, circa 1877.

Stoker's theatre criticism in Dublin routinely presents women as virtually disembodied voices, faces, and hands that mostly serve as vessels for violently primal emotion. When Kate Bateman performed in the biblical drama *Leah*, Stoker noted that "in scenes of passionate invective, Miss Bateman has no peer on the British stage," displaying a visage that "might well serve a painter for the study of a head of a Fury. Every feature seems almost radiant with the inspiration of hate—the brows and wide-spread quivering nostrils, the burning eyes and the mouth opening almost into a square, in true tragic style."

Stoker's description anticipates that of *Dracula*'s vampire Lucy Westenra, also to be described in terms of classical mythology and the theatre: Lucy's brows aren't merely "corrugated" but "wrinkled as though the folds of the flesh were the coils of Medusa's snakes," while her "lovely, blood-stained mouth grew into an open square, as if in the passion masks of the Greeks and Japanese."

As Medea, Adelaide Ristori (Genevieve Ward's celebrated Italian acting coach) elicited Stoker's admiration for "the savage glitter of the eye, the wildly vindictive gesture, and the incisive harness of the voice"; her performance was "almost beyond belief in its expressiveness" as her brain bypassed her body and communicated directly to her hands: "Whilst telling how her brother hurled the blood from his dripping wound at his murderers, her hand, her face, every gesture seems to repeat the action, so that when, as if with a dying effort, she dashes forth her open hands, the audience involuntarily recoils." And virtually every appraisal of Ward during her own Dublin engagements expresses an awestruck wonder at her fearful transfixing gaze, like that of Medusa or a basilisk.

Whereas men can be praised for intellectuality, complexity, and nuance, women are best appreciated by Stoker at their polar reaches. On Bateman, for instance: "She is best in those scenes which have no medium tones—where the extreme of emotion of one kind or another are portrayed." Actresses specializing in virago roles are especially praised when they soften the blood and thunder with diametrically opposite infusions of maternal tenderness. Stoker's work has frequently been cited for its reliance on impossibly virtuous women (for instance, Katey in *The Primrose Path*), while also containing some of the most misogynistic imagery in fiction (*The Lair of the White Worm* has some of the worst examples).

Whither this profound ambivalence about women? Part of the answer may lie in Stoker's early years, when he would have witnessed his own mother's distraught emotions over his frustrating illness like some looming theatrical performance. The show went on for seven years, until he was well enough to take instruction like a normal child—intense instruction, given the years he had lost and had to recover. Any little boy with an exacting taskmaster for a mother knows full well the paralyzing power of the well-aimed female gaze.

Charlotte Stoker's formidable personality remains legendary in her descendent family. Is it any wonder that a steely, survivalist-approach outlook might have risen from her own frightening childhood, steeped as it was in plague and approaching death? It would have taken the protective instincts of a she-wolf—or a Lady Macbeth—to hack off a dying man's hand at the height of the 1832 famine, if that's what was required for her family to go on living. As for angry emotions, Charlotte's simmering frustration and rage, held in check by Christian propriety but palpable to all around her, would be the stuff of grand opera.

Charlotte was a woman of unrealized talent and potential, arguably a proto-feminist, a writer and reformer who had nonetheless directed the energy of her prime years into near-continuous pregnancy, while her husband's ambition and income failed to keep up with the growing size of their family. Chased out of home after home by financial necessity, she shepherded her flock endlessly from one Dublin neighborhood to another, the better to make do. She kept track of her food purchases down to the penny.

Projecting one's own unrealized dreams onto one's children is rarely a happy strategy. And if Charlotte "didn't care a tuppence" for her daughters' education, perhaps it was because she wanted to spare them her own bitter disappointment.

Had she been so inclined—and her own interest in frightening, supernatural subjects suggests that she could have been—Charlotte herself might well have written Gothic novels. But the only work she actually published consisted of two reform pamphlets. In 1873 Bram asked her to put to paper the account of the cholera epidemic she had told so many times. She did so in chilling detail, pouring out the tale from her exile in Caen, France—but she left out the grisly and unflattering detail about the cholera victim's severed hand. It remains her only piece of autobiographical writing.

Only a handful of letters from Abraham Stoker to his son have survived,

interesting enough for their surface content, and even more for their judgmental undertones. On the matter of his son's possible ambitions beyond
the civil service, the father drew a comparison between the two men, suggesting Bram's impracticality, and even ingratitude.

> I know your present income is not by any means a liberal one, but still it
> is an increasing one, and your prospect of succeeding to a better class is
> not by any means hopeless. I was eighteen years in the civil service before
> I had as good a salary as you have now. You must know that there are few
> men of your standing now in the castle who have a larger income—and
> you can also guess how many competitors there would be if a vacancy took
> place in your office.

But when Stoker actually applied for the job of city treasurer, perhaps even aided by a letter of recommendation from Lady Wilde ("He
never gets into debt," she told Oscar, "and his character is excellent"), his
father slapped him down with a tone of cynical defeatism and religious
prejudice—an outlook that may have hampered his own escape from
Dublin Castle: "Any trouble you may take in looking for the vacancy will
only be lost time," he wrote. "An outsider has no chance, particularly
when there is a member of their own body looking for it, and even if
there were not, I should say none but an advanced Liberal or a Roman
Catholic would be elected."

Both Abraham and his wife clung to their anti-Catholic sentiments.
Stoker noted a certain hypocrisy on Charlotte's part: believing all cabmen
to be villains, she would take the precaution of ordering the driver to stop
near a policeman or a convent. "She is a Protestant & believes the worst of
the whole Catholic world," Stoker wrote in his journal, only slightly disguis-
ing his mother's identity, "but she seeks the sanctuary of the convent."

Dublin Castle provided a kind of sanctuary against Catholicism for
conservative men like his father. Stoker didn't share Lady Wilde's romantic,
even Gothic view of the institution: "Strange scenes, dark, secret, and cruel,
have been enacted in that gloomy pile," she wrote. "No one has told the full
story yet. It will be a Ratcliffe [sic] romance of dungeons and treacheries,
of swift death or slow murder." But the idea of a slow death by bureaucracy
must have crossed his mind. The underlying message of Abraham's advice
was clear. *Stay in the Castle, son, exactly like I did. Don't judge my own failures by*

succeeding where I did not. It was classic, passive-aggressive parent-speak. *Stay in the Castle—and rot.*

On his son's specific aspirations in the theatre and his heavy fraternization with theatre people, Abraham was far more direct. "I am sure you will not think that I want to dictate to you as to the class of acquaintances which you ought to make," he wrote, then went on to do more or less exactly that, offering "some experience of my own early life, which was very varied, and during which I was acquainted with both actors and actresses." Did he now regret having introduced his son to the fairy charms of Christmas pantomimes as a child? It was an early gift that kept on giving. Despite all his admiration for the likes of the famous Irish tragedian Barry Sullivan, Abraham feared (read: adamantly believed) that performers offstage were different creatures entirely:

> Although I am ready to admit that in many instances their society was very agreeable, still I don't think they are altogether desirable acquaintances to those not connected with their own profession (if I may call it,) because it may involve expense and other matters which are not at all times advantageous. Under all the circumstances I believe such acquaintanceship is better avoided.

One of Abraham's last communications with his son, the letter was the sort of thing Stoker probably had in mind when he wrote elsewhere of a "latest move on the family chessboard." Other than his theatre reviews and story-scribbling, Stoker made no real move toward independence from Dublin Castle during the remainder of his father's life, which wasn't long. Abraham Stoker took ill in mid-1876, and on October 12, at the age of sixty-seven, he died in Cava de' Tirreni, Italy. With his brother Thomas, Stoker made a trip to the Continent to arrange the funeral. Charlotte and her daughters decided to remain.

Margaret and Matilda would eventually marry—Matilda also becoming an occasional writer on art and fashion, her work admired by Oscar Wilde—but Charlotte extended her self-imposed exile for another nineteen years, not returning to Dublin until 1885. What she and her husband thought about living in the overwhelmingly Catholic countries of Italy and France, with only Switzerland offering some religious balance, is not recorded. Neither is it known why she decided to keep a two-decade physical distance between herself and her sons. Perhaps she felt she had sacrificed enough for her male children and now deserved an independent life, even if it meant being surrounded by Catholics.

The full substance of Charlotte's bitterness was never recorded, but had Stoker lived into the next theatrical century, we can easily imagine him identifying with Tom Wingfield, the aspiring writer in Tennessee Williams's *The Glass Menagerie*, and his mother's angry parting words: *Go to the moon—you selfish dreamer!* Years later, a London periodical would fancifully caricature Stoker as a man in the moon with "immortal longings."

Stoker lost two fathers in 1876, if Sir William Wilde is considered a surrogate parent. Replacement parents are a common theme in fairy tales, and fairy tales were, not insignificantly, a special interest for both men. In April, Wilde had succumbed after a long illness. His own medical practice had begun a slow downhill slide following the Mary Travers rape accusation, and at his death his cash assets had been severely depleted, with several properties heavily mortgaged. His fame was sustained not by any continuing achievements but by the prominence of his wife and the persistent stories of sexual transgression. A rumor circulated that Lady Wilde had permitted a heavily veiled woman to maintain a death vigil at the Merrion Square house, and it was true. The woman's identity was never revealed, but speculation was fueled. Was she a previously unknown mistress? The mother of those illegitimate, incinerated daughters? Or of the young Dublin eye specialist Henry Wilson (or "Will's Son"), another out-of-wedlock but better-known child that William Wilde educated and supported?

Although it is inconceivable that Stoker did not attend the funeral and interment at Mount Jerome Cemetery (which would also be a Stoker family burial place, and home to the graves of J. Sheridan Le Fanu and other Dublin luminaries), no mention at all of the Wildes appears in Stoker's surviving Dublin journal. Is it possible that he didn't record the highly quotable quips of Lady Wilde at the salons he regularly attended? Or Sir William's fascinating thoughts on Egyptology and Irish folklore? Or Oscar himself, inviting a fellow student to one of his mother's salons at Merrion Square, explaining that "she and I have founded a Society for the Suppression of Virtue"?[1]

The Wildes warranted a journal all their own. And they may have had

---

[1] Wilde is lampooning the Society for the Suppression of Vice, founded in 1802.

one. There is at least one piece of evidence that Stoker wrote of the legend-ary Wilde salons in a journal, letter, or some other unpublished document that was lost or destroyed—along with all other references to the Wilde family. In his book *Speranza* (1951), Horace Wyndham refers to Stoker's obviously written account of her droll comment when the young writer introduced a young woman as "half English and half Irish," and Speranza replied, "Glad to meet you, my dear. Your English half is as welcome as your Irish bottom." The original document has never been found. But the anec-dote has the same tone and style of his humorous journal entries, as well as the many unsigned sketches he contributed to the *Irish Echo* during his half-year tenure as editor.

Had Stoker kept the job at the *Echo*, he would have had a larger plat-form to celebrate the return of Henry Irving to Dublin in 1876. Instead, he used the *Mail* to give the Irving visit an unusual number of column inches. At the end of November Irving brought in his London productions of *Hamlet, The Bells*, and *Charles I*. Although Stoker had not seen him act in five years, he had followed the stunning rise of his reputation in London with many reviews that compared him favorably to theatrical legends David Garrick and Edmund Kean. But a dissenting critical cadre continued to loathe him.

British actors of the period were largely self-taught, learning their craft by observing other performers and through the lessons of simple trial and error. England had no national theatre, such as France's Comédie-Française, to uphold rigorous standards of diction and deportment. The English stage was a free-for-all in the matter of technique. Raucous audiences in London and the provinces winnowed out the most resilient actors, who often devel-oped trademark tics that may or may not have actually helped their profes-sional survival. Irving had some riveting peculiarities that focused attention more through their oddness than their aptness and became ingrained mannerisms. If something seemed to work, why let go of it?

Three basic criticisms of Irving's acting would dog him for his entire career. First was his less than powerful physique, with a strange gait often referred to as a "dragging leg," a trait not observed off the stage. Why he consciously, or unconsciously, would do such a thing is an almost impen-etrable question. Self-sabotage? An involuntary manifestation of some buried sense that he might be artistically "crippled"? Or just a variation on the old trick of waving a handkerchief—a cheap but effective way to draw attention if all else failed? A phalanx of armchair psychologists might never get to the bottom of it. A particularly venomous 1877 pamphlet, *The Fashionable Tragedian*, published anonymously in Edinburgh, described it thusly: "In walking, he plants one foot upon the stage as if his whole 'eminence' depended on its firmness, and then drags the other leg after it in a limp and nerveless fashion, which cannot be described, and must be seen to be appreciated,—all the while working spasmodically with his shoulders, and very often nodding his head backwards and forwards in a manner which is positively painful to contemplate."

Second, he had a vocal style that could be almost as odd as his stride. In moments of great excitement, he would fall into something like a Midlands or North Country accent; the word "God" he often produced as "Gud," a phrase like Shylock's "cut-throat dog" would come out as "cut-thrut dug,"

Postcard caricature of Henry Irving as Mathias in **The Bells.**

and in *The Bells*, "take the rope from my neck" became "take the rup from mey nek," and the word "rich" was pronounced as "ritz." The American impresario Augustin Daly found "farceur's tricks" in Irving's speech. "The peculiarity of his voice . . . consists of sudden and unexpected and some-times absurd rises and falls—and I can only compare it to a man speaking half a long sentence while drawing *in* his breath and letting the other half fly out while he expels the breath."

One of the only verified captures of Irving's voice is a wax cylin-der recording of the "Now is the winter of our discontent" speech from *Richard III*. Even allowing for the primitive sound technology, the voice has nothing of the mellifluous sonority we associate with twentieth-century Shakespeareans like Laurence Olivier, John Gielgud, or Derek Jacobi. According to *The Fashionable Tragedian*, Irving's "naturally harsh voice is rendered still more unpleasant by his trick of alternating between basso profundo and falsetto, like a ventriloquist imitating a conversation between the Giant Cormoran and Jack the Giant-Killer." There was no more surefire way of skewering a "serious" actor than to evoke pantomime.

The third criticism, embracing the previous ones and adding more, concerned his tendency toward general grotesquerie—a guaranteed if cheap method of satisfying any actor's look-at-me propensities. As the critic E. A. Baughan recalled Irving, "His intensity hypnotized me, but I was awed by his weirdness and strangeness rather than moved by the emotional appeal of his acting. Everything helped this magnetic power—Irving's strange voice, fantastic bearing, ascetic face, and curious, compelling eyes."

Irving used those eyes masterfully to register an inner, contemplative gaze so convincing it made audiences believe that . . . well, that they might be having deep thoughts, too. It was a novel way of playing to the crowd—the new, self-aggrandizing middle-class audience so necessary to Irving's project of elevating the social estimation of the stage. If only the critics would let him.

"Apart from his fatal mannerisms of motion and speech," the *Tragedian* continued, remorselessly,

he has physical defects which nothing but the most marked genius could hide. A weak, loosely-built figure, and a face whose range of expression is very limited, are the two principal disadvantages under which he has had to labour. Abject terror, sarcasm, and frenzy are the only passions which

Mr. Irving's features can adequately express. When he drops his lower jaw and turns up the whites of his eyes, he certainly looks as if some direful ghost had been freezing his young blood . . . and when he raises his chin, curls his under-lip, and elevates his eyebrows, the sneer so produced is inexpressibly diabolic.

The passage concluded with the observation that "some of Mr. Irving's most effective attitudes might well be taken for a representation of the final stages of Asiatic cholera—that is, total collapse." And if that jab didn't penetrate deeply enough, the authors addressed the frequent praise accorded Irving for being "picturesque": "There are those who would discover picturesqueness in the writhings of the octopus at the Brighton Aquarium."

The Fashionable Tragedian stung Irving at least as much as the merciless rejection he had received in Dublin years earlier. Fearing a lawsuit, the authors withdrew their pamphlet, but its ripples continued. Irving even stooped to defending himself in print—anonymously. "It was all very tiresome," wrote Laurence Irving. "If he was perpetually to be engaged in a war of pamphlets and *démentis* in his own defense, he would be forced to find a henchman who, skilled in the arts of publicity, could handle these matters for him." Upon Irving's arrival in Dublin with a program headlined by *Hamlet*, Bram Stoker was in a unique position to go to battle. He had championed Walt Whitman, and he would now champion Henry Irving. He used florid metaphors of war to describe the actor's ascendancy, "a hard fight, for there were some violent and malignant writers of the time who did not hesitate to stoop to any means of attack. It is extraordinary how the sibilation of a single hiss will win through a tempest of cheers! The battle, however, was being won."

Stoker's ability to look past the well-enumerated vagaries of Irving's performances may have stemmed from the fact that the conventions of melodrama and the grotesque were so ingrained in the theatre of his own mind that Irving's histrionic excesses attracted rather than repulsed him. He tempered his first-night appraisal with a mild acknowledgment of some of the actor's more problematic qualities, the better to inoculate readers against dissent and win them over to alternate criteria of judgment.

Mr. Irving's very appearance sets him at once above his fellows as no common man; but his physique is somewhat too weak for the heavy work he has to go through. Thus at times there is a variance between voice and gesture, or expression, which is manifestly due to a want of physical power. . . . The voice lacks power to be strong in semitones, and in moments of intense passion that speech loses its clearness, and becomes somewhat inarticulate. . . The tone broadens, and some words are tinged with a strong provincial accent.

Stoker concluded that Irving "had by nature a certain peculiarity of voice which despite training, manifested itself in moments of excitement."

Hamlet appealed to Stoker on a number of levels. A classic study in indecision, the play has always struck a particular note for young men arriving at adult crossroads. Stoker's decisions were both professional and personal. Would he remain at Dublin Castle, or follow his deepest longings to become part of the theatre? Would he seek a true romantic partnership (whatever that meant for him), or settle for a pragmatic marriage at the expense of an emotional connection?

The play is also a story about the impossibility of heterosexual love. As his friend and mentor Edward Dowden wrote, "It is the strangest love story on record. Never throughout the play is there one simple and sincere word uttered by lover to lover." Dowden observes that the "ruin of an ideal" leaves Hamlet "cruelly unjust to the creature of flesh and blood."

A woman's body, therefore, doesn't satisfy the tragic prince's true notion of love, and certainly can't achieve Stoker's Whitmanesque ideal of "a father and brother and wife to my soul." Hamlet's mother's marriage is a hollow sham based on a murder. His famous observation "Frailty, thy name is woman" neatly encapsulates the ensuing disappointment. All of Hamlet's references to heterosexual marriage are rants calculated to disgust: his explosive pronouncements (most to his own mother) are heavy with words and phrases like "corruption," "satyr," "incestuous sheets," and "reechy kisses"; he directs Gertrude to "let the bloat king tempt you" to "the rank sweat of an enseamèd bed" (that is, one altogether greasy from use), and, of course, "there will be no more marriages." Hamlet's sturdy friendship with Horatio, with whom he bonded at Wittenberg University, is the only solid relationship in the play. Only male friendship is honest and true—it is only Horatio who stands with him unto death. Critics have long debated whether Hamlet's love for Ophelia was based on real passion and whether it was ever physically consummated.

Stoker's relationships are equally murky. There is nothing to indicate that Stoker socialized one-on-one with women—or men, for that matter—outside of Lady Wilde's salons, the structured interaction of the Hist and the Phil, and the pleasant public impression he made on Dublin dance floors. But aside from the two-word description of a new family maid as "very pretty," virtually all the women described in his journal are crones or flibbertigibbets. If there were any fair Ophelias in Stoker's formative Dublin life, none have ever come to light, via Stoker or anyone else.

Hamlet is a drama driven by supernatural agency, a mature theatrical meditation on the otherworldly themes of the pantomimes and fairy tales that enthralled Stoker as a child. The ghost of Hamlet's father, who sets the story in motion, appealed especially to his fascination with the possibility of occult forces, along with the possibilities of stagecraft in conjuring them. He had already seen Barry Sullivan's striking production, which employed a large angled sheet of glass to produce the appearance of a transparent spectre—an impressive effect that endures to this day in the see-through phantasms of Disneyland's Haunted Mansion. Irving's production avoided such tricks and kept its evocation of supernatural forces subtle.

Hamlet's funereal dress echoed the somber attire of Le Fanu's Uncle Silas, Maturin's Melmoth, and other compelling characters out of sensation fiction and the Gothic. Modern literature's only other enduring figure in black, inextricably linked to the grave and the afterlife, is Stoker's Count Dracula. Although Shakespeare never used the word "vampire" (it didn't appear in English until the eighteenth century), there could not be a better overall description of a thirsty nocturnal revenant than in Hamlet's third-act pronouncement:

> 'Tis now the very witching time of night,
> When churchyards yawn, and hell itself breathes out
> Contagion to this world. Now could I drink hot blood
> And do such bitter business as the day
> Would quake to look on.

Other critics took Irving to task for his cerebral, inward-gazing portrayals, which flew against all established convention and additionally felt self-serving or pretentious. But Stoker used a kind of critical jujitsu to find a deeper, quasi-religious aspect to Irving's interiority.

The great, deep, underlying ideal of Hamlet is that of a mystic. In several passages Mr. Irving seems to have a tendency toward this rendering: when with far introspective gaze he appears on the scene; when he delivers the words, "In my mind's eye, Horatio," whenever his thoughts turn toward suicide and the mystic's psychic sensibility recognises a danger and a purpose far away; and noticeably in his rendering of the debated passage, "Look upon this picture, and upon this." In this latter he leaves aside the idea of corporeal pictures, either hanging on walls or in lockets, and sees the stern reality of the peopled air above and around him.

From his first essay of the role at the Manchester Theatre Royal in 1863, Irving's Hamlet forever after wore a black-plumed hat in the graveyard scene, the inky feather drawing a subliminally suggestive line from the book and volume of Hamlet's brain up into the nineteenth century's magnetic, mesmeric ether. Hats and headdresses have always had magical/mystical associations, from the pointed caps of wizards and witches to the upward-jutting cock's feather sported by Mephistopheles in Gounod's opera *Faust*, which Stoker attended several times in Dublin. In a few years, Irving himself would adopt the traditional plume, called by one critic "the defiant cock's feather" and "a quick ensign of fiendhood," for his own interpretation of the devilish tempter. Stoker ultimately saw Irving's *Faust* performed nearly eight hundred times.

Irving's personal interest in the preternatural extended no further than a "lingering methodism," according to his grandson. Stoker's thoughts, however, were interesting, and seized upon the public's perpetual fascination with the occult, which could hardly be bad for the box office, and could perhaps even help it. As a practical matter, a mystical aura could only add value to his celebrity. When you were already bigger than life, where else was there to go except into a larger reality?

Irving did have one experience, although with a most unpleasant professional outcome, having to do with séances and spiritualism. While working at the Manchester Theatre Royal, the year following his first performance there as Hamlet, he was offended by the positive public reception given to a visiting American table-rapper named Davenport. "Toward the end of 1864," Laurence Irving wrote, "England had been swept by one of its epidemic fevers of spiritualism." Davenport had been riding a similar tide back home, where the massive casualties of the Civil War produced

Henry Irving as Hamlet. Manchester, 1864.

among the grieving a huge market, cynically exploited, for reassuring contact with the recent dead.

Irving watched Davenport's performance, appalled as much at the credulity of the audience as at the trappings of Christian devotion (including a live endorsement by a local clergyman) that struck him as blasphemous.

With the help of some other actors, Irving staged a cutting parody of Davenport's routine at a local hall, exposing the charlatan's stage tricks. Audiences enjoyed the debunking as much as they had the original deception. When Irving refused his producer's request to reproduce the stunt at the Theatre Royal—thereby curtailing legitimate productions and the opportunity to really act—he was promptly fired. There followed several seasons of less-than-steady employment, and roles far beneath a young actor who had won plaudits for his Hamlet.

His professional reputation reestablished, Irving limited his dabbling in stage supernaturalism to works of literary merit. He was never again called upon to perform cheap magic tricks or reprise otherworldly roles like Venoma the Spiteful Fairy, a transvestite part he had performed early in his career in an Edinburgh Christmas pantomime of *Sleeping Beauty*. Nonetheless, such folderol had given him the experience of acting in elaborate makeup—"astonishingly correct," one critic wrote, whatever that might mean for a character that doesn't actually exist—accompanied by demonic red lighting.

The ghosts in *Hamlet* and *Macbeth* were always crowd-pleasers. In the scene between Hamlet and his revenant father, Irving intensified the mise-en-scène by shutting down all extraneous lighting on the stage or in the theatre, including the house lights. These ordinarily were kept low but still functioning at a time when theatregoers expected to be seen themselves almost as much as they wanted to see the play. It was an extraordinary novelty.

After his second appraisal of *Hamlet* appeared, Stoker was told by theatre management that Irving would like to meet him. If he had any other plans that night, they were promptly canceled. He was introduced to Irving in his dressing room before the play and asked to supper afterward.

Like everyone else, Irving was struck by Stoker's physical presence: imposingly tall, with the still-powerful body of the college athlete he had been. And yet, behind the muscle and the beard and penetrating blue eyes was an incongruous personality, childlike in its enthusiasms and vulnerable in its insecurities. The twenty-seven-year-old tried to hide any signs of weakness behind a thin veil of affected erudition, a not uncommon trait in university men, and in Stoker's case more endearing than annoying. And that athletic mass of him was a defensive costume—a barricade of body armor, fashioned from his own flesh.

Irving, too, had his insecurities ("An actor *never* forgets a hiss!" Stoker wrote) and understood the creative frustrations of an expressive soul struggling to escape the provinces. Irving realized quickly that Stoker was no ordinary sycophant. In addition to his voluminous newspaper writing and his aspirations as a writer of fiction, he seemed to have an encyclopedic knowledge of the theatre, and a mind that absorbed information like a vacuum pump. He could express himself in the written word with a quick and uncanny facility that might be likened to the "automatic writing" of a trance medium. His job at Dublin Castle required meticulous attention to detail and extraordinary organizational skills. He had been entrusted with a book-length project for Dublin Castle, to be called *The Duties of Clerks of Petty Sessions of Ireland*. A drier subject could not be imagined, but it involved a formidable ability to assimilate and manage information. Stoker was a man who could be trusted with serious responsibilities.

The evening concluded with another invitation to supper, and this one would be accompanied by a most theatrical finish. Stoker wanted something mystical? An otherworldly experience? Irving knew just the thing to give him.

Not many years later, when he returned to Dublin with *The Bells*, a newspaper would cartoon Irving transfixing his audience with hypnotism. It might have just as easily described another ready recitation he had perfected over several years, as a curtain raiser, a curtain call, and an occasional piece for audiences of all sizes and in all locations, including private homes. Jessie Millward, a member of Irving's acting company in the 1890s, experienced the performance a number of times. As a child she "would peep over the banisters to watch the famous ones arrive and depart, and when all was safe steal downstairs and crouch outside the drawing-room door and listen to Mr. Irving as he recited 'The Dream of Eugene Aram.'"

Written in 1810 by Thomas Hood, "Eugene Aram" was sturdy melodrama, recounting a grisly murder, its concealment, and the long-delayed confession and justice that followed. Millward's parents felt the poem was too much for a young child, but that only caused little Jessie's curiosity to grow. When she was "a little older and allowed inside the sacred room," Millward wrote, she finally beheld Irving in full performance. "I can see him now, stretched on the rug before the fire, his body slightly raised on one shoulder, and his wonderful face resting on his hand, while his eyes shone in the firelight like burning coals."

Charles Dickens's daughter-in-law Marie was also witness to a "weird and thrilling" at-home performance. "I had heard Irving recite 'The Dream of Eugene Aram' many times in public," she wrote, "but the thrill of that first occasion, when he did it at my old home in Cadogan Gardens, is a memory I shall always carry with me."

The recitation at the Shelbourne Hotel would be similarly intimate and memorable. Irving omitted the come-hither fireplace posturing he had burned into Jessie Millward's brain. The guests sat, and Irving stood before them in evening clothes. He began speaking in a kindly, gentle tone.

'Twas in the prime of summer-time
An evening calm and cool,
And four-and-twenty happy boys
Came bounding out of school;
There were some that ran and some that leapt,
Like troutlets in a pool.

"Eugene Aram" had been a perennial favorite among students; Stoker himself commented that he and the other guests "had all been familiar [with it] from our schooldays," and "most if not all of us had ourselves recited [it] at some time." Stoker had, in fact, appreciatively reviewed a performance of the poem in Dublin two years earlier and offered suggestions on how the delivery should best be modulated. For any performer, Hood made memorization easy, writing his verses in the same infectious meter Lewis Carroll employed for "The Walrus and the Carpenter" (1871). But the invigorating headlong rhythm only belied a swelling display of mortal terror to come.

Like sportive deer they coursed about,
And shouted as they ran,—
Turning to mirth all things of earth,
As only boyhood can;
But the Usher sat remote from all,
A melancholy man!

The Usher—an assistant schoolteacher—happens upon a serious, solitary boy poring over a book. One imagines Irving turned to address the following lines directly to Stoker. After all, they could have been *about* the young Stoker and his imaginative, morbid interests.

"My gentle lad, what is't you read—
Romance or fairy fable?
Or is it some historic page
Of kings and crowns unstable?"
The young boy gave an upward glance—
"It is 'The Death of Abel.'"

The Usher recoils, but then, as if fired by the boy's morbid state of mind, launches into an escalating monologue about murder, beginning with Cain. "That I knew the story and was even familiar with its inalterable words was nothing," wrote Stoker. "The whole thing was new, recreated by a force of passion."

> He told how murderers walk the earth
> Beneath the curse of Cain,—
> With crimson clouds before their eyes
> And flames about their brain:
> For blood has left upon their souls
> Its everlasting stain!

Finally he tells the boy of the murder he himself committed, at first describing it as a dream. According to Marie Dickens, Irving "made you actually see the corpse of the murdered man—as though you were hypnotized."

> "I took the dreary body up,
> And cast it in a stream,—
> A sluggish water, black as ink,
> The depth was so extreme:
> My gentle boy, remember this
> Is nothing but a dream!"

For Stoker the experience was much more than a reverie. It was a demonstration of Irving's "incarnate power, incarnate passion" as the room "became non-existent" and "recurring thoughts of self-existence were not at all." As the murderer recounts repeated attempts to conceal the body, only to have it surface, the narrative becomes a figurative ghost story. In his guilty mind, the dead man relentlessly returns.

> "So wills the fierce avenging Sprite,
> Till blood for blood atones!
> Ay, though he's buried in a cave,
> And trodden down with stones,
> And years have rotted off his flesh,—
> The world shall see his bones!"

"Here indeed was Eugene Aram as he was face to face with his Lord," Stoker would write, describing Irving's "nervous eloquent hands slowly moving, outspread fanlike, round the fixed face . . . [with] eyes inflexible as Fate. . . . One instinctively quivered with pity."

> "Oh God! that horrid, horrid dream
> Besets me now awake!
> Again—again, with dizzy brain,
> The human life I take:
> And my red right hand grows raging hot,
> Like Cranmer's at the stake."[2]

As Irving's impassioned recitation reached its climax, "the ghost in his brain seemed to take external shape before his eyes, and enforced on him that from his sin there was no refuge."

> "And still no peace for the restless clay,
> Will wave or mould allow;
> The horrid thing pursues my soul—
> It stands before me now!"

Stoker may not have fully heard the quieter, resolving verses in which the killer is taken away in manacles. Regressed into the fearful boy of the poem, he trembled at the awesome, overpowering tale. He sat dumbstruck while Irving, having completed the recitation, "collapsed, half-fainting."

Irving's semiprostration may well have been a practiced part of the act, the sort of trick guaranteed to generate sustained applause while the actor "recovered" his strength sufficiently to take a bow. For Stoker, however, doubt was not an option. He remembered having "no adequate words" for what happened next. In his first jotting down of the event he wrote, "I can only say that after a few seconds of stony silence following his collapse, I burst into a violent fit of hysterics."

He didn't mean he was laughing. In the Victorian era, the colloquial use

---

[2] Richard Cranmer, archbishop of Canterbury and Protestant martyr, burned at the stake by Queen Mary Tudor in 1556. Cranmer first thrust his own "guilty" hand—the one that had written false declarations of loyalty to the Catholic crown—into the fire, charring it to a stump.

Henry Irving as Eugene Aram.

of "hysteria" to describe out-of-control emotions didn't completely obscure the then-prevalent clinical definition associated exclusively with bizarre behavior in women, believed to arise from uterine dysfunction. For a man to be hysterical was unseemly, if not unmanly. Essentially, Stoker is saying that Henry Irving turned him into a sobbing woman. In his published version of the event, Stoker's reaction is milder and less definite: "I burst into *something like* a fit of hysterics" (emphasis added). Whatever the intensity of his behavior, it was startling. He admitted, with no small understatement, that the outburst was "distinctly a surprise" to the party assembled. Much later, in more measured language, Stoker described his emotional epiphany:

> Art can do much; but in all things even in art there is a summit somewhere. That night for a brief time in which the rest of the world seemed to sit still, Irving's genius floated in blazing triumph above the summit

of art. There is something in the soul which lifts it above all that has its base in material things. If once only in a lifetime the soul of a man can take wings and sweep for an instant into mortal gaze, then that "once" for Irving was on that, to me, ever memorable night.

Seeing the effect he had elicited in the shaken young man, Irving excused himself, went to his room and shortly returned with an inscribed photograph: "My dear friend Stoker. God bless you! God bless you!!"

The invocation added a religious dimension to an occasion already heavy with initiatory significance. "In those moments of our mutual emotion he too had found a friend and knew it," Stoker wrote. "Soul had looked into soul! From that hour began a friendship as profound, as close, as lasting as can be between two men."

Two souls may indeed have glimpsed each other. But whether they saw the same thing is another question entirely. Irving's written sentiment hid an unspoken realization, one that might best be expressed by the first line of dialogue Stoker would indicate fourteen years later in his working notes for *Dracula*:

This man belongs to me I want him.

Nothing in Irving's life indicates a personality needing or craving friendship, especially close male friendship in the way Stoker dreamed of it. His soon-to-be leading lady Ellen Terry would be brutally honest in her appraisal of Irving's sealed-off personality and its shortcomings: "His worst is his being incapable of caring for people, sons, friends, anyone, and his lack of enthusiasm for other people's work or indeed for anything outside *his own* work."

Irving's grandson saw the "Eugene Aram" business as deliberately calculated. "The effect of his recitation upon Stoker was all that Irving had hoped—as welcome as the effects of the 'Murder of Gonzago' on his uncle were to Hamlet." More to the point, the Danish prince also called the play-within-a-play "The Mouse Trap," calculated to snare Claudius and reveal his true nature. Stoker's hysterics, to Laurence Irving's mind, marked the moment his grandfather realized the full power and potential of his hold on Stoker.

In the first days of their acquaintance, there was no thought of Stoker potentially aiding Irving professionally in any other capacity than as a cheer-leading newspaper critic who effectively did the double duty of unofficial press agent for Ireland. A young journalist named Hall Caine in Liverpool had served much the same function for the North Country. Though his reputation was growing exponentially in London—at the Lyceum Theatre, under the management of the transplanted American actor-manager Colonel Hezekiah Bateman and his wife—Irving fared much better with provincial critics, and it was prudent to have them on his side (especially in Dublin, where, as a purely personal matter, he would never forget being hissed). In London, he felt his performances were too frequently under-mined; the Batemans often cut corners, and his supporting casts were not always what they ought to be. Audiences and reviewers on tour were much more forgiving, and, with a little care and some judicious ego feeding, Stoker could always guarantee him large audiences in Dublin, the largest and most profitable venue outside London.

It's hardly surprising that Stoker's review of *The Bells*, published two days after the "Eugene Aram" recitation, dispensed with any critical qual-ifications. "Anything more splendid than Mr. Irving's performance would be hard to conceive," he wrote. "It is no easy task for an actor to render duly the expression of terror that is purely subjective." He cited the supernatural terrors experienced by Macbeth and Hamlet as touchstones for an appreci-ation of Irving's Mathias, and communicated his own fascination with ethe-ric influence through an unusually long and detailed synopsis of the play's mesmeric machinations. For *Charles I*, he declared Irving's acting "princely; it is noble, single-purposed, and self-contained as a prince should be."

He reported on Irving's final *Hamlet* performance, a Saturday "University Night" at the Theatre Royal, ostensibly as an objective journal-ist, but could not disguise his personal pleasure at the thundering ovation the actor received. He also didn't identify himself as one of the prime orga-nizers of the event, or mention that he stayed at Irving's side, glowing in reflected adulation, as nearly a thousand Trinity men escorted him—that is, them—the several blocks to the imposing Shelbourne Hotel following the performance. And they didn't just walk the newly minted couple home. "They had come prepared with a long, strong rope, and taking the horses from the carriage harnessed themselves to it," Stoker recalled many years later. "There were over a thousand of them. . . . The street was a solid mov-ing mass and the wild uproar was incessant."

In his next-day column, Stoker left out the human horses but did write about the rhapsodic final curtain call (in operatic fashion, Irving actually took several, one at the end of each act), projecting himself into the crowd, much as he had while describing the audience at a pantomime:

> Hats and handkerchiefs were waved, and cheer upon cheer swelled louder and louder as the player stood proudly before his audience, with a light upon his face such as never shone from the floats. It was a pleasant sight to behold—the sea of upturned faces in the pit, clear, strong young faces, with broad foreheads and bright eyes—the glimpse of colour as the crimson rosettes which the students wore flashed with their every movement— the moving mass of hats and handkerchiefs, and above all the unanimity with which everything was done.

If Stoker's masculine ideal—at least as embodied in the imposing person of Henry Irving—was mature, commanding, and controlling, Oscar Wilde was cultivating a very different standard for male adoration.

Like Stoker, Wilde left Trinity College without taking final examinations. Unlike Stoker, he had at least the reason of having won a scholarship in classics at Oxford's Magdalen College in 1874. While still in Dublin he had shown a burgeoning interest in aesthetics, an attraction that would swell into a full-fledged creed under the tutelage of Oxford dons John Ruskin and Walter Pater. A doctrine of "art for art's sake," aestheticism had close ties to the Pre-Raphaelites, extolling standards of beauty drawn from antiquity and medievalism. Wilde's pilgrimage to Greece with J. P. Mahaffy would certainly have involved some consideration of the idyllic male love Wilde had helped his mentor usher into public discussion with *Social Life in Greece.* Barbara Belford notes that the difference in Wilde's and Mahaffy's ages—fifteen years—was exactly the temporal distance Wilde would keep with the young men whose ill-advised company would ultimately destroy him. At Oxford, Wilde wrote a poem, "Choir Boy," which went unpublished in his lifetime but makes clear his interest in Ganymede-like youths had distinctly unsublimated aspects:

> See what I found in the street
> A man child lusty and fair
> With little white limbs and little feet
> A glory of golden yellow hair

Oscar Wilde as an undergraduate at Oxford.

The poem roughly coincided with a school holiday in 1876, when Wilde attended the theatre in Dublin and noticed another student from Oxford occupying a private box along with a local choirboy. The theatre was most likely the Gaiety, the site of the Wills-Ward-Stoker *Sappho* the year before, whose boxes had a reputation for semidiscreet male-male occupancy. He immediately wrote to his friend William Ward with the news, and his belief that the student "only mentally spoons the boy, but I feel he is foolish to go about with one, if he *is* bringing this boy about with him," and concluded the gossipy report telling Ward that he was "the only one I would tell about it, as you have a philosophical mind"—the word "philosophical" being a common euphemism describing homosexuality or people open to discussing the topic. He cautioned his friend emphatically not to discuss the other friend and his boy with anyone, as it would do no good for any of them.

Stoker, who was then attending both the city's major theatres several

Florence Balcombe, about the time she met Oscar Wilde. Unknown photographer.

nights a week, would have had considerably more opportunity to observe such same-sex outings. As his reviews repeatedly demonstrate, he had a keen eye for the audience as well as the performance.

On one of his visits or summer vacations in Ireland, Wilde made the acquaintance of an "*exquisitely pretty girl*" (emphasis Wilde's) of seventeen, he wrote to a classmate. Though unnamed in the letter, she has generally been identified as Florence Anne Lemon Balcombe, one of eight children (six of them daughters) of Army Lieutenant-Colonel James Balcombe and his wife, Phillipa Anne. By family tradition, she had been named after Florence Nightingale, an inspirational fixture of the Crimean War, in which James Balcombe had served. Wilde described Florence as having the "*most perfectly beautiful face I ever saw and not a sixpence of money.*" He escorted her to an afternoon service, presumably at the ancient Christ Church Cathedral in central Dublin, which had only very recently been restored to a fashionable semblance of its medieval glory. It may have been there that he made her a Christmas gift of a small gold cross engraved with his name.

Although Wilde would have made nothing of the fact, had he even known it, the Balcombe family lived on the same townhouse block in Clontarf where Bram Stoker had been born, but not until years after the

Stokers had departed the neighborhood. Wilde had no reason to imagine that the Trinity alumnus and drama critic who was a friend of his brother's and a regular at his mother's salons and soirées might ever have anything to do with his relationship with Florence—much less be centrally involved in its eventual dissolution.

At five foot eight, the willowy Florence was a good match for the six-foot-two Oscar, at least for the purpose of Sunday promenades, and Merrion Square was a favorite outdoor location for regular romantic parading. The gated gardens, then accessible by key only to the adjacent residences, was a haven from the often unpleasant sights and persons of Dublin's city core. The best homes pushed up against the worst slums, and the neighborhood was rife with beggars. A quarter century before, the back garden of the Wildes' house was opened as a soup kitchen in the difficult times after the famine, but now that was private, too. Lady Wilde could barely afford her salons, much less feed the poor.

Not long before meeting Florence, Oscar had developed a close attachment to an Oxford alumnus, the artist Frank Miles. He was the son of a clergyman and the protégé of Lord Ronald Gower, a self-taught Scottish sculptor (most famously responsible for the Shakespeare memorial at Stratford-upon-Avon) and a leading figure of London's homosexual demimonde. Gower is generally understood to be Wilde's model for Lord Henry Wotton, the Mephistophelian omnipresence of *The Picture of Dorian Gray*. Miles was described by Wilde biographer Rupert Croft-Cooke in rather blunt terms for a 1971 book:

> George Francis Miles was one of those sophisticated queers who tell women what they should wear, have rather exaggerated good manners and camp outrageously, preferably among titled people. He was frivolous and amusing and inherited from his mother some rather facile artistic gifts which he (at the time he met Wilde) was already devoting to pastel portraiture, chiefly of famous beauties and well-known actresses.

Florence soon became one of Frank's sitters—he also drew a doe-eyed portrait of Wilde—and she would have been flattered to join the company of the celebrated faces that graced his sketchbooks. Through their London connection with Ronald Gower, Oscar and Frank were already hobnobbing in artistic circles with the likes of actress Lillie Langtry, and undoubtedly

Frank Miles. Undated photograph.

told Florence that her looks simply destined her for the stage. Although she was beautiful, intelligent, and fluent in French, there is no evidence she had been active in even amateur theatricals or possessed a particular aptitude for performance. But receiving such flattering attention from a pair of older, sophisticated men must have been exciting indeed. Wilde made his own, remarkably evocative pencil sketch of Florence, which bolsters the idea that Miles's work was facile. Frank's portrait of Florence is pretty in a conventionally flattering way; Wilde's is truly soulful, suggesting Modigliani in a wistful mood.

Oscar also presented Florence with one of his delicate watercolors, depicting Moytura House, his family's country retreat in County Mayo. It was the place he had taken Frank Miles for at least one private retreat. Wilde's recent biographers have concluded, rather convincingly, that Frank was indeed Oscar's real love interest at the time he courted Florence. As Neil McKenna observed in *The Secret Life of Oscar Wilde*, "Women were half

Oscar Wilde and Florence Balcombe, as sketched by Frank Miles.

of the question of love: they represented purity and freshness, safety and security, and sometimes even sanctuary: boys and young men, on the other hand, were on the dangerous and dark side of the erotic moon, where forbidden pleasures tasted so much sweeter."

For Victorian connoisseurs of harmony and beauty, the idea that a woman could provide a necessary aesthetic balance to the life of a man who loved men was nothing new. It had its roots in the Attic Greeks who seemed to effortlessly juggle marriage and pederasty, and was clearly reflected in the bottomless pansexual yearnings of Bram Stoker as expressed in his letters to Walt Whitman. But some men, like Ronald Gower and Frank Miles, had no sexual use for women and no interest in maintaining the appearance. Gower regularly guided his adventurous protégé into the lunar penumbra of sexual slumming and rough trade, where Wilde, for all his reverence for purity and beauty, would eventually follow. Their adventures would form the essential substrata of *Dorian Gray*.

At least some of Wilde's drift toward Catholicism may have been prompted by the tacit understanding that its monasteries and convents had always provided safe harbor for erotic minorities of both sexes; the veneer of celibacy barely concealed a same-sex nirvana, only intensified by guilt and penitence. As Dorian Gray himself experienced the Catholic ritual, "The fuming censers, that the grave boys, in their lace and scarlet, tossed into the air like great gilt flowers, had their subtle fascination for him. . . . He used to look in wonder at the black confessionals, and long to sit in the dim shadow of one of them and listen to men and women whispering through the worn grating the true story of their lives."

Unlike Wilde, and in spite of any shared predilections, conventional Protestants like Gower had no use for the guilty contortions of the Church over sex. When Lord Ronald was first introduced to Wilde, he described him as "a pleasant cheery fellow, but with his long-haired head full of nonsense about the Church of Rome. His room full of photographs of the Pope and Cardinal Manning."[3] In June or July of 1877 Oscar sent Florrie a copy of his sonnet "Urbs Sacra Aeterna" ("Sacred and Eternal City"), a paean to the spirit of Rome, which had been published in the *Illustrated Monitor: A Monthly Magazine of Catholic Literature.*

> And now upon thy walls the breezes fan
> (Ah, city crowned by God, discrowned by man!)
> The hated flag of red and white and green.
> When was thy glory! when in search for power
> Thine eagles flew to greet the double sun,
> And the wild nations shuddered at thy rod?
> Nay, but thy glory tarried for this hour,
> When pilgrims kneel before the Holy One,
> The prisoned shepherd of the Church of God.

Florence responded with an appreciative note, written in her large, girlish hand: "It was so very good of you sending me the Monitor, your sonnet is sublime & I can quite understand the priests going into ecstasies over it—the idea of the 'prisoned shepherd of the Church of God['] is perfect. We want to hear you read it yourself to us." She expressed mild amusement at his having sent it to "a good Protestant house," but asked him to come

---

[3] "The Pope" was Pope Pius IX. Edward Manning was the archbishop of Westminster, and himself a convert from Anglicanism.

round, if he could, the following evening, and signed the note "Believe me / ever yours / Florrie."

Whether Florence, or her parents, considered him as a harmless diversion rather than a serious suitor is a point to be pondered. If Florence was penniless, Wilde was getting close himself. His family's finances were in tatters, and the Wilde name itself had had a dodgy reputation ever since the Mary Travers affair. Despite Sir William's knighthood and genuine medical accomplishments, as he withdrew from his practice and public life, his image had taken on a bizarre taint. W. B. Yeats recalled a bizarre, folktale-like story that circulated about the surgeon. For Wilde to work his eye-doctor magic, it was said, he first had to remove your eyes from their sockets. Then he would place them on a plate on a table, where his prowling cat was sure to eat them.

Beyond such wild stories, there was more that could be directly observed, and shuddered at. That painted clown of a mother. The drunken brother, Willie. And then there was Oscar himself, presenting his affected person on their Protestant threshold, spouting florid Catholic sympathies as if he were on the verge of conversion. Alternately, Lieutenant-Colonel Balcombe and his wife may have regarded Wilde as a useful distraction for their daughter, his foppish, effeminate presence safely shielding the beautiful girl from the less aesthetic interests of other Dublin men.

Richard Ellman, Wilde's most noted biographer, places the crucifix gift at Christmas 1875, even though the letter describing the *"exquisitely pretty girl"* as "just seventeen" was written in the summer of 1876, when Florence had just turned eighteen. Either Wilde was mistaken, or Ellman moved the year back to coincide with her actual age. Or, since the 1876 letter doesn't mention the girl's name, it is completely possible he is describing someone else entirely, because Wilde is known to have flirted with other Dublin girls as well. In any event, if he wasn't describing Florence in 1876, he certainly was in 1877, when he wrote to the same friend that "Florrie is lovely as ever."

There is a gap in Wilde's correspondence with and about Florence until the following year, which may indicate missing letters, an actual lapse of contact, or possibly a bit of both. It was, in any event, a period of personal upheaval for Wilde. According to Ellman, "It was at Oxford that an event occurred that was to alter his whole conception of himself. Wilde contracted syphilis, reportedly from a woman prostitute. As a doctor's son, he had come to minimize illness, so this came as an especially crushing blow."

Ellman's diagnosis remains controversial, though it stems from some of the earliest Wilde biographies and people who knew the writer well.[4] Arthur Ransome's *Oscar Wilde: A Critical Study* (1912) was published under the close supervision of Robert Ross, one of Wilde's closest friends and one of his earliest lovers. Ransome wrote, with Ross's full approval, "His death [in 1900] was hurried by his inability to give up the drinking to which he had become accustomed. It was directly due to meningitis, the legacy of an attack of tertiary syphilis." Ross also oversaw the 1916 publication of Frank Harris's *Oscar Wilde*, which also referenced syphilis, albeit euphemistically. Another Wilde friend and confidante, Robert Sherard, stated in a letter that Wilde "knew himself to be syphilitic." He amplified the account to biographer Boris Brasol, who wrote in 1935, "While at Oxford, [Wilde] had contracted syphilis for the cure of which mercury injections were administered."

Mercury—ingested, injected, or rubbed on the skin—was a time-honored treatment, known even by the Greeks and Romans, and the source of the mordant adage "One night with Venus, a lifetime with Mercury." It actually cured nothing and had toxic side effects. As Ellman wrote, "The main physical effect of mercury on Wilde was to turn his slightly protrusive teeth black, so thereafter he usually covered his mouth with his hand while talking." Other accounts confirm the unsightliness of his teeth—if not blackened, they are described as greenish—and Andre Gide, meeting Wilde in exile near the end of his life, observed that "his teeth were horribly decayed."

Although there is a single recollection of Wilde having noticeably white teeth—an account used to discredit the syphilis claim—it does not take into account that nineteenth-century barber-dentists offered a primitive form of teeth bleaching using a caustic wash of nitric acid. The results did not last, and ultimately aggravated decay by destroying dental enamel. But just as today, there were always people vain enough to take serious health risks for temporary cosmetic advantage. A preening figure like Wilde would have been an ideal candidate. And a disfiguring change in his appearance would do much to explain breaking off contact with Florence Balcombe.

---

[4] On the centenary of Wilde's death, Merlin Holland, the writer's grandson and the leading authority on his life and work, told an interviewer for the BBC that "around 25% of Victorian men had syphilis and he may have had it, too—we'll never know." A few years earlier Holland wrote the introduction to a new edition of the much-maligned Frank Harris biography, arguing for its positive reappraisal.

The standard medical prescription for syphilitics in 1878 combined sexual abstinence and the delay of any marriage for at least two years, while mercury (and sometimes arsenic) treatments were administered.

A diagnosis of syphilis did not merely disrupt relationships—it often led to radical life changes, sometimes including religious conversion. In April 1878, Wilde sought the counsel of Father H. Sebastian Bowden at the sumptuous, Italianate Brompton Oratory, the most fashionable Catholic church in London, just a few blocks from Harrods (then commonly known as "the Stores") on Brompton Road in Knightsbridge. It was not exactly the pretext for conversion Jane Wilde had in mind for her son. Although Wilde kept in touch with his mother regularly from Oxford, none of their correspondence on the matters of Florence, Father Bowden, or his illness (during the acute early stages of which he had been confined to bed) has survived.

What has survived is the letter written to Wilde by Father Bowden subsequent to their meeting. "Whatever your first purpose may have been in your visit yesterday there is no doubt that as a fact you did freely and entirely lay open to me your life's history and your soul's state," wrote the priest, strongly implying that Wilde had made a Catholic confession, or its equivalent. He continued, telling Wilde, "You have like everyone else an evil nature and this in your case has become more corrupt by bad influences mental and moral, and by positive sin," and assuring him that "as a Catholic you would find yourself a new man. . . . I trust then that you will come on Thursday and have another talk; you may be quite sure I shall urge you to do nothing but what your conscience dictates. In the meantime pray hard and talk little."

It is unlikely Wilde talked much. "The word 'syphilis' was taboo in nineteenth-century society: rarely written, either in correspondence or in print, and even more rarely spoken, and then only to a few intimate friends of the poor victims, with an implicit agreement that it was never to be repeated," writes the medical and cultural historian Deborah Hayden in *Pox: Genius, Madness, and the Mysteries of Syphilis.* In Wilde's case, it is hardly surprising to find circuitous language, and suspiciously missing letters.

The circumstances of Wilde's infection have generated warring speculation. In several accounts, the presumed prostitute was "Old Jess," a well-worn veteran of the Oxford sex trade, who has also been suspected as the source of Lord Randolph Churchill's ultimately fatal encounter with syphilis. Churchill (the father of Winston) was a contemporary of both Wilde and Stoker, born in 1849, two years after Bram and five years before Oscar. At Oxford, a drunken Churchill was allegedly delivered unconscious into the bed of an aging and repulsive syphilitic whore by pranking school chums. He woke to two unpleasant surprises, one immediate and another a short while later. Churchill died in his forties from what many (including his son) believed was tertiary syphilis, though today there are many skeptics.

In various accounts of "Old Jess" encounters, the prostitute is also characterized as Oxford's only pay-for-play option for randy young men, which strains belief. The number of prostitutes per capita was extraordinarily high in Victorian England; by some estimates, as many as one in ten London women resorted to selling sex at some point when all other means of support failed. Oxford, not far from the capital, had a population in 1878 of nearly forty thousand—a large percentage, of course, being single young males in their sexual prime. Upon the most cursory analysis, "Old Jess" would seem to be something of a Victorian urban legend, and a very unlikely candidate for a monopoly practitioner of Oxford vice.

The Jess story, however, has a certain dubious utility. It helps bolster the narrative—a debatable and, at root, homophobic narrative—that Wilde must have been sexually interested in women at least until after his marriage. That is, that he was normal until he wasn't normal. That no one could be born "that way." That there is some basic problem with even imagining Wilde exploring and acting upon his strongest feelings at an early age. In 1877, the same year he sent Florence Balcombe his poetic paean to Catholic Rome, he published another sonnet in the Trinity College magazine, *Kottabos*, which he didn't send her. It was called "Wasted Days" and reflected his predominant attraction to all things Uranian:

> A fair slim boy not made for this world's pain,
> With hair of gold thick clustering round his ears,
> And longing eyes half-veiled by foolish tears
> Like bluest water seen through mists of rain;
> Pale cheeks whereon no kiss hath left its stain . . .

A few years later, Wilde would rewrite the poem as "Madonna Mia," changing the subject to a young girl. He never explained his reasons, but the desire to achieve harmoniously "balanced" relations with both sexes was an aesthetic ideal. The resulting ambiguity of poetic intention was similar to those sexually baffling verses in Stoker's poem "Too Easily Won."

Leaving aside obvious questions about bisexuality and its many gradations, in the question of female prostitutes, Wilde's passionate commitment to aestheticism makes it inconceivable that this lover of all things beautiful would have chosen a snaggle-toothed crone for his sexual initiation. We already know of his revulsion at the profligate drinking and whoring of his classmates at Trinity College. As for possible sexual hazing at Oxford, the only prank Wilde is said to have endured at Magdalen College involved his thwarting an attempt by upperclassmen to smash the collection of china he kept in his rooms.

If not talked about publicly, the dangers of syphilis privately haunted young men like Wilde and Stoker in their first bloom of manhood. It provided macabre imagery and metaphor for poets like Baudelaire (himself a victim of the disease) and, as the late Victorian age progressed, was explicitly acknowledged in art and literature, as in J. K. Huysman's commonplace book of decadence, *A rebours* (1884; usually translated into English as *Against the Grain*). At one point, the novel's neurasthenic protagonist, Duc Jean Des Esseintes, confronts syphilis personified as a spectre with "pricked ears, two rows of yellow teeth, [and] nostrils breathing clouds of vapor that stank of phenol."

> His blood gave one bound within him and he remained nailed to the spot in utter horror. The ambiguous sexless creature was green, and from under purple lids shone a pair of pale blue eyes, cold and terrible, two arms of inordinate leanness, like a skeleton's bare to the elbows, shaking with fever, projected from ragged sleeves. . . . In an instant he knew the meaning of the appalling vision. He had before him the image of the Pox.

The "sexless," living-dead thing morphs into something unmistakably female, fixing him with an uncanny, penetrating gaze. "He sank to the earth, abandoning all resistance or even of flight; he shut his eyes so as not to see the dreadful eyes of the Syphilis glancing at him through the wall, which nevertheless forced their way under his lids, glided down his spine, enveloped his body."

Whether in poetry, prose, or painting, Victorian personifications of syphilis were always female, and usually blended with the image of the prostitute. Dirty, druggy whores provided an easy, class-marginalized scapegoat for a disease spread equally by men and women of all social strata. The unquenchable demand for extramarital sex was, of course, driven by men themselves and not the prostitutes who served them. In Wilde's case, the "Old Jess" legend perpetuates the same antifeminine bias, never taking into account that Wilde, given his predilections, could have easily been made sick by another man. Although syphilis can lie dormant in an infected person for decades—as many as half of all cases never even progress to the tertiary stage—ten years before the most devastating symptoms manifest is a normal course for the disease.

"Mors Syphilitica," engraving by Félicien Rops (1892).

Even allowing for the possibility that Wilde didn't have syphilis, he moved in circles where the danger was real, and may well have believed he was infected. Sexually transmitted diseases like chanchroid, for instance, had not yet been differentiated from syphilis and were treated as such—naturally giving false credence to the curative power of mercury and other nostrums.

For Oscar Wilde, Bram Stoker, and countless other men of their generation in Europe and America, the threat of syphilis was a constant cultural subtext. As the historian Patrick Wald Lasowski commented on the pervasiveness of the disease in French literature, "Many Demons and Divinities vie with each other as to who can claim to inspire the nineteenth century, to preside over its terrors and delights, to rule its ecstasies. . . . The most important is Syphilis."

Given its many mysteries, it is not surprising that disease would almost effortlessly inform supernatural metaphor. The signature fictional works of both Wilde and Stoker would be fin-de-siècle horror stories easily interpretable as syphilis parables. The secret, corrupted painting in *The Picture of Dorian Gray* emblemized the process of a hideously insidious disease rising from sensuality and vice. *Dracula* similarly fixated on a corruption of the blood, pseudoscientific remedies, and the anxious anticipation of telltale marks on the skin. Each book illuminates the other, just as the lives of Stoker and Wilde provide endlessly reciprocal insights.

The events of 1878 were hardly the last time the shadow of syphilis would enter the life stories of Oscar Wilde and Bram Stoker.

After flirting with Catholic conversion at the Brompton Oratory, Wilde never again met with Father Bowden. On the appointed day, he sent the priest a spray of lilies instead. Like the sunflower, the lily was a blossom closely linked to the aesthetic movement. But, like one of Baudelaire's *fleurs de mal*, it was also the flower most traditionally associated with death.

In 1877 the prospect of Henry Irving running his own theatre was still something of a pipe dream. But, like Stoker, he knew full well the powerful attraction of London for stifled creative people in the provinces, and did what he could to encourage his potentially very valuable Dublin asset to relocate, even if only for extratheatrical employment.

Stoker's dreams still centered on writing, not theatre management. He was eligible for a master's degree from Trinity College in 1875 (by way of purchase, not additional study) and took advantage of the opportunity, although an M.A. was of little or no value to a writer of fiction or to a man of the theatre. His immediate reason was more likely to please his unpleasable parents with the seeming prospect of civil service advancement—or something else respectable.

For the 1877 holidays, Stoker visited London, ostensibly to take in the seasonal Handel festival, but of course he spent time with Irving nearly every day of the trip. Irving made him a personal introduction to James (later Sir James) Knowles, editor of the just-founded *The Nineteenth Century*, a literary and philosophical monthly.

Knowles and many of his contributors were members of the multidenominational Metaphysical Society, which had for more than a decade presented papers on such topics as "The Theory of a Soul," "Is God Unknowable?" and "What Is Death?" Stoker himself had not ventured into such waters as a writer, though his deeply ingrained metaphysical and supernatural interests had begun their literary manifestation in a cycle of original fairy tales he was assembling, without any idea how or where they could be published. The fact that they all circled back on themes of childhood and death gave them a certain quaint gravitas, but they held no particular cachet for the British intelligentsia who might read *The Nineteenth Century*.

So it wasn't surprising that Knowles had no immediate assignments to offer. He deflated Stoker's expectations—and presumably those of Irving as well—by encouraging him to stay in Dublin and write from there. "Oh!" Stoker replied, "I could write well enough, but I have known that game for some time. I know the joy of the waste-paper basket and the manuscript returned—unread." And in terms of arts and culture, there was no way he could write about anything but drab, provincial Dublin if he remained in Ireland. Everything important originated in London. He had no proximate model for Irish literary "success" other than J. Sheridan Le Fanu, who ended up an unhappy, shuttered recluse—hardly a consummation to be wished.

Knowles gave assurances that he would personally read anything Stoker chose to send him. The two men became friends, although Stoker would not publish anything in *The Nineteenth Century* until 1890. Oscar Wilde would beat him to the punch, placing his celebrated essay "The Decay of Lying" with the publication in 1889.

Although Irving may have been disappointed not to lure Stoker onto

London turf by his dream of becoming a writer, he drew Bram more into his confidence (if information calculated to manipulate and control can ever be considered a true confidence). Over a private supper in Stoker's rooms on St. Stephen's Green, he hinted at the life—that is, the professional life—they might have together. As if Bram the emotional man-child made much distinction.

"We were quite alone and talked with the freedom of understanding friends," Stoker recalled. And, indeed, Irving understood perfectly what Stoker needed to hear. "He was quite frank as to the present difficulties, although he put them in the most kindly way possible," said Stoker, although one can wonder whether Irving really shared the full extent of his difficulties with the Batemans. Friends and critics alike were suggesting, increasingly, that his potential as an actor was being stifled by the inferior talent that surrounded him under the present Lyceum management.

"He spoke of the future and of what he would try to do when he should have a theatre all to himself where he would be sole master," Stoker wrote, adding that he had "a sort of dim idea of where events were moving" when Irving raised, explicitly for the first time, "the possibility of my giving up the post I then occupied in the Public Service and sharing his fortunes." It was not a firm offer, but nonetheless a pivotal and, for Stoker, an emotional moment. "The hope grew in me that a time might yet come when he and I might work together to the one end we both believed in and held precious in the secret chambers of our hearts."

The lopsided romance would not reach its pseudo-consummation for another year, but Stoker was still moved to make a three-word entry in his diary: "London in view!"

It was the night of Thursday, November 22, 1877. The next twelve months would be a period of suspense, anxiety, and, above all, intense and unforgettable excitement. It was the same exquisite tension described by Stoker's fictional alter ego Jonathan Harker, not knowing what to expect of an approaching vampire, yet unable to resist: "I closed my eyes in a languorous ecstasy and waited—waited with beating heart."

Bram Stoker was not Irving's only target for seduction in 1877 and 1878. He badly needed a new leading lady, a personality strong enough to complement him without posing distracting competition. It was a delicate

Ellen Terry, early in her stage career.

balance, but his search finally focused upon a rising London actress, ten years his junior, with whom he first acted in David Garrick's 1756 abridgment of *The Taming of the Shrew*, called *Katherine and Petruchio*, a decade earlier. Her name was Ellen Terry. More recently, she had drawn considerable praise in W. G. Wills's *Olivia*, a popular adaptation of Oliver Goldsmith's *The Vicar of Wakefield*. Terry was physically striking, with golden hair and the strong-jawed warrior-saint profile made iconic by the Pre-Raphaelites. She radiated an innate, effortless grace that could not have been more opposite to Irving's self-conscious and self-serving contortions. In truth, neither performer was very good in *Katherine and Petruchio*; Terry recalled that Irving "could not speak, he could not walk. . . . His amazing power was imprisoned, and only after long and weary years did he succeed in setting it free."

Terry's actor-husband, Charles Wardell (professionally, Charles Kelly), was not a dependable theatrical partner. What he really excelled at was drinking, accompanied by angry bouts of jealousy. And Terry may have given her husband some cause for concern. She had a rather checkered—and, to some, confusing—past, starting with her child-bride marriage to the painter G. F. Watts, from whom she separated after less than a year, though they did not divorce. There followed an adulterous, country-cottage cohabitation with the architect Edward Godwin, who would father her two illegitimate children, later known as Edith and Edward Gordon Craig. When Godwin left her, she finally divorced Watts and married Charles Wardell, giving herself and her children a modicum of respectability. But in the end Terry was a woman constituted to flout convention and live as she chose. Playfully and charmingly transgressive, flitting from man to man, she may well have been on Stoker's mind when he created *Dracula*'s Lucy Westenra, who resents having to choose between suitors and exasperatedly asks her friend Mina Murray, "Why can't they let a girl marry three men, or as many as want her?" Ellen Terry had already had three men, and she wasn't finished.

Wardell was offended by Irving's approach to his wife, which at first was all professional blandishments with no firm contract offer. And it was the pugnacious Wardell (whom Terry once likened to a bulldog) who pressed her to demand a "definite" commitment in writing. Wardell may have been additionally irked by the fact that Irving was not extending an invitation to him as well. Irving was adept at thinking several steps ahead, and there was nothing to be gained through daily professional proximity to Terry's ill-tempered husband. Especially if there was a possibility of cuckolding him. Adultery, after all, was the only sexual outlet for a man who wouldn't divorce his wife, and, no doubt, Irving understood this and behaved accordingly.

Irving was not yet free of the Batemans and did not yet have title to a theatre, or even working capital. What he did have was a bottomless belief in his own manifest destiny in the theatre. For the moment, it was not enough to secure the cooperation of the woman he had already mentally claimed as his own.

Wagner's 1843 opera *The Flying Dutchman* did not have its London premiere until 1870, in French, and was revived in English at the Lyceum in 1876, where it was a great success. Colonel Bateman, shortly before his death in 1875, felt that a drama based on the Dutchman legend would suit Irving admirably. Irving agreed. The role of the Dutchman, a sea captain cursed to pilot a phantom ship forever (unless a virginal woman breaks the spell by declaring her eternal fidelity), was a brooding, highly romantic part. Bateman commissioned a problematic script from Percy Fitzgerald, a prolific if dilettantish writer and artist. The attempt fell flat. Bateman asked W. G. Wills to assist, but collaboration proved futile. Finally, three years after Bateman's passing, Wills produced his own complete script, but the opera-based story without Wagner's soaring score simply couldn't fly.

The *Times* did not mince words, judging *Vanderdecken* to be "one of the dullest and most uninteresting performances it has ever been our lot to witness. . . . Unfortunately, such a play is calculated to accentuate all Mr. Irving's worse qualities as an actor."

It must have come as a shock for Stoker to see his idol stumble so badly in a mismanaged production, especially as he was on the verge of walking away from a steady job with a guaranteed pension. And Irving would certainly have understood that *Vanderdecken* was hardly a performance with which to cement a firm commitment from Stoker.

The fiasco also underscored the difficulties of Irving's strained relationship with Mrs. Bateman, her management of the Lyceum, and her family. To top the whole mess, Bateman's daughter Isabel, known more familiarly as "Bella," had revealed her long-smoldering infatuation with Irving, which he was in no position, or mood, to reciprocate. Besides, he had an extremely low opinion of her as an actress. Horrifyingly, her mother actually suggested that Isabel and Irving might simply live together while he arranged to divorce his estranged wife, something he had no intention of doing. And if Bella's unwanted affections weren't enough, her sexual distress had a countervailing, alternate obsession: the recurring desire to enter a convent. This was one Ophelia who didn't need an admonishment to get herself to a nunnery. She had already taken that option under advisement.

Irving was trapped in a state of personal and professional limbo, which may have colored Stoker's estimation of the actor in his own review: "In his face is the ghastly pallor of the phantom Captain and in his eyes shines the wild glamour of the lost—in his every tone and action there is the stamp of death." Stoker felt it was "marvellous that any living man could show such eyes. They really seemed to shine like cinders of glowing red from out the marble face."

Beyond the ability of Irving to appear convincingly undead, Stoker had little else to praise in the production in the *Evening Mail*, save the stage effect of Irving's first appearance, seemingly out of nowhere, "the most startling and striking thing I ever saw on the stage." The trick was most likely achieved by some shrewd lighting and/or the use of a vampire trap in the scenery. Stoker fails to mention another ingenious stage contrivance, which the *Times* singled out as one of the few high points in an otherwise hopeless production: Vanderdecken tussles with his mortal romantic rival and is thrown into the sea, which rejects the cursed wanderer and

Henry Irving as the Flying Dutchman in **Vanderdecken** *(1878).*

heaves him back onto the shore for more earthly punishment. "A more cleverly-managed [effect] than this was, perhaps, never seen within the walls of a theatre," the *Times* opined, "and credited almost the only applause heard during the evening."

The illusion was achieved by scenic designer Hawes Craven and property master A. Arnott by means of a revolving tube, three or four feet in diameter, running the width of the stage and painted with ocean waves that blended into a scenery drop of the roiling sea. At the appropriate moment Irving set himself upon the turning cylinder and was pulled back onto the stage, as if being disgorged by a crashing wave. "The play proved less buoyant than its hero," wrote Laurence Irving, "and sank slowly with all hands during its brief run of a month."

Irving certainly knew the play was hopeless, but, in a move possibly calculated to reengage Stoker's attention and commitment, asked him to collaborate on (or at least observe) some judicious play-doctoring. No doubt he was already aware of Stoker's heady, ego-inflating experience with Genevieve Ward and *Sappho*, even though his contribution was pitifully small. But if he thought he could actually fashion a play for Henry Irving, why not let him think so?

Irving's personal estimation of Stoker's gifts as a creative, as opposed to a useful, writer, was never what Stoker imagined it to be. The oft-repeated story that Irving dismissed *Dracula* with one word—"Dreadful!"—may be apocryphal, but in a letter to the editor of the American magazine *Theatre*, which Stoker (mercifully) would never see, Irving once revealed his true feelings. In response to some complimentary remark the editor had made, Irving wrote, "You are quite wrong," he said, going on to say Stoker knew "as much about theatre as the man in the moon."

Stoker's own part in *Vanderdecken* was likely little more than that of a secretary for Irving's own alterations; if he contributed anything really substantial, surely Stoker would have told us about it. "I spent hours with Irving in his rooms in Grafton Street helping him to cut and alter the play," Stoker recalled, conveniently without specifics. "We did a good deal of work on it and altered it considerably for the better I thought."

It was his first visit to Irving's Mayfair residence, at the corner of Grafton and Old Bond Streets near Berkeley Square. The seal of the sanctum sanctorum had been broken, and that was the real importance of the occasion. Another visitor described Irving's lair as a "mysterious-looking house" located at "the corner where the traffic of Bond-street ebbs and flows past picture exhibitions and jewelry stores." The house's "basement [the ground floor] was occupied by a trunk store. From the second floor to the top were Irving's chambers." In total, the actor occupied three levels of the building. Six years earlier, following the separation from his wife, he had moved in with almost nothing but his books and pictures, only gradually adding furnishings.

Stoker was to be his latest acquisition.

On Monday, June 10, Stoker breakfasted with Irving, and, "after another long spell of work on the play, I went with him to the Lyceum to attend the rehearsal of the altered business." Both he and Irving felt the play was improved "so far as was possible to a performance already so complete," at least in Stoker's judgment. No one else seemed to think so. After the performance, both men supped at the Devonshire Club, followed by another long conversation in Irving's rooms, which lasted nearly till dawn.

"The next day I went to Paris," Stoker wrote (he had a standing invitation from Genevieve Ward and her mother), "but on my return saw *Vanderdecken* again and thought that by practice it had improved. It played 'closer' and the actors were more at ease—a most important thing in an eerie play!"

In his subsequent *Evening Mail* review, Stoker was pretty much alone in his praise of the production, and what admiration he put to paper comes across as a bit forced. As with *Sappho*, he did not share with his readers the fact of his backstage involvement. Nonetheless, the eeriness of *Vanderdecken* had a lasting impact on his imagination. It added to his already resonant store of macabre and fantastical nautical imagery: the "coffin ships" of the famine years, in which the passengers arrived dead; the supernaturally driven shipwreck of Shakespeare's *The Tempest*; Coleridge's "Rime of the Ancient Mariner" (directly quoted in *Dracula*); and the ship disaster and storms that punctuate the rambling pages of *Varney the Vampyre*—like the strange ruminations of his sickly childhood, these images, too, "would be fruitful in their kind."

It cannot be precisely determined when in 1878 Oscar Wilde learned of Florence Balcombe's engagement to Bram Stoker, but most chroniclers have placed the betrothal in late spring or early summer, shortly after Wilde had sent her a note from Bournemouth, saying he was sorry that he was not in Dublin and reminding her of the Easter card he had received from her "over so many miles of land and sea" while traveling in Greece the previous year. Evidently, he hadn't received anything this time around. The unresolved nature of their relationship was underscored by a puzzling sentence: "The weather is delightful and if I had not a good memory of the past I would be very happy." If Florence responded at all, she said nothing about the engagement.

The circumstances of the first meeting between Bram and Florence are even more unclear than her first introduction to Wilde. Since it is impossible that Oscar didn't show her off at one of his mother's salons—Lady Wilde was an inescapable fact of the Dublin social whirl—it's completely conceivable Oscar made the introduction himself. Bram, after all, dined regularly at Merrion Square and had become one of his mother's favorites. When Oscar matriculated at Oxford and couldn't return for Christmas, Stoker was a houseguest of the Wildes, figuratively standing in for their absent son.

But one of the most glaring gaps in the surviving papers of the Stokers and the Balcombes is the absence of a single journal notation or any correspondence pertaining to the courtship or engagement. This is especially peculiar given that Florence saved her letters from Wilde. Dubliners, in the days before the telephone, depended on written communications delivered overnight, and even the same day, by a notably efficient postal service as well as foot messengers and cabbies. The premarriage correspondence of the Stokers must have been considerable and, since Bram was a writer, quite expressive. On the other hand, Victorians were notorious for editing their lives through the selective destruction of letters. This might also explain the nonsurvival of all but one of Stoker's Dublin diaries.

But what of Bram's decision to marry in the first place? His published references to his wife are so rare, and so cursory when they do appear, that the idea that their union grew from a passionate romantic attraction seems small. Victorians frequently married for reasons of practicality and economic stability more than sexual attraction, or even sexual compatibility. Perhaps Florence wanted to get away from Dublin as much as her husband did. And, given all the indications of Stoker's sexual ambivalence, it is possible that he, like Wilde, craved the balance offered by "aesthetic marriage," or what was recommended to conflicted young men as the "marriage cure"? If only the doomed hero of Stoker's *The Primrose Path* had had a "pretty little wife" at his side in theatrical London, perhaps his catastrophe could have been prevented.

At the end of September 1878, Irving barnstormed Dublin for a fortnight, reprising *The Bells* and presenting the Irish premieres of *Richelieu* and *Louis XI*. A local paper cartooned Irving in *The Bells* hypnotizing a captivated audience. The essence of hypnotism, of course, is concentrated focus, to which end Irving strategically employed stage lighting in *Louis XI*. Augustin Daly, who saw the production in Liverpool just after its Dublin engagement, described "one of his stage tricks" as

> very effective but quite unworthy a great artist. He is fond, whenever the
> scene permits, of shutting down every light—leaving the stage in utter
> darkness, lit only by the solitary lamp or dull fire which may be in the

room; while he has directed from the prompt place or the flies a closely focused calcium—which shines only and solely upon *his* face and head; so that you can only see a lot of spectral figures without expression moving about the scene—and one ghostly lighted face shining out of the darkness; an expressive face to be sure—but after all the entirety of the drama disappears and a conjurer-like exhibition of a sphinx-head wonder takes its place.

Irving also managed to captivate Stoker's immediate family. Irving lodged with Stoker's brother Thornley instead of at the Shelbourne. Stoker recalled that the actor had become "great friends" with both his brother and sister-in-law, with whom he dined, along with Bram, almost every day. Irving would have been intent on ingratiating himself with those who might have some sway over Stoker's decision. He also met Florence (how could he not?), and knew exactly how to deliver the sort of compliments that might reinforce her belief that she, too, just might have a theatrical future in store. It was a highly pressured two weeks, "an intensive period of probation," according to Laurence Irving. Stoker still had his six-day-a-week job at Dublin Castle, plus his deadline commitments at the *Evening Mail*. Nonetheless, "Irving kept him at his side during performances and rehearsals at the theatre and rarely dined or supped except in his company."

Stoker painted this "probation" as something else entirely, "a sort of gala time to us all, and through every phase of it—and through the working time as well—our friendship grew and grew," to the point that they "understood each other's nature, needs and ambitions, and had a mutual confidence, each towards the other in his own way, rare amongst men." At least that was the way Stoker saw things. Irving himself never wrote or uttered any such understanding. He left town, still not having made Stoker an offer. Languorous ecstasy was reaching a crisis. By this point he could have told Stoker that he had, more than a month earlier, finally secured an agreement with Ellen Terry and finalized arrangements with Mrs. Bateman for a transfer of the Lyceum lease. But then he would have been obligated to make Stoker a binding offer as well. He preferred to prolong the torture.

And therein is contained the central dynamic between Bram Stoker and Henry Irving, hinted at every time Stoker describes the actor's "commanding force," transcendent authority, and power. Domination requires a weaker personality, eager and ready and willing to be commanded. Stoker's essentially masochistic nature explains much: the self-punishing work, the self-punishing athletics, the overwhelming propensity for "hero worship" and the self-deprecation such worship implies. Henry Irving was the master he had been searching for all his life, a formidable personality who would make more overwhelming and exhausting demands on Stoker than anything he could inflict upon himself. Irving would make him whole. And Stoker's devotion to the man would be the exquisite ecstasy of a martyr.

Six weeks after Irving departed Dublin, Stoker "received a telegram from him from Glasgow, where he was then playing, asking me if I could go to see him at once on important business." The game of cat and mouse would continue until the next night, following what must have been an exhausting journey from Dublin to Liverpool by night mail and from Liverpool to Glasgow by train. Then, finally, Irving told him in person that he had finally captured the Lyceum. "He asked me if I would give up the Civil Service and join him; I [was] to take charge of his business as Acting Manager."

Stoker accepted "immediately," with no indication of any discussion or negotiation of a salary, nor a consideration of the costs of living in London compared to Dublin, or anything practical at all. The next morning, by telegram, he resigned his job and, also by telegram, made "certain domestic and other arrangements of supreme importance to me at the time," including the rushed scheduling of his marriage, which had been planned for a year later. The new season at the Lyceum would begin at the end of the year, and there was no time to be wasted.

Upon Stoker's return to Dublin, a marriage license was hurriedly taken out. Florence gave her official address as Thornley's, the place she and Bram would spend their wedding night. The license also listed her "occupation," rather quaintly, as "spinster." Their marriage at St. Ann's Church on Dawson Street near the Trinity campus on December 4 was a small affair, attended by the families and close friends. Among those not present was Oscar Wilde, whose home on Merrion Square was only several blocks away. He was in Dublin settling his family's affairs and preparing for his own move to London, along with his mother. Lady Wilde could no longer afford her expensive life in Dublin, but both her sons seemed to have prospects in the British capital. Oscar requested that Florence at least return the gold cross he had gifted her. After all, he wrote, the fact that it bore his name made it impossible for a married woman to ever wear.

> Though you have not thought it worth while to let me know of your marriage, still I cannot leave Ireland without sending you my wishes that you may be happy; I at least cannot be indifferent to your welfare; the currents of our lives flowed too long beside one another for that. . . . We stand apart now, but the little cross will serve to remind me of the bygone days, and though we shall never meet again, after I leave Ireland, I shall still always remember you at prayer.

Wilde's attempts to retrieve the cross apparently continued past the actual wedding. In a presumably lost communication, she must have suggested that he fetch it at Thornley's. Wilde expressed his umbrage and made the ridiculous demand that she meet him at her mother's home in Clontarf, where he had originally made the gift—and where, of course, she might still appear as the unbetrothed virgin she had been. To cross her marriage threshold to retrieve a romantic trinket would be positively indecent.

Whether the cross ever found its way back to Wilde is not known. It never surfaced among any of his effects, or among Florence's. Stoker himself may have advised her to finally give up the trinket. There were ample reasons for Stoker to think Oscar was unsavory, or somehow unclean. If you threw a crucifix at him, perhaps he would just go away.

One is tempted to believe that Stoker relished the aptness—however overreaching—of having his last Dublin theatre review on November 26 be that of *The Tempest* at the Theatre Royal. "Whatever difference of opinion may exist in the chronological order of Shakespeare's plays," the notice reads, "it is admitted that *The Tempest* is one of the very last of his masterpieces." The idea that Shakespeare's plays were informed by the stages and events of the Bard's actual life was a central point of Edward Dowden's criticism, and Stoker may have allowed himself to be his mentor's mouthpiece on any number of occasions in the previous seven years. The *Tempest* review contains Stoker's typical appreciation of stagecraft and mise-en-scène. The famous storm and shipwreck, driven by a nobleman in exile possessed of supernatural powers, who also controls an animal-like slave, added to the growing storehouse of images that would fuel the nascent dream ultimately given form as *Dracula.*

Commanded by his own Prospero, Stoker sailed through a stormy December sea to meet the master on his island, and began a twenty-seven-year-long adventure more consuming and challenging than anything he had read or imagined.

Bram and Florence canceled their plans for a honeymoon, and never rescheduled. What would be the use? In the final analysis, they were both marrying Henry Irving.

CHAPTER FIVE

LONDONERS

I LONG TO GO THROUGH THE CROWDED STREETS
OF YOUR MIGHTY LONDON, TO BE IN THE MIDST
OF THE WHIRL AND RUSH OF HUMANITY,
TO SHARE ITS LIFE, ITS CHANGE, ITS DEATH,
AND ALL THAT MAKES IT WHAT IT IS.

—Count Dracula

In a period of six months between December 1878 and May 1879, the Stokers and the Wildes all journeyed to London to pursue what they hoped would be their good and lasting fortunes. But the Irish, even the Protestant Irish, were not necessarily welcome in Britain's capital city. Had Bram, Florence, Lady Wilde or her sons been looking for menial work or employment as domestic help, they would likely have been rebuffed at most approaches; NO IRISH was a tediously common message on hiring signs.

Dublin was gritty, but London was filthy. The industrial soot and chemicals that descended everywhere and on everything were the driving ingredients in the city's legendarily thick and enveloping fogs. By the late nineteenth century London's population was nearly five million, and coal drove almost every aspect of life: factories, steam-powered transportation,

A first night at the Lyceum Theatre epitomized the social whirl of Victorian London. Irving and Terry in the triumphant 1878 production of Hamlet.

and residential heating churned out unimaginable amounts of smoke, and other industrial toxins only worsened the airborne miasma. Ash and horse dung commingled on the cobblestones in a thick, sickening paste. Women wore black, and shoe scrapers were ubiquitous. The chemically fueled fogs were famously called "pea-soupers," as much for their consistency as their color, which could range from strange reddish yellows and murky browns to a bilious green. Claude Monet recorded an even wider spectrum in his paintings of the city and, remarking that "the fog in London assumes all sorts of colors; there are black, brown, yellow, green, [and] purple fogs."

London fogs could turn day into night, make it literally impossible to see one's hand before one's face, and completely disrupt inner-city traffic. Lanterns were often needed to lead lorries and trams. Anyone and anything could appear from and disappear into swirling, sulphuric mist. Pickpockets and thieves, of course, had a field day, and their presence added an extra, anxious sense of menace. Today these fogs are de rigueur in film adaptations of mystery-laden stories of Sherlock Holmes, Dr. Jekyll and Mr. Hyde, Dorian Gray, and Dracula, even though their authors referenced fog glancingly, if at all. They didn't have to. Their readers were fully and painfully aware of the condition of London air, its ability to assault their throats and sear their eyes, and its ever-present association with respiratory failure and fatality among the infirm. The worst fogs on record were still to come; in 1952, choking fog would be held responsible for four thousand unnecessary London deaths.

The first few years of the Stokers' marriage would be spent in almost chained proximity to the Lyceum, on the top floor of a mixed-use building in Southampton Street. Their son would later claim to have been born in Bloomsbury, but he may have confused his birthplace with that district's far more exclusive Southhampton Row—or simply led to believe that by his increasingly status-sensitive parents. A short block and a half from the theatre, it was presumably found for them by someone connected to the Lyceum, since the couple did not arrive in London until December 14, having been in perpetual motion with the tour. Not only was it impossible for Bram and Florence to have a honeymoon—there was no real time to deal with the practicalities of relocation, either.

The final touring week in Birmingham was "child's play compared with the next two weeks in London," Stoker wrote. "The correspondence alone was greater; but in addition the theatre which was to be opened was in a state of chaos. The builders who were making certain structural alterations had not got through their work; plasterers, paper-hangers, painters, [and] upholsterers were tumbling over each other. The outside of the building was covered with men and scaffolding. The whole of the auditorium was a mass of poles and platforms. On the stage and in the paint-room and the property-rooms, the gas rooms and carpenter's shop and wardrobe-room, the new production of *Hamlet* was being hurried on under high pressure." As Irving's grandson would write, "Bram Stoker had to exert all his physical and mental energy in order to master the intricacies of theatre management while dealing with the immediate problems that arose from hour to hour."

The Lyceum property had been previously used for a variety of entertainments, including opera, phantasmagoria (supernaturally tinged magic lantern shows), and, in 1802, the first London exhibition of Madame Tussaud's waxworks. After a fire in 1830 (one of several in its history), it reopened in 1834 as the Royal Lyceum and English Opera house. By the time of the Batemans' stewardship it had become decidedly worn and dingy. But it was Irving's theatre now, and it would have Irving's stamp, on stage and off. The stately portico entrance remained, but interior architectural alterations were extensive. Attention was given to improved seating in the dress circle and the stalls, and the plain benches that lined the pit and gallery were, for the first time, given backrests—a nod of respect to the ordinary theatregoers who often stood outside all day, waiting for unassigned, inexpensive seats. A new color scheme of sage green and turquoise transformed the auditorium.

Stoker occupied a work alcove off the main office where Irving's desk faced that of his stage manager H. J. Loveday. A stage manager, in Irving's time, assumed much of the work done by a producer or director today, even if actor-managers like Irving largely directed their own performances. Loveday, not Stoker, was Irving's true right-hand man, a distinction made clear by the position of Stoker's desk and his being barred from using the door and passageway that connected the office directly to the stage; this was reserved for Irving and Loveday alone. If Stoker needed to talk to either man during a rehearsal, he would have to enter the auditorium from the back of the house, and return to the office in the same circuitous manner. Readers of Stoker's Irving memoir would scarcely believe he could have ever been treated in such a petty way, but it was typical

The Lyceum Theatre, at the height of Irving's reign.

behavior on Irving's part to keep even loyal associates not quite sure of where they stood. *Hamlet,* with a new Ophelia in the person of Ellen Terry, was an unqualified triumph for Irving. But Terry, largely ignored by Irving in rehearsal, and slyly undermined in matters like her costume choices, felt—quite wrongly—that her own first-night performance was a disaster. She left shortly after the curtain and rode despondently in a cab up and down the Embankment. Despite all the charisma he radiated, and no matter how much devotion he inspired, somehow Henry Irving knew exactly how to make you feel miserable and drained, alone and empty . . . and always ready for more.

Lady Wilde, still lingering in Dublin long after the *Hamlet* debut, wrote to Oscar in London about her own relocation anxieties. "I don't know what to do. The Bram Stokers have six rooms unfurnished lodging and attendance [household staff, presumably a cook and a maid] in Southampton Street for £100 a year. . . . What am I to do? Meanwhile, I know nothing of Willie's wishes—is the furniture to be sold or brought over? I know not—I think I'll die and end it—I'm sick and weary—meantime I have a dozen trunks of books to be put somewhere—but where?"

Her histrionics gradually subsided, and she arrived at last in May. Almost immediately she set about the project of reviving her Dublin salon in Covington Square, and in two more residences she and Willie would share. She was now nearing sixty, and her taste for shadows and soft candles had only increased; guests sometimes nearly stumbled trying to find chairs. She had brought trunks full of her trademark costumes from Dublin, among them ball dresses twenty years out of date, accessorized with brooches, scarves, streamers, and beribboned headdresses. Frankly, she didn't have money for a new wardrobe. But to expect literary London to embrace the eccentricities to which Dublin had become inured only after decades of relentless exposure was a mile too far. Comments aimed in her direction were often barbed. Yet at least one visitor was impressed that her "faded splendor was more striking than the most fashionable attire. . . . She wore that ancient finery with a grace and dignity that robbed it of its grotesqueness." On the other hand, George Bernard Shaw called the London incarnations of her Merrion Square salon "desperate affairs." Nonetheless, she continued to maintain a public profile, living frugally and earning money from essays and articles, and a new project of assembling her late husband's voluminous notes on Irish folklore and editing them for publication. Willie, in turn, would depend mostly on her.

There had never been talk of Lady Wilde living with Oscar. It seemed foreordained that he and Frank Miles would require bachelors' quarters of their own. The men set up housekeeping at 15 Salisbury Street, barely a block away from the Stokers on the other side of the Strand. Because of its view of the river, they called the rental property Thames House. The view was marred by dirty haze, but Wilde preferred to think of choking pollution in aesthetic terms. In his poem "Impression du Matin," he watched as "The yellow fog came creeping down / The bridges, till the houses' walls / Seemed changed to shadows and St. Paul's / Loomed like a bubble o'er the town."

Whatever people might have thought privately of their relationship, Oscar and Frank presented themselves as a bachelor social couple—and a socially very ambitious pair, at that. One of their mutual adorations was the actress Lillie Langtry, whom Oscar would flatter (he inscribed his first book to her, "To Helen formerly of Troy, now of London") and whom Frank would paint.

At Oxford, a friend once asked Wilde for his goal in life, and he replied that he wanted to be famous or, that failing, notorious. He would become both, in spades, but his first years in London were spent social-climbing. Although he had published almost nothing, and was still finishing his first volume of poetry, he had internalized his mother's belief that "epigrams are always better than argument in conversation" and that "paradox is the very essence of social wit." He perfected a trademark style of wicked flippancy that never failed to delight people who were worth knowing with quips that were worth repeating. In a Victorian sort of way, he simply "went viral" in London society. Oscar Wilde has often been called one of the first persons to have become famous for being famous, and in the early years of the 1880s he was a ubiquitous self-created celebrity and a sought-after guest. An invitation to a soirée hosted by Oscar and Frank was equally coveted. They moved within a few years to a house in Tite Street, Chelsea, which they extensively renovated with funds provided by Frank's well-to-do father, Canon Robert Henry William Miles of Nottinghamshire. Here in Chelsea their neighbors included the artistic likes of James McNeill Whistler—the leading exponent of the aesthetic creed—and John Singer Sargent.

The new residence, called Keats House (not after the poet but as word-play on the name of some former residents named Skeates), was much better suited for entertaining than Salisbury Street. The painter Edwin A. Ward recalled Miles as "a kindly, handsome fellow, and his little house became the haunt of great folk in society with the Prince of Wales's set as hallmark. The Prince himself was a frequent visitor, and Miles was bombarded with commissions for pencil portraits from every fashionable beauty of the day." As for his partnership with Wilde, Ward remembered Wilde's "instanta-neous and astounding social success" and how the painter and poet "were seen everywhere; no fashionable function was complete without them, and their parties in Tite Street became the rage."

One of the most colorful get-togethers transpired in the spring of 1881, when Oscar and Frank invited an exclusive group to a demonstration of "thought reading" by an American stage mentalist who, as if in anticipation of Harry Houdini's similar efforts, debunked the claims of phony spiritu-alists through an entertaining demonstration of the fraudulent methods frequently used by mediums and psychics. His name was Washington Irving Bishop, and he claimed to be the godson of the writer Washington Irving. It was only appropriate that one of the guests was Henry Irving, named himself after the American storyteller. Irving had reveled in exposing a fraudulent medium act in Manchester early in his career, and no doubt provided some memorable anecdotes. The other guests included the Prince of Wales, Lillie Langtry, James Whistler, the actor Edwin Booth (John Wilkes Booth's brother, in London to alternate the roles of Othello and Iago with Irving at the Lyceum, a successful publicity gambit if not a complete artistic success—Booth made the better Moor), and a number of titled personages. Bishop made quite a career bursting ectoplasmic bubbles, but met a truly spooky personal end in 1899, when he collapsed during a demonstration at the Lambs Club in New York and appeared to be dead. Attending doctors hastily performed an autopsy, and were accused by Bishop's family of never reading a note in his pocket stating that he suffered from catalepsy and under no circumstances should be dissected or interred. Although no such note was ever produced, Bishop's mother cried murder anyway, and spent the next three decades unsuccessfully filing lawsuits and publicly demanding justice. She insisted that her son be buried in a windowed

Washington Irving Bishop, "thought reader" for Oscar Wilde, Frank Miles, and their guests, in a postmortem publicity photograph with his mother. She charged doctors with murder for presuming her son dead and performing a too-hasty autopsy, even though he was a known cataleptic.

coffin to clearly show the world the ghastly scar that encircled his forehead and skull—his brain having been removed, examined, and unceremoniously sewn up in his chest cavity. The word MARTYR was carved at the top of his headstone.

At the height of his London visibility in 1881, Wilde chose to self-publish his book of poetry—a strategic decision, but one that backfired badly. The book was not favorably received at the Oxford Union (the university debating society), which had previously requested a copy for its library, only to decline it on the basis of its unoriginality. London reviewers went so far as to charge plagiarism, and even indecency, creating a contretemps that escalated into attacks on Wilde's moral character while at Oxford. An undergraduate journal made it clear that the simmering animus toward Oscar was beginning to boil. "If a man leads an evil life in the University, even though he may not suffer for his acts at the time, yet his character will not have escaped the notice of his colleagues." Wilde was not named and the acts not described, though it is easy to imagine what they might have been, or were insinuated to be.

Frank's father became alarmed by the controversy, especially the charges of indecency, which centered on the poem "Charmides," about a young man who makes love to a marble statue of Athena. It was tame stuff compared to the truly transgressive work of the French decadents, but, according to Edwin Ward, "the old-fashioned cleric became alarmed. . . . He wrote to his son expressing his horror at the suggestions contained in the lines he had read; in fact he insisted that it was impossible for a son of his to continue under the same roof with a man capable of holding such views." Ward acknowledged that Miles was placed in a difficult and unpleasant situation, but "his devotion to his father left him no alternative and he felt compelled to place the whole embarrassing position before his friend. . . . Wilde, livid with rage, flew into a furious passion and demanded to know if Frank Miles intended to act upon so outrageous a breach of all the ties of their long friendship. Miles protested that much as it grieved him, he had absolutely no alternative."

As reported to Ward by the servant at Tite Street, Wilde said, "Very well, then. I will leave you. I will go now and I will never speak to you again as long as I live." Then, Ward wrote, "he tore upstairs, flung his few belongings into a great travelling trunk, and without waiting for the servant to carry it downstairs, tipped it over the bannisters, whence it crashed down upon a valuable antique table in the hall below, smashing it into splinters. Hailing a passing cab, he swept out of the house, speechless with passion, slamming a door he was never to darken again."

Wilde's final words to his friend anticipated a famous scene he would write almost a decade later for *The Picture of Dorian Gray* (1890–91), in which Dorian issues his own ultimatum to the artist Basil Hallward, who has adored him, and painted a portrait supernaturally preserving his youth while the painting itself manifests all the evidence of corruption and debauchery he conceals from the world. "If you try to look at it, Basil, on my word of honour I will never speak to you again as long as I live. I am quite serious. I don't offer any explanation, and you are not to ask for any. But, remember, if you touch this screen [that hides the painting], everything is over between us."

Commentators have speculated extensively on Wilde's possible source of inspiration for the cursed portrait, but none to date have wondered about Frank Miles and a terrible secret he was hiding from the world. Miles created unusually flattering portraits that froze his subjects in time, idealizing and commemorating their beauty in a particularly mesmerizing way. Women clamored for sittings, for the chance to be expertly frozen by the unmistakable Miles touch. But beneath his facility for capturing the surface loveliness of others on canvas and his skill at projecting his own charming façade was a dark, gnawing fact: Frank Miles had syphilis. A poem about a statue was hardly enough for Canon Miles to hurl a lightning bolt down at a friendship he had condoned for at least five years. Wilde's poetry was only a pretext to act on knowledge that couldn't be written down, or even spoken aloud. Whenever and however the father learned the truth, his son had contracted an incurable disease at some time during his friendship with Oscar Wilde—whether from a direct infection or through some contact encouraged by Wilde's questionable company didn't matter.

Frank continued his career as an ornament to society lives, though without the added benefit of Oscar's seemingly effortless ability to attract attention and clients. He continued for the next few years as a fixture of Whistler's Chelsea coterie and as a society pet, sketching the rich and beautiful until the ravages of syphilis began to affect his mind and he was no longer pleasant company at parties. Canon Miles had died in the meantime, and his degree of support was not continued by Frank's successful but unsympathetic brothers, who were both worth millions. Miles was already

*Frank Miles (right) had an artistic circle of Chelsea friends including
James McNeill Whistler (center). This photograph was taken in 1891, the same year
as Miles's acrimonious breakup with Oscar Wilde.* (Library of Congress)

the black sheep of his family. Entranced by aestheticism above practical values, he surrounded himself with the trappings of art but never managed to make a secure life for himself. In 1886 he wrote a less than coherent letter to the wife of the painter George Boughton that seemed to permanently disavow his aesthetic principles: "Tell George I have given up his idea and Oscars—and Jimmy [Whistler] long ago—that art is for art's sake. . . . [If] some unfortunate accident happens of its doing some harm to somebody why it is the artist's fault." The following year he was committed to Brislington House, an asylum near Bristol, where he died a lunatic in 1891 from general paresis of the insane. The destructive onset of neurosyphilis in a typical case is about ten years, placing contraction squarely around the time of Wilde's likely infection at Oxford, the height of his early friendship with Frank, and the breaking of his engagement to Florence Balcombe. While Wilde would draw on other real-life models to populate his preternatural masterwork, Frank Miles's tragedy and its fashionable art-world setting were the primary sources for the central, syphilitic metaphor of *The Picture of Dorian Gray.*

Hamlet played for a hundred performances, and toward the end of its run in the spring of 1879, Florence Stoker conceived with her husband their only child, Irving Noel Thornley, who was born on December 30. Henry Irving was the godfather and namesake, but Noel would never call himself anything except Noel. Stoker let friends in Dublin know of his impending fatherhood late in 1879, eliciting a warm response from one of his closest Trinity friends, John Joseph Robinson, with whom he shared interests in literature, athletics, and debate, and who followed him as president of the Phil from 1874 to 1877 and who was now a Dublin clergyman. In regard to the Stokers' new arrival, Robinson wrote, "The more I think of it, the more wonderful and strange the gift of a child seems." He recommended that Stoker read Samuel Taylor Coleridge's "well-put" sonnet on a new-born child.

Stoker in his early London years. (John Moore Library)

Stoker must have sent several telegrams to Dublin on New Year's Eve announcing his son's birth. Robinson's reply the following day was particularly emotional. "My very dear Boy," it began,

> I must lose not a moment in sending you most hearty congratulations. May God's blessing rest from the very first on your little son. Is it not a wonderful & mysterious thing altogether old man that gift of Fatherhood in which we perhaps we come nearest to what is divine. Don't you find that there are stirrings of you know not what in your heart that were never there before. You will find too that there are tones in your wife's voice, as soon as she gets strong enough to talk to her baby, the sacred Mother tones, which you never heard before. And so God bless you & your family & your work old boy. You in your work and & I in mine, & keep us both in love & brotherhood to one another which no distance or diversity of interest can diminish.

Robinson closed, "And so the Church sends New Year's greeting to the drama. I wish I were near enough to baptize your baby."

Robinson's gushing sentiments apparently struck the wrong tone. A week later he wrote again, dampening his emotionality considerably. "You did not answer my letter. I hope that does not mean you are offended with me for writing as I did, but only that you are very busy. I don't think you are a likely man to be offended if I know you at all, though probably you did not agree with me. A very happy new year to you & the wife & the child. Is there any chance of your being over here if so do come and see me."

There is no evidence Stoker ever communicated with Robinson again. Perhaps his letters had threatened to reawaken a previous degree of intimacy with which Stoker was no longer comfortable. It is also possible Robinson's recommendation of the Coleridge sonnet hit too close to home. Coleridge had written of a melancholy new father, restored to good cheer by watching his wife's nurturing maternal behavior. This did not necessarily describe Florence. According to Stoker's second biographer, his great-nephew Daniel Farson, "My family, speaking of her, gave me the impression of an elegant, aloof woman, more interested in her position in society than she was in her son." He then recounted a conversation with Noel's daughter, Ann, in which she told him Florence "was cursed with her great beauty and the need to maintain it. In my knowledge now, she was very antisex. After having my father in her early twenties, I think she was quite put off."[1]

Florence may also have had quite enough of commercial Southampton Street, with its noise, its smells, and the whores at night, not to mention the complete lack of charm and amenities. It was no place to raise a child. And its proximity to the Lyceum only encouraged Bram to never come home except for meals and sleep. In addition to working in the office all day, he oversaw the box office at night and greeted important audience members, of which there were many. Irving held court at late-night suppers for guests and visiting dignitaries given in the Lyceum's Beefsteak Room, where Stoker was expected to be on hand as well, in addition to accompanying the Governor (as Irving liked to be called) to all manner of other social events. It would be understandable if Florence was also sick of living almost literally under the shadow of a theatre that she had made part of her personal dreams as an aspiring actress, a theatre that had failed her. Yes, Henry Irving had given her *one* part on the stage—a vestal virgin, one of a hundred supernumeraries in a crowd scene for Tennyson's *The Cup*, its production designed by the Pre-Raphaelite master Edward Burne-Jones, who had personally sketched her profile in pencil. It was a small consolation prize for a stage career that was never to be. And to think that they had actually listed her occupation as "artist" for the London census!

Although in the end it was wishful thinking to think Bram would ever really cut back on his working days and nights, no matter where they lived, the Stokers made a dramatic change in their living situation sometime around 1881. They relocated to Chelsea, one of the most desirable districts in London, an area known for its exclusivity since the Tudor era. In the late 1800s Chelsea retained an English village charm despite the density of its population, and was London's prime neighborhood for artists, writers, and high-end bohemianism generally. The home at 26 Cheyne Walk was—and still is—a gated, four-story, graciously terraced redbrick corner house with a garden and an idyllic view of the Thames. The riverfront street had been the creative epicenter of the Pre-Raphaelite movement; the house occupied

---

[1] Ann Stoker Dobbs denied she made these statements to Farson in a 1999 conversation with the fourth Stoker biographer, Paul Murray. Farson was dead by that time, and no further clarification was or is possible. It seems odd, however, that Farson would invent a lie and then attribute it to the very person to whom the book was dedicated. It is more reasonable to conclude that seeing an honest family conversation appear in print simply caused her embarrassment.

Top: Henry Irving's residence in Mayfair.
Bottom: The Stokers' first Chelsea residence as it appears today. (Photograph by the author)

by both Dante Gabriel Rossetti and Algernon Charles Swinburne was only a few blocks east.

For artsy, arriviste pretension they couldn't have done better. The question is, how on earth could they manage it? Even Henry Irving, the West End's greatest star, lived in three floors above a trunk shop. Houses like the one on Cheyne Walk were expensive leaseholds, not rentals, and required a substantial amount of upfront money. It is not likely that the ever-subservient Stoker demanded a raise. But did he borrow from (and thereby mortgage himself to) the Lyceum? Debt of some kind must have been taken on, and a lot of it. Owing to the Byzantine security built into the Lyceum bookkeeping system (devised by Stoker to keep the overall ebb and flow of the theatre's finances known only to himself), no one has been able to draw a clear picture of Stoker's or Irving's actual ongoing compensation, nor any possible cash advances or loans from the Lyceum's treasury. Irving believed in paying bills in gold sovereigns—a strategic policy that assured loyalty among vendors and suppliers but also made definitive tracking of the theatre's cash problematic. As Noel would recall, "To attain the necessary degree of secrecy, my father laid out the accounting system so that no one knew more than the portion allotted to him."

Just as Loveday was the stage manager, Stoker was the house manager. Noel remembered that "he used to arrive at the Lyceum long before the doors were opened. When the time came, he would go out into the still deserted stalls and call out to each of the ushers by name. 'Mr. Jarvis' and there came back 'Here, Sir' from the dress circle, and so on, until the 'Here, sir,' came down from the usher in charge of the gallery. Then, my father would shout at the top of his powerful voice, 'Open.' I once asked him, why he did this; and the answer was, 'So that, in the case of fire or any other emergency, they will know my voice.'" Stoker could be impressively stentorian when he needed to. He was said to have once stopped a train leaving without him with nothing but a full-throated roar.

Under Irving's management, the Lyceum never produced Christmas pantomimes. But in December 1881, Stoker himself produced what amounted to his own toy-theatre variation, in book form. *Under the Sunset*, published in a sumptuous illustrated edition by the London publisher Sampson Low, Marston, Searle & Rivington contains seven fairy tales, ostensibly for children, that he had been writing since his Dublin days. The manuscript consists of stories written in ink and pencil on different sizes of

Preliminary sketches by William Fitzgerald for **Under the Sunset.** (John Moore Library)

paper (the earliest being the smallest), with sheets evidently in short supply; Stoker wrote to the very edges of the paper, though later he would come to realize the value of margins for editing and notes. Only one of the stories had been previously published, the central tale called "The Castle of the King," which had appeared in the *Warder*, a newspaper covering Dublin and Waterford, in 1876.

The book was illustrated by two artists. W. V. Cockburn was assigned the steel-engraved frontispiece and several story scenes. The other artist, who worked in pen and ink and was based in Dublin, was William

Fitzgerald, a good friend of Stoker's at Trinity. He made a number of pre-liminary sketches, many of them quite evocative and haunting. Fitzgerald also liked to decorate his letters with sketches of strange creatures and droll characters whose faces were apparently inspired by some of the more colorful Trinity dons. Fitzgerald and Stoker had a good rapport and shared a wicked sense of humor, particularly in a letter the artist illustrated with a cartoon of Stoker, hurrying along the street, literally reduced to a skeleton doing the bidding of Henry Irving.

Traditional Irish fairy tales evolved and existed side by side with Christian theology, but in Stoker's stories biblical imagery and cadences mix freely with the author's own eclectic imaginings. Angels and evil spirits of a kind that never appear in the Bible interact like good fairies and bad fairies in the manner of Celtic legend. He dedicated the book

TO

MY SON

WHOSE ANGEL DOTH BEHOLD THE FACE

OF

THE KING

The meaning of the dedication isn't fully clear until one begins to read the stories, in which it becomes apparent that the king is the King of Death, and that nearly all the stories involve mortality in some way: the coming of death, the fear of death, and the reversal of death. The *Dublin Evening Mail* (reviewing its own reviewer for the first time) noted, tactfully, that the doom-saturated holiday book was "somewhat out of keeping with the popular conception of Christmas." As Stoker explains in the book itself, "It is whispered that Death has his kingdom in the Solitudes beyond the marshes, and lives in a castle so awful to look at that no one has ever seen it and lived to tell what it is like. . . . All the evil things that live in the marshes are the disobedient Children of Death who have left home and cannot find their way back again." The most frequently reproduced illustration from *Under the Sunset* is Cockburn's impression of King Death's castle, with a huge skull superimposed on its shadowy entrance.

The Demon King of the Christmas pantomimes yielded the King of

Some of Fitzgerald's fanciful character concepts are believed to be based on the faces and personalities of certain Trinity College dons, known to both the artist and Stoker.

Irving exits the Lyceum for a cab,
Stoker hurrying behind.

William Fitzgerald's satiric cartoon of Stoker,
reduced to a walking skeleton under the
demanding employ of Henry Irving.
(John Moore Library)

Death in *Under the Sunset*, and he would eventually and inexorably reemerge in *Dracula*. A poem in "The Castle of the King" anticipates the peasants' warnings to Jonathan Harker, urging him to stay at the inn and proceed no further in the direction of the Count's abode:

> Pass not the Portal of the Sunset Land!
> Pause where the Angels at their vigil stand.
> Be warned! And press not though the gates lie wide,
> But rest securely on the hither side.
> Though odorous gardens and cool ways invite,

The architecture of death. William Fitzgerald's macabre illustration for "The Castle of the King" in **Under the Sunset** *(1884).* (John Moore Library)

Beyond are the darkest valleys of the night.
Rest! Rest contented.—Pause whilst undefiled,
Nor seek the horrors of the desert wild.

One of the most affecting stories, "The Shadow Builder," needs no deep psychological exegesis to be understood as Stoker's dream-account of the mortal terrors attending his own sickly childhood, and the difficulty of separation from an emotional and protective mother. "The Wondrous Child" similarly involves the death of a baby and its miraculous restoration to life. "The Invisible Giant" is a truly remarkable transformation of Charlotte Stoker's account of the cholera scourge into a towering spectral metaphor of mortality.

Many reviewers wondered if the darker stories were a bit over the heads of the intended readers. *Punch* called *Under the Sunset* "a charming book . . . though, perhaps, somewhat above the heads of those who are only three and a-half high." According to the *Morning Post,* "If, as in the 'Castle of the King,' the allegory occasionally seems too deep for child-minds, that is no

Charlotte Stoker's chilling memories of the 1832 cholera epidemic informed her son's story "The Invisible Giant," in which a deadly plague is personified. (John Moore Library)

Frontispiece for **Under the Sunset** *by W. V. Cockburn.*

drawback—the boys and girls will enjoy the pretty story, and can wait a while to fully understand it." The *Norfolk News* discerned rumbling undercurrents: "Under the pleasant stories, told in such felicitous language, rhythmical in its flow, lies a deeper meaning. It is as if while the reed pipes of an organ were singing pleasant melodies, the pedal pipes sounding far below were stirring up half slumbering memories, awakening deeper thoughts and teaching stronger lessons." The *Spectator* opined, quite flatteringly, that Stoker "is upon the same ground as Nathaniel Hawthorne, and it is no slight praise for his work to be able to say that he does not suffer by the comparison."

Henry Irving's personal secretary, Louis Frederick Austin (with whom Stoker had a sometimes prickly, rivalry-fueled relationship), alleged that *Under the Sunset* was a vanity project, for which the author paid Samson Low £700, a huge sum. This may or may not be true, or only partly true (in substance as well as in the figure). It is understandable that Stoker was dying to be published. Before he left Dublin, he thought he would be able to juggle the Lyceum *and* a sideline writing career. That had not happened. The year

1881 marked the fourth Christmas since he had arrived in London, but he was an unknown commodity in the book world, and it's quite plausible the book's publication was subsidized in whole or part, and not necessarily by Stoker alone. All writers yearn to make a splash with their first book. But the extravagant presentation of *Under the Sunset* is hardly the sort of thing a publisher would lavish upon an untested author.

Stoker presented a copy of the first edition to the Evelina Hospital for Sick Children in Southwark Bridge Road, London, inscribed to "The Sick Children / with Bram Stokers love / January 1882." According to Dublin collector John Moore, present owner of the signed volume, "The plight of the hospital's sick children would have resonated heavily with Stoker himself, whose early childhood was blighted by a mysterious illness that confined him to bed for a number of years." Stoker's affinity for children is also recorded in the *Dublin Freeman's Journal* review, which described *Under the Sunset* as "a book as kind, and genial, and thoughtful to our children as Mr. Bram Stoker has ever known how to be. The honest ring of his voice is almost audible from the words as they lie silent on the page."

Noel Stoker never made any reference to or comment about *Under the Sunset*. His childhood amounted to its own shadowy fairy tale. His earliest recollections of his father were as "a red-bearded giant" who would "lie at full length on the drawing room carpet, and let me climb about his chest. Later, I used to join him when he was getting into his dress suit, and listen to tales about pixies." However, as with parents and parental

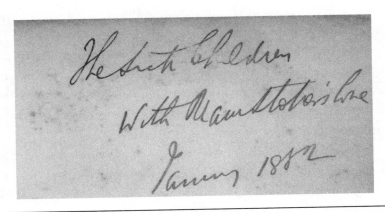

Stoker's inscription of **Under the Sunset** *to the Evelina Hospital for Sick Children.*
(John Moore Library)

Florence and Noel Stoker in the early 1880s. Unknown photographer.

figures in fairy stories from time immemorial, there was a dark side as well. Noel encountered this aspect of his father on a summer holiday on the beach at Whitby, North Yorkshire, where Bram decided to give his son an impromptu swimming lesson—the sink or swim variety. Noel flailed helplessly in the deep water as his father walked backward away from him. The only lesson he learned was the terror of parental abandonment and threat of infanticide that were always lurking behind the supposedly children-friendly tales of the Brothers Grimm. According to his daughter, Noel never did learn how to swim.

If Bram was a two-faced giant in his son's imagination, Florence Stoker was a mirror-gazing Snow Queen. She might well have been put off not so much by motherhood itself as by the physical effects of childbearing. Despite her beauty, she was not petite; her height of five feet eight inches may have already made her feel ungainly and self-conscious in comparison to the sylphlike Victorian ideal promoted everywhere around her.

Women's fashion advertisements in the 1880s and '90s were relentless in their emphatic insistence on tiny waists. There were no fashion photographers then, and illustrators had the latitude to depict waistlines that went beyond a mere "hourglass" look to visions resembling the midsections of famished wasps, or daggers driven down into the pelvis. The reviled Barbie-doll template of the female form, an impossible standard excoriated by feminists since the mid-twentieth century, had far worse precursors in the corseted Victorian age. And whatever the era, being the child of a vain woman who blames you in any way for ruining her figure cannot be a happy position.

It may also be a mistake to constantly speculate about Florence's supposed frigidity, as argued by Farson and others, without considering how she really may have felt about the opposite sex. Sexual disinterest in men is not necessarily the same thing as sexual dysfunction. And although the term "lipstick lesbian" is recent, the reality of beautiful women drawn to other women is a story as old as time, or at least Sappho's time. Genevieve Ward's reaction to Florence's legendary attractiveness would be fascinating to know, especially as Ward remained close to the Stokers and was a steady social fixture in their lives until Bram's death.

For whatever reasons, or whatever resentments, there are no warm remembrances of Florence by Noel Stoker or anyone else in the family. By one account, a wet nurse "starved" him. He spent so much time with a French governess that his first language was French instead of English, acquired so well that he could be mistaken for a native French speaker as an adult. In a *Punch* cartoon by George du Maurier, showing the Stoker family at a backyard garden party, the accompanying text speaks volumes. Under the heading A FILIAL REPROOF the caption reads, "Mamma to Noel, who is inclined to be talkative, 'Hush, Noel! Haven't I told you that little Boys should be *Seen* and not *Heard?*'" Noel's reply: "Yes, Mamma! But you don't *Look* at ME!" And, for the record, Florence—projecting, perhaps?—could be angrily critical of the lack of attention her husband showed her son. She reputedly said he would be more upset if Irving died than he would over losing his own son. Stoker is said to have snapped back that a child could be replaced—but Henry Irving couldn't.[2]

---

[2] It is hardly surprising that this unflattering exchange, included in a letter from Noel Stoker to his father's first biographer, Harry Ludlam, in 1959, was not quoted in Ludlam's book

"Children should be seen and not heard." **Punch** *cartoonist George du Maurier memorably recorded Noel Stoker's difficulty engaging his mother's attention at a Chelsea garden party.*

Unmoored from Frank Miles, Oscar Wilde was restless. The next chapter in his life opened unexpectedly, though perhaps not unpredictably. He had been working too hard on his own self-promotion for a major new opportunity not to present itself. W. S. Gilbert, the librettist partner of composer Arthur Sullivan, was annoyed at the pretensions and posturing of the aesthetic movement and went about skewering them as best he could in the book and lyrics of *Patience; or, Bunthorne's Bride,* a comic opera that had its London premiere in April 1881. Gilbert didn't particularly have Oscar Wilde in mind when he created the character of the "fleshly poet" Bunthorne—Swinburne and Rossetti were closer to the mark—but there was enough of Wilde in Bunthorne's velvet breeches and languid flower-waving that the producer of the upcoming American tour asked Wilde

---

A Biography of Dracula, the following year. The unusually revealing letter is conspicuously missing from the Stoker/Ludlam correspondence Bram's great-nephew Noel Dobbs sold to the Trinity College Library Dublin in 1999.

Oscar Wilde strikes a classically aesthetic pose for the American photographer Napoleon Sarony.

if he would tour the United States as a paid advance man for the show, delivering lectures on aesthetics, giving interviews to the press, and sometimes simply making an appearance at the back of a train to show the rubberneckers at the whistle-stop exactly what one of these aestheticians was about, the better to ready them for *Patience* when it inevitably came to town.

Wilde didn't hesitate, and in January 1882 embarked on what would balloon into an eleven-month stay in America. His arrival in New York was the apocryphal occasion when he supposedly told a customs official "I have nothing to declare but my genius." No one knows who really said it, or wrote it, but Wilde had no reason to disavow such an inspired line. Nor did he chafe or complain when newspapers caricatured him as a monkey or a missing link, or let their readers know, as did the *Kansas City Star*, that "Oscar Wilde, the long-haired what-is-it, has finally reached Kansas City, and the aesthetic noodles and blue-china nincompoops are in the seventh heaven of happiness." Wilde was one of the first celebrities to understand that there was really no such thing as bad publicity—except, of course, *no* publicity.

The tour, however, was more than nonstop buffoonery. He gave serious, substantial lectures, sometimes disappointing audiences who were expecting something a good deal more Barnumesque. His ideas made a genuinely positive impression on coal miners in Leadville, Colorado. He undertook literary pilgrimages to such places as the house in the Hudson Valley where Edgar Allan Poe wrote "The Raven," as well as a visit to a living poetic monument—Mr. Walt Whitman, of Camden, New Jersey.

It was a meeting Bram Stoker had always imagined for himself but would not be able to realize for another two years. No doubt he read press accounts of Wilde's visit—they were plentiful—and as Irving's continued and growing success at the Lyceum began to generate talk of an American tour, the possibility of meeting his literary hero in the flesh began to seem like a probability.

In the company of his Philadelphia publisher friend J. M. Stoddart, Wilde was welcomed by Whitman in the house he shared with his brother and sister-in-law. Both men were masters of self-promotion, both had published controversial poetry, both had a special appreciation of the same sex, but in other ways they couldn't have been more different. Wilde was a clean-shaven dandy. Whitman couldn't care less what he wore, and he sprouted a massive unruly beard. And yet they impressed each other most favorably. Whitman later told an interviewer that "I don't see why such mocking things are written about him," calling his visitor "frank and outspoken and manly." For his part Wilde called his host "the grandest man I have ever seen" and "one of those wonderful, large, entire men who might have lived in any age and is not peculiar to any people. Strong, true, and perfectly sane: the closest approach to the Greek we have yet had in modern times." After finishing a problematic bottle of homemade elderberry wine ("If it had vinegar I would have drunk it all the same, for I have an admiration of the man I can hardly express"), Wilde was invited by Whitman to his dusty, cluttered, private den, where they could be on "thee and thou terms" and discuss Swinburne, Tennyson, and Whitman's impressions of aestheticism.

According to Stoddart, "In free conversation with intimate friends, the poet did not trouble to conceal his liking for handsome youths." Stoddart's told-to version of the private audience with Whitman described how, "after embracing, greeting each other as 'Oscar' and 'Walt,' the two talked of nothing but pretty boys, of how insipid was the love of women, and of what other poets, Swinburne in particular, had to say about these tastes." Wilde had no doubts about the tastes of Walt Whitman, and later suggestively told another friend, George Ives, that "I still have the kiss of Walt Whitman on my lips."

While Wilde was still busy conquering America, Henry Irving had begun to mount more new productions in addition to the revivals of his earlier, Bateman-era hits like *The Bells* and *Louis XI*, which formed the backbone of the first two Lyceum season repertories under his own direction. *The Corsican Brothers*, a strange, swashbuckling spectacle *après* Dumas, which saw Irving in the dual role of conjoined twins who were separated at birth but nonetheless can still feel each other's pain, was given an especially splashy production. For an elaborate masked ball enacted on the stage of the Paris Opera, the Lyceum audience saw what could be its own mirror image at the back of the stage. "The Opera House was draped in crimson silk," Stoker remembered, and "the boxes were practical and contained a whole audience, all in perspective. The men and women in the boxes near the footlights were real; those far back were children dressed like their elders. Promenading and dancing were hundreds of persons in striking costumes. It must be remembered that in those days there were no electric lights, and as there were literally thousands of lights in the scene it was a difficult one to fit. Thousands of feet of gas-piping, the joining hose being flexible, were used and the whole resources of supply were brought into requisition."

The Corsican Brothers is the only production in which Stoker is known to have taken part as an extra, and it was also the closest thing to performing in a pantomime he would ever know. "The Masked Ball was a scene which allowed of any amount of fun," he wrote, "and it was so vast that it was an added gain to have as many persons as possible in it. To this end we kept a whole rack in the office full of dominoes [half-masks], masks, and slouched hats, so that any one who had nothing else to do could in an instant make a suitable appearance on the scene and not be recognized." Stoker made his Lyceum stage debut a few nights after the opening. It was a dizzy-making experience, but it must have transported him back to his first Christmas panto at the Theatre Royal Dublin, where every imaginative child longed to be part of the action.

*Stoker availed himself of the Lyceum's wardrobe for a costume ball (date unknown),
where he was photographed with Mrs. Henry Dickens.*

We had amongst others engaged a whole group of clowns. There were
eight of them, the best in England; the pantomime season being still far
off, they could thus employ their enforced leisure. . . . When I ventured
amongst them they recognized me and made a ring around me, dancing like demons. Then they seized me and spun me round, and literally
played ball with me, throwing me from one to the other backwards and
forwards. Sometimes they would rush me right down to the footlights and
then whirl me back again breathless. But all the time they never let me
fall. . . . I could not but admire their physical power as well as their agility
and dexterity.

Romeo and Juliet, starring Irving and Terry in the third season, was a
more problematic production, but it continued the remarkable attention to
scene painting and virtuoso illumination that were becoming the Lyceum's
signature. Irving avoided electrical lighting as long as possible, continuing

Henry Irving and Ellen Terry in the final act of Romeo *and* Juliet *(1884).*

to use gas and limelight even as other theatres were completely electrified, and thereby achieved subtle and painterly effects beyond the reach of other producers. The crypt setting by Hawes Craven for *Romeo and Juliet* was a Gothic extravaganza, the kind of thing that might have inspired the art directors of the classic Universal and Hammer horror films in the next century, had they only seen it. Shakespeare's story, of course, climaxes with the discovery in a tomb of a maiden who is not exactly living or dead, and how she comes to be truly dead. One wonders how many times Stoker watched the grim but exquisitely staged tableau, and about the effect it may have had on his own Gothic imaginings. Stoker's strong eye for theatrical scenery, evident in his Dublin theatre reviews, carried over to his fiction, wherein he characteristically lingered over descriptions of landscapes and other locations.

Irving was unsure how Romeo was to follow the stage direction "He bears the body of Paris to the tomb" and asked Stoker, as a former athlete, to demonstrate how he might best carry a corpse. Loveday obliged by playing dead. "Standing astride over the body I took it by the hinches—as wrestlers call the upper part of the hips—and bending my legs whilst at the same moment raising with my hands, keeping my elbows down, and swaying backwards I easily flung it over my shoulder." Irving approved and asked to stand in for the corpse himself, the better to understand the action. "I did so several times," wrote Stoker. "Then I lay down and he lifted me, easily enough, in the same way. It must have required a fair effort of strength on his part; for he was a spare, thin man whilst I was over twelve stone."[3] Irving thought the technique "looked all right" but might be a strain in performance.

A second experiment in corpse lifting occurred ten days later, with the help of Bram's physician brother George, who had been a surgeon in the Turkish service all throughout the Russo-Turkish war of 1877–78, there gaining "about as much experience in the handling of dead bodies as any man wants." This time, Irving was curious about the *easiest* method. Stoker was the dead man this time. George spread his brother's legs and, facing away, rested them on his own shoulders at the knees. "Then, catching one of my ankles in each hand, he drew my body up till the portion of my anatomy where the back and legs unite was pressed against the back of his neck. He then straightened his arms and rose up, my body, face outward, trailing down his back and my arms hanging limp." Stoker described the result as looking exactly like a butcher lugging a sheep carcass. Yes, it did seem to be the simplest way to carry a body, "but its picturesque suitability for stage purpose was another matter." Irving laughed heartily and decided that dragging the body to the entrance of the tomb would be the best solution of all. "He would then appear in the next scene dragging the body down the stone stair to the crypt. To this end a [dummy] body was prepared, adjusted to the weight and size of Paris so that in every way *vraisemblance* was secured."

If Irving was willing to cheat a bit with Romeo's exertions, the same could not be said about the extras, representing the angry Capulet and Montague factions, who were given the prompt-book direction "Enter Several Persons of both Houses, who join in the Fray: then enter Citizens and Peace Officers, with their Clubs and Partisans." As Stoker described it, "They used to pour in on the scene down the slope of the bridge like a released torrent, and for a few minutes such a scene of fighting was enacted

---

[3] Twelve and a half stone equals 172 pounds. At six foot two, Stoker was rather trim himself, at least during the 1881–82 Lyceum season.

as I have never elsewhere seen on the stage. The result of the mighty fight was that during the whole run time of the play there was never a day when there was not at least one of the young men in hospital." Despite efforts to keep the performers strictly to the safety-assuring fight choreography they had been given, "one side or the other would grow so ardent that a nightly trouble of some kind could be counted on."

As a physical production, *Romeo and Juliet* was extraordinary, but it had one glaring problem in performance. Henry Irving was forty-four and Ellen Terry was thirty-four, and even the softest gaslight failed to make them believable teenagers in love. For Irving it was strictly a vanity performance. He had never played the role when he was young, and it was a deficiency he was determined to correct. But he succeeded mostly in dragging down Ellen Terry, of whom the reviews were especially critical. As a writer for the *Academy* put it, Terry's later scenes "are wanting in the imagination of tragedy. Nothing is called out of the depths. The actress deals with tragedy like an eighteenth-century portrait painter. . . . The first word is grace—but so is the last."[4]

There was trouble of a kind Stoker never could have anticipated the night of September 14, 1882. Following the performance of *Romeo and Juliet* (and whatever unrecorded injuries it may have wrought), he headed home to Chelsea on the ferry steamer *Twilight*. While approaching the Oakley Street pier, an elderly, never-identified passenger attempted suicide by jumping over the rail. Stoker managed to grab the old man's coat, but he was intent on death and kept his face underwater. Stoker released him, stripped off his own dress coat and vest, and dove into the Thames. Noel Stoker later described his father as an "intrepid swimmer" and recalled his seashore holiday fondness for diving into giant waves. "They seemed to me to be over ten feet high!" Here, he may also have been impulsive and reckless—both he and the drowning man could easily have been pulled under by the steamer's propellers. After five minutes, Stoker managed to

[4] Irving often chose roles to show himself off at Terry's expense, and avoided plays in which she truly might shine on her own. The public waited expectantly for her to essay Rosalind in *Twelfth Night*—many felt it was the role she was simply born to play—but Irving was no Orlando, and the part of the philosophical commentator Jacques, which would have suited him beautifully, he apparently thought was too small. Why he never cast himself and Terry as Oberon and Titania in *A Midsummer Night's Dream*—perfect roles for them both, the king and queen of the theatre as the king and queen of the fairies—was likely because the roles took a back seat to the play's quartet of young lovers.

have the man, still breathing but just barely, back on deck. Florence Stoker was startled a few minutes later when a party of men including her husband burst into 26 Cheyne Walk with the waterlogged victim, whom they laid out on the mahogany dining table. A doctor was called, but he pronounced the man dead.

"Unfortunately," wrote Noel Stoker, "the recollection of a clammy corpse in the dining room made my mother take a dislike to the house." The family version of the story has Florence, unable to dismiss the dead body from her mind, pressure Bram into another move, but this seems unlikely. The move would take place three years after the man died in their dining room, more than enough time for Florence—hardly a wilting flower—to process the unpleasantness of a single night, and it's difficult to see what there was to "dislike" about the home, other than its mounting expenses. As always in Stoker family relocations, money was the most probable determinant this time as well. Beyond the cost of their exclusive address, the Stokers entertained frequently as Florence's stifled artistic dreams were redirected into the role of society hostess, with all the attendant pressure to impress. But they couldn't live in a manner significantly grander than Bram's employer indefinitely, at least not without significant additional income. *Under the Sunset*, however politely received, and even after two printings, had hardly been a best-seller, and Stoker's responsibilities at the Lyceum were so overwhelming he would not have the time to publish fiction again for nearly a decade. In 1885 they moved to a Chelsea neighborhood farther inland. Number 17 St. Leonard's Terrace was a rather nondescript house compared to the showplace on Cheyne Walk. It faced a park and shared a carriage turnaround with a nicer house, number 18, which today bears a handsome plaque identifying it as the home of the author of *Dracula*. The novel would actually be completed while the Stokers were still occupying the adjacent residence.

The Lyceum's first excursion to North America finally took place in the autumn, winter, and spring of 1883–84, with Stoker responsible for almost all the logistics. Irving's first offering in New York, at the Star Theatre on Thirteenth Street on the night of October 29, was his old warhorse *The Bells*. The opening performance was complicated by a torrential downpour that snarled transportation, but even more by an enterprising ticket scalper who had virtually bought out the house, reselling $2 seats for as much as $15 to a soggy, angry crowd. Irving found the merely polite applause at

Stoker completed Dracula *at 17 St. Leonard's Terrace, though its writing is commemorated on a plaque at number 18, where the Stokers subsequently moved.* (Photograph by the author)

each act curtain ominous. In the privacy of his dressing room he railed at his first Yankee audience, calling them "icebergs, blocks, stone. . . . I might as well play to a churchyard!" He was unaccustomed to American audiences holding full judgment until the end of the piece, at which time their approval of *The Bells* was overwhelmingly enthusiastic. The other New York offerings were *Charles I* (in which Ellen Terry made her American debut), *Louis XI*, and *The Merchant of Venice*. He saved *Hamlet* for Philadelphia, a city commonly regarded as having the most intellectually discriminating audiences and critics, and the reception was effusive. The company had filled six train coaches, two boxcars, and an enormous scenery gondola for the Philadelphia stop, but it was quickly apparent that the load simply was too unwieldly to be lugged to the remaining destinations: Boston, Baltimore, Chicago, St. Louis, Cincinnati, Columbus, and Washington. Stoker sent word ahead that scene carpenters and drop painters would be required to re-create much of the scenery in each city. Eighty flats, twenty-five drops, sixty wings, and twenty set pieces were stored in New York, allowing the company to travel and function far more nimbly.

On March 20, 1884, near the end of the tour when the company was traveling back up the northeastern corridor, Stoker accompanied Irving to the

W. V. Cockburn's illustration for the story "The Rose Prince' in **Under the Sunset.**

Philadelphia home of Thomas Donaldson, a noted collector of Americana for the Smithsonian, for a long-awaited meeting. As Stoker described the occasion, there was seated in the parlor an "old man of leonine appearance. He was burly, with a large head and high forehead slightly bald. Great shaggy masses of grey-white hair fell over his collar. His moustache was large and thick and fell over his mouth so as to mingle with the top of the mass of the bushy flowing beard."

"Mr. Irving," Donaldson said, "I want you to know Mr. Walt Whitman."

Irving quickly crossed the parlor. The two shook hands. Stoker watched in awe as the two great idols of his life met. "When my turn came and Donaldson said 'Bram Stoker,' Walt Whitman leaned forward suddenly, and held out his hand eagerly as he said: 'Bram Stoker[.] Abraham Stoker is it?' I acquiesced and we shook hands as old friends as indeed we were."

Whitman was most taken with Irving's gentlemanly mien. "Be it remembered," wrote Stoker, "that Walt Whitman was fond of the theatre and went to it a good deal before he was incapacitated by his paralysis; but he did not like the vulgarity of certain actors in their posing off the stage. In his day in parts of the Southern States and even to this day with a certain class of actors in some places a travelling company on its arrival had a 'parade.' They all had loud costumes for the purpose, and the whole company, men and women, would strut through the streets. It was most undignified, and naturally offended one who, like the Poet, had the real artistic sensitiveness." However, when Whitman "met the great actor with whose praise the whole country was then ringing and found that he was gentle and restrained and unassuming in manner the whole craft rose in his estimation."

When it was time for Stoker to take part in the conversation, he found Whitman "all that I had ever dreamed of, or wished for in him: large-minded, broad-viewed, tolerant to the last degree; incarnate sympathy; understanding with an insight that seemed more than human." It was no accident, Stoker thought, that Whitman had been so effective and inspiring as a field nurse in the Civil War, and "made a place for himself in the world of aid to the suffering which was unique. No wonder that men opened their hearts to him told him their secrets, their woes and hopes and griefs and loves." Stoker indeed knew what it was like to open his heart to such a

Walt Whitman in later life. (Library of Congress)

Pencil sketch of Florence Stoker by Edward Burne-Jones, circa 1882.

man. "To me he was an old friend, and on his part he made me feel that I was one. We spoke of Dublin and those friends there who had manifested themselves to him. He remembered all their names and asked me many questions as to their various personalities. Before we parted he asked me to come to see him at his home in Camden whenever I could manage it. Need I say that I promised."

Henry Irving's first tour of the United States was filled with memorable incidents, but the most colorful one involving Stoker occurred on the return trip to Liverpool aboard *The City of Chester* out of New York. Irving and Ellen Terry sailed separately—at least from the rest of the Lyceum company—on the *Aurania*. Stoker's duties on tour would involve making discreet arrangements for the couple's lodgings. Connected hotel suites with separate entrances were usually enough, but in cities with especially nosy press people, a show of different hotels sometimes had to be made. Two company members on board *The City of Chester* were in a similar situation, but their relationship would never require Stoker's vigilance. William Terriss, also known as "Breezy Bill," was best known as the handsome leading man in Adelphi Theatre melodramas. He had joined the Lyceum family along with the young actress Jessie Millward, his constant companion in spite of his being a married man. Terriss sometimes played the offstage part of Irving's brash jester, the only company member unafraid to disagree with the Governor, who regarded the younger man with amused tolerance, if not encouragement. Once Terriss wondered if he might have a larger share of the blue spotlight that followed Irving alone during a swordfighting scene. Wouldn't moonlight illuminate the entire stage? His rationale was so disarmingly logical that Irving could do nothing but concede the point and share the light.

Terriss was fond of pranks. "Hypnotism was at that time a fashionable craze," wrote Millward, "and one day in the smoke-room Terriss declared that he possessed great and mysterious hypnotic powers, the extent of which even he himself did not understand." Both Millward and Stoker were in on the joke, and they arranged a follow-up scene. As Millward recalled in her memoir, "One morning when I was sitting on deck Terriss kept passing to and fro in front of me, glaring fiercely each time he passed, and naturally soon attracted the attention of a good many passengers. Poor old Mrs. Pauncefort, who was sitting beside me knitting, became quite alarmed, thinking perhaps he had temporarily gone off his head, and every time he approached with a ferocious stare she would whisper timidly: 'Oh, here he comes again ! Don't look at him, my dear ! Don't look at him!'"

Millward feigned falling into a prearranged mesmeric stupor; "it was not until Terriss had made some mysterious passes over my face that I was supposed to come out of the trance." Onlookers "were tremendously impressed, and to his secret horror Mr. Terriss was approached by a deputation who formally invited him to give a lecture on hypnotism in the salon." The joke was clearly getting out of hand. "This was rather more than he had bargained for," Millward wrote, "but it was too late for him to back out, and with the assistance of Bram Stoker a lecture was hurriedly concocted, and delivered with immense success, the 'demonstrations' being particularly impressive. Needless to say, the 'subjects' were carefully chosen and had also been carefully rehearsed, thus carrying out to the last the 'Lyceum thoroughness' which had so impressed America."

Two years later, during an 1886 trip to New York and Philadelphia to plan the 1887 tour of Irving's *Faust,* Stoker at last had the chance to visit Whitman at home, again in the company of Thomas Donaldson.

His house, 328 Mickle Street, was a small ordinary one in a row, built of the usual fine red brick which marks Philadelphia and gives it an appearance so peculiarly Dutch. It was a small house, though large enough for his needs. He sat in the front room in a big rocking chair which Donaldson's children had given him; it had been specially made for him, as he was a man of over six feet high and very thick-set. He was dressed all in grey, the trousers cut straight and wide, and the coat loose. All the cloth was a sort of thick smooth frieze. His shirt was of rather coarse cotton, unstarched, with a very wide full collar open low very low in the neck and fastened with a big white stud. . . . His hair seemed longer and wilder and shaggier and whiter than when I had seen him two years before. He seemed feebler, and when he rose from his chair or moved about the room did so with difficulty. I could notice his eyes better now. They were not so quick and searching as before; tireder-looking, I thought, with the blue paler and the grey less warm in colour. Altogether the whole man looked more worn out. There was not, however, any symptom of wear or tire in his intellectual or psychic faculties.

Stoker felt Whitman was "genuinely glad" to see him. "He was most hearty in his manner and interested about everything. Asked much about London and its people, specially those of the literary world; and spoke of Irving in a way that delighted me." The conversation drifted to the subject of Abraham Lincoln, "for whom he had an almost idolatrous affection. I confess that in this I shared; and it was another bond of union between us." Stoker had read with great interest Whitman's account of the assassination, "so startlingly vivid that I thought that the man who had written it could tell me more. So I asked him if he were present at the time." No, Whitman said, he wasn't, but he was "close to the theatre and was one of the first in when the news came." Members of the President's Guard personally told him how, upon receiving the terrible news, they stormed the house with fixed bayonets. "It was a wonder that there was not a holocaust," Whitman said, "for it was a wild frenzy of grief and rage." The celebrated author of "O Captain! My Captain" likened the grief over Lincoln to an ancient saga, awakened, of a Viking chieftain rising to Valhalla, surrounded by a legion of attending spirits.

"The memory of that room will never leave me," Stoker wrote. Whitman found the visit equally memorable and later told Donaldson, "Well, well;

what a broth of a boy he is! My gracious, he knows enough for four or five ordinary men; and what tact! Henry Irving knows a good thing when he sees it, eh? Stoker is an adroit lad, and many think that he made Mr. Irving's path, in a business way, a smooth one over here. . . . See that he comes over again to see me before he leaves the country. He's like a breath of good, healthy, breezy sea air."

Unfortunately, Stoker was not able to return during that trip, but he traveled again to Camden with Donaldson just before Christmas of 1877, when *Faust* was playing Philadelphia. The previous year he had had dinner with a mutual friend, Talcott Williams, editor of the *Philadelphia Press*, who was not only a friend of Whitman's and a staunch public defender of his poems but also the model for the reclining nude in Thomas Eakins's 1884–85 canvas *The Swimming Hole*, something of a scandal in its time but today considered an iconic masterpiece of American painting. It is perhaps not surprising that *The Swimming Hole* has been used quite effectively to illustrate modern editions of *Leaves of Grass*. Williams had introduced Eakins to Whitman, whom he also painted, albeit fully clothed. At the dinner, Stoker and Williams "agreed that it was a great pity that [Whitman] did not

Idyllic male bonding, classically captured in Thomas Eakins's The Swimming Hole *(1884–85). The model for the reclining nude was Stoker's Philadelphia friend Talcott Williams.*

cut certain lines and passages out of the poems. Talcott Williams said he would do it if permitted, and I said I would speak to Walt Whitman about it whenever we should meet again." Stoker breakfasted with Williams just a few days before the 1877 trip to Camden, and they once more talked about the proposal to sanitize *Leaves of Grass* in what Stoker described as "much intimate conversation."

It seems a bit startling that Stoker and Williams, previously vociferous defenders of Whitman's poetry, would even consider censoring *Leaves*. To what end? Just to sell more books? Perhaps they felt Whitman's message to broadminded men like themselves needed to be closely held, esoteric knowledge—a hidden arcana about men, maleness, and manly affection that the general public was never going to comprehend.

Stoker and Donaldson found Whitman "hale and well. His hair was more snowy white than ever and more picturesque." Stoker thought he looked rather like King Lear. Then he finally raised the touchy subject of making "certain excisions" to Whitman's masterwork. Stoker explained, "If you will only allow your friends to do this—they will only want to cut about a hundred lines in all—your books will go into every house in America. Is not that worth the sacrifice?"

Whitman had heard it all before and responded bluntly. "It would not be any sacrifice. So far as I am concerned they might cut a thousand. It is not that—it is quite another matter." His voice and expression grew solemn. "When I wrote as I did I thought I was doing right and right makes for good. I think so still. I think that all that God made is for good that the work of His hands is clean in all ways if used as He intended! If I was wrong I have done harm. And for that I deserve to be punished by being forgotten! It has been and cannot not-be. No, I shall never cut a line so long as I live!"

"One had to respect a decision thus made and on such grounds," Stoker concluded. "I said no more."

It was the last time the men met, but not the last time Whitman thought of Stoker. On February 19, 1889, Whitman gave Horace Traubel, his amanuensis and chronicler, some pinned-together correspondence. They were the letters Bram had written in 1872 and 1876 and a draft of Whitman's reply. He said, "I want you to read it all to me: there are three letters: you have heard of Bram Stoker—Irving's man: he took a shine to me over there in Ireland when he was in college: wrote me from there—but was afraid to mail the letter: the second letter tells about it: he has been here: I value his good will highly: he seems to have remained of the same mind, mainly in substance, as at first."

As Trauble read, Whitman commented. "He was just about a boy back in those days: now it was fifteen years ago: he has been here: I think the man Stoker repeats, fulfils, the boy: I never quite think of myself as being the subject of such utterances. There's one sentence in his letter which hit me hard." Traubel said, "I'll bet I know which one it is." Whitman nodded. "I'm rather persuaded that you do: which?" Traubel began to read: "I write this openly—" and Whitman immediately interrupted. "That's it: that's me, as I hope I am: it's Leaves of Grass if Leaves of Grass is anything: 'I feel that with you one must be open': that explains Children of Adam, everything."

As Trauble continued with Stoker's entreaties that Whitman should burn his letters, the poet noted that "he was a sassy youngster: as to burning the epistle up or not—it never occurred to me to do anything at all: what the hell did I care whether he was pertinent or impertinent? he was fresh, breezy, Irish: that was the price paid for admission—and enough: he was welcome!" When Stoker wrote "You have shaken off the shackles and your wings are free," the incapacitated Whitman parried with "My wings may be free but the same can't be said of my backside!" As the letter rambled on, Whitman chuckled. "The boy fires off a hell of a big prologue— eh?" and "Come, Mr. Bram Stoker: get down to business: this is all only preliminary!" At the young man's detailed self-description: "And a mighty graphic picture it is too: I seem to see you not as in a glass darkly but as in the broad day lightly: I do, I do!" Overall, Whitman found Stoker's 1872 letter "an extraordinary occurrence: that he should have let himself go in that style: or do you argue that it's all studied out—even the spontaneity? It all sounds easy and informal to me—not verbally stiff in the joints anywhere: I was, I am, inclined to accept it for just what it pretends to be. I may be gullible, deceived, fooled: yet I am confident I have made no mistake." And apropos Stoker's most striking disclosure, "How sweet a thing it is for a strong healthy man with a woman's eyes and a child's wishes to feel that he can speak so to a man who can be if he wishes father, and brother and wife to his soul," Whitman mused, "How sweet, indeed! where there is love, why not? why not?"

Walt Whitman died on March 26, 1892, and Stoker did not travel to Philadelphia again until January 4, 1894, when he spent an afternoon at Donaldson's home. "Shortly after I came in he went away for a minute and came back with a large envelope which he handed to me," saying it was from Whitman. He had been keeping it for Stoker's next visit.

The envelope, described by Stoker, "contained in a rough card folio pasted down on thick paper the original notes from which he delivered his lecture on Abraham Lincoln at the Chestnut Street Opera House on April 15, 1886." It was the same theatre in which Henry Irving had introduced his *Hamlet* to America. A letter from Whitman to Donaldson read, "Enclosed I send a full report of my Lincoln Lecture for our friend Bram Stoker."

"This," wrote Stoker, many years later, "was my Message from the Dead."

Back in London after nearly a year in America, Oscar Wilde decided to marry. His fiancée was Constance Lloyd, a well-bred young woman who had grown up in an artistic environment, and to whom he had been introduced in the summer before his American odyssey. They were the very model of an "aesthetic" couple, and in both their minds ideally matched. Cynics believed a major consideration could have been Constance's money, for she came from a wealthy family, and there probably were some purely practical calculations on Oscar's side. He was in considerable debt, more than £1,500, but Constance's grandfather approved the engagement and established a trust for the couple. They were married in May 1884 and had their first child, Cyril, the following June. A second son, Vyvyan, arrived in 1887.

And then everything changed.

Constance's pregnancies disgusted him. "When I married," Wilde told his future biographer Frank Harris, "my wife was a beautiful girl, white and slim as a lily, with dancing eyes and gay rippling laughter like music. Within a year or so the flower-like grace had vanished; she became heavy, shapeless, deformed. She dragged herself about the house in uncouth misery with drawn blotched face and hideous body, sick at heart because of our love. It was dreadful. I tried to be kind to her, forced myself to touch and kiss her; but she was sick always and—oh! I cannot recall it, it is all loathsome. I used to wash my mouth and open the window to cleanse my lips in the pure air."

Wilde's Oxford mentor, John Ruskin, despite his high achievements as a critic, may be best remembered today as being the Victorian so repulsed by the discovery of his wife's pubic hair that he was unable to consummate the marriage. While the anecdote may be to some degree apocryphal, it

Constance Wilde and her son Cyril.

underscores the sometimes absurd degree to which Victorian women were categorized at polar extremes: virgin/whore, spirit/flesh, angelic/demonic, inspiring/disgusting—or just hairless/hairy. Wilde's poem "The Harlot's House," written immediately after his marriage, illustrates the tragic descent of ethereal love into rank carnality, a transition Wilde explicitly associates with death:

> Then turning to my love I said
> "The dead are dancing with the dead,
> the dust is whirling with the dust."
> But she, she heard the violin,
> And left my side, and entered in;
> Love passed into the house of Lust.

Constance watched helplessly as Oscar withdrew from the family, spending more and more time with an ever-expanding coterie of young men, finding excuses to be away from home, living in hotel rooms for weeks at a time. All for the sake of his writing. All for the sake of his art. Ten years after their romantic misunderstanding in Dublin, Oscar and Florence Stoker became friends again. He attended her Sunday at-homes, and she exchanged social notes with Constance. Like Bram, Oscar had published a book of fairy tales, and in 1887 he sent Florence an inscribed copy of *The Happy Prince*: "I hope you will like them, simple though they are," he wrote, adding his "kind regards to Bram." He did not make a favorable impression on Noel, who, decades later, remembered how Wilde "used to call occasionally in my pre-boarding school days [up to 1889] and left the impression on me that he was intensely self-satisfied, which I did, and do, dislike."

Before being sent away to school (banishment, it should be noted, is an ever-recurring fairy tale theme), Noel would accompany his mother on an ill-fated excursion to France. On April 13, 1887, the steamship *Victoria* was approaching Dieppe when its hull was suddenly ripped open by fog-shrouded rocks. As Florence described the wreck, the "whole forepart of the boat was underwater, which seemed creeping steadily on towards us. The part we were on was high out of the water. We heard agonizing shrieks from the second and third class passengers, who were still below, and in the grey light of dawn saw dim figures climbing the rigging. . . . They allowed the first boat to fill before she touched water and it upset." A young girl clutching an oar was rescued, but there was no room for an old man flailing in the water. Florence remembered his cries as "heart rending," but there was nothing to do except watch him drown. Florence wrote about the experience for the *Dublin Evening News*. In all, 20 of 120 passengers died. Noel would never mention the ordeal at all, although watching a helplessly pleading man perish must have left a traumatic impression on the boy, especially given his terrifying experience with swimming lessons. Crew members rowed ceaselessly, but it was low tide and they could find no entrance to a harbor. Finally, after seven hours, the survivors were rescued by a steam tug.

"I was dripping wet; my dress torn, and trailing; my hair over my face," Florence told the *Evening News* readers. Noel had lost one shoe but was uninjured. When her luggage was finally returned to her, Florence's trunk had been broken into and ransacked. "Of course my dresses were spoiled by salt water; half my linen stolen, and everything of value gone," she wrote. Fortunately, she had secreted money in her corset. She telegraphed Stoker, but he never received the wire, and remained in a state of unrelieved panic for two days until his family was reunited. She made some intemperate comments to the press about the French crew's competence, or lack thereof, which necessitated retractions to spare the Lyceum embarrassment.

The incident coincided with a period of great professional stress, enough for him to seriously consider other career options. Stoker's story is usually told as three decades of unstinting devotion to Henry Irving, but in 1886 he had decided to qualify for the London Bar, Inner Temple. Being a barrister would be of no practical use in his duties at the Lyceum, but it could provide an escape hatch if and when he decided one was necessary. The process required considerably more effort than purchasing a master's degree—four years of part-time study and preparation, which must have occupied a good portion of his August holidays, a time he later would devote to writing. His decision was reported in the press, with the assurance that his decision would not impact his work for Henry Irving in any way. Was Florence pressing him? Were their finances becoming impossible? In the end, after becoming a barrister, he never practiced. Instead, he would throw himself into earning additional money by the sheer force of his mind and imagination as he had never done before.

His pressured state of mind is well reflected in a letter he wrote to one J. B. Pond on August 13, 1887. "I feel somewhat like a guilty man beginning a letter to you," he said, "for I feel that my correspondence is shamefully in arrears. You have no idea of how I have been overworked in the last six months." In addition to the stress of preparing for tours in England and America, "in April my wife and I were wrecked in the Victoria off the French Coast—this involved great delay in business as well as terrible anxiety and took me twice over to France." The letter is significant in being perhaps the only document in which Stoker complains of overwork, so much apparently that he conflated himself with his wife and son on the wrecked ship.

Seventeen years later, following a life-ruining public disgrace, Oscar Wilde would propel himself into self-exile on precisely the same route from Newhaven to Dieppe. But that would be a different kind of shipwreck entirely.

CHAPTER SIX

PANTOMIMES FROM HELL

'TIS THE EYE OF CHILDHOOD
THAT FEARS A PAINTED DEVIL.

—Lady Macbeth

One night in the 1880s—or so a story goes—during an otherwise unevent-ful evening at the Lyceum Theatre, a couple sitting in the dress circle glanced down into the stalls and were startled to see an elderly woman holding in her lap a man's grinning, severed head.

Alarming though the sight was, the couple chose not to cause a scene, or even quietly alert theatre personnel to summon the police. Instead, with all the British reserve and self-reliance and restraint they could muster, they waited until the intermission to venture downstairs and investigate for themselves. Alas, both the lady and the head that had glared up at them had disappeared. It is a shame they didn't inform Bram Stoker, always on duty during performances to handle such exigencies. The paranormal nature of the incident surely would have interested him, though whether he could have actually apprehended the spectral vision is another matter. It would, however, have been another colorful anecdote to add to his bot-tomless hoard of stories about the Lyceum's unstopping parade of eccentric personalities, droll production mishaps, near-fatal accidents, and visiting

Henry Irving as Mephistopheles in **Faust** *(1886). Illustration by Bernard Partridge.*

dignitaries almost wandering out onstage during performances. (The clue-less Chinese ambassador in flowing yellow robes who very nearly interrupted Hamlet and Ophelia's "Get thee to a nunnery" scene may be the best of all.)[1]

In fact, Stoker biography and commentary is often swamped and deflected by the sheer volume of Lyceum lore. Stoker himself emerges from history as a barely glimpsed spectre, lurking in Irving's shadow. Until the mid-1880s, little of Irving's work sparked Stoker's own creativity, and just dealing with Irving's output was a constant impediment to his writing. But now, supernatural happenings at the Lyceum—if only on the stage and not in the stalls—were becoming more frequent, and giving Stoker ideas. Previously, subjects like ghosts and mesmerism had been confined to *Hamlet* and *The Bells*. Irving, at the age of forty-seven, dropped the prince of Denmark (along with his revenant father) from the Lyceum repertoire in the spring of 1885. But it was quickly replaced with even more satur-nine characterizations—Mephistopheles in *Faust* (1885) and the title role in *Macbeth* (1887) opposite Ellen Terry. These productions powerfully inter-sected with Stoker's early passion for the Christmas pantomimes, works that turned and soared on fearful fantasy and wondrous spectacle, and both *Faust* and *Macbeth* would be dramatically reflected and refracted in *Dracula*.

Bram Stoker and Johann Wolfgang von Goethe both discovered Mephistopheles innocently, in the entertainments of childhood. Stoker first encountered the character as the omnipresent Demon King of pan-tomimes around the age of eight; Goethe's introduction came at the age of four at a traveling puppet-show rendition of the medieval Faust legend, about an alchemist who unwisely sells his soul to the devil for knowledge and power. The prince of darkness would preoccupy each author, in his own way, for the rest of his life and figure prominently in both writers' mas-terworks. Goethe began work on his verse drama in 1773 and published the first part of *Faust* in 1808 and the second near the end of his life, in 1832. The towering meditation on man's quest for knowledge and the nature of good and evil is an achievement so massive that it has only rarely been

---

[1] As told by Stoker, who physically blocked the ambassador from stumbling into the limelight: "Under ordinary circumstances I think I should have allowed the contretemps to occur. Its unique grotesqueness would have ensured a widespread publicity not to be acquired by ordi-nary forms of advertisement. But there was a greater force to the contrary. The play was not yet three weeks old in its run; it was a tragedy and the holy of holies to my actor-chief to whom full measure of loyalty was due; and beyond all it was Ellen Terry who would suffer."

staged. *Faust* gained a much-amplified cultural currency through operatic adaptations, especially Charles Gounod's opera *Faust* (1859) and Hector Berlioz's *The Damnation of Faust* (first performed in 1846, though not successfully or regularly until 1877). The dramatic adaptation by W. G. Wills, produced by Henry Irving in 1885, would be the Lyceum's greatest commercial success and have an outsized impact on Stoker's imagination vis-à-vis all things diabolical, and is therefore an important key to *Dracula*'s meaning and importance.

W. G. Wills was the West End's lucky penny, a reliable source of successful if often formulaic historical plays and adaptations for himself and others since the Bateman years, including *Charles I* (1872) and *Eugene Aram* (1878). *Olivia* (1878) was the dramatization of *The Vicar of Wakefield* that had originally showcased Ellen Terry and brought him to Irving's attention; the Lyceum's 1883 revival would star both Irving and Terry and have an especially successful run. Only Wills's *Vanderdecken* (1878) had been a fizzle, but the actor liked the spooky leading role (Stoker, of course, adored it) and hadn't given up on another possible dramatization of the Flying Dutchman story. The Lyceum coffers were fairly flush after the first few seasons, and Irving paid Wills the handsome sum of £600 to write *Mephisto*, based on the first part of Goethe's *Faust* and tailoring the part of Mephistopheles to Irving's most sardonic and saturnine side. Purists would shudder at the kind of wholesale cuts the German masterpiece would endure, including the elimination of Goethe's sixty-page prologue and its monumental debate between Mephistopheles and God. There were no waltzes by Gounod to set audiences humming, and Wills's blank verse was pedestrian indeed compared to the complicated German rhyme scheme of the original and the ambitious 1835 English verse translation of John Anster, which could have been freely adapted, but wasn't.

But, as the actor's grandson observed, "Irving's intuition as a showman had not failed him. Although the inadequacy of the text was plain to all, although Irving's most ardent admirers admitted that his demon teetered dangerously on the edge of pantomime, and although the whole affair offended the genuine and professed students of Goethe, this consummate confection of villainy and piety, of beauty and fearsome hideousness, of claptrap and culture, was the greatest financial success Irving ever had. For many years it was a seemingly inexhaustible source of wealth which subsidized his other more admirable but less rewarding ventures."

As Stoker related, "When Irving was about to do the play he made a trip to Nuremberg to see for himself what would be most picturesque as well as suitable." It's not at all clear that a research dig was even necessary. A single photographer on assignment could have provided more than enough scenic and architectural references. Instead, Irving, Terry, Stoker, Loveday, and scenic designer Hawes Craven embarked on what was much less a business trip than a holiday junket, one that afforded Irving and Terry a relatively private vacation in Bavaria, far from prying eyes and gossiping tongues. Although Prime Minister William Gladstone had wanted to give Irving a knighthood in 1883, advisers cautioned him that it might be inadvisable, given scandalous whisperings about Irving's ambiguous relationship with his leading lady. Irving preferred to say he had declined the honor out of modesty, rather than propriety.

However much or little the trip to Germany informed *Faust*, it definitely inspired one of Stoker's most chilling short stories, "The Squaw" (1893), in which a young English couple on their honeymoon—possibly fictional stand-ins for Bram and Florence on the honeymoon they never had—stumble upon an old German torture chamber, now a tourist attraction, where an obnoxious, talkative, pistol-packing American named Elias P. Hutcheson relates a story about the grisly revenge taken by a Native American woman for the abduction and murder of her child. The foreshadowing is more than a bit over-obvious as Hutcheson accidentally drops a rock on the head of a frolicking kitten, smashing out its brains. The kitten's mother flies into a demoniacal rage and pursues the tourists into the torture exhibition, where the American insists on being bound inside the "Nurnberg Virgin," the notorious spiked sarcophagus more famously known as an Iron Maiden, its heavy lid lined with deadly spikes. As the exhibit's custodian slowly lowers the lid toward the morbidly delighted thrill-seeker, the mother cat reappears and hurls herself not at Hutcheson but at the custodian, clawing his face and causing him to drop the rope. "And then the spikes did their work," Stoker's first-person narrator tells us. "Happily the end was quick, for when I wrenched open the door they had pierced so deep that they had locked in the bones of the skull which they had crushed, and actually tore him—it—out of his iron prison till, bound as he was, he fell at full length with a sickly thud upon the floor, the face turning up as he fell." The cat takes her place on the dead American's head, lapping the blood that wells from the emptied eye sockets. "I think no one

Set rendering of German village for Irving's **Faust.**

will call me cruel," the narrator tells us, "because I seized one of the executioner's swords and shore her in two as she sat."

Bavaria is also home to Munich, a reasonable place for additional exploration on a research holiday. For Stoker, a side trip may have uncovered additional horrors to fuel his fiction. His preliminary notes for *Dracula* make reference to the notorious Munich "Dead House," a municipal morgue to which, partly for sanitary reasons but also as a gruesome kind of entertainment, all the city's dead, rich and poor, from infants to the aged, were taken for voyeuristic public viewing, as well as to be monitored, via electrical wires attached to a ring on each corpse's finger, for any sign of life that may have been missed. The terror of premature burial was still alive and well forty years after Edgar Allan Poe raised the alarm on a peculiar and stubbornly persistent nineteenth-century phobia.[2] As described by the *American Magazine* in 1892, the Deadhouse (as the periodical spelled it)

---

[2] The magazine also related, "upon authority not traceable, that years ago a Munich butcher came out of a trance in the middle of the night and found himself in the Deadhouse. The shock this discovery gave him is said to have entirely shattered his nerves and though still alive, he is a nervous wreck."

was "a spectacle sufficiently ghastly to cause any foreigner to grow faint. It is an awful and repulsive sight."

> On each side of the rectangular room is arranged a row of slightly inclined biers, on which rest the yellow-covered coffins containing all that is mortal of from twenty to forty human beings. The faces of the emaciated old women with their sharp, cronelike chins and sunken eyes, their open mouths disclosing one or two discolored teeth, are enough to sicken most spectators at a glance. Indeed, the Müncheners regard going to the Deadhouse on holidays as a standard recreation, and always recommend it to visitors with a weird sort of pride.

In his undated *Dracula* notes, Stoker has his protagonist, Jonathan Harker, visit both Munich and its morgue: "Sees old man on bier, describe— then to babies—then hears talk & listens—man went to fix corpse—place taken—returned on inquiry & find corpse gone—Harker has seen the corpse but does not take part in discussion." The corpse, of course, is the Count himself, who has found the perfect place to hide in plain sight as he makes longer and bolder exploratory trips from Transylvania in anticipation of his triumphant relocation to England. The incident does not appear in the finished book, but a deleted line later in the Dracula typescript—"and he thought now the Man of the Munich Dead House and Count Dracula were one"—is clear evidence that the morgue episode was part of an major excision early in the book, only a hint of which survives in Stoker's posthumously published short story "Dracula's Guest" (1914).

The Faustian theme in *Dracula* emerges when Van Helsing informs his fellow vampire hunters that the Dracula family "had dealings with the Evil One. They learned his secrets in the Scholomance, amongst the mountains over Lake Hermanstadt, where the devil claims the tenth scholar as his due." Why the nine other students got a free education in evil isn't explained, but the arrangement is described in greater detail in Emily Gerard's article "Transylvanian Superstitions" (1885), a primary reference for Stoker. According to Gerard, the Scholomance is a "school supposed to exist somewhere in the heart of the mountains, and where all the secrets of nature, the language of animals, and all imaginable magic spells and charms are taught by the devil in person. Only ten scholars are admitted at a time, and when the course of learning has expired and nine of them are released to return to their homes, the tenth scholar is detained by the devil as payment, and mounted upon an *Ismeju* (dragon) he becomes henceforward the devil's aide-de-camp, and assists him in 'making the weather.' That is to say, preparing the thunderbolts." The name Dracula derives from *drac*, or dragon, and Stoker dramatized the vampire's power to drive storms in the *Tempest*-like manner by which he shipwrecks himself in Whitby Harbor.

A moment more derivative of the Wills *Faust* can be found in Stoker's final *Dracula* typescript, though not in the finished book. During the notorious scene in which Van Helsing and Seward, bearing crucifixes, barge in on the bloody ménage à trois between Dracula, Mina, and Jonathan, Stoker deleted Seward's line "Even then at that awful moment with such a tragedy before my eyes, the figure of Mephistopheles in the Opera cowering before Margaret's lifted cross swam up before me and for an instant I wondered if I were mad." Here, despite the opera reference, Stoker is referring not to Gounod's *Faust* but to the Wills version, wherein Margaret (Marguerite in Gounod) is menaced by Mephistopheles while at her spinning wheel:

MAR. [*Aside. Stopping her spinning*].
　　Sooth, this man is an enemy to God,
　　With every shuddering instinct I can feel it.
MEPHIS. But if you disobey my counsels, maiden,
　　And talk of the redemption, faith, and prayer,
　　Your happiness will turn to must and blight:
　　Despair, disgrace, and ruin will o'ertake you,
　　Then, should you turn for help—
[MEPHIS. *Sees her cross, his eyes fix on it, and he half-rises to move away.*]
MAR. [*Observing, starts up*]
　　If you are evil, and God's enemy,
　　Then let this holy symbol drive thee hence.
[*She stands up, and lifts cross. He cowers away out of the door, looking devilishly, behind.*]

When Faust enters, Margaret informs him of what the audience already knows about the crucifix's power.

MAR. Part from that man—that demon—part from him.
Before you came he sat there by my side,
I felt like a poor bird before a snake,
But when I lifted up this sacred cross,
He shrank away, unmasked, and horrible.
He is a devil, and God's enemy!

Prior to *Dracula*, there were many folkloric testimonials to the power of religious objects against evil, but the specific image of a crucifix held aloft to stop the approach of evil was not a set piece in vampire fiction until Stoker, and the place it came from was Irving's *Faust*. Both the cross and holy water—each also effectively employed by Van Helsing in *Dracula*, along with the communion wafer—are referenced in the dramatic clash at the end of act 2, when Mephistopheles forbids Faust from seeing Margaret again.

FAUST. By what pretence canst thou forbid me, fiend?
MEPHIS. Thou answer'st me
As if I were some credulous, dull mate.
I am a spirit, and I know thy thought.
You think you may be fenced round by-and-by
With sprinkled holy water, lifted cross—
While you and your pale saint might hold a siege
Against the scapegoat—'gainst the devil here.
Ere that should be I'd tear thee limb from limb,
Thy blood I'd dash upon the wind like rain,
And all the gobbets of thy mangled flesh
I'd scatter to the dogs, that none should say
This carrion once was Faust!
Yon cottage would I snatch up in a whirlwind,
At dead midnight, like a pebble in a sling,
And hurl it leagues away, a crumbled mass,
With its crushed quivering tenant under it.
Dost know me now?
FAUST. Fiend, I obey.
MEPHIS. When hell's aroused in me, beware!

Although Ellen Terry admitted she "never cared much for Henry's Mephistopheles, a twopence colored part, anyway," she did single out the ultimatum given to Faust as a particularly hair-raising moment. On the booming declaration "I am a spirit," she recalled, "Henry looked to grow a gigantic height—to hover over the ground instead of walking on it. It was terrifying."

To one degree or another Irving was always playing some version of himself, so it isn't surprising that another celebrated role could be discerned around the edges of Mephistopheles's aura. Wills could only have had Irving's Hamlet in mind during the scene in Faust's study where he peers at an iconic prop from under his long-plumed, princely hat. But unlike Hamlet, Irving's devil doesn't waste time brooding over the mysteries of mortality.

FAUST . . . See here this skull—
    Canst thou set eyes within these hollow sockets,
    Give it a tongue to tell its earthy secret?
MEPHIS. *[taking skull]* Who knows? I might,
    If these two jaws could wag again to words.
    There is no secret worth the telling. Merely
    'Twould say—"Doctor, I'm dead and damned."

Although Wills considered the Anster translation so fine as to be "unapproachable," and claimed to have worked directly from Goethe's original text with the aid of a German dictionary, he had no qualms about lifting rhymes verbatim from Anster when it suited him, and blank verse be damned, as when Mephistopheles summons vermin to eat away the edge of a chalked pentagram in which he is trapped:

MEPHIS. The lord of the frogs and the mice and the rats,
    Of the fleas and the flies and the bugs and the bats,
    Commands you with your sharp tooth's saw
    The threshold of this door to gnaw.

Stoker never gave an opinion for the record on the quality of Wills's script, but his handwritten corrections appear all through a printer's proof of the play, which was subsequently published and may also have been used

Ellen Terry as Margaret in **Faust**.

in printed form by the Lyceum company, which, for *Faust*, included hundreds of technicians and extras in addition to twenty-three speaking parts. Hand-copying scripts for all who needed them would have been a daunting task, but Irving had the money available for typesetting. It's impossible to know whether Stoker had actual creative input or was recording changes requested by Irving and/or Wills. The latter makes more sense. Since he claimed to have helped Irving improve *Vanderdecken*, surely he would have tried to snare some credit for *Faust*, but he never did. The most substantial material in Stoker's hand is a revision of the Brocken scene opening, deleting Mephistopheles's lines to Faust as they climb to the summit: "Dost thou not wish you had a broomstick, friend? / I wish I had a tough he-goat to ride! / Hark! to the crashing woods! / The affrighted owls are on the wing; / Oohoo! Shoohoo! Oohoo! Shoohoo! / Cling to my cloak—fear nothing." Stoker begins the scene with "Grasp my shirt and fear nothing," allowing the flying witches and owls to speak for themselves.

Whatever editing he may or may not have contributed, Stoker worried justifiably about the production's viability. "I began to have certain grave doubts as to whether we were justified in the extravagant hopes which we had all formed of its success," he wrote. "The piece as produced was a vast and costly undertaking; and as both the decor and the massing and acting grew, there came that time, perhaps inevitable in all such undertakings of indeterminate bounds, as to whether reality would justify imagination." His doubts were only deepened after a partial dress rehearsal that ran long into the night. "It was then, as ever afterwards, a wonderful scene of imagination, of grouping, of lighting, of action, and all the rush and whirl and triumphant cataclysm of unfettered demoniacal possession. But it all looked cold and unreal—that is, unreal to what it professed." By the time the devilish revels ended, the gray morning was breaking (rather appropriately, given the scene just rehearsed). "I talked with Irving in his dressing-room, where we had a sandwich and something else, before going home. I expressed my feeling that we ought not to build too much on this one play. After all it might not catch on with the public as firmly as we had all along expected— almost taken for granted. Could we not be quietly getting something else ready, so that in case it did not turn out all that which our fancy painted we should be able to retrieve ourselves. Other such arguments of judicious theatrical management I used earnestly."

After weighing Stoker's points, Irving was not swayed. "That is all true," he said, "but in this case I have no doubt. I know the play will do. To-night I think you have not been able to judge accurately. You are forming an opinion largely from the effect of the Brocken. As far as to-night goes you are quite right; but you have not seen my dress. I do not want to wear it till I get all the rest correct. Then you will see. I have studiously kept as yet all the colour to that grey-green. When my dress of flaming scarlet appears amongst it—and remember that the colour will be intensified by that very light—it will bring the whole picture together in a way you cannot dream of. Indeed I can hardly realise it myself yet, though I know it will be right. You shall see too how Ellen Terry's white dress and even that red scarf across her throat will stand out in the midst of that turmoil of lightning!"[3]

---

[3] Although one is tempted to read "scar" as a typographical error for "scarf," Ellen Terry's appearance as a vision was intended to foreshadow Margaret's death; in Wills's script, Faust explicitly wonders "what means that slender scarlet line / Around her throat—no broader than

Poster for the original production of Irving's **Faust.**

To others, Irving would bemoan the fact that, being caught up in the middle of it, he would never personally be able to witness the finished effect. His vanity was such that he never even considered the eminently practical solution of simply having a costumed stand-in demonstrate the spectacular stage picture. Company members recalled Irving as more than usually autocratic, impatient, and demanding during the play's preparation. Alice Comyns Carr, wife of the critic, playwright, and gallery owner J. Comyns Carr, was an author in her own right, as well as a costume consultant, who had traveled with the company on the German research trip. Now, with *Faust* in rehearsal, she was appalled at the Jekyll-and-Hyde transformation

---

a knife." In Goethe, Mephistopheles goes further, comparing her to the beheaded Medusa: "Be not surprised, if you should see her carry / Her head under her arm—'twere like enough; / For since the day that Perseus cut it off, / Such things are not at all extraordinary."

that had overtaken him. "Gone was the debonair, cheery, holiday companion," she remembered, "and in his place was a ruthless autocrat, who brooked no interference from anyone, and was more than a little rough in his handling of everyone in the theatre." The roughness included the actual hitting and slapping of other actors.

Irving had intended to unveil *Faust* early in the season, in September instead of around Christmas (which might have deflected at least some of the inevitable pantomime comparisons), but the physical production was on a scale the Lyceum had never attempted. "Many of the effects were experimental and had to be tested; and all this caused delay," wrote Stoker. "As an instance of how scientific progress can be marked even on the stage, the use of electricity might be given." Gilbert and Sullivan's *Patience* had been the first stage production entirely lit with electricity, but Irving still relied primarily on gas and limelight, saving electricity for lightning and other special effects. Like Nikola Tesla, that supreme showman of the early electrical age, he understood the value of exploiting electricity for its theatrical rather than utilitarian qualities.

The sword fight between Faust and Valentine (Marguerite's brother, outraged after Faust impregnates her) employed an "invisible" Mephistopheles as a third participant. A century before the dawn of lightsabers, Irving's *Faust* startled audiences (and at times the actors) with electrified swords that threw off blue sparks when they touched. "This effect was arranged by Colonel Gouraud, Edison's partner, who kindly interested himself in the matter," Stoker remembered. "Two iron plates were screwed upon the stage at a given distance so that at the time of fighting each of the swordsmen would have his right boot on one of the plates, which represented an end of the interrupted current. A wire was passed up the clothing of each from the shoe to the outside of the indiarubber glove, in the palm of which was a piece of steel. Thus when each held his sword a flash came whenever the swords crossed." A certain number of shocks to the actors were unavoidable, but when they happened Irving would just ad lib a delighted cackle.

In addition to the sparks, there was a startling variety of sudden blue flames that erupted periodically throughout the show, and which Stoker surely remembered when he sent Dracula looking for treasure-heralding blue fire during a coach stop in the Borgo Pass—fire that rendered him transparent when he walked in front of it. "The arrangement of the fire which burst from the table and from the ground at command of Mephistopheles

The Witches' Kitchen scene from **Faust** *(1886).*

required very careful arrangement so as to ensure accuracy at each repetition and be at the same time free from the possibility of danger," Stoker noted. "Altogether the effects of light and flame in *Faust* are of necessity somewhat startling and require the greatest care. . . . The methods of producing flame of such rapidity of growth and exhaustion as to render it safe to use are well known to property masters. By powdered resin, properly and carefully used, or by lycopodium[4] great effects can be achieved."

Beyond pyrotechnics, Stoker noted that "steam and mist are elements of the weird and supernatural effects of an eerie play." In the 1880s, dry ice and chemical fog had not yet been developed for stage effects, but there was still a trusty standby. "Steam can be produced in any quantity, given the proper appliance," Stoker wrote. "But these need care and attention, and on a stage, and below and above it, space is so limited that it is necessary to keep the tally of hands as low as possible. . . . Inspecting authorities have become extra careful with regard to such appliances; nowadays they

---

[4] Flash powder, commonly used in magic acts, derived from the flammable dried spores of the lycopodium plant, a kind of clubmoss.

require that even the steam kettle be kept outside the curtilage[5] of the building." Steam also had the drawback of making noise as it was produced, but except for the less than satisfactory use of scrims and dim lighting, fogs were otherwise impossible to reproduce, or even indicate. There was a certain kind of hissing in the theatre Irving would simply have to endure.

Fortified with a battery of stage tricks unparalleled outside of pantomime, *Faust* premiered on December 19, 1885, with every seat taken; the Prince and Princess of Wales were among the first-nighters. According to Stoker's meticulous record keeping, between 1885 and 1902, the play "was performed in London five hundred and seventy-seven times; in the provinces one hundred and twenty-eight times; and in America eighty-seven times. In all seven hundred and ninety-two times, to a total amount of receipts of over a quarter of a million pounds sterling."

Such impressive statistics meant little to critical observers like the British-American writer Henry James, who was already predisposed not to like Wills's work. In 1878, he had written that the popularity of *Olivia* "could only be accounted for by an extraordinary apathy of taste on the part of the public, and a good-natured disposition in the well-fed British playgoer who sits in the stalls after dinner to accept a pretty collection of eighteenth-century chairs, buffets, and pottery . . . as a substitute for dramatic composition and finished acting." As for *Faust*, he found it baffling that, to Henry Irving, so many of the play's essential aspects simply "wouldn't matter."

> It wouldn't matter that Mr Wills should have turned him out an arrangement of Goethe so meagre, so common, so trivial (one must really multiply epithets to express its inadequacy), that the responsibility of the impresario to the poet increased tenfold, rather than diminished. . . . It wouldn't matter that from the beginning to the end of the play, thanks to Mr Wills's ingenious dissimulation of the fact, it might never occur to the auditor that he was listening to one of the greatest productions of the human mind. It wouldn't matter that Mr Irving should have conceived and should execute his own part in it the spirit of a somewhat refined extravaganza; a manner which should differ only in degree from that of

---

[5] The land area immediately surrounding a structure.

the star of a Christmas burlesque—without breadth, without depth, with little tittering effects of low comedy.

James thought it best to "confess frankly that we attach the most limited importance to the little mechanical artifices with which Mr. Irving has sought to enliven *Faust*."

We care nothing for the spurting flames which play so large a part, nor for the importunate limelight which is perpetually projected upon somebody or something. It is not for these things that we go to see the great Goethe, or even (for we must, after all, allow for inevitable dilutions) the less celebrated Mr Wills. We even protest against the abuse of the said limelight effect: it is always descending on some one or another, apropos of everything and of nothing; it is disturbing and vulgarizing. That blue vapors should attend upon the steps of Mephistopheles is a very poor substitute for giving us a moral shudder.

At times, though, James was willing to admit—however grudgingly—that Irving did manage to achieve a few "deep notes."

The actor, of course, at moments presents to the eye a remarkably sinister figure. He strikes us, however, as superficial—a terrible fault for an archfiend—and his grotesqueness strikes us as cheap. We attach also but the slenderest importance to the scene of the Witches' Sabbath, which has been reduced to a mere hubbub of capering, screeching, and banging, irradiated by the irrepressible blue fire, and without the smallest articulation of Goethe's text. The scenic effect is the ugliest we have ever contemplated, and its ugliness is not paid for by its having a meaning for our ears. It is a horror cheaply conceived, and executed with more zeal than discretion.

James's thoughts on *Faust*'s leading lady were more gently put, though just barely. "It seems almost ungracious to say of an actress usually so pleasing as Miss Terry that she falls below her occasion, but it is impossible for us to consider her Margaret as a finished creation. Besides having a strange amateurishness of form (for the work of an actress who has had Miss Terry's years of practice), it is, to our sense, wanting in fineness of conception, wanting in sweetness and quietness, wanting in taste."

It may have been James's review, and many similar harsh appraisals, that prompted Irving to take the unusual step of defending his *Faust* publicly at a meeting of the Goethe Society at the Madison Square Theatre on March 15, 1888, and in populist terms that no doubt scandalized many Germanists in attendance. "Goethe endeavored to give practical life to an ideal which still haunts many earnest minds—the ideal which places the functions of the stage entirely beyond and above the taste of the public. That," Irving insisted, "is impossible." In the actor's view, Goethe erroneously dismissed the popular desire for amusement as "degrading," and therefore his conception for staging *Faust, Part I* was a completely misguided attempt to elevate ordinary human passions

> into a rarefied region of transcendental emotion; and the actors, who naturally found some difficulty soaring into this atmosphere, he drilled by the simple process of making them recite with their faces to the audience, without the least attempt to impersonate any character. His theory, in a word, was that the stage should be literary and not dramatic, and that it should hold up the mirror, not up to nature, but to an assemblage of noble abstractions. It is needless to say that this ideal was predoomed to failure.

Irving insisted "that there is a great popular demand for a kind of entertainment which would have excited Goethe's disgust, and which does not appeal very strongly to your sensibilities or to mine." Stoker's very probable hand in writing this speech is evidenced by a digressive defense of popular fiction, in which Stoker had a far stronger interest than Irving.

> You sometimes hear to-day that the popularity of entertainments which are not of the highest class is evidence of the incurable frivolity, or coarseness, or ignorance of the vast mass of playgoers. I always wonder why the argument is applied only to the stage. You never hear any pulpit orator denounce the enormous sale of fiction which appeals to the ineradicable taste for exciting narrative. . . . No rational being believes that imaginative literature is hopelessly degenerate because the best novels are not as widely read as their inferiors.

Irving's impersonation of Mephistopheles brought the devil down to earth and made him accessible in a way Goethe simply didn't. "He is without the traditional horns and tail; and cloven feet. . . . He is not the Satan of Milton, but a 'waggish knave.' He represents not the grandeur of revolt against the light, but everything that is gross, mean and contemptible. He delights not in great enterprise but in perpetual mischief. Sneering, prying, impish, he is the heartless skeptic of modern civilization, not the demon of medieval superstition."

Members of the Goethe Society might have easily retorted that Irving was playing Mephistopheles to his audience as much as to his Faust, tempting them with a crude approximation of high culture and laughing as they congratulated themselves on their sense of being elevated. If Irving's devil sneered, some of the sneers were directed at audience members themselves. He didn't claim their souls, but at least he collected their money, and in a crass bourgeois sense, perhaps it was the same thing. However, on a completely different level, the enormous popularity of *Faust* in England and America spoke to its spectacular, if kitschy, reaffirmation of God, the devil, and the possibility of an afterlife in the face of the nineteenth century's materialist juggernaut. Spiritualism attracted followers for similar reasons. And so, of course, would *Dracula*.

As Stoker attested, Irving never forgot a slight—or a hiss—and many of his critics were canny in their perception that he might be treating his audiences badly with *Faust*, if not with outright contempt then at least with some level of condescension. He had keenly felt the sting of audience disapproval while learning his trade in the provinces, and never really trusted the public. His grand goal of raising the standards of British audiences also amounted to withering judgment on the taste and intelligence of those audiences. Irving's inability to let go of a grudge was seen nowhere as vividly as in the treatment of his estranged wife, Florence. After she responded to his breakthrough triumph in *The Bells* by asking him if he intended to make a fool of himself forever, he broke off all communication with her and their children, one not yet born. Although he eventually reconciled with his sons, Harry and Laurence, and saw to their educations, he condemned his marriage to Florence to a living death. Now that he was successful, she craved the shared public spotlight of her husband's fame, even as she hated him, and missed no opportunity to ridicule him to their boys. She could

Program for Irving's Faust.

call herself "Mrs. Henry Irving" as much she liked and be received socially as such, but never again in his company. No doubt she was aware that others knew the truth. As part of her separation agreement she was always assigned an opening-night box; this was in addition to her "allowance"—polite terminology for ongoing blackmail payments made on the condition that she never speak of Irving's relationship with Ellen Terry. It fell to Stoker and Irving's secretary L. F. Austin to greet the ogress at openings, show her to the box, coo over the children, and conduct backstage tours.

Florence Irving loathed Stoker and Austin at least as much as the men loathed each other. About eight months before, Austin had prepared an address for Irving to deliver at Harvard University—one he said brought tears to the actor's eyes when it was read to him—but to his horror he discovered, and disclosed to his wife in a letter, "That idiot Stoker wrote a speech for the same occasion and I was disgusted to find it on the Governor's table. When I read mine to Henry, he said: 'Poor old Bram has been trying *his* hand but there isn't an idea in the whole thing.'" Austin replied, "I should be very much surprised if there was." To his wife, he went on:

The fact is Stoker tells everybody that he writes Henry's speeches and articles, and he wants to have some real basis for this lie. This is why he worried H.I. into putting his name to an article which appeared in the *Fortnightly Review*, a fearful piece of twaddle about American audiences that B.S. was three months in writing. . . . I am not vindictive, as you know, but such colossal humbug as this . . . makes me a little savage. The misfortune is that in my position as a *very* private secretary compels me to keep in the background. I cannot tell the truth about my own work for that would not be right. Luckily, I have a faithful friend and ally in [George] Alexander, who knows everybody in London worth knowing and will prick Stoker's bubble effectively.

George Alexander had replaced H. B. Conway as Faust after a disastrous opening, at least for the actor. Conway, hampered by illness, played the character like a deer in the headlights, tears welling in his eyes as he struggled through. It was testimony to the degree to which the title role was overshadowed by Irving, the stage effects, and the general hoopla surrounding the production that Conway's performance itself drew little fire except within the Lyceum, where he was literally fired. Alexander would go on to greater fame as a major West End producer, whose stagings of *Lady Windermere's Fan* and *The Importance of Being Earnest* (in which he also starred) propelled Oscar Wilde to his greatest fame.

That there was no love lost between Stoker and Alexander is evident between the lines of one of Stoker's anecdotes about *Faust*. "One night early in the run of the play there was a mishap which might have been very serious indeed," Stoker wrote. "In the scene where Mephistopheles takes Faust away with him after the latter had signed the contract, the two ascended a rising slope. On this particular occasion the machinery took Irving's clothing and lifted him up a little. He narrowly escaped falling into the cellar through the open trap— a fall of some fifteen feet on to a concrete floor." It is interesting that Stoker fails to mention that George Alexander was also dangerously swept off the stage and faced the same potential fate. Perhaps, as Austin hinted, Alexander had indeed been popping Stoker's bubble around town.

Faust was the highlight of the Lyceum's third American tour, in the fall and winter of 1887–88. Despite her dreadful experience in the shipwreck off the French coast earlier in the year, Florence Stoker accompanied her husband on the transatlantic voyage, only to face a particularly turbulent crossing on the *City of Richmond* in late October. She was distraught the entire trip and never again traveled to America. The weather didn't improve, and the opening night of *Faust* at the Star Theatre on November 7 coincided with New York's worst blizzard ever recorded. Most of the sold-out audience managed to get to the theatre anyway.

The production was a huge draw throughout the entire tour, despite some very frank appraisals. "Mr. Irving's 'Faust' was viewed by a very large audience at the Star Theatre with admiration, but also with disappointment last evening. That is the plain truth, and it may as well be admitted at the start," said the *New York Times.*

> It is a good thing to be courteous to distinguished foreigners, and the courteous attentions (and money) American playgoers have hitherto bestowed upon Henry Irving have not been misapplied; but the expectations derived from the statements of English newspapers, from cable dispatches, and from the effusive descriptions of enthusiastic people who have been abroad concerning this drama, were not fulfilled on the occasion of its first presentation in this country. The scenic effects are often handsome, the groupings picturesque, the dresses suitable, and the changing calcium lights as pleasing and ingenious as all of Mr. Loveday's efforts in that line. . . . On the other hand, the scenes of magic and mystery are all somewhat ludicrous, and not a bit thrilling. They recall the old comic pantomimes of the Lauri family and Tony Denier.[6]

Aside from the electrical swordplay and the "impressive and artistic" reproduction of sunset and moonlight, the *Times* found almost everything that had been praised elsewhere sadly lacking in the first American presentation. The effect of Faust's rejuvenation was "clumsily managed." The witches' revels were presented "with stronger effect" in two different productions of Gounod's opera recently staged in New York.

> The vision of Margaret in the episode, of which so much has been said in praise, was merely Miss Terry walking across a plank like Amina in "La Sonnambula." The yells of the spirits did not produce a sensation of

---

[6] Charles Lauri was famous for his animal impersonations in pantomimes at the Drury Lane Theatre in London; Tony Denier produced Christmas pantomimes at the Adelphi.

horror; the temptation of Faust by two or three ordinary-looking girls was neither picturesque nor convincing, and the spectacle of Mr. Irving holding up the corners of his red cloak and gazing about him with a sardonic smile while the supernumeraries jumped and shouted did not inspire awe.

Even though the physical effects were "all good enough," the *Times* wondered how the production had been "lauded as the finest spectacle of the age. Hence some of the disappointment." George Alexander's Faust was "a mere puppet" who treated the role "in a sing-song, monotonous way." Irving's acting was found to be facile: "[He] walks quickly, with a very decided limp, and is fond of stretching his arms before him, as if superintending an incantation. The familiar vocal tricks of the actor are all exaggerated in the character." And, perhaps most damning of all, "If Mr. Irving's rank as an actor depended upon his Mephistopheles alone, we do not think, judging from a first view of this work, that he would be the foremost man on the stage of England."

Happily for the Lyceum coffers, *Faust* was critic-proof. Stoker felt that American religious attitudes were to be thanked. "In New York the business with the play was steady and enormous. New York was founded by the Bible-loving righteous-living Dutch." New England was similarly predisposed toward morality tales. "In Boston, where the old puritanical belief of a real devil still holds, we took in one evening four thousand five hundred and eighty-two dollars—$4,582—the largest dramatic house up to then known in America. Strangely the night was that of Irving's fiftieth birthday. For the rest the lowest receipts out of thirteen performances was two thousand and ten dollars. Seven were over three thousand, and three over four thousand." In Philadelphia, "where are the descendants of the pious Quakers who followed Penn into the Wilderness, the average receipts were even greater." In Stoker's description, the clamor for tickets approached the frenzy of a religious revival run riot.

Indeed at the matinee on Saturday, the crowd was so vast that the doors were carried by storm. All the seats had been sold, but in America it was usual to sell admissions to stand at one dollar each. The crowd of "standees," almost entirely women, began to assemble whilst the treasurer, who in an American theatre sells the tickets, was at his dinner. His assistant, being without definite instructions, went on selling till the whole seven

Mephistopheles on the Brocken. Painting by Amédée Forestier (1886).

hundred left with him were exhausted. It was vain to try to stem the rush of these enthusiastic ladies. They carried the outer door and the check-taker with it; and broke down by sheer weight of numbers the great inner doors of heavy mahogany and glass standing some eight feet high. It was impossible for the seat-holders to get in till a whole posse of police appeared on the scene and cleared them all out, only re-admitting them when the seats had been filled.

Chicago was a completely different matter, a city that "neither fears the devil nor troubles its head about him or all his works," and where "the receipts were not much more than half the other places."

No matter where *Faust* played, picture postcards of Irving's counte-nance and costume followed. Always camera-shy, Irving sat for only one photographic portrait, and surviving copies of the resulting postcard show him made up as an archetypal stage villain, with a widow's peak, exaggerated eyebrows, and sharp, shifty eyes—almost uncannily the image of a twentieth-century movie vampire (though nothing like Stoker's novelistic description of Dracula). If not inspirational, Stoker found the face of Irving's Mephistopheles compelling, noting that

> there is for an outsider no understanding what strange effects stage make-up can produce. When my son, who is Irving's godson, then about seven years old, came to see *Faust* I brought him round between acts to see Mephistopheles in his dressing-room. The little chap was exceedingly pretty—like a cupid—and a quaint fancy struck the actor. Telling the boy to stand still for a moment he took his dark pencil and with a few rapid touches made him up after the manner of Mephistopheles; the same high-arched eyebrows; the same sneer at the corners of the mouth; the same pointed moustache.[7] I think it was the strangest and prettiest transformation I ever saw. And I think the child thought so, too, for he was simply entranced with delight.

Noel Stoker never mentioned the incident, so we can't be sure exactly what he thought. However amusing, there is also something profoundly ambivalent in the act of literally demonizing a child, especially a child whose parents already gave him so many mixed messages about their affections. As if underscoring the point, Stoker published a ferocious short story about demoniacal children in the 1887 Christmas issue of the *Theater Annual*. Called "The Dualitists: or, The Death Doom of the Double-Born," the tale concerns two little psychopaths, Harry Merford and Tommy Santon, morbidly and mutually obsessed with knives—more than a decade before Sigmund Freud began talking about the symbolism. "So like were the knives that but for the initials scratched in the handles neither boy could have been sure which was his own," wrote Stoker. "After a little while they began mutually to brag of the superior excellence of their respective weapons. Tommy insisted that his was the sharper, Harry asserted that

---

[7] No images survive of Irving wearing a mustache for the role, but it is quite possible he saw fit to add one in later seasons. The only representations of Mephistopheles—one photograph, one oil painting, several watercolors, and numerous drawings—all seem to have been created for the inaugural production.

his was the stronger of the two. Hotter and hotter grew the war of words. The tempers of Harry and Tommy got inflamed, and their boyish bosoms glowed with manly thoughts of daring and of hate."

The boys join forces in a game they call "Hack," which at first involves terrorizing neighborhood girls. As Stoker explains, "It was a thing of daily occurrence for the little girls to state that when going to bed at night they had laid their dear dollies in their beds with tender care, but . . . when again seeking them in the period of recess they had found them with all their beauty gone, with arms and legs amputated and faces beaten from all semblance of human form." In the time-honored manner of budding serial killers, they escalate to attacking and killing neighborhood pets. The animal kingdom thus decimated, they turn their malignant attention upon a pair of baby twin boys named Zacariah and Zerubbabel Bubb, whom they lure to a stable roof, where Harry and Tommy promptly begin smashing in their little faces. The Bubb parents, horrified and enraged, take aim with a shotgun at the monsters, but blow the heads off their own children instead. The boys play catch with the decapitated twins, then hurl the corpses down upon the mother and father, who are also killed. The parents are posthumously found guilty of murder, buried in unhallowed ground with stakes driven through their hearts, while Harry and Tommy are knighted for bravery.

"The Dualitists" is more disturbing than the darkest tales in *Under the Sunset* and, like "The Squaw," hints at an increasingly dark side of Bram Stoker, bubbling like a witch's brew during the years Irving achieved his greatest successes. These triumphs coincided with unprecedented pressures on Stoker's time and finances, to the point that a second career as a barrister may have seemed a necessary and reasonable exit strategy—or at least some light at the end of the gravelike tunnel in which all of his own creative aspirations seemed destined to be interred.

One might expect, when it came time for the Lyceum to resurrect *Macbeth*, that the old superstitious custom of calling the production "the Scottish play" backstage, and never by its actual name, would be a tradition strictly enforced. However, as Shakespeare historian Paul Menzer reveals in *Anecdotal Shakespeare: A New Performance History*, no "curse" was attached to *Macbeth* until the early twentieth century, whereupon it arrived with "a fake genealogy" invoking various disasters attending productions dating back to

Shakespeare's time, none of them documented. "The history of *Macbeth*'s run of bad luck is a lie that sounds like the truth," Menzer writes. The play has actually been quite lucky for companies that produce it, a perennial crowd-pleaser. Nonetheless, sometime between the First and Second World Wars—the same time, it might be noted, that King Tut's curse was all the rage—a set of ritual beliefs and practices emerged, including not only the injunction against speaking the name "Macbeth" outside of rehearsal or performance, but an effective "remedy to undo the spell should one transgress," requiring the violator to "leave the building, spin around three times, spit, curse, and then knock to be let back in." Given the surprisingly recent nature of the belief, we can safely assume that Henry Irving and all in his company were free to shout or mutter "Macbeth!" as much as they liked and wherever they liked without fear of supernatural retribution.

Even if not cursed, *Macbeth* is still considered Shakespeare's darkest play, and draws at least some of its shadowy glamour from being one of the Bard's handful of late works performed indoors by candlelight, and thereby open to a degree of mysterious atmosphere and illusion impossible at the open-air Globe Theatre, where night could be only roughly indicated by dialogue and props—torches, candles, and lanterns. Indeed, *Macbeth* was premiered at the Globe in 1603, after the ascension of King James I—it is generally believed that the supernatural element in the play was a nod by Shakespeare to the king's personal belief in witchcraft—but after 1609 it was also performed at the Blackfriars Theatre, a former priory hall that became the winter home for Shakespeare's company. Unlike the Globe with its noisy pit, the Blackfriars was an elite playhouse that made use of rapidly advancing stage technology for previously impossible effects like the magical visions Shakespeare imagined in *The Winter's Tale* and *The Tempest*.

Stoker had been familiar with *Macbeth* since his Dublin years, and he had favorably reviewed both the acclaimed Irish actor Barry Sullivan and the equally laureled Italian tragedian Tommaso Salvini in the role. In October 1873, reviewing Sullivan, he noted that " 'Macbeth' occupies a peculiar position amongst plays—a melo-drama by its action, and more especially by its finale; and a tragedy by its underlying idea. It is no wonder that it is one of the most popular plays performed. What it must have been in the seventeenth century, when the belief in witches still existed, we can understand, when we consider the rapt attention of the nineteenth century audience at the incantation scenes."

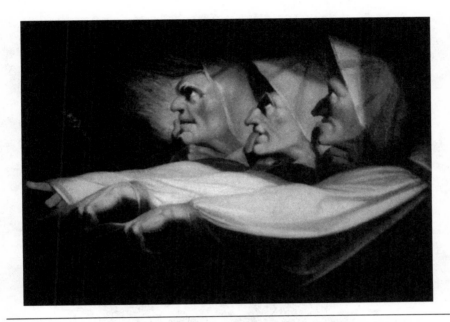

Irving's weird sisters took inspiration from Henry Fuseli's famous painting of 1783.

The three witches, virtually synonymous with the play itself in the public mind, interested Stoker enough that he would invoke them as the hungry wives of Dracula who materialize out of moonlit dust to gloat over Jonathan Harker. Even without *Macbeth*, the world's mythologies and folklores overflow with triadic female entities; the Gorgons, Fates, Furies, Hours, and Graces, for instance, were all supernatural sisters who traveled in threes. And Stoker needn't have gone further than his alma mater, Trinity College, to make a basic imaginative connection between things mystical, mysterious, and triplicated.

Stoker found Macbeth an especially, and essentially, sympathetic character. "We sympathize with him as we do with Faust, who, deluded by the powers of Evil, awakes too late to the awful knowledge that diabolical promises are based on sand. . . . The tragedy of 'Macbeth' consists in the way in which Fate closes round the hapless Thane, slowly but surely darkening his path by degrees, like the shades of evening." In a later appreciation of the Sullivan production, he was especially taken with the stagecraft employed in representing Dunsinane Castle. "It was supposed to be vast, and occupied the whole back of the scene. In the centre of the gate, double doors of a Gothic archway of massive proportions. In reality it was quite

Cartoon of Henry Irving as Macbeth.

eight feet high, though of course looking bigger in perspective." Sullivan entered "thundering" his speech as the huge entranceway effortlessly flew open. "Now this was to us all very fine, and it was vastly exciting. None of us ever questioned its accuracy to nature. That Castle with the massive gates thrown back on the hinges by the rush of a single man."[8]

Where Barry Sullivan was powerful and impassioned, Salvini's Macbeth was morally weak. Describing the April 1876 performance, Stoker noted

---

[8] There is no better location than a castle to divert the imagination and assist the suspension of disbelief. It has been repeatedly asserted that Castle Dracula was inspired by Slains Castle, a landmark at Cruden Bay, Scotland, where Stoker spent holiday time while writing the novel, but to anyone growing up in England or Ireland, real castles were just part of the ordinary landscape, and they had always been central to the virtual landscape of fairy tales. By the time Bram Stoker was in his forties, he hardly needed the poke of inspiration to realize a haunted castle might be a good location for a scary story.

that "his dagger soliloquy is done in a much quieter manner than is usual, and in nowise does he confound, as too many tragedians do, the air-drawn dagger with a real thing. He knows throughout that it is a phantom, and no more tries to clasp it than he would seek to wrestle in actual combat with the ghost of Banquo." As he approaches Duncan's chamber for the murder, "the thought of fear, awakened by conscience, suddenly strikes him, and he looks round with the glare of a wild animal at bay and then, suddenly finding his resolution, quickly enters with a gesture of impatience at his own weakness."

Henry Irving had first played Macbeth at the Lyceum in 1875 for the Batemans and, except for the new staging, held to his earlier essaying of the role for his new production in 1887. It was an interpretation both eccentric and, for the actor, more than a little self-serving. Instead of a vacillating thane, goaded by his far more resolute consort to kill King Duncan and take his throne, Irving's Macbeth is determined from the start. Ellen Terry described him as looking like "a famished wolf" in the part. The witches' prophecies and his wife's encouragement merely reinforce the

Ellen Terry as Lady Macbeth.

Irving encounters the witches in the Lyceum production of **Macbeth.**

plans he has already formed. This approach, of course, drains the menace out of the witches by making them cheerleaders rather than agents of fate. Worse, it effectively eviscerates the character of Lady Macbeth, reducing her to a swept-along accomplice, a supportive spouse in the middle-class Victorian mold rather than the cold-blooded avatar of feminine evil—a quasi-vampiress—that has traditionally made the role an especially coveted assignment for actresses. Once more, Irving's willingness to undermine Ellen Terry and relegate her to a less showy part was evident. Terry would still receive plaudits, of course, for her "womanliness" in a role better defined by lines like "Spirits that tend on mortal thoughts, unsex me here." Unfortunately, this Lady Macbeth would be forced to sleepwalk on more than one level.

But on the level of memorable iconography, Terry fared far better than Irving, owing to a stunning costume designed by Alice Comyns Carr. Loosely crocheted from green yarn and blue tinsel to create the appearance of chain mail, and bordered with Celtic designs, the dress was finally gold-embroidered and ornamented with a thousand iridescent wings of the green "jewel beetle," *Sternocera aequisignata.* Comyns Carr felt the decoration "would give the appearance of the scales of a serpent." (Perhaps Stoker still held the image in mind when he concocted a formidable snake-woman for his final novel, *The Lair of the White Worm*.) A heather-colored cloak decorated in a griffin motif completed the apparel, and Terry additionally wore a massive red wig, its long braids enlaced with spiraling ribbons. As Terry described the look to her daughter, "The whole thing is Rossetti—rich stained-glass effects."

Oscar Wilde, by then editor of the periodical *The Woman's World*, where he gave expert advice on all matters pertaining to decorating and fashion, quipped to his readers, "Lady Macbeth seems to be an economical

Henry Irving as Macbeth.

John Singer Sargent's 1906 memory impression of Ellen Terry in **Macbeth.**

housekeeper and evidently patronizes local industries for her husband's clothes and the servant's liveries, but she takes care to do all her own shopping in Byzantium."

The painter John Singer Sargent, who attended the opening night, was immediately enthusiastic about the visual impression Terry made, and he proposed to commemorate Lady Macbeth on canvas. Wilde, who watched Terry arrive to pose at his neighbor's Tite Street studio, commented, "The street that on a wet and dreary morning has vouchsafed the vision of Lady Macbeth in full regalia magnificently seated in a four-wheeler can never again be as other streets: it must always be full of wonderful possibilities." Sargent and Terry conspired on a pose that never appeared in the production but restored Lady Macbeth to full strength and volition as she raised the slain Duncan's crown above her head in a triumphant self-coronation.[9] Before eventually moving to its permanent home at the Tate Gallery, the life-sized portrait would hang for many years in the Lyceum's Beefsteak Room, near to some charming but soon

[9] Sargent's painting is reproduced in the color plate section of this book.

to be forgotten landscapes of Frank Miles, that painter now sadly removed from the London art world and languishing in an asylum, waiting for death.

Despite the narcissistic way in which Irving undermined Shakespeare's conception of *Macbeth*, the images of an unquenchable evil spawned by the play haunted Stoker powerfully as he gestated his most famous novel: the desolate castle, the three weird sisters, the revenant dead, disturbed sleep and somnambulism, and indelible spots of blood everywhere. Lady Macbeth's famous comment on the dead king Duncan might well serve as an observation on Dracula himself, in both his supernatural aspect and his cultural longevity: "Yet who would have thought the old man to have had so much blood in him?"

Macbeth: *Duncan's fatal arrival at Dunsinane Castle.*
A souvenir program illustration for Irving's production by John Jellicoe.

CHAPTER SEVEN

THE ISLE OF MEN

HEAVEN SAVE ME FROM THIS FIEND THAT TAKES
HOLD OF ME AND POSSESSES ME!
—Hall Caine, *Drink*

Bram Stoker and Thomas Henry Hall Caine met for the first time at the glittering premiere of *Hamlet* at the Lyceum on December 30, 1878. Caine, an ambitious twenty-six-year-old journalist and budding novelist from Liverpool who had been one of Henry Irving's most vocal public supporters in the provinces, had received a note earlier that day from stage manager Henry Loveday. "Delighted to see you tonight," it read. "See Mr. Bram Stoker—he has a seat in a box for you. Come round later."

Caine was in good company. Among those assembled to bear witness to the christening of Henry Irving's new temple of culture were the Prince and Princess of Wales (and, seated quite separately, the prince's mistress, the actress Lillie Langtry), the politicians Benjamin Disraeli and William Gladstone, the painters James McNeill Whistler and John Everett Millais, and the writers Algernon Charles Swinburne and Alfred, Lord Tennyson. Oscar Wilde, who had not yet officially relocated to London but was nonetheless in town to get a start on his social climbing, was also there, only a few weeks after Stoker's Dublin marriage to Florence Balcombe, a social

---

Greeba Castle on the Isle of Man, private lair of novelist Hall Caine (on staircase).

ceremony he pointedly did not attend. There is, sadly, no record of what interesting words of greeting may have transpired between Wilde and Stoker. It is highly unlikely that Stoker arranged for Wilde's ticket, and more plausible that he attended as the guest of Mrs. Langtry.

Irving's courtesy to the Liverpool theatre critic was both gracious and strategic; like Stoker, Caine had provided Irving with invaluable press agentry in the guise of theatre criticism on the pages of the Liverpool *Town Crier* and might well be very useful again. There were so many parallels between Stoker and Caine that it is surprising they didn't meet much earlier. Dublin and Liverpool were sister cities on opposite sides of the Irish Sea, and between them was the Isle of Man, Caine's ancestral home, where he spent large stretches of his boyhood. For both young men, an early interest in folk and fairy lore led to a bottomless appetite for books and a special fascination for the theatre. In the 1870s they saw all the same touring productions at roughly the same time; because of their geographical proximity, a theatre company's stop in Dublin was often followed by one in Liverpool, or vice versa. They were both admirers of Henry Irving, Whitman, Swinburne, Rossetti, and Edward Dowden—Stoker's mentor and Caine's correspondent. Stoker was born sick, and Caine grew up thinking he was sick; hypochondria and vague nervous complaints dogged him all his life, sometimes prompting him to seek out dubious cures.

Where Stoker's major interest in fairy tales rose from his exposure to Christmas pantomimes, Caine attributed his own baptism in folklore to his Manx grandmother. "She believed in every kind of supernatural influence," wrote Caine. "I think of her now feeding the fire with the crackling gorse[1] while she told me wondrous tales." She claimed to have seen fairies with her own good eyes as a girl, and told how, in the light of the moon, she was beset by a "multitude of little men, tiny little fellows in velvet coats and cocked hats and pointed shoes, who ran after her, swarmed over her and clambered up her streaming hair." It was Caine's grandmother who gave him the Manx nickname "Hommy Beg," meaning "Little Tommy."

For all the similarities between Stoker and Caine, there was one major difference, which must have been all the more exaggerated as Caine ascended the dozen carpeted, brass-railed steps that led to the Lyceum

---

[1] A spiny, yellow-flowered weed, prolific in Great Britain and France, where it is commonly used for burning; its bursting seed pods give off a crackling sound.

Hall Caine as a rising author.

main lobby—an architectural feature that always reminded audiences, at least on a subliminal level, that they were meant to have an elevated experience. But there was nothing subliminal about Stoker's imposing presence. He was a big, bearded bear of a man over six feet tall, while Caine was nervous, slight, and diminutive—five feet three inches tall by some accounts, five-four by others. "Little Tommy" was right. Their first encounter at the theatre must have been like a scene between a giant and a dwarf in a pantomime. Had *Punch* cartoonist Harry Furniss been there, his efforts, no doubt, would have resulted in something very much like his satirical sketch of Lady Wilde and Sir William.

Caine's first impression of Stoker may have been a bit like that recorded by author Horace Wyndham, even if, on this particular night, his gatekeeper persona had yet to be buffed to a high polish. "To see Stoker in his element was to see him standing at the top of the theatre's stairs, surveying a 'first night' crowd trooping up them," wrote Wyndham. "A Lyceum

opening could be counted on to draw an audience that was really representative of the best of the period in the realms of art, literature, and society.
Admittance was a very jealously guarded privilege. Stoker, indeed, looked
upon the stalls, dress circles and boxes as if they were annexes to the Royal
Enclosure at Ascot, and one almost had to be proposed and seconded
before the coveted ticket would be issued."

Although both men were status conscious and relished elbow-rub-
bing with the glitterati, in 1879 they were still in the early stages of their
writing careers. People were struck with Caine's resemblance to certain
portraits of William Shakespeare, and he enjoyed the comparison (what
young writer wouldn't?), trimming his beard and brushing his hair back
from his high forehead accordingly. The look became a central part of
his self-presentation, so much so that when a shipboard barber once took
a bit too much off his beard, he hid in his cabin for the duration of the
trip. Caine had published essays on the supernatural element in poetry and
Shakespeare. Neither had published a novel, but Caine would beat Stoker
to the punch beginning in 1885 with a well-received first thriller, *The
Shadow of a Crime*, quickly followed by *She's All the World to Me: A Manx Novel*
(1885), *A Son of Hagar* (1886), and the best-selling *The Deemster* (1887). His
Recollections of Dante Gabriel Rossetti (1882) and *Life of Samuel Taylor Coleridge*
(1887) did not fare as well. Oscar Wilde had taken no note of Caine at
the *Hamlet* premiere, but later as a reviewer dismissed the Rossetti memoir
out of hand, and wrote of the Coleridge biography, "So mediocre is Mr.
Caine's book that even accuracy couldn't make it better." Wilde complained
that "never for one single instant are we brought near to Coleridge[;] the
magic of that wonderful personality is hidden from us by a cloud of mean
details, an unholy jungle of facts. . . . Carlyle once proposed to write a life
of Michael Angelo without making any reference to his art, and Mr. Caine
has shown that such a project is perfectly feasible." On another occasion
Wilde's contempt was far more general and sweeping: "Mr. Hall Caine, it
is true, aims at the grandiose, but he writes at the top of his voice. He is so
loud that one cannot hear what he says."

For a pair of men who would be remembered legendarily as closest
friends and confidantes, Caine and Stoker seem to have remained only
acquaintances during the 1880s. Bram and Florence were nearly Caine's
neighbors when they moved to Chelsea. At 10 Cheyne Walk, Caine lived with
the declining Rossetti, serving as secretary, companion, and drug-dispensing

nurse (a chronic insomniac, Rossetti was hopelessly addicted to chloral hydrate) until the death of the painter in 1882, shortly before the Stokers relocated to number 26. Caine provided Bram with some secondhand intimacy to one of the most ghoulish episodes in art history. Rossetti had founded the Pre-Raphaelite Brotherhood, and his mistress Elizabeth Siddal was one of the movement's more important models, helping to define for the Victorian mind how, exactly, medieval maidens ought to look. In 1862, not long after she finally married Rossetti, Siddal died of a laudanum overdose. She was buried in Highgate Cemetery with a notebook of her husband's unpublished poetry, with a strand of what William Michael Rossetti described as her "lavish heavy wealth of coppery golden hair" wrapped around it before the coffin was closed. Seven and a half years later, Rossetti wanted the poems back. Friends oversaw the exhumation by torchlight, and as legend tells it, Siddal's corpse was like that of an uncorrupted saint, and her beautiful hair had continued to grow, filling the casket. The fact that the notebook was drilled through with wormholes argues against a flawless state of preservation—one explanation, that she had been essentially pickled by laudanum use, was scientifically absurd. In all likelihood the story was told to Rossetti to assuage the guilt of a grave robber. If the body was beatific, it could be, perhaps, a sign of approval from the beyond.

Stoker would echo the incident in two pieces of fiction. In *Dracula*, Lucy Westenra, with her "sunny ripples" of hair, is interred in a cemetery very much like Highgate, and when the vampire hunters open her coffin, her features still have the blush of life. In Stoker's short story "The Secret of the Growing Gold" (written circa 1897, published 1914), a murdered woman's shorn golden hair continues to grow, pushing up through fireplace stones beneath which it lies buried, causing the killer husband to die of fright. The vengeful undead propensities of blond female hair were also prominent in Magyar folktales Stoker consulted while researching *Dracula* and appear in Irish legends as well.

We don't know when Stoker first heard the exhumation story from Caine, and he almost certainly first heard it somewhere else. Although Caine was a notorious pack rat—nearly ninety years after his death, an enormous volume of his personal papers has yet to be cataloged by its repository, the Manx National Heritage Library and Museum. At the personal request of the present author, in 2010 the library conducted a half-year effort, including the aid of volunteers, to uncover previously unknown correspondence

The Rossetti gravesite, Highgate Cemetery. It was here that Dante Gabriel Rossetti
exhumed his wife, Elizabeth Siddal, to retrieve a book of poetry he had buried with her.
(Photograph by the author)

between Stoker and Caine. Although scores of new letters and some telegrams were found, almost none include personal or literary revelations
about Stoker, and they are overwhelmingly about Caine's publishing interests, for which Stoker acted in a significant way as adviser, editor, and agent.
The letters also reflect a shifting intimacy. Sometimes Stoker opens his correspondence with stiff formality ("My dear Hall Caine," "Dear Caine," or
just "Caine," even after he has begun making jokes and using the salutation
"Hommy Beg," alternately "Hommybeg"). Stoker's astute contract advice,
supplementing any opinion Caine received from his own lawyer, begins
in 1887, before Stoker has negotiated any novel contract on his personal
behalf—but exactly during the period he was reading for the London bar
and completing his own first novels. Since it is impossible to believe Stoker
worked for free or waived commissions on Caine's increasingly substantial
earnings—how could he afford to?—we are led to only one conclusion:
that Stoker's income from literary management and editing was sufficiently

Illustration for Stoker's "The Secret of the Growing Gold" from **Famous Fantastic Mysteries** *(1947).*

lucrative and flexible to preclude choosing between his Lyceum job and conventional, day-consuming work as a barrister.

In early 1887, Stoker pointed out to Caine that he had made ill-advised concessions to a newspaper syndicate for serial rights and subsequent hardcover options for his first books, and suggested remedies for his forthcoming novel, *The Deemster* (the Manx term for "judge"; the book dealt with hothouse criminal intrigue on the Isle of Man, where it created an uproar, even though Caine set it in the eighteenth century to avoid controversy).

In a long typewritten letter dated February 1887, Stoker concludes, "You see, my dear Hall Caine, that I write on the typewriter so that you may be able to follow the important business without stopping to swear—necessarily— at my calligraphy!" It is a rare, and perhaps the only, acknowledgment of the frequent illegibility of his rushed, headlong handwriting, which was surely a chronic symptom of the difficulty Stoker had simply keeping up with his own thoughts.

The Deemster was a bona fide best seller, and Caine immediately set about dramatizing it. Irving wanted to produce the play but was too late in making an offer, and it was successfully staged at the Princess Theatre instead of the Lyceum. This led to Caine and Irving discussing a variety of projects on which they might collaborate. According to Stoker, "the conversation tended towards weird subjects." It was only appropriate, since today both Hall Caine and Henry Irving are summoned forth from their graves by the public mostly because of their association with Stoker and *Dracula*. When, one night in the Beefsteak Room, Caine told of having once seen in a mirror a reflection that wasn't his own, Irving responded by telling how an accidental effect in a mirror gave him an inspiration for the materialization of Banquo's ghost in *Macbeth*. As Caine later wrote, "During many years I spent time and energy and some imagination in an effort to fit Irving with a part. . . . I remember that most of our subjects dealt with the supernatural, and that the Wandering Jew, the Flying Dutchman and the Demon Lover were themes around which our imagination constantly revolved."

Irving, always thinking big, thought the prophet Mohammed might be an excellent part. He engaged Florence Stoker, fluent in French from her Dublin education, to translate Henri de Bornier's successful play *Mahomet* for Caine to review. Although a paying job for the Lyceum, it was hardly the kind of artistic employment she had once expected from Irving, but on which she had long given up. Caine didn't find the de Bornier play useful and came up with his own scenario, which he preferred to perform for Irving rather than submit a preliminary script. The night before, staying with Bram and Florence Stoker, he memorably rehearsed his pitch. As Stoker described the recital:

> Now in the dim twilight of the late January afternoon, sitting in front of a good fire of blazing billets of old ship timber, the oak so impregnated with salt and saltpetre that the flames leaped in rainbow colours, he told the story as he saw it. . . . That evening he was all on fire. His image rises now before me. He sits on a low chair in front of the fire; his face is pale, something waxen-looking in the changing blues of the flame. His red hair, fine and long, and pushed back from his high forehead, is so thin

that through it as the flames leap we can see the white line of the head so like Shakespeare's. . . . His hands have a natural eloquence—something like Irving's; they foretell and emphasize the coming thoughts. His large eyes shine like jewels as the firelight flashes. Only my wife and I are present, sitting like Darby and Joan[2] at either side of the fireplace. . . . We sit quite still; we fear to interrupt him. The end of his story leaves us fired and exalted too.

Irving liked it as well, but an actual production was never to materialize. "I spent months on 'Mohammed,'" Caine wrote, "and think it was by much the best of my dramatic efforts; but immediately it was made known that Irving intended to put the prophet of Islam on the stage, a protest came from the Indian Moslems, and the office of the Lord Chamberlain intervened. This was a deep disappointment to Irving, for the dusky son of the desert was a part that might have suited him to the ground."

Caine proposed a stage adaptation of his poem "Graih my Chree" (Manx for "Love of My Heart"), a retelling of the Scottish legend "The Demon Lover," about an unhappily married woman who takes to the sea with a former suitor, only to learn he is a cloven-hoofed demon who offers hell in place of a honeymoon. The actor thought the part would be too young for him. Could Caine do something with the similar Flying Dutchman story instead? He still wanted to redeem the failure of *Vanderdecken*. Caine tried, but to no avail: "In spite of the utmost sincerity on both sides, our efforts came to nothing, and I think this result was perhaps due to something more serious than the limitation of my own powers." He felt that Irving had become so used to playing the part of "Henry Irving" that "it stood in the way of his success in a profession wherein the first necessity is that the actor should be able to sink his own individuality and get into the skin of somebody else."

The American actor Richard Mansfield was a performer who had no difficulty changing his skin, as he proved with the great stateside success of his adaptation of Robert Louis Stevenson's 1886 novella *Dr. Jekyll and Mr. Hyde*. Irving rented him the Lyceum in the late summer and early autumn of 1888 to present the show in London while *Faust* toured the provinces. Mansfield shapeshifted in plain view of the audience, using colored lighting that made his preapplied reddish makeup, imperceptible under warm

---

[2] A pair of devoted homebodies in an eighteenth-century poem.

Souvenir postcard of Richard Mansfield in **Dr. Jekyll and Mr. Hyde,**
produced at the Lyceum at the time of the Jack the Ripper murders.

illumination, horrifying apparent as the light shaded toward blue. Irving
himself had passed up the chance to perform the dual role himself, though
his son H. B. Irving would make a hit of it years later. Mansfield's production
was terribly ill timed. Only a few weeks after it opened, East London experienced the first of what would initially be called the Whitechapel Murders—
and then, as the body count of gutted prostitutes relentlessly increased, the
perpetrator would be immortally christened as Jack the Ripper.

The events in Whitechapel quickly dampened the public's appetite
for imaginary horrors, and Lyceum box office receipts fell precipitously.
Mansfield himself came under suspicion—at least by one impressionable
theatregoer who wrote to the London police that he "went to see Mr
Mansfield Take the Part of Dr Jekel & Mr Hyde I felt at once he was the
Man Wanted & I have not been able to get this Feeling out of my head.

. . . I thought of the dritfull manor we works himself up in his part that It might be possible to work himself up So that he would do it in Reality." Professional critics weren't quite so suggestible. "There is but little scope for acting in what has been described as Mr. Stevenson's 'psychological study,'" opined the *Times*. "Mr. Mansfield's appearances, now in the one part and now in the other, involve no more psychology than the 'business' of a 'quick-change artiste' in the music halls." The *Times* reviewer cited Henry Irving's role in *The Bells* as a far superior study in divided psychology.

For all the publicity it generated, the Mansfield engagement at the Lyceum was not lucrative, and the actor ended up heavily indebted to Irving. Some commentators worried that the grisly play itself had inspired a real-life madman, while the *East End Advertiser* felt the public was affected "the same way as children are by the recital of a weird and terrible story of the supernatural." In a piece called "A Thirst for Blood," the paper observed that "the mind turns unnaturally to thoughts of occult force, and the mysteries of the Dark Ages rise before the imagination. Ghouls, vampires, bloodsuckers, and all the ghastly array of fables which have accrued throughout the course of centuries take form, and seize hold of the excited fancy."

The Ripper targeted prostitutes, at first in dark alleys, cutting their throats (which silenced them instantly) and then mutilating their bodies, especially their bellies. Eleven crimes between April 1888 and February 1891 were classified by police as the Whitechapel Murders, but over time experts have come to consider only five of them—the so-called canonical five—as committed by the Ripper. The first two occurred nine days apart, on August 31 and September 8, when Mary Ann Nichols and Annie Chapman both had their throats cut and abdomens torn open; Chapman's uterus was taken as a souvenir. The murderer struck for the third and fourth times on the same night, September 30. Elizabeth Stride suffered a cleanly sliced throat with no mutilations, and it was theorized the killer was simply interrupted. (Some modern investigators feel, however, that Stride's murder may have been a coincidence rather than an unfinished Ripper outrage.) Catherine Eddowes, the night's other fatality, was attacked far more savagely, and her left kidney went missing, along with most of her uterus.

On November 9, the most horrific killing took place in the shabby boardinghouse room of Mary Jane Kelly, giving the murderer the luxury of time to complete his desecrations unobserved. She was completely disemboweled; her uterus and breasts were arranged behind and about her head

The murder of prostitute Mary Jane Kelly, the Ripper's last victim, was especially ghastly.

and body, and the flesh from her thighs was heaped on a bedside table. The face, hacked to the bone, was virtually beyond recognition as human. On this night the Ripper made a new choice of bloody keepsake—Mary Jane Kelly's heart.

Neither of the missing uteruses, nor the heart, was ever found, but half of an alcohol-preserved left kidney was sent in a small cardboard box to George Lusk, chairman of the Whitechapel Vigilance Committee, on October 16 with a short letter. Return-addressed "From hell," it read:

> MrLusk
> Sir
>   I send you half the Kidne I took from one women
> prasarved it for you tother piece I fried and ate it was
> very nise. I may send you the bloody knif that took it
> out if you only wate a whil longer.
>   Signed Catch me when you can
> MISHTER LUSK

All over London, women were terrified, regardless of class or location. In the East End, the fear was understandably immediate and visceral. In the West End, women like Florence Stoker were not in danger of being literally gutted; still, their midsections daily endured the assault of the corset, and the murders could only reinforce a more general sense that every pre-suffrage woman was chattel, always at risk of having her life emptied and diminished by the actions of men.

The Ripper was never caught, but in the ensuing century and a quarter nearly a hundred suspects or theories have been proposed, perhaps none so intriguing as the case made against a Canadian-born American quack doctor, Francis Tumblety, who had both the opportunity and a misogynistic psychological profile that was disturbingly on point. Born in 1833, the son of an Irishman, Tumblety claimed to have studied medicine at Trinity College Dublin—he claimed a lot of things, as quack doctors usually do—but the essence of his education consisted of peddling pornography on the Erie Canal when he was fifteen. A Rochester acquaintance described him as "a dirty, awkward, ignorant, uncared-for, good-for nothing boy." After an apprenticeship in Rochester with a back-alley abortionist who employed both surgical and medicinal means, Tumblety styled himself as an "Indian Herb Doctor," and thereafter took his show on the road in Canada and the United States, bilking the public with cure-all elixirs and nostrums and often finding himself just a few steps ahead of the law. The chase seemed to excite him. He made enough money to affect the trappings of wealth and sported phony military garb and decorations. His most prominent feature was an enormous mustache that overpowered his lower face. In 1865 he was accused of aiding John Wilkes Booth in the assassination of Abraham Lincoln; although the charge was false, he relished the publicity.

In short, Francis Tumblety was a character who might have been invented by Mark Twain. He did, in fact, navigate the Mississippi, using St. Louis as a base of operations for a period. In hindsight, the world would have been a better place had his existence been confined to humorous fiction.

First, there was his hatred of women. It was said he was betrayed by a woman he married, who turned to prostitution, although this cannot be documented. According to Colonel C. A. Dunham, a New Jersey lawyer who knew Tumblety in Washington, D.C.:

Francis Tumblety, notorious American quack doctor, and an unhealthy controlling presence in Hall Caine's early life. In addition to a predatory taste for young men, the Tumblety style included phony military affectations and dress.

Someone asked why he had not asked some women to his dinner. His face instantly became black as a thunder-cloud. He had a pack of cards in his hand, but he laid them down and said, almost savagely, "No, Colonel, I don't know any such cattle, and if I did I would, as your friend, sooner give you a dose of quick poison than to take you into such danger." He then broke into a homily on the sin and folly of dissipation, fiercely denounced all women and especially fallen women.

Then, for an unexpectedly grisly nightcap, he invited the guests into his office. "One side of this room was entirely occupied by cases, outwardly resembling wardrobes," Dunham wrote. "When the doors were opened quite a museum was revealed—tiers of shelves with glass jars and cases, some round and others square, filled with all sorts of anatomical specimens. The 'doctor' placed on a table a dozen or more jars containing, as he said, the matrices [uteruses] of every class of woman. Nearly one half of one of these cases was occupied exclusively with these specimens."

No one knows, or ever asked, where the uteruses came from.

After a while, Tumblety's ongoing games of cat-and-mouse with the authorities over his dubious medical activities escalated to the point that prosecution and imprisonment were real possibilities. Like a certain Transylvanian vampire, having exhausted the possibilities of his native land, Francis Tumblety set sail for England. When he set up shop in Liverpool in 1874, he advertised as usual and attracted customers as usual, many of them suffering from "nervous" complaints, as well as hypochondriacs with their multiform attendant anxieties. From a business standpoint, bottom-less issues were always the best.

Since Tumblety advertised himself as an "electric physician" of inter-national renown, we can comfortably assume hypnosis was also found in his bag of tricks, along with the "blood purifiers," "pimple-banishing" oint-ments, and the like. Mesmeric or not, he was a forceful magnet for young men, and an attractive coterie inevitably clustered around him when he arrived in a new city. "He had a seeming mania for the company of young men and grown-up youths," observed the American lawyer William P. Burr, who added that "once he had a young man under his control he seemed to be able to do anything with the victim."

One of these young men was Hall Caine, who sought out Tumblety's services in 1874 and quickly became one of his favorite pets. Opinion is nearly universal among Caine's chroniclers that the relationship was both sexual and exploitative. Caine had girlfriends, none that lasted, but at least one friend from childhood, William Tirebuck, who showed signs of hav-ing been romantically fixated on him. Tirebuck knew about Tumblety and expressed some mild jealousy about his friend's relationship. Following whatever "medical" advice or treatment Caine received, Tumblety found his new conquest especially useful for writing pamphlets and letters in his defense, for no matter where the herb doctor went, angry criticism and denunciation were sure to follow.

Considering the older man's overbearing sociopathy, it is doubtful the affair left Caine with idealized notions about the Whitmanesque possi-bilities of romance between men. Whitman didn't eroticize master-slave arrangements, or manipulative blandishments meant only to keep the weaker party in control. "Your letter just received is full of philosophy,"

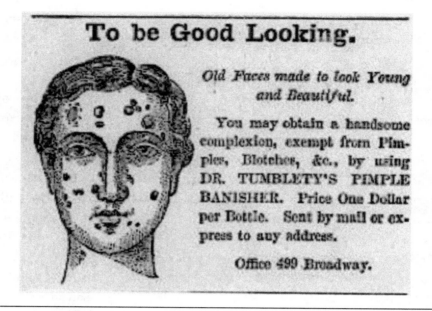

Advertisement for Tumblety's "pimple banisher," a typical quack cure of the time.

reads a typical, unctuously flattering letter from London in April 1875. "I should dearly love to see you I want to talk to you so much. . . . An empty mind is the Devil's workshop it is hard to stand the temptation and the fascination which surrounds one here." He doesn't describe these London temptations, but it is Caine, apparently, who keeps him from partaking. "When you visit America with me I shall be able to introduce you to some of the leading newspaper people of that country and I think you will be able to make terms with them to suit yourself, you are an ambitious enterprising journalist of the first order, and your genius & talent will be appreciated in America. . . . I am interested in everything that concerns your welfare. . . . I have taken pleasure in showing your letter to literary gentlemen of your own profession and you are an ornament to it. The newspaper people here want to see you."

From London, Tumblety repeatedly asked Caine to be his traveling companion in America, invitations he diplomatically evaded. Meanwhile, Caine saw more and more of Tumblety's darker side. When he balked at the propriety of a requested financial transaction, Tumblety exploded. "Don't trifle with my patience any longer, send me two pounds & our friendly correspondence will go on independent of the little financial matter, nobody

One of Tumblety's unctuous, ingratiating letters to Hall Caine. (Courtesy of Manx National Heritage)

else knows anything about it, there is no fraud being committed on you, and I am not in the habit of telling people my private affairs." Telegraphs were even less diplomatic: "Dear boy wire at once . . . wire forty wire wire wire wire wire wire." Or the simple command, with the implicit, imperious understanding that it will not—cannot—be disobeyed: "Come here tomorrow evening. I must see you."

The final piece of surviving correspondence from Tumblety to Caine is

"Don't trifle with my patience any longer." When flattery failed,
Tumblety turned imperious and demanding. (Courtesy of Manx National Heritage)

dated May 31, 1876, and was mailed from St. Louis. The racism and misogyny alone would have been ample cause for Caine to bring the relationship
to an end. Writing of his recent experiences in the West, Tumblety rants

about the country being overrun by "Asiatic hoards," which he compares unfavorably to insects.

> The chinamen are as nasty as Locust, they devour everything they come across, rats and cats, and all sorts of decomposed vegetable matter. . . . The Chinese that are now being landed on the Pacific shelf are of the lowest order. In morals and obscenity they are far below those of our most degraded prostitutes. Their women are bought and sold, for the usual purposes and they are used to decoy youths of the most tender age, into these dens, for the purpose of exhibiting their nude and disgusting persons to the hitherto innocent youth of the cities.

Tumblety, whose return to America somehow didn't land him in jail, nonetheless grew restless and in time went back to England. As crime historians Stewart Evans and Paul Gainey describe it, "Travel for Tumblety was not a source of amusement or of intellectual enrichment; it was a disease. . . . There was no cure. For most of the rest of his life Tumblety was a man on the run. He behaved like a hunted fugitive even when the police had stopped looking for him. Indeed, he seemed almost to invite their attentions, relishing the role of an international outlaw." He arrived at Liverpool in the summer of 1888, made his way to London, and secured lodgings in Batty Street in the East End, at the very epicenter of the murders. He drew the suspicion of investigators early in the case, but they only had evidence to charge him in an unrelated matter: acts of gross indecency with four men. He was in custody only a few days when he made bail, just before the Kelly murder. Perhaps knowing he was being trailed, the killer executed his gruesome pièce de résistance indoors. The next day Tumblety was arrested on suspicion of being the Ripper, but again there was no real evidence. It's not surprising. Modern forensic tools were nonexistent; even fingerprinting would not enter into criminal investigations for another three years.

While awaiting trial on the sex charges, Tumblety broke bail, fled to France, and from there returned to New York City. The eviscerations in Whitechapel stopped. Acts of gross indecency were not extraditable offenses, and he had never been charged with anything else. Tumblety attracted widespread press attention and gave interviews complaining of his mistreatment at the hands of the incompetent London police force. By

"KIDNAPPING"
of

Dᴿ. TUMBLETY.

BY ORDER OF THE SECRETARY OF WAR OF THE U.S.

*A self-published, self-serving pamphlet showcasing Tumblety's ability
to attract and maintain public attention.*

1893 he was living again in Rochester, with his sister, and he died ten years later in St. Louis, a wealthy man.

By late 1888 Stoker and Caine were fast friends, and it is inconceivable they didn't discuss the Ripper, especially after Tumblety's escape to America was extensively covered in the press. Even without a close connection to the case, everyone in London had something to say about what remains one of the most notorious crime sprees of all time. Scotland Yard was deeply embarrassed at letting Tumblety get away, and it is perhaps not surprising that the original dossier outlining their suspicions has never been found.

The idea that Jack the Ripper influenced Stoker's creation of *Dracula*

Spring-Heeled Jack was a frightening urban legend in Victorian England, which influenced the public's response to Jack the Ripper, as well as its receptivity to **Dracula.**

has been put forward a number of times. Certainly, the simple idea of a bloodletting monster at loose in Victorian London is suggestive enough. A terrifying entity known as Spring-Heeled Jack was a widespread urban legend in Victorian times that theoretically could have been the Ripper's namesake and have given Stoker a few ideas as well.[3] Spring-Heeled Jack wore a batlike cloak, appeared out of nowhere, and disappeared just as quickly. He attacked women and men alike, had blazing red eyes, and was said to breathe blue fire. A popular penny-dreadful account of Jack's exploits was serialized in 1886.

The opening chapters of *Dracula*, in which Jonathan Harker is held prisoner in the castle, have often been interpreted as a conscious or

---

[3] "Jack" was not a name invented by the police but first appeared in a gloating letter sent to a London newspaper, purportedly from the killer. It was signed "Yours truly, Jack the Ripper."

Few images of Francis Tumblety exist, but they all accentuate one feature:
a prominent, overpowering mustache that nearly conceals his mouth.
Stoker described Dracula as having a similar appearance.

unconscious representation of Stoker's hostagelike relationship with Henry Irving, but he could have had Hall Caine's personal incubus on his mind when he imagined a tall, thin man with a drooping mustache commanding Harker to write letters in a strange castle where women are banished monsters and the master of the house claims the male guest as his special tool and possession.

Stoker and Caine shared an interest in mesmerism, and Stoker could not have been unaware of a magazine serial his friend published around 1890, called *Drink: A Love Story on a Great Question.* Sixteen years later, it would be published as a slim illustrated book, the story unchanged. Heretofore, *Drink* has not been mentioned among the literary works having influenced *Dracula,* but the story has a striking number of similarities to Stoker's novel, and Caine published it roughly the same year Stoker began his *Dracula* notes. Robert Harcourt (his surname a near-homonym for Harker) travels to the ancestral home of his fiancée, Miss Lucy (Clousedale, in place of Westenra) in the Cumbrian village of Cleaton Moor. En route, he receives ominous warnings about a family curse, which may be descending on Lucy, who has undergone a strange personality transformation. To his horror, Harcourt learns that his beloved suffers the terrible night-thirst of alcoholism, and discovers how she crawls out her window in disguise to seek shameful liquid sustenance in the village below. Confronted, Lucy admits her secret; because of her uncontrollable behavior brought on by polluted blood—her condition is indeed a hereditary, blood-based scourge—their marriage can never be. (At a similar point in *Dracula*, Mina fearfully renounces her own marriage: "Unclean! unclean! I must touch him or kiss him no more.")

Harcourt makes the acquaintance of a French mesmerist, Professor La Mothe, who at "a place of popular entertainment" puts people into a blissful suspended animation for periods of a week or more. Although the sleep is peaceful, the trappings are macabre.

> It was still an hour earlier than the time appointed for the experiment, but I found my way to the sleeper. He was kept in a small room apart, and lay in a casket, which at first sight suggested a coffin. There were raised platforms at either side, from which the spectator looked down at the man as into a grave. . . . I sat on a chair on the platform and looked down at the sleeper. And as I looked it seemed at last that it was not a strange man's face I was gazing into, but the beautiful face that was the dearest to me in all the world. Suddenly a thought struck me that made me quiver from head to foot. What if Lucy could sleep through the days of her awful temptation? What if she could be put into a trance when the craving was coming upon her? Would she bridge over the time of the attack? Would she elude the fiend that was pursuing her?

After the performance, at the end of which the refreshed sleeper "vaulted" from the coffin, Harcourt visits the hypnotist in his dressing room. "Dr. La Mothe," he asks, "has artificial sleep ever been used for the cure of intemperance?" Since La Mothe is a Parisian, Harcourt needs to repeat the question in French. "In the school of Nancy," he says, "the cure of alcoholism by suggestion is not unknown." Does he know the form of drinking mania in which the desire is periodical? "Certainly." Harcourt then puts forth his thesis. "Do you think if a patient were put under artificial sleep when the period is approaching, and kept there as long as it is

Caine's Drink *advocated hypnosis for the treatment of alcoholism, but the technique was more often used for the control of "contrary sexual instinct."* (Courtesy of Manx National Heritage)

usual for it to last, the crave would be past and gone when the time came to awaken him?" La Mothe is startled and fascinated. "With a proper subject it might be—I cannot say—I think it would—I should like to try."

The mesmerist agrees to attend Lucy. Harcourt is overjoyed. "Is it too much to say that I went home that night with the swing and step of a man walking on the stars? If I had found a cure for the deadliest curse of humanity, if I had been about to wipe out the plague of all races, all nations, all climes, all ages, I could not have been more proud and confident. Hypnotism! Animal magnetism! Electro-biology! Call it what you will. To me it had one name only—sleep. Sleep, the healer, the soother, the comforter—."

As an awe-inspiring if overcredulous fictional demonstration of hypnotic power, Caine's story bore a surface resemblance to "The Facts in the

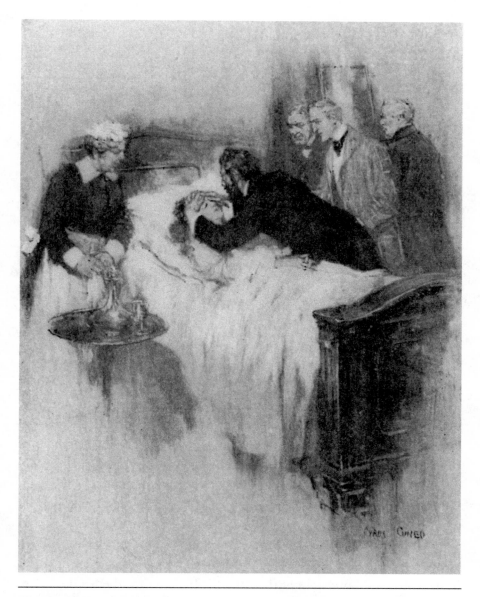

Illustration for **Drink**: *Miss Lucy's uncontrollable night-thirst yields readily to mesmeric suggestion.*
(Courtesy of Manx National Heritage)

Case of M. Valdemar." Indeed, had he intended a perverse lampoon of Poe, upon awakening, poor Miss Lucy might easily have been reduced to a reeking puddle of gin. But mesmerism won the day, at least within the sunnier universe of Caine's imagining, aided by a narrative structure drawn from classic wonder stories. Not unlike Sleeping Beauty or Snow White, Lucy wakens from her deathlike sleep free from the curse, ready and eager to marry the prince who brought her a cure. Caine describes drink itself as "the great hypnotizer," but its awful power is banished and can no longer sap the maiden's soul. George Cruikshank couldn't have written a better fairy tale.

Caine's motivation for publishing *Drink* is puzzling, because there is nothing to suggest that he had personally struggled with alcohol. He had watched, of course, as Rossetti's drug addiction was compounded by the alcohol he additionally drank to mask the taste of chloral hydrate, and his writer friend Wilkie Collins[4] had a truly frightening capacity for laudanum. But Caine never advocated conventionally for temperance, on behalf of his friends or the public. When *Drink* was published, Caine received testimonials from several doctors, attesting to the efficacy of the pseudoscientific treatment. According to Stoker, the 1906 book version sold a hundred thousand copies, but no stampede to hypnotists followed. The public responded to it as melodramatic entertainment, not as medical advice.

Drink was an eccentric outlier among the many books advocating the medical use of hypnosis in the fin de siècle and early twentieth century. If alcohol is even mentioned in the literature, it is mentioned only rarely. The predominant application of hypnosis put forward by medical men, as opposed to novelists, was in the treatment of sexual complaints. In women, the problems inevitably rose from "hysteria," that catchall condition encompassing everything from frigidity to nymphomania, and supposedly emanating from the uterus. In men, the issues centered largely on controlling masturbation and reversing "contrary sexual instinct." Books like *Therapeutic Suggestion in Psychopathia Sexualis* (1895), by Dr. A. Von Schrenck-Notzing, were translated from German into English for medical professionals on both sides of the Atlantic. In America, the leading advocate was Dr. John D. Quackenbos of Columbia University—an occultist as well as a physician—who described his success in mesmerizing away "sexual perversions" as well as smoking, dishonesty, "dangerous delusions," and "willfulness, disobedience, and untruthfulness in children."

---

[4] Collins, whose seminal novel *The Moonstone* (1868) was a clever arrangement of diaries and letters, is generally believed to have inspired Stoker's similar use of the epistolary technique in *Dracula*.

In 1899, he presented some of his case studies to the New Hampshire Medical Society. "A gentleman of twenty-five, occupying a position of great trust with one of our great life insurance companies, came to me, and wept with mortification as he recounted the story of his abnormal attachment to handsome young men," wrote Quackenbos. "As he described it, nature had given him a woman's brain." Schrenck-Notzing borrowed language from Krafft-Ebing to describe such cases as "psychical hermaphrodites." Quackenbos gave hypnotic suggestions to the young man that "portrayed 'unnatural lust' as moral, mental and financial ruin, and the results of a happy marriage were depicted as involving the greatest human happiness."

After only a few treatments, the insurance agent "felt no longer drawn toward a fellow clerk who had previously caused him a great deal of trouble" and "was enabled to throw off the influence with comparative ease. The object of treatment to come will be to eradicate it completely." Schrenck-Notzing recounted a more colorful patient. "In one case of complete effem-ination," he wrote, hypnosis was followed by "an unmistakable weakening of feminine peculiarities. Powder and paint were no longer used; the pic-tures of urnings disappeared from the wall; the feminine articles of toilet were given away."

Stoker had used alcohol euphemistically in his novelette *The Primrose Path* to work through his anxieties about what temptations might await a young man who leaves his Dublin wife and mother for a curiously all-male theatre world where actresses almost don't exist. So, too, does Caine seem to be making an argument about something that doesn't seem to really be the point, but a subject that could not be spoken about openly in com-mercial fiction of the 1890s. In *Maurice*, a novel written in 1913 but not published until 1971, E. M. Forster draws honestly from his own experi-ence as a turn-of-the-century Oxford undergraduate. The title character, madly in love with a classmate, confesses to a conventional doctor that "I'm an unspeakable of the Oscar Wilde sort" but receives no useful advice or information. He tries again with a hypnotist, Lasker Jones,[5] who gives him the suggestion to visualize the portrait of an imaginary beautiful woman and eroticize it. The session ends with Maurice in tears, and he has the good sense to abandon the treatments entirely and get on with the life he has, not the one he thinks he should have. According to the historian

---

[5] Memorably played by Ben Kingsley in the Merchant Ivory film adaptation of 1987.

Graham Robb, in *Strangers: Homosexual Love in the Nineteenth Century*, "These hypnotic cures sometimes lasted several years and more than 100 sessions. They were the Victorian equivalent of long-term, voluntary psychoanalysis. Their apparent popularity is understandable: the price of normality was always just out of reach, and the length, cost and futility of the treatment gave patients a good reason to feign success." As Robb notes, "The idea that homosexuals were constitutional liars was usually set aside when they claimed to be cured."

Caine's biographer Vivien Allen notes that the Isle of Man was a small community, prone to small-town gossip. It was good that he married a decade before acquiring the turreted, faux-medieval island residence known as Greeba Castle; the odd circumstances behind the marriage would have truly set tongues wagging. Caine had been more or less blackmailed by the stepfather of a pregnant thirteen-year-old girl, Mary Chandler, to take her off his hands. Caine wasn't the father, but the girl delivered meals to his rooms at Clement's Inn, and he was friendly toward her. He was an easy target and yielded easily to pressure. Caine lied about Mary's age, saw to her education, and let people assume they were married for several years. While he didn't mind the comparisons to Shakespeare, he didn't need to be likened to Edgar Allan Poe and his legendary child bride, Virginia Clemm. Caine and Mary had one child of their own out of wedlock before finally tying the knot in 1886. She was seventeen, but the marriage certificate said she was twenty-three. After they had a second child, their marriage became a largely companionate affair. Mary would never feel she was part of his real life, his literary life, and his obvious preference for the company of other men was a sore spot for decades. Eventually she would have her own house in London, on Hampstead Heath.

As the Caines' frequent separations became more evident, Allen notes, the whole island suspected that Caine "was conducting a series of torrid love affairs, of which there is no evidence whatsoever, but many of the Manx—and some folk from further afield—thought Caine lived the love scenes and romances he wrote about. More sophisticated people noted the stream of male visitors to Greeba Castle when Mary was not present and drew other conclusions." No one has ever suggested any physical intimacy between Stoker and Caine, and it is far easier to imagine them intimately and endlessly commiserating about their mutual attraction to men than actually doing anything about it. Caine, Stoker, Wilde, and many other

Hall Caine's highly strung personality is well captured in a bug-eyed caricature for **Vanity Fair.**

youthful acolytes of Walt Whitman had, by the 1880s and 1890s, made their compromises with middle-class respectability and settled into marriage and parenthood, however problematic. The Criminal Law Amendment Act of 1885 had greatly expanded the range of homosexual behavior that could be prosecuted in England by only vaguely defining what constituted "gross indecency." In this light, Stoker's appeal to Whitman to censor his work begins to make some sense. Let there be two Walt Whitmans—a sanitized one for the masses, but, *entrez nous,* a more rarified and private understanding.

The friendship between Bram Stoker and Hall Caine will forever be to some degree impenetrable because so many letters that should exist between them appear to no longer exist. It was not uncommon for "very private" Victorians to edit their lives for posterity by destroying their letters, but it is still the bane of biographers. One of the few appreciations of Stoker and his friendship was put to paper by Caine on the dedication page of his 1893 novel *Cap'n Davy's Honeymoon*:

To Bram Stoker

> When in dark hours and in evil humours my bad angel has sometimes made me think that friendship as it used to be of old, friendship as we read of it in books, that friendship which is not a jilt sure to desert us, but a brother born to adversity as well as success, is now a lost quality, a forgotten virtue, a high partnership in fate degraded to a low traffic in self-interest, a mere league of pleasure and business, then my good angel for admonition or reproof has whispered the names of a little band of friends whose friendship is a deep stream that buoys me up and makes no noise; and often first among these names has been your own.

The upswing in Caine's career buoyed both men, though neither could imagine that a decade later the sales of Caine's books would be exceeded only by Dickens and Thackeray. In addition to assisting Caine, Stoker returned to work on his own languishing projects and began new ones. His first full-length novel, *The Snake's Pass*, his only novel set in Ireland, appeared as a serial in 1889 and as a book in 1890.

Sharing in Caine's productive energies stimulated his own creativity, and his mind was newly awash with ideas for stories. One was an especially strange dream fueled by the love of folklore and the supernatural he shared with his friend, as well as a storehouse of images and ideas dating to his babyhood: children spirited away by dark entities, revenants in haunted castles, mesmerism and deathlike sleep, shipwrecks, storms, and coffin-ships. The battle between science and religion—a fantastical dream-world anchoring Darwin's magical pantomime theatre, where animals could become human or slide back again. The fear that there might not be anything beyond death. And the even more terrifying possibility that there might. And above all there was the magic of blood, the mysteries of blood, the dangers of blood . . .

Out of the dream-maelstrom coalesced an archetypal, beckoning

The Snake's Pass *(1890) was Stoker's only novel with an Irish setting..*

figure dressed completely in black. Tall, thin, waxen-faced, and cadaverous, it approached with a singularity of purpose, sweeping away three weird women with voluptuous red lips who bestowed their languorous kisses on the throat instead of the mouth. *Old Count interferes—rage & fury diabolical—This man belongs to me I want him.*

Bram Stoker, the boy who went away with the fairies and never completely returned, had finally been chosen by the Demon King himself to write *Dracula.*

CHAPTER EIGHT

A LAND BEYOND THE FOREST

You go into the woods, where nothing's clear,
Where witches, ghosts and wolves appear.
Into the woods and through the fear,
You have to take the journey.

—Stephen Sondheim and James Lapine, *Into the Woods*

There are many stories about how Bram Stoker came to write *Dracula*, but only some of them are true.

According to his son, Stoker always claimed the inspiration for the book came from a nightmare induced by "a too-generous helping of dressed crab at supper"—a dab of blarney the writer enjoyed dishing out when asked, but no one took seriously (it may sound too much like Ebenezer Scrooge, famously dismissing Marley's ghost as "an undigested bit of beef, a blot of mustard, a crumb of cheese") But that hasn't stopped the midnight snack of dressed crab from being served up as a matter of fact by countless people on countless occasions. While the nightmare aspect may well have some validity—Stoker's notes at least suggest that the story *might* have had its genesis in a disturbing vision or reverie—it exemplifies the way truth, falsehood, and speculation have always conspired to distort *Dracula* scholarship. An unusually evocative piece of storytelling, *Dracula* has always excited

---

Frontispiece of Sabine Baring-Gould's **The Book of Were-Wolves** *(1865).* (John Moore Library)

more storytelling—both in its endlessly embellished dramatizations and in the similarly ornamented accounts of its own birth process.

Some *Dracula* creation myths are easier to believe because they contain partial truths, although they quickly begin to enable improbabilities and impossibilities. For example, it is an undisputed fact that Stoker spent at least seven years working on *Dracula,* from conception to publication, but this leads to a number of unsupported assumptions. First, that it was his masterwork largely *because* he spent seven years on it, and that the book is deservedly renowned for the endless care Stoker took in its crafting. Second, that a work span of seven years indicates, ipso facto, unusually painstaking and authoritative research, which uncovered, among other things, the grisly true story of a bloodthirsty fifteenth-century Wallachian warlord, Vlad Tepeş, "the Impaler," who was also known as Dracula. The name was not well known outside Romania, but Stoker would make it world-famous as the historical source and embodiment of the vampire mythos. In reality, Vlad's connection to Stoker's character was more fortuitous than inspirational, and the author's research was surprisingly thin, but over time, and especially with the release of Francis Ford Coppola's misleadingly titled film *Bram Stoker's Dracula* (1992), Vlad's story is now universally misunderstood as Stoker's central source and impetus, and the novel itself as an overheated romance about Dracula's quest over the centuries for the reincarnation of his long-lost love. The motif appears nowhere in Stoker's book or his foundational notes.

Like the unending parade of dramatists and filmmakers who have not been able to resist tinkering and altering and "improving" his story, Stoker initially had trouble recognizing the essential elements that would make his tale click. The reason *Dracula* took seven years to write was that Stoker had great difficulty writing it, especially cutting through the overload of his own imaginative clutter. The process was twisted, arduous, and constantly interrupted. He stopped to write other books. He questioned himself. He censored himself. He had second, even third thoughts about almost everything.

In the end, he wondered if the book would even be remembered.

Apart from his long-standing interest in the occult, the best reason we can deduce for Stoker's apparently sudden interest in writing an out-and-out supernatural novel at the end of the 1880s was his working association with Hall Caine. Since they had many discussions about legends of living death, demonic love, and life unnaturally prolonged as possible stage vehicles for Henry Irving, it is not surprising that Stoker began mulling over a similar theme. Caine may even have suggested a modern-day vampire adventure as something with a good chance for commercial success. Traditional Gothic novels were always set in the past, or at least stripped of the trappings of modernity. But what if the present was pitted against the past? No one had attempted such a thing, and there was a good chance it might catch the public's fancy. The literary vampire canon then extant was fairly small, comprising familiar works like Polidori's tale "The Vampyre," wherein a vampire sets up shop in London society; *Varney the Vampyre*, the rambling penny dreadful serial in which key scenes in *Dracula* have obvious antecedents; *Carmilla*, of course; and the sometimes overlooked but nonetheless strong inspiration of the German short story "The Mysterious Stranger" (1844) by Karl von Wachsmann, best known from its anonymous English translation of 1854.

While we have no letters from Stoker to Caine asking for editorial advice on any of his books, since Caine was already highly successful and would soon be the best-selling British novelist of his time, Stoker would have taken any recommendation seriously. So perhaps their discussions of wandering Jews and demon lovers did stray into vampire country. We do know, at least, that the beginning of his professional relationship with Caine coincided with his own renewed determination to become a successful novelist. Around the time he began making notes for the yet-untitled vampire story, Stoker had finished and was in the process of publishing *The Snake's Pass*, a straightforward romantic melodrama, well paced and still entertainingly readable. The villain is Black Murdock, a "gombeen man," or shady moneylender, who wants to foreclose on a certain property because he knows something its cash-strapped owner does not: the land (situated on the pass to the sea through which St. Patrick drove out Ireland's snakes) contains a hidden treasure. The property is also surrounded by a dangerous, all-engulfing peat bog, which catches up with Murdock when he ignores its perils in his greedy quest for gold.

Then the convulsion of the bog grew greater; it almost seemed as if some monstrous living thing was deep under the surface and writhing to escape. By this time Murdock's house had sunk almost level with the bog. He had climbed on the thatched roof, and stood there looking towards us, and stretching forth his hands as though in supplication for help. For a while the superior size and buoyancy of the roof sustained it, but then it, too, began slowly to sink. Murdock knelt and clasped his hands in a frenzy of prayer. And then came a mighty roar and a gathering rush. The side of the hill below us seemed to burst. Murdock threw up his arms—we heard his wild cry as the roof of the house, and he with it, was in an instant sucked below the surface of the heaving mass.

The cataclysm strongly recalls the climax of Poe's "The Fall of the House of Usher," which Stoker admired and always thought might be an excellent basis for an opera. The image of a domicile being engulfed in geological turmoil was one he would revisit more than once in his writing.

Although work for Irving and Caine was already threatening to swallow Stoker himself up, in London, on Saturday, March 8, 1890, he found time to write the first of only two dated notes for the new novel's plot.[1] A certain "Count _____" in Styria, who wishes to buy property in England, has written the president of the Incorporated Law Society, who refers the matter to the solicitor Abraham Aaronson, who in turn selects an unnamed but "trustworthy" young lawyer who

> is told to visit Castle—Munich Dead House—people on train knowing address dissuade him—met at station storm arrive old castle—left in courtyard driver disappears Count appears—describe old dead man made alive waxen colour dead dark eyes—what fire in them—not human—hell fire—Stay in castle. No one but old man but no pretence of being alone—old man in waking trance—Young man goes out sees girls one tries to kiss him not on lips but throat Old Count interferes—rage & fury diabolical—This man belongs to me I want him. A prisoner for a time . . .

[1] Stoker's working notes for Dracula, long available to scholars at the Rosenbach Museum & Library in Philadelphia, have also been published in an indispensable volume annotated and transcribed by Robert Eighteen-Bisang and Elizabeth Miller, *Bram Stoker's Notes for* Dracula: *A Facsimile Edition* (Jefferson, NC: MacFarland, 2008).

The notes contain three separate references to the Old Count's inten-tion to possess his male visitor; in addition to the March 8 "This man belongs to me I want him," a March 14 notation reads "Loneliness" followed by "the Kiss—'This man belongs to me.'" When he begins to formally out-line his chapters, he identifies Dracula's brides as "the visitors," followed by "is it a dream—woman stoops to kiss him—terror of death—suddenly Count turns her away—'This man belongs to me.'" The importance of the line to Stoker is also evidenced in the novel's final typescript, where the typist has mistakenly entered something other than the word "man" and Stoker has emphatically restored it—the largest, boldest single-word hand emendation in the final typesetter's manuscript.

In the published book, Dracula additionally says to his wives, "Back, back to your own place! Your time is not yet come. Wait. Have patience. To-morrow night, to-morrow night is yours!" In the 1899 American edition, Stoker changed the last sentence, rather significantly, to "To-night is mine. To-morrow night is yours!" There can be no doubt that the Count intends to make a very personal claim on Harker. On the way to his room, Harker notes that "the last I saw of Count Dracula was his kissing his hand to me; with a red light of triumph in his eyes." The Count has already told his wives that "when I am done with him you can kiss him at your will." Dracula's parting gesture—his own gloating kiss blown to the young man—makes his intentions fairly explicit. Christopher Craft, in his frequently cited essay "Kiss Me with Those Red Lips: Gender and Inversion in *Dracula*," suggests that the whole novel "derives from Dracula's hovering interest in Jonathan Harker; the sexual threat that this novel first evokes, manipulates, sustains but never finally represents is that Dracula will seduce, penetrate, drain another male."

In the end Dracula never touches Harker—it is Harker who, searching for a key, touches the Count's body, which is tumescent and blood-gorged, like a postmortem erection. Harker might as well be looking for the key to his own sexual ambivalence; his repulsion for the act is matched only by his compulsion to carry it out. "I shuddered as I bent over to touch him, and every sense in me revolted at the contact," Harker writes in his journal, "but I had to search, or I was lost. The coming night might see my own body a banquet in a similar way to those horrid three." Has he already forgotten the exquisite sexual thrill, the "languorous ecstasy," he experienced during the vampire woman's oral ministrations? Harker continues: "I felt all over the body, but no sign could I find of the key. Then I stopped and looked at the Count. There was a mocking smile on the bloated face which seemed to drive me mad."

If the homoerotic dimensions of *Dracula* are largely subliminal, a matter of Stoker's "unconscious cerebration" (the pre-Freudian term for involuntary thought processes operating beneath the level of awareness), several earlier works consciously presented vampires frankly attracted to the same sex. The lesbian intrigue of Le Fanu's *Carmilla* is front and center, at least to modern readers, and almost certainly to Stoker. Karl Heinrich Ulrichs's short story "Manor," published in Germany in 1885, concerns the love of a dead sailor (the title character, turned into a vampire at the age of nineteen) for a younger boy who equally adores him. There is nothing at all malignant about Manor—Ulrichs was a pioneering crusader for homosexual rights—and the real villains are the townspeople who dig up the beach to locate his resting place and destroy him and his relationship. Ulrichs's story was not translated into English during Stoker's life, and he was unlikely to have even heard of it. Far more accessible to Stoker was Count Stanislaus Eric Stenbock's "A True Tale of a Vampire," included in his 1894 collection *Studies in Death*, which frankly equated vampirism with pederasty. The story opens with a clear reference to the setting of *Carmilla*: "Vampire stories are generally located in Styria; mine is also." Stenbock was a well-known figure to literary London, if only because he pursued the grotesque with an almost religious fervor. Arthur Symons recalled him as "one of those extraordinary Slav creatures, who, after coming to settle down in London after half a lifetime spent in traveling, live in a bizarre, fantastic, feverish, eccentric, morbid and perverse fashion. . . . He was one of the most inhuman beings I have ever encountered; inhuman and abnormal; a degenerate, who had I know not how many vices." In life, Stenbock seems to have preferred adult men over boys, but the monstrous Count Vardalek of "A True Tale" would have been perfectly at ease dragging children home in bags to satisfy his appetites.

Since Stoker's time, vampires have reliably aligned themselves with changing fashions in sexual and social transgression. In folklore, simply existing outside the tribe in any discernable or annoying way could be enough to stoke suspicions of vampirism or witchcraft. The village idiot, the village drunk, the village whore—all were excellent candidates for supernatural scrutiny and scapegoating, especially when the crop failed, or mysterious illnesses transpired. Stoker told an interviewer that he had always been interested in the vampire legend, because "it touches both on mystery and fact." He went on to explain how prescientific peoples might conjure vampires to explain poorly understood natural phenomena. "A person may have fallen into a death-like trance and been buried before the time. Afterwards the body may have been dug up and found alive, and from this a horror seized upon the people, and in their ignorance they imagined that a vampire was about." Those prone to hysteria, "through excess of fear, might themselves fall into trances in the same way; and so the story grew that one vampire might enslave many others and make them like himself."

Almost every culture has some variation of the myth of the hungry dead, and the rules by which these creatures are created and killed are so varied and diverse that no work of fiction could utilize them all and remain coherent or plausible, even taking into account a heavy dose of suspended disbelief. Stoker wisely steered clear of some of the more ludicrous beliefs (for instance, that vampires, seemingly driven by obsessive-compulsive disorder as much as by bloodlust, could be stopped by strewing poppy seeds in their path, which they would be compelled to individually count—a laborious process sure to last until dawn). In order to create at least a degree of believability, Stoker judiciously adapted the basics of vampirism as set forth in the accounts of eastern European vampire panics by the French biblical scholar Dom Augustin Calmet in *Dissertations sur les apparitions des esprits et sur les vampires* (1746, translated as *The Phantom World* in 1850). Here he found the time-honored methods of vampire disposal, actually used on suspicious corpses: a sharp stake through the heart, decapitation, and cremation. Variant methods included the removal of the heart rather than its staking. These were all physical measures taken against a physical threat. For the most part Stoker intended his vampires to be reanimated corpses, not (as some traditions held) the body's astral projection of its ghostly double, which in its nocturnal wanderings collected blood that was somehow dematerialized and physically reconstituted in the grave-bound corpse. The 1888 edition of the *Encyclopedia Brittanica* presented this view, but Stoker went his own way; he retained the vampire's power of dematerialization but never raised the conundrum of blood transport. He gave Dracula the ability to shapeshift into a bat (or batlike bird), a trait not found in folktales, and the additional ability to assume the form of a wolf, something he found in Sabine Baring-Gould's *The Book of Were-Wolves* (1865). Baring-Gould described the Serbian *vlkoslak*, a vampire-werewolf hybrid, and related the Greek belief that werewolves became vampires after death. Stoker was sufficiently impressed by some of Baring-Gould's descriptions of werewolf traits that he incorporated them almost verbatim into his description of Dracula. (Baring-Gould, for instance, says the werewolf's "hands are broad, and his fingers short, and there are always some hairs in the hollow of his hand"; Dracula's hands "are rather coarse—broad, with squat fingers. Strange to say, there were hairs in the centre of the palm.") Baring-Gould also gave Stoker his descriptions of werewolf eyebrows meeting above the nose and sharp white teeth protruding over the lips. A blurred boundary between human and animal forms was especially resonant for late Victorian readers, still reeling from Darwin's unsettling theories.

Since so many film adaptations of *Dracula* have depicted the vampire being incinerated by sunlight, readers are often surprised that in Stoker's novel the Count walks the streets of London by day, unscathed, although his powers are diminished in the light. In folklore, the vampire, like other evil spirits, retreats into hiding by day but is never destroyed by the sun. This particular vulnerability made its first appearance in F. W. Murnau's unauthorized *Dracula* adaptation, the German Expressionist classic *Nosferatu: Eine Symphonie des Grauens* (*Nosferatu: A Symphony of Terror*) in 1922. Stoker discovered the curious word *nosferatu* in Emily Gerard's 1885 essay "Transylvanian Superstitions," which first appeared in the journal *The Nineteenth Century* and was later included in her book *The Land beyond the Forest* (the title refers to Transylvania's literal meaning, "across the forest"). Although she claimed the word as the Romanian term for vampire, *nosferatu* appears in no Romanian dictionary, or any dictionary in any language. To date, it has been found in only two other published sources, a German account of Transylvanian traditions published in 1865 by Wilhelm Schmidt, and an 1896 article by the Hungarian-Romanian folklorist Heinrich von Wlislocki, in which it appears in the variant, capitalized form *Nosferat*, describing an illegitimate child of illegitimate parents, who becomes a bloodsucking spirit. The word's elusive etymology has prompted numerous origin theories, none completely convincing.[2]

---

[2]Wilhelm Schmidt, "Das Jahr und seine Tage in Meinung und Brauch der Rumänen Siebenbürgens," *Österreichische Revue* 3, no. 1 (1865): 211–26, trans. Andrea Kirchhartz. Heinrich von Wlislocki, "Torturing Spirits in Romanian Folk Belief," *Am Ur-Quell* 6 (1896): 108–9. This

Folklorist Emily Gerard.

At roughly the same time Stoker made his earliest notes, Oscar Wilde delivered a handwritten manuscript of his own horror story to Miss Dickens's Type Writing Office, just a block away from the Lyceum on Wellington Street. Ethel Dickens (granddaughter of Charles) would produce the typescript for the first version of Wilde's only novel, *The Picture of Dorian Gray*, which appeared in the July 1890 issue of *Lippincott's Magazine*, an American periodical distributed simultaneously in England.

The title character is a privileged young man "of extraordinary personal beauty." His portrait has been painted by a society artist, Basil Hallward, whose admiration of his model borders on obsession. The portrait's subject, however, has an unexpected reaction to the canvas. "How sad it is! I shall grow old, and horrible, and dreadful. But this picture will remain always young," Dorian pouts. "If only it were the other way! If it were I who was to be always young, and the picture that was to grow old! For that—for that—I would give everything! Yes, there is nothing in the whole world I would

---

author has found only one Romanian word, the adjective *nesuferit* (meaning "annoying" or "insufferable") that has any possible relevance.

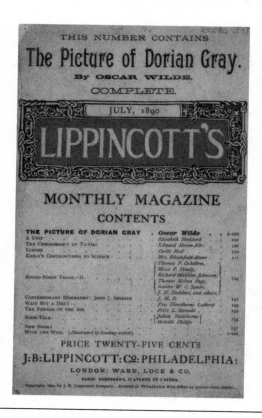

THIS NUMBER CONTAINS

The Picture of Dorian Gray.

By OSCAR WILDE.

COMPLETE.

JULY, 1890

LIPPINCOTT'S

MONTHLY MAGAZINE

CONTENTS

PRICE TWENTY-FIVE CENTS

J:B:LIPPINCOTT:Cᵒ:PHILADELPHIA:

LONDON: WARD, LOCK & CO.

PARIS: BRENTANO'S, 17 AVENUE DE L'OPÉRA.

Copyright, 1890, by J. B. Lippincott Company. Entered at Philadelphia Post-Office as second-class matter.

The Picture of Dorian Gray *caused a furor when it first appeared
in the July 1890 edition of* **Lippincott's Magazine.**

not give! I would give my soul for that!" There is a convenient stand-in for Mephistopheles at hand, Lord Henry Wotton, who doesn't directly broker the deal but tacitly approves Dorian's descent into darkness with an engulfing tsunami of cynical epigrams. ("The only way to get rid of a temptation is to yield to it. Resist it, and your soul grows sick.") Wilde saw himself in all three characters: "Basil Hallward is what I think I am: Lord Henry what the world thinks me: Dorian is what I would like to be." There is also more than a hint of Frank Miles in the doomed, fictional Hallward; both painters are killed, in their own ways, in the pursuit of masculine beauty.

As Dorian retains his youth, the painting begins to show signs of both age and moral corruption, until at last it resembles a hideous, ancient satyr and has to be shut away in an attic room. Meanwhile, Dorian callously drives an actress who loves him to suicide, but mostly he ruins the lives and reputations of other males. "Why is your friendship so fatal to young men?"

Basil demands, after he has aged eighteen years and Dorian none at all. "There was that wretched boy in the Guards who committed suicide. You were his friend. There was Sir Henry Ashton, who had to leave England, with a tarnished name. You and he were inseparable. What about Adrian Singleton, and his dreadful end?" The list goes on and on. Like a vampire, Dorian feeds on the lives of others to maintain his unnatural existence. When Basil Hallward finally discovers the secret of the painting, its original beauty eaten away by "the leprosies of sin," he begs Dorian to pray with him for mutual forgiveness. "The rotting of a corpse in a watery grave was not so fearful" as the cursed, corrupted painting he had created. Instead Dorian stabs the artist to death and arranges for his corpse to be destroyed by acid.

In the end he has covered all his crimes. The painting is the only witness. In a final frenzy, he stabs the canvas, somehow imagining the act will set him free. It does, but not in the way he hoped. The painting returns to its unblemished state, and Dorian lies dead before it with the knife in his own heart, "withered, wrinkled, and loathsome of visage."

The critical reaction to *Dorian Gray* was swift and savage. The London *Daily Chronicle*'s notice amounted to a neat distillation of the general outrage that descended on the book. "It is a tale spawned from the leprous literature of the French *Décadents*—a poisonous book, the atmosphere of which is heavy with the mephitic odours of moral and spiritual putrefaction—a gloating study of the mental and physical corruption of a fresh, fair and golden youth, which might be horrible and fascinating but for its effeminate frivolity, its studied insincerity, its theatrical cynicism, its tawdry mysticism, its flippant philosophisings, and the contaminating trail of garish vulgarity."

The *New York Times* Sunday correspondent reported how *Dorian Gray* "had monopolized the attention of Londoners who talk about books. It must have excited vastly more interest here than in America simply because [of] last year's exposure of what were euphemistically styled the West End scandals." Also called the Cleveland Street affair, the scandals were a series of trials involving sensational charges against high government officials for covering up a male brothel in Cleveland Street, which procured telegraph boys for wealthy and aristocratic clients. As the *Times* correspondent explained, "Englishmen have been abnormally sensitive to the faintest suggestion of pruriency in the direction of friendships. Very likely this bestial

The artist Majeska illustrated Horace Liveright's 1932 deluxe
edition of **The Picture of Dorian Gray.**

suspicion did not cross the mind of one American reader out of ten thousand, but the whole town here leaped at it with avidity."

For most of August 1890, Bram, Florence, and Noel vacationed in the picturesque fishing village of Whitby, North Yorkshire. Vacation may not be the best word to ever describe Bram's time away from the Lyceum, for as usual he was still preoccupied with work—his writing—and he spent uncounted hours taking notes from books at the local museum and subscription library. It is not inconceivable that Whitby was chosen for the holiday because Bram had already decided it might make an ideal location in his novel, the English port of entry for his still unnamed vampire menace; he had first chosen Dover, then wisely reconsidered. Whitby provided a more surreptitious route, and considerably more atmosphere. Stoker came alone to Whitby for the first week, and it was therefore likely that he did the bulk of his research and note taking then. Not far from the guesthouse was the storefront studio of a local photographer, Frank Sutcliffe, who sold prints and postcards of Whitby and environs. His sepia-toned views

The ruins of Whitby Abbey, photographed by Frank Sutcliffe in the 1880s.

of the abbey and the adjacent church and cemetery overlooking the sea were especially striking, but the Sutcliffe photo that commanded Stoker's attention depicted the dramatically beached wreck of the Russian schooner *Dmitry*, run ashore in Whitby on October 24, 1885. (Henry Irving was in rehearsals for *Faust* at the time.) His curiosity piqued, Stoker sought out and had a conversation with a Coast Guard boatman, William Petherick, who gave him details on various wrecks, including the *Dmitry*, and seems to have transcribed a complete account of the incident from official records and given it to Stoker. If the idea of Count Dracula arriving via a deliberate shipwreck, instead of merely by sea, had never occurred to him before, it did now. He only slightly disguised the name of his fictional vessel, the *Demeter.*

Whitby's harbor is situated at the mouth of the River Esk, which divides the town into two promontories, east and west. The Stokers stayed at an

Top: Stoker was fascinated with the wreck of the Russian schooner Dimitri *near Whitby in 1885. His name for the vampire-haunted ship in* Dracula *was the* Demeter. *Below: Max Schreck, the first screen Dracula, takes to the sea in F. W. Murnau's* Nosferatu *(1922).*

ideally located guest house at 6 West Crescent owned by a Mrs. Veazy, with
an excellent view of both the harbor and the east cliff dominated by the
imposing ruins of Whitby Abbey, founded in 1078 on the site of an original monastery dating to the year 657 and destroyed by Viking invaders in
the late ninth century. The ghost of its medieval abbess, Saint Hilda, was
believed to haunt its empty windows and is mentioned in passing by Mina
Harker in *Dracula*.

In addition to a location, Whitby afforded Stoker some of his most profitable research. It was his only known visit to the town, and he made the
most of it. At the Whitby Museum, he found a glossary of Whitby localisms, a
good number of which found their way into his finished book. The museum
building also held the Whitby Subscription Library, where he requested an
1820 volume by William Wilkinson, *An Account of the Principalities of Wallachia
and Moldavia: with Various Political Observations Related to Them*. In this book
Stoker momentously encountered the name "Dracula," the sobriquet given
to the Wallachian warlord Vlad Tepeş (1431–76), legendary for protecting
the region from Turkish invasion, and a folk hero in Romania to this day.
Stoker paraphrased Wilkinson in his notes and added emphatic capitaliza-
tion: "DRACULA in Wallachian language means DEVIL. Wallachians were
accustomed to give it as a surname to any person who rendered himself
conspicuous by courage, cruel action, or cunning."

Wilkinson erred slightly. "Dracula" in Romanian means "Son of the
Devil" or "Son of the Dragon"; Vlad's father was called "Dracul," which
means both "devil" and "dragon." There is no evidence Stoker was aware
of the warlord's reputation as Vlad the Impaler, so-called for his favorite
and extraordinarily sadistic method of dispatching enemies. On one particularly atrocious occasion, twenty thousand Turkish captives were exter-
minated in this manner and displayed in a mile-long semicircle outside
the capital city of Târgovşte. It is nothing but a gruesome coincidence that
stakes are also used to kill vampires. And there is no documentation that
Stoker ever came across a German pamphlet describing Dracula dining
beneath his writhing victims and dipping his bread in their blood. But,
since wooden stakes and blood were highly suggestive of vampires, enthusiastic modern scholars have repeatedly asserted that Stoker was far more
knowledgeable about Vlad than he actually was, even maintaining that the
historical Dracula was the primary inspiration for the fictional one. This is
patently untrue; Stoker's notes show that the book had taken considerable

AN

ACCOUNT

OF

THE PRINCIPALITIES

OF

WALLACHIA AND MOLDAVIA:

WITH

VARIOUS POLITICAL OBSERVATIONS

RELATING TO THEM.

By WILLIAM WILKINSO[N]

LATE BRITISH CONSUL RESIDENT A[T]

Dobbiamo considerare queste due provincie, Wa
guisa di due nave in un mar' tempestoso, dove-
tranquilita e la calma.   DELCHIARO—*Revo*

LONDON:

PRINTED FOR LONGMAN, HURST, REES, OR
PATERNOSTER-ROW.

1820.

WALLACHIA AND MOLDAVIA.   **19**

the Archipelago, afforded them a new opportunity of shaking off the yoke. Their Voïvode, also named Dracula *, did not remain satisfied with mere prudent measures of defence: with an army he crossed the Danube and attacked the few Turkish troops that were stationed in his neighbourhood; but this attempt, like those of his predecessors, was only attended with momentary success. Mahomet having turned his arms against him, drove him back to Wallachia, whither he pursued and defeated him. The Voïvode escaped into Hungary, and the Sultan caused his brother Bladus to be named in his place. He made a treaty with Bladus, by which he bound the Wallachians to perpetual tribute; and laid the foundations of that slavery, from which no efforts have yet had the power of extricating them with any lasting efficacy. The following is the substance of the treaty:—

* Dracula in the Wallachian language means Devil. The Wallachians were, at that time, as they are at present, used to give this as a surname to any person who rendered himself conspicuous either by courage, cruel actions, or cunning.

c 2

Bram Stoker discovered the name "Dracula" in this book, which he found at the Whitby Susbcription Library while on holiday. (John Moore Library) shape in his mind before he struck out his first idea for his monstrous villain's name—the all-too-obvious "Count Wampyr"—and replaced it with the three crackling, undulating syllables that would forever define the idea of vampirism in the public mind. Professor Van Helsing, enumerating historical documents, notes that "in one manuscript this very Dracula is spoken of as 'wampyr,' which we all understand too well." This is Stoker's invention; there has been found no manuscript or historical book in any language using the German word for "vampire" in connection with Vlad.

If Stoker hadn't taken *Lippincott's Magazine* with him to Whitby, he certainly carried the imprint of *Dorian Gray* in his mind. The firestorm of moral outrage at the book already threatened to make Stoker's concept of Dracula as an archetypal Gothic novel villain problematic at best. Dorian Gray's sins, never explicitly identified, paled before the lurid transgressions described in meticulous detail in Gothic novels like *The Monk* and *The Italian*. These villains, whose hawklike profiles and blazing eyes made them perfect physical templates for Dracula, were also unashamed sexual predators, their overt, libidinous behavior exceeding anything even hinted at by Wilde. Stoker's notes indicated Dracula's power to implant "immoral thoughts" in his victims, and this idea of moral pollution was precisely what critics objected to in *Dorian Gray*.

Stoker's first instinct may have been to increase his cast of characters, the better to distract the reader from thinking about matters that were increasingly unspeakable. And so an early page of notes headed "Dramatis Personae" contains a painter, Francis A. Aytown; a "Deaf Mute Woman" and "Silent Man," both servants to the Count; an unnamed "Texas inventor;" a detective named Cotford; a "Psychical Research Agent" named Alfred Singleton; and a "German Professor," Max Windshoeffel. These last three seem to have been merged later into one character, the vampire hunter Abraham Van Helsing. It is interesting indeed that Stoker named a discarded preliminary character "Adrian Singleton," more than slightly similar to Wilde's "Alfred Singleton." In *Dorian Gray* he is one of the title character's victims, a degraded denizen of a vice den. It is exactly the kind of place Hall Caine described disapprovingly in *Drink* and claimed to have personally visited—purely in the interest of research, of course. Perhaps Stoker accompanied him.

People have long sought a specific real-world model for Dracula, a part most frequently assigned to Henry Irving, but other candidates have been nominated, some of them less than convincingly. The elderly Franz Liszt visited the Lyceum, and he was a dramatic-looking old man who had composed "The Mephisto Waltz." (To paraphrase Tennessee Williams, sometimes there was Dracula—so quickly!) Slightly better nominees for Stoker's prototype have included the Greek-born French actor Jacques Damala, Sarah Bernhardt's husband at the time she was in London as Irving's guest in 1882. According to Stoker, the twenty-seven-year-old morphine addict "looked like a dead man. I sat next to him at supper and the idea that he was dead came strong on me. I think he had taken some mighty dose of opium, for he moved and spoke like a man in a dream. His eyes, staring out of his white waxen face, seemed hardly the eyes of the living."

In seven more years Damala would indeed be dead, from the effects of morphine mixed with cocaine. But that night in 1882 during which she entranced Stoker, the Divine Sarah herself might have been actively auditioning for the role of Lucy Westenra, or at least one of Dracula's Transylvanian brides. In Paris, she had just posed for a series of photographic souvenir postcards showing her sleeping in a coffin. The public had come to expect her dying onstage—her signature roles were tragic heroines, often suicides, including the likes of Phèdre, Cleopatra, Lady Macbeth, and Tosca. The coffin photograph was an inspired publicity ploy, trading on the popularity of Victorian postmortem photography, but also serving another ritual function. At thirty-eight she was precariously close to the dreaded "certain age" of forty. The coffin photo was Bernhardt's Dorian Gray portrait in reverse, allowing her to freeze her beauty, stage-manage her "funeral," and have her own last laugh on mortality .

The spectre of aging haunted Victorians almost as much as death. In *Aging by the Book: The Emergence of Midlife in Victorian Britain*, the historian Kay Heath notes, "The fin-de-siècle preoccupation with degeneration in individuals and the general population also increased age anxiety. Age itself could be considered definitive evidence of degeneration as the human body began to dissolve before one's eyes, a miniature version of the regression of the populace which was becoming feared." Bernhardt had been consumptive, or was thought to have been, in her teens. While she mysteriously outgrew her bloody cough, an aura of deathliness still clung to her, and she consciously cultivated it for public attention. A talented sculptress, Benrhardt modeled a bronze inkwell incorporating her own sphinxlike head flanked by bat wings. She was also said to have worn a stuffed bat as a fashion accessory.

While Bernhardt's eccentricities were morbid enough, her ghoulishness never prompted public objection, perhaps because the unhealthy sexual overtones weren't sufficiently pronounced. But on March 13, 1891, almost exactly a year after Stoker made his first notes for *Dracula*, London experienced its worst eruption of censorship hysteria since *Dorian Gray* when the first English performance of Henrik Ibsen's *Ghosts*, denied a public license by the Lord Chamberlain, was given a legal but private performance at the Royalty Theatre, Soho. The critic William Archer, recounting the event for the *Fortnightly Review*, recorded "a few of the choice epithets"

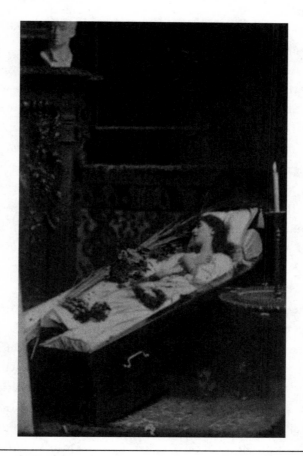

Sarah Bernhardt, in one of her celebrated coffin portraits,
sold as souvenir postcards to morbid admirers. Since so many of Bernhardt's
most famous roles were tragic, audiences expected to see her die onstage.

the press had hurled at the Norwegian play: "Abominable, disgusting, bestial, fetid, loathsome, putrid, crapulous, offensive, scandalous, repulsive, revolting, blasphemous, abhorrent, degrading, unwholesome, sordid, foul, filthy, malodorous, noisome. Several of the critics shouted for the police."

The story recounted the horrible choice faced by the long-suffering Mrs. Aveling, whose husband has finally died from his endless dissipations, when her grown son, Osvald, returns with the news that he has been diagnosed with a hereditary "softening of the brain"—that is, advanced syphilis. He pleads with his mother to take the life she has given by mercifully administering an overdose of morphine. The play ends with the mother's horrible choice hanging unresolved, forcing the audience to make a decision of its own. In *Dracula*, the mercy-killing theme is raised when Mina secures the promise from her protectors to take all appropriate steps if vampirism engulfs her.

The *Sporting and Dramatic News* claimed that "ninety-seven percent of the people who go to see *Ghosts* are nasty-minded people who find the discussion of nasty subjects to their taste, in exact proportion to their nastiness." The *Daily Telegraph* called *Ghosts* an "open drain," a "sore unbandaged," and "a dirty act done publicly." The periodical *Truth* decried the private audience as a pack of "muck-ferreting dogs" and seemed to have Oscar Wilde and other transgressive company in mind when they decried the (assumed) appeal of *Ghosts* to "effeminate men and male women," the "socialistic and the sexless," and, heaping on some gratuitous misogyny, "unwomanly women, the unsexed females, the whole army of unprepossessing cranks in petticoats. All of them—men and women alike—know that they are doing not only a nasty but an illegal thing."

Stoker needn't have seen the performance; just reading the reviews and letters to the editor may have prompted him to ask himself if it was really the right time to resurrect an archetypal Gothic villain, his moral outrages made all the worse by way of vampirism, and drop him down into a modern London, especially *this* modern London, where a reactionary moral crusade was taking hold. Apropos of *Ghosts*, *The Picture of Dorian Gray* reads today as an almost transparent syphilis parable, an interpretation first put forth by Wilde's preeminent biographer, Richard Ellman. Stoker may have dialed back a full elaboration of his vampire's sins, but *Dracula* would also contain a discernible allegory of syphilis as its characters, terrified of a blood-borne contagion, obsessively examine the skin for telltale lesions,

As depicted in the 1945 MGM film version,
Dorian's portrait was a perfect picture of syphilitic corruption.

with pseudoscientific cures like garlic wreaths and wolfbane sprigs in lieu of mercury treatments and "blood purifiers."

The first of two documented social encounters between the creators of Dorian Gray and Dracula, at least during the developmental stages of Stoker's book, took place in 1889. Wilde had written a note to Stoker: "My dear Bram—my wife is not very well and has gone to Brighton for ten days rest, but I will be very happy to come to supper on the 26th myself. Sincerely yours, Oscar Wilde." He had been accepting many social invitations on his own, and his wife's illness may have been, in part, a reaction to the stress of their leading increasingly separate lives. Since the birth of their sons, Constance Wilde had had to cope with an increasing parade of attractive young men at Tite Street, apparently blind to the extent of Oscar's involvement with them. One, Robbie Ross, is thought to have been his first extramarital male lover. (The idea, put forth in earlier biographies, that he was Oscar's first male lover, period, today seems rather quaint.) Robbie remained a close family friend to the very end. But Constance's denial was so deep she confided to a friend that she was struggling with feelings of jealousy for a woman she suspected might be her husband's mistress. And she doesn't seem to have suspected anything about another frequent visitor, Lord Alfred Douglas, the son of John Sholto Douglas, the Marquess of Queensberry. Pale, blond, and strikingly beautiful, Alfred—more familiarly known by his childhood nickname, "Bosie"—was a twenty-one -year-old Oxonian and a budding poet of some talent.

The supper to which Wilde had been invited by Stoker would have been held in the Lyceum's Beefsteak Room, one of its paneled walls then dominated by John Singer Sargent's life-sized canvas of Ellen Terry as Lady Macbeth. Some of Frank Miles's landscapes also hung there, even as the artist was dying in an asylum, very much in the same wretched manner described by Ibsen in *Ghosts*. Miles would finally succumb to brain syphilis in July 1891.

With the Banquo-like presence of the doomed artist hovering in the

Oscar Wilde and Lord Alfred Douglas.

air, what literary matters might have been discussed that night? The year of 1889 would culminate in Wilde's outpouring of *Dorian Gray*, and Stoker, no doubt, was at least beginning to mull over the possibilities of literary vampires. Irving had not yet given up the idea of resurrecting the living-dead Vanderdecken. If the conversation turned to such matters, Wilde's thoughts about vampirism would have been fascinating to know. He would have been quick to notice the inherent paradoxes of being simultaneously dead and alive, and could anyone have better encapsulated the transgressive erotics? The subject lends itself easily to an imagined, wickedly Wildean epigram: "The vampire's mouth—such an ambiguous orifice! So soft and sensual, yet so hard and penetrating . . ."

Stoker may well have been reading Wilde's poetry as well as *Dorian Gray* in preparation for *Dracula*. In his opening chapter, upon glimpsing the sharp-toothed coachman who meets Jonathan Harker at the Borgo Pass, a fellow traveler nervously whispers, "Denn die Todten reiten schnell," a slight misquote of a line from Gottfried Bürger's death-and-the-maiden ballad "Lenore" (1774), famously and accurately translated as "For the dead ride fast" by the American romantic poet James Russell Lowell in 1846. Though "Denn" does not appear in Bürger, Stoker translates the line as "For the dead travel fast," as if taking a cue from Wilde's poem "Fabien dei Franchi," dedicated in 1882 "To my friend Henry Irving" and named after one of the actor's dual roles in *The Corsican Brothers*: "The dead that travel fast, the opening door / The murdered brother rising through the floor." Stoker certainly knew Wilde's poem—it was too cloyingly flattering to Irving for anyone to forget. Because of the fame of *Dracula*, the line from Bürger's ballad is now almost always quoted in English the way Wilde and Stoker, and not James Russell Lowell, chose to present it.

The next time we can place Wilde and Stoker in the same room is three years later, at the West End debut of Oscar's *Lady Windermere's Fan*, his first theatrical success. The play is a sparking comedy of manners about a young wife confronting the possibility that her husband has been leading a double life. The presumed dalliance is ultimately revealed to be harmless, but the theme reflected Constance Wilde's anxieties about the state of her marriage that could not be explained away. Her husband would spend more and more time with Bosie, often in hotels, and later with lower-class rent boys, for whom Bosie had a special appreciation.

According to Wilde biographer Neil McKenna, "The audience on that memorable night of *Lady Windermere's Fan* constituted an emotional and sexual autobiography for Oscar. There were lovers past, present and even future seated in the auditorium." Bosie, along with Bram and Florence Stoker, and a host of celebrities, attended the premiere. Oscar had ordered a dozen or so carnations dyed a bright green and distributed them among selected friends. The actor Ben Webster, playing an epigram-spouting, Wilde-like bachelor named Cecil Graham, also sported a green flower in his lapel when he delivered such quips as "We're all in the gutter, but some of us are looking at the stars." In Paris, green carnations had replaced green cravats as signals between members of the homosexual demimonde, and Wilde had learned of the trend. He knew Londoners would talk, and they did, even if they didn't really know what they were talking about.

Following the curtain call, Wilde strolled languidly onstage, a cigarette dangling between what one critic described as his "daintily gloved" fingers, and the green carnation affixed to his lapel. "Ladies and gentlemen," he said, "I have enjoyed this evening *immensely*. The actors have given us a *charming* rendering of a *delightful* play, and your appreciation has been *most* intelligent. I congratulate you on the *great* success of your performance, which persuades me that you think *almost* as highly of the play as I do myself." Some were amused, but many others were revolted by what they regarded as an arrogant breach of decorum—especially smoking in front of the ladies. And that was the least of Wilde's gender transgressions that night, and in general. Everyone understood that those green flowers *meant* something . . . something that mocked and subverted traditional notions of masculinity.

We don't know what words Wilde exchanged with the Stokers that night, but we can assume he always thought of Stoker as something of a prig—the priggishness covering a submerged self Wilde could imagine all too well. It would have been so very easy, at the interval, while complimenting Florence on what a newspaper described as her "marvelous evening wrap of striped brocade," to discreetly slip a carnation into Bram's pocket to be discovered later. When he undressed.

It is difficult to understand how Stoker ever found time to write *Dracula*. In addition to Irving's London seasons and provincial tours, and a command performance of *Becket* for Queen Victoria at Windsor Castle, there were two more Lyceum tours to America, one in 1893–94 and another in 1895–96. Beyond theatre commitments was his continued involvement in Hall Caine's literary affairs, including preparing for publication and writing introductions for reprints of Caine's books. These were part of an ambitious enterprise headed by the publisher William Heinemann called the English Library, which invited established writers in England and America to distribute their work in continental Europe. Stoker was a partner in the imprint, along with publisher Wolcott Balestier and journalist W. L. Courtney. English Library authors included Rudyard Kipling, Arthur Conan Doyle, J. M. Barrie, and, at Stoker's personal invitation, Mark Twain, who later became a friend when he lived with his family in London.

A letter written by H. P. Lovecraft in 1932, and first noted by Raymond T. McNally and Radu Florescu in 1979, claimed that "Stoker was a very inept writer when not helped out by revisers. . . . I know an old lady who almost had the job of revising 'Dracula' back in the early 1890s—she saw the original ms. & says it was a fearful mess. Finally someone else (Stoker thought her price for the work was too high) whipped it into such shape as it now possesses." The explosive implications were not well received by Stoker aficionados, and the letter has routinely been dismissed as one of Lovecraft's strange imaginings; the writer's eccentricities have been exhaustively documented. However, Lovecraft told variants of the same story on at least three other occasions. As early as 1923, in a letter to writer Frank Belknap Long, he named the would-be book doctor as Edith Miniter. "Mrs. Miniter saw Dracula in manuscript about thirty years ago. It was incredibly slovenly. She considered the job of revision, but charged too much for Stoker." A letter to Donald Wandrei in 1927 offered more information, and gave another decidedly negative appraisal of Stoker as a writer:

Have you read anything of Stoker's aside from *Dracula?* . . . Stoker was absolutely devoid of a sense of form, and could not write a coherent tale to save his life. Everything of his went through the hands of a re-writer and it is curious to note that one of our circle of amateur journalists, an old lady named Mrs. Miniter, had a chance to revise the *Dracula* manuscript (which was a fiendish mess!) before its publication, but turned it down because Stoker refused to pay her the price which the difficulty of the work impelled her to charge. Stoker had a brilliant fantastic mind, but was unable to shape the images he created.

Finally, in a lengthy and heartfelt appreciation of Miniter written following her death in 1934, but not published until 1938, Lovecraft offered a different reason for her rejecting Stoker's offer. "Notwithstanding her saturation with the spectral lore of the countryside, Mrs. Miniter did not care for stories of a macabre or supernatural cast; regarding them as hopelessly extravagant and unrepresentative of life," Lovecraft wrote. "Perhaps that is one reason why, in the early Boston days, she had declined a chance to revise a manuscript of this sort which later met with much fame—the vampire novel *Dracula*, whose author was then touring America as manager for Sir Henry Irving."

Edith Dowe Miniter (1867–1934) was a New England journalist and amateur fiction writer who published one commercial novel, *Our Natupski Neighbors* (1916). The amateur press movement to which Miniter belonged emerged after the Civil War as a serious hobby for people interested in writing, editing, and letterpress printing. Its small-circulation newspapers and journals served as social hubs, often extending to regional and national conventions. H. P. Lovecraft became active in the movement in 1920, the year he met Miniter, and the spirit of amateur journalism went

Boston journalist Edith Miniter, who refused Stoker's offer to edit and revise **Dracula.**

on to significantly drive the growth of fantasy and science fiction fandom throughout the twentieth century.

If Stoker offered Mrs. Miniter the job of revising *Dracula*, how and when did he meet her? When Henry Irving's 1893–94 American tour reached Boston in January, Miniter had just joined the editorial staff of the *Boston Home Journal*, a lively arts and literary weekly. "Its Editorials are pungent and straightforward," a typical advertisement for advertisers enthused. "Its Society News tells your doings and those of your friends. Its Fiction is of the highest order. Its Dramatic Criticisms are scholarly and its Musical Melange is sparkling. It is as full of interest as an egg is of meat. There is no doubt of the value of an 'ad' in the Boston Home Journal."

The paper obviously had a good opinion of itself, and the promised editorial pungency came out in its reviews. The Lyceum was traveling with nine productions that season: *The Merchant of Venice, Olivia, Nance Oldfield, The Bells, Becket, Louis XI, Charles I, The Lyons Mail,* and *Henry VIII.* Early during the three-week engagement, the *Journal* showed it knew how to damn with faint praise. On the topic of Ellen Terry, an anonymous writer opined, "She is not a great actress in the sense of the word as usually applied to actresses of broad intellectual power and vivid passion—the Medeas and Lady Macbeths of the stage; she does not belong to their rank and fails to suggest even vaguely the scope and splendor of their geniuses. But with those who have seen her, she remains in the memory a dream of youth, beauty and sweetness." Like Philadelphia, Boston was known for tough, skeptical critics; this may be a reason Broadway producers chose both cities as the most useful out-of-town venues in advance of New York.[3]

Stoker was the company's press contact, and he also bought the advertising. One can imagine he had some diplomatic words to share with the *Journal* editors, especially after the paper's appraisal of *The Merchant of Venice* near the end of the Boston stay. Of Irving's portrayal of Shylock,

---

[3] The critic for the *Boston Evening Transcript,* in an otherwise positive assessment of Irving, seemed constitutionally incapable of resisting some lacerating digs: "Mr. Irving . . . held you fast from beginning to end; there was an indescribable element for greatness in his performance. *Indescribable* is the right word for it. Here is this wonderful man, chock full of mannerisms, and pretty ungainly mannerisms at that; at times hardly speaking what can rightly be called English; with scarcely any power of climax, reading his lines in a way that seems most cunningly devised to conceal their meaning; and yet, with and in spite of all this, producing an impression of force, dignity, and beauty such as one hardly imagined surpassed."

the reviewer did not mince words, calling the performance a "grotesque caricature."

> In representing, or attempting to represent, the racial characteristics of Shylock, Mr. Irving goes too far in a line that most actors do not go far enough in. Mr. Irving's Shylock is the kind of a Jew that in our day we would expect to see upon the streets with a tray hung about his neck whereon would be displayed suspenders, buttons, combs, and other small articles, to say nothing of shoe strings. He is the kind of Jew that one would find in the lowest dives of the North End, by no means the Jew who could bring forth a daughter who could win the sympathy that Jessica demands.

The last comment was presumably a crumb thrown to Terry, who played Shylock's daughter. But the attack on Irving continued with relish: "He is a dirty Jew, withal, one who deserves the contempt that is heaped upon him, not for his religion or belief, but for his own repulsiveness. . . . It is easy to see how Mr. Irving's Shylock would be spurned as a rodent, as an unclean thing." The reviewer also complained that Irving delivered the "Hath not a Jew" speech like "a second-hand clothing dealer disposing of a suit of clothes."

Although Stoker might well have objected to the review as an affront to Irving—according to almost all other accounts, Irving played the always-problematic role with great restraint and dignity—the degree to which he was offended by the reviewer's attitude toward Jews is a matter for debate. The great Gothic character then taking shape in Stoker's mind has, in recent years, been criticized as an anti-Semitic stereotype, and perhaps deservedly. The simple idea of a hook-nosed foreigner who steals babies for their blood, of course, comes straight out of the time-dishonored playbook of the blood libel, not to mention the recoiling from Christian symbols. Stoker drops some casual anti-Jewish sentiment into Jonathan Harker's journal entry of October 30, when it is discovered that a cargo receiver facilitating Dracula's escape back to Transylvania in his earth-box is one Immanuel Hildesheim, "a Hebrew of rather the Adelphi Theatre type, with a nose like a sheep, and a fez. His arguments were pointed with specie [money in coin]—we doing the punctuation—and with a little bargaining he told us what he knew."

Antisemitic Victorian architypes. Top: George du Maurier's "Filthy black Hebrew," Svengali.
Below: Henry Irving as Shylock.

Shylock was part villain but mostly victim. If Stoker needed a model for a thoroughly evil Jew, he needn't have looked any further than a book he would have known well since childhood. Charles Dickens's *Oliver Twist* (1838) introduced the repellent character Fagin, who preys on children by turning them into thieves, with nowhere to go outside of his protection. He doesn't abduct them in bags, but they are held hostage nonetheless, with the threat of a blood sacrifice hovering; when Oliver wakes after the first night in the thief's house, a suspicious Fagin almost immediately threatens him with a knife. That it is described by Dickens as a bread-knife only intensifies a subliminal connection to the ancient calumny about the blood of Christian children being used to prepare Passover bread.

But the question remains: was Stoker himself anti-Semitic or racist? Probably not beyond the norm for Victorian England, where a basic distrust of foreigners and ideas about racial purity and the great hovering bugaboo of "degeneration" were so fully ingrained into daily life that they were deployed almost unconsciously. His 1886 pamphlet *A Glimpse of America* makes no mention of slavery or the Civil War, the unresolved social issues of Reconstruction, or the impact of race on American culture and character. He mentions blacks only in the context of being well represented as domestic servants, with the men being subject to immediate lynching if they commit an outrage upon a white woman. The lynched men are grouped by Stoker with a category of "tramps, and other excretions of civilization." Near the end of his life, Stoker would turn again to the "American Tramp Question" and recommend the establishment of remote labor camps, as well as branding (or, as he put it, "marking the ear"). His final novel, *The Lair of the White Worm* (1911), would feature a frightening, subhuman manservant, Oolanga, whose fondness for wearing dress coats only underscores his apelike animality. The casual, recurrent use of the word "nigger" throughout the narrative is still a bit startling. Until the end of his life, Stoker's library contained a history of the Ku Klux Klan's first incarnation in the 1860s and 1870s.

It may have been in Boston, following the volley of undeserved critical abuse hurled at Irving, that he decided to write an essay on "Dramatic Criticism" and publish it in the *North American Review* while the American tour was still ongoing. He succeeded only in prompting the *New York Times* to spend more time in a Sunday column attacking Stoker than it

The ruins of St. John the Baptist Church, site of Bram Stoker's baptism, in Clontarf, Dublin. (*Photograph by the author*)

Anti-crown sentiment in Ireland caricatured as "The English Vampire" in the *Irish Pilot*, November 7, 1885.

Early twentieth-century postcard of the main entrance to Trinity College Dublin, unchanged since Stoker's student days of the 1860s.

Lady Jane Wilde, a.k.a. "Speranza," seen here in a crayon portrait by J. Morosini, circa 1870, was one of Stoker's Dublin mentors.

Oscar Wilde, son of Lady Jane and Sir William Wilde, matriculated at Trinity before moving on to Oxford. He would remain Stoker's lifelong, hovering acquaintance.

ctress Genevieve Ward, one of Stoker's
losest friends, from a painting by Hugh
3. Riviere.

op right: The best-selling Victorian
ovelist Hall Caine, to whom *Dracula* was
edicated, was Stoker's most intimate
riend. Right: The Hall Caine Memorial on
he Isle of Man. (*Photograph by the author*)

Left: Ellen Terry as Lady Macbeth, painted by John Singer Sargent (1889). Right: Henry Irving as Macbeth, painted by James Archer (1875). Below: Henry Irving as Mephistopheles in the Witches' Kitchen scene from *Faust* (1886), painted by William Henry Margetson.

The Lyceum Theatre interior as it appeared in the 1890s.

The Lyceum Theatre today. (*Photograph by the author*)

Whitby Abbey, North Yorkshire, a major inspiration and prominent location for *Dracula*, as captured in an 1890 mist by photographer Frank Sutcliffe.

Whitby Abbey today. (*Photograph by the author*)

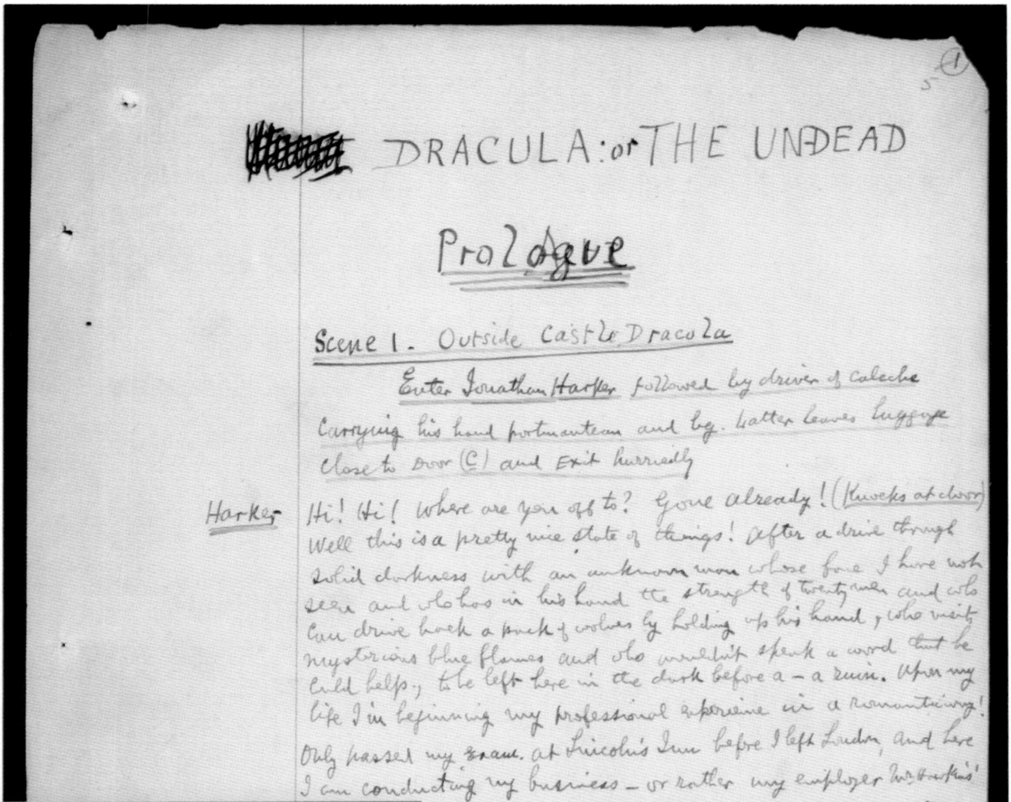

DRACULA: or THE UNDEAD

Prologue

Scene I. Outside Castle Dracula

Enter Jonathan Harker followed by driver of caleche carrying his hand portmanteau and bag. Latter leaves luggage close to door (C) and Exit hurriedly

Harker   Hi! Hi! Where are you off to? Gone already! (Knocks at door) Well this is a pretty nice state of things! After a drive through solid darkness with an unknown man whose face I have not seen and who has in his hand the strength of twenty men and who can drive back a pack of wolves by holding up his hand, who visits mysterious blue flames and who wouldn't speak a word but he cried help; to be left here in the dark before a – a ruin. Upon my life I'm beginning my professional experience in a romantic way! Only passed my exam. at Lincoln's Inn before I left London, and here I am conducting my business – or rather my employer Mr Hawkins' ...

Dracula's 1897 publication was preceded by a marathon reading at the Lyceum for purposes of theatrical copyright. Above: The opening page of Stoker's script at the British Library. Left: Poster for the staged reading.

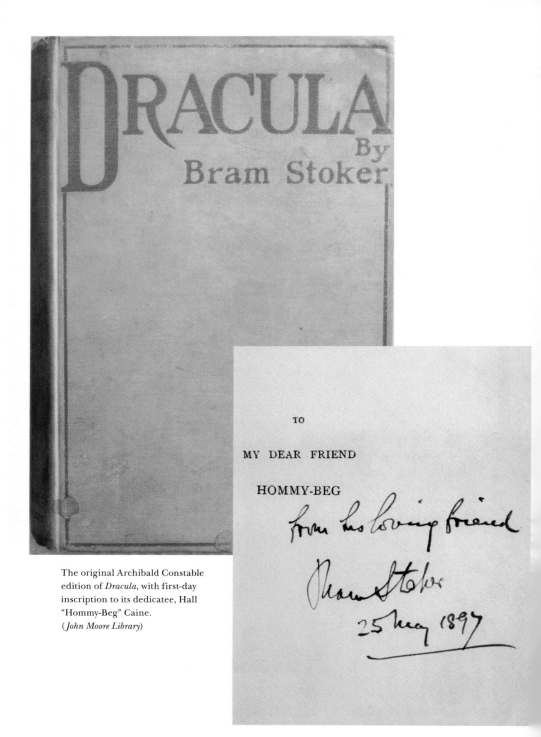

TO

MY DEAR FRIEND

HOMMY-BEG

from his loving friend

Bram Stoker

25 May 1897

The original Archibald Constable
edition of *Dracula*, with first-day
inscription to its dedicatee, Hall
"Hommy-Beg" Caine.
(*John Moore Library*)

Opposite: A representative sampling from *Dracula*'s publication history. Top row, left to right: First American edition,
Doubleday & McClure, 1899; second Doubleday edition, 1902; William Rider & Son (UK), 1912. Middle row: Grossett
& Dunlap, 1928: Modern Library, 1932; second Modern Library edition, 1940, cover design by Edward McKnight
Kauffer. Bottom row: Dell Books, 1965, illustration by Paul Davis; New American Library/Signet Classics, 1965;
Doubleday, 1975, illustration by Ben Feder. (*John Moore Library*)

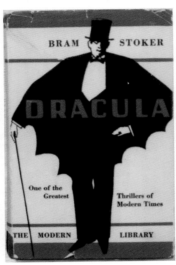

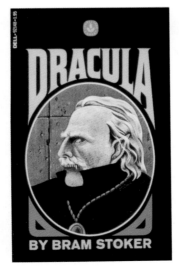

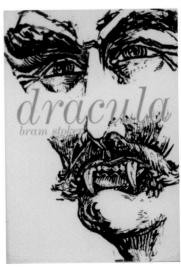

Pamela Coleman Smith, noted designer of the Waite tarot card deck, provided color illustrations for the first edition of *The Lair of the White Worm* (1911). Right: Lady Arabella March goes into her snake dance. Below: Stoker's fondness for hawk-faced villains reached a new high in the shadow-visage of Edgar Caswall. (*John Moore Library*)

Actress Amanda Donohoe, as Lady Sylvia Marsh, slithered her way through *The Lair of the White Worm*'s over-the-top 1988 screen adaptation by director Ken Russell. (*Vestron Picture*)

A pair of piracies. F. W. Murnau's classic of German Expressionism, *Nosferatu* (1922), blatantly plagiarized *Dracula* and set off an international legal battle with Stoker's widow, who succeeded in having the film removed from general circulation. (*Courtesy of Ronald V. Borst/Hollywood Movie Posters*) At right: The pirated 1926 Hungarian translation could not be legally challenged; Hungary had not yet joined the Berne Copyright Convention.

Above: Raymond Huntley, the original stage Dracula in London's West End, reprised the role on tour in America for producer Horace Liveright.

Above right: The original London program for *Dracula* at the Little Theatre (1927).

Right: Artist Vernon Short's startling poster for Horace Liveright's Broadway production of *Dracula* in 1927 and his touring productions from 1928 to 1930.

"Better Than 'The Bat'"
N.Y. HERALD-TRIBUNE

DRACULA

THE WORLD FAMOUS
VAMPIRE THRILLER

The most iconic *Dracula* film adaptation was the 1931 classic produced by Universal Pictures, starring Bela Lugosi and directed by Tod Browning. A simultaneously produced Spanish-language version (below) was equally successful in Mexico, Central and South America, and Spain.

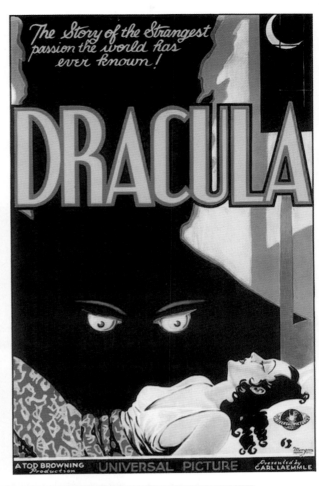

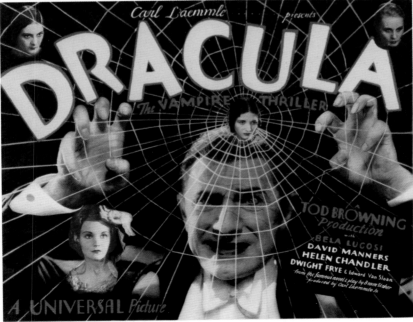

Dracula's Daughter (1936), also produced by Universal, demonstrated the coded manner in which sexual minorities were sometimes depicted under the restrictions of the Production Code.

"Bosie with fangs": David Peel's undead baron in Hammer Films' The Brides of Dracula (1960) had serious mother issues along with his unnatural appetite.

The BBC television miniseries Count Dracula (1977) starred Louis Jourdan in what remains the most faithful adaptation of Stoker's novel.

Three of the most iconic post-Lugosi screen Draculas: top, Christopher Lee in Hammer Films' *Dracula* (1958; US title, *Horror of Dracula*); center, Frank Langella in Universal's 1979 remake; bottom, Gary Oldman in Columbia Pictures' *Bram Stoker's Dracula* (1992), directed by Francis Ford Coppola.

Top: Bram Stoker's burial urn, Golders Green Crematorium, London. (*Copyright © Brian J. Showers*) Bottom: Bust of Bram Stoker by artist Beatrice Stewart, displayed at a public memorial service marking the centenary of his death, at St. Ann's Church, Dublin, 2012. (*Photograph by the author*)

did covering the appearance of Irving and Terry. The piece is remarkably vicious and personal.

> Who said anything about dramatic criticism? Who asked Bram Stoker to write anything about it? Of course, everybody knows Bram Stoker's name, for it has been in print before, and it is a name one never forgets, like Dodge Orlick or Quentin Durward. But few persons in this country have ever associated the name with a clearly-defined personality. If any of the John Smiths or William Browns of the American public, who read the North American Review to learn what public characters do not know about the questions of the hour, have thought of Bram Stoker at all, they have merely thought it was odd that any contemporary human being should be so named, and, being so named, should not ask legislative permission to change his name.

The *Times* conceded that "he is a gentlemen amply qualified to inform the world on some important subjects, such as the difficulty of keeping one's temper when selling theatre tickets through a peephole to ungrateful and inquisitive people, and the quickest way to stick up a four-sheet poster on a windy day." The writer predicted that "sometime in the twentieth century—I trust well along in that century—Mr. Bram Stoker will be of much interest to the biographers of Henry Irving. They will go to him for facts about the distinguished gentleman who employed him, as to his clothes and his food and his dependence on the advice of Bram Stoker." As to Stoker's perceived general grievance against drama critics on both sides of the Atlantic, the *Times* speculated that "perhaps they have too frequently neglected to mention in their notices that during the performance the money at the box office was counted, with his accustomed skill, by Mr. Bram Stoker, who also, after the play, and with great delicacy of touch, filled his hand-wash basin and laid out the towels for Mr. Irving to remove his 'make-up.'"

In his essay, Stoker had quoted an anonymous British critic who wondered if actors should be considered parasites, since they lived off plays, playwrights, and producers. The *Times* jumped at the chance for a delicious, gratuitous coup de grace: "We can imagine what such a critic, who holds an actor to be a parasite, would call an actor's business agent. He might even be rude."

The anonymous *Times* writer wanted to land a punch, and succeeded. The column was both a merciless caricature of Stoker as Irving's fawning factotum and a direct attack on his abilities as a writer. He had, of course, seen Irving endlessly assailed and ridiculed, but he was not at all accustomed to being on the receiving end himself. It's hard to imagine Stoker having knowingly snubbed or otherwise displeased anyone at New York's leading newspaper, but someone in the employ of the Gray Lady had obviously been offended somehow, and expressed his umbrage in the most humiliating way possible. The attack was so personal that it pricks curiosity about the nature of Stoker's friendships (and possible intimacies) in America, which almost by necessity would have overlapped with his theatrical responsibilities, and perhaps compromised or complicated them.

For Stoker, the winter of 1894 was not a happy season. Aside from a personal but very public slap in the face from the *New York Times*, the vampire novel was tied in knots he would have to untangle himself, and his summer holiday would be devoted to yet another book, *The Watter's Mou'*, set in Cruden Bay, Scotland, which he had visited for the first time the previous year. As a fallback, he dusted off a short historical novel, *Seven Golden Buttons*, which he had finished in 1891 but never submitted for editorial consideration. After returning to London he offered it to the Bristol publishing house J. W. Arrowsmith, but it was rejected.

As for the vampire book, it is not known whether Edith Miniter gave him any kind of detailed critique, but from his notes we can surmise the manuscript was likely a now-lost first draft titled either *The Dead Un-dead* or *The Un-Dead*. "Undead" was an existing word, derived from the Middle English *undedlic* but having no supernatural connotation; it was merely a roundabout locution for being alive, that is, "not dead." Stoker's hyphenated coinage was the first known use of the term in its now-familiar revenant sense. He must have had the work-in-progress already transcribed by a typing service, in manifold (a precursor to the carbon paper process), since it is inconceivable he would leave the only copy of a handwritten draft in America, even if Miniter had accepted the book-doctoring assignment. And it's a fair assumption the "fearful mess" of the manuscript resulted from what is apparent in Stoker's notes: far too many characters with overlapping identities and functions, and a surfeit of subplots. It was the most complicated and ambitious piece of fiction he had ever attempted, but his ambition simply outpaced his technical ability to manage and channel his own imagination.

In order to conceptualize (or at least roughly imagine) what the manuscript that ultimately became *Dracula* might have looked like in early 1894, it is useful to flash forward six years to Reykjavik, Iceland, when a novel called *Makt Myrkranna* (or *Powers of Darkness*) was published under Stoker's name as a magazine serial in 1900 and as a book in 1901, an apparent translation of *Dracula*. The translator was Valdimar Ásmundsson, a well-regarded Icelandic journalist and author, but with no other known connection to supernatural fiction. Since the rest of the book was far shorter than the 1897 Archibald Constable edition, it had until recently been assumed that the novel had been abridged. A previously unknown introduction to the book, signed by Stoker, caused stirs in *Dracula* circles when it was retranslated into English in 1986, largely because it made a tangential reference to the Jack the Ripper murders, sparking overheated speculation about a substantial, inspirational link to the Whitechapel crimes and perhaps even clues to the killer's identity.

In 2014, the Munich-based Stoker scholar Hans C. de Roos revealed that *Makt Myrkranna* was in fact a radically different telling of *Dracula*, 80 percent of its action taking place during Harker's visit to Transylvania. Dracula is "the leader and financier of an international elitist conspiracy," according to Roos, who, at the time of this writing, is preparing a full English version of the Icelandic text. Ásmundsson, whose other writings covered both socialism and anarchism, "puts the fiend in the corner of reactionary social-Darwinist forces as the arch-enemy of egalitarianism, at the same time linking him to vile murder, sexual libertinage, incestuous degeneration and satanic cult: at Castle Dracula, Harker sees the Count leading a kind of black mass." Once Dracula is in England, his home is not a ruin but a splendidly appointed showplace where the Count (under the adopted name of Baron Székély) entertains a band of glamorous and aristocratic co-conspirators who have enabled his relocation from Transylvania.

Could such a strange, truncated and bastardized version of *Dracula* have actually been approved by Stoker? Roos seems to think so, but there are other factors and possibilities that need consideration. To begin with, why was this text created in Iceland? Stoker had no known contacts or correspondents there. But Hall Caine did. He knew the country extremely well and had friends there, and it provided a major setting for his novel *The Bondman* (1890). As Stoker wrote in his 1895 introduction to the book's reissue as part of Caine's collected works, "Iceland and the Isle of Man are so closely linked by far-back associations, that one cannot deeply study the history of one without being somewhat fascinated by the other." In *The Essential Dracula*, Raymond McNally and Radu Florescu first floated the possibility that Caine himself might have been the "someone else" whom H. P. Lovecraft mentioned as having "whipped [*Dracula*] into such shape as it now possesses." Given the extent of Caine's own publishing commitments between 1894 and 1897, this is highly unlikely. But Caine could have given Stoker advice, or recommended another writer to help revise the book. A writer, perhaps, who lived in Iceland.

While no correspondence between Caine and Ásmundsson has yet surfaced, a surprisingly large percentage of Caine's papers has yet to be sorted or cataloged, and may yet yield surprises about the Icelandic connection to *Dracula*. Nonetheless, we can be confident that Ásmundsson somehow had access to an early version of the manuscript. The evidence is contained in Stoker's preliminary notes. The Icelandic book contains a character named Barrington, who does not appear in the finished novel, but does appear in the notes. Likewise, a deaf-mute housekeeper, and a dinner party at which Dracula is the final guest to arrive. None of these elements were available to Ásmundsson via the published version of Stoker's novel. The retranslated version of the Icelandic introduction reads suspiciously like Stoker's bloated, overstrained first draft of the terse prefatory note that effectively opens the book as we know it today.[4]

---

[4]Following is the full author's preface to *Makt Myrkranna*, retranslated into English, as it first appeared in *A Bram Stoker Omnibus*, edited by Richard Dalby (London: Foulsham, 1986):

> The reader of this story will very soon understand how the events outlined in these pages have been gradually drawn together to make a logical whole. Apart from excising minor details which I considered unnecessary, I have let the people involved relate their experiences in their own way; but, for obvious reasons, I have changed the names of the people and places concerned. In all other respects I leave the manuscript unaltered, in deference to the wishes of those who have considered it their duty to present it before the eyes of the public.
>
> I am quite convinced that there is no doubt whatever that the events here transcribed really took place, however unbelievable and incomprehensible they might appear at first sight. And I am further convinced that they must always remain to some extent incomprehensible, although continuing research in psychology and natural sciences may, in years to come, give logical explanations of such strange happenings, which, at present, neither scientists nor the secret police can understand. I state again that this mysterious tragedy which is here described is completely true in all its external respects, though naturally I have reached a different conclusion on certain points than those involved in the story. But the events are

Is it possible that Ásmundsson, on Caine's recommendation, took on the formidable job of revising *The Un-Dead*? And that *Makt Myrkranna* was the bizarre, off-the-rails, and ultimately rejected result? Even without Stoker's early draft for comparison, this makes far more sense than the idea that Stoker actually approved the Icelandic adaptation—which, at least according to Roos's synopsis, reads like a piece of unauthorized fan fiction, with scant regard to the original author's vision. But no regard or respect was needed. Iceland had not yet joined the Berne Copyright Convention. Neither Ásmundsson nor his publishers needed to seek permission from Stoker or any other foreign national for publication. Their works could be pirated with impunity. Indeed, the initial installment of the serialization

---

incontrovertible, and so many people know of them that they cannot be denied. This series of crimes has not yet passed from the memory—a series of crimes which appear to have originated from the same source, and which at the same time created as much repugnance in people everywhere as the notorious murders of Jack the Ripper, which came into the story a little later. Various people's minds will go back to the remarkable group of foreigners who for many seasons together played a dazzling part in the life of the aristocracy here in London; and some will remember that one of them disappeared suddenly without apparent reason, leaving no trace. All the people who have willingly—or unwillingly—played a part in this remarkable story are generally known and well respected. Both Jonathan Harker and his wife (who is a woman of character) and Dr. Seward are my friends and have been so for many years, and I have never doubted that they were telling the truth; and the highly respected scientist, who appears here under a pseudonym, who will also be too famous all over the educated world for his real name, which I have not desired to specify, to be hidden from people—least of all those who have from experience learnt to value and respect his genius and accomplishments, though they adhere to his views on life no more than I. But in our times it ought to be clear to all serious-thinking men that

"there are more things in heaven and earth
than are dreamt of in your philosophy"

London, —— Street,
August 1898

B.S.

By contrast, Stoker's opening note in *Dracula* is a model of simplicity, a matter-of-fact statement that accomplishes much more than the Icelandic preface, simply by doing less: "How these papers have been placed in sequence will be made manifest in the reading of them. All needless matters have been eliminated so that a history almost at variance with the possibilities of latter-day belief may stand forth as simple fact. There is throughout no statement of past things wherein memory may err, for all the records chosen are exactly contemporary, given from the standpoints and within the range of knowledge of those who made them."

in the January 13, 1900, weekly magazine *Fjallkonan* contains no notice of copyright, describing the work only as "Novel. After Bram Stoker."

Without the literary equivalent of a major international archaeological dig—funded, exactly, by whom?—the truth may never be known. But there can be no doubt that Ásmundsson had access to some of the earliest notes or drafts of Stoker's book, upon which he constructed a uniquely curious fantasia. The fact that *Makt Myrkranna* gives so much play to the Transylvania chapters may indicate that Harker's visit to Transylvania was the most coherent section of the lost draft, and that Stoker may have had as much trouble getting out of Castle Dracula as a writer as Jonathan Harker did as a character.

Victorian writers were bedeviled by literary piracy, which they rightly considered parasitism—a charged word with many other associations apart from intellectual property theft. In the hierarchy of social Darwinism, the poor, foreigners, the weak, and the infirm were all perceived as sapping power and money from the middle and upper classes. For nervous men, women's growing independence was experienced as a kind of sexual energy siphon. Arthur Conan Doyle's novella *The Parasite* (1894) presented a psychic female vampire: a self-employed, self-possessed, and sexually self-directed occultist who used her powers to seduce and destroy.

Parasitism was also a concern of degeneration theory. In *Dracula*, Stoker drops the names of two leading degenerationists, the Italian criminologist Cesare Lombroso (1835–1909), author of *Criminal Man* (1876), and the German cultural critic Max Nordau (1849–1923), author of *Degeneration* (1892–93; English translation 1895). Lombroso would have interested Stoker because of his own long-standing interest in phrenology and physiognomy, but Lombroso's direct influence on *Dracula* has been consistently exaggerated. *Criminal Man* put forth Lombroso's taxonomy of the physical characteristics of people he claimed were "born criminals," and these characteristics, or so it is said, formed the basis of Stoker's description of Dracula. In fact, Stoker's vampire bears little resemblance to any of Lombroso's examples, save for his claim that murderers tended to have hawklike noses, a trait already supplied for Dracula's villainous precursors in fiction, and that the eyebrows above such noses grew together (as did those of the evil Ambrosio in Lewis's *The Monk* and the werewolf as described by Baring-Gould). Lombroso also mentions, almost in passing, that a small protuberance atop the criminal ear is the vestige of an animal's pointed ear. Dracula, of course, has fully pointed ears—something Stoker had seen on imaginary beings since childhood, when he first beheld the costumes for beloved pantomime characters like the Wolf, Puss in Boots, and Dick Whittington's Cat. The goat god Pan and the satyr in general were common subjects of nineteenth-century academic painting, reflecting a general cultural delirium about reverse evolution and animal tendencies in humans. Lombroso's criminal types lacked mythic resonance; they had jug ears, asymmetrical features, prognathous jaws, and receding brows with small craniums—quite unlike Dracula's "lofty domed forehead," clearly intended by Stoker to signify superior intelligence and cunning. We can safely conclude that Stoker invoked Lombroso merely as a contemporary, authoritative reference to bolster verisimilitude, however pseudoscientific. Stoker's description of Dracula's face ultimately owed much more to Baring-Gould and to his own imagination than to Lombroso.

Nordau's *Degeneration*, though formally dedicated to Lombroso, was more concerned with finding evidence of mental and moral decay in cultural productions, not in somatotypes. There was almost nothing in fin-de-siècle arts and letters that met with Nordau's approval. Pre-Raphaelitism, aestheticism, symbolism, realism, naturalism, mysticism, and everything from the philosophy of Nietzsche to the theatre of Ibsen—for Nordau, all were clear signs of creeping hysteria and insanity, both in their creators and in the public that accepted them. Nordau actually believed that both visual art and the written word had the power to reverse human evolution. "When under any kind of noxious influences an organism becomes debilitated," he wrote, "its successors will not resemble the healthy, normal type of the species, with capacities for development, but will form a new sub-species." Degeneration was a contagious disease, even if Nordau could identify no particular agent of contagion. His book was basically a scream against the miasma of modernism in all its forms. In literature, among many other things, Nordau objected to exactly the kind of "rationalized" horror fiction Stoker was writing. According to Nordau, "Ghost stories are very popular, but they must come on in scientific disguise, as hypnotism, telepathy, somnambulism." Stoker was using precisely these elements, widely accepted as scientific in the 1890s, to give his novel-in-progress credibility.

It should not be surprising that Nordau also had a specific distaste for Oscar Wilde.

"Where, if not from the Impressionists, do we get these wonderful brown fogs that come creeping down our streets, blurring the gas-lamps and changing the houses into monstrous shadows?" Wilde had written. "The extraordinary change that has taken place in the climate of London during the last ten years is entirely due to this particular school of Art." Nordau was appalled, and completely insensate to Wilde's humor. "He asserts that painters have changed the climate," he sputtered. Nordau felt that Wilde's degeneracy rose from "a malevolent mania for contradiction" and a "purely anti-socialistic, ego-maniacal recklessness and hysterical longing to make a sensation."

Wilde, of course, reveled in public attention, all the more so with the increasing success of his drawing-room comedies: *Lady Windermere's Fan* (1893), *A Woman of No Importance* (1894), and *An Ideal Husband* and *The Importance of Being Earnest* (both 1895.) But his private life was increasingly disordered and indiscreet. He was seen everywhere dining extravagantly with Bosie, while privately he endured torrents of Douglas's rage and emotional abuse—which he always forgave, like a clueless battered spouse.[5] Other companions lacked Bosie's pedigree, comprising a shifting entourage of scruffy young men whose most valuable assets, no doubt, included the endless supply of engraved silver cigarette cases Oscar had given them.

Unlike Stoker, Wilde had never been a college athlete, but from his early years there remain descriptions of a powerful, imposing physique. However, by the early nineties, after more than a decade of gastronomic indulgence and dissipation, he had morphed into a corpulent caricature of himself, subject to the kind of merciless lampooning his mother had endured in Dublin. There can be no doubt that his physical presence caused many people to shudder. The American novelist Gertrude Atherton, in London during the early nineties, turned down the chance to meet him solely on the basis of her visceral reaction to a photographic portrait— the very daguerreotype of Dorian Gray, at least in Atherton's description. "His mouth covered half his face," she recalled, "the most lascivious coarse repulsive mouth I have ever seen. I might stand it in a large drawing room,

---

[5] John George Littlechild, the Scotland Yard chief inspector who strongly suspected that Francis Tumblety was Jack the Ripper, made the following unrelated but intriguing statement about Wilde's masochistic streak: "It is very strange how those given to 'Contrary sexual instinct' and 'degeneration' are given to cruelty, even Wilde liked to be punched about."

HOW FAR IS IT FROM

THIS

TO

THIS?

A **Washington Post** *caricature of Wilde as the Missing Link.*

but not in a parlor eight-by-eight lit by three tallow candles. I should feel as if I were under the sea pursued by some bloated sea monster of the deep, and have nightmares for a week thereafter."

For all his intellectual brilliance, Wilde set off atavistic, Darwinian anxieties in his detractors, as well as in his partisans. Again and again he was described as pale and bloodless, a kind of fleshy, engulfing amoeba. Even his admirer Richard Le Gallienne admitted to a "queer feeling of distaste, as my hand seemed literally to sink into his, which was soft and plushy." "The face was clean-shaven, and almost leaden-coloured," recalled Horace Wyndham in *The Nineteen Hundreds*, "with heavy pouches under the eyes, and thick blubbery lips. Indeed he rather resembled a fat white slug, and even to my untutored eye, there was something curiously repulsive and unhealthy in his whole appearance." Alice Kipling, Rudyard's sister, quickly detected signs of invertebrate life: "He is like a very bad copy of a bust of a very decadent Roman Emperor, roughly modeled in suet pudding. I sat opposite him and could not make out what his lips reminded me of—they are exactly like the big brown slugs we used to hate so in the garden." Whistler once caricatured Wilde as a pig. As early as his 1882 American tour, the *Washington Post* had depicted him outright as an evolutionary throwback, "the Wilde Man of Borneo," foreshadowing ridicule to come. And capitalizing on the Wildean fondness for the sunflower as an aesthetic prop, many graphic satirists chose to go even further, casting Wilde lower than the animal realm as a human sunflower—a droopy, half-vegetable monstrosity.

As Irishmen in London, Stoker and Wilde were keenly aware of the pernicious and deeply ingrained stereotype of the Irish as brutish, drunken, and subhuman. The shiftless stage Irishman was already a sturdy convention of comedy. It was a caricature often deepened and darkened elsewhere, as in the pages of *Punch* by artists like Sir John Tenniel ("the Irish Frankenstein," looking more like a simian Mr. Hyde). The magazine once featured a "satirical" piece called "The Missing Link," informing readers that "a creature manifestly between the Gorilla and the Negro is to be met in some of the lowest districts of London." The Hibernian ape stereotype originated before Darwin but quickly drew additional noxious energy from evolutionary theory. Following a visit to Ireland in 1860, the Cambridge historian Charles Kingsley wrote to his wife, "I am haunted by the human chimpanzees I saw along the hundred miles of horrible country." The Famine years had stoked intolerance as well; if the Irish seemed animalized by hunger, it was because they were animals to begin with.

In the face of British power and intolerance, Wilde's mother had always asserted her Irish identity. Oscar, by contrast, ingratiated himself with the enemy, shedding his Irish accent at Magdalen College and arriving in London with a comprehensive plan for social climbing. Lady Wilde's surrogate son Bram Stoker made no such move toward assimilation and retained his rich and musical brogue for life. Unlike his own parents, he supported home rule. Perhaps part of the reason for the *New York Times*'s personal attack on him was unvarnished antipathy for his nationality. Like their counterparts in London, many New Yorkers in the 1890s reacted to Irish immigrants with a visceral revulsion.

Stoker, of course, never sought the spotlight like Lady Wilde's real son. Through Henry Irving and his rabid detractors, he became well acquainted

with the dark and vicious flip side of public acclaim. Even as Wilde's sparkling plays earned plaudits and applause, the public sensed his shadow
side the way sharks smell blood. Wilde was a constant topic of increasingly
nasty gossip, fueled in no small part by a scandalous roman à clef by Robert
Hichens, *The Green Carnation*, published anonymously in 1894. Hichens
had slyly penetrated Wilde's circle the year before and observed Oscar and
Bosie at close quarters; in the book he gave them the fictional names of
Esmé Amarinth and Lord Reginald (Reggie) Hastings. In a scene parody-
ing the dyed-boutonniere opening night of *Lady Windermere's Fan*, a young
lady, recently arrived in London, notices the green flowers and comments
that "all the men who wore them looked the same. They had the same
walk, or rather waggle, the same coyly conscious expression, the same wavy
motion of the head. . . . Is it a badge of some club or society, and is Mr.
Amarinth their high priest?" The *Saturday Review* was not so naïve as the
naïf and duly made note of the novel's "allusions, thinly veiled, to various
disgusting sins."

Lord Alfred Douglas's father had introduced the Queensberry rules
of boxing, but the marquess had a personality sufficiently pugnacious to
ignore any rules of engagement he didn't care for. Especially when he felt
certain his opponents were guilty of disgusting sins. To the marquess, paranoia came easily; the Douglas clan had a history of psychological instability.
By the early 1890s Queensberry was thought by some—perhaps especially
those who were scandalized by *Ghosts*—to be yet another sad victim of
long-simmering syphilis. It was not an outlandish idea. He was obsessed to
the point of derangement with the idea that the soon-to-be prime minister
(Archibald Primrose, the 5th Earl of Rosebery) was having an affair with
his eldest son, Francis, who served as Rosebery's personal secretary. Francis
Douglas died in an 1894 "hunting accident" that many suspected was a suicide but has never been proven as such. Queensberry threatened to thrash
Rosebery in public and even carried a riding crop to be on the ready.

It's quite possible that Queensberry's animus toward Rosebery was
deflected by the Crown's willingness to offer up an alternate, sacrificial
scapegoat. Bosie's father abruptly shifted his fixation from Rosebery to
Wilde. He would later claim that Wilde fell into the "booby trap" intentionally set for him. The first step involved goading Wilde into a foolish move. On February 18, 1895, at the Albemarle Club, where both he
and Wilde were members, Queensberry left his card scrawled with the

now-infamous if barely legible and badly spelled missive, "For Oscar Wilde posing Somdomite." Wilde rashly responded by charging Queensberry with criminal libel, a move he was advised against by everybody except Bosie and his family, who absolutely loathed their patriarch. They intimated they would even pay for Wilde's court costs, which (of course) they never did. Bosie hated his father and invoked vampiric metaphor when he called Queensberry "an incubus" who had abused and tormented him all his life. Despite their prestigious educations at Oxford, neither Bosie nor Oscar comprehended the nature or possible ramifications of the legal action. Bosie was excited that all his father's defects of character would be exposed, humiliating him before the world. Oscar somehow never considered that Queensberry was fully entitled to a defense of justification and already had a team of investigators tracking down, coercing, and even bribing witnesses who could testify that Queensberry's calling card had been no libel. "Blindly I staggered," he later wrote, "as an ox into the shambles."

To the degree he did think through his testimony, Wilde expected to charm the courtroom with witty ripostes and the natural superiority of an acclaimed apostle of art over an uncouth if wealthy Philistine. But from the start, it was clear that the plaintiff was doomed to be the defendant. The tables turned abruptly and alarmingly on the first day of the trial, catching Wilde off guard. He had never anticipated being forced to answer questions, as pointed as they were endless, about a long string of relationships with questionable young men, and certainly didn't plan to commit perjury, as he did repeatedly in a futile attempt to portray his compulsive sexual slumming as platonic mentoring. And he could hardly be the only literary man in London taken aback when *The Picture of Dorian Gray* was hauled into court and used against the author. Never before or since has a work of fiction—supernatural or not—been presented as evidence in a nonliterary criminal proceeding. There was a ghostly surreality to the notion that imaginary characters, having no substance beyond the words and ink with which they were constructed, might be called to testify about events in the real world. The idea itself was the stuff of a weird tale.

Queensberry's defense, and soon to be Wilde's archnemesis, was Edward Carson, a Dublin contemporary of both Wilde and Stoker active in the Trinity College debating societies. Carson called *Dorian Gray* an "immoral and obscene work" that was "designed and intended by Mr. Wilde, and was understood by the readers thereof, to describe the relations, intimacies and passions of certain persons of sodomitical and unnatural habits, tastes and practices." There was, of course, nothing explicitly sexual in the story. "Each man sees his own sin in Dorian Gray," Wilde had written to a newspaper. "What Dorian Gray's sins are no one knows. He who finds them has brought them." But in front of a jury, the argument fell short. Wilde denied that the book was in any way obscene; he contended that it was, in fact, a morality tale. This was true. But it was also true that the author had pressed a multitude of invisible green carnations between its pages, and had described a particular demimonde with great precision.

Queensberry's plea of justification ultimately prevailed, and the jury found for the defense. And now the Crown had amassed all the evidence it needed to prosecute Wilde criminally. Among the few people who urged Wilde *not* to immediately flee England was his own mother. Lady Wilde's nationalist pride overtook her common sense; somehow this was all about the Crown attacking Ireland, and she was Speranza again, rejuvenated like the painting in her son's book, or at least in her own mind. She was now in her seventies and barely subsisting on a civil list pension. Willie's marriage to the wealthy American heiress Mrs. Frank Leslie had collapsed under the weight of his drinking, adultery, and indolence, and with the divorce came the end of desperately needed income. Mother and son and his new wife, Lily, now lived together in a small rented house in Oakley Street, a few blocks from Oscar, who paid many of her bills but never arranged for an allowance, despite his spending lavishly on Bosie—something he estimated at £5,000 over the course of their relationship, including the payment of his gambling debts. Bosie was rich and didn't need Oscar's money. He expected it anyway. "I see little of him," Speranza sadly told a visitor of her son not long before the Queensberry affair. "He is so very busy. He is always working, and the world will not let him alone. No one in London is so sought after as Oscar." She had no idea at the time of how frightfully he was about to be pursued.

Lady Wilde's grandson Vyvyan remembered her as "a terrifying and severe old lady seated bolt upright in semi-darkness," even as the sun beamed brightly outside. "She was dressed like a tragedy queen, her bodice covered with brooches and cameos. The curtains all through the house remained permanently drawn, and the drawing-room was lit by guttering candles arranged in the corners of the room, as far away from my grandmother as possible, so that the heavy make-up with which she tried to

The last known photograph of Lady Wilde—a "terrifying old lady," according to her grandson.

conceal her age could not be detected. I protested strongly every time I was taken to pay her a duty visit."

In her memoir *Adventures of a Novelist,* Gertrude Atherton recalled her own visit to Lady Wilde's cramped and crepuscular house, where the gas evidently had been turned off. "The room was close and stuffy, the furniture as antiquated as herself; the springs could not have been mended for forty years," Atherton wrote. Speranza's person fared no better. "In her day she must have been a beautiful and stately woman; she was still stately, heaven knew, but her old face was gaunt and gray, and seamed with a million criss-crossed lines, etched by care, sorrow, and, no doubt, hunger." She was dressed in "a relic of the sixties, gray satin trimmed with ragged black fringe over a large hoop-skirt. As her hair was black it was presumably a wig, and it was dressed very high, held in place by a Spanish comb, from which depended a black lace mantilla." When the candlelit apparition extended "a claw-like hand" in Atherton's direction, she "wondered if I were expected to kiss it," but in the end "gave myself the benefit of the doubt."

> To her present circumstances she made no allusion, and the walls seemed to expand until the dingy parlor became a great salon crowded with courtiers, and the rotting fabric of her rag-bag covering turned by a fairy's wand into cloth of gold, shimmering in the light of a thousand wax candles. But the dream faded. Once more she was a laboriously built up terribly old woman who subsisted mainly on indigestible cake contributed by the few friends who remembered her existence.

There is no record of any contact between Lady Wilde and the Stokers after 1884, when she wrote to a friend in Dublin, "Bram is always very attentive and kind when I meet him at the theatre," but Florence Stoker never visited her. In late life Lady Wilde does not seem to have socialized much outside of her rooms. The only hint we have of Stoker's possible behavior vis-à-vis his onetime mentor in the immediate aftermath of the libel trial is the curious fact that a watercolor portrait of Lady Wilde—her favorite likeness, painted in 1864 by Bernard Mulrenin and exhibited at the Royal Hibernian Academy—came into Bram and Florence's possession. No matter how fond Speranza had been of Stoker in Dublin, it is inconceivable that such a cherished heirloom was ever gifted to him. But might it have been acquired in the frenzied bankruptcy auction of all Wilde's personal property at Tite Street? The drastic action was forced immediately by Queensberry to recover court costs for the libel trial as his vindication shifted into triumphal vindictiveness. The public sale was held on Friday, May 24, and liquidated Wilde's furniture, books, manuscripts, artwork, and other property, including his children's toys. Was Stoker there that fateful Friday? On his own volition? At Florence's suggestion or request? The Mulrenin portrait of Lady Wilde was still in the possession of Stoker's granddaughter as late as 1997.[6]

Blind to the enormity of Oscar's loss, Bosie told Wilde he thought bankruptcy was a "splendid score," a clever way of writing off a debt to his detested father and thereby having the last laugh. Bosie didn't understand

---

[6] The painting appears as a color illustration in Merlin Holland's *The Wilde Album* (1997), with credit given to Stoker's granddaughter Ann Dobbs.

the implications of bankruptcy, just as he didn't comprehend the magnitude of the situation his friend and benefactor now faced. Despite being at the center of the whole disaster, Bosie was never called to testify, and never charged with a crime that by definition could only have been committed mutually. Queensberry, however, had the prosecution in his pocket from the outset—or under his heel, given all the allegations against Rosebery and other liberals of high position he was willing to make public.

Queensberry was one of those paranoid personalities who sometimes choose to obsess over plots and conspiracies that actually have merit. Freud explained paranoia as rising from latent homosexual desires; if this theory is applied to Queensberry, the Wilde imbroglio becomes a true psychosexual rabbit hole. That Queensberry himself had complicated sexual issues is bolstered by his first wife's divorcing him for whoring and his second wife's obtaining an annulment on the basis of nonconsummation due to a never-explained "malformation of the parts of generation" and impotence. The atmosphere of near-hysteria surrounding the Wilde prosecution was bound up in a more general crisis of masculinity, including but hardly limited to the visibility of men who loved men. Male power and privilege appeared to be under relentless assault by economic and cultural forces. A depression that had lasted more than a decade had reduced England's per capita output to a fraction of France's, Germany's, or America's. Empire was waning. The influx of foreigners, experienced almost viscerally as an invasion, was an especially unwelcome kind of penetration—a reverse colonization. The increased visibility and assertiveness of women was a direct challenge to men's virility and to their sexual prerogatives. Wilde's public persona was mocking, flabby, and effeminate—in short, a classic scapegoat for a threatened patriarchy.

Following Queensberry's exoneration, Wilde had only one night of freedom before being arrested the next day and officially charged with acts of gross indecency—not sodomy, which under British law described anal penetration exclusively (to all accounts, Wilde's sexual tastes were predominantly oral) and was punishable by life imprisonment. He was arraigned at the Bow Street police station in Covent Garden and remanded without bail.

There followed not one but two sensational trials. The first ended in a hung jury, after which Wilde briefly obtained bail. He quickly found that no hotel in London would admit him. Like a character created by Bram Stoker, he encountered the equivalent of garlic or wolfsbane at every door. Finally, he sought refuge in Oakley Street's cramped confines. "Willie, give me shelter or I shall die in the streets," he implored his brother. Willie acceded, but nonetheless passed a drunken judgment: at least his own vices were "decent." As J. B. Yeats recalled it, "His successful brother who had scorned him for a drunken ne'er-do-well was now at his mercy." It was still possible for him to escape to France. Bosie was already there. Constance had taken the children to Switzerland, where they would all change their names. He would never see his sons again. Friends had arranged for a private yacht to cross the Channel, and offered him money, even ordered the champagne for the trip, and yet he refused. In Yeats's recollection, his mother had given him a simple choice—or no choice. "If you stay, even if you go to prison, you will always be my son," she said. "It will make no difference to my affection. But if you go, I will never speak to you again." According to Frank Harris, however, Willie used more than emotional blackmail. Oscar was convinced his jealous, vindictive brother would personally tip off the police if he made the slightest move to jump bail. He was already a prisoner. Many notes of sympathy and encouragement arrived, but Willie screened anything that urged Oscar to flee. Among the missives was an unsigned note of support from Henry Irving and Ellen Terry, delivered with a spray of violets by a veiled woman said to be Terry herself. But after a few days, Wilde did flee—for the kinder sanctuary offered by a friend, Ada Leverson.

From the beginning of the second trial, which commenced on May 20, the writing was already on the wall. In truth, the conclusion had been determined from the moment the libel suit was lost. The same witnesses were paraded out—mostly blackmailers and rent boys who seemed, to many observers, far more deserving of prosecution than Wilde. In the end, Wilde and codefendant Alfred Taylor were found guilty. Taylor was the procurer whose male brothel was the scene of numerous alleged assignations (and who frequently goes unmentioned in condensed accounts of the trials). The judge called it "the worst case I have ever tried" and declared Wilde to "have been at the centre of a circle of extensive corruption of the most hideous kind among young men."

The sentence was imprisonment at hard labor for two years, the maximum punishment allowed under law. Wilde struggled to respond. "And I? May I say nothing, my lord?" The judge dismissed the convicted man with a disgusted wave of his hand.

Bram and Florence had followed every moment of the trial—who in London hadn't?—but seem to have kept their thoughts and feelings to themselves. Before *An Ideal Husband* and *The Importance of Being Earnest*, Wilde's name was removed from their playbills and programs. Anyone connected to Wilde became suspect. One of the casualties was the artist Aubrey Beardsley; he was never accused of any personal impropriety, but his illustrations for Wilde's controversial play *Salome* (1894) associated him too closely in the public mind with a newly minted social pariah. At the height of his career, he became suddenly unemployable. In his novel *The Confessions of Aubrey Beardsley*, Donald S. Olson evocatively imagines the artist's recollections: "It is quite impossible to convey the atmosphere of London during that time," he tells the priest who hears his testament.

> One half-expected to see witches flying past the chimneypots and people being burned at the stake in Trafalgar Square. People became beasts. Everything that had been progressive and modern in the world of art and literature was suddenly suspect. . . . Panic spread amongst the inverts of London. Today it was Oscar, but who would it be tomorrow? If evidence had been obtained by threats, bribes, blackmail and stolen address-books, who was safe? What other names would come out in cross-examination? Incriminating letters were burned, certain books and journals disposed of, bachelor households dissolved, and hasty marriages arranged. Those who could afford to fled the city. The boat-trains to Calais and Dieppe were filled with nervous gentlemen whose blood turned to ice every time they saw a grim-faced official.

Stoker needn't have feared unwelcome attention himself. After all, he was married to one of the most beautiful women in London, even if they saw little of each other during waking hours. Much of the time they did share was public—Lyceum openings and Florence's Sunday at-homes. To a certain degree, even to an essential degree, the Stokers had a marriage for show. And why not? They were an extraordinarily handsome couple. Bram was strikingly good-looking—burly, bearded, with piercingly blue eyes and retaining the imposing build of the athlete he once was. Almost coinciding with the Wilde trials, a stunning, just-commissioned portrait of Florence adorned a wall at the Royal Academy's summer exhibition. It was painted by the well-known Dublin artist Walter Frederick Osborne,

Irish painter Walter Frederick Osborne's ravishing oil portrait of Florence Stoker,
exhibited in 1895 at the time of the Wilde trials.

a master of plein air, or natural lighting effects.[7] Even though the word
"heterosexual" had yet to be coined, Mr. and Mrs. Bram Stoker presented
a seemingly unassailable picture of an idealized Victorian union. For
Florence, there still may have been a hidden Wildean connection. It is said
she vowed never to be photographed or painted after she turned forty,
and in 1895 she was only a few years away from the point of no return.
Walter Osborne may not have been a Basil Hallward, but his portraiture
managed, in its own nonsupernatural way, to effectively suspend the aging
process of a woman who might have married the creator of Dorian Gray
but chose the author of *Dracula* instead.

There was no reason for Stoker to make any comment on Wilde's tragedy, and he didn't. Other writers, like Hall Caine, were openly unnerved.

---

[7] Osborne also painted Bram's father (from a photograph) and his mother (from life), though
judging from an apologetic letter from the artist, Charlotte Stoker was not completely pleased
with her likeness.

"It haunts men," Caine said, "like some foul and horrible stain on our craft and on us all, which nothing can wash out. It is the most awful tragedy in the whole of literature." At the time of the trial H. G. Wells was revising *The Island of Dr. Moreau,* published the following year. Like *Dracula,* it featured shapeshifting animals—beasts who became people—and responded to the era's preoccupation with evolution and its fearful double, degeneration. In a later reference to Wilde's ordeal and the writing of *Moreau,* Wells remembered "the graceless and pitiful downfall of a man of genius" and said the "story was the response of an imaginative mind to the reminder that humanity is but animal rough-hewn to a reasonable shape and in perpetual instinct between instinct and injunction."

Philip Burne-Jones, son of the Pre-Raphaelite painter Sir Edward Burne-Jones, was an artist himself and creator of a scandalous 1897 canvas called *The Vampire,* the exhibition of which practically coincided with the publication of *Dracula.* The painting was accompanied by a poem by the artist's cousin Rudyard Kipling, also entitled "The Vampire," that began with the famous line "A fool there was . . ." In the painting the lovestruck fool is represented by an unconscious male figure straddled in bed by a gloating woman in a nightgown who has left an ominous wound over his heart. The painting was deemed scandalous because of gossip that Burne-Jones based the female figure on the actress Mrs. Patrick Campbell, who had badly used him. Whatever the truth, both artist and involuntary subject greatly enjoyed the flood of public attention that ensued. The reviewer of *Dracula* in the *Weekly Sun* related that "it was not until I had read Mr. Stoker's book that I grasped the full meaning and weirdness of that painting." We will never know Stoker's reaction to either the painting or the poem, and whether he identified in any conscious way with Kipling's lines:

> The fool was stripped to his foolish hide
> (Even as you and I!)
> Which she might have seen when she threw him aside—
> (But it isn't on record the lady tried)
> So some of him lived but the most of him died—
> (Even as you and I!)

If Philip Burne-Jones had seen fit to paint an emotionally honest canvas of Florence and Bram—he masochistically drained, devitalized by work

"A fool there was . . ." Philip Burne-Jones's scandalous painting The Vampire *(1897).*

and wife—the result might have been a compelling Dorian Gray portrait of the Stoker marriage itself.

Stoker knew Burne-Jones personally and sent him a copy of *Dracula*, which the artist gratefully acknowledged: "Your most kind promise of the other evening was most pleasantly fulfilled to-day, when your book arrived." The artist had earlier been quite the acolyte of Oscar Wilde, inviting him to the rambling family homestead, the Grange, and hanging on his every word. At dinner, his cousin Alice Kipling was not so impressed with "Phil's latest adoration"—it was she who likened Wilde's lips to garden slugs. After Oscar's downfall, Burne-Jones switched his allegiance to the traumatized Constance Wilde, offering her what assistance he could.

On July 16, nearly eight weeks after his brother's incarceration, Willie Wilde wrote to Stoker. "Bram, my friend, poor Oscar was *not* as bad as people thought him. He was led astray by his Vanity—& conceit, & he was so 'got at' that he was weak enough to be guilty—of indiscretions and follies—that is *all*. . . . I believe this thing will help to *purify* him body & soul. Am sure you and Florence must have felt the disgrace of one who cared for you both sincerely." Stoker's response, if he had one, has never surfaced. But in all likelihood he never wrote back to Willie, and Oscar's conviction likely marked a complete and final break with the Wildes. More than a decade later, when Stoker wrote his biography of Henry Irving, he would omit the names of both Oscar and his mother from the extensive list of distinguished guests at the Lyceum. Wilde's omission was rather more understandable than the slighting of Lady Wilde, to whom Stoker was genuinely close in Dublin.

But 1895 was a rather busy year for Stoker, and it is possible that many letters went unanswered. On the very day of Wilde's conviction, announcement was made of Henry Irving's impending knighthood—the first for an English actor. Irving had been considered for the honor a decade earlier, but, contrary to Stoker's later account, the prime minister had qualms about Irving's adulterous relationship with Ellen Terry. In Stoker's telling, Irving refused the offer as being extravagant and premature. In any event, the new prime minister, Lord Rosebery—the very bane of Queensberry— hardly regarded the Irving and Terry liaison as a controversy, perhaps because of the far weightier sex scandals that never stopped swirling around him personally. Bram's brother Thornley Stoker, by then the president of the Royal College of Surgeons in Dublin, was also knighted in 1895, for his distinguished contributions to medicine. Stoker acknowledged the honor in the dedication of *The Shoulder of Shasta*. Throughout the summer, preparations were being completed for another North American tour, with *Faust*'s Montreal opening in September.

And still, there was the damned unfinished book.

While Stoker may have worried about having his novel linked to Wilde in any way, there were commercial considerations as well as personal ones. Whatever else his motivations were as a writer, he wrote for money, and the public downfall of Wilde might as well have been market research. As it stood, by the summer of 1895, anything that was left of the art world subplot, and paintings of Dracula that looked like other people despite the artist's best efforts—all the remaining vestiges of *Dorian Gray* simply had to go. The spectacle of Queensberry's defense going savagely after the content of Wilde's book as if words were forensic facts was alarming to any writer paying attention. And we can assume that this was also the point at which Dracula's London social calendar was completely scrubbed, his dinner party invitations torn up, and the character began to take a snarling step back into the shadows. Just as Wilde was silenced at the end of his trial, Stoker muted Dracula before he ended his book.

And yet Wilde's ghostly imprint still lingers in the pages of *Dracula*. Jonathan Harker's visceral disgust at the Count's swollen, blood-bloated body ("he lay like a filthy leech") echoes countless descriptions of Wilde, and Harker's fear that Dracula will spread "an ever-widening circle of semi-demons" finds a parallel in the sentencing judge's characterization of Wilde as "the center of a hideous circle of corruption." During the trial, a Savoy Hotel chambermaid had testified to the excrement-streaked sheets removed from Oscar's rooms while he and Bosie were in residence; just as the vampire rested on a bed of his native earth, Wilde, too, seemed to sleep in proprietary dirt.[8] Both Dracula and Wilde maintained multiple residences around London to avoid detection of their activities. Both depended on the bodies of the young and the vital to procure the fluids that satisfied their unconventional appetites. Both had made a sea voyage from their land of origin, relocating in London—only to be destroyed. The true story of Wilde and the fictional story of Dracula both emphasize the importance and primacy of bonding between males. As Nina Auerbach, author of *Our Vampires, Ourselves*, explains it, *Dracula* "abounds in overwrought protestations of friendship among the men, who testify breathlessly to each other's manhood. In fact, Van Helsing should thank the vampire for introducing him to such loveable companions. Borrowing the idiom of Oscar Wilde's letters to Lord Alfred Douglas, he declares himself to Lucy's former fiancé, 'I have grown to love you—yes, my dear boy, to love you.'"

In the Norton Critical Edition of *Dracula*, Auerbach notes that the Wilde trials gave Victorian England "a new monster of its own clinical making" in a medicalized paradigm for homosexuality that "stigmatized not acts, but essence; like the vampire this creature was tainted in its desires, not its deeds. This pariah, more dangerous than the New Woman because more insidiously pervasive, cast a shadow not only over the theatrical community but over all men." Stoker, meanwhile, also medicalized

---

[8] Although this evidence would seem to suggest sodomy under the British legal definition, the prosecution didn't press the matter, possibly because it knew the sheets in question were used by Bosie and another party, and it was understood that the son of Queensberry was not to be prosecuted for any reason.

and technologized his monster, containing and controlling and repelling the arch-pariah Dracula with up-to-date blood transfusions, phonograph diaries, and the typewriter. The legal thresholds that defined Wilde's transgressions were as pseudoscientific as the superstitious thresholds that defined vampirism.

Wilde's residual spectre would not be commented upon at the time of the book's publication, or for almost a century afterward. As the novelist Fay Weldon notes in her introduction to *Bram Stoker's Dracula Omnibus*, in the 1890s "who'd ever heard of a sub-text?" Witness Edward Carson's mind-numbingly literal reading of *Dorian Gray*.

Stoker's book was ending up quite unlike the lurid sensation novel he had first envisioned. In making his final revisions, he fell back instinctively, if perhaps unconsciously, on the sturdy substructure of the literary form that had sustained him since childhood: the fairy tale. The plot took on an archetypal simplicity, drawing on the folktale motif of abused and abandoned children. An orphan (Jonathan Harker, bereft of parentage like most of the main characters) ventures into the woods and is confronted with a terrifying demon king, who chases him home, but the young hero must return to the dreaded place to destroy the monster and restore moral order. Among the many classic tales evoked are "Bluebeard" (the castle with locked rooms and bloody secrets), "Jack the Giant Killer" (the ogre who chases the protagonist to his homeland and is slain), and "Little Red Riding Hood" (explicitly cited in Stoker's text and mimicked when a wolf crashes through a bedroom window to menace Lucy and her mother). In short, for *Dracula* to be saved as a publishable tale, it had to be shrunken, collapsed, and dwindled down into a bedtime story of childhood abandonment and rescue.

As argued by Jarlath Killeen, "The novel is deeply involved in the metaphysical orphanage that nineteenth-cetury Britain had become, due to the crisis of faith and the apparent withdrawal of God," who is replaced by a threatening ogre straight out of a pantomime. Indeed, the characters "all appear to have arrested development, and lack the ability to grow up," a point well illustrated by the numerous occasions when the grown men of *Dracula* simply break down and cry.

Instead of stabilizing Stoker's finances, the vampire book had only complicated things by sapping Stoker's time over seven long years without any return. In fairy tale terms, seven years was a magical span. In terms of

Dracula, the magic took on the dimensions of a curse. On June 3, 1896, he wrote Caine on the letterhead of the Adelphi Hotel, Liverpool:

> My dear Hommy Beg,
>
> There is a matter which I want to ask you about and I write instead of speaking as I wish you to be quite free in the matter. Though I would like to make it a matter of business it is a matter entirely between friends also, and I would rather if I might, ask you than anyone I know. I have to borrow some money—£600—as I have to pay an old debt which I intended paying some time ago and which in any case I would have cleared off in the immediate future had not the call come rather sooner than I expected and I want to know if you would care to lend me the amount. The Heinemann & Balestier enterprise took so much more than I intended investing—£800 in all—it left me rather short, and a year ago I bought the lease on my house leaving me with a rental of only £10 a year for the next eleven years. This cost me £600 which I got from Coutts giving them a security some £800 worth of stocks all good paying things which it would not be wise to sell. . . . I am glad to hear Heinemann and Balestier is getting all right but at present the money is laid up & is not available.
>
> Now my dear old fellow if you would rather not do this do say so freely for I would not for all the world have you let anything to do with money (of all things) come in any way between us. I only mention this matter to you at all because you are closer to me than any man I know, and I prefer to ask my own kind who are workers like myself rather than rich men who do not understand. Any time within a month (or even longer) would do me to have the money but I'd like to be in time in such matters and if the matter is settled it will be a certain ease to me in the mist of much

work and after a long and trying year. Of course if the
new book comes out well at all the first money I get
will go to pay the debt. . . .

This is a long letter but I want you to quite
understand and honestly hope that if you do not care
to go into the matter you will treat me as a friend and
say so frankly—as frankly as all things have been—
and please God ever shall be between you and me. In
any case you must not let the matter worry you by a
hair's breadth.

Yours always,
BRAM STOKER

The mail between Liverpool and the Isle of Man was quick, and without a moment's hesitation Caine posted Stoker a check, which he received
at the Adelphi on June 6. "My Dear Hommy Beg," he responded. "Your letter is like yourself and that is saying all. I won't say much about it as I know
you do not like it[.] I feel truly grateful all the same—and I am rejoiced that
I was right in thinking or rather knowing that I might speak to you frankly.
. . . And believe me my dear old fellow I shall not forget your brotherly gesture." But as warm as his emotions were, and despite the familiar greeting,
he nevertheless signed the letter with his usual, inexplicably stiff formality:
"Yours Always, Bram Stoker."

He would ultimately repay Caine not with vampire money but with a
cashed insurance policy, the same move made by Abraham Stoker to fund
his sons' educations. The loan released the debt pressure and presumably
allowed him to devote a concentrated amount of time to finishing the
book in the summer of 1896. The previous year had been the Lyceum's last
American tour until 1899, so he was free of that particular pressure. But
that didn't mean he wasn't anxious to finish the project. He had published
two books in 1895, but none in 1896, despite mounting financial concerns.
Noel recalled him being "very testy" during the completion of the novel,
withdrawing from Florence and himself, and told biographer Harry Ludlam
that Stoker always "used to seek complete isolation" while writing. Cruden
Bay had become the family's regular summer holiday destination—if "holiday" is ever the accurate word for an unreformed workaholic's leave-taking.

Stoker's begging letter to Hall Caine, asking for money to complete **Dracula.**
(Courtesy of Manx National Heritage)

Noel remembered his father "striding out on long walks" and "stabbing at the sand with his strong walking stick, and at other times sitting for hours perched on the rocks off shore like some giant seabird, his notebook on his knee," and being "inclined to be short-tempered if interrupted." But, according to Florence, once he came out of his writing trance, Stoker "used to read his stories over to me as they were written, and 'Dracula' was by no means least among those which revealed to me the supernormal imagination of the author."

Unlike some of his later manuscripts, which had entries meticulously dated, with *Dracula* it is impossible to determine exactly when any particular passage was composed or revised. The final typescript has numerous cut-and-paste revisions, and the pagination indicates that whole chapters were shuffled around like cards. But whenever they occurred, many of the revisions are quite fascinating. For example, at some point before typesetting, Stoker struck out a dramatic description of Castle Dracula's seeming self-destruction, immediately following its owner's dusty demise. From Mina Harker's final journal entry: "As we looked there came a terrible convulsion of the earth so that we seemed to rock to and fro and fell to our knees. At the same moment, with a roar that seemed to shake the very heavens, the whole castle and the rock and even the hill on which it stood seemed to rise in the air and scatter skywards in fragments while a mighty cloud of black and yellow smoke volume on volume of rolling grandeur was shot upwards with inconceivable rapidity." The return of the debris to earth is rendered in tortured syntax that might have warranted deletion on that basis alone: "Then down in a mighty ruin falling whence they rose came the fragments that had been tossed skyward in the cataclysm."[9] Then, Mina writes, "it seemed as if the one fierce volcano burst had satisfied the need of nature and the castle and the structure of the hill had sunk again into the void."[10] Again? When had the hill or castle previously been in "the void"?

In any event, the demolition order on Castle Dracula was likely rescinded not because words failed Stoker but on account of a last-minute idea that the story might not be finished after all, or at least might rise again. The American writer and former Massachusetts state senator and assistant attorney general Roger Sherman Hoar claimed that "Stoker told me that he planned to bring Dracula over to America in a new story."[11] This might

---

[9] If "ruin" is taken as the typist's mistaken transcription of Stoker's handwritten "rain," the sentence suddenly makes sense.

[10] Here Stoker may be taking a cue from a similarly cataclysmic, and much better written, climax by Poe: "My brain reeled as I saw the mighty walls rushing asunder—there was a long tumultuous shouting sound like the voice of a thousand waters—and the deep and dank tarn at my feet closed sullenly and silently over the fragments of the '*House of Usher.*'"

[11] Hoar reportedly met Stoker as a seventeen-year-old Harvard freshman working as a local stage extra for Irving's December 1903 engagement at the Tremont Theatre in Boston. Could Stoker have already been thinking of a sequel, even while struggling with the original manuscript? Before his political career, Hoar wrote pulp fiction under the pseudonym Ralph Milne Farley. His two-part serial "Another Dracula?" appeared in *Weird Tales* for September–October 1930. It was a Stoker-like tale set in the United States, and lifted Stoker's description of the

also explain why Dracula's bloodless "death"—a crumbling into dust, when we already know the Count has the ability to transform himself into dust motes—is so different from those of the four other vampires killed in the book. Lucy and Dracula's brides all die gruesomely; Van Helsing describes the dispatching of the latter three women as "butcher work" with a "horrid screeching as the stake drove home." Ancient like Dracula, they, too, crumble into their native dust—but only after they scream through "lips of bloody foam" and put on a show. Another reason to suspect Stoker considered a sequel is a press clipping, included with his notes, titled "Vampires in New England" and dated 1896—too late to be of use in *Dracula*, but of great potential utility in a follow-up book set in America.

There was no advance announcement of the book, save Stoker's cryptic comment to an Atlanta journalist, who told readers in January 1896 that Stoker's "next book is going to have ghosts in it." Sometime later that year Stoker delivered a final, professionally typed and hand-emended manuscript called *The Un-dead* to Archibald Constable & Company. That the penultimate title was a last-minute decision is indicated by Stoker's handscrawled title page, added to the typescript. For seven years of work, he received no advance, only a guaranteed first print run of at least three thousand copies and a payment of one shilling for each copy sold. No one knows when the title was changed to *Dracula*, or at whose inspired suggestion. The final title was assigned by the end of the previous summer at the very latest, far earlier than is usually assumed. A bookseller's advertisement for "New Books" in the September 11, 1896, issue of the Cape of Good Hope's *Cape Illustrated Magazine* includes "Dracula by Bram Stoker." This can only be an advance announcement of the Hutchinson Colonial Library edition of the book (very likely delayed; the magazine didn't publish its review until September 1897), licensed by Constable and printed in London from the original typesetter's plates. A strangely after-the-fact contract between Stoker and Constable, prepared and signed in May 1897, retains his original title, *The Un-Dead*, which raises a question never asked before: Did Stoker possibly *object* to the new title, rather than propose it himself? His seemingly obstinate clinging to the first title tends to bolster the idea that the change might have been Constable's and not Stoker's.

Count verbatim to describe a character who ultimately was revealed to be not a vampire, but rather the unfortunate victim of a sun-sensitivity disease.

Page from the typescript of Dracula, *describing the Count's first appearance.*

In any event, typesetting of *Dracula* could not have been complete before March 1897. Stoker must have been making final galley corrections when he wrote to Hall Caine on March 2.

I was thinking, if you would not object, to dedicate
the book to you—may I? If so how would it do to put it
                To my dear friend
                Hommy-beg?
or would it be better to note the name more
formally—if the book is ever worth remembering it
will be well understood what is meant.

I saw Mrs. Caine at the theatre. . . . Florence is in
Ireland has been almost a month and I am all alone at
home. When do you come in?

                            Yours ever
                            BRAM STOKER

On May 18, 1897, the week before *Dracula* appeared in bookstalls, Stoker held a staged reading of the book for dramatic copyright purposes at the Lyceum. Theatrical piracy was a thorn in the side of many nineteenth-century writers, most famously Charles Dickens and Mark Twain, and although there is no evidence that copyright readings actually prevented unauthorized stage adaptations, they were nonetheless a common practice. Programs were printed, placards posted, and a token admission was charged to make the event an official, commercial endeavor (the Stokers' cook, Maria Mitchell, was the only known paying customer). Fifteen actors from the supporting ranks of the Lyceum company participated in the reading, and Ellen Terry's daughter, Edith Craig, took the role of Mina. Dracula was played by a now-obscure actor named T. Arthur Jones. The ritual lasted over four hours, and because it would have been impossible for Stoker to have created multiple copies of the complicated cut-and-paste script (which utilized galley proofs of the novel and connective material handwritten by the author), the performers must have been seated on the stage behind a lectern to which they rose to read from a single script.

Although Stoker really did believe *Dracula* had theatrical possibilities, his adaptation was perfunctory and his dramaturgy not quite ready for prime time. The breathless exposition he puts in the mouth of Jonathan Harker to avoid the difficulties of putting a carriage ride through the Carpathian Mountains on a proscenium stage is a prime example. "Well, this is a pretty nice state of things," Jonathan exclaims after being dropped

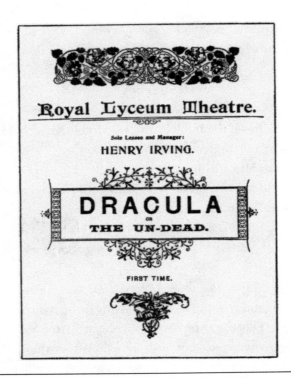

Program for the copyright reading of Dracula,
performed on the Lyceum's stage to protect the book's theatrical rights.

off on Dracula's doorstep. "After a drive through solid darkness with an unknown man whose face I have not seen and who has in his hand the strength of twenty men and who can drive a pack of wolves by holding up his hand; who visits mysterious blue flames and wouldn't speak a word that he could help, to be left here in the dark before a—a ruin. Upon my life I'm beginning my professional experience in a romantic way!" The theatrical shortcomings of the piece were clear enough to Henry Irving. Asked by Stoker what he thought of the effort, Irving reportedly had a one-word reply: "Dreadful!"

No doubt, Stoker knew this wasn't real theatre. Any kind of representation of the book would do. Because the reading required an official license from the censor's office, Stoker was cautious in the treatment of certain elements. For instance, he self-censored Lucy's death scene, or any description of it, from the cobbled manuscript submitted to the Lord Chamberlain. A gap appears instead of the following:

The Thing in the coffin writhed; and a hideous, blood-curdling screech came from the opened red lips. The body shook and quivered and twisted in wild contortions; the sharp white teeth champed together until the lips were cut, and the mouth was smeared with a crimson foam. But Arthur never faltered. He looked like a figure of Thor, his untrembling arm rose and fell, driving deeper and deeper the mercy-bearing stake, whilst the blood from the pierced heart spurted up around it.

Stoker also eliminated most of the bloody ménage à trois involving Dracula, Mina, and Jonathan, luridly played out in the Harkers' bed:

With his left hand he held both Mrs. Harker's hands, keeping them away with her arms at full tension; his right hand gripped her by the back of the neck, forcing her face down on his bosom. Her white nightdress was smeared with blood, and a thin stream trickled down the man's bare breast which was shown by his torn open dress. The attitude of the two had a terrible resemblance to a child forcing a kitten's nose into a saucer of milk to compel it to drink.

All that remains of this scene in the play script is the stage direction "See Dracula holding Mrs. Harker's face to his breast." It is a bloodless pantomime; once more Stoker avoids staging any action or image the Lord Chamberlain might find objectionable. Mina does recount the details of the blood communion with her rescuers, but it is only a description, if still a gruesome one: "He pulled open his shirt, and with his long sharp nails opened a vein in his breast. When the blood began to spurt out, he took my hands in one of his and held them tight and with the other seized my neck and pressed my mouth to the wound, so that I must either suffocate or swallow some of the—Oh my God! My God! What have I done?"

"What have I done?" could have been a question in Stoker's own mind as he waited for reactions to the book. He could not have been unhappy with the first reviews, though he might have been surprised, given the doubt expressed to Hall Caine that he had written anything memorable. Although a great number of sources have described the overall critical response to *Dracula* as "mixed," outright pans of the book were exceedingly rare, and the overwhelming majority of notices were enthusiastically supportive. However, since a great number of the positive reviews also adopted

8 (4)

"You shall, I trust, rest here with me a while, so that by our talking I may learn the English intonation ; and I would that you tell me when I make error, even of the smallest, in my speaking. I am sorry that I had to be away so long to-day ; but you will, I know, forgive one who has so many important affairs in hand."

Harker — I am quite at your service. When you are away may I come into this room.

Drac —
"You may go anywhere you wish in the castle, except where the doors are locked, where of course you will not wish to go. There is reason that all things are as they are, and did you see with my eyes and know with my knowledge, you would perhaps better understand."
"We are in Transylvania, and Transylvania is not England. Our ways are not your ways, and there shall be to you many strange things. Nay, from what you have told me of your experiences already, you know something of how strange things here may be."

Harker — May I ask you about some things which have puzzled me.

Drac — (bowing) Go on. I shall try to answer.

Harker — Last night your coachman several times got down to look at places where blue flames rose from the ground, though there were wolves about and the horses were left uncontrolled. Why did he act thus.

Drac — These flames show where gold has been hidden. I see you do not understand. I shall then explain.

St George's day It is commonly believed that on a certain night -last night, in fact, when all evil spirits are supposed to have unchecked sway—a blue flame is seen over any place where treasure has been hidden. "That treasure has been hidden," "in the region through which you came last night, there can be but little doubt; for it was the ground fought over for centuries by the Wallachian, the Saxon, and the Turk. Why, there is hardly a foot of soil in all this region that has not been enriched by the blood of men, patriots or invaders. In old days there were stirring times, when the Austrian and tne Hungarian came up in hordes, and the patriots went out to meet them, men and women, the aged and the children too, and waited their coming on the rocks above the passes, that they might sweep destruction on them with their artificial avalanches. When the invader was triumphant he found but little, for whatever there was had been sheltered in the friendly soil."

Harker — "But how," "can it have remained so long undiscovered, when there is a sure index to it if men will but take the trouble to look?"

Drac — "Because your peasant is at heart a coward and a fool. Those flames only appear on one night, and on that night no man of this land will, if he can help it, stir without his doors. And, dear sir, even if he did he would not know what to do. Why, even the peasant that you tell me of who marked the place of the flame would not know where to look in daylight even for his own work. You would not, I dare be sworn, be able to find these places again."

Harker — "There you are right," "I know no more than the dead where even to look for them."

Drac — But "Come," "tell me of London and of the house which you have procured for me."

Harker — Pardon my remissness [Gets papers from his bag whilst his back is turned Dracula removes food or a lighted lamp]

---

*For the staged reading, Lyceum actors read from Stoker's cut-and-paste script, assembled from **Dracula's** printer's proofs.* (The British Library) a tongue-in-cheek tone, it is understandable that these appraisals might be perceived as ambivalent.

The *Daily Mail* set a high bar in its baseline literary comparisons: "In seeking a parallel to this weird, powerful, and horrible story, our minds revert to such tales as 'The Mysteries of Udolpho,' 'Frankenstein,' 'Wuthering Heights,' 'The Fall of the House of Usher,' and 'Marjery [*sic*] of Quelher.' But 'Dracula' is even more appalling in its gloomy fascination than any of these!" The *Bookman* was similarly admiring:

> Since Wilkie Collins left us we have had no tale of mystery so liberal in manner and so closely woven. But with the intricate plot, and the methods of the narrative, the resemblance to stories of the author of "The Woman in White" ceases; for the audacity and the horror of "Dracula" are Mr. Stoker's own. A summary of the book would shock and disgust; but we must own that, though here and there in the course of the tale we hurried over things with repulsion, we read the whole with rapt attention. It is something of a triumph for the writer that neither the improbability, nor the unnecessary number of hideous incidents recounted of the man-vampire, are long foremost in the reader's mind, but that the interest of the danger, of the complications, of the pursuit of the villain, of human skill and courage pitted against inhuman wrong and superhuman strength, rises always to the top.

The *Athanaeum* was the only British periodical to discern a creeping zeitgeist quality in *Dracula*. "Stories and novels appear just now in plenty stamped with a more or less genuine air of belief in the visibility of supernatural agency. The strengthening of a bygone faith in the fantastic and magical view of things in lieu of the purely material is a feature of the hour, a reaction—artificial, perhaps, rather than natural—against late tendencies in thought. . . . Mr. Stoker has got together a number of 'horrid details,' and his object, assuming it is ghastliness, is fairly well fulfilled." One through-line in all the contemporary reviews was praise to Stoker for his cleverness in juxtaposing medieval legend with up-to-date modernity. We have become so accustomed to thinking of *Dracula* as a "period" novel that it is easy to forget that in its time, the book was set in an immediately recognizable present day.

Noel Stoker, then studying at Winchester College, sent his father a note of congratulations. In one of the few recorded instances of a warm or humorous communication between father and son, Bram replied, "Dear Sir—let me thank you for your most kind appreciation of my last book. May I ask, as you have perused my previous books, if you enjoyed reading my first book, 'The Duties of Clerks of Petty Sessions in Ireland.' If you have not already read it let me advise you to do so, as you will find it interesting and amusing and that the continuous nature of the narrative is instructive—Believe me, yours faithfully, Bram Stoker."

Bram, Florence, and Noel vacationed again in Scotland in the summer of 1897, and this visit concluded with a three-day stay at Slains Castle as the guests of the French artist Henri Rivière and his wife, who were in turn the guests of the Earl of Erroll, whose family had owned the castle for three hundred years. Today it resembles a medieval ruin (leading some to mistakenly think it provided some measure of inspiration for Castle Dracula), but in the late nineteenth century it was sumptuously appointed, and the earl entertained many celebrities. The Rivières and their daughter had been Irving's guests at the Lyceum, and Stoker obviously made a good impression. Rivière was well known for his cleanly drafted landscapes of the coast of Brittany, but also for the unique shadow puppet theatre he devised for the legendary Parisian cabaret Le Chat Noir. The silhouetted figures and shapes were placed at various distances behind the screen, creating a gradated tonality of shadows and a remarkable illusion of depth. Rivière's dramatic compositions and penumbral mise-en-scène could easily have qualified him to illustrate *Dracula*. Could it be possible Stoker's just-published book was not a topic of conversation that weekend?

Stoker's fears of piracy were almost immediately validated when an unauthorized Hungarian translation appeared in Budapest in 1898 as *Drakula* (subtitled *Angol Regény*, or "English Novel.") Like Iceland, Hungary was not yet a member of the Berne Convention, and British books provided ridiculously easy targets. There is no evidence, however, that Stoker knew of the theft. The American publisher Doubleday & McClure brought out the first authorized foreign edition of *Dracula* as a holiday book in 1899, but not without delay and frustration. According to the New York trade publication *The Bookman*, *Dracula* "had some curious vicissitudes in the United States. At first no American publisher would take it and Bram Stoker went to considerable expense in copyrighting it in this country. Time went on, and it looked as if this money—hard-earned, as was all Stoker's money—would be utterly wasted. Then suddenly a publisher took the book and from the very first its sales were enormous, not only in the States, but Canada also."

The American copyright formalities were handled not by the publisher as such but by the firm's partner S. S. McClure personally. McClure was considered a brilliant publisher—he would become a major player in muckraking journalism—but an erratic businessman, and his joint venture with Frank Nelson Doubleday was coming to an end in 1899, after only three years. His more enduring enterprises included *McClure's Magazine* and the McClure Newspaper Syndicate, which maintained an office in London and had introduced a number of British writers, including Rudyard Kipling and Arthur Conan Doyle, to American readers through popular newspaper serializations of their books. Like Stoker, McClure had been born in Ireland.

The copyright registration made by McClure in Stoker's name on March 10, 1899, was not for the Doubleday & McClure book but rather for a newspaper serialization, deposit copies of which were received "in parts" between March 10 and April 10—exactly twenty-seven publication days (excluding Sundays), corresponding precisely to the twenty-seven chapters of the novel. These deposit copies no longer exist at the Library of Congress, and no correspondence regarding the matter was officially preserved. To date, an extensive search of newspaper microfilm and digital databases, conducted by the present author and others over a period of many years, has not revealed the identity of the periodical in which *Dracula* first appeared in America in the spring of 1899. But a confirmed weekly serialization in the *Charlotte Daily Observer* (titled *Dracula: A Strong Story of the Vampire*) followed from July 16 to December 10, and a subsequent 1900 serial in the *Buffalo Courier* included the first known illustration for the book, depicting Harker at the Transylvanian inn, receiving a letter from the Count. With an increasing array of digitized historical papers becoming available each year, the number of discovered serializations may well grow; it would, in fact, be quite surprising if they didn't.

But what about Stoker's "considerable expense" in securing an American copyright? It seems that McClure arranged for book publication only after *Dracula* had proved its viability in regional papers, and Stoker was expected to assume a portion of the financial risk for typesetting. Syndication was profitable because a book only needed to be set in hard type once. Daily

Irregularities abounded in Stoker's registration of **Dracula** *with the U.S. Copyright Office. Had anyone challenged the matter, the American copyright claim could never have been enforced.*

(Photographs courtesy of Elias Savada)

DRACULA

A STRONG STORY OF THE VAMPIRE.

By Bram Stoker, the Dramatic Critic,
Theatrical Manager and Author of "Miss
Betsy," "Under the Sunset," and Other
Books.

Copyright, 1897, by Bram Stoker.

CHAPTER I.
JONATHAN HARKER'S JOURNAL.

3 May. Bistritz.—Left Munich at 8:35
p. m. on 1st May, arriving at Vienna
early next morning. Buda-Pesth seems
a wonderful place, from the glimpse
which I got of it from the train and
the little I could walk through the
streets. I feared to go very far from
the station, as we had arrived late and
would start as near the correct time as
possible. The impression I had was
that we were leaving the West and entering the East, the most western of
splendid bridges over the Danube,
which is here of noble width and depth,
took us among the traditions of Turk-

Stoker personally covered typesetting costs for an American newspaper serialization of Dracula,
which appeared in the **Charlotte Observer** and other papers.

(Courtesy of Paul S. McAlduff)

newspapers that accepted syndicated material utilized columns of a standard width and were accustomed to receiving lightweight, easily shipped
papier-mâché molds known as stereotypes,[12] into which they poured their
own hot metal to produce printing plates. Stoker must have truly run out of
publisher options when he accepted McClure's deal. From the very beginning, he had warned Hall Caine of the financial disadvantages of accepting syndication offers tied to book publication, but now he found himself
in the position of signing exactly such a contract or not being published in
the United States at all.

---

[12] Printing stereotypes were first used in the early nineteenth century, and by the mid-1800s the
word "stereotype" began to accrue its modern, metaphorical meaning from the predictabil-
ity and standardization inherent in mass production. Similarly, *cliché* was originally a French
printer's term for the frame that held the *stéréotype* in place on the press.

HE WENT, BUT IMMEDIATELY RETURNED WITH A LETTER.

Top: The first known illustration for
Dracula, *depicting Jonathan Harker and the*
Transylvanian innkeeper, appeared in the
Buffalo Evening Courier *in 1900.*
(Courtesy of Paul S. McAlduff)
Right: The Count himself was first visualized
on the cover of Constable's abridged
paperback in 1901.

Stoker entrusted the copyright paperwork for the published American book to William Carey, a friend and fellow Walt Whitmanite based in New York. Whitman supplemented his income by selling autographed portraits of himself and had designated Carey as sales agent for engravings based on the 1887 "Laughing Philosopher" photograph taken by George Collins Cox. Except for their mutual interest in Whitman, and the fact that they both worked in publishing, little else is known about Carey and Stoker's relationship. Carey worked for the *Century Magazine*, America's most widely circulated monthly, with offices overlooking Union Square. Carey's name and his business address are penciled under the formal entry in the Copyright Office ledger: "Library of Congress, to wit: be it remembered, That on the 19th day of March, 1897, Bram Stoker of London, Eng., has deposited in this office the title of a Book the title or description of which is in the following words: Dracula By Bram Stoker."

It is not clear that this registration carried legal weight. No deposit copy of the Constable edition was provided to the library—the line for that information is blank—but even that wouldn't have satisfied the standing requirement that a copyrighted work by a foreign national needed to be manufactured in America. Further, the registration of a title is not the same thing as the copyright in a published work, and titles alone have never been eligible for copyright. Stoker probably made the registration only to meet Constable's contractual requirement that he copyright the work in the United States as a prior condition of British publication, even though this was technically impossible.

McClure broke with Doubleday near the time the American *Dracula* arrived in bookstores, and he never sent the Copyright Office the two printed copies required upon publication. Someone—possibly Stoker, Carey, or the new firm of Doubleday, Page & Company—deposited two cloth copies on September 28, 1901, almost two years after any reasonable definition of timely compliance. The Copyright Office is a registry only, and any challenge to the validity of a copyright certificate is a matter for the courts, not the Library of Congress. There were enough irregularities in Stoker's two registrations to invalidate his claim on *Dracula*. Fortunately, no one ever did.

Why Stoker wasn't more vigilant on copyright matters we may never know. *Dracula*, in the end, may simply have exhausted him. He staged one more "copyright reading" at the Lyceum, for his novel *Miss Betty* in 1898, and obtained a Lord Chamberlain's license for a staged reading of *Mystery of the Sea* in 1902, but never followed through with the performance.

Stoker would not live long enough to see *Dracula* achieve media superstardom in America, but the initial critical response to the book was mostly positive, and sometimes more insightful than the original British notices. A long and perceptive review in the *Brooklyn Daily Eagle* sensed the author's affinity for fairy tales, mixed with a revulsion at the dehumanizing effects of a purely scientific worldview. "Upon an age of materialism, the book flashes a light of faith. On a time of fads and fakirs, it pours the results of an imagination that is as facile and familiar with marvels as children are made from nurses' lips." The reviewer found the novel's "persuasive audacity" to be "a rare fact and find." The worst condemnation on either side of the Atlantic ran in the *San Francisco Wave*, which titled its notice "The Insanity of the Horrible." "When an Englishman, or, for that matter, anyone of Anglo-Saxon blood, goes into degenerate literature of his own

An engraved portrait of Bram Stoker published in 1897, the year of Dracula's *debut.*

sort, he reveals a horrible kind of degeneracy. The works of the French degenerates possess a verve, a Gaelic attractiveness, indefinable but definite. . . . The difference is that between Whitechapel and the Moulin Rouge." But even this hatchet job ended with a left-handed compliment. "If you have the bad taste, after this warning, to attempt the book, you will read on to the finish, as I did—and go to bed, as I did, feeling furtively of your throat."

Henry C. Dickens (1882–1966), Charles's grandson, was one of the longest-living persons with a clear memory of Stoker at the time he wrote *Dracula*. In response to a 1959 *London Observer* piece by Maurice Richardson, drawing from his essay "The Psychoanalysis of Ghost Stories," in which he likened reading the book to "entering a twilight borderland, a sort of homicidal lunatic's brothel in a crypt, where religious and psychopathological motives intermingle," all culminating in "a kind of incestuous, necrophilous, oral-anal-sadistic wrestling match." Dickens wrote to the *Observer* editor and told him Stoker would have laughed at the assessment. "He wrote his book as an unashamed horror story (which it undoubtedly was) and hoping it to become a best-seller (which it did) and he wrote it in any case as a joke." According to the drama critic Frederick Donaghey, "He knew he had written, in 'Dracula,' a shilling shocker, however successful a one, and was frank about it." And no less an authority than Hall Caine wrote that Stoker "took no vain view of his efforts as an author. . . . He wrote his books to sell. . . . He had no higher aim."

In the final analysis, the most frightening thing about *Dracula* is the strong probability that it meant far less to Bram Stoker than it has come to mean to us.

Georg Sylvester Viereck:
Das Haus des
Vampyrs

CHAPTER NINE

UNDEAD OSCAR

FOR HE WHO LIVES MORE LIVES THAN ONE,
MORE DEATHS THAN ONE MUST DIE.

—Oscar Wilde, "The Ballad of Reading Gaol"

On May 18, 1897, no one noticed that the fictional monster Count Dracula
had been formally released into the world at almost the precise moment the
public monster Oscar Wilde had been officially returned to the world. By
an eerie coincidence, Wilde was released from Reading Gaol within hours
of Bram Stoker's marathon copyright reading of *Dracula* at the Lyceum
Theatre. Not that the event would have interested him. *The Picture of Dorian
Gray*, of course, was the superior meditation on the theme of supernatural
energy transference and moral corruption. As far as Wilde was concerned,
the theme would never need to be revisited. Besides, he had no time for
theatre now. He would never again set foot in the West End, never write
another play or even a work of fiction.

The epigrams he had left would be few, and mordant.

A few hours after the Lyceum actor Wallace Widdecombe read the
dying words of the American vampire slayer Quincey Morris, which closed
Stoker's play—"Now God be thanked that all has been not in vain. . . .

---

*Seven years after his death, Oscar Wilde was resurrected as a fictional vampire
by an obsessive admirer.*

The curse has passed away"—Wilde was given new street clothes, along with the precious manuscript on which he had labored for months (with the warden's hard-earned approval) that would ultimately be known as *De Profundis*. Under police escort, he was taken by train to Pentonville Prison, where he would spend the night. The stop at Pentonville spared him any chance of being recognized while waiting on a connecting train platform, as he had been at Clapham Junction on his initial transfer to Reading. Then, a crowd had jeered at him, as if he were a chained sideshow ape.

Arriving by train in London the morning of May 19, he was whisked by cab to a friend's house in Bloomsbury to change clothes and have his hair waved, and to taste coffee for the first time since his imprisonment. But he also received a major disappointment in the form of a letter his friends were holding for him. Wilde had hoped, perhaps, to spend a year in religious contemplation, but his last-minute application to a Catholic monastery had been denied on the basis of timeliness. He wept at the news. The Catholic Church had not only failed him—it was, in effect, barring his entry onto sacred ground, like some foul creature from Stoker's fevered imagination.

There was no question of Wilde's remaining in London. Personally, socially, and professionally, he was ruined. His exile and new identity had been prearranged as a rough Victorian equivalent of a witness protection program. He would take the night boat across the channel to Dieppe, France, to be met by his friends Robbie Ross and Reggie Turner. He was provided bags bearing the monogram initials "S. M."; at Robbie's suggestion he assumed the ironic cover name of "Sebastian Melmoth." St. Sebastian was a classic icon of male beauty and stoic martyrdom, as well as Wilde's favorite saint; the surname came from the title character of the Gothic novel *Melmoth the Wanderer*, written by his great-uncle Charles Robert Maturin in 1820. Maturin's Melmoth was an ambitious hybrid creation, part Faust and part Mephistopheles, his soul in a strange limbo that anticipated Dorian Gray's, and a traveler through the centuries in the manner of the Wandering Jew, Cagliostro, and Dracula.

It was only natural for Wilde to assume the aspect of a Gothic revenant. He already had a deeply ingrained belief in the supernatural. Like so many other Irish (including Bram Stoker's mother), he was convinced he had heard the wail of the banshee as a child, although at the time he believed it was the howl of a dog being beaten. He cried at the sound, wanting the terrible cruelty to stop. In 1893, at an opening night party for *A Woman of No Importance*, he was given a reading by the famous palmist Cheiro.[1] Guests presented their hands through a curtain, lest knowledge of their identity influence the reading. Cheiro claimed to have not recognized Wilde's particularly plump hands, although his identity ought to have been obvious, given the purpose of the gathering. Nonetheless, Cheiro was prescient. The lines of the hands diverged portentously. "The left hand is the hand of a king, but the right is that of a king who will send himself into exile." When was this to happen? In about two years, the seer replied. In other words, the exact year of his downfall. Wilde was shaken and left the party abruptly. He approached another fortune-teller the following year, a society Sybil called Mrs. Robinson. "I see a very brilliant life for you, up to a certain point," she told him. "Then I see a wall. Beyond the wall I see nothing."

Both Wilde and his mother were attracted to palmistry, divination, and the occult. According to Oscar, in 1896, the night before she died, a vision of Lady Wilde appeared in his jail cell, and he knew that she was dead even before his wife, Constance, arrived at Reading with the news. After his release, when Constance herself unexpectedly died—in European exile with her children under the assumed name "Holland"—her own ghost was said to have manifested before him. Wilde begged it to leave him alone.

The title character of *Melmoth the Wanderer* also wanted to be left alone by the supernatural entities with whom he had made a Faustian bargain. *Melmoth*, like *Dracula*, had been published by the venerable firm of Constable. The publisher assigned Maturin the title when he couldn't decide on one, just as the firm may have suggested *Dracula* as a title to Stoker in place of his generic (and somewhat perplexing) first choice, *The Un-Dead*. Both titles were the kind of simple solution—using the name of a central, supernatural character—that is sometimes obvious to everyone but the author. *Melmoth* is a complicated structure of stories within stories, a bit like *The Arabian Nights*, beginning with the efforts of John Melmoth, a student at Trinity College (Maturin, like Stoker and Wilde, was Trinity educated) to solve the mystery of a namesake forbear who has apparently survived for more than a century after his last recorded appearance. It

---

[1] The adopted professional name—from the old term "cheiromancy," meaning palmistry—of the Dublin-born occultist William John Warner, who also used the pseudonym Count Louis Hamon.

"Sebastian Melmoth": Oscar Wilde in exile.
Photograph possibly taken by Lord Alfred Douglas.

is ultimately revealed that the first Melmoth made a deal with the devil for a life extension of 150 years, the return of his soul predicated on his finding a successor who would accept the same terms. But, wander as he might, Melmoth is unable to find such a person, and suffers the hellish consequences.[2]

The book contains many horrific prison scenes that echo in Wilde's final work, "The Ballad of Reading Gaol," written shortly after his release. One of the poem's most famous lines, "Each man kills the thing he loves," has a chilling cannibal/vampire elaboration in Maturin as he describes the sights and sounds of a man and woman dehumanized in their cruel confinement: "The shriek of the wretched female—her lover, in the agony of hunger, had fastened his teeth in her shoulder;—that bosom on which he had so often luxuriated, became a meal to him now."

---

[2] Balzac wrote a parody of Maturin's novel, and suggested that if Melmoth was really serious about finding people willing to pawn their souls, he should have simply come to Paris.

Wilde didn't witness the eating of flesh in prison—cannibalism would have been a nourishing luxury—but he did see and experience the degradation of the human body every day. The strictly enforced official policy of "hard labour, hard fare, and a hard bed," combined with the unofficial but nonetheless omnipresent reality of dysentery and other intractable diseases, created an environment calculated to break the body and soul, and if it happened to prove fatal ... well, it must have been God's will. Prison officials knew that a man of Wilde's background, completely unaccustomed to inadequate nutrition and punishing work, might not live long even if he survived his term. No doubt this truth informed the judge's decision to inflict the maximum sentence.

The first part of Wilde's sentence was served at the facility in Pentonville, where, weakened by the poor food, he collapsed in the prison chapel, striking the side of his head. He developed a severe ear infection and spent two months in the prison infirmary. Without the benefits of antibiotics, yet to be developed, the injury never completely healed. Upon his transfer to Reading Gaol, the full reality of the conditions of his incarceration became clear. Prisoners lived in solitary confinement, slept on bare planks, were forbidden to talk, and were subjected to endless rounds of hard labor with no useful purpose. Climbing the steps of a creaking treadwheel, he made a daily virtual ascent of more than a mile. Endless hours were spent marching in circles, turning heavy cranks that themselves turned nothing, or shredding rope fiber with one's bare, bleeding fingers. Food was edible in only the narrowest physical sense.

In a post-imprisonment letter to the *Daily Chronicle*, Wilde deplored the conditions of the British penal system, which "seems almost to have for its aim the wrecking and the destruction of the mental faculties. ... Deprived of books, of all human intercourse, isolated from every humane and humanising influence, condemned to eternal silence, robbed of all intercourse with the external world, treated like an unintelligent animal, brutalised below the level of any of the brute-creation, the wretched man who is confined in an English prison can hardly escape becoming insane." In other words, the British criminal code was designed to create the very conditions of degeneration and evolutionary regression Victorian society pretended to fear and abhor, but found fascinating as cathartic entertainment in books like *The Picture of Dorian Gray, The Island of Dr. Moreau,* and *Dracula.*

An unverifiable yet fascinating story passed down through the Stoker family is that Bram and/or his wife assisted Wilde financially, either in prison or in exile. In *Children of the Night,* an inventive 2011 chamber musical about Stoker and Henry Irving, the composer and lyricist Scott Martin includes a scene in which Stoker visits the imprisoned Wilde, who encourages his long-time acquaintance to finally admit the actual nature of his slavish devotion to the charismatic actor. In reality, Wilde in 1897 was so thoroughly broken by his experiences "feasting with panthers" and the punishment that followed that he would be the last person to encourage others to flaunt unconventional passions. In retrospect, Wilde is indeed a great martyr to the cause of modern gay liberation, but he was hardly a crusader in his own time. In the musical, Wilde also ponders another point of similarity between Stoker and himself. Commenting on the imminent publication of *Dracula,* and in silent reference to *The Picture of Dorian Gray,* Wilde wonders, "What is it about the macabre that comes so naturally to us? Was there something tainted in the Dublin water supply when we were children?"

While it is next to impossible for either of the Stokers to have made such a prison visit—audiences with inmates were doled out quite sparingly, following a formal application process that would have left some record—the idea of some contact with Wilde in France, or a clandestine gift to him there, is not so farfetched, especially if instigated by Florence, who never quite relinquished a what-if fantasy about her near-marriage to one of the most brilliant celebrities of the age. And, of course, she was never at a loss in finding ways to dispose of her husband's money.

But had the Stokers given any cash to Wilde, it would have undoubtedly been squandered, if not on boys then most assuredly on drink. Paris, where he had settled, was known as the City of Light but had an omnipresent and liquid dark side. The liquor that flowed during the Belle Epoque was enough to flood the celebrated subterranean catacombs that underpinned the aboveground Parisian glamour. Like Dracula, Wilde in Paris was a creature in a self-imposed exile, driven by a terrible thirst. But unlike Dracula, the thirst was never limited to the night. Innumerable accounts of his final years describe him making ceaseless rounds of Left Bank bars and cafés, even when he had no money at all, leading to sad, humiliating scenes. Alcohol had always been a family weakness. In just a few years it would kill his brother, Willie, and even now was doing its part to gnaw away the precarious health Oscar had left. In sufficient quantities, alcohol will not only "create all the effects of inebriation," as per Wilde's famously flippant quip;

ultimately, it can negatively impact every system and organ in the body. Nonetheless, he continued to engorge himself with prodigious quantities of champagne, as well as a bubbling greenish mixture of champagne and absinthe, long after he was warned of the medical dangers, even when he was told outright that he was killing himself. He threw away even more money on a series of boulevard boys, many of them rough and with criminal backgrounds. "I cannot bear being alone . . . ," he said. "My companions are such as I can get, and of course I have to pay for such friendships."

With Maurice Gilbert, a less mercenary but nonetheless very popular new adoration (who shared himself with Robbie, Reggie, and even Bosie at one point), he managed to visit Auguste Rodin's studio, where the master sculptor personally showed him his monumental bronze doorway, *The Gates of Hell.* Since he had already been to hell, or at least its earthly approximation, one can imagine him complimenting Rodin with some darkly insightful observations on damnation. But there was little humor in one of his actual comments: "I will never outlive the century; the English people would not stand for it." He spent his last year doing everything he could to guarantee they wouldn't have to.

In November 1900, just weeks before the twentieth century officially began on January 1, 1901, he developed an infection of his prison-injured ear, resulting in a painful abscess requiring surgery. The operation did not relieve the underlying infection, which escalated into bacterial meningitis, as untreatable as syphilis was in the pre-antibiotic age. The question of syphilis and its role in Wilde's death continues to be controversial, though at this late date it shouldn't. As in arguments about the purported syphilitic deaths of many famous people, the questions "Did he die of syphilis?" and "Did he have syphilis?" are too often ignorantly conflated. As Wilde's grandson, Merlin Holland, told a BBC interviewer, "Around twenty-five percent of Victorian men had syphilis, and he may have had it, too—we'll never know—but one thing that's almost certain is that he didn't die of it."

Like all medical conditions, syphilis can coexist with, complicate, and even mimic a myriad of other diseases. In a significant number of cases, the condition does not even progress to its terminal, tertiary stage but instead remains dormant, deep in the body. Further complicating detection and assessment is the fact that subsequent, additional infections of *Treponema pallidum* can confer a partial immunity that suppresses primary symptoms. For individuals like Wilde, an active member of a highly promiscuous subculture in which untreated (and untreatable) sexually transmitted diseases were already rife, superinfection was not only possible but almost inevitable. He could well have been harboring a dormant case contracted at Oxford, and a later case when he began straying from his marriage.

In any case, Wilde believed he had syphilis and likely assumed it was taking his life, and his friends believed this, too. He may also have been secretly convinced it had killed Constance Wilde. The medical historian Deborah Hayden makes a strong case that the creeping spinal paralysis that took Constance Wilde's life may itself have been an expression of tertiary syphilis. Wilde learned of her spinal problems shortly after being released from prison, exactly the period in which he wrote "Each man kills the thing he loves." Robert Sherard remembered seeing a letter from Constance in which she wrote, "And you know that you made me ill."

As his own health worsened, his dream life followed suit. "I dreamt I was supping with the dead," he told Reggie Turner and Robbie Ross. Turner replied, "My dear Oscar, you were probably the life and soul of the party." It was the last laugh the three men would have together.

The story that Wilde made a deathbed conversion to Catholicism has been repeated so often it is usually taken as gospel, but a close reading of the supporting documents yields far less certainty. In Paris, Oscar talked about his desire to convert, more or less in the dilettantish way he had talked about it for most of his life. Robbie Ross, himself a lapsed Catholic, told Oscar he couldn't support him in the matter if he wasn't completely serious. But when Oscar began slipping away, Robbie—probably guilt stricken over not having given his friend more encouragement while he was still able to make such decisions—managed to find an Irish Passionist priest, Father Cuthbert Dunn, willing to come to the hotel. While Father Dunn was convinced that the delirious, semiconscious patient finally accepted the Church, Ross would on at least one occasion admit that he didn't truly know what had happened. Officially speaking, the sacrament was "conditional" and not subject to earthly verification.

Wilde lingered overnight, but the coming of dawn was the beginning of the end. "After 5:30 in the morning a complete change came over him," Ross wrote, "the lines of the face altered, and I believe what is called the death rattle began, but I had never heard anything like it before; it sounded like the horrible turning of a crank, and it never ceased until the end." Death, like a demanding, uncontrollable, and monstrous child, would be seen as well as heard. "Foam and blood came from his mouth, and had to be wiped away by someone standing by him all the time. . . . The painful noise from the throat became louder and louder." The end came in the early afternoon. Ross noticed that "the time of his breathing altered. I went to the bedside and held his hand, his pulse began to flutter. He heaved a deep sigh, the only natural one I had heard since I arrived, the limbs seemed to stretch involuntarily, the breathing became fainter; he passed at 10 minutes to 2 p.m. exactly."

Unpleasant though it was, the account was sanitized. Wilde's actual moment of death might have been imagined by Poe—something akin to the shocking conclusion of "The Facts in the Case of M. Valdemar." Ross and Turner told friends privately what really transpired, as reported by Wilde's biographer Richard Ellman: "He had scarcely breathed his last when the body exploded with fluids from the ear, nose, mouth, and other orifices. The debris was appalling."

The bedding had to be burned. The body was washed, bound, and dressed in a clean nightshirt. Father Dunn placed palm fronds on the corpse. Ross hung a rosary around the neck. According to one account, the proprietor of the hotel removed Wilde's dentures; the gold fittings would partially offset a sizable sum still owed the establishment.

By registering at the Hotel d'Alsace under a false name, Wilde had broken French law, raising the possibility that he would be taken as an ordinary unidentified corpse to the morgue. In operation since 1865 just behind the Cathedral of Notre Dame, the Paris Morgue was a ghastly tourist attraction where unidentified bodies (or body parts), many pulled from the Seine, were put on ammonia-refrigerated public display, ostensibly to be identified and claimed by loved ones, although in reality only a very small percentage of visitors—the daily attendance record was forty thousand—came on missions of care. Most were there to be morbidly entertained. Wilde had visited the carnivalesque charnel house himself, and near his death wrote, "The Morgue yawns for me. I go and look at my zinc bed there." Bram Stoker's working notes for *Dracula* refer to the even more grisly Munich "Dead House" for an unrealized scene wherein the Count, experimenting with travel beyond Transylvania, hides in plain sight among the openly displayed German dead. But a notorious dead celebrity like Oscar Wilde could expect no such anonymity.

When the district doctor, or medical examiner, arrived at the Hotel

Oscar Wilde in death, Paris, 1900.

d'Alsace, he wanted to know whether the dead man had committed suicide or had been murdered. According to Ross, "After examining the body, and, indeed, everybody in the hotel, and after a series of drinks and unseasonable jests, and a liberal fee," the official signed the papers necessary for Wilde's burial.

Wilde and Ross had discussed Oscar's wish to be buried at Père Lachaise, the largest cemetery within Paris and the resting place of choice for prominent Parisians, including creative giants like Molière and Chopin. But the arrangement was impossible on short notice. As a temporary concession, Ross took out a five-year renewable lease on a cemetery plot in the commune (or township) of Bagneux, about eight miles south of central Paris. A more appropriate site, and fitting monument, would have to wait. Ross's own finances were depleted, and he would spend several years settling Wilde's estate and paying off accumulated debt.

"When preparing the body for the grave," Harris wrote in his Wilde biography, "Ross had taken medical advice as to what should be done to make his purpose [eventual reinterment] possible. The doctors told him to put Wilde's body in quicklime." According to Harris, the doctors offered assurance that quicklime "would consume the flesh and leave the white bones—the skeleton—intact, which could then be moved easily." This was not scientifically accurate, but Ross may well have been additionally persuaded by Wilde's own writing. "The Ballad of Reading Gaol" described the quicklime interment of the executed prisoner Trooper Charles Woodridge:

> And all the while the burning lime
> Eats flesh and bone away,
> It eats the brittle bone by night,
> And the soft flesh by the day,
> It eats the flesh and bones by turns,
> But it eats the heart away.

Another purpose of the powder was simply to mask stench, for which it had a proven efficacy, both in funerary matters and in latrines. Ross was urged to seal the body in its coffin quickly, before decomposition began.

Bosie had been contacted, but not in time for him to reach Paris before Wilde's coffin had been screwed shut. The two men had made a disastrous attempt at reconciliation in Naples after Oscar's release from Reading, and their relationship had continued for the most part at a prickly distance. Bosie sent Wilde small gifts of money, grudgingly, but after he came into a substantial inheritance upon the death of the Marquess of Queensberry in early 1900 and Wilde asked if some regular allowance might be arranged to supplement the not-lavish income from his wife's estate, Bosie responded with the reflexive instinct of an adder. Wilde was "like an old fat prostitute" for even asking. "I can't afford to spend money on anything but myself," Bosie claimed. These expenses included a race stable in Chantilly, gambling, and many other extravagant pursuits. "He has left me bleeding," Wilde told Frank Harris.

On the cold, rainy morning of December 2, the coffin was drawn by horses to a funeral mass at the ancient Left Bank church of St. Germain de Prés. The service was austere, unaccompanied by music, and attended by a small number of friends and acquaintances. After the long muddy journey to Bagneux, the burial ceremony, by one account, was marred by a heated argument over who, exactly, would officiate as chief mourner: Robbie Ross or Lord Alfred Douglas? Bosie had paid for the funeral, conducted very noticeably on the cheap. In the ugly confrontation, it was said, he was very nearly knocked into the open grave. Or perhaps he just slipped in the mud. But on one level he truly did fall into a pit, where he would spend the rest

Wilde's first grave, at Bagneux, outside Paris.

of his life wrestling with his revenant lover, who would drain his energies and sap his soul.

While Wilde still rested in his temporary grave in Bagneux, a young German American devotee in New York was determined to resurrect him by any means necessary.

Even if that meant turning him into a vampire.

But first, in a strange and breathless 1905 letter to the American literary journal *The Critic*—it had been turned down elsewhere—the twenty-year-old poet and essayist George Sylvester Viereck, still a student at the City University of New York, reported a "rumor afloat so sensational that I hardly dare express it, namely, that the author of 'De Profundis' is not dead at all, but that he either lives the life of a recluse in the bosom of the all-embracing Church, or, according to another version, that he is at this very moment in the city of New York." Viereck admitted that "what I shall say has the thrill of the melodrama, and for that reason will be doubted by many who do not know the truth of the old platitude that truth is stranger than fiction and that, though it may imitate art, it often surpasses the latter."

During intermission at a fashionable New York theatre, Viereck reported, the conversation had "for some reason" turned to the topic of Wilde. "A very charming and clever woman, well known in the circles of the Sunrise Club, spoke to me softly: 'and have you not heard . . . they whisper . . . among those who know . . . that Oscar Wilde is not dead at all . . . that the monks in a Spanish cloister have taken him under their shelter . . . that he is dead to the world only . . . but . . . ' and she raised her finger to her lips . . . 'they whisper. . . .' I was speechless."

Was such a thing possible? Not long after, while in conversation with a Manhattan bookseller, he couldn't resist broaching the subject. "I said significantly, as it were in italics: '. . . It is said that Wilde has not died at all. . . .' When I had said these words the young man looked at me curiously. Then he said, as if confident that I was one of the partakers of a great secret: 'I know, for I saw him only two weeks ago.' 'Is it possible? But where?' 'Right here in New York.' 'On the street?' 'No, not on the street.' 'Did you try to speak to him?' 'I did, for ten minutes. And I have hardly ever heard a talker more brilliant, or one more sparkling with wit.' 'Are you sure that it was he?' 'It could have been no other, but I asked no questions. . . . ' My curiosity seemed to arouse his suspicions. 'You want to establish the facts in the case, I see.' And from that moment it was impossible to draw another word from him."

Viereck claimed to have discovered, in a truncated German edition of *De Profundis*, recently published, a passage in which Wilde described himself "as a revenant, in the French phrase, as one whose face has become gray and distorted with pain. Terrible as are the dead when they rise from the graves, the living that come back from the grave are far more terrible." Though convincingly Wildean in cadence, these lines appear nowhere in the original manuscript. Fortunately for Viereck, no one at the time questioned the hoax. "There would have to be accomplices, of course," he admitted, then posited a conspiracy, for "we know that only a few friends attended his funeral. His family took no part in it. And so it is possible that under that grave in Paris . . . sleeps some poor beggar or honest bourgeois who never dreamed that he should rest in a poet's tomb." Viereck closed his missive with an apotheosis formed as a rhetorical question:

> Was not this brilliant lover of the paradoxical capable of making his very life and death a paradox, and in the phrase of a Greek poet, "to be and not to be, not being to be."[3] And was not the Unexpected, the Sensational, the element in which he loved to move in life and art? And would it not be quite in accordance with his character to carry to the last point of consistency the Christ pose, blasphemous perhaps, which he adopted especially in his last book, . . . and from his tomb to roll the stone and rise from the dead?

Readers were puzzled, to say the least. Who on earth was this George Sylvester Viereck person, and where did he get such crazy ideas?

Born in Munich to a cultured family on the last day of 1884, Viereck was already recognized as a literary wunderkind when his family moved to New York in the late 1890s. Like Bram Stoker, he possessed extraordinary verbal gifts and expressed them early, even alarmingly. Like Stoker, he relished befriending famous, powerful people. Where Stoker cultivated favor with the artistic likes of Walt Whitman, Henry Irving, Hall Caine, and Mark Twain, and could drop the names of countless others, Viereck sought out a broader trophy list: George Bernard Shaw, Albert Einstein, Nikola Tesla, Theodore Roosevelt, and, most improbably, Sigmund Freud.

Also in common with Stoker, he had significant early anxieties about death—like both Stoker and Stoker's mother, Charlotte, he was fascinated by Poe—and as a child became fantastically obsessed with discovering a formula for immortality. Eventually, he must have realized that a highly eccentric, self-consciously cultivated literary reputation was the closest approximation he was going to achieve. The word "prodigy" was originally used to describe sideshow monsters, and the freakish talents of young Viereck established him as an enfant terrible, a formidable monster of the literary midway. Barely out of grammar school, he espoused outlandish opinions, wild even by adult standards, and was writing and translating

---

[3] The "Greek poet" is the Eleatic philosopher Parmenides, whose work both anticipated and influenced Heidegger's phenomenology.

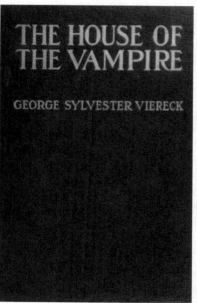

THE HOUSE OF
THE VAMPIRE

GEORGE SYLVESTER VIERECK

Left: George Sylvester Viereck, German American prodigy of the perverse.
Right: American edition of House of the Vampire *(1907).*

poetry with ease, even before puberty. His first published verses, in German, appeared in New York newspapers when he was thirteen.

Viereck was also sexually precocious. His friend and biographer Elmer Gertz noted (with cushioned understatement) that "his amorous tastes were dubious, and troubled a few of his peers and elders." These predilections revolved around a "too rabid admiration for Wilde" and for "the roses and raptures of Swinburnian vice." One of his youthful, unpublished opuses was a massive manuscript in German called *Elinor: The Autobiography of a Degenerate.* He reveled in the works of Havelock Ellis, Krafft-Ebing, and Sade. Eventually he would declare himself a "sexual relativist," an erotic omnivore who would proclaim, "There is no such thing as a perversion," defining the concept as "what the other fellow does and we don't like," a statement roughly in the style of (though not quite so memorable as) Wilde's epigrammatic definition of wickedness: "a word invented by good people to account for the curious attractiveness of others."

"Wilde is splendid," Viereck wrote. "I admire, nay I love him. He is so deliciously unhealthy, so beautifully morbid. I love all things evil! I love the splendor of decay, the foul beauty of corruption." As if in preparation for his own foray into Wilde-related vampirism, he hated "the freezing rays of the sun. Day is nausea, day is prose. Night, Beauty, love, splendor, poetry, wine, scarlet, rape, vice and bliss! I love the night—*und Meschugge ist Trump!* [Craziness trumps all!]"

Little more than a year after Wilde's death, the seventeen-year-old Viereck was startled and excited to learn Lord Alfred Douglas himself was in New York (ostensibly to find a suitable heiress with whom to settle down, as Wilde's dust did the same.) After virtually stalking Douglas, leaving fever-ish notes and missing him three times at his hotel, Viereck was rewarded with a luncheon date with Bosie himself. Viereck's biographer encapsulated the boy's reaction as the "glorious feeling" of meeting "one who had clasped the hand of god and known and loved him in the flesh!" A more neutral observer might detect something more akin to necrophilia by proxy.

Since lunch would be a blind date, Viereck told Douglas he could be recognized by his fur coat and clean-shaven face. What fully transpired between the boy and Wilde's now thirty-one-year-old angel of destruction isn't known, but Viereck was adventurous, and Bosie was still the person whose own insatiable appetite for men went miraculously unmentioned in the Wilde trials. The upshot of their meeting was an apparently affec-tionate friendship, and they would remain off-and-on correspondents until the older man's death in 1946. He wrote to Viereck before leaving New York, without an heiress. As he told Olive Custance, the boyish and lesbian-leaning woman with whom he would enter an ultimately unsuccessful mar-riage, "It might have been different if I had met a nice heir. But apparently there are none." Had he, perhaps, met some less-than-nice ones? He wrote to Viereck, "I have met many charming people here and seen many inter-esting and wonderful things in this country and not the least of my plea-sures was meeting you." He concluded wistfully: "You are too clever not to make your mark some time or other. I hope you will have more luck and make a better business of your life than I have done with mine."

Douglas was no doubt unusually surprised to make the acquaintance of anyone who viewed his relationship with Wilde in a positive, much less an overtly worshipful, light. Viereck met him just as the full consequences of the scandal—and it was *the* scandal of the age—had begun making them-selves clear. While visiting Washington, DC, during this very trip, he had been unceremoniously asked to leave his guest lodgings at the Metropolitan

Club after it received a complaint about his connection to "objectionable persons." He responded with a withering sonnet dedicated to, or aimed at, the club, printed prominently in the *New York Herald*.

Viereck may have intuited Bosie's burgeoning resentment and sense of victimization over the Wilde affair, which would only increase. This was supremely ironic, since he had emerged legally unscathed by Oscar's trials. When he met Viereck at the end of 1901, he still was unaware of the explosive contents of *De Profundis*, in which Wilde excoriates his former lover unmercifully, with accusations that both his finances and his creativity had been drained away by their relationship.[4] Not all of Wilde's indictments are deserved, and Douglas was not quite the soulless, predatory monster described in the letter. But there was enough truth to really sting. As delineated by Wilde, Douglas is a spoiled parasite who exerts an irresistible and nearly preternatural hold on his victim. A century later, he could have provided (and possibly did provide) a template for one of Anne Rice's beautiful, golden-haired bloodsuckers, and it is easy enough to imagine a *Dorian Gray*–like story in which both men are condemned to a querulous undead eternity, where the bitchy recriminations never stop. The strong supernatural potential of Douglas's personality was pointedly raised in the *London Evening Standard* review of the 1960 Hammer film *The Brides of Dracula*, in which the blond and well-preserved vampire Baron Meinster (David Peel) is likened to "Bosie with fangs."

Was there something about Wilde and Douglas that might be suitable for a fictional treatment in the decadent mode of which Viereck was so fond? Something weird and unworldly? Perhaps even . . . vampiric? Nothing in that line had yet been done in the United States. The best-selling novelist Owen Wister, author of *The Virginian*, announced his intention to write an American epic of the undead in 1902. Philip Burne-Jones, painter of *The Vampire*, expressed his willingness to illustrate it. Neither Stoker's nor Wister's book materialized, which was a shame, because a vampire novel set firmly in the robber-baron era would have had enormous thematic possibilities. However, a good deal of short vampire fiction blossomed in

---

[4] *De Profundis* was first published by Robert Ross in 1905 in a shortened version with all references to Lord Alfred Douglas redacted. This material would have continued to be suppressed, under the threat of a libel action, until it was forced into evidence in another suit Douglas unwisely instigated in 1912, and thereby made public.

Scene from Edgar Allan Woolf's **The Vampire,** *the 1909 stage adaptation of Viereck's novel.*

Dracula's transatlantic penumbra at the turn of the century. Much of it is still worth reading, including the New England tale "Luella Miller" (1901) by Mary E. Wilkins-Freeman, and "Count Magnus" (1904) by the British ghost story master M. R. James.

But no one since Stoker had ventured to essay another vampire novel. George Sylvester Viereck believed he was fated to the task. The result of his efforts was a short novel, *The House of the Vampire*, published in 1905. The book was issued simultaneously in English and German, the latter edition stamped with an unmistakable cover image: the livid face of Oscar Wilde.

The novel introduces Reginald Clarke, a charismatic American luminary of literature and the arts with the power to absorb the talent and creativity of others—a psychic vampire capable of entering minds to steal intellectual property, even before the original owner has put pen to paper. He lives in imposing, sumptuously appointed rooms that frown down upon Riverside Drive as if it were the Borgo Pass, and offers hospitality to a series of unsuspecting, talented young men, sacrificial protégés who will never, of course, realize their own artistic dreams. After he has drained the seminal source of their talent, they believe they are going mad. Early in the story, Reginald summarily dismisses Abel Felton, his latest, exhausted conquest who mourns his bled-away inspiration. "It will come again, in a month, in a year, two years," Reginald assures him.

> "No, no! It is all gone!" sobbed the boy.
>
> "Nonsense. You are merely nervous. But that is why we must part. There is no room in one house for two nervous people."
>
> "I was not such a nervous wreck before I met you."
>
> "Am I to blame for it—for your morbid fancies, your extravagance, the slow tread of a nervous disease, perhaps?"
>
> "Who can tell? But I am all confused. I don't know what I am saying, Everything is so puzzling—life, friendship, you. I fancied you cared for my career, and now you end our friendship without a thought!"

Following a round of epicene fireworks, Abel is quickly replaced by Ernest Fielding, another young man with the requisite amount of aesthetic baggage, notably an androgynous friend named Jack, an inseparable soulmate with long eyelashes who, alas, is now gone away to Harvard, leaving open a vampiric approach. (The names Jack and Ernest, of course, are a somewhat less than subtle evocation of John "Jack" Worthing and his alter ego in *The Importance of Being Earnest.*) Ernest has in mind a strange but monumental drama, a compelling admixture of *Hamlet* and *Salome,* which the vampire can read in his mind and decides to take as his own. When Ernest sees Abel leaving the house, he remembers that the boy is an aspiring writer and inquires about the progress of his latest work. "I am not writing it," Abel says, smiling sadly. "Not writing it?" Ernest asks. "Reginald is," Abel says. "I'm afraid I don't understand," Ernest replies. "Never mind," Abel says in parting. "Some day you will."

When Ernest realizes that the readings Reginald begins giving during his elegant evening salons are based on the play he is still only in the process of imagining, he consults a former disciple, Ethel Brandenbourg, who, the reader can assume, escaped Reginald's thrall largely because she was a woman; men are the monster's preferred tidbits and toys. Ethel succeeds in making him realize Reginald's full demonic power. Ernest believes he is falling in love with Ethel, but it is only Reginald's invading mind, seeking to possess her once again. Ethel firmly resists, and encourages him to seek additional support from his trusted friend Jack, to whom he immediately writes. But it is too late. Reginald has already summoned him and selected him as Ernest's replacement. Following a tense confrontation between vampire and victim, Reginald declares his triumph and mentally sucks out the contents of Ernest's brain, like marrow from a bone. Ethel arrives at the house and sees "something that resembled Ernest Fielding" emerge from the door, gibbering like an idiot, "a dull and brutish thing, hideously transformed, without a vestige of mind."

Although Viereck had envisioned Wilde while writing *The House of the Vampire*, another great writer lent some inspiration as well. Clarke describes Honoré de Balzac's genius at "absorbing from life the elements essential to his artistic completion." Evil attracted Balzac especially, the vampire explains. "He absorbed it as a sponge absorbs water; perhaps because there was so little of it in his own make-up. He must have purified the atmosphere around him for miles, by bringing all the evil that was floating in the air or slumbering in men's souls to the point of his pen."

With his first piece of book-length fiction, Viereck took aim not just at Stoker but at the looming white whale of literary accomplishment as well. "You've heard of the 'great American novel'? Well, I've written it," he proclaimed to an interviewer with characteristic immodesty. "The hero is a vampire. In every age there have been great men—and they became great by absorbing the work of other men." Napoleon appropriated power. Shakespeare ransacked lesser, earlier works for his own, transcendent glory. John D. Rockefeller, "by his great genius, has acquired material wealth by absorbing smaller capitalists. . . . My vampire is the Overman of Nietzsche. He is justified in the pilfering of other men's brains."

If such an overwrought love letter to the privilege and entitlement of great men sounds like a horror novel imagined by Ayn Rand, it is only because Viereck beat her to the punch. In his swooning surrender to authoritarian energies, he echoes Stoker's weakness for the domineering likes of Henry Irving. But where *Dracula* exorcised—or at least bargained with—Darwinian anxieties about the survival of the fittest, *The House of the Vampire* gave them all a big, hearty welcome. Not surprisingly, Viereck's passion for Great Men and All Things German led inevitably to his idolization of Kaiser Wilhelm, and later Adolf Hitler. Viereck's work as an obsessive propagandist for Germany would be understandably controversial during World War I, and would actually land him in prison during World War II for violations of the Foreign Agents Registration Act.

Critics of *The House of the Vampire* were relentlessly skeptical, refusing to concede the birth of a new Melville. "Except in the final scene, where its extravagances are in keeping with the subject," opined the *New York Times*, "the style of the book is quite impossible. 'The House of the Vampire' may be described as a tale of horror, keyed from the first word to the last in the highest pitch of tragic emotion." The *Nation* concurred. "The difficulty with Mr. Viereck's treatment lies in purely melodramatic conception of character, an utter lack of subtlety in dealing with the whole situation, and a distressing congestion of large words."

Nonetheless, the novel contains some genuinely chilling moments, as when Clarke, slumming at a downscale variety show, detects the one trace of real talent in an otherwise mediocre singer—a distinctive tremolo, her only grace—and casually snatches its expressive quality for his own. Her livelihood evaporated, she has no choice except to become one of the prostitutes glancingly encountered by Ernest and Jack, and described as pathetic "creatures who had once been women." A particularly inventive note is that Clarke's vampirism is omnivorous, making no distinction between the art forms upon which it feeds. The literary can feed the visual, and vice versa. "But what on earth could you find in my poor art to attract you? What were my pictures to you?" asks Ethel, whose talent as a painter waned under his malignant influence. "I needed them, I needed you," he replies. "It was a certain something, a rich colour effect, perhaps. And then, under your very eyes, the colour that vanished from your canvases reappeared in my prose."

But reviewers were right in taking the author to task for campy overkill in his treatment of Reginald's final triumph over Ernest. "He stood up at full length, the personification of grandeur and power. A tremendous force trembled in his very fingertips. He was like a gigantic dynamo, charged with the might of ten thousand magnetic storms that shake the earth in its orbit and lash myriads of planets through infinities of space." The vampire, whose powers Viereck likened favorably to the monopoly might of Standard Oil, gloats over his puny victim, who should be grateful that his meager talent is being absorbed into a greater, glorious power. "Look at me, boy! As I stand before you I am Homer, I am Shakespeare. . . . I am every cosmic manifestation in art. Men have doubted in each incarnation of my existence. Historians have more to tell of the meanest Athenian scribbler or Elizabethan poetaster than of me. The radiance of my work obscured my very self. I care not. I have a mission. I am a servant of the Lord. I am the vessel that bears the Host!"

If it is difficult to see any of Oscar Wilde in this monomaniacal portrait of Nietzsche's *Übermensch* morphed into a Christian-inflected black hole, it's because there really isn't much to see. Wilde may have been egotistic, but he didn't believe in eating his inferiors. He was the compassionate author of "The Soul of Man under Socialism," and a crusader for prison reform in the deeply empathic "Ballad of Reading Gaol," works that would surely repel any self-respecting sociocultural vampire like Clarke as effectively as a brandished Bible. As Lord Alfred Douglas would much later (and very gently) tell Viereck, apropos of some of the young writer's other excited musings, they didn't necessarily see eye to eye on the subject of Oscar. In *The House of the Vampire* Viereck takes both sides—admiring Clarke/Wilde and justifying the terrible trouble he causes a young man, yet sympathizing with Ernest/Bosie for getting involved with him in the first place.

Viereck obviously couldn't have written *The House of the Vampire* without the prior existence of *Dracula*. The American edition had been in print for five years, and a steady seller, crystalizing vampires in the public imagination like nothing before or since. The idea was sufficiently familiar for Viereck to float his own imaginative variation on an already imaginative theme. Ethel's explanation for Reginald's existence is a virtual précis of Van Helsing's argument that vampires could be understood in the context of revealed modern science. "Our scientists have proved true the wildest theories of modern scholars. The transmutation of metals seems to-day no longer an idle speculation. . . . Life was become once more wonderful and very mysterious. But it also seems that, with the miracles of the old days, their terrors, their nightmares and their monsters have come back in a modern guise."

The concept of psychic vampirism had been essayed even before *Dracula*, in stories like Arthur Conan Doyle's *The Parasite* (1894), playing to the fascination with psychic phenomena and spiritualism as expression of a new kind of science, if one not yet completely comprehended. The broad renown of *Dracula* made Viereck's variant premise understandable to general readers. Also available to Viereck were some of the same sources that preceded and informed Stoker, especially the German sources, including von Wachsmann's "The Mysterious Stranger" and the libretto of Heinrich Marschner's opera *Der Vampyr* (1828), a standard work in the German repertoire for most of the nineteenth century.

Actor John Kellerd, cast in **The Vampire** *because of his striking resemblance to Oscar Wilde.*

In 1909 Viereck allowed, or presumably allowed, the playwright Edgar Allan Woolf (best known today for his contributions to MGM's *The Wizard of Oz*) to adapt *The House of the Vampire* for the New York stage, with a number of significant alterations. First, and for no discernible reason, the names of the characters were all changed: Reginald Clarke became Paul Hartleigh, Ernest Fielding transmogrified into Caryl Fielding, and Ethel Brandenbourg was alliterated into Allene Arden. Unlike Ethel, Allene was the vampire's ward and unrequited love interest, not his brain candy. Strangest of all was the play's climax, in which Allene and Caryl play a bit of psychic jujitsu, confronting the vampire and forcing him to relinquish his powers. While this confusingly contradicted Viereck's whole triumphal concept of the *Übermensch*, it provided a more or less "happy" ending, a concession likely demanded by the commercial producers.

A concerted effort must have been made to find the actor in New York most resembling Oscar Wilde, and success came in the person of the veteran performer John E. Kellerd, who couldn't have looked more like Wilde in his prime. The role of the first, discarded victim was considerably expanded and played by the young Warner Oland (later Charlie Chan of movie fame),[5] whose Neronian bangs made him also appear like Wilde, in his early aesthetic period. Oddly, none of the New York reviewers talked about Wilde at all. He may still have been a subject that prompted reticence. When the *New York Times* reviewed the first American revival of *The Importance of Being Earnest* in 1902, its notice had the most lugubrious preamble imaginable for a comedy, lamenting that the play was "inextricably associated with the saddest and most revolting scandal in the history of the English drama—perhaps of all drama," and that it was "impossible to forget the broken and almost abandoned man of genius who crept away to a by-street in the Latin Quarter, to die like a rat with a broken back in an alley." One reviewer of *The Vampire* described Kellerd simply as "a clean shaven Svengali," leaving it to the editorial cartoonist to capture the essences of both Wilde and Dracula, adding to the villain's Noël Cowardish dressing gown a pair of flapping bat wings.

It was only appropriate that a play about supernatural plagiarism faced charges of copyright infringement itself from a number of parties. Arthur Stringer, author of the 1903 novel *The Silver Poppy*, claimed that *The Vampire* stole its theme and filed suit. Stringer's book was a story about a very different kind of literary imposture, and contained a metaphorical passage about a pterodactyl-like creature from the Amazon who perishes with its biologist captor. The strange fusion of human bones and what appear to be gigantic bat wings is taken as evidence of a Dracula-like vampire's existence. Viereck happily told the press, "I am really sorry the charge is not true, because in that case it would be conclusive proof that my theory of thought absorption is true." He continued, more or less adopting the Reginald Clarke persona, "Even if I had absorbed ideas from works ojf an inferior quality I still would feel justified in using them, but, unfortunately, I have not done anything of the kind." Two other complainants said they had registered *The Vampire* title with the Copyright Office, even though a title alone was never subject to legal protection.

In the fascinating analysis by Paul K. Saint-Amour in *The Copywrights: Intellectual Property and the Literary Imagination*, the whole issue of copyright

---

[5] Oland also appeared in Universal's *Werewolf of London* (1935) as Dr. Yogami, an Asian (and rather Wildean) lycanthrope who warns another shapeshifter that "each man must kill the thing he loves."

A newspaper cartoon of **The Vampire** *employed bat imagery found nowhere in the play.*

is examined from the "hauntological" perspective of an author's legal ability to survive death and keep feeding, at least monetarily. "Without ever mentioning the word 'copyright,'" Saint-Amour writes, "Viereck's novel and play had tapped into a vein of contemporary discourse about both the power and the limits of intellectual property law." An opponent to expanded author protections, he notes, "could interpret *The Vampire* as a cautionary tale about the appropriations and erasures licensed by a law that treated ideas and experiences like objects." Similar issues (and metaphors) were raised in the landmark legal case *Lugosi v. Universal Pictures*, argued from 1972 to 1979, which set important precedents in the areas of celebrity likeness and trademark, all stemming from the question of whether or not Bela Lugosi's famous Dracula persona could survive Lugosi's actual death in the realm of living commerce. Informal, meta-phorical references to blood and bloodsucking are also quite common in issues of property law generally, as well as in innumerable crass jokes about lawyers.

After providing some publicity, presumably gratifying for both sides, the lawsuit hoopla over the Woolf and Viereck play evaporated when the New York production, presented at Hackett's Theatre on Forty-second Street, closed after only a few weeks. Then, after rematerializing for a handful of touring engagements in New England, *The Vampire* itself vanished. No copy of the script or promptbook has ever been unearthed. While hardly commercial successes, both the novel and stage adaptation were harbingers of a greater interest in vampires to come. The year 1909 also marked the appearance of *A Fool There Was*, a runaway success onstage based on a best-selling novel, both inspired by the 1897 Philip Burne-Jones painting *The Vampire* and its accompanying Rudyard Kipling poem. The debut of the painting and poem shared a publicity sphere with *Dracula*, and *A Fool There Was* crystallized the image of the femme fatale vampire, or "vamp," which launched the career of the silent movie actress Theda Bara when the story was filmed in 1910.

Viereck's psychic vampire feeds on his victims' creativity instead of their blood.

Dracula had set in motion a variety of derivative metaphors, rippling outward over an ever-widening pool of blood that would captivate the twentieth century, and in which Dracula himself would continue to thrive. Viereck's Reginald Clarke in particular provided an important bridge between the secretive, reclusive, crepuscular Count and the evolving conceit of vampires as creatures of taste, refinement, and conspicuous consumption—an appetite extending beyond the mere consumption of human blood. Stoker's Dracula stuffed gold into his clothing as if into a miser's mattress and maintained a lair in London devoid of objets d'art, with little more than a bloodstained water basin for furniture. Commenting on the showier, emboldened decadence of the undead in the Edwardian era, Nina Auerbach, in *Our Vampires, Ourselves*, observes that "homosexuality clung to them in the sickeningly sinister form it assumed after the imprisonment of Oscar Wilde. Dracula was one particularly debased incarnation of the fallen Wilde, a monster of silence and exile, vulnerable to a legalistic series of arcane rules." The new century, however, opened the coffin-closet more than a crack. "As Dracula, Wilde could be isolated by diagnoses and paralyzed by rules, but as the psychic vampire Reginald Clarke, Wilde's image, ungovernable and cosmic, rules the world."

Once upon a time in Dublin there lived a wondrous child named Hester Dowden. She had dark hair and large, intelligent eyes that could absorb printed words that her mind understood magically, as if she were already an adult. At the age of four, she astonished grown-ups with her ability to read and comprehend Goethe's *Faust*, in German as well as English. While other children still languished with fairy tales, she could read Grimm in the original language if she wanted to, but instead was drawn to more challenging supernatural tales. *Faust* was about a most attractive devil who could bestow uncanny gifts upon mortals, including the power to perceive the spirit world and all the fantastic beings that lived there.

Hester lived in a fine house filled with books. The books belonged to her father, Edward Dowden, a very wise man who wrote books himself about the famous playwright Shakespeare and taught literature at the great university around which all the people and activities of Dublin revolved.

As a child, her affection for her father was real and reciprocal. When she was only eight years old he wrote letters to her while on literary business in London telling her about his pleasure at viewing Sir Isaac Newton's man-uscripts and death mask, explaining what the Poets' Corner at Westminster Abbey was, or describing to her amazing drawings by William Blake he couldn't wait to tell her more about. All in all, he seemed eager to encour-age her precocious interest in the world of arts and letters. But almost simultaneously he could drop into an essay for the *Contemporary Review* his casually misogynistic disdain for women's efforts to express themselves like men. He deplored the "crew of disorderly persons, often of the fair sex, each of whom, more perhaps through weakness than wickedness, has been guilty of bringing into the world a novel in three volumes." He called upon critics to "administer justice of the rough and ready kind," because "the female novelist, having once erred, is lost to all sense of shame."

According to her biographer Edmund Bentley, "The great quad of Trinity College, with its grey stone buildings and magnificent oaks, impressed Hester up to a point. But she felt that it contained a world of men . . . beyond her orbit or province." Bram Stoker was one of those men who regularly visited the Dowdens' suburban home, probably since the time of her birth. He was a favorite of her father's, and would have seen her grow from infancy into the attractive young girl memorably captured on canvas by John Butler Yeats, the artist brother of William Butler Yeats. Local celeb-rities like Lady Wilde or the occasional visiting actress like Ellen Terry or Genevieve Ward were only exceptions that proved the rule. Men were the people who really mattered, to her father and to the world.

Edward Dowden was a failed poet, who, despite his many achievements and accolades, harbored a gnawing resentment for the academic life and privately conceded that he didn't really consider it an honor to have been named Trinity's first professor of English literature. He thought he deserved another life entirely. His ambivalence about his daughter increased as she got older, and when she fell in love with a young poet, one seriously consid-ered poet laureate material, he refused the marriage proposal. The reason, supposedly, was the difference in their ages (only ten years, and a rather common arrangement). The men had a difference of political opinion over the Boer War, which provided another pretext. But the real reason was that the poet was competition—a reminder of the life Dowden couldn't have for himself, and his daughter would not have without him.

When Hester's mother, Mary Clerke Dowden, died in 1892, Hester gave up music studies she had begun in London and returned to Dublin to care for her father and siblings. One of her "great friends" during 1891 and 1892 was Bram Stoker, who had been a natural contact for her in London, since he and her father had remained on close terms ever since their Trinity days. No correspondence between them has survived, but it was precisely the same time he was researching *Dracula* in earnest. It can be reasonably assumed that Hester would have been invited to the Stokers' Sunday at-homes, and there met a fairly amazing cross-section of cultural London, including one of Florence Stoker's regular and favorite guests, Oscar Wilde. The initial storm of public outrage over *The Picture of Dorian Gray* in 1890 had all but subsided. Wilde seemed to have drawn power from all the negative attention and turned it to his advantage, honing the trademark outrageous public persona that made its effective debut with the notorious "green carnation" premiere of *Lady Windermere's Fan*.

When the Wilde scandal broke in 1895, Hester had been back in Dublin nearly three years. The story exerted the same lurid front-page fascination there as it did in London, and all throughout the world. The vicarious drama came within Hester's close purview when her father refused W. B. Yeats's plea that he add Dowden's name to a petition of support from Irish literary men for one of Dublin's most illustrious sons. Dowden wanted nothing to do with it. The Wilde affair also coincided with Dowden's remarriage, hardly a happy occasion for Hester, who felt that both she and her mother were being summarily replaced. She clashed with the new wife, who resurrected some of the fairy tale coloration of her childhood—only this time more darkly, as a classically wicked stepmother.

Hester left her father's house to marry Dr. Richard Travers Smith, to all accounts a rather unromantic catch who at least offered money and stability. He was a dermatologist specializing in eczema and varicose veins and had a large, established practice. There were no grounds, invented or otherwise, for her father's opposition. She settled into a pampered bourgeois lifestyle, dutifully had two children, and for the next twenty years gave up all her creative dreams, which, following the aborted music career, included an interest in writing and criticism. These literary pursuits withered as well.

Edward Dowden died in 1913. Hester believed she had an uncanny premonition of the event. Of course she did, but it was nothing uncanny. Dowden had been in steadily failing health for years, and there was no need for a crystal ball, much less a banshee's wail. But the thought remained with her: Was it possible that she actually *did* have unusual powers? Was there

Hester Dowden, the spirit medium daughter of Stoker's Trinity College mentor Edward Dowden.

actually something beyond the earthly plane? Beings? Forces? Possibilities? Like many other middle-class women of the Victorian and Edwardian eras, when traditional notions and practices of spirituality were at a low ebb, Hester felt increasingly that she was buried by materialism and money. The Travers Smiths spent, entertained, and traveled lavishly, but their marriage was passionless. Her husband's nationalist politics irritated her. Her boredom was almost unbearable. Even at the height of the Easter Rebellion in 1916, partly in rebuke to her husband, she decided to go shopping. There had to be something beyond *this* life. A life that was being drained out of her by forces she could not control.

The Irish rebellion coincided with World War I, and her son was joining the army. The threatening spectre of death that overshadowed Europe had reached Hester's Dublin. Sometime during the conflict, she came to the belief that dead soldiers were speaking to her. It wasn't a particularly strange idea in a time when spiritualism enjoyed a large middle-class following, on both sides of the Atlantic. Everywhere, people were experimenting with divination boards and conducting séances. Hester met a number of people—many from the prestigious Society for Psychical Research—who encouraged her to hone her skills. And finally she realized that not only was there another *side*, there was another *life*—for her. The fairy folk could have spirited her away as a child but chose not to. But as an adult she could rely on a different kind of supernatural entity for rescue. Spirits that tended on mortal thoughts could unsex her—or at least release her from the constrained sex role that had made her life intolerable.

While her husband was away working as a field doctor, she filed her petition for separation. A few years later a divorce would be finalized. In the meantime she moved to London and set up practice in Chelsea Gardens. As concisely described by Helen Sword in *Ghostwriting Modernism*, spirit mediumship was "one of the relatively few means by which women of virtually any social or educational background could earn money, engage in high-profile careers, lay claim to otherworldly insight and subvert male authority, all while conforming to normative ideals of feminine passivity and receptivity." Denied a voice of her own, the medium could take on the voices of others. After all, weren't women supposed to live selflessly, for and through other people?

It is not clear exactly why Hester decided to contact the ghost of Oscar Wilde. If she met him in London in 1868, had he made an especially favorable impression? Had she objected to her father's turning his back on him during the trials? Around the same time as the Viereck hoax, in 1905, an after-dinner séance was conducted in the home of André Gide by "an intellectual lady who acted as writing medium," according to Robert Sherard in *The Real Oscar Wilde*. Indeed, Hester knew of this event, just as she knew about Viereck's strange claims in the *Critic*, published at nearly the same time as the séance chez Gide. "Wilde's wraith was evoked from the Yonder-Land," wrote Sherard, "and the first thing he commented [to an Italian guest] was: '*Doriano mi ha tradito*' (Dorian has betrayed me). Gide asked him his opinion about his trial, and Wilde said: 'It was typically English. Perjurers. Hypocrites. Puritans.'" When asked to describe life beyond the grave, Wilde called it "A chaotic confusion of fluid nebulosities. A *cloaque* [sewer] of souls and the essences of organic life." To Gide's query about the existence of God, the ghost replied, "That is still for us the great mystery."

At least one account maintains, without documentation, that Hester's first attempt to contact Wilde's ghost after World War I was at his family's

Dorothy "Dolly" Wilde, Oscar's niece, was a prominent social fixture of the lesbian Left Bank.

request, but there was practically no one left in Wilde's family to ask. His mother, brother, and wife were long dead; his older son, Cyril, had been killed in the war; and his younger son, Vyvyan, had distanced himself utterly from anything regarding his father. The only conceivable relation who might have been interested in the otherworldly Wilde was his lesbian niece, Dorothy "Dolly" Wilde, who bore such an amazing resemblance to her uncle that people actually wondered aloud about reincarnation. According to her biographer Joan Schenkar, "Wherever Dolly went, whatever social performance she was giving, someone in the charmed circle of her listeners was certain to be watching for traces of Oscar Wilde; trying to see the uncle *through* the niece, trying to see the uncle *in* the niece, trying to see the uncle somewhere *near* the niece."

Dolly's life could be described as a marathon séance. She divided her time between London and Paris in the 1920s, taking the shadow of Oscar Wilde with her. At one otherwise listless party, her arrival was said to electrify the room as she quipped, "You all look as if you were waiting for the coffin to be brought in." One only wishes she had been wearing some bat-winged gown, designed in gold lamé, by Erté.

Dolly was as well known on the Left Bank as she was in Hester's Chelsea. Dolly's world, especially in Paris, was openly lesbian, while the world of mediumship was tacitly. Hester met another Irish medium, Geraldine Cummins, who introduced her to the ways of Ouija on a visit to Paris. They would live together in Chelsea for several years, until Cummins moved in with a wealthy female patron.

Radclyffe Hall, the British author of the 1928 lesbian classic *The Well of Loneliness*, became an acolyte of mediumship following the death of her lover, Mabel "Ladye" Batten. A new lover, Una Troubridge, became her partner in a séance-obsessed folie à deux, in which the approval and advice of the dead woman came to control and dominate their lives. Radclyffe was also a devoted Catholic, and spiritualism brought her to loggerheads with the father confessor of the Brompton Oratory. But since she was independently wealthy and donated generously to the church, her eccentricity was tolerated. Her wealth also allowed her to dress and behave with aggressive mannishness. Who would stop her? She was active in the Society for Psychical Research, but her appointment to its governing board was blocked on the basis of her lack of moral fitness. She sued for libel and, in a complete reversal of the Wilde trial dynamic, won for damages, though she was never able to collect; since lesbianism wasn't illegal in Britain, the society could not defend its discrimination against her in any way that would stand up in court. Radclyffe Hall achieved a permanent postmortem connection to Bram Stoker when she was interred in Highgate Cemetery, the atmospheric inspiration for the cemetery called Kingstead in *Dracula*, where the vampire Lucy Westenra wandered nightly from her tomb.

The war years opened up extraordinary opportunities for mediumship. Mass death always did. The postwar artistic ferment in Europe fueled expressionism, especially in Germany, where strange images of living death fascinated the audiences of *The Cabinet of Dr. Caligari* and *Nosferatu*, F. W. Murnau's famously unauthorized adaptation of *Dracula* that benefited significantly from spiritualist interest and financing. The public couldn't get enough of the Other Side, and Hester Travis Smith had become a shrewd and independent businesswoman. Her 1919 book *Voices from the Void* had greatly increased her reputation and demand for her services. Wherever the idea came from, reaching out to Oscar Wilde was another inspired business plan.

Hester made her first contact with Wilde through the Ouija board, comprising an alphabet covered with plate glass and a pointing device—known alternately as a traveler or planchette—on which she rested her fingers. Various spirit guides would act as intermediaries with individual discarnate entities, and guide the medium's hands from letter to letter, which an assistant transcribed. Later, as the messages became longer and more complex, she would collaborate with a transcribing "automatist," to whom she could relay messages directly, simply by resting one of her hands on his or hers. After a few rusty initial tries, and some purgatorial complaining from the dead man, his familiar voice, witty and flippant as it had ever been in life, spoke confidently in cursive script.

> Being dead is the most boring experience in life. That is, if one excepts being married or dining with a schoolmaster. Do you doubt my identity? I am not surprised, since sometimes I doubt it myself. I might retaliate by doubting yours. I have always admired the Society for Psychical Research. They are the most magnificent doubters in the world. They are never happy until they have explained away their spectres. And one suspects a genuine ghost would make them exquisitely uncomfortable. I have sometimes thought of founding an academy of celestial doubters . . . which might be a sort of Society for Psychical Research among the living. No one under sixty would be admitted, and we should call ourselves the Society of Superannuated Shades.

His evocation of the afterlife was quite a bit more colorful and specific than when he spoke to André Gide. His boredom was palpable. "I am doing what is little better than picking oakum in gaol. There, after all, my mind could detach itself from my body. Here, I have no body to leave off. It is not by any means agreeable to be a mere mind without a body. That was a very decorous garment, that made us seem very attractive to each other; or, perhaps, supremely the opposite. Over here that amusement is quite out of

---

Inset: Radclyffe Hall, pioneering lesbian novelist, who may have taken some inspiration for **The Well of Loneliness** *from Stoker's novel* **The Man.** *Below: The tombs of the Lebanon Circle, Highgate Cemetery, Hall's final resting place. Highgate was Stoker's model for Kingstead Cemetery in* **Dracula,** *the site of Lucy Westenra's horrific destruction.* (Photograph by the author)

the question, and we know far too much about the interiors of each others' ideas." In no way could the spirit plane be called blissful. Instead it entailed "the dimming of the senses and the stultifying of the brain from lack of light and colour."

Asked for some verifiable biographical details, he recalled his dreary days at Trinity College Dublin, before Oxford opened his eyes to the world. "I almost forget that time when I was chained within the walls of the university. I was a carrier pigeon who had flown by mistake into a nest of sparrows. These Dublin students could see such a short distance. I was a giant among pigmies." Pressed to explain the appeal of George Sylvester Viereck's survival hoax, he had a quick answer. "Men are ever interested, dear lady, in the remains of those who have had the audacity to be distinguished, and when, added to this, the corpse has the flavor of crime, the carrion birds are eager to light on it." He found it "delightful to think that after the carcass has been conveyed to its modest hole a legend is woven round its decaying particles. You, I am sure, give me credit for the fact that I really accomplished the feat of dying when I was supposed to die. I did not fly from the world a second time in order to create fiction."

With the assistance of Geraldine Cummins, Hester also claimed to have downloaded from Wilde a new play completely composed in the otherworld, a comedy of manners she first called *The Extraordinary Play* but later (and perhaps more realistically) referred to as *Is It a Forgery?* The script was never produced or published, and no copy has ever been found. Hester claimed to have sent it to the prominent actor Gerald du Maurier, who rejected it for unstated reasons.

Hester's second book, *Oscar Wilde from Purgatory*, appeared in 1924 and generated interest throughout the world. It also generated imitators. In 1928, the New York publishing house Covici-Friede brought out *The Ghost Epigrams of Oscar Wilde*, channeled by a medium known only as "Lazar." The slim volume featured some convincing approximations of Wilde's ironic wit, including such examples as "Charity begins at home and generally dies from lack of out-of-door exercise" and "Woman begins by resisting man's advances and ends by blocking his retreat." But the book's entertainment value is marred by a relentless streak of mean-spirited misogyny: "Woman spoils her first lover and practically ruins the rest," "Only an idiot doubts the sincerity of a stupid woman," and "Woman has never created anything as beautiful as she has destroyed" are just a few examples.

In contrast, Hester's conversations with Wilde yielded many positive estimations of the fair sex. He admitted, however, that women of the flapper age were not to his taste. "The women of my time were beautiful, from the outward side at least. They had a mellifluous flow of language, and they added much to the brilliant pattern of society. Now woman is an excrescence, she protrudes from social life as a wart does from the nose of an inebriate." Nonetheless, and in contrast to his well-known passion for beautiful young men, he assured Hester, and her readers, that his "sensations were so varied with regard to your sex, dear lady, that you would find painted on my heart—that internal organ so often quoted by the vulgar—you would find every shade of desire there—and even more." Women, in fact, were the wellspring of his creativity; just forget all those golden-haired Ganymedes. "Woman was to me a colour, a sound. She gave me all. She gave me first desire, desire gave birth to that mysterious essence which was within me, and from that deeply distilled and perfumed drug my thoughts were born; and from my thoughts words sprang. Each word I used became a child to me. . . . I nurtured them, and in their fullness brought them forth as symbols of the woman."

To Hester, he made a bold and parasitic proposition. He wanted to "crawl into your mind like a sick worm and try to bore a hole above the earth that I may once more look at the sun." Would she allow him to enter her mind, body, and brain and experience London once more? It was a strangely exciting idea. An erotic idea, though a curiously disembodied one. Like being possessed by an incubus, but without the sex. Like being penetrated by a man without being touched. They went to the theatre, where Oscar saw and heard, through Hester's physical senses, a revival of *The Importance of Being Earnest.* Back in the Ouija room, he offered a detailed critique, and even gave notes to the actors. He critiqued recent literature as well, and was especially caustic about James Joyce's *Ulysses* and the controversy it stirred. "It is a singular matter that a countryman of mine should have produced this great bulk of filth. . . . In 'Ulysses' I find a monster who cannot contain the monstrosities of his own brain. The creatures he gives birth to leap from him in shapeless masses of hideousness, as dragons might, which in their foulsome birth contaminate their parent. . . . It gives me the impression of having been written in a severe fit of nausea. Surely there is a nausea fever. The physicians may not have diagnosed it. But here we have the heated vomit."

To put things politely, since it is somewhat less than likely that Hester actually conversed and interacted with the sentient ethereal residue of Oscar Wilde, much less went with him on a theatre date in the West End, the question immediately arises: Was she a conscious fraud? Even today, people are just as willing to believe "six impossible things before breakfast" as they were in the days of Lewis Carroll. And, while it's easy to conclude that mediums were nothing more than cynical charlatans, offering a cruelly phony kind of amateur grief counseling for profit, the reality is more complicated. Many practitioners were convinced, if only through multiple veils of delusion, that their powers were real. They received constant reinforcement in their belief from prominent, educated people. Some were genuinely empathic and highly intuitive, and learned to read their clients' almost subliminal expressions and body language to prompt seemingly uncanny responses (in carnival parlance, this skill is called "cold reading"). And some, like Hester, had already demonstrated extraordinary verbal gifts early on, which found an unexpectedly viable outlet in automatic writing. Her friend Bram Stoker might well have made an outstanding spirit medium himself. He wrote fiction and nonfiction with such breathtaking speed he might as well have been taking dictation from the void. Both, in their own ways, were word freaks. But Bram was a man, permitted to move freely in the world, attend Trinity College, and publish books as he wished.

After early success, a medium might begin to cheat in various ways, rationalizing that the gift was not always reliable, but that didn't mean it wasn't real. There were appearances to be kept up, and bills to be paid. William Butler Yeats, himself an ardent spiritualist, took a rather jaundiced view of Hester in his 1934 play *Words upon the Window-Pane*, perhaps after reading the transcript of her Wilde conversations, in which the dead man described Yeats as "a fantastical mind, but so full of inflated joy in himself that his little cruse of poetry was emptied early in his career." In the play, Mrs. Henderson (a barely disguised Hester Dowden), a famous Irish medium based in London, returns to Dublin for a séance in which the personal questions of those attending (who have been admonished not to expect much) are simply ignored. Instead, Henderson/Hester becomes the mouthpiece of a great Irish author—not Wilde but Ireland's other great wit, Jonathan Swift—for a highly detailed dialogue with the woman who yearns to marry him about his overwhelming fear of passing on hereditary madness. It is quite a performance. As the other guests file out, they leave tributes of money, despite their individual disappointment and over the medium's protestations. Yet she makes furtive glances to see exactly the amount they have left. Yeats's skeptical alter ego approaches her. "I have been deeply moved by what I have heard," he says. "This is my contribution to prove I am satisfied, completely satisfied." He places a note on the table. She is stunned: "A pound note—nobody ever gives me more than ten shillings, and yet the séance was a failure." The young man explains himself further. "When I say I am satisfied I do not mean I am convinced it was the work of spirits. I prefer to think you created it all, that you are an accomplished actress and a scholar." She claims never to have heard of Jonathan Swift. At the end Yeats adds a note of humorous ambiguity. After the last visitor leaves, she is once more suddenly possessed by Swift's voice, then wakes, seemingly unaware of what has happened.

Whatever Yeats thought of her, Hester was by then a well-established social figure in Chelsea. She had achieved for herself more than she would have thought possible as an unhappy housewife in Dublin. The time had finally come for her to settle a special score with the man who discouraged her music, her writing, any kind of expression or real existence. The man who had betrayed her mother, and betrayed her.

As a Shakespearean scholar, Edward Dowden was particularly irritated and bedeviled by the "authorship question," which, since the mid-nineteenth century, had encompassed a constellation of theories alleging that the Bard of Avon was not the true author of the plays attributed to him. Shakespeare was considered too rustic and uneducated to have written such fine language, even if he had produced the plays, one fact that seemed incontrovertible. Alternate candidates included Sir Francis Bacon; Edward de Vere, the Earl of Oxford; Christopher Marlowe; Sir Walter Raleigh; Thomas Kyd; and, in one particularly ludicrous concoction, Queen Elizabeth herself, evidently in her spare time. All the theories turned on complicated conspiracies and implausibilities, including hidden ciphers in the texts of the plays themselves that could reveal the truth to the world, if anyone would only listen. The doubters were driven and obsessive—as many of them are to the present day. They rankled Dowden because much of his reputation rested on his "personalist" interpretation of Shakespeare; that is, the idea that the plays were best interpreted as products of distinct stages of William Shakespeare's own life.

Hester remembered well how much her father hated these people.

Therefore, when the chance finally presented itself, she took sides with the enemy. And never looked back.

Her first client in the campaign against her father was a man named Alfred Dodd, who was visited in a dream by Shakespeare's ghost, which led him to believe there was a vast Rosicrucian plot to hide the truth of authorship. For Dodd, unraveling the plot became a cause and a creed. He passionately believed that the real author was Francis Bacon, and Hester obliged him via a spirit guide named Johannes who provided Dodd with clues and keys to the Baconian conclusions he sought. For another seeker, Percy Allen, a proponent of the Edward de Vere theory, Johannes explained that "Bill Shakspere had a lot to do with the gist of [the plays], but did no finished work." Johannes told Allen de Vere did the bulk of the writing, sometimes employing other writers, including Bacon from time to time. Hester made no apologies for such yawning discrepancies. Offering assistance to anyone who wanted to undermine her father's authority was what really mattered.

In the last years of her life, Hester dropped her married name and was known again as Hester Dowden . . . *the* Dowden, more famous than her father. Edward Dowden, literary mentor of the man who wrote *Dracula*, had now been in his grave for thirty years. But at long last she had managed to have her revenge, eclipse his legacy, challenge and delegitimize his life's work—and drive a pointed Ouija planchette through his moldering and hideous heart.

There were so many ways for Oscar Wilde to join the ranks of the walking dead that it was almost inevitable that he would. Like Wilde, vampires traditionally inhabited the borderlines of social and sexual propriety. Suicides were the classic candidates, and Wilde's actively self-destructive final years certainly qualified him. Folklore also worried about people who had unfinished business with the living, especially their surviving lovers. Heresy was a surefire ticket to Transylvania, and Wilde was a master heretic in secular matters and manners. In certain Slavic traditions, alcoholics and homosexuals also made the cut, along with the marginalized and miscreant, and anyone generally despised. Outsiders among the living became excellent outsiders postmortem. It was only natural for Wilde's memory to merge with that of the unnatural Count Dracula, and all the hungry revenants who had fed before him.

And nine years after his burial at Bagneux, Oscar Wilde actually did come out of his grave.

In 1909, after settling Wilde's estate and paying his debts, Robbie Ross finally secured a fitting final burial place at the prestigious Père Lachaise cemetery, and the necessary disinterment of Wilde's body was arranged in Bagneux. As Frank Harris described the scene, "To his horror, when the grave was opened, Ross found that the quicklime, instead of destroying the flesh, had preserved it. Oscar's face was recognizable, only his hair and beard had grown long."

The idea that quicklime would reliably reduce a corpse to bones had little basis but was widely believed. In fact, quicklime could have quite the opposite effect, drying and preserving tissue instead of destroying it. But Harris exaggerates when he talks about Wilde's hair and beard. The belief that hair keeps growing after death is an old wives' tale, biologically impossible, yet kept alive in fiction like Bram Stoker's "The Secret of the Growing Gold," and the legendary account of Elizabeth Siddall's exhumation by Dante Gabriel Rossetti. The postmortem shrinking of skin, however, easily creates the appearance of fresh stubble. Teeth can appear lengthened as the gums recede. And for unfortunate cataleptic persons buried alive—a widespread fear in the nineteenth century—hair and nails *did* keep growing. The frightful appearance of these suffocated souls, discovered when their graves were disturbed, along with the signs of their final thrashing moments, seemed to prove the existence of the living dead and contributed to the amply documented waves of vampire panic that swept Europe in the eighteenth century.

Upon seeing the disturbing condition of the body, Ross immediately shielded the sight from Wilde's son Vyvyan Holland, whom he had brought to Paris for the ceremony. "At once Ross sent the son away," Harris wrote, "and when the sextons were about to use their shovels [to lift the corpse], he ordered them to desist and, descending into the grave, moved the body with his own hands into the new coffin in loving reverence."

Ross may have had deep regard for Wilde, but not for this particular coffin. He had personally ordered a sumptuous tribute casket, only to be rebuffed by cemetery officials who insisted that any container used for exhumation and reburial had to be crafted by Bagneux workers, a regulation "doubtless invented as a perquisite for someone," according to Holland. To add insult, the box they cobbled for the purpose had a silver plate misspelling Wilde's name as OSCARD. "This was the last straw and I

Jacob Epstein, sculptor of the Wilde monument at Père Lachaise,
in his studio with the finished work in 1910.

thought Ross was going to explode," Holland wrote. The undertaker used
a chisel to make a crude correction.

Ross had obtained funds from a wealthy benefactor to commission a
young sculptor, Jacob Epstein, to create a fitting monument. The design
was controversial from the outset. Epstein sculpted an angular, stylized
angel in a style that echoed the art of Egypt and Assyria and at the same
time anticipated the machine-tooled lines of Art Moderne. The angel was
male, evidenced by a stone penis and pendulous testicles, which raised eyebrows and for a time prompted the addition of a fig leaf. Ultimately the sex
organs were broken off by vandals and never recovered or replaced. From a
Freudian perspective, the unconscious mind makes no distinction between
acts of castration and decapitation. The defacing of a tombstone's genitals to insult or exorcise the grave's occupant was the symbolic equivalent
of cutting off the head of a vampire, that time-honored remedy so vividly
commemorated by Bram Stoker.

Wilde personally disliked his new home. He told Hester Dowden, via the Ouija board, that the Epstein monument didn't contain "an atom of that power which came to me direct from my great ancestors" and that "the monstrous creature shaped by Mr. Epstein does not express the soul of Oscar Wilde. . . . My wings were spread, ready to carry me away into the heavens, not lying slack and lifeless."

Even in death he misunderstood the real purpose of funerary sculpture. It was never meant to set him free. One of the oldest, most primitive purposes of placing a heavy stone on a grave was not only to mark the place of burial but to keep the restless dead underground. Weighed down by Jacob Epstein's massive block of marble, Oscar Wilde never emerged from his grave again. But by the end of the century he knew he could never inhabit, an uncountable number of adoring visitors from all over the world would make a ritual pilgrimage to Père Lachaise, there to leave indelible stains of their voracious red mouths, male and female alike, on the body of an emasculated angel.

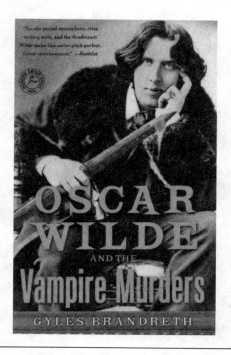

Oscar Wilde's association with the undead persists to the present day, as evidenced by Gyles Brandreth's mystery novel Oscar Wilde and the Vampire Murders *(2011), depicting Wilde as an amateur detective in the Agatha Christie mold.* (Touchstone Books)

CHAPTER TEN

MORTAL COILS

THE WHOLE PLACE LOOKED AS IF A SEA OF BLOOD
HAD BEEN BEATING AGAINST IT.
—Bram Stoker, *The Lair of the White Worm*

Seven months after the publication of *Dracula*, a stealthy shadow began its slow encircling of the Lyceum family. The novel that would come to be regarded as Stoker's masterpiece, the climax of his literary energies (whether or not he regarded it as such), was also a tale of enervation, decay, and death. With grim irony, *Dracula* coincided with the arrival of an increasingly dark and tumultuous period in the theatre's history, as well as for Irving and Stoker personally, and everyone else who had been involved in the grand, glamorous, almost quixotic project of reclaiming the lost dignity of the British theatre.

By the end of 1897, the actor William Terriss, one of Irving's favorites and the player who eventually had assumed the mantle of Faust against his Mephistopheles, was a star in his own right and had moved on to being a leading man and main draw at the Adelphi Theatre on the Strand. A true matinee idol (known to fans as "Breezy Bill"), the handsome actor appealed to audiences of all ages. Stoker's son, Noel, fondly recalled

The last known photograph of Henry Irving and Bram Stoker together.

William Terriss and Jessie Millward were an attractive couple onstage,
and an adulterous one privately.

Terriss's swashbuckling presence in Adephi melodramas. But on Thursday, December 16, all that would end—with a ghastly melodramatic flourish.

The Lyceum actress Jessie Millward had followed Terriss to the Adelphi—not just as his leading lady, but his mistress as well. Their long-standing relationship despite Terriss's marriage was well known, but happily overlooked by an appreciative public; they were like Irving and Terry, writ only slightly smaller.

The previous night, or the night before, Millward had heard a man sharing angry words with Terriss in his dressing room. He was preparing for that night's performance with Millward in William Gillette's Civil War romance *Secret Service*. In the corridor she saw the actor with an individual she remembered as "a former super" (a supernumerary, or extra), whom she recalled previously "posing about the stage." His name was Richard Archer Prince, described by Millward as "a short, thin, dark man, with a

pronounced squint." Indeed, he was derisively called "Squinto" by detractors, of whom there were many. Millward asked Terriss what was causing
the dressing room ruckus. "'This man is becoming a nuisance,' he told me,
and I guessed that it was a case of begging," she wrote.

It was much more than that, as Millward horrifyingly learned Thursday
night, when her hansom cab pulled up at the Adelphi stage entrance on
Maiden Lane. Both stars had keys to the private door Queen Victoria
had installed at the back of the theatre to allow her quiet access when she
needed it. There, by the door, was Prince again, impossible to miss—he
had donned a theatrical cloak as street wear. As Millward remembered,
"Just as I reached the pass door Prince came towards me, and I half thought
of giving him some money so that he should not delay Mr. Terriss when he
arrived, but as he came towards me there was something in the man's face
that frightened me, and instead of waiting to open the pass door I rushed
to the stage door, and on entering my dressing-room I told my maid, Lottie,
of my encounter with Prince. In the midst of my dressing I heard Mr. Terriss
put his key in the pass door, and then there was a strange silence."

The familiar sounds of the door opening and closing never came.
"Something has happened!" Millward cried to the maid, and the two
women rushed down the stairs. "Mr. Terriss was leaning against the wall,
near the door. 'Sis,' he said faintly, 'Sis, I am stabbed.'" Prince had carried a long knife concealed under his cloak, which he plunged into Terriss
three times, twice in the back, and then, as he turned around, fatally, in
the heart. Millward reached out to support him, but they fell to the floor
together. Terriss died in her arms. She later recalled that "the murderer
had rushed into Maiden Lane, flourishing a long knife, my faithful Lottie
clinging to him until the police seized him. When he was told Mr. Terriss
was dead: 'Yes,' he said; 'and I meant to kill Miss Millward, too.'"

With his cape and bloody knife (which he himself offered up to the
police, who had failed to notice it dripping under the cloak), Prince closely
resembled cartoon conceptions of Jack the Ripper put forth by the tabloid
press nine years earlier, images he may well have seen and remembered.
Born Richard Archer in Dundee, the aspiring actor had upgraded himself to royalty. He had been a bit-part actor in the long-running Adelphi
production *The Harbour Lights* (1885), in which Terriss had costarred with
Millward. (Oddly enough, George R. Sims, playwright of *The Harbour Lights*,
was also an obsessive amateur criminologist and journalist whose columns

on the crime were so vividly detailed that some wondered if he might be the Ripper himself.) Because of some offensive comment about the leading man, relayed to Terriss, Prince was dismissed from the company for reasons then unexplained to him. Due to his off-putting personality—he had been considered strange since childhood—Prince had difficulty finding and maintaining employment, and after finally learning Terriss was responsible for his firing at the Adelphi (where, of course, he was destined for greatness) he harbored a festering grudge forevermore. Prince returned to Dundee, finding sporadic work, more often as a laborer than onstage. He appeared in public sporting bizarre, affected garb and became a notorious pest at the local theatre, where he clapped inappropriately and talked back to the performers. He believed people were trying to poison him. He was subject to what his family called, almost romantically, "fits of passion," even if these involved chasing his mother out of the house and threatening his brother with a knife and a poker.

The theatre has always been a haven for misfits, and these have always included a certain number of mental misfits. Prince still believed he was an underappreciated genius and inevitably fell once more into the gravitational pull of London, the only place his delusional self-conception might be realized. At the beginning of November 1897, he presented a note addressed to Terriss at the Adelphi stage door and was granted a meeting. The substance of this charged encounter is not recorded, but for reasons of guilt, pity, or a simple act of kindness, Terriss gave his supplicant a letter addressed to the Actors' Benevolent Fund, a charity for which Bram Stoker had helped to draft the bylaws: "I have known the bearer, Mr. Richard Archer Prince, as a hardworking actor for many years. William Terriss." A complete lie, of course. It's not even clear Terriss remembered him at all, but he may have been dispensing with an unpleasant situation in the most expeditious way possible. It was a mistake he would not live to regret.

Prince was given money by the Benevolent Fund four times over the next several weeks, but this did not prevent a threat of eviction from his current lodgings in a boardinghouse. A final, desperate approach to the charity in mid-December was refused on the basis that its committee could not meet that day, but more likely because the applicant was so obviously unhinged. As Millward recalled, "I was told afterwards that for a week before his crime he had been strutting about the Strand boasting that in a few days his name would be on everybody's lips." By then, Prince's deadly rendezvous with the object of his obsession was as inevitable as the fated course of a Greek tragedy.

Late on the night of the crime, when Jessie Millward finally left the theatre to walk home to Hanover Square with her maid, she cringed at the newsboys already running along Regent Street, yelling excitedly, "Murder of William Terriss! Murder of William Terriss!"

Henry Irving, deeply shocked that his friend, and his Faust, had been taken from the world by a seemingly demonic killer, was deeply cynical about the course of justice that was to come. "They will find some excuse to get him off," Irving said bitterly. Instead of holding Prince truly culpable, he predicted, "they would say 'mad' or something." The reason? "Terriss was an actor," and therefore "his murderer will not be executed." Clearly, the first knighted actor had no illusions about how far he had raised the estimation of "strolling players" at large.

Prince was arraigned at the Bow Street police station next to the Covent Garden opera house, the same brig to which Oscar Wilde had been dragged following his arrest two years earlier. Stoker described the angry crowd that assembled there: "When he was placed in the dock, with one impulse they *hissed* him!" As Stoker recalled from Irving's struggling days, and his lifelong observation of theatre people, "to an actor nothing is so deadly as to be hissed. Not only does it bar his artistic effort but it hurts his self-esteem. Its manifestation is a negation of himself, his power, his art. It is present death to him *quâ* artist, with the added sting of shame." In Stoker's opinion, the actors who crowded the Bow Street court behaved quite admirably.

The funeral created a difficult situation for Jessie Millward. While she had been Terriss's close companion for fifteen years, she was not his wife, and her presence would be extremely awkward. However, Henry Irving came to the rescue. He would personally escort her, and dare anyone to say an unkind word. Irving, of course, knew how to manage the mistress game. With Ellen Terry's departure from the Lyceum company, he acquired a new extramarital companion, the socialite Mrs. Eliza Aria. Florence Irving, now Lady Irving and happy only with the title, was still persona non grata in his personal life. Mrs. Aria could be extravagantly adoring, as in her recounting of Irving's kindness to Miss Millward. "Irving was Christ," she wrote in her memoirs, "protector of the weak, a shelter against slander, a solace for the sorrow-stricken, a standby for an afflicted people. . . . There was not a member in the theatrical world in the crowd which followed the murdered man to his last resting-place who did not fall in worshipful admiration of Irving when they noticed the tenderness that went to his shepherding."

Tens of thousands of people lined the streets for the funeral procession to Brompton Cemetery. There were nearly a hundred carriages, including two additional hearses carrying flowers only. As per Irving's prediction, in January 1898 the murderer was judged insane and sentenced to life imprisonment at the Broadmoor Criminal Lunatic Asylum. There he conducted the hospital orchestra and directed inmate performances, in the legendarily macabre manner of the Marquis de Sade at the Asylum of Charenton. In London, he achieved a theatrical presence, of sorts, as a crowd-drawing exhibit at Madame Tussaud's Chamber of Horrors. Richard Archer Prince died at Broadmoor in 1937.[1]

Outside the madhouse, life continued. A year later, Stoker's publisher, Constable, published a Terriss biography, and the fifth edition of *Dracula* was advertised in its back pages, with fulsome blurbs. The *Christian World* called it "One of the most enthralling and unique romances ever written," and *St. Paul's* opined that "the idea is so novel that one gasps, as it were, at its originality. A romance far above the ordinary production." *Dracula* was indeed gaining steam, although Stoker never dreamed of the extent to which his own humble production, a "shilling shocker," would be recognized the world over, while the theatrical efforts of Victorian superstars like Irving and Terriss would, over time, fade from the popular mind like ghosts.

Interestingly enough, William Terriss became one of the most talked-about revenants ever to haunt the West End. A plaque at the Adelphi still commemorates his murder, and for over a century his restless, costumed apparition has been regularly reported haunting the theatre and its environs, including many impromptu ectoplasmic appearances (and

---

[1] In April 1899, Stoker responded to a press report that Prince had sent a letter to Henry Irving, threatening the actor with assassination if he were ever released from Broadmoor. The death threat was not true, although a disturbing letter had indeed been sent. Stoker called the report "an evident exaggeration of some one who got hold of a bit of the story. The fact is that three months after he was sent to Broadmoor, Prince by some means posted a letter to Sir Henry, in which he libeled and abused several people, members of the profession and others. Of course Sir Henry took no notice of these incoherent ramblings of a lunatic, but as he thought it was not right that inmates should be able to send out letters unknown to the Governor, the contents of which might cause pain to others, he mentioned receipt of this communication to the authorities with a view to preventing the repetition of such an occurrence."

vanishings) performed busker-like upon the platforms of the Covent Garden Underground station, with no donations required or expected.

Almost exactly eight weeks after the attack on Terriss, another omen, this one threatening the Lyceum's basic ability to perform, manifested like a bad dream. "At ten minutes past five on the morning of Friday 18th February 1898, I was wakened by a continuous knock at a door somewhere near my house in Chelsea," Stoker wrote. "I soon discovered it was at my own house." Always a night person and never an early riser, Stoker groggily "went downstairs and opened the door, when a muffled-up cab driver gave me a letter. It was from the police station at Bow Street telling me that the Lyceum Storage, Bear Lane, Southwark, was on fire. The four wheeler was waiting and I was soon on the way there as fast as the horse could go."

When he arrived at the storage facility, a huge converted vault under the arches of a railway overpass, not far from the original location of Shakespeare's Globe, firefighters had given up trying to control the fire and could do nothing except supervise the burning-out. "The fire was so fierce," Stoker recalled, "that it actually burned the building of the railway arches three bricks deep and calcined the coping stones to powder." In all, two thousand pieces of scenery and "bulky properties without end" were destroyed. The painted drops and flats from forty-two productions were lost, including all of Irving's major successes—*Faust, The Bells, Macbeth, Hamlet*—along with the rest of the Lyceum's Shakespearean settings, not to mention the exquisite and completely irreplaceable productions of *King Arthur* and *The Cup* designed by Sir Edward Burne-Jones. The scenery had been insured for £6,000, only a fraction of its original, unappreciated value—£ 30,000—because everyone involved perceived a very low fire risk. In the end, the brick, stone, and slate of the great room proved indeed fireproof, but acres of paint-covered canvas did not. "But the cost price was the least part of the loss," Stoker wrote. "Nothing could repay the time and labour and artistic experience spent on them. All the scene painters in England working for a whole year could not have restored the scenery alone."

The effect of the fire was to checkmate any plans Irving had to revive most of his repertory or preserve the executed designs for posterity. His longtime refusal to have his actual productions photographed would consign the full achievement of his finished work to living memory alone, and to fleeting impressions that might be gleaned from preliminary sketches and models that survived.

Charlotte Stoker had returned to Dublin in the mid-1880s after about a dozen years abroad in France, Switzerland, and Italy. A decade of independence from her sons and their families had apparently agreed with her, and she chose to live alone in a modest brick row house at 72 Rathgar Road, south of the city center and not far from the family's first south-of-the-Liffy residence on Orwell Road. In Rathgar, she had no daily obligations to anyone but herself. Her daughters were married and her grown sons beyond the tight control she had exerted when they were young. She had done her best, but she always thought Bram could have done better. Charlotte never had a good thing to say about Henry Irving, much less her son's career in the theatre. She may have isolated herself; Stoker's dedication to her of his 1895 novel *The Watter's Mou'* read, rather glumly, "To My Mother, in her loneliness." But finally, with *Dracula*, her son had produced something that resonated with her own passion for the Gothic novels of her girlhood, and it may have partially closed an emotional chasm. It seems to have cheered her. "My dear it is splendid, a thousand miles beyond anything you have written before, and I feel certain it will place you very high in the writers of the day," she wrote. "No book since Mrs. Shelley's 'Frankenstein' or indeed any other at all has come near yours in originality, or terror—Poe is nowhere. I have read much but I have never met a book like it at all. In its terrible excitement it should make a widespread reputation and much money for you."

But a later letter reflected a return to darker moods. "I have not been well at all lately, time tells very severely upon me and even the drops in my eyes begin to lose their effect. I only hope God will be good enough to take me home before I get quite blind. Situated as I am it is a terrible look forward for me but I can't complain. I have had a happy and healthy life and must take the bad as well as the good. If I had lost my sight in the early part of my life, when it needed me to be useful, how much worse it would have been."

Charlotte died in Dublin on March 15, 1901, three months short of her eighty-third birthday. Bram received the news while on a provincial tour with the Lyceum company. Stoker's biographer Paul Murray reports the cause of death as heart failure following influenza, with only Charlotte's "illiterate maid" in attendance at her Rathgar home. But the earlier biographer Barbara Belford makes an extraordinary suggestion—that her suffering was ended by a mercy killing. Immediately following her presenting the fact of Charlotte's death, Belford inserts, with no further elaboration, Dr. Seward's opinion from *Dracula*: "'Euthanasia' is an excellent and comforting word! I am grateful to whoever invented it." The term "euthanasia," in its original Victorian coinage, described the use of morphine to relieve pain in the final stages of terminal illness; there was a very fine line between aggressive palliative care and the actual termination of life, and doctors understood there was a potent power at their discreet disposal. However, the *Dracula* quotation Belford uses appears in the context of Dr. Seward's considering a fail-safe plan for killing Mina Harker if her teeth begin to sharpen—and not with a morphine injection. "If this change should come, it would be necessary to take steps!" writes Seward. "We both know what those steps would have to be, though we do not mention our thoughts to each other. We should neither of us shrink from the task—awful though it be to contemplate." Decapitation and heart-staking had already been established as the optimal means, and Mina has already asked explicitly for the procedures if or when they are needed.

Was Charlotte Stoker delivered a "mercy-bearing stake" in the form of a morphine syringe, by or under the supervision of one of her physician sons? Awful though it might be to acknowledge, such a compassionate action would never appear on a death certificate, though the tightly held truth might be passed down privately by the family. Whatever the immediate cause of Charlotte's death, the loss of sight in a woman who, above all, prized reading and literacy her entire life, would have made her final illness a cruel personal hell. She was buried in a family plot at Mount Jerome Cemetery, also the resting place of Dublin luminaries Sir William Wilde and J. Sheridan Le Fanu. When her son Thornley (along with his wife, Emily) joined her, a headstone was erected commemorating Abraham Stoker as well, though his ashes remained permanently interred in Italy.

If Bram did not witness his mother's last days, the same cannot be said of his ringside seat at the sorry spectacle of Irving's declining health, a creeping process spread over several years. Rumors about the actor's weakened stamina and impending retirement began not long after the scenery fire, and Stoker was forced to refute them in the press. The first chink in Irving's stage armor came on the opening night of the 1896 revival of *Richard III*, when, following the performance, he stumbled at home and tore ligaments in his knee. As Ellen Terry recalled, "With characteristic fortitude, he struggled to his feet unassisted and walked to his room. This made the consequences of the accident far more serious, and he was not able to act for weeks."

Two years later, a graver health challenge made a most unwelcome entrance. According to Terry, "when we were on tour, he caught a chill. Inflammation of the lungs, bronchitis [and] pneumonia followed. His heart was affected. He was never really well again. . . . The seriousness of his illness in 1898 was never really known. He nearly died."

The inflammation Terry described was pleurisy. In Glasgow, halfway through a performance of *Madame Sans-Gêne* (in which Irving played Napoleon with oversized furniture intended to reduce the actor's considerable stature to Napoleonic proportions), Irving summoned Stoker to his dressing room. "I think there must be something wrong with me. Every breath I take is like a sword-stab." He may well have been exaggerating, since he went on with the performance, but the pain was real, and Stoker had a doctor waiting after the curtain call.

Four decades before penicillin, the complication of pneumonia was extremely dangerous. Irving remained in Glasgow for seven weeks under the care of two nurses while the tour continued without him, at his insistence. Stoker monitored his employer anxiously. "At first, of course, he got worse and worse; weaker, and suffering more pain. He had never in his life been anything but lean, but now as he lost flesh the outline of his features grew painfully keen. The cheek and chin and lips, which he had kept clean shaven all his life, came out stubbly with white hair. At that time his hair was iron-grey, but no more." In *Dracula*, Stoker had reversed the aging process in the Count, his appearance dramatically changed by blood rejuvenation. "There he lay looking as if youth had been half-renewed," observed Jonathan Harker, specifically noting that Dracula's hair had "changed to dark iron-grey." If Dracula was in any way inspired by Irving, might Stoker have been entertaining, on some partly conscious level, a magical reverie about extending the actor's life? By 1897, when the novel was published, Irving was already slowing down.

With an understudy instead of Irving, tour attendance plummeted, but seventy loyal people were dependent on Irving's payroll and couldn't

One of Henry Irving's last photographic portraits.

survive without the promised provincial engagements. The ten weeks of the tour cost Irving "a very considerable sum of money," said Stoker. The cost of re-creating sets for performances in London and on the road was another unplanned and ongoing expense; new flats and drops now cost three times their original prices. The Lyceum's finances were severely strained, and, even with Irving performing, the first nights no longer had the social cachet of earlier decades. "At the turn of the century, the theatrical conditions which prevailed while Irving conquered and finally dominated the London stage had gone forever," wrote his biographer grandson. "Now he had to face vigorous competition not only from rival actor-managers, but from new styles of entertainment. The public still looked at him affectionately as the grand old man of the theatre—but they no longer gravitated instinctively to the box-office of the Lyceum."

Irving also had some costly flops, such as *Coriolanus* (1901) and especially *Dante* (1903), which fared poorly in London and had to be entirely removed from the touring repertory in New York after a disastrous opening night. "Both plays were out of joint with the time," wrote Stoker. "In both pieces Irving made a personal success; it was the play in each case that was unpopular. . . . Whenever any other play was put up the house was crowded." It was remarkable that Irving, following his near-fatal illness, was able to recover sufficient stamina for two more American tours, played largely in the dead of winter.

Did Stoker offer any advice to Irving on his choice of plays? It was during one of the last tours that the Chicago drama critic Frederick Donaghey recalled a bold if self-serving suggestion. "Bram Stoker told me that he had put in endless hours in trying to persuade Henry Irving to have a play made from *Dracula* and to act in it[;] he added that he had nothing in mind save the box office," Donaghey wrote. "'If,' he explained, 'I am able to afford having my name on the book, the Governor can certainly afford, with business bad, to have his name on the play. But he laughs whenever I talk about it; and then we have to go out and raise money to put on something in which the public has no interest.'" How might Irving have essayed the part? "The Governor as Dracula would be the Governor in a composite of so many of the parts in which he has been liked—Mathias in *The Bells*, Shylock, Mephistopheles, Peter the Great, the bad fellow in *The Lyons Mail*, Louis XI, and ever so many others, including Iachimo in *Cymbeline*. But he just laughs at me!"

Here, several things come across, none of which is a confirmation of the legend that Stoker wrote *Dracula* specifically for Irving. Not one of the characters he enumerates—including Mephistopheles—is anything at all like Stoker's concept of the vampire (save Dracula's basic supernaturalism), so we can surely chalk up at least some of this as old-fashioned blarney. His concern for the box office, however, was sincere. But given the furious financial pressure on him to continue moonlighting, Stoker also understood that such a production, however unlikely, could provide a significant personal windfall. After all, didn't Irving pay W. G. Wills £600 for *Faust*? Stoker had helped Irving revise and shape the problematic script, which had gone on to become one of the actor's greatest successes—but, as usual, he received no overtime compensation.

Freelance writing was now a necessity for Stoker, and not a choice; from the time Henry Irving began to falter ominously, he carved out more and more time for fiction. After *Dracula*, he reworked his earlier, rejected novel called *Seven Golden Buttons* as *Miss Betty* and sold it to the publisher C. Arthur Pearson Limited, which issued the book in 1898. *Dracula*'s encouraging initial sales may have prompted Pearson to take a chance based on Bram's name recognition, but any reader approaching it on that basis would be sorely disappointed. *Miss Betty* was not *Dracula*, despite the fact that Stoker gave both novels a full copyright reading on the Lyceum stage. *Miss Betty* remains one of his weakest efforts. Interestingly enough, it was also the only book he ever dedicated to his wife.

Between the last two American tours, Stoker published *The Mystery of the Sea* (1902). It played unabashedly to the escapist expectations of a youthful male audience. As the *New York Tribune* noted, "The story is not saturated with the weird horror that held us in 'Dracula,' but it has enough of the supernatural for due glamour and thrill. . . . One parlous[2] episode succeeds another; ancient documents, secret passages, rising tides, play significant parts; the lovely girl is always brave and sweet, the splendid hero is always full of resource."

A briskly moving boy's adventure tale with every stock character and clichéd situation imaginable tossed into the campfire stew, *The Mystery of the Sea* opens on a supernatural note, as our hero Archibald Hunter arrives at Cruden Bay for a summer holiday, much in the manner of Stoker himself.[3] At the seashore, Archie begins to have strange visions of the dead and meets an imposing Gypsy-like seer named Gormala who informs him that he, too, has the "second sight." His gift comes in and out of play after he meets (and marries) a plucky American heiress named Marjory Drake, who lives in an ancient castle, faces a kidnapping plot, and becomes involved in the search for a lost treasure from the Spanish Armada. Stoker anticipates the cliffhanger conventions of Saturday matinee movie serials yet to come as both hero and heroine locate the Armada gold in a coastal cave, only to be trapped by the inrushing tide. "Marjory, my wife, the end is close!" Archie cries. "I fear we may not both live. In a few minutes more, at most, the water will be over my mouth. When that time comes, I shall sink over the pile of treasure on which we rest. You must then stand on me; it will raise you sufficiently to let you hold out longer." The wincingly awkward dialogue brings to mind the stilted exposition of radio drama, a medium for which Stoker would actually have been well suited. "You are saved! You

---

[2] Obsolete form of "perilous"; could also mean "clever."

[3] The reviewer for the *Daily Mail* erred by calling Stoker's Archie an "autobiographical hero," although on one level the book might well be considered a memoir, of sorts, since it recapitulates all the thrills and pleasures of Stoker's own boyhood reading.

are saved!" Marjory tells the reader/audience, not her husband, though both already know that the threatening tide is receding. "The water is falling," Marjory observes, redundantly.

Also in the fashion of future radio shows, *The Mystery of the Sea* came with its own early version of a "decoder ring"—several pages in the back of the book dedicated to the encryption tables of the "biliteral cipher" (that is, a code based on the double-letter substitution formula first developed by Sir Francis Bacon, a pioneer in cryptography and secure communications), which the reader could use to personally create impenetrable communications like the ones used in the story's treasure hunt. On a theatrical note, the *Glasgow Herald* suggested that the code "may be of some interest to the cranks who contend for Bacon against Shakespeare."

Despite being shot through with shadows, *The Mystery of the Sea* would be Stoker's last book to put forth anything like a sunny worldview. "Through it all beams the breezy personality of Bram Stoker" was the judgment of *Punch*, though "once over lightly" might better describe the book's overall style and attention to characterization. Perhaps as a holdover reflex from an old fascination with the revelations of physiognomy, his sinister characters repeatedly take the form of human raptors. Their faces first entered his imagination by way of villainous characters in Gothic novels like *The Monk* ("His nose was aquiline, his eyes large, black, and sparkling"), which he later resurrected in the cadaverous visage of the revenant jurist in "The Judge's House," who steps out of a painting to demonstrate his reputation as a hanging judge ("His face was strong and merciless, evil, crafty, and vindictive, with a sensual mouth, hooked nose of ruddy color, and shaped like the beak of a bird of prey"). Next came Count Dracula, he whose "nose was a strong—a very strong—aquiline" upon his midnight introduction, and later, in broad daylight, just "beaky." Then, in *The Mystery of the Sea*, Stoker re-created the face on the seeress Gormala, a "great-eyed, aquiline-featured, gaunt old woman" who at first seems menacing but is ultimately benevolent. Even a redeemed villain, Don Bernadino, descending from the family that lost the Armada treasure, arrives equipped with the same Gothic face, demonstrated by "his high aquiline nose and black eagle eyes of keenness." It is sometimes hard to determine whether Stoker was invoking a persistent archetype or just indulging in lazy writing. But even when he resorted to descriptive shorthand, as in *Mystery*, he summoned durably demonic imagery that would stubbornly resist exorcism in the popular imagination. And some of Stoker's most indelible images were yet to come.

Since *Dracula* had been in print for over five years, it made sense for Stoker and his publisher to make another commercial bet on the walking dead, this time a resurrected Egyptian mummy in *The Jewel of Seven Stars* (1903). In Dublin, Stoker had known Sir William Wilde, whose ethnographic and archaeological studies had taken him to Egypt in 1838, where, in Saqqara, he unearthed a mummy, which he hauled back to Merrion Square. What subsequently happened to the relic is anyone's guess; had it been displayed in the Wilde home, it would have assuredly been mentioned as an especially atmospheric prop in accounts of Lady Wilde's candlelit soirees. Previous Stoker biographies and critical studies have assumed, without evidence, that Stoker's presumed Dublin conversations with Sir William about Egyptology directly inspired *The Jewel of Seven Stars*. But Wilde was in poor and ever-worsening health during the handful of years Stoker attended the salons at Merrion Square, and his days as a lively raconteur were long past. Guests who attended Lady Wilde's Sunday at-homes in the 1870s never mention his attendance, and there are no Stoker papers in which Sir William's name even appears, except for one of his books, *The Narrative of a Voyage to Madeira, Teneriffe, and Along the Shores of the Mediterranean* (1840), owned by Stoker and describing Wilde's excursions in the classical world, including Egypt. Although Noel Stoker had no clear recollection of his father ever talking about the Wildes, Harry Ludlam asserted the inspirational link in his 1960 book *A Biography of Dracula*, and like so many other Stoker factoids, it has been accepted as true, and relentlessly embellished upon ever since.

In reality, Stoker needed no research or creative stimulation from Sir William Wilde to write *The Jewel of Seven Stars*. "Egyptomania" was a public preoccupation—a veritable craze—far beyond Wilde's purview, beginning in the early nineteenth century and continuing even beyond the discovery of Tutankhamun's treasure in 1922. Egyptomania had a strong visual influence on design and fashion; its stylized lines were evident in both Art Deco and Art Moderne, and strongly felt in Jacob Epstein's monumental grave marker for Oscar Wilde. Along with pyramids, obelisks, and ankhs, mummies were prime avatars of a neo-Gothic fascination with the long-dead past that had the power to touch the living.

Revived and/or oracular mummies made their first literary appearances in works like Jane Loudon's *The Mummy! A Tale of the Twenty-Second Century* (1827), which mixed the sensibilities of the Gothic and science fiction. In Théophile Gautier's "The Mummy's Foot" (1840), the curio-shop customer who buys an ancient princess's relic is stalked by its reawakened original owner. Poe's satirical sketch "Some Words with a Mummy" appeared in 1845, and in 1892 Stoker's friend Arthur Conan Doyle published "Lot No. 249," about a student who revives a mummy in his rooms at Oxford and sends it forth to wreak havoc on his enemies.

Stoker may well have discussed Egyptian mummies with his friend Mark Twain, who, on top of what he actually knew about the subject, was happy to share invented information as well. In *The Innocents Abroad* (1869) Twain put forth the satirical idea that mummies were so plentiful in Egypt that an eminently practical use had been found for them in the country's ever-expanding, British-built system of railroads: the trains' fuel, Twain reported, "is composed of mummies three thousand years old, purchased by the ton or by the graveyard for that purpose, and . . . sometimes one hears the profane engineer call out pettishly, 'D—n these plebeians, they don't burn worth a cent—pass out a King!'" Twain added, with a wink, that "I only tell it as I got it. I am willing to believe it. I can believe anything." Nonetheless, it is still easy to find any number of sources where the joke is repeated as fact.

If Victorian mummies didn't actually stoke steam engines, they did fuel the public's interest in *The Jewel of Seven Stars*. The *Reader* magazine assured its followers that "this book is not a shilling shocker—it is a dollar-and-a-half Egyptologic nightmare and 311 pages of gooseflesh and cold chills." A much darker exercise than *Mystery*, with enough imagistic appeal to eventually inspire five screen adaptations, *Jewel* has proved Stoker's most media-genic work of fiction after *Dracula*.[4]

The Jewel of Seven Stars opens, in the manner of a classic Sherlock Holmes puzzler, when the young barrister Malcolm Ross is called to the home of Abel Trelawny, a renowned Egyptologist, whom his daughter, Margaret, has found badly beaten and insensate in a room to which there was no

---

[4]The first dramatization was made for British television in 1970, under the title *Curse of the Mummy*, part of the *Mystery and Imagination* series that had already produced *Dracula* in 1968. Next was the Hammer film *Blood from the Mummy's Tomb* (1971), followed by *The Awakening* (1980), *The Tomb* (1980), and *Bram Stoker's Legend of the Mummy* (1998). A radio adaptation, called simply *The Mummy*, was produced in 1999.

apparent means of access. It is gradually revealed that Margaret's mother died in childbirth during the opening of the tomb of Queen Tera, and the daughter is somehow possessed by the soul of the ancient monarch, preternaturally intent on walking the earth once more. Malcolm and Margaret are romantically involved, which blinds him to the possibility that she might be responsible for the repeated mysterious attacks on her father. When Trelawny, released from his comatose trance, unwraps Queen Tera, her impossibly uncorrupted body shows her to be the very image of Margaret, who has indeed been functioning as the mummy's projected, astral form. The novel has two endings. In 1903, the experiment in resuscitation ends with everyone dead except for Malcolm. A revised text published in 1912 ends with the queen destroyed and Margaret and Malcolm married, a conclusion echoing the finale of *Dracula*, in which domesticity and parenthood restore the world to balance after the vanquishing of an ancient monster. As in *Dracula*, Stoker's unease with the idea of the New Woman is still palpable; as Margaret becomes increasingly empowered and assertive under Tera's influence, Malcolm feels threatened, even "unmanned."

The Jewel contains other parallels to Stoker's magnum opus as well. *Dracula*'s invasion of England has been endlessly dissected as a guilty imperialist parable of exceptionally bad national karma, manifested as the popular-culture fixation on "reverse colonization" by the alien other. The motif was hardly limited to Stoker's novel. For example, in *War of the Worlds* (1895), H. G. Wells's Martians were literal space vampires, eager to siphon English blood. The figure of the Egyptian mummy was especially effective bait for gnawing English anxieties about the limits of Empire. The Victorian occupation of Egypt had proved particularly difficult. As summarized by Kate Hebblethwaite, the astute editor of the Penguin Classics edition of *The Jewel*—the only edition to contain both endings—"British attitudes towards Egypt, reflecting those of the West towards the East generally, were characterized by both attraction and revulsion. On the one hand, Egypt was the imaginative nexus of savagery, rebellion, licentiousness, moral degeneration and otherness; on the other, it was an exhilarating, exotic, passionate playground." Mummies who wouldn't stay dead were dreamlike representations of an entire people who wouldn't play dead in the face of Britain's imperialist aggression.

Like séances, Egyptomania provided a novel way to explore alternate conceptions of an afterlife to fortify, or even displace, the embattled

Christian version. As the Great Pyramid of Giza amply attests, there has been no other civilization so monumentally obsessed with the realm of death as ancient Egypt. The public unwrapping of mummies was a recurrent ritual that always drew fascinated Victorian audiences, despite the truly unpleasant smells released by bandage removal. Gautier, in his non-fiction *Romance of a Mummy* (1842), described one such event:

> Strange indeed was the appearance of the tall rag-doll, the armature of which was a dead body, moving so stiffly and awkwardly with a sort of horrible parody of life. . . . Our curiosity was becoming feverish, and the mummy was being turned somewhat quickly. . . . A sudden storm was lashing the windows with heavy drops of rain that rattled like hail; pale lightnings illumined on the shelves of the cupboards the old yellowed skulls and the grimacing death's-heads of the Anthropological Museum; while the low rolling of the thunder formed an accompaniment to the waltz of Nes Khons, the daughter of Horus and Rouaa, as she pirouetted in the impatient hands of those who were unwrapping her.

Stoker, too, gave his unwrapped Queen Tera the semblance of life, but it was nothing like Gautier's mechanically balletic danse macabre—death doing a dusty striptease—except for the fact that both scenes are accompanied by the melodramatic window dressing of electrical storms. Unlike Dracula's dessicated body and buried libido, Queen Tera's uncorrupted body illustrates the inherent forbidden eroticism of all fantastic beings who return from their graves. Like other sensual transgressors, the living corpse craves taboo experience—the simple, erotic state of being and feeling alive. As Malcolm describes the scene, "We all stood awed at the beauty of the figure which, save for the face cloth, now lay completely nude before us. Mr. Trelawny bent over, and with hands that trembled slightly, raised this linen cloth. . . . As he stood back and the whole glorious beauty of the Queen was revealed, I felt a rush of shame sweep over me. It was not right that we should be there, gazing with irreverent eyes on such unclad beauty: it was indecent; it was almost sacrilegious! And yet the white wonder of that beautiful form was something to dream of. It was not like death at all."

Henry Irving, while still a living person, was hardly so well preserved as Stoker's Queen Tera, and people who never liked him in the first place considered him a fossilized relic. "Moving so stiffly and awkwardly with a sort of horrible parody of life" is almost exactly the way his detractors had described him from the very beginning. Stoker kept an obsessively detailed account of the actor's failing health in his diary, with acute observations of the subtlest changes in his physiognomy and physique. "There was a certain shrinkage . . . only too apparent to the eyes of those who loved him," Stoker wrote. "Irving had been working now for forty-two years, strenuously for twenty seven of them. . . . Labour so exacting and so prolonged increases vastly the wear and tear of life." In 1903 Irving was sixty-five years old, but to Stoker he was "actually older than his years. . . . Every little ailment told on him with undue force."

Stoker's hovering descriptions of Irving's physical decline may amount to a consolation prize for a more corporeal intimacy that never was. But he projects a tone of self-flagellation that may reflect his own personality more than his employer's. "Each day, each hour had its own tally of difficulty to overcome—of pain or hardship to be borne—of some form of self-denial to be exercised."

Ever since the 1898 illness, Irving had suffered from a worsening case of what he and his doctors considered "clergyman's sore throat," common enough among actors and public speakers, and coughing up increasing amounts of what appeared to be phlegm. How he managed to suppress the reflex during performance is a mystery. It must have been a supreme exercise of willpower. Nevertheless, "month by month and year by year the weakening expectoration increased, till for the last three years he used some *five hundred* pocket-handkerchiefs in each week. Such a detail is a somewhat sickening one even to read—what must it have been to the poor brave soul who through it all had to present himself so as to conceal it from the world. . . . It was not until February 1905 when after a hard night's work he fell fainting in the hall-way of the hotel at Wolverhampton that the true cause of his weakness was diagnosed. . . . For more than six years, ever since his attack of pleurisy and pneumonia—Irving had been coughing up pus from an unhealed lung. I ask no pardon for giving these medical details. It was prudent to be silent all those years; but the time has gone for such reticence." Like Oscar Wilde, whose long-festering ear injury had tormented him the last five years of his life, Irving suffered from the suppurating persistence of an old malady. Without antibiotics, the only prescription was rest. Sometimes it helped, sometimes it didn't. It is appropriate that one of his last roles was Dante Alighieri, since Stoker encapsulated Irving's career almost as a series of friezes from the descending, punishing rings of the Inferno. In *Personal Reminiscences*, he summed up Irving's energies in almost superhuman terms. The actor simply could *not* stop performing.

> Day or night; in stillness; in travel; in tropic heat such as now and again is experienced in early summer in America; through raging blizzards; in still cold when the thermometer registered down to figures below zero which would kill us in a breath did we have it in our moist atmosphere; in dust storms of rapid travel; in the abounding dust of many theatres, the man had to toil unendingly. For others there was rest; for him none. For others there was cessation, or at worst now and again a lull in the storm of responsibility; for him none. Others could find occasional seclusion; for him there was no such thing, His very popularity was an added strain and trial to increasing weakness and ill-health. But in all, and through all, he never faltered or thought of faltering.

Stoker, of course, was the one who had spent his days bearing the weight of the world, but in this passage, in repeated rhythms of almost biblical cadence, he achieves the transcendent fusion of souls he always sought by projecting his own driven, self-punishing personality onto a transfigured and Christ-like Irving. "He made throughout years a great fortune, but nearly all of it he spent as it came in on his art, and in helping his poorer brethren. His own needs were small. He had no vices that I know of; he was not extravagant; did not gamble, was not ostentatious even in his charities." More typical appraisals of Irving paint him as a supreme narcissist incapable of playing any role but himself, an autocratic egoist without equal.

As Camille Paglia has aptly observed, "The great stars are sacred monsters, amoral vampires who drain those around them to feed the world." Henry Irving was a vampire, no doubt. And he certainly drained Bram Stoker. But the deeply ingrained myth that Dracula represented Stoker's conscious or unconscious revenge on the man who had stifled and smothered and stolen his life is, in the end, a facile untruth that ignores some obvious psychological realities. Irving *did* recognize and honor Stoker—as a slave. In the time-honored protocols of domination and submission, the controlling partners are never resented; quite to the contrary, they're eternally worshipped. Enslavement is the masochist's ultimate validation and gratification. Stoker played the role without the need of actual ropes or restraints, or locks and chains. But he played it all the same, and he always played it to please.

Stoker's subservient devotion to a monster in failing health may have pushed Florence Stoker to the end of her endurance. She had withstood a quarter century of marriage to a man who had spent literally years away from home on tours to the provinces and America, and for all practical purposes lived at the Lyceum when he was home. The end of Irving's reign would also be the end of the family's precarious, overleveraged position in London society. Irving would have no successor. Bram's employment would end. He had no other real ambitions besides his writing and the unpredictable income that came with it. How would he provide? After all that preparation, why *hadn't* he become a practicing barrister? She had always been told that her extraordinary beauty destined her to soar in the theatre. She might have been another Lillie Langtry. Fame might have made her life secure. But dull marriage, dull motherhood, and Irving's unforgivable indifference to her potential had killed that dream. She had been cheated, and the clawing bitterness would persist to the end of her life.

Florence often thought of Oscar Wilde. Bram was earnest and kind, but, truly, he was never meant for greatness. What would a life with Oscar have been? Certainly not the disastrous death sentence it became with Constance at his side. Pretty, yes, but such a timid mouse, and no match for his weaknesses. Oscar needed a lioness for a wife. She and Oscar had recognized fire in each other. His "Catholic" poetry had scandalized her family in Dublin, but she liked it, and he knew she liked it. At heart they were both secret transgressors. Who better than she, therefore, to have kept his most dangerous impulses in check?

A religious crisis overtook Florence, but today there is no one alive in the Stoker family who knows the details.[5] In their private Dublin moments Wilde may well have told her something of his own spiritual struggles, though almost certainly not the terrifying medical problem that precipitated his pilgrimage to Father Sebastian Bowden at the Brompton Oratory. But it does not seem a coincidence that Florence knew exactly where to find

---

[5] Ann Stoker Dobbs, the Stokers' granddaughter, died in 1999. Although she was interviewed for three Stoker biographies, and knew Florence well in her childhood and adolescence, no questions about her grandmother's religious beliefs were ever asked.

Father Sebastian Bowden of the Brompton Oratory,
confessor to Oscar Wilde, Lord Alfred Douglas, and Florence Stoker.

the priest who had almost succeeded in converting her onetime suitor to Catholicism—and who had also served as confessor to Bosie Douglas.

Sometime during the year 1904, she completed the act that Wilde had left unfinished and was received into the Church of Rome. Her husband's and son's reactions are not known, but they were not inclined to follow, and a permanent shadow of religious estrangement, unexplained to the present day, descended with finality on the house of Stoker.

The Lyceum was planning a provincial tour for the spring of 1905, to be followed by a final American expedition in the autumn. But Irving "had become so alarmingly ill that we were very seriously anxious," Stoker wrote, noting in his diary after a precarious performance of *The Lyons Mail* at Boscombe, "H.I. fearfully done up, could hardly play. At end in collapse. Could hardly move or breathe." The month was March, and the weather was frigid, with snow. Irving recovered enough to charge on through the next engagement, in Bath, but during the following stop in Wolverhampton, a strenuous performance of *The Bells* was simply too much, and for the first time in his life, Irving fainted at the entrance to his hotel. In the morning he had no recollection of what had happened. After two more touch-and-go performances, of *Becket* ("comparatively light work for him") and *The Merchant of Venice*, a doctor's notice was posted for the company: "It is imperatively necessary that Sir Henry Irving shall not act for at least two months from this date." The remainder of the tour was canceled. "In the meantime," wrote Stoker, "I had seen Charles Frohman and postponed our American tour for a year."

Irving played a short, six-week season in London at the Drury Lane, then made his final London appearance in *Waterloo* as a benefit for his actor friend Lionel Brough at His Majesty's Theatre in June. A provincial farewell tour commenced in October, beginning in Sheffield. At the next stop, Bradford, Stoker accompanied him to a tribute luncheon at the Town Hall, where Irving employed a face-saving trick to cover his infirmity. "He had become adept at concealing his weakness on such occasions," Stoker wrote. "He would seize on some point of local or passing interest and make inquiries about it, so that by the time the answer came he would have been rested." He was able to finish that night's performance of *Louis XI*, but the following evening's staging of *The Bells* was so difficult that the production was banished from the tour and the scenery ordered back to London. On Friday, October 13, Stoker sat with him to deliver the news that the American tour was being abandoned. He acquiesced easily, with a mordant quip: "A kindly continent to me, but I will not leave my bones there if I can help it."

During Friday's performance of *Becket*, the company was startled at his improvising certain lines and bits of action. They were used to his never varying the smallest aspect of his speech and presentation. It was especially disturbing when, near the end of the play, he changed a key line about being ready to die, delivering "God's will be done" as "God is my judge." Finally came the climax, with Becket's assassins moving in for the kill.

BECKET (*falling on his knees*).
    At the right hand of Power—
Power and great glory—for thy Church, O Lord—
Into Thy hands, O Lord—into Thy hands!——
              (*Sinks prone.*)

Irving had edited Tennyson, who followed Becket's death with the outbreak of a thunderous storm (believed to have been a historical fact) and the assembling of mourners around the body. But Irving was not one to be upstaged by the weather. It was he, after all, who was expected to provide the blood and the thunder.

When Irving fell, the curtain did as well.

As soon as it rang down, Loveday and an assistant rushed onstage to help the actor to his feet and off the stage, something that in earlier years had never been necessary.[6] And for the first time in any performance of the play, Irving had collapsed with his head not downstage, toward the audience, but instead upstage, toward the steps of the cathedral transept where he had been attacked. It was as if he were trying somehow to hold on, cling to the scenery, and stay in the play.

As described by the *Bradford Daily Telegraph*, "At the close last night the audience were most unwilling to part with the great actor and four times did the curtain rise, to discover Irving standing by one of the Cathedral pillars, motionless and exhausted. The audience determined that, if possible they would have a few words more from his lips, and after long sustained applause, the curtain rose upon an empty stage. Stepping out from a door on the side, Sir Henry waited until the rapturous welcome had subsided. In a voice that betrayed some signs of emotion he thanked them for the great reception of the noble and beautiful work of the great poet Tennyson, and expressed the deep sense of gratitude felt by his company and himself at the splendid reception accorded them."

Stoker went to Irving's dressing room and congratulated him on the performance. Now that the strenuous demands of *The Bells* had been removed from the tour, he said, Irving would surely regain his strength. The actor agreed, smiling. "I stood up to go and he held out his hand to say good-night. Afterwards, the remembrance of that affectionate movement came back to me with gratitude, for it was not usual; when men meet every day and every night, handshaking is not a part of the routine of friendly life. As I went out he said to me:

"'Muffle up your throat, old chap. It is bitterly cold to-night and you have a cold. Take care of yourself ! Good-night ! God bless you!' "

---

[6] Assisting Irving at this performance was the veteran Lyceum actor George Belmore, whose son Lionel played one of Becket's enemies. In Hollywood, twenty-six years later in 1931, Lionel Belmore would essay the memorable role of the burgomaster in James Whale's *Frankenstein*, while his sister Daisy appeared as an English coach passenger in the opening scene of Tod Browning's *Dracula*.

What happened next, when Irving left the theatre for the hotel, was told to Stoker, who re-created the scene in his memoir. "When he got into the carriage he had sat with his back to the horses; this being his usual custom by which he avoided a draught. He was quite silent during the short journey. When he got out of the carriage he seemed very feeble, and as he passed through the outer hall of the hotel seemed uncertain of step. He stumbled slightly. . . . Then when he got as far as the inner hall he sat down on a bench for an instant."

That instant proved fatal.

"In the previous February at Wolverhampton," wrote Stoker, "when he had suffered from a similar attack of weakness, he had fallen down flat. In that attitude Nature asserted herself, and the lungs being in their easiest position allowed him to breathe mechanically. Now the seated attitude did not give the opportunity for automatic effort. The syncope grew worse; he slipped on the ground. But it was then too late. By the time the doctor arrived, after only a few minutes in all, he had passed too far into the World of Shadows to be drawn back by any effort of man or science. The heart beat faintly, and more faintly still. And then came the end. . . . The actual cause of Irving's death was physical weakness; he lost a breath, and had not strength to recover it." Stoker's basic understanding of a heart attack was a bit fuzzy, but at least it was poetic.

Irving's valet sat sobbing on the floor over the body. Stoker stared. "[Irving's] face looked very thin and the features sharp as he lay there with his chest high and his head fallen back; but there was none of the usual ungracefulness of death." Here Stoker may be spinning things. Collapsing in a chair and falling dead on the floor cannot be fairly called a graceful act. "The long iron-grey hair had fallen back," Stoker continued, "showing the great height of his rounded forehead. The bridge of his nose stood out sharp and high." Early in their relationship, during the production of *Vanderdecken*, Stoker marveled at Irving's ability to appear simultaneously living and dead. Now things had come full circle. As for the iron-gray hair, lofty forehead, and prominently bridged nose, except for the use of the word "aquiline," the descriptions remarkably matched his visualized physiognomy of Dracula.

"I closed his eyes myself," wrote Stoker, "but as I had had no experience in such a matter I asked one of the doctors, who kindly with deft fingers straightened the eyelids." Closing a dead person's eyes is not as simple as

Commemorative postcard of the hotel lobby where Irving died.

the gentle finger stroke usually depicted in film and television—modern undertakers use glue—but Stoker may have been additionally unnerved by the unexpected reality of actually touching the face that he worshipped in his dreams but that in life was forever beyond his reach. He helped move Irving's body, first to a couch on the hotel mezzanine and then to his room. Stoker was up all night. "I had to send a host of telegrams at once to inform the various members of his family and the press. The latter had to go with what speed we could, for the hour of his death was such that there was no local information." By the time the last notices were sent, it was nearly dawn. "Before I left the hotel in the grey of the morning I went into the bedroom. It wrung my heart to see my dear old friend lie there so cold and white and still. It was all so desolate and lonely, as so much of his life had been. So lonely that in the midst of my own sorrow I could not but rejoice at one thing: for him there was now Peace and Rest."

A bit later he oversaw the blanking out of the Theatre Royal's playbills. There is a haunting photo of Stoker crossing the street in front of the theatre that morning. At first glance it seems to be a candid moment, fortuitously captured, at least until one realizes that this is not a snapshot but a carefully posed and planned image made by a large-format camera on a heavy tripod positioned in a window above street level, or on a roof

Stoker exits the Bradford Theatre Royal the morning after Irving's death.
(John Moore Library)

across the street. Stoker had never sat for a formal portrait with Irving, but he stage-managed a final, memorably poignant picture on the subject of Irving and himself.

On Saturday morning an undertaker arrived; the body was embalmed and prepared for an afternoon viewing by the whole company. "At seven o'clock in the evening," Stoker recalled, "the body was placed in the lead coffin. I was present alone with the undertakers and saw the lead coffin sealed. This was then placed in the great oak coffin—which an hour later was taken privately through the yard of the Midland Hotel by a devious way to the Great Northern Station so as to avoid publicity; for the streets were thronged with waiting crowds." It would not be the last bit of chicanery involving the casket Stoker would witness.

On Sunday, in his exhausted hurry to return to London, he left behind at the hotel a suitcase with BRAM STOKER, ESQ. engraved on the lid. It remains in Bradford to this day.

"No one could deny Stoker's signal devotion to Irving's interest—that was there for all to see and admire," wrote Sir John Martin-Harvey of his days at the Lyceum. But while the funeral arrangements were being made, a certain brusque insensitivity toward members of the company was evident. The actors had always resented "a tendency on his part to herd us here and there in our travels like helpless sheep; which indeed we often were—but we didn't like the fact being rubbed in!" In their moment of shock and grief, "Stoker strongly fortified the barriers which kept us away from our Guv'nor." From Walter Collinson, Irving's valet and dresser, Martin-Harvey learned that "Stoker was responsible for the order which prevented any member of the company viewing our dead master's coffin, as it lay in his rooms at Stratton Street."[7]

---

[7] Martin-Harvey didn't long hold a grudge. As he explains in his *Autobiography*, "I set out to speak the truth in this book, and I hope, when this is said, that I shall not have hurt anyone's feelings, seeing that I have so much to say on the other side. It always thawed any resentment I might feel against Bram Stoker when I noted the conspicuous courtesy with which he always treated my wife, even when she was merely a very obscure little member of the company, and noted, too, the many little considerations he showed her which were scarcely warranted by her modest position there. It was rather pleasant to see his hat fly off whenever he met her as a small girl. I owe him, too, one of the greatest compliments I ever received in my life—of course ill-deserved—for, when some conjectures arose on a certain occasion as to who in the far future would wear the mantle of Irving, he roared in his attractive Irish brogue—'You're all wrong, it will be Martin-Harvey.'"

One reason Stoker kept mourners away from Irving's rooms was that they were simply too cramped to accommodate the large number of people expected to pay their respects. Another location had to be found. Over six hundred floral tributes had already been delivered, and the place was overflowing. Additionally, it was not immediately clear where England's first knighted actor would be buried. Most accounts of Irving's death present his interment at Westminster Abbey as a more or less foregone conclusion. In reality, it was a fallback choice, and one not without complications. A group of Irving's friends and associates, headed by the actor-producer George Alexander and the actor Norman Forbes-Robertson, approached the dean of St. Paul's Cathedral. The request was quickly refused. St. Paul's had accepted many artists, but never an actor. Westminster was the only alternative, especially after a snub of such magnitude. Although David Garrick had been laid to rest in Poets' Corner in 1779 (Geoffrey Chaucer was the first actual poet, in 1556), and a memorial statue of Sarah Siddons stood in St. Andrew's Chapel, Irving himself doubted he could be buried in such company. As he had told Mrs. Aria, "There will be nothing of the sort this century; no actor will be buried in Westminster Abbey."

And he very nearly wasn't. The dean of Westminster, Joseph Armitage Robinson, was bedridden in a darkened room, in danger of losing his sight and attended by an oculist. His sister, puritanically suspicious of actors, proved a buffer to be reckoned with. When Alexander and some of Irving's friends arrived, with a petition signed by many luminaries to press Irving's case, she made her objections forcefully clear: "No actors—no actors!" Irving had been prescient about official resistance to his eternal rest. As Irving's grandson noted, "the old prejudices against players and playhouses lingered," and that was putting it mildly.

Meanwhile, Alexander had hurriedly engaged the noted sculptor George James Frampton to take a death mask of Sir Henry. Frampton, later knighted himself, was well known for his royal commissions and would be especially remembered by the general public as creator of the beloved Peter Pan monument in Kensington Gardens, commissioned by J. M. Barrie, as well as the famous pair of lions guarding the north entrance to the British Library.

The details of the death mask's manufacture are sketchy. As a major theatrical producer, Alexander was a formidable personality used to getting what he wanted—he had snapped up the performance rights to *The Importance of Being Earnest* and *Lady Windermere's Fan* for a song when Oscar

Wilde's property was sold at auction[8]—and may well have presented the project to Stoker as an imperious and acquisitive fait accompli. Or Stoker may himself have made the request to Alexander. What is clear is that the private ceremony of the mask was intended to create a privately held trophy—not something for public commemoration or appreciation. The first and finest positive cast from the original mask (the actual plaster applied to the face) was to remain Alexander's; two second-generation copies made from the original would be given to Ellen Terry and to Stoker. In Stoker's case, it is not at all clear whether the gift was in recognition of his service to Irving or simply of the help he gave Alexander in acquiring the main prize.

The logistics were impossible. Primary among these was scheduling enough time to allow the public to pay their respects.

If Frampton did his mask work at Stratton Street, as is most likely the case, it would have been more than enough reason to turn away visitors, and the real reason Martin-Harvey and others were turned away. The lead coffin, ceremonially sealed in Bradford, would be unceremoniously opened. Irving's body would be removed from the coffin and propped upright, the head held in place by a two-piece wooden stock, which looked remarkably like the kind employed in the guillotine. Positioned horizontally, the wood provided a surface on which thick wet plaster could be worked and applied to the dead man's face, which had first to be slathered with mineral oil to facilitate the dried mold's smooth removal and to prevent pulling of the hair and eyebrows. Today, death masking is a decidedly antique art, akin to postmortem photography. Yet it still stirs the memory of Egyptian funerary rituals, in which mummy cases were decorated with masks of the deceased. In modern times, quick-drying materials are frequently used to capture the facial contours of living persons, usually for the creation of special effects makeup for film or television, or the ritual re-creation of celebrities in wax museums. But in 1905 it was all done with plaster, which required time to set. Stoker must have been sleepless and exhausted. But can there be any doubt he would have wanted to watch the bestowal upon Irving of the odd kind of immortality—call it undeath—that only a postmortem mask could provide?

---

[8]Alexander, who had produced both comedies, promised Wilde some voluntary payments during his penury in France, but the plays were never again produced during Wilde's lifetime. Royalties were, however, subsequently assigned to the playwright's sons. Once, while bicycling in Paris, Alexander spotted the exiled Wilde on the street, but after a startled meeting of their gazes, the producer quickly pedaled on.

Death mask of Henry Irving (Gwen Watford
Collection/Lebrecht Art and Music)

*A plaster death mask in the making, circa 1910.
Unknown subject.* (Library of Congress)

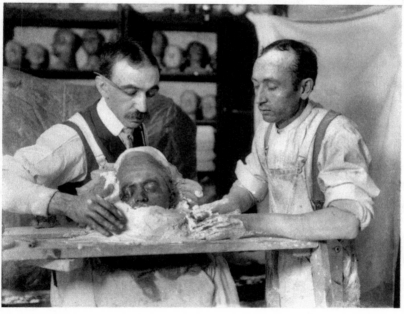

If so, it would be the last time Stoker ever laid eyes on his employer,
or participated significantly in the memorial rites. George Alexander, in
league with Irving's sons, blocked both Stoker and Loveday, the actor's
longest, closest Lyceum associates, from acting as pallbearers. They were
always regarded as servants, never equals. Stoker was also excluded from
any other aspect of the funeral planning, and even before the burial the

heirs demanded that all of Irving's papers and records be handed over to them. Since the actor's death the previous Friday, Stoker had worked tirelessly, handling all the arrangements in Bradford, dealing with the press, and sending an uncounted number of telegrams to people all over the world. These essential tasks completed, he was kicked to the curb. Ellen Terry expressed her regret to Stoker, writing, "That you and poor L[oveday] were not more closely associated with the last scene . . . grieves me."

Others made sure they got their piece of the dead man. In addition to the striking of the death mask, no time had been wasted in the acquisition of other delectable memento mori. The playwright and actor Seymour Hicks told Jessie Millward how, by shrewd action, he had come into possession of the very chair in which Irving had died. "The chair was marked in pencil by the hall porter, there being twelve others like it at the hotel, and was initialed by the directors at my request," he boasted. A commemorative medal was issued. The Bradford hotel soon began selling souvenir postcards showing Irving as Becket, inserted into a photograph of the entry hall where he died.

Permission for burial was finally granted by Westminster Abbey, but not without more high drama. In *Personal Reminiscences*, Stoker dissembles in his statement that the petitioners were so prestigious that approval was essentially rubber-stamped. "So important were the signatories that no difficulties were experienced," he wrote. A half century later, Laurence Irving would reveal that George Alexander had to finally ask Armitage Robinson's eye doctor, Sir Anderson Critchett, to intercede, pressuring the dean to ignore his sister's shrill objections for the simple reason that he was indebted to the doctor for having saved his sight. The doctor was now calling in the debt and dictating the terms. Payment for his eyes would be the burial of Henry Irving in the Abbey. An official statement glossed over any hint of grave wrangling: "The Dean of Westminster, having received a request signed by leading members of the dramatic profession, and by other persons of distinction has consented to the interment of the late Sir Henry Irving in Westminster Abbey." It was further announced that all inquiries and applications for tickets should be addressed to the honorary secretaries, Alexander and Forbes-Robertson. By Tuesday night, fifty thousand requests were received for the twelve hundred places available. Meanwhile, the Baroness Burdett-Coutts and her husband offered the convenience of their palatial Mayfair house at

1 Stratton Street, only about a block and a half from Irving's flat, as a place for the lying-in-state.

Permission to inter at Westminster had come with one proviso: Irving would have to be cremated. The abbey's foundations could not withstand any further excavation for full-sized graves. Irving's family found the requirement unseemly and did what they could to deflect public attention. The nearest facility was the City of London Crematorium, but Irving's body could not be transported there without drawing crowds. The only other practical choice was the Golders Green Crematorium in North London, a significant trek in a time before motorized hearses, and when the fastest steam-powered street conveyances were legally limited to nearly walking speed. Even today, bus connections from Stratton Street to Golders Green can take nearly an hour. One-way transport in 1905 could take three, about the same time as the actual cremation required, not including cooling of the ash and residual bones, which then had to be raked into a cremulator, or grinder, to eliminate any trace of the skeleton that might remain, and usually did remain. All in all, from door to door and dust to dust, it was a process requiring almost an entire day. Most likely, the initial transport took place under the cover of night. While the cremation was hardly a state secret, the *New York Times* reported that the family did not want the fact publicized. (Any connection drawn between the macabre game of hide-and-seek over Irving's coffin and the efforts of the supersecretive creature of Stoker's imagining to move and hide his boxes around London will not be resisted here.)

On Thursday morning the coffin, now containing Irving's urn, was taken to the Burdett-Coutts home, its stately dining room transformed into a *chapelle ardente* where what remained of Irving could rest from ten in the morning until four in the afternoon. The occasion was intended not for the general public but for the social and cultural elite. Florence Irving, the termagant as always, looked for a way to oppose the Westminster burial, until she was gently advised—by George Bernard Shaw—that taking such a stand might jeopardize her chances for any widow's pension or other consideration for which she might qualify. For his own part, Shaw refused to attend the service. He called Irving "an illiterate mutilator of every piece of fine dramatic literature he laid his hands on." However much she hated her husband (an "implacable Irish hatred," according to Shaw), the widow still enjoyed, or at least coveted, the privileges of being Lady Irving. These did not include being remembered in her husband's will, which was one final thing not to forgive. She sat in the Burdett-Coutts house in full mourning, glowering at the extravagant floral tributes that had arrived, especially one that upstaged them all. Dominating the back wall, and soon to all but smother the casket itself, was a flowing pall of thousands of fresh laurel leaves that Eliza Aria had hired two dozen florists to sew. Mrs. Aria had signed the card "Anonymous," but that only served to set tongues wagging.

Feeling slighted and overshadowed, Irving's widow had her solicitor draft a public letter. "Now that the excitement of Sir Henry Irving's funeral is over," he wrote, "it may not be amiss to inquire how it is that in the midst of this enthusiastic display no mention that I have seen has been made of his wife. . . . It may interest many of your readers that Lady Irving is in excellent health, notwithstanding the shock and excitement of the last few days." As for Mrs. Aria, it would be many years before she refuted the persistent gossip that she had personally created the pall with her own grief-trembling hands as a final labor of love. Stoker never mentions Lady Irving or Mrs. Aria in his reminiscences, nor the death mask, and barely mentions George Alexander. Sometime after Alexander was knighted, Lady Alexander would present the final mistress with the precious original casting. Aria thereafter carried it wherever she traveled, displaying the ghostly face on a blue velvet cushion for anyone who cared to look at it. Its ultimate resting place would be the Victoria and Albert Museum.

On Thursday night, the coffin was driven slowly in a glass hearse through the streets from Piccadilly to Westminster, where uncounted throngs witnessed Irving's last transit through London. The coffin was laid overnight in the abbey's Chapel of St. Faith. The next morning, thousands upon thousands of people lined up for the five hundred public tickets, and thousands were disappointed.

According to the English correspondent for the *France Times*, who managed to secure a prime seat, "At a quarter past eleven Sir Frederick Bridge played Chopin's *Funeral March* on the organ[;] I have never heard a more magnificent and impressive rendering of that grand music. Purcell's funeral music for trumpets and trombones came next, followed by Schubert's *Marche Solennelle.* Just before noon when everyone had taken their seat, there were some appreciable minutes of silence, real absolute silence, such as one seldom meets with. Then far away in the distance came the faint sound of a pure voice, like a bird singing; it became more

Irving's funeral at Westminster Abbey, as depicted in the **Illustrated London News.**

distinct, and every one seemed to hold their breath in rapt attention. The voice rose clearer and more powerful, swelled into many voices, until it filled the building with melody and harmony." The pallbearers were Sir Squire Bancroft, Lord Aberdeen, Lord Tennyson, Sir Charles Wyndham, John Hare, Lord Burnham, Sir Alexander Mackenzie, George Alexander, Herbert Beerbohm Tree, Sir James Dewar, Norman Forbes-Robertson, Albert Wing Pinero, Arthur Collins, Sir Lawrence Alma-Tadema, RA, and William Burdett-Coutts, MP.

As the processional choir sang the hymn "Brief Life Here Is Our Portion," and the casketed urn was borne from the cloisters to a pedestal before the high altar, the full impact of Mrs. Aria's floral offering could be appreciated. "Surely such a pall was never before seen," wrote Stoker. "It was so large that at the funeral when fourteen pall-bearers marched with the coffin it covered all the space and hung to the ground, before, behind, and on either side." In one sense it was Mrs. Aria herself, brazenly clinging to the coffin. Lady Irving must have been seething. She would continue to seethe for a very long while, living to ninety. Some say she died mad.

The day was cold and cloudy, almost lugubriously so. Both Stoker and Ellen Terry (and, no doubt, everyone else in attendance) took note when a decidedly theatrical turn of the weather occurred, almost on cue. "As from the steps of the Sanctuary came the first words of the Service for the Burial of the Dead," Stoker recalled, "a bright gleam of winter sunshine burst through the storied window of the Southern Transept and lit up the laurel pall till it glistened like gold."

When it came time for the actual burial ceremony, the coffin was carried to Poets' Corner and laid next to the grave of Garrick and at the foot of Shakespeare's memorial. "The family and the pall bearers alone moved to the grave, after the Dean and Canons, the congregation being requested to keep their seats," reported the *France Times*. In other words, the vast majority of those assembled never saw the urn. In death Irving had accomplished a coup de theatre. Most of the people who had lined the streets and crowded the abbey believed they were still in the physical presence of one of the greatest actors who ever lived. For the dead man, however, it was a fitting vanishing act for one who had engineered some of the Victorian theatre's most astonishing stage magic.

As Mina Harker writes in her journal at the conclusion of *Dracula*, "It was like a miracle. . . . The whole body crumbled into dust and passed from our sight."

In 1989, the ashes of Sir Laurence Olivier were interred next to Sir Henry's. The spirit medium Hester Dowden interviewed the ghost of Dame Ellen Terry following the release of Olivier's acclaimed film version of *Hamlet*, and asked for her opinion on the Olivier performance vis-à-vis Irving's. Terry, in the spirit world, seems to have become a veritable Pauline Kael, and she had a surprising amount to say for one who had died before the advent of talking cinema. Nonetheless, Dame Ellen judged Olivier's brooding Prince of Denmark against Irving's, and in her opinion Lord Larry fared very well indeed.

The loss of all theatre income pushed Stoker immediately into a necessary whirlwind of literary production. Using the meticulous diaries he had kept over twenty-seven years in Irving's employ—Noel Stoker recalled that they filled a room—he set about the huge project of *Personal Reminiscences of Henry Irving* (1906), a two-volume biography-as-memoir. Since the lengthy work was published within a year of Irving's death, it is a virtual certainty he had begun the book while the actor was still alive, and perhaps even years earlier (the idea that he might be immortalized as Irving's Boswell surely occurred to him early on). The month following Irving's death, it was announced to the press that the actor had designated his sons as official biographers; since Laurence and H. B. were hardly Stoker's favorite people, he may have been especially motivated to beat them to the punch. In the end the sons never did write their book.[9]

Personal Reminiscences was politely received in Britain and America, with one recurring critical caveat. The *New York Times*'s London book correspondent wired home: "Almost every one criticizes it here because, though it is called a book about Irving, it is really a book about Stoker and Irving. There is something naïvely appealing in the way Mr. Stoker seems to suppose the public will be equally interested in himself and the great actor."

Mid-list authors like Stoker usually received no publisher's advance, but their books at least began to earn money without delay upon publication. Stoker's novel *The Man* (1905) had been published shortly before Irving's death and so provided at least a small income stream at the time his salary evaporated. Read today almost exclusively by Stoker scholars, *The Man* is a provocative romance about gender ambiguity with a few Gothic flourishes. Stephen Norman is a woman named and raised as a boy to satisfy her dying mother's wish for a son. At first, her unusual degree of self-assertiveness at the age of eleven gets her into trouble when she disobeys authority and goes exploring a crypt, unaware that it contains the coffin of the mother she never knew. She faints dead away at the discovery but is rescued by the orphaned boy Harold An Wolf, whom her father has taken in to raise as his own, and who will eventually become her major love interest. She clings to Harold as she relives the horror.

> Oh, Harold! It was too awful. I never thought, never for a moment, that my poor dear mother was buried in the crypt. And when I went to look at the name on the coffin that was nearest to where I was, I knocked away the dust, and then I saw her name: "Margaret Norman, aetat 22." I couldn't bear it. She was only a girl herself, only just twice my age—lying there in that terrible dark place with all the thick dust and spiders' webs.

---

[9] In 1951, Irving's grandson, the second Laurence Irving, would publish *Henry Irving: The Actor and His World*, a truly magisterial theatrical biography owing a substantial debt to Stoker and his obsessively worshipful record keeping.

Oh, Harold, Harold! How shall I ever bear to think of her lying there, and that I shall never see her dear face? Never! Never!

The terrifying encounter with the reality of death serves at once as the end of Stephen's innocence and as a coming-of-age initiation that foreshadows her eventual marriage to Harold. There is much consideration of how female dominance and male submissiveness might be balanced, without the New Woman hysterics of *Dracula*, in which Lucy shocks propriety by suggesting a woman might propose to a man and is summarily cursed with living death. In *The Man*, Stephen Norman does propose to a man, with consequences far less severe. But the opening cemetery atmosphere signals a Gothic undercurrent, that signature admixture of eros and thanatos that bubbles up whenever Bram Stoker decides to tell a story. *The Man* would not be the last time Stoker would put a problematic woman in a crypt.

That Stoker was still casting about—anywhere—for steady work is supported by an April 1, 1906, piece in the *San Francisco Chronicle*. "Stoker, for many years, directed the business end of Irving's tours. There has never been word of Stoker's having taken more than casual interest in the actual staging of plays, yet it is said, and apparently in good faith, that he has been invited to become the stage manager of one of the 'artistic' theatres which 'society,' in the whirligig of its jealousies, plans to build in this city." The *Chronicle*, however, was skeptical of the ability of San Francisco to support such an enterprise. "Before Stoker is pressed for a contract it might be profitable [for him] to come here and report on conditions as they exist. . . . But Mr. Stoker has a weakness for a joke that may lead him to accept the offer. . . . His geniality would add to the diversion which the public is already finding in these proposed temples of high art."

Two and a half weeks later, any such offer was summarily canceled with the complete destruction of San Francisco by an earthquake no theatrical effect could rival in replication. It is doubtful, though, that Stoker even responded to the proposal. In early 1906 he suffered what he described as a stroke, which left him unconscious for twenty-four hours. In the account approved by his son, it was the beginning of "a painful illness that dragged on for weeks, robbing his robust frame of much of its boundless vitality and leaving his eyesight impaired."

"Stroke" has never been a precise medical term, although today it is used as universal shorthand for vascular blockage and/or bleeding in the

brain. In Stoker's time it was used far more loosely, and sometimes euphemistically. The 1913 edition of *Webster's Dictionary* defines "stroke" in the
medical sense as "a sudden attack of disease; especially fatal attack; a severe
disaster; as, a *stroke* of apoplexy; the *stroke* of death." "Apoplexy," from a
Greek word meaning "to be struck down by a sword," was used before the
twentieth century interchangeably with "brain attack" to describe a variety of conditions, including emotional and psychological breakdowns as
well as "hysterical" paralysis, aphasia, and blindness. These ischemic, or
transitory, strokes generally last no more than twenty-four hours and do
not result in permanent tissue damage. Stoker's incident, though, seems to
have permanently affected his eyesight and was the beginning of a six-year
downhill slide.

In June 1907, the *Grand Magazine* published "In the Valley of the
Shadow," an anonymous story that has been attributed to Stoker. The
strange narrative recounts a medical crisis that may well be autobiographical, given the startling developments in Stoker's health just the year before.
The story opens with the narrator being taken by stretcher into a hospital, not knowing where or who he is or why an ambulance has deposited
him in a place where there are faces in the curtains. His mood swings
between ecstasy and despair. Moving, changing religious messages appear
around the room's cornices. His bed has the power to pass through walls
and enter into neighboring houses. He begs a nurse for pen and paper "to
write not only this particular tale, but a complete account of my visions. Of
course, I was not permitted, and now, alas! It has gone to join that great
company of magnificent-seeming but elusive ideas one has in dreams." He
refuses medicine, which he believes is whiskey. "Surely you know I am a
Mussulman and forbidden to drink spirits?" When the nurse persists, he
dashes the glass to the floor. "Devil in human form, you tempt me to my
destruction. Begone and let me die in the true faith." He tries to flee and is
overpowered. Rather than take alcohol, he realistically feigns death. When
they give him an injection, he believes it is whiskey being pumped forcibly
into his veins. "I sit up in bed, and glare at them with concentrated hatred,
then I fall back, heartbroken at my forced abjuration, sobbing, sobbing."
Suddenly, then,

> I am alone on a flat desert plain. I am sitting with my back against one
> of the stone pillars of a huge closed gateway reaching to the sky. In front

of me is proceeding a cinematographic entertainment on a stupendous scale. I cannot now remember much about it, but the series was long and of an appalling character. Below each picture was a placard stating the subject of the next one. I had the feeling that they were not pictures at all, but real events in the process of happening; further that by answering a question put to me by a mysterious voice I could bring the series to an end, but, though I knew the answer, it was quite beyond my power to give it.

The story echoes Stoker's earlier fairy tale "The Castle of the King" from *Under the Sunset*, in which the Valley of the Shadow is repeatedly invoked.

From the shadow of his own medical problems, Stoker's health improved sufficiently that 1908 could be an especially busy year. His journalism included a January interview with Winston Churchill, who told him, "I hate being interviewed, and have refused altogether to allow it. But I have to break the rule for you, for you were a friend of my father." "Then," Stoker reported, "he added gracefully another reason, personal to myself: 'And because you are the author of "Dracula." '" Churchill had been twenty-two years old when the novel was published, and, according to Stoker, "it appealed to his young imagination." Bram and Florence would both attend Churchill's wedding on September 12 at St. Margaret's Church, Westminster.

Throughout the year Stoker also continued to work tirelessly (or exhaustedly) as Hall Caine's literary agent, as well as the editor of his 1908 autobiography, *My Story*, from which he had the thankless task of cutting over fifteen thousand words at Heinemann's insistence. Stoker's correspondence with Caine over the project shows that he took on the work with great good humor. These letters are among the last documents in which Stoker communicates anything like a buoyant mood.

Stoker continued his apparent truce with assertive female characters in his romantic novel *Lady Athlyne*, about Joy Ogilvie, a high-spirited American woman who, on a lark, assumes the identity of the eponymous lady, to the great consternation of the actual, unmarried Lord Athlyne. Using an alias of his own, he tracks her down in New York, and the inevitable real romance ensues. But beneath the mistaken-identity romantic-comedy trappings, Stoker continues his personal wrestling match with the whole question of, and quest for, the magic formula for heterosexual harmony. Athlyne's ruminations on the topic are taken directly from formulas advanced in Otto Weininger's *Sex and Character* (1906). As filtered through Stoker, Athlyne closely parrots Weininger, positing that "each individual must have a preponderance, be it ever so little, of the cells of his own sex; and the attraction of each individual to the other sex depends on its place in the scale between the highest and lowest grade of sex. The most masculine man draws the most feminine woman, and so down the scale till close to the border line is the great mass of persons who, having only development of a few of the qualities of sex, are easily satisfied to mate with anyone."

Weininger's sexology reeks of eugenics, which was only beginning its long dark march to the Holocaust, not to mention a misogyny reflected in its emphasis on the importance of masculine willpower to conquer the female's inherent "chaos, mystery, and darkness." Weininger also posits androgyny and bisexuality as natural states that must be overcome through male effort and vigilance. Despite its sunny surface plot, *Lady Athlyne* has a palpable shadow side.

Also published in 1908, Stoker's story collection *Snowbound: A Record of a Theatrical Touring Party* would be his only book other than *Personal Reminiscences* devoted to the theatre, and the first and only time after his Dublin days that he would evoke the Christmas pantomime, that life-restoring epiphany of his sickly childhood ("the greatest event in the life of a child . . . the real world in which the dawning imagination has sought and found a home"). Now, during his own life's final act, his view of the holiday ritual was becoming jaundiced and cynical. In "A Star Trap," a story darkly echoing an episode from *The Primrose Path*, an actor playing Columbine is unparalleled for his skill in shooting up through the stage like an acrobatic cannonball, delighting both children and adults. A star trap employed a kind of vertical catapult that hurled performers up through a trapdoor made of triangular sections resembling the points of a star. These would fall safely shut just as the actor reached his airborne apex above the stage. In "A Star Trap," Stoker wrote, "Something was wrong. The trap didn't work smooth, and open at once as the harlequin's head touched it. There was a shock and a tearing sound, and the pieces of the star seemed torn about, and some of them were thrown about the stage." The colorfully costumed and spangled figure shoots into the air, but limply, and topples on its side as it falls to the boards. The audience shrieks. The actor's fatal mistake had been making love to the wife of the company's master carpenter, who sealed the hinged wooden panels of the trapdoor just enough to create a catastrophic barrier for the actor's head, rocketed upward by the falling of heavy counterweights under the stage. Breaking the clown's neck like Prospero's staff, Stoker had, in effect, drowned his book, and, as in *Lear*, hanged the Fool.

Beginning in late 1907 Stoker signaled a major break from his earlier, liberal attitude vis-à-vis the controversies over sensation fiction. Now, with a series of public speeches that continued into 1908, he lashed out at indecent writing. His turnabout passion was sudden and startling, and was reported by newspapers as far-flung as the *Los Angeles Times*:

DENUNCIATION
PRURIENT NOVEL IS CONDEMNED
•

BRAM STOKER OPENS CRUSADE IN LONDON
•

Famous Irish Critic Declares in White Friar's Club That
Objectionable Fiction in Vogue in Britain and America
"Must Be Stamped Out Like a Pestilence."

LONDON. Oct. 19—[Exclusive Dispatch.] At last night's meeting of the White Friar's Club, Bram Stoker, the famous critic and writer, started a crusade against the prurient novel.

Stoker's outspoken address, teeming with specific references to objectionable fiction, created a sensation and provoked keen discussion.

"This abomination—the foully conceived novel," cried Stoker, "has great vogue in Britain and America and belongs to that category of pestilences which must be stamped out.

"We journalists and authors have the deepest responsibility in the matter. Our responsibility is equaled by that of the publishers."

At the close of the meeting, Stoker, whose Irish brogue gave a peculiar charm to his address, was surrounded by a throng of writers who showered him with congratulations.

Given Stoker's longtime fascination with sensation novels, his 1908 essay "The Censorship of Fiction," published in *The Nineteenth Century and After*, is a stunning repudiation of his previous liberalism. Censorship was needed in the cause of "perpetually combatting human weakness," which manifested in two forms, "the weakness of the great mass of people who form audiences, and those who are content to do base things in the way of catering for these base appetites." To Stoker, the situation represented "the degradation of humanity; another instance of the war between God and the devil. The vice of many of the audience in this case is in yielding to the pleasant sins or weaknesses of the flesh as against the restraining laws made for the protection of higher effort. The vice of the few who cater is avarice pure and simple. For gain of some form they are willing to break laws—call them conventions if you will, but they are none the less laws." The process was insidious. "It creeps in by degrees, each one who takes a part in it going a step beyond his fellows, as though the violation of law had become an established right by its exercise. . . . It shows to any eye, even an unskilled one, a startling fact of decadence." Then, from his fiery and puritanical pulpit, Stoker laid down the law. Censorship, he demanded, "must be continuous and rigid. There must be no beginnings of evil, no flaws in the mason work of the dam."

The author of *Dracula* was a natural authority on what he called the "evils of the imagination." What might these be? "We shall, I think, on considering the matter, find that they are entirely limited to evil effects produced on the senses," he wrote, harking back to his Trinity days when the doctrine of "sensationism" in philosophy and sensationalism in literature held sway. Finally, he put forth his most significant and revealing conclusion: "A close analysis will show that the only emotions which in the long run harm are those arising from sex impulses, and when we have realised this we have put a finger on the actual point of danger."

In his strident lashing out at fictional indecency, Stoker was an isolated voice in 1908. There was no general outcry then against indecent novels; the fin-de-siècle panic over decadent fiction had cooled, and the great censorship controversies over D. H. Lawrence's *Lady Chatterley's Lover*, Radclyffe Hall's *The Well of Loneliness*, and James Joyce's *Ulysses* would not begin to explode for another decade. The only publisher of the period who might have irritated Stoker was the British expatriate Charles Carrington, whose *Catalogue of Rare and Curious Books Both English & French, Offered in*

Many Cases, at Sweeping Reductions off Cost Prices was now issued in Paris. Carrington offered a selection of classics—Aristophanes and others—as a commercial cover for his real bread and butter. Among his most popular titles of 1907 were *The Beautiful Flagellants of New York* by Lord Drialys (under the staid-sounding Carrington imprint the Society of British Bibliophiles) and *Sadopaideia: Being the Experiences of Cecil Prendergast Undergraduate of the University of Oxford Shewing How He was Led through the Pleasant Paths of Masochism to the Supreme Joys of Sadism.* The last was published anonymously but sometimes attributed to Swinburne. If it is not already clear, Carrington specialized in one kind of erotica: spanking and flagellation. Why this particular fetish would have attracted Stoker, only to elicit his self-righteous repulsion, is an open question. Since he was a self-punishing person all his life, it would not be at all surprising that masochistic surrender might be a prominent aspect of his sexual imagination. It is still surprising that the bloody three-way vampire orgy between Mina and Jonathan Harker and Dracula was never condemned as obscene. But for the simple substitution of a body fluid (or the addition of one), the scene could have been plucked straight from a novel by Sade.

But one thing about the censorship crusade is undeniably palpable, if not perfectly clear: *something* about sex and its dreadful consequences had begun eating away at Bram Stoker, and eating at him badly.

Sex cooled by the semblance of undeath was a repeated image in Stoker's penultimate novel. *The Lady of the Shroud* (1909) traded heavily on the reputation and familiarity of *Dracula,* and for a while its story seems to promise a direct revisiting of that novel's supernatural universe. Like *Dracula,* it unfolds through journals and letters, primarily those of Rupert Sent Leger, the heir to a fortune in the Balkans who must reside in his family's castle for a year as a condition of his uncle's will. Since the inheritance is worth more than £1 million, Rupert is highly motivated. But once ensconced in the mountains, he begins to have night visitations from a strange figure.

> There, outside on the balcony, in the now brilliant moonlight, stood a woman, wrapped in white grave-clothes saturated with water, which dripped on the marble floor. . . . Attitude and dress and circumstance all conveyed the idea that, though she moved and spoke, she was not quick but dead. She was young and very beautiful, but pale, like the grey pallor

of death. Through the still white of her face, which made her look as cold as the wet marble she stood on, her dark eyes seemed to gleam with a strange but enticing lustre.

Rupert invites her inside to warm herself by his fire. She doesn't speak, and leaves before morning. But her enigmatic visits recur. "It was all like a dream," Rupert writes in his journal. "It was not possible to doubt that the phantom figure which had been so close to me during the dark hours of the night was actual flesh and blood. Yet she was so cold, so cold! Altogether I could not fix my mind to either proposition: that it was a living woman who had held my hand, or a dead body reanimated for the time or the occasion in some strange manner."

Ruling out all other possibilities, he finally concludes that she must be a vampire, and seems to confirm his suspicions by entering the crypt of a local church, where he discovers a stone sarcophagus covered with a sheet of movable plate glass. "Within, pillowed on soft cushions, and covered

A make-believe vampire: Stoker's **The Lady of the Shroud.** (John Moore Library)

with a mantle woven of white natural fleece sprigged with tiny sprays of pine wrought in gold, lay the body of the woman—none other than my beautiful visitor. She was marble white, and her long black eyelashes lay on her white cheeks as though she slept." The scene recalls Jonathan Harker's discovery of Dracula's daytime hiding place, and his instinctive reaction. Like Jonathan, Rupert flees the crypt. Unlike Jonathan, he finds himself falling in love. Underscoring the particular affinity of Stoker's horror fiction and fairy tales, the scene's use of a glassed coffin can be nothing but a barely veiled invocation of "Snow White."

Despite all the practical difficulties that might be expected in a vampire-human marriage, Rupert Sent Leger and Teuta Vissarion become man and wife, but Rupert's heart is nearly broken when, following the ceremony, Teuta disappears once more into the shadows. But he ultimately learns that she is not a vampire after all but the living daughter of the ruling voivode (military governor); recovered from a catalyptic trance mistaken for death, she has adopted the ongoing pose of a vampire to keep the restive populous at a frightened distance from her father's endangered rule. Unfortunately, the revelation comes along with the news of her kidnapping by Turks. Rupert kills her takers and rescues his wife, only to find that her father has been kidnapped as well. With the aid of a silent-running airplane and bulletproof clothing, Rupert stages a stealthy airlift and saves them both. His secret marriage to Teuta is revealed, welcomed, and celebrated, and the novel ends with a striking endorsement of traditional sex roles in matrimony.

Stoker's liberal meanderings into submissive manhood in *The Man* and *Lady Athlyne* were apparently not meant to be taken seriously. Teuta makes an impassioned speech in which she denigrates "an age when self-seeking women of other nations seek to forget their womanhood in the struggle to vie in equality with men." There can be little doubt that Stoker has finally come to the end of his struggle with the "woman problem," at least in fiction. Teuta acts as his mouthpiece: "I speak for our women when I say that we hold of greatest price the glory of our men. To be their companions is our happiness; to be their wives is the completion of our lives; to be the mother of their children is our share of the glory that is theirs." Teuta is more than happy to be a doll in a box, and doesn't have to be staked and decapitated to stay there.

In early 1910 Stoker had another medical setback, which has been described as a stroke or, more ambiguously, as some kind of "breakdown." Hall Caine was both alarmed and concerned. "My Dear Bram," he wrote, "I've been thinking about you a good deal since we parted last night & have come to the conclusion (a) that your best chance of staving off your new attacks is to make up your mind & do not work & to think of no work for, say, six months, & (b) that in order that you may do this you ought to permit a friend to help you in some small way to dismiss the thought of mere domestic needs during that time." Clearly, a new course of medical attention had already been researched, and decided. Caine continued: "You will go down to Deal tomorrow & as you say it won't cost very much to keep things going, if Mrs. Stoker is able to get along under such different & perhaps rather depressing circumstances—during the first months at all events."

Deal is a seaside town in Kent, northeast of Dover. Its dreary history included an unsavory eighteenth-century reputation as a smuggling port. In 1823, the British journalist William Cobbett had called Deal "a most villainous place. It is full of filthy looking people. . . . Everything seems upon the perish. I was glad to hurry along through it." Charles Dickens, in *Bleak House* (1852–53), describes "the narrow streets of Deal, and very gloomy they were." By the turn of the century, however, Deal was transforming itself into a resort town, and Stoker had spent several weeks there in 1904, recuperating from an attack of gout at the Fairlight Lawn holiday cottages. But that was when he was still in Irving's employ and could afford such a luxury. It is completely possible Caine and Stoker were now talking about not a cottage but the Victoria Cottage Hospital, a charity facility that offered an alternative to the free medical care that was available in cities to the desperate, but resented by the healthy and wealthy who insisted that even the poorest patient pay something. Cottage hospitals required that patients, after being recommended and approved by committee, contribute a regular, token amount of money, sometimes just a few shillings. The remaining funds came from charitable donations and insurance subscriptions, enough to deliver a thrifty, no-frills, yet humane and dignified level of care.

Cottage hospitals flourished in smaller towns, providing services in simple, repurposed, whitewashed buildings. Beds were limited, sometimes to just a dozen or so, but the problems of crowded urban hospitals were avoided. The amount of a patient's financial contribution was determined by his or her nominating sponsor, and in Stoker's case it could have been

Caine, who wrote, "May I not help a little towards this small expense by asking my banker to pay you (in any way you wish) a couple of pounds (£2) a week during the six months I suggest? It is only a little assistance, but I trust you will take it, for it will give one much more pleasure to give it than it could possibly give you to receive it." The amount was much more than many patients paid, and this was probably a face-saving strategy. Stoker need not appear completely impoverished. As Caine continued, "I know it may be just a little hurtful to you to take help like that, but in the first place no human creature need know anything about it except ourselves, & I shall not even tell my wife, & you need not tell your wife. The money can be passed weekly from my bank to your bank, or sent to you in any other way you may direct."

In fact, there were no decisions for Stoker to make, as Caine quickly explained. "Indeed I have taken your permission for granted & have settled the little matter personally with the manager of this bank," he wrote, referring to an enclosed card, "so that all that remains is that you should write to him when you reach Deal, say what you would wish to be done. If you don't write to him I shall perfectly understand if I am not necessary, & in any case you need not write to me." He asked that Stoker excuse "the form of payment I suggest—it enables me to take the money out of income. Don't let yourself be hurt by that. All you need to say to the manager is that you wish the money I am to pay you to be, etc." He closed with "affectionate greetings & best wishes for your quick recovery, believe me my dear Bram, Yours, Hall Caine."

We don't know how much time Stoker actually spent at Deal; aside from the publication of *Famous Impostors* and its attendant publicity, the year 1910 is not heavily documented. He did spend one last holiday in Cruden Bay, where he walked with difficulty on the beach, exhibiting a peculiar, stamping gait. He wrote his brother Thornley, "I can stand now for a few seconds on the one leg," and lamented that "happy memories are all anyone can ask for."

A letter from Florence Stoker to Thornley late in the year indicates at least some respite from an otherwise relentless decline. "Poor old Bram is no worse," Florence wrote, adding that "this wet weather stiffens him up so it makes it so hard for him to get about. He is an Angel of patience, & never complains, & it is so hard for him being so helpless." Thornley was struggling with health and money problems of his own in Dublin, and would ultimately outlive his brother by only six weeks. His wife, Emily, had spent decades as a schizophrenic recluse, shut off in a separate wing of the house and requiring full-time care. Once, during a dinner party that became notorious, she burst into the room completely nude, running around the table pursued by attendants, exclaiming, "I like a little intelligent conversation!" If nothing else, she certainly generated talk.[10]

Florence's letter to Thornley had been a message of condolence on Emily's death in November. Bram's physician, Dr. James Browne, ordered him not to attempt the cold, damp sea voyage to Dublin for the funeral. Browne had been prescribing arsenic treatments, avoidance of meat, and sturdy soups, but nothing really improved Stoker's condition. In December he complained to Thornley that he had only earned £80 in royalties for the last year ("Not much for a living wage, but there is hope we can manage"). He continued to let his significantly more prosperous brother know of his financial woes, but there is no indication Thornley even considered giving him money. In some ways he was still the family's designated black sheep. In January Bram wrote again, "It is harder on poor Florence (who has been an angel) than on me. She had to do all the bookkeeping and find the money to live on—God only knows how she managed."

Stoker's next-to-last book, the nonfiction *Famous Impostors*, was commissioned and published simultaneously in London by Sidgwick & Jackson and in New York by Sturgis & Walton. As a work-for-hire, he wrote it for a flat fee and received no royalties. He needed money badly, and in the short run it made sense to accept a flat fee up front, even though a royalty arrangement could possibly earn more money over time. Stoker maintained he had significant input into the chapter topics, so it should be no surprise that a significant part of the book was devoted to dubiously "undead" figures like Cagliostro and the Wandering Jew, both purported to have cheated death and lived for centuries.

But Stoker's recurring preoccupation with gender ambiguity and reversal predominated. The section "Women as Men" covers four historical females who managed to pass as male. The most colorful had been the real-life inspiration for Théophile Gautier's novel *Mademoiselle de Maupin*, a woman whose inner man simply wouldn't be contained after she mastered

---

[10] Belford notes that Thornley's marital situation mirrors that of Abraham Van Helsing, who describes "my poor wife" as "dead to me, but alive by Church's law, though no wits, all gone."

fencing. According to Stoker, "For some years she flourished and exercised all the tyrannies of her own sex and in addition those habitual to men which come from expert use of the sword. Thus, she went attired as a man to a ball given by a Prince of the blood. In that garb she treated a fellow-guest, a woman, with indecency; and she was challenged by three different men—all of whom, when the consequent fight came on, she ran through the body, after which she returned to the ball."

La Maupin's swashbuckling escapades and narrow escapes find a reverse mirror in Stoker's account of the Chevalier d'Eon, a male transvestite and a favorite in the court of Louis XV, who conducted delicate missions of diplomacy in which he was presumed to be female. "His clean shaven face, his personal niceties, the correctness of his life, all came to the aid of that supposition," wrote Stoker. "In England bets were made and sporting companies formed for the purpose of verifying his sex."

But Stoker saved his biggest volley for an in-depth examination of the "Bisley Boy," a persistent conspiracy theory that Queen Elizabeth I was actually a man, the real princess having died at an early age with only a male substitute quickly available to fool Elizabeth's visiting father, the enormously volatile King Henry VIII. No one, the story went, was willing to risk their head by telling the King the truth. Thereafter the boy was raised as a girl in all respects, the secret guarded by each successive high-security squadron of loyal ladies-in-waiting. Elizabeth's real sex was the explanation for her purported mannishness, keen military instincts, legendary refusal to marry, and fondness for wigs and thick lead makeup.

Even in 1910, the whole story could have been readily debunked. For instance, on the occasions when offers of marriage were being considered, doctors were called upon to certify the Virgin Queen as fully intact. The real Elizabeth was also fond of occasionally displaying her bosom in décolletage that might be considered daring even today. Stoker simply ignored facts that weren't useful in creating a strong circumstantial case, and almost no one in the press called him out. On October 20, the Sunday *New York Times* gave the book a very large, illustrated preview with the banner headline WAS QUEEN ELIZABETH A "FAMOUS IMPOSTOR"? The tone was serious and credulous, and was backed up with extended quotations from the text. A few months later, however, when the *Times* evaluated the published book, the reviewer had to officially dismiss the Bisley Boy as "tommyrot." The book was otherwise shrewdly well publicized in America with a strategic splashy Sunday feature (prepared, no doubt, by the publisher and inspired by the *New York Times* piece) called "Was Queen Elizabeth a Man?" that appeared in six papers across the country on February 19, 1911—the *Cleveland Plain Dealer,* the *Denver Post,* the *Lima* (Ohio) *Daily News,* the *New Orleans Item,* and the *San Antonio Light & Gazette*—and a week later, on February 26, in the *Fort Worth Star-Telegram* and the *Seattle Daily Times.*

Did Stoker actually believe the story? Though ultimately dismissive of the impersonation plot, the *New York Times* reviewer assured readers that "Mr. Stoker is not indulging—consciously at least—in any mere romance; he is not giving us another 'Dracula,' but a serious interpretation of certain historical facts backed up by documents and 'evidence' of a sort, from all of which it appears that, whether his readers follow him or not, Mr. Stoker, for one, believes that Elizabeth, in spite of her little flirtations with Leicester, Essex, and the rest of them, was a man forced by a cruel fate to masquerade as a woman." Had he wanted, Stoker could have taken a cue from his friend Mark Twain and added that trademark wink that accompanied his more outrageous tall tales, but if Stoker intends humor, it is humor of a decidedly deadpan kind. To the reader, the author seems genuinely convinced, or at least mesmerized. It was as if the Bisley Boy were an image he had been waiting for his entire life, ever since his sickly childhood in skirts when he gazed upon the androgynous Christ-fairy, crucified in a woodcut illustration. In a sense, the Bisley Boy was the guiding presence, the invisible chaperone at his first pantomime, where he wondered at the spectacle of bigger-than-life women who were really men. And what woman was bigger than Queen Elizabeth?

However much the subject engrossed him, Stoker had considerable difficulty completing the book. The handwritten draft of the preface dated August 18 and 19, 1910—only three months before publication—is a rambling, often incoherent document that gives strong evidence that Stoker's facility for one-draft composition failed him. While his hand is steady, the mind that guides the hand is not. Circular trains of thought, often abstruse and disjointed, make for a sad reading experience. "The subject of Imposture is ~~a never-ending one~~ ever new. It is based on principles of human nature and so long as social life works within the broad lines a, demarcation can never have an end," the manuscript confusingly begins. A bit later, Polonius-like, he strays from the main point of his sentence into a detour on the meaning of an adjective, and never gets back to his central point. "Imposture is in truth an unorganized war on society. The word unorganized must be taken in a collective sense; for though forethought must not be taken as synonymous with organization both efforts thus implied are requisites. Or to put it differently forethought is implied in all matters of organization. Though organization cannot exist without forethought, the contra is not equally true."

We never do get back to the very interesting idea of imposture as an act of war; what follows is bursts of undeveloped ideas and prolixity with no beginning, middle, or end. The writer cannot find a through-line for his argument, if indeed there even is a main point. While the failure of the piece does not come close to suggesting dementia, it shows at the very least a sudden, serious inability to concentrate.

The published preface, though signed "B.S.," was clearly the work of someone else, who discards almost everything in Stoker's draft save for some scattered phrases, but reasonably approximates Stoker in a more lucid frame of mind. "The histories of famous cases of imposture in this book are grouped together to show that the art has been practiced in many forms—impersonators, pretenders, swindlers, and humbugs of all kinds; those who have masqueraded in order to acquire wealth, position, or fame, and those who have done so merely for the love of the art." Ghostwriters, wags will note, are never mentioned at all.

Although he stumbled in the book's final execution, Stoker's attraction to the Bisley Boy came from a place very deep inside himself, the place that harbored the old Irish changeling stories, and memories of the fantastic character transformations in classic fairy tales. For what was the Bisley Boy if not a variation on Cinderella, a favorite inspiration for the Christmas pantomimes of his childhood? In this case, the child who became a princess, and later a queen, just happened to be a boy in the first act. In *Famous Impostors*, Stoker gave his last tribute to the world of the panto by casting Queen Elizabeth as the greatest travesty dame of all time—a sacred hermaphroditic monster with a livid, painted face.

On or about February 20, 1911, the week before the syndicated newspaper feature on *Famous Impostors* appeared all over America, Florence Stoker appealed to a friend and neighbor, Lady Anne Ritchie (the eldest daughter of the novelist William Makepeace Thackeray, author of *Vanity Fair*) for assistance in obtaining charity support for Bram. The elderly Ritchie had already asked Florence, "as a favor," if she would be willing to read to her in the evenings for a few shillings per sitting, but more substantial assistance was needed. Ritchie wrote to Arthur Llewelyn Roberts, chairman of the Royal Literary Fund. She was evidently a reliable go-to person for this kind of assistance. "I wrote you only yesterday with a petition," she told Roberts, "and now by chance—which indeed often happens in life—I come with something which affects me very much for it concerns some kind old friends I have known for years & about who I feel very sad." She laid out the basic facts of Bram's case. "He has published Sir H. Irving's life & written a great deal. He is now attacked by a terrible illness he is gradually losing the use of his limbs and can hardly walk even with a stick. He is wonderfully brave and cheerful, but he can no longer work & things are more and more difficult. . . . [A] cruel fate is upon him. They are trying to let their house— it is too large for their one servant—I do not know the exact details but as he can't earn & as Sir Henry left nothing a little help *now* might perhaps enable him to try measures of relief and get away."

Ritchie requested a meeting with Llewelyn Roberts "at any time you would be able to see me for a few moments for I want to be advised to whom to go to bring the case forward." She suggested Sir Frederick Pollock, a well-known jurist and author, as "a likely person to put forward Mr. Stoker's case." In another note she suggested Henry Charles Dickens and James M. Barrie as potential sponsors. Five days later, February 25, 1911, Stoker wrote personally to the Committee of the Royal Literary Fund, "stating the facts of my working and of my long illness, and suggesting reason why I might ask for your aid":

> I spent thirteen years in the Civil Service (Petty sessions branch of the Irish Chief Secretary's office.[)]
> I entered in 1865 and left in 1878 to become acting manager for Henry Irving who had just taken the Lyceum Theatre. With him I remained till his death in 1905. In addition to my business of this kind I followed a literary career in my spare time, At Sir Henry Irving's death I devoted myself to literature entirely.
>
> At the beginning of 1906 I had a paralytic stroke was not a bad one and in a few months I resumed my work. Just a year ago I had another breakdown from overwork which has incapacitated me ever since. The

result of such a misfortune shows at its worst in the case of one who has to depend on his brain and his hands. For a whole year already I have been unable to do any work with the exception of completing a book begun some time before and the preparatory study for which had largely been done. This book "Famous Imposters" [*sic*] has just been published but I shall not derive any substantial benefit from it for about a year.

At present I do not know whether I can in the future do much, or any, literary work. I am emboldened to look to my fellow craftsmen in my difficulty.

I may say that I have already written fifteen books besides many articles for magazines and newspapers and a number of short stories as well as doing a fair share of ordinary journalism.

I am a Barrister at Law (Inner Temple)[.] I am a Medalist of the Royal Humane Society.

> I am gentlemen
> Yours faithfully
> BRAM STOKER

On the accompanying formal application, he gave his total income for the previous year as £166—twice what he reported to his brother in his clumsy, indirect appeal for benevolence. Among the letters of support Stoker provided was one from W. S. Gilbert, who wrote, "I have enjoyed the privilege of Mr. Bram Stoker's friendship for about twenty five years, during portion of which period he has devoted himself earnestly to literary pursuits. I am intimately acquainted with his many works. . . . For the last twelve months he has been unable to follow his profession owing to a distressing and wholly incapacitating illness, [and] his case is eminently deserving of the consideration of your Committee." Gilbert's endorsement came none too soon. Four months later he died of a heart attack while attempting to rescue a neophyte swimmer in his private lake. Another friend, Henry F. Strickland, wrote to give his "warm support" to Stoker's request. "This is not a mere formal backing on my part but I desire to support his application to the fullest possible extent with the utmost sincerity and belief in the soundness of his claim."

Ultimately, the fund made Stoker a grant of only £100. Despite his disappointment at the sum, he accepted it gracefully and gratefully. "This, I fancy, is as much as is ever given except under special circumstances," he told Gilbert in a letter.

On March 9, Florence declined a gallery invitation for both herself and her husband, adding that "I am looking forward to going *myself* on Saturday, but perhaps you haven't heard that Bram is ill and has been a semi-invalid since March last he is a little better but not able to do any work yet."

In reality, on the very same day Stoker felt well enough to begin writing what would be his final novel. He had in mind a story that would, somehow, involve a great onslaught of birds. His original title was *Rushing Wings*. But the story he wrote, as if taking it down by dictation, began to drift. The birds remained as a secondary element, but at some time during the novel's composition he went back to the first page, crossed out the title, and replaced it with a new one: *The Lair of the White Worm*.

Because the novel contains some of the sickest and most wildly unhinged imagery in all of Stoker's work, many commentators have concluded that the author must have been sick while writing it. Indeed, he was very ill. The manuscript itself, however, written in a more legible hand than is usual for Stoker, indicates a remarkable degree of control and intention. Each day's work is methodically dated and flows clearly.

The lead character and hero, Adam Salton (whose original first name was the exceedingly odd Elbur, changed by Stoker almost immediately), is a well-to-do Australian who returns to his ancestral estate in Derbyshire, where his great-uncle, Richard Salton, intends to make him heir. The two men are the only remaining members of the Salton family line. The neighboring estates, Castra Regis and Diana's Grove, are inhabited by two bizarre characters, Edgar Caswall and Lady Arabella March. Edgar presides over Castra Regis like a standard-issue Gothic villain, the latest of an ancient line of "dominant" and "masterful" Caswall forbears. "The aquiline features which marked them seemed to justify every personal harshness," observes Richard Salton's Van Helsingish friend Nathaniel de Salis. "The pictures and effigies of them all show their adherence to the early Roman type. . . . The most remarkable characteristic is the eyes. Black, piercing, almost unendurable." When he practices mesmerism (a fairly standard activity in this kind of novel) Edgar's eyes "glowed with a red fiery light. He was still the old Roman in inflexibility of purpose; but grafted on the Roman was a new

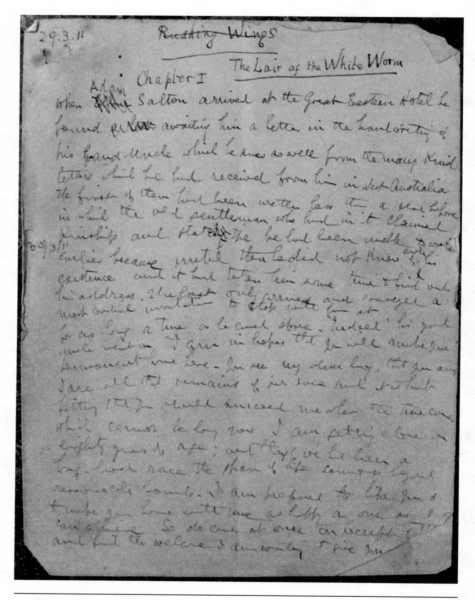

Stoker's manuscript for **The Lair of the White Worm,** *originally titled* **Rushing Wings.**
(Courtesy Fales Manuscript Collection, Fales Library, New York University)

Berserker fury." Caswell's African servant, Oolonga, takes Stoker's obsession with physical typing and evolutionary backsliding to the lowest, most
racist point in his oeuvre. Dressed ludicrously in ill-fitting evening clothes,
Oolonga is a "negroid of the lowest type; hideously ugly, with the animal

The manservant Oolanga in **The Lair of the White Worm** *is one of Stoker's worst racial stereotypes. Illustration by Pamela Coleman Smith.* (John Moore Library)

Pamela Coleman Smith's illustration for the original British edition of
The Lair of the White Worm. (John Moore Library)

instincts developed as in the lowest brutes; cruel, wanting in all the mental and moral faculties—in fact, so brutal as to be hardly human."

Lady Arabella, who may have designs on the ladyship of Castra Regis— she's a widow, and the upkeep of Diana's Grove is expensive—is the stranger of the two householders. As Adam observes:

Her dress alone was sufficient to attract attention. She was clad in some kind of soft white stuff, which clung close to her form, showing to the full every movement of her sinuous figure. She was tall and exceedingly thin. Her eyes appeared to be weak, for she wore large spectacles which seemed to be made of green glass. Certainly in the centre they had the

effect of making her naturally piercing eyes of a vivid green. She wore
a close-fitting cap of some fine fur of dazzling white. Coiled round her
white throat was a large necklace of emeralds, whose profusion of colour
quite outshone the green of her spectacles—even when the sun shone on
them. Her voice was very peculiar, very low and sweet, and so soft that the
dominant note was of sibilation. Her hands, too, were peculiar—long,
flexible, white, with a strange movement as of waving gently to and fro.

Arabella is indeed one slinky lady, with fingers only a snake charmer
could love. Soon, she reveals aspects that are not only strange but disturbing. When Adam employs a mongoose to deal with an infestation of snakes,
Arabella stops by to observe. "Hitherto the mongoose had been quiet, like
a playful affectionate kitten; but when the two got close he was horrified to
see the mongoose, in a state of the wildest fury, with every hair standing on
end, jump from his shoulder and run towards Lady Arabella." Adam cries
out a warning, but the mistress of Diana's Grove "looked more than ever
disdainful and was passing on; the mongoose jumped at her in a furious
attack. Adam rushed forward with his stick, the only weapon he had. But
just as he got within striking distance the lady drew out a revolver and shot
the animal, breaking his backbone." As if this weren't enough, "she poured
shot after shot into him till the magazine was empty. There was no coolness
or hauteur about her now. She seemed more furious even than the animal,
her face transformed with hate, and as determined to kill."

A second encounter, with a replacement mongoose, leaves the animal
ripped in two by snakelike hands. And then there are the lady's nocturnal peculiarities. "In the uncertain, tremulous light which fell through the
treetops, it was hard to distinguish anything clearly, and as Adam looked it
seemed to him that Lady Arabella was actually dancing in a fantastic sort
of way. Her arms were opening and shutting and winding about strangely;
the white fur which she wore round her throat was also twisting about, or
seemed to be."

In the pages of the *Occult Review*, Stoker credited the story's genesis
to a pair of fairy tales drawn from English folklore: "The Worm Well of
Lambton Castle" and "The Laidly Worm of Spindleston Heugh." "In both
of these legends," Stoker said, "the 'worm' was a monster of huge size and
power—a veritable dragon or serpent, such as legend attributes to vast fens
or quags, where there was illimitable room for expansion." The second

For his final novel, Stoker took significant inspiration from the Northumbrian legend of the "Lambton Worm."

story, Northumbrian in origin, features a princess turned into a snake-thing by her wicked stepmother, who also happens to be a wicked witch. The curse is canceled only after her brother bravely bestows some semi-incestuous kisses upon the scales of his monstrous sibling.

As always, Stoker was primally inspired by fairy tales, but could not have been unaware of the astonishing profusion of snake-women in fin-de-siècle art. Eve, Lilith, Lamia, and Salammbo were all associated with serpents, when they weren't physically fused with them by Symbolist painters and poets. Medusa had gone mainstream; readers and audiences no longer needed even a soupçon of classical education to immediately recognize her stony stare. The idea of women as snake monsters was so commonplace that Oscar Wilde could elicit an easy laugh in *The Importance of Being Earnest* with Jack Worthing's observation, "I don't really know what a Gorgon is like, but I am quite sure that Lady Bracknell is one. In any case, she is a monster, without being a myth, which is rather unfair."

Reptilian womanhood in visual art was hardly a late nineteenth century invention of the Symbolists. As early as 1597 Carvaggio had produced a nightmarishly realistic portrait of Medusa, soon eclipsed in gruesomeness by Rubens in 1616–17. In literature, John Keats's "Lamia" (1820) poetically immortalized a scaly succubus of antiquity. In the context of Stoker, it is surely significant that the resurrected, destroyed, and re-resurrected wife in Johann Ludwig Teick's "Wake Not the Dead" (1800), often cited as the first example of a vampire in fiction, assumes the shape of a giant snake in her final incarnation, crushing her husband in her coils.

Given Stoker's gift of near-photographic memory, Shakespeare's plays, or at least their major speeches, would have been fairly burned into his brain. Stoker knew *King Lear* well. He had greatly admired Barry Sullivan's 1873 performance in Dublin—Irving's, at the Lyceum, had been a misfire—and especially praised the delivery of Lear's curse on Goneril. The misogynistic excesses of *The Lair of the White Worm* are amply foreshadowed in Lear's denunciation of his wicked daughters, women repeatedly compared to vipers and adders, their famous ingratitude "sharper than a serpent's tooth." Goneril and Regan are described as devolved, chimerical animals, their sexuality concentrated into something like Lady Arabella's noxious snake-hole. Below his daughters' waists, Lear declares, "There's hell, there's darkness, there's the sulphurous pit; burning, scalding, stench, consumption."

In *Lair*, the subterranean tunnel that harbors Arabella's reptile form is simultaneously vaginal and phallic, and one of the most disgusting figurative representations of sexual revulsion in the history of literature: "The open well-hole was almost under his nose, sending up such a stench as almost made Adam sick, though Lady Arabella seemed not to mind it at all. It was like nothing that Adam had ever met with. He compared it with all the noxious experiences he had ever had—the drainage of war hospitals, of slaughter-houses, the refuse of dissecting rooms. None of these was like it, though it had something of them all, with, added, the sourness of chemical waste and the poisonous effluvium of the bilge of a water-logged ship whereon a multitude of rats had been drowned."

In the end, the strategic application of dynamite and the fortuitous action of lightning bring Arabella's serpentine reign to a well-deserved end. The subterranean scene

> looked as if a sea of blood had been beating against it. Each of the explosions from below had thrown out from the well-hole . . . a horrible repulsive

slime in which were great red masses of rent and torn flesh and fat. As the explosions kept on, more and more of this repulsive mass was shot up, the great bulk of it falling back again. Many of the awful fragments were of something which had lately been alive. They quivered and trembled and writhed as though they were still in torment, a supposition to which the unending scream [of Lady Arabella] gave a horrible credence.

In a brutal eruption conflating violent coitus and catastrophic birth,

some mountainous mass of flesh surged up through the narrow orifice, as though forced by a measureless power through an opening infinitely smaller than itself. Some of these fragments were partially covered with white skin as of a human being, and others—the largest and most numerous—with scaled skin as of a gigantic lizard or serpent. . . . The seething contents of the hole rose, after the manner of a bubbling spring, and Adam saw part of the thin form of Lady Arabella, forced up to the top amid a mass of blood and slime, and what looked as if it had been the entrails of a monster torn into shreds.

This would seem to be quite enough, already making Dracula's demise look like painless euthanasia. But, like Henry Irving ill-advisedly milking an encore, Stoker refuses to let his scotched snake lie, and ratchets the imagery up to a delirious, even Lovecraftian level:

After a few minutes of watching, it became apparent to the three men that the turmoil far below had not yet ceased. At short irregular intervals the hell-broth in the hole seemed as if boiling up. It rose and fell again and turned over, showing in fresh form much of the nauseous detail which had been visible earlier. The worst parts were the great masses of the flesh of the monstrous Worm, in all its red and sickening aspect. Such fragments had been bad enough before, but now they were infinitely worse. . . . The whole mass seemed to have become all at once corrupt! The whole surface of the fragments, once alive, was covered with insects, worms, and vermin of all kinds. The sight was horrible enough, but, with the awful smell added, was simply unbearable. The Worm's hole appeared to breathe forth death in its most repulsive forms.

The climax recalls Stoker's redacted destruction of Castle Dracula, as well as Poe's obliteration of the House of Usher, which, in his Dublin years, Stoker thought might figure in a splendid opera. But some cataclysms, like the ones coming down upon the abodes of Dracula and Usher, and Casta Regis, would not be practical on the stage during Stoker's lifetime and were better left to the theatre of the mind.

> At last the explosive power, which was not yet exhausted, evidently reached the main store of dynamite which had been lowered into the worm hole. The result was appalling. The ground for far around quivered and opened in long deep chasms, whose edges shook and fell in, throwing up clouds of sand which fell back and hissed amongst the rising water. The heavily built house shook to its foundations. Great stones were thrown up as from a volcano, some of them, great masses of hard stone, squared and grooved with implements wrought by human hands, breaking up and splitting in mid air as though riven by some infernal power.

The Lair of the White Worm received the most mixed reviews of Stoker's career. On one hand, the *Daily Telegraph* positively reveled in the novel's excesses. "Mr. Bram Stoker has a genius for the gruesome, and in the contrivance of nightmare his imagination knows no limit," wrote the anonymous author of the "Current Literature" column. "The White Worm of his story is not the humble, wholesome creature such as makes the early blackbird's meal on dewy lawns but a vast, appalling, age-old, intolerable monstrosity, lurking in the dark and slimy recesses of a pestiferous pit, and by some awful metabolic mystery it is also the Lady Arabella March." Within the fevered plot, "events move as in a dream, a very vivid and exciting dream." Following a very detailed synopsis, the *Telegraph* cautioned that its précis might well lack precision. "Whether we have stated events accurately and in chronological order we cannot be sure. Nightmares are not easily remembered in detail. Let no one read this book before going to bed, still less look at its illustrations, for Mr. Bram Stoker is a magician, an illusionist, and weaver of fearsome spells." But the *Times Literary Supplement* would have none of it. "In attempting to exceed the supernatural horrors of *Dracula*, Mr. Stoker has in his latest book degenerated into something very like nonsense. No one asks for probability or even possibility, but coherence is a necessity."

Amanda Donahoe in Ken Russell's film version of **The Lair of the White Worm.**

Of all the contemporary criticisms leveled at *Lair of the White Worm*, none detected even a whiff of the grotesque sexual symbolism or the nearly hallucinogenic level of misogyny that spur most commentary on the novel today. As in *Dracula*, the psychological and cultural horror was allowed to hide in plain sight—a purloined, encrypted letter yet to be deciphered by Freudian sensibilities. It would take the completely unanticipated cultural cataclysm of World War I for a jolted public to begin to dig deeper.

By the new year, Stoker was sicker than ever. Hall Caine wrote him from Switzerland on January 16, 1912.

> My dear Bram,
> Since coming to St. Moritz I have often thought of you
> & wondered how you are. I am afraid the shocking
> weather of this terrible winter has been much against
> you, & that you have been a great deal indoors. I wish
> you could be here in the bright warm sunshine we
> have at least occasionally. There has been much snow
> & little hard frost but during the past week we have
> had the true Engadine weather. It has done one good

& I think would have been good to you. But you have
your compensations. You are at least enjoying your
charming & comfortable home & the society of your
dear wife. I am denied those inestimable advantages
& sometimes my exile in search of health goes a little
hard with me. On the whole I have been having a
pleasant & happy time, & am certainly much rested.

I hope all goes as well with you as we could wish.
I trust you are not thinking of work. Don't do that
unless you feel really fit for it. You have done a long
& good day's work & deserve a thorough rest. Be sure
your friends always remember you with a very deep &
true affection. At least be certain that I always do. I
often think of you & recall with great pleasure many
memories of past days.

I got to work on my new book to-day. It is likely to
be another "Manxman" with the difference that the
woman is the central figure throughout. Give my love
to your wife, & don't answer this letter until you feel
entirely in the mood to do so. I shall feel quite sure
that you are answering me as you read. Your message
will come to me whether you pen it or not.
With warm affection.

> Yours,
> HOMMY.

In his last communication with his friend of nearly thirty years, Caine
ended on a note of mystical bonding. It was only fitting for two men who
had, in their own ways, "gone with the fairies" together to part on a supernatural plane. The book Caine referred to was *The Woman Thou Gavest Me*,
published in 1913, a curious experiment in the sexual transmigration of
souls, at least from a literary perspective. A polemical treatment on divorce
law reform and the consequences of illegitimacy, the novel was written by
Caine in the first-person voice of a woman, a technique unheard of at the
time. The book was highly controversial, but women readers were largely
of the opinion that Caine had succeeded admirably in channeling the soul
of a woman through the mind of a man. Although Stoker frequently read

drafts of Caine's work, and no doubt would have been captivated by such a tour de force of gender transgression, Caine this time gave a manuscript to Florence Stoker, perhaps as much to take her mind off Bram as to get her opinion. "My dear friend," she wrote him, "I thank you for the privilege you accorded me in letting me read enclosed scenario of your new book, it's a wide subject, & me, I can see you will treat it with great art, & tact, & you can give all the horror, & brutality of her early experience, just as delicately, & convincingly *all* the tragedy."

The next three months after Caine's letter are not directly documented; as Caine himself would remember, "Of the devotion of his wife during these last dark days, in which the whirlwind of his spirit had nothing lost to it but the broken wreck of a strong man, I cannot trust myself to speak. That must always be a sacred memory to those who knew what it was. If his was the genius of friendship, hers must have been the genius of love."

Meanwhile, the world continued to turn. Roald Amundsen discovered the South Pole. The first parachute jump from an airplane was made. Then, on April 15, the RMS *Titanic* struck an iceberg and sank near Newfoundland while on its maiden voyage. If Stoker was conscious, and not sedated with morphine (as was mostly likely the case), Florence could have told him the electrifying news, which dominated world news coverage for the following week. If nothing else, it would have been a chilling reminder to her of the frightening, near-fatal shipwreck she experienced with her son so many years before. Stoker sank more slowly than the *Titanic*, but there was no doubt about his approaching end. He left the world as he had entered it, incapacitated by daunting illness, helpless as the paralyzed child that had entered the world sixty-four years before. He took his last breath at home on April 20, in the company of his wife, son, and physician.

Four days later, Bram Stoker was cremated at Golders Green, as Irving was seven years earlier. No death mask was taken, or considered. The mourners included Florence and Noel, Hall Caine, Genevieve Ward, Laurence Irving, Ford Madox Hueffer (later Ford Madox Ford), and the writer Violet Hunt. Ellen Terry and the playwright Arthur Wing Pinero sent tribute wreaths. A service was conducted by the Reverend Herbert Trundle. Obituaries appeared widely, all cut from the same cloth, emphasizing his long service to Irving and barely mentioning his writing. *Dracula* was cited in only a handful of notices. The *Times* additionally described him as "the master of a particularly lurid and creepy kind of fiction."

The most personal and eloquent appreciation came from Hall Caine, who prepared a piece for the *Daily Telegraph* to run on the morning of the funeral. It was entitled "Bram Stoker: The Story of a Great Friendship." "Bram Stoker is to be buried today," it began. "Only the friends (and there are many) who know and loved him will be there when the last offices are done, and that will be enough. He could have desired no more and no better. The big, breathless, impetuous hurricane of a man who was Bram Stoker had no love of the limelight," and he was "a man of the theatre only by the accident of his love for its leader."

The real Bram Stoker, Caine wrote, could best be glimpsed outside of the theatre, and would "occasionally reveal itself among the scarcely favourable conditions of a public dinner, when, as speaker (always capable of the racy humor which is considered necessary in that rather artificial atmosphere), he would strike, in the soft roll of his rich Irish tongue, a note of deep and almost startling emotion that would obliterate the facile witticisms of more important persons." As for his literary work, Caine stated, "I cannot truly say that this deeper side of the man ever expressed itself in his writings. He took no vain view of his efforts as an author. Frankly, he wrote his books to sell, and except in the case of one of them (his book on Irving), he had no higher aims. But higher aims were there, and the power of realizing them had not been denied to him." Caine specifically regretted that his friend had never written his own autobiography, with celebrity anecdotes unfiltered through the life of another. Stoker had "a vast store of memories which the public would have welcomed if he had written them down. He never did write them, and the world is poorer for want of his glimpses, however brief and casual, of some of its great souls in their happiest hours."

Caine concluded by remembering Stoker as "a massive and muscular and almost volcanic personality" with a special "genius for friendship" unknown to all but "the friend to whom, under various disguises (impenetrable to all except themselves), he dedicated in words of love some of his best known works (*Dracula* in particular).[11] . . . I can think of nothing—absolutely nothing—that I could have asked Bram Stoker to do for me that he would not have done. It is only once in a man's life that such a friendship

---

[11] Despite Caine's claim, a search of all Stoker's first editions reveals no work except *Dracula* including a veiled dedication.

comes to him, and when the grave is closed on the big heart which we are to bury to-day, I shall feel that I have lost it."

Stoker was well remembered in America, where Boston's Irish Catholic newspaper, the *Pilot*—apparently ignoring Stoker's lifelong Protestantism—took umbrage that he had been described elsewhere as an "English author." "English forsooth!" the unsigned piece began, in a warmhearted rant. "Someone once said that when an Irishman did anything creditable he was English; when he did the opposite, then he was Irish. Constantly is the effort made to rob Irish brains and genius and courage of the credit their due. Bram Stoker was a fine Dublin man, six feet three and as brainy as he was big. He was really a rabid home ruler and keenly sensitive of the good name of his native land, which he loved with a rare devotion. . . . Mr. Stoker never let anyone, even when the occasion called for a declaration, forget that he was Irish through and through without one tittle of Angloism. . . . He would be the first to declare that he was an Irishman, Irish educated, too, and that whatever talents he possessed were due his Irish birth and Irish environment."

At his death, Stoker's estate was valued at £4,664—a startling figure, the equivalent of over half a million American dollars in 2016, quite surprising for an individual who sought charity assistance only a year before he died. The Royal Literary Fund, however, asked no questions about Stoker's assets, only his income, which at the end was sufficiently pitiable to earn their support. Since Stoker's bank records are unavailable and presumably long lost, we need to reinterpret what little we do know about his finances, if only to make sense of them. There is a clue in Anne Ritchie's letter to the committee, in which she writes that the Stokers are considering letting their Durham Place home. And of course this is exactly what they must have done. Stoker was chronically house poor. Three decades of his slaving, scrimping, and moonlighting must have been largely in the service of punishing leaseholds, which often left Stoker without ready cash but at least guaranteed his family a legacy. He had watched his parents flee like refugees from one temporary Dublin home to another—with nothing to show for it in the end.

Besides his will, another revealing document was left. Stoker's death certificate was first alluded to in 1960 in *A Biography of Dracula: The Life Story of Bram Stoker*, by Harry Ludlam, who mentioned almost in passing that the word "exhaustion" was given as a cause, intimating that a lifetime of unselfish hard work and devotion to others simply caught up with him, and death was somehow a well-earned rest. It was hardly a medical diagnosis, but inasmuch as Noel Stoker vetted the manuscript for the explicit reason of excluding any material of which his parents would not approve, it is not surprising. Fifteen years later (and fifteen years after Noel's death—he never lived to see Ludlam's book published) Stoker's grandnephew Daniel Farson published *The Man Who Wrote "Dracula"* (1975), in which the information contained in the certificate was reported for the first time.

"Bram died of tertiary syphilis," wrote Farson.

And so began a long-running controversy. The full cause of death certified by James Browne, MD, was "Locomotor ataxy 6 months Granular Contracted Kidney. Exhaustion." A physician consulted by Farson told him, quite correctly, that locomotor ataxy (or locomotor ataxia, both meaning irregular, impaired motor function) was the standard description for the effects of tabes dorsalis, the most common form of tertiary neurosyphilis. In addition to tabes, neurosyphilis can include general paresis (often called "general paralysis of the insane"), in which neuromuscular symptoms are followed by progressive psychosis, dementia, and death. Just as syphilis overall has primary, secondary, and tertiary stages, so too have both forms of neurosyphilis. Farson erred in calling tabes and paresis identical (they are discrete conditions, though closely related), but he did accurately understand the simple fact that locomotor ataxy indicated advanced syphilis, and had no other useful diagnostic meaning.

Additional research for the present book has included the examination of an original copy (preserved, appropriately enough, at the Trinity College Dublin Library) of the most comprehensive and authoritative British medical guide on the topic, published around the time of Stoker's final decline and regularly updated. The 1910 edition of F. J. Lambkin's *Syphilis: Its Diagnosis and Treatment* supports Farson's basic conclusion: "Tabes, tabes dorsalis, or locomotor ataxia, is an affliction characterized clinically by sensory disturbances, incoordination, trophic discharges and involvement of special organs, particularly the eye. . . . At the present time, tabes is looked on as essentially a syphilitic disease." Lambkin's conclusions were drawn from his longtime work as a colonel in the Royal Army Medical College, where he treated and monitored generations of syphilitic soldiers in optimally controlled conditions. As to the interpretation of "Granular Contracted Kidney," Lambkin notes that in tertiary syphilis, "nephritis is of the chronic interstitial variety, and leads to the granular contracted kidney presenting the usual symptoms of that condition." Kidney disease need not wait until the tertiary stage of syphilis but can be an early presentation; as Lambkin writes, "there is no doubt that early, and sometimes rather late in the secondary stage, a mild or severe form of nephritis may occur." Bright's disease—an archaic name for chronic nephritis—has also been associated with syphilis, and can be an ironic side effect of mercury treatments for the disease as well. As for the stamping walk Stoker exhibited in 1910 at Cruden Bay, Lambkin describes "the characteristic gait of ataxia," including the foot coming down "with a sudden stamp caused by the entire sole striking the ground at once."

Syphilis: Its Diagnosis and Treatment enumerates several other indications of the disease that match aspects of Stoker's illness. As to Dr. Browne's arsenic prescriptions, Lambkin notes that "the Arylarsonates [arsenicals] have a distinct specific effect in clearing up syphilitic symptoms, both in early and late syphilis, there can be no doubt," but acknowledges the limitation of their use, and regrets to report that "eighteen months ago one had much hope of their being able to effect a final cure; however, since Wasserman's reactive test became more familiar to us, this assumption, to say the least, has become doubtful."

As for Stoker's stroke, or strokes, "As a cause of aneurysm syphilis stands pre-eminent. . . . The frequency of aneurysm in locomotor ataxy . . . is now known to be almost solely of syphilitic origin." Lambkin also offers a response to the common assumption that syphilis always manifests on a predictable timetable (an idea that has often been spuriously invoked to prove or disprove syphilis in biographical subjects), noting that "one patient may become hopelessly ataxic in a twelve-month, whereas another may be able to walk about and attend to his business for twenty or thirty years." As with Oscar Wilde, Stoker's infection could have occurred anytime over a very long period—in Stoker's case, between the alleged cessation of sexual relations with his wife (around 1882) and the turn of the century.

The Stoker family was infuriated at Farson's revelations and his insinuations, and some of their animus simply arose from a personal dislike of the man. Already a designated black sheep of the family for his homosexuality and alcoholism, Farson incurred additional enmity for selling family heirlooms—in particular, Oscar Wilde's Dublin letters to Florence when she was a girl—just to settle a drinking tab (see chapter 4).

But if Stoker had syphilis—and it now seems inconceivable that he didn't—how and when did he contract it? Daniel Farson speculated, "His wife's frigidity drove him to other women, probably prostitutes among them. . . . Possibly the disease was contracted in Paris, where so many 'faithful' husbands, such as Charles Dickens and Wilkie Collins, had gone for discreet pleasure before him." This comports with the traditional British description of syphilis as the "French disease" (the French liked to talk about "*la maladie anglaise*") but assumes the need for unnecessary travel. The Lyceum Theatre is located at the edge of Covent Garden, a notorious red light district in Stoker's time, and had he been interested in the services of female streetwalkers, they would have been available at all times, merely steps away. For other sexual possibilities, male brothels had been driven further underground by the Wilde and Cleveland Street scandals, but telegraph boys were still ubiquitous and could be had cheaply. Closer to home, the theatrical profession itself teemed with the possibility of discreet male contacts. Whatever Stoker desired, or actually did, the simple fact of acquiring a sexually transmitted disease signifies a single unlucky encounter with an infected person, male or female, not necessarily an ingrained pattern of behavior. And it should be considered that uncountable numbers of men contracted disease from female prostitutes they engaged to "cure" tormenting homoerotic desires they never, or rarely, acted upon.

The year following her husband's death, Florence sold at auction the bulk of his books, papers, and personal effects. The auction drew attention as far away as America, where the *New York Sun* noted, "Among the treasures which will go to the highest bidder are a very important collection of letters and manuscripts of David Garrick, as well as letters of celebrated persons to him. Also, the Dryden copy of the first folio Shakespeare, a copy of the second folio, expurgated by the Spanish inquisition; Hazlitt's 'Life of Napoleon' with nearly 2,000 extra illustrations, and copyrights of many distinguished authors of the eighteenth century will be sold under the hammer." Special comment was given to Stoker's collection of Whitmaniana, including "the sheaf of original notes of Walt Whitman's lecture on Abraham Lincoln. But this is not all about Lincoln in the library, for Mr. Stoker and Henry Irving joined with eighteen others in the purchase of moulds of the death mask and hands of Abraham Lincoln from the son of the sculptor [Leonard W.] Volk. Augustus Saint Gaudens cast

these in bronze and the twenty subscribers each received a copy. Doubtless
Mr. Stoker's will sell for very high prices." Among the items not mentioned
were Stoker's working notes for *Dracula* and the manuscripts for *Under the
Sunset, The Lair of the White Worm,* and *The Lady of the Shroud.*

The auction proceeds did not live up to expectations. Still, Florence
was happy to tell a friend "I made £400 on the 'Bram Stoker Library,'" a full
quarter of which she called "rubbish."

Not included in the first-day auction, but sold sometime thereafter, was
a manuscript called *The Russian Professor,* probably the only known piece of
unfinished fiction by Stoker. Apparently the opening of a novel, it begins
with two creative young men, a writer and a painter, enjoying an idyllic seaside holiday, reminiscent of the real-life vacation time Stoker once shared
with the playwright W. G. Wills in France.

> Two persons have hitherto watched the coming storm with rapt attention.
> One of them has been seated on a campstool before an easel, painting a
> headland where the jagged rocks run far out and where there is a cease-
> less eddy round the point. The other is lying on the crisp dry grass beside
> him making notes in shorthand. The men are both young and somewhat
> representative of their respective crafts. The artist—Oswald Croft, is of
> medium size and delicate build. His face is fine and chiseled—with clean
> cut nose and sensitive nostrils of the poet and the big eyes of the dreamer.

His counterpart is distinctly different, suggesting that the pair somehow constitute a completion, or gestalt.

> Richard Power, the journalist, is tall, strong built and wiry—every move-
> ment is instinct with intention; even his lazy repose has an abandon of
> rest—the purposeless purpose which is the true relief to high wrought
> energies. Power's face is that of a sturdy Englishman, Saxon in its confor-
> mation—in its full lines and masterful strength—the sort of face which
> when seeing we expect the full-throated voice and energy of Command
> to follow. It is only when he smiles that we see a reason why his profession
> is not that of a soldier. The smile changes the whole man; it is soft and
> full of humor and enjoyment—a voluptuous smile which springs from
> boundless capacities of enjoyment both intellectual and physical. With
> such expression habitual, though a man may become great, he cannot

be a true and steadfast Master of men—a Captain of his age. Truly ste[a] dfast purpose is the Conquerer's baton, if genius be his crest.

Stoker's use of the word "voluptuous" in describing Power's mouth is interesting, and highly charged; the adjective is used repeatedly in *Dracula* to evoke dangerous, seductive sexuality in women. Power is androgynous, and so is the sensitive, slightly built Oswald. We have no way of knowing where Stoker would have taken this story. We can roughly date it to the period between the Wilde trials and the publication of *Dracula*, because the type characters closely resembles dated Stoker typescripts of the period. If not created by the same machine, they do appear to be from machines by the same manufacturer; in other words, from one of several machines owned or rented by a typing service like Miss Dickens's. That it was transcribed by a service is evidenced by spaces inserted where the typist could not decipher Stoker's handwriting, something also obvious in the *Dracula* typescript.

Why was *The Russian Professor* abandoned? If Stoker indeed intended to explore the homoerotically nuanced theme at which the opening chapter hints, the wake of the Wilde scandal would have been reason enough not to publish a book about grown men with sensitive nostrils and voluptuous mouths who go off on dreamy holidays together. If he began work on it, he may simply have not had the strength to go on. Either way, there is enough in the fragment to suggest the story would go on to develop the theme of a close bond between two men being disrupted by the presence of an archetypically mysterious woman. Unfortunately, we will never know what happened.

But it may be worthwhile to examine the work of another British novelist who, less than a decade after Stoker's death, took up the Whitmanesque ideal of a man seeking pansexual fulfillment. *Women in Love* by D. H. Lawrence (1920) explores the psychology of Rupert Birkin, a school inspector wrestling with the themes suggested by Stoker's life: the frustrating inability to love a woman passionately, and the impossibility of consummating that passion with another man despite every fiber of his being pushing him in that direction.[12] Lawrence's novel, highly controver-

---

[12] In Ken Russell's 1969 film version of *Women in Love*, Birkin was quite effectively portrayed by Alan Bates, who, in his prime, would have been a most interesting choice for Stoker, had a biographical film ever been made.

sial in its time, was part of the great artistic ferment propelled by World War I when unprecedentedly visceral emotions and ideas exploded in literature, theatre, and film, partly in response to the apocalyptic assault on human life and culture from 1914 to 1918. The characters in *Women in Love* (a novel in which the words "horror" and "death" occur with more frequency than in the most frightening scenes of *Dracula*) engage in a kind of panic sex set against the industrial-scale annihilation taking place in Lawrence's world, if not in the novel itself. *Dracula's* characters also panicked over sex roles at the end of an industrialized, despiritualized century devoted to the annihilation of the soul. Significantly, the refusal to accept "annihilation" was a constant refrain of the spiritualist quest, both in Stoker's time and in Lawrence's. In *Women in Love*, Lawrence longed to fuse the animal and the spiritual. Stoker did something similar with *Dracula's* dream of a Darwinian substitute for the traditional Christian afterlife.

In the self-suppressed prologue to the novel, Lawrence is far more explicit about Birkin's sexual duality than in the published book: "Although he was always drawn to women, feeling more at home with a woman than a man, yet it was for men that he felt the hot, flushing, roused attraction which a man is supposed to feel for the other sex. . . . The women he seemed to be kin to, he looked for the soul in them. The soul of a woman and the physique of a man, these were the two things he watched for, in the street." Birkin has a tormented physical relationship with Hermione Roddice, who is to him a mostly mental construction, a woman without a body. "To be spiritual, he must have a Hermione, completely without desire; to be sensual he must have a slightly bestial woman, the very scent of whose skin soon disgusted him. . . . He could not save himself from these extreme reactions, the vibration between two poles." This is a fair description of the classic madonna/whore schism Stoker delineates most memorably in the women of *Dracula*.

In the published version of *Women in Love*, Rupert's essential dilemma is summed up in his final conversation with his wife, Ursula, following the death of Gerald Crich, his male object of obsession. "Aren't I enough for you?" Ursula asks. No, he says. In order to be happy and complete, he wants "eternal union with a man too: another kind of love." The novel concludes at a famous literary impasse:

"I don't believe it," she said. "It's an obstinacy, a theory, a perversity."

"Well—" he said.

"You can't have two kinds of love. Why should you!"

"It seems as if I can't," he said. "Yet I wanted it."

"You can't have it, because it's false, impossible," she said.

"I don't believe that," he answered.

Florence Stoker never heard from Hall Caine again. Perhaps, after a time, she finally had a candid conversation with Mary Caine, who had left her husband to live in London after decades of marriage, because he simply preferred the company of men. And perhaps Florence finally read the voluminous personal correspondence that must have existed between her husband and Caine during their intimate, decades-long friendship, the kind of letters that can only be written between two mutually trusting confidants looking for fathers and brothers and wives to their souls.

And then, perhaps, she burned them.

CHAPTER ELEVEN

THE CURSE OF DRACULA

. . . PAINTERS CANNOT PAINT HIM—THEIR
LIKENESSES ALWAYS LIKE SOMEONE ELSE . . .
—Bram Stoker's working notes for Dracula

Shall we pity Bram Stoker?

No, but he at least deserves a big warm hug, in recognition of a singular life lived at a fevered, exhausting pitch, a life spent wrestling consciously/unconsciously with the greatest questions and conflicts of his time and distilling them into a resilient modern folklore by which we may begin to understand our own age, if through a glass darkly. At this writing, his most celebrated novel—and the most famous horror novel of all time—has been in print for almost 120 years, and the recognition factor of Stoker's name nearly rivals that of his undying creation. No longer consigned to the academic shadows, *Dracula* is now a standard Victorian text, studied in elite universities and community colleges alike. No less august an institution than the New York Public Library has named it among the one hundred most influential books of the twentieth century. As a media superstar Dracula is rivaled only by Sherlock Holmes, and he supports a similar, obsessively dedicated fan base throughout the world. The Transylvanian

---

As Dracula, the Hungarian actor Bela Lugosi, who never escaped the curse of typecasting.
(Courtesy of Ronald V. Borst / Hollywood Movie Posters)

count has become a Hollywood star in his own right, resurrected hundreds of times on film and television, and an icon evoked in all manner of communications and advertising and merchandise and food, ranging from the droll to the ludicrous to the downright grotesque. What would Bram Stoker make of such developments as a breakfast cereal called Count Chocula, transmogrified further into a rubber-fanged masturbation toy called Count Cockula?

It has become a standard, pedantic refrain among fans and academics alike that no stage or screen adaptation of *Dracula* has ever been truly faithful or done justice to Stoker's vision; even the versions that hew most closely to the original story cannot resist taking major creative liberties. The overriding curse of *Dracula*, as intuited by Stoker in his working notes for the book, is that the master vampire's true self would never be accurately reflected by painters or photographers (whose images would appear skeletal, like x-rays), or, by an extension of dream logic, producers and playwrights, screenwriters and filmmakers, or composers and choreographers. Stoker wondered whether his book would be remembered, and on this point he was prescient: a great deal of it *was* doomed to be forgotten, ignored, altered, and/or mutilated—or left otherwise lifeless on the cutting-room floor.

The pile of dust Stoker left us at the end of his novel has never been acceptable. That is why Dracula always gets another chance, a media-franchise afterlife that truly goes on forever.

Make no mistake. *Dracula* is an important book, but ordinary standards of literary criticism have never satisfyingly pinned down the authorial intent or larger meaning of a novel that has been an object of continuous popular fascination—if not downright obsession—in the nineteenth, twentieth, and twenty-first centuries. It has been dissected as the supreme embodiment of the late English Gothic, a veritable Rosetta Stone of Victorian anxieties, a Freudian primer, and a critique of British colonialism; it has been condemned as a profoundly misogynistic diatribe and praised, topsy-turvy, as a secret document of female empowerment. Is it a Marxist fable about predatory capitalism? A veiled attack on Darwinism? Or a defeated acceptance of the same? A key to the Tarot? A quasi-Gnostic, coded revelation of the real story of Jack the Ripper?

With so many possible interpretations, it is hardly surprising that *Dracula* has fired the imaginations of filmmakers and other creative artists. Even the misfires are fascinating, the failed attempts often as interesting as the ones that came to fruition. *Dracula* is surely unique in narrative history, with its origins in oral folklore, its longevity in print, and its apparently unstoppable afterlife in the realm of the moving image. Like Dracula himself, the story's ability to endlessly shapeshift is the essential key to its immortality.

Since Dracula has already clocked so much screen time—in their fascinating compilation *Dracula in Visual Media*, John Edgar Browning and Caroline Joan (Kay) Picart include more than seven hundred citations of films, television programs, comic books, and electronic games—it may be useful to consider his many absences from the picture: he was already an offstage (but always anticipated) character for most of Bram Stoker's novel, and the story of his many failures to be conjured onscreen, and elsewhere, amounts to a chronicle in itself. The history of *Dracula* has also been one jinxed by nonpresence, missed chances, grand plans, failures, invisibility, and unaccountability. Stoker himself was only dimly aware of the emerging technology of the motion picture, but believed that his book should be theatrically performed. Ambivalence has been at the core of this devilish game of approach/avoidance; one might say that dramatic adaptations of *Dracula* have all constituted a protracted state of "development hell" now lasting well over a century.

Assuming that the Icelandic *Makt Myrkranna* was a free-form piracy, Ásmundsson's "translation" uncannily anticipated the kind of wholesale liberties with the text that would dominate the Dracula mythos in the century to come. First, however, his widow would begin steering and shaping the mythos, even if she let some major distortions slip by in the process.

Late in his career, Stoker began worrying about his literary legacy, adding clauses to his publishing contracts reserving the unrestricted right to publish an edition de luxe of his collected works, much like the *Works of Hall Caine* to which he had contributed appreciative introductions in 1905. But the publishing world was only interested in a small sliver of his total work postmortem. In 1914 Florence authorized publication by George Routledge & Sons of his only story collection, *"Dracula's Guest" and other Weird Stories*,[1] to which she added a personal note of introduction:

---

[1] It is not known how much material Florence Stoker submitted to Routledge, but the publisher's initial offer of publication was for one volume of six stories. The book ultimately contained nine: "Dracula's Guest," "The Judge's House," "The Squaw," "The Secret of the Growing Gold,"

PREFACE

A few months before the lamented death of my husband—I might say even as the shadow of death was over him—he planned three series of short stories for publication, and the present volume is one of them. To his original list of stories in this book, I have added an hitherto unpublished episode from "Dracula." It was originally excised owing to the length of the book, and may prove of interest to the many readers of what is considered my husband's most remarkable work. The other stories have already been published in English and American periodicals. Had my husband lived longer, he might have seen fit to revise this work, which is mainly from the earlier years of his strenuous life. But, as fate has entrusted to me the issuing of it, I consider it fitting and proper to let it go forth practically as it was left by him.

FLORENCE A.L. BRAM STOKER.

26, ST GEORGE'S SQUARE
LONDON, S.W.

Stoker had left tear-sheets of printed stories from newspapers and magazines, obviating the need for any typesetter to decipher his illegible hand. But the precise evolution of the title story—which was never intended by Stoker to be a part of the collection—has never been satisfactorily answered. No manuscript or typescript of its final version is known to exist, and it could not be a cleanly deleted portion of the full typescript for *The Un-Dead*, which has an epistolary format with clearly identified "authors." "Dracula's Guest" has an anonymous narrator with no given reason for his trip to meet Count Dracula, and more has been removed than simply the chapter heading "Jonathan Harker's Journal." If the narrative, or something like it, originally opened the novel, basic information would have been confusingly absent. In short, it cannot be a simple excision. Florence Stoker also authorized its publication in the June 1914 issue of the *Story Teller* as "Walpurgis Night," a decision likely made to give Routledge exclusive use of a title containing the name "Dracula."

"A Gipsy Prophecy," "The Coming of Abel Behenna," "The Burial of the Rats," "A Dream of Red Hands," and "Crooken Sands."

Dracula's Guest, *Stoker's posthumous collection of short stories,* *was published by his widow in 1914.* (John Moore Library)

According to Noel Stoker, his mother received valuable assistance in the preparation of *Dracula's Guest* and other matters from a man named Jarvis, formerly the ticket taker for the Lyceum's dress circle, whom she trusted. Did Jarvis have skills as a writer or editor? The story "Dracula's Guest" is a notably polished piece of prose, free from the clumsy syntax that often mars Stoker's writing, including *Dracula.* Did Stoker himself really craft the unused material into a classically crafted mood piece "even as the shadow of death was over him"? More important, why would he bother if he had no plans to publish a collection called *Dracula's Guest?* Jarvis's or not, another editorial hand is likely.

As Florence gradually assumed the role of a literary executor, she relied on business advice from her accountant son, as well as the City of London law firm E. F. Turner & Sons, which negotiated her contract with Routledge for *Dracula's Guest.* It included some shrewd provisions, especially pertaining to dramatization and cinema rights (Florence retained all), the addition of a prominent advertisement facing the title page that listed all of Stoker's available books from other publishers, and a guaranteed advance (that is, nonrefundable even if the book sold poorly) of twenty-five pounds on publication, and the same amount six months after. Fifty pounds in 1914 is worth nearly $9,500 in 2016, a rather respectable advance for a volume of reprinted stories from a backlist author. *Dracula* was still selling steadily but in no way could be considered a bona fide Victorian best seller, the category that Hall Caine's books more or less defined in the 1890s. Specious comparisons are sometimes made between the popularity of Stoker and of Stephen King, although there is really no comparison. Victorian horror fiction was a niche category, and *Dracula*'s phenomenal sales were achieved only over time.

The backlist advertisement in *Dracula's Guest* was a particular sticking point for Florence, who hoped, quite unrealistically, that public interest in her husband's novels other than *Dracula* might rebound and generate significant royalties after the publication of the collection. Routledge was reluctant to contract for an indefinite term for the ad, which occupied the space ordinarily given to a frontispiece, and did not want to permanently rule out the possibility of an illustrated edition, but did give her extracontractual assurance that her husband's other works would appear opposite the title for the first edition and subsequent printings, at least for the foreseeable future.

Florence was suspicious, however. It was finally necessary for one of the Turner sons to have an additional phone conversation with Noel, who agreed that she would be wise to accept Routledge's "honourable understanding," especially in light of other concessions they had made. Noel asked Turner to urge his mother (mother and son seem to have been on rather strained speaking terms) to do so. She finally agreed, still miffed that the publisher would not give her more than six printed books gratis.

It was just the beginning of endless matters regarding *Dracula* in which Florence would feel somehow cheated or aggrieved. Her resentments may have had something to do with the marked decline of her public persona, which once effused the reflected glamorous glow of Henry Irving, Ellen Terry, and first nights at the Lyceum. Now, more than anything, she was associated with—if not chained for life to—the noxious perambulations of a living corpse. "She was teased mercilessly about being Dracula's wife," recalled her granddaughter, Ann, adding that "it really wasn't fair."

She was now in her fifties, and for the rest of her life people would remark on how well she retained her beauty. Of course, it was almost always a backhanded compliment, qualified by some condescending variation on "for a woman of her age." Could any woman still be called truly beautiful at fifty? Or sixty, or seventy? Conventionally beautiful, Florence believed conventional things. There was a reason she stopped allowing her image to be captured at forty. Unlike Dracula, or Dorian Gray, she had no prospects, supernatural or otherwise, for eternal youth or even its convincing simulacrum. On this level, the age of Victorian supernaturalism had failed her badly.

To maintain herself in old age, it would be necessary for Dracula to remain robust and employed. In the early 1920s she was able to place the French and Italian rights, for small money. In 1908, Bram Stoker himself had sold German translation rights to Max Altmann, a Leipzig publisher who specialized in Theosophical tracts, among other spiritual esoterica and exotica. Altmann, a distinctly prickly personality, would give Florence endless grief by not providing regular statements of account, much less royalties. She frankly thought him to be a thief, and it's not surprising she initially believed him to be the instigator of Murnau's pirating the novel for his *Nosferatu*. Altmann, it was discovered, had nothing to do with the 1922 German film, but he would later aggravate the widow further by refusing to give up his publishing contract—in spite of many violations—when another German house made an attractive offer for *The Lair of the White Worm*, but only on the condition that they publish it in tandem with *Dracula*.

Unable to implicate Altmann, Florence moved aggressively on her own against *Nosferatu*, which was blatant copyright infringement by any standard. After two years of rancorous litigation with the aid of the British Society of Authors, she succeeded in having the German courts order the already bankrupt company Prana Film to destroy all prints and negatives.[2] There is no record she actually saw *Nosferatu*, or ever felt the need to. Had she bothered to look, she would have seen firsthand the opening titles proclaiming that the film was "freely adapted from *Dracula* by Bram Stoker," an incriminating admission that was shamelessly brazen, or just incredibly

---

[2] For a highly detailed account of Florence Stoker's legendary holy war against *Nosferatu*, see this author's *Hollywood Gothic: The Tangled Web of "Dracula" from Novel to Stage to Screen* (New York: W. W. Norton, 1990; revised edition, New York: Faber & Faber, 2004).

Nosferatu: In a scene taken directly from Stoker's novel, the frightened castle visitor comes face-to-face with Dracula's unnatural proclivities.

stupid, since both England and Germany were members of the Berne Copyright Convention. However badly Stoker had mangled his American copyright registration, the book was fully protected elsewhere. Calling the film *Nosferatu* instead of *Dracula*, and simply changing the names of the characters (the Count became Graf Orlok, Harker was reborn as Hutter, Mina as Ellen, and so forth) didn't make it any less a piracy, or elevate it to an homage. Yet many critics consider it the greatest *Dracula* film of them all.

As in Stoker's book, a real estate representative (Hutter, played by Gustav von Wangenheim) makes a journey to Transylvania to conclude a nobleman's purchase of a house in Hutter's hometown, Wisborg. The nobleman, Graf Orlok (Max Schreck), is revealed as a sexually omnivorous vampire who partakes of his male visitor's neck, even as he ogles a photograph of the young man's wife—who, of course, also has a "lovely throat." Hutter escapes the vampire's castle; Orlok travels to Wisborg with boxes of his native earth, terrorizing and killing a ship's crew in the process, then takes up residence in the house he has purchased, directly across from Hutter's.

A terrible plague ensues, and the streets of Wisborg are soon filled with funeral processions. Hutter's wife, Ellen (Greta Schroeder), welcomes home her delirious husband, and finds in his possession "The Book of Vampires," wherein she learns that the only way to destroy Nosferatu is for a virtuous woman to invite the monster to her bed, and keep him there until the rays of the morning sun destroy him. The strategy succeeds but is self-sacrificial; the blood-drained Ellen is also destroyed, expiring in her husband's arms.

Nosferatu unreels like a stark Germanic fairy tale, and on this level it is more faithful to Stoker's inspirational roots than any other adaptation. Murnau never gave an interview or any written account of his involvement in the project, and all evidence points to Prana's producer and art director, Albin Grau, as the driving creative force. Grau was the sole press spokesman for the film, and one of his advance essays recounted his personal experience in the World War I trenches, where he heard a Serbian villager's account of vampire legends. Grau likened the recently ended conflict to supernatural horror. "Suffering and grief have shaken men's hearts and have, little by little, suspended their desire to understand the cause of the monstrous events that had depleted the world like a cosmic vampire, drinking the blood of millions and millions of men."

And so, with *Nosferatu* and the mass death of World War I, the Dracula story took on additional curses—the burden of politico-cultural metaphor and the cloak of artistic pretension. Within a few years, horror movies would forget about their arty European origins and sink into a decades-long coma born of commerce, but later the sleeping hunger for critical and academic respectability would reassert itself with a terrible vengeance. In the brief shining heyday of German Expressionism, however, all manner of grotesquery was welcome at the table of high culture.

The most memorable thing about *Nosferatu* for most audiences is the ghastly makeup worn by Max Schreck—his real name, which means "terror" in German—which kept Stoker's description of pointed ears while swelling the "lofty domed forehead" into something like a hydrocephalic skull, with the "peculiarly sharp white teeth" lengthened into a pair of jumbo rat's incisors. The rodent association linked Orlok with pestilence, and quite successfully. The final touch was the addition of clawlike finger extensions (likely inspired by similar appliances employed two years earlier by John Barrymore in *Dr. Jekyll and Mr. Hyde*, widely seen in Europe). Stoker's Dracula had sharpened nails at the end of "broad, squat" fingers,

The former Kinnerton Studios, Florence Stoker's mews residence in Knightsbridge,
where she waged a battle to the death over the piracy of **Nosferatu.** (Photograph by the author)

but *Nosferatu* evoked the penny-dreadful horror of *Varney the Vampyre*'s opening chapter, in which the monster's nails memorably seem to hang and clatter from bony fingers tapping at a window.

If Schreck was more hideous than anything described by Stoker, his appearance had a good deal in common with the repulsive, pointy-eared satyr Oscar Wilde envisioned for Dorian Gray's portrait when the haunted canvas finally hit bottom. It is unlikely Wilde would have approved of Stoker's vampire, or Murnau's. Dorian, his own, more nuanced conception of a vampirish monster, presented an irresistibly attractive exterior. Wilde died too early to experience *Nosferatu*, but his friend André Gide saw the film in Paris and described his own Wildean response. If he were to remake the film, Gide wrote, the vampire would be depicted as "an inoffensive young man. . . . Wouldn't it be much more frightening if he were first presented to the woman in such a charming aspect? It is a kiss that is to be transformed into a bite."

By contrast, Stoker would have had a rollicking good time watching Schreck's ghastly comings and goings. Although many critics have argued (with some cause) that Graf Orlok is an anti-Semitic caricature in the theatrical tradition of Shylock, and thus a harbinger of horrors to come in Germany, they overlook his more obvious roots in children's theatre, especially in the heavily made-up pantomime ogres that Stoker loved, and even more particularly in the centuries-old puppet character Punchinello. Viewed in profile, Nosferatu and Mr. Punch register the same beaked-nosed image—one disturbingly grim and one almost malevolently cheerful, a perverse variation of the classic masks of comedy and tragedy.

There has been much speculation about Murnau's acknowledged homosexuality having possibly flavored the film. After all, there are no vampire brides at the castle, and Hutter's neck like his bed, is violated by the Count himself. But Murnau didn't write the film (the scenarist was Henrik Galeen, who had written Paul Wegener's *The Golem* two years earlier), and the male-male blood contact was probably just an expeditious device to eliminate unnecessary extra characters. That said, the homoerotic tension of the Transylvanian scenes in the novel is fairly close to the surface, and Galeen might well have discerned it.

Galeen's script for *Nosferatu*, preserved at the Cinémathèque Française, gave Murnau a clear narrative structure, though described rather impressionistically. The film was shot largely on location in Czechoslovakia, and lacked the theatrical settings of Robert Weine's 1919 *The Cabinet of Dr. Caligari*—the highly influential German Expressionist template of modern horror movies—but cameraman Fritz Arno Wagner compensated with boldly composed visuals. Prana Film was not well capitalized, and some of the more ambitious concepts could not be easily realized on location sets, including the scripted action of Hutter entering the castle with Orlok and passing by an ancient portrait, its eyes following them uncannily. The film's single most memorable pair of images, comprising two shots of Orlok's shadow—first creeping up the stairs to his victim's bedroom, then reaching out its penumbral claw toward her door—was not scripted. Galeen originally intended the vampire to jump from the street to the second-story window Ellen has just thrown open, an action that would have been awkward to stage and probably more funny than frightening. Even if it breaks the viewer's natural expectation of an entrance by casement, the compromise solution contributed one of the most frighteningly famous visions in cinema history.

In America during the silent film era, supernatural-seeming creatures were almost always revealed to be phony, typically criminals using scare techniques to pull off a crime. It was a formula drawn from popular drawing-room mystery melodramas in the theatre, like *The Cat and the Canary* (1927). *Dracula*, however, intrigued filmmakers even earlier, despite the American public's resistance to frankly supernatural themes.

When Carl Laemmle founded Universal Pictures in 1915, prominent on its wish list of productions was Stoker's novel, until a studio memo pointed out that *Dracula*'s American copyright was "clouded." Only five years later, the studio floated a news item that one of its rising directors, Tod Browning, was ready and eager to produce *Dracula*, but once again the interest cooled. It was true that Universal, or any other studio, could produce a film version of Stoker's book with impunity in the United States, but since silent cinema was an international medium, with as much as half a studio's revenue being generated overseas, there was no compelling reason to challenge a copyright for a film that would necessarily have severely limited distribution. No copy of Stoker's American publishing agreement with Doubleday & McClure has yet surfaced, but if the language of the agreement assigned publication rights for the duration of copyright, the publisher would have been within its rights to cancel the royalties while continuing to issue the book. Of course, such a move would open the floodgates to myriad American editions of *Dracula*, which would hardly be in Doubleday's interest. Royalties were a very small part of the total cash flow generated by the novel, and a reasonable price to pay for an exclusive franchise.

Early in her campaign against *Nosferatu*, Stoker's widow maintained that she had been involved in motion picture negotiations "for some time"; this might have been bluster, but it is also possible that unspecified silent filmmakers besides Universal had their own ideas brewing.

One curiosity of the period is a Hungarian silent entitled *Drakula halála* (*The Death of Drakula*), directed by Károly Lajthay in 1921. A lost film (only a short novelization and a handful of tantalizing photos survive), Lajthay's effort was the first media appropriation of Stoker's title, but hardly an adaptation. Instead, "Drakula" is the delusional alter ego of a former music teacher committed to a mental institution. When the heroine, Mary Land (Margit Lux), arrives at the asylum to visit her dying father, she first encounters this madman (Paul Askonas), whom she remembers as her one-time singing instructor. Now he wears, and even sleeps in, a black cloak, all the while insisting that he is Drakula, the immortal. "I have been alive for a thousand years, and I will live forever. . . . People will die, the world will be destroyed, but I shall keep on living!"

Deeply shaken, Mary is approached by another mental patient, this one dressed as a doctor, who insists she has a serious eye disease and, if not operated upon at once, will go blind. A second doctor-impostor helps bind her to an operating table, and the crazy pair come close to cutting into her eyes when they are interrupted by the asylum's real director and Mary is saved. Shortly thereafter she falls into a deep sleep and dreams of being abducted by Drakula and spirited to his mysterious castle, where she is to be made into one of his undead brides. Drakula twice cringes at the sight of a crucifix she carries. After an escape and additional melodramatic jeopardy, Mary wakes in the asylum, wondering if she too is mad. There is no doubt, however, that Drakula is insane. His life comes to an abrupt end when, throroughly convinced he is unkillable, he dares another patient with a loaded revolver to shoot him.

Although the film's title, the central motif of a haunted castle and undead brides, and crucial action transpiring in a madhouse all link *Drakula halála* to Stoker, other influences are discernible. *The Cabinet of Dr. Caligari* was also set in a mental lock-up and included a nightmarish abduction. André de Lorde's Parisian stage adaptation of Poe's 1845 short story "The System of Doctor Tarr and Professor Fether," in which lunatics take over an asylum, had been a sturdy part of the Grand Guignol repertory since 1903. And the plot element of a crazy musician abducting a protegée was central to Gaston Leroux's 1910 novel *The Phantom of the Opera*.

Is it possible Prana Film had knowledge of, and had been emboldened by, the Hungarian film? Lajthay was openly exploiting the name, if not the plot, of Stoker's novel and had not been challenged. Moreover, Hungary had not yet joined the Berne Convention, and literary works from Britain could be appropriated with impunity. A pirated Hungarian translation of the book (also spelled *Drakula*) appeared in 1926, perhaps based on an equally unauthorized serial in Budapest around the turn of the century. The 1926 book cover illustration was clearly influenced by ship-sequence images from *Nosferatu*, the vampire resembling a blend of Max Schreck and the nightmarish figure in Edvard Munch's painting *The Scream*.

Drakula halála would hardly be the last dramatization to capitalize on the fame of the title *Dracula* while at the same time throwing the book under the bus. Badly in need of money, and also eager to establish a stage copyright, Florence Stoker herself betrayed the novel when, in 1924, she agreed to the proposal of a provincial actor/manager named Hamilton Deane to adapt the book for his touring repertory company. Florence asked Deane to retain as much of the original dialogue as possible but otherwise washed her hands of creative input. Honestly, she could barely stand the book. In another life, she might well be collecting the royalties from *The Importance of Being Earnest* and basking enviably in its reflective brilliance. Having to depend on *Dracula* was rather like being like Mina Harker, forced to guzzle blood from an open wound.

In time, she would live to regret the contract with Deane. The only thing they shared in common was a desire to make money. A former bank manager from Dublin, he had been a member of the Henry Irving Vacation Company (a troupe in which Irving did not perform) at the turn of the century. According to the *Stage*, Deane "lived and breathed and looked theatre. Clichés of acting seemed to whirl off him," yet he "had the power to rivet attention and to create an audience into which audiences were drawn without resistance." Audiences simply flocked to him, whether he was starring in a play, guest-delivering a sermon, or even judging a beauty contest. Although he would often claim in interviews that he had known Stoker personally (he later confessed that the acquaintance had been a glancing one at best), Deane had never actually talked to the author of *Dracula* about his most famous book, or any book. He was also a bit confused about Florence Stoker's still-unsettled lawsuit over *Nosferatu*, assuming she was talking about a German stage piracy, not a film.

Did Florence Stoker place her own curse on *Dracula*'s legacy? Even if she didn't formally approve some of Deane's wholesale changes, she tacitly permitted them. Conceivably, she even liked Deane's major departure from her husband's vision: the complete transformation of Dracula from a degenerate denizen of the shadows to a well-dressed, cultivated aristocrat who could at least pretend to observe social niceties. Deane, not Bram Stoker, was responsible for outfitting the vampire in a high-collared black cape that has since come to instantly signify the whole Dracula mythos—a supernaturalized synecdoche, universally understood by young and old. Stoker mentions the garment only once, in connection with the Count's Transylvanian wall-crawl ("his cloak spread out around him like great wings"). Deane wanted to open his play with a silent prologue enacting this dark descent, with a wire-reinforced cape opening like bat wings—essentially a big flapping umbrella suit. The ambitious effect proved impractical and was never staged, but Deane used the image on his touring poster and settled for an Episcopalian priest's traditional funeral cape for the show proper, its large collar stiffened with wire, with a red satin lining added. The collar framed the actor's face in a way that at least suggested a bat. The costume, resembling the clichéd attire of a music-hall magician or hypnotist, was especially appropriate for a production employing a variety of effects drawn from stage magic, including flash-bombs, secret panels, and, in the final scene, a coffin tricked out like a magician's cabinet, in which Dracula would vanish beneath folding boards in a cloud of agitated fuller's earth.

Stoker, of course, never envisioned Dracula as a toff-about-town in elegant evening dress. But in productions of Gounod's *Faust*, Mephistopheles usually dressed formally, sometimes with an opera cape, a tradition Deane would have known well. Deane emphasized a devilish *Faust* connection by giving Dracula a dark wig with curling white streaks resembling horns.

Deane first wanted to play Dracula himself, until he finished the script and realized Van Helsing had the lion's share of dialogue. When the production debuted at the Grand Theatre in Derby on May 15, 1924, playing for three nights only, an actor named Edmund Blake had the distinction of being the first authorized Dracula of the legitimate theatre. Little known today, Blake—whose real name was Frederick Alkin—appeared in several silent films (directing at least one, *Flotsam*, filmed in 1921 on the Isle of Man) and had also played Sax Rohmer's supervillain Dr. Fu Manchu onstage. Deane remembered that Blake had a glittering gold front tooth that effectively enhanced his demonic grimace.

The *Derby Telegraph* reported that *Dracula* was "a show which causes the imaginative spectator to grab his seat and gurgle with nervous anticipation as thrill succeeds thrill. One forgets the absolute twaddle to which one is listening. The utter drivel of werewolves, vampires and undead, which provokes nothing but laughter in the sa[n]e light of day, becomes dreadful reality in the awful semi-darkness of the stage." As to the first stage Dracula himself, "Edmund Blake has the more difficult task in creating such a role as that of the undead Count. His every appearance throughout the piece is stamped with the hallmark of finish and his disappearance in a puff of smoke at the close of the third scene is a remarkable example of ingenious stagecraft."

Among the many other actors who played Dracula for Deane were John Laurie, Keith Pyott, Frederick Keene, and W. E. Holloway, but the performer with the most longevity in the role was Raymond Huntley, who would go on to play it in the West End and on tour in America. Huntley would later become a beloved fixture of British film and television, most famously as the family lawyer on the long-running series *Upstairs, Downstairs.*

Business was so good that at one point Deane was simultaneously touring three different troupes, known as the Red, the White, and the Blue companies. After a while, Deane admitted, "I was simply coining money." But before the production was a proven hit, he tried to save money wherever he could. For instance, the scene in which Van Helsing confronts Dracula about his absent reflection in the mirror could be performed two ways, depending on the box office. Dracula could smash the mirror, incurring the cost of a nightly glass replacement, or he could angrily raise a candlestick to strike, only to regain his composure at the last, thrifty moment.

Company members recalled many mishaps during the touring years. The flying bat, with battery-charged green lights for eyes, once broke from its wire and lodged in the footlights, staring at the audience and making Dracula's entrance a trifle awkward. And not all the unexpected happenings were onstage. By two different accounts, a woman actually gave birth during a performance. The actress Vera Raven recalled this happening "in the ladies'," while Noel Stoker remembered "signs" of a baby being born— presumably the afterbirth—being discovered in the auditorium stalls.

Despite provincial success, London terrified Deane. He very correctly feared that the critics would eat him alive, or try to. *Dracula,* in the final analysis, was country-bumpkin entertainment, and his barnstorming style an uneasy fit amid the self-consciously sophisticated offerings of the West End. But he was convinced to take a chance at the Little Theatre, a very accurately named venue in the Adelphi, off the Strand, that had had a string of good luck with mysteries and melodramas. José Levy, the theatre's proprietor, had already presented Sybil Thorndike in a short but successful season of grisly Grand Guignol plays there, and attracted attention by

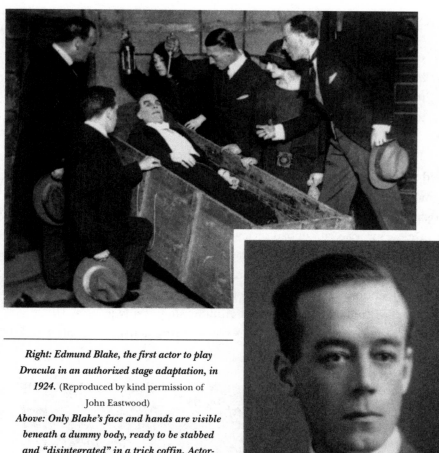

Right: Edmund Blake, the first actor to play
Dracula in an authorized stage adaptation, in
1924. (Reproduced by kind permission of
John Eastwood)
Above: Only Blake's face and hands are visible
beneath a dummy body, ready to be stabbed
and "disintegrated" in a trick coffin. Actor-
manager Hamilton Deane (at right) played
Van Helsing, wrote the original script,
and directed.

positioning a nurse in the lobby for every performance. Deane repeated
the Barnumesque stunt, thereby giving audience members a perfect excuse
to get into the act. At many performances, women screamed and fainted,
and men grew nervous. Luckily, fortifying brandy was readily available.
The element of audience participation had already been an important part
of the touring production. People looked forward to return visits of the
play, especially Deane's curtain speech.

Just a moment, Ladies and Gentlemen! Just a word before you go. We hope the memories of Dracula and Renfield won't give you bad dreams, so just a word of reassurance. When you get home tonight and the lights have been turned out and you are afraid to look behind the curtains and you dread to see a face appear at the window . . . why, just pull yourself together and remember that after all, *there are such things!*

The audience relished the chance to join in on the portentously delivered final line, exactly as generations of children at Christmas pantomimes had done, happily shouting *"Look behind you!"* to characters in mock jeopardy.

Deane's worries about bad reviews were realized—in spades. Notice after notice dripped with condescension, taking Deane to task for his wandering Dutch accent, the "appallingly pompous" dialogue, the amateurish acting and its elocutionary excesses, the cheap stage effects, and, most memorably, the "ill-fitting mask" Raymond Huntley supposedly wore as Dracula— which prompted Huntley to send the complaining newspaper a letter, which

Cast of the original West End production of **Dracula** *at the Little Theatre, 1927.*

it printed. Although he had no quarrel with the critic that the face might indeed be ill-fitting and mask-like, "I should be glad of the hospitality of your column to assure him that at least it is my own," the actor wrote.

The reviewer for *Punch* threw the publication's usual supercilious punches:

> The late Mr. Bram Stoker's *Dracula*, which I understand has for many years been a cause of frequent nightmares in the unsophisticated, has been done into a play by Mr. Hamilton Deane, and I am bound to say he has made a mirth-provoking affair of it—in parts. It is true this vampire business is not primarily designed for mirth, and no doubt the apparatus of suddenly-opened doors, clocks that tick eerily, howling lunatics who eat flies and white mice, pink-eyed bats (not induced by alcohol), magnesium flashes, swirling mists which don't smell at all like mists, pale-faced aristocratic aliens whose bodies are not reflected in plane mirrors and whose hair is twisted into devilish horns may well be very more seriously alarming between the pages of a book than they are in the three-dimensional medium of the stage. If this had all been played in a full-blooded transpontine manner, and if everything hadn't been said seven times, laughter would have been even more easy, though I admit there was something especially diverting in watching a company of grave conscientious actors in the West End manner heroically pretending to take it all seriously.

The casual dismissal of Stoker's novel was a harbinger of future adaptations, which would reject any bookish buildup of atmosphere in favor of startling stagecraft. As another reviewer quipped, "There is very little of Bram Stoker in it. But most of us jumped in our seats at least once in every act."

Coincidentally, the New York publisher and producer Horace Liveright was in London the month *Dracula* opened. By 1927, the year usually regarded as the height of the Jazz Age, he was already a legendary figure. With his partner Albert Boni, Liveright permanently revolutionized the way books were sold and promoted in America—even if the previously genteel business had to be forcibly pulled into the twentieth century, writhing and screaming. The cofounders of the Modern Library were the first publishers to make acclaimed literary works available in attractive, inexpensive volumes, aggressively advertised and readily available. Although his critics (and there were many) loathed the idea of literature being suddenly treated as a commodity—and by *a failed toilet paper salesman,* no less!—Liveright, the public face of the business, knew how to move books. By offering generous advances, he was able to attract major authors, even if their agents—like Ezra Pound's—considered Liveright "vulgarity personified." Nonetheless, his stable of writers included seven future Nobel Prize winners. He published Ernest Hemingway's first book, as well as Dorothy Parker's, and year after year showcased the likes of T. S. Eliot, E. E. Cummings, Eugene O'Neill, and Djuna Barnes. He conveniently popularized the writings of Sigmund Freud in a decade in which free sex became fashionable. The midtown offices of Boni and Liveright were famous for wild parties, usually held in the firm's reception area, where rum-runners could outnumber writers. In short, Liveright seemed to embody everything that was creative, controversial, or scandalous about New York in the Roaring Twenties. His office was outfitted with a secret room reached through a revolving fireplace, ideal for illicit trysting. He made a lot of money and spent a lot of money. And one of his favorite money holes was the theatre. As described by his biographer Tom Dardis,

> Liveright's critics considered a book publisher's involvement with Broadway as beneath contempt. They were equally outraged by Horace's constant Wall Street speculations that bled the firm of its money on a regular basis. In July 1928, his company achieved the peculiar distinction of having six out of the ten best-selling books in the United States on its list yet having no ready cash with which to pay its bills. With sales exceeding a million dollars a year, the firm produced only paper-thin profits of a few thousand or none at all.

John L. Balderston, London correspondent for the *New York World,* had the task of squiring the visiting Liveright around town in February 1927 when they happened upon the Little Theatre production, which had just opened. Despite withering notices, the play was a hit, even if (or simply because) much of the audience found it a fashionable goof. Balderston recognized the play's glaring deficiencies—could anybody really miss them?—but Liveright saw potential box office gold. Under all the amateur theatrics something else was pulsating. Something unusual. Something attention grabbing. And yes, dammit, something strangely sexy. To Liveright, one of the play's central, recurrent images—the girl laid out on the couch, ready to be spooked—looked a heck of a lot like a woman being psychoanalyzed. Didn't Freud talk about the death wish?

As for all the bad reviews, Liveright was way ahead of the game in recognizing that bad publicity was an oxymoron. He also knew that novelty, especially weird novelty, could be easily marketed, especially in America. One of his best-selling authors was Gertrude Atherton—the same writer who thought Oscar Wilde looked like a sea monster—whose 1923 blockbuster *Black Oxen* was all about a mysterious countess who keeps herself unnaturally young through glandular treatments and x-rays. If he could sell Atherton, he could sell Stoker, even as refracted and transformed by this scenery-chewing Hamilton Deane person.

Of the two men watching *Dracula* play out at the Little Theatre that cold winter night, Balderston had the stronger interest in the occult. He

Hamilton Deane.

John L. Balderston.

had adapted Henry James's time-travel romance *The Sense of the Past* as the play *Berkeley Square* (1926), a hit in London and New York, made into a film in 1933, and remade in 1951 as *I'll Never Forget You* (the play also very loosely inspired the 1965 musical comedy *On a Clear Day You Can See Forever*). As a London-based journalist, he had covered the opening of King Tut's tomb in 1922, which ten years later informed his screenplay for the Boris Karloff film *The Mummy*. Liveright was not himself drawn to the supernatural apart from its commercial potential, and *Berkeley Square* had struck a productive mother lode. Could Balderston do anything with *Dracula*? Yes, but he made it clear Deane's script was "illiterate" and, while he would share a byline, he wouldn't collaborate. Liveright agreed; as a concession, Deane was to receive first billing as author, even though almost none of the final dialogue was his, or even resembled his. Next, Florence Stoker would have to be persuaded to sign a three-way contract.

The widow disliked Liveright, and people who didn't like him usually loathed him, often for ethnic reasons. One detractor called him "a Jewish Edgar Allan Poe," and after *Dracula* there would come unflattering comparisons to the Count as well, with additional shadings of Shylock and Svengali. If there was any anti-Semitism in Florence's estimation of Liveright, it was the banal, unacknowledged prejudice of the decade in which *Dracula* had been written, when suspicions about "degenerate" foreigners were just part of the air middle-class, middlebrow people breathed. They didn't use outright ethnic slurs. They were just prone to calling people of a certain religious persuasion crass, vulgar, and money-grubbing. Balderston, as a long-transplanted American, understood British people and manners. Nonetheless, managing a prickly holdover of the Victorian age was a special challenge. But in dealing with Florence, he was deftly able to play the good cop to Liveright's bad.

One of the first performers to be cast, as Lucy Seward, was Liveright's girlfriend, Dorothy Peterson (his pending divorce—long simmering in order to maintain loans from his wife's wealthy father—would not be finalized for another year.) Bernard Jukes, the manic Renfield of both the provinces and the West End, gladly signed. Two experienced character actors who would eventually follow the production to Hollywood were Edward Van Sloan and Herbert Bunston as Van Helsing and Dr. Seward, respectively. Soon, according to John Balderston Jr., "they had cast everybody but the Count. And they were out of money." Raymond Huntley turned down

Liveright's offer of $125 a week to reprise the role of Dracula in New York. He had been playing it for three years and felt that further identification with the part was simply not in his interest. He had trained in London with the likes of John Gielgud and was understandably worried that *Dracula* might turn out to be a "youthful indiscretion" preventing his working with experienced London actors in "real" plays and generally advancing his career. A few years later, he would accept a more favorable offer from Liveright for the national tour in America, but that didn't help Horace Liveright Theatrical Productions in the summer of 1927.

Then came Béla Blaskó. The forty-eight year-old actor from Lugos, in Transylvanian Hungary, had worked professionally as Lugosi Bela in Europe, and Bela Lugosi in America. He was a political expatriate, and his English was very poor. But he was tall and imposing with a compelling combination of dark hair and penetrating, sapphire-colored eyes. He had a baritone voice with an odd inflection that was less Hungarian-accented English than the sound of a Hungarian reciting English phonetically. Fortunately, according to Balderston, he could understand French, as could the director, Ira Hards. After *Dracula*, Lugosi's sonorous voice would become one of the most readily identifiable and most frequently imitated in theatrical history.

Lugosi accepted $100 a week, which is not what one would think adequate pay for a former romantic lead at the National Theatre in Budapest. He had, in fact, worked quite extensively there, but always in supporting roles. Nonetheless, he could truthfully claim to have done *Hamlet*—and conveniently omit the information he had played Horatio, and not the prince.

Only days before the New York opening, Liveright and his general manager, Louis Cline, hired Guy Jarrett, the legendary stage magician, to devise a showstopping illusion for Dracula's third-act escape. During the out-of-town previews in Hartford, New Haven, and Stamford, Connecticut, Dracula's disappearance was achieved as it had been by Hamilton Deane: a distracting flash pot in the fireplace (the effect was called "fireworks" in one British review), followed by a brief blackout in which Lugosi slipped out of the cape and through a hidden panel, leaving the actors playing Harker and Seward holding an empty cloak and trying to look astonished. The audience wasn't astonished at all. The trick (if it could even be called a trick) was so transparently obvious it was almost insulting.

Jarrett's challenge was not to create a world-class illusion (of which he

*Cornered by his enemies, Bela Lugosi prepares for a theatrical vanishing act,
designed by the great stage magician Guy Jarrett.*

was an acknowledged master) but to devise a flashy, surprising effect that
could be carried out by ordinary actors with minimum rehearsal. He built
a special cape for the scene, about six inches longer than Lugosi's usual costume, in order that it could brush the floor. The shoulders were reinforced
with a stiff wire frame that retained its shape even without an actor wearing
it. A second loop of wire supported a dark, tight-fitting, hoodie-like cowl
that would stay rigid without a head inside.

The third device employed was an elevator trap, more or less the reverse
of the star trap through which demons and fairies made their gymnastic
entrances in Christmas pantomimes. Bram Stoker's fascination with trapdoors is evidenced by incidents in *The Primrose Path* and his *Snowbound* story
"A Star Trap." No doubt this illusion would have fascinated him—even as
he would likely have been appalled by what his widow had allowed to be
done with the rest of his story.

The trick was set up during the climactic scene in which Dracula has
been cornered before dawn in Dr. Seward's study. Unlike in the novel (and
Deane's play), Renfield is not killed by Dracula but used as bait to trap him.
Harker and Seward hold the Count at bay with their crucifixes while Van
Helsing counts down on his watch the minutes and seconds before the sun

will rise. Dracula, having rebounded from his animalistic attempt to strangle Renfield, takes it all in stride.

DRACULA: [*Calmly, suavely again.*] I thank you for reminding me of the time.
VAN HELSING: Harker, open the curtains. [HARKER *opens curtains. Red light of approaching dawn outside.*] That is the East. The sun will rise beyond the meadow there.

Dracula reacts, raising his cape against the light while simultaneously, and unnoticed by the audience, pulling up the small cowl. We do not see his face again—only the back of the hood, which, in the dim light and partially covered by the cape's large collar, appears to be the top of the actor's head.

SEWARD: [*Glancing behind, leaves wolfsbane on the desk as he looks up at window.*] The clouds are coloring.
HARKER: God's daybreak.
   [HARKER *leaves crucifix on desk.* VAN HELSING *checks watch.* SEWARD *and* HARKER *step in.*]
DRACULA: [*Coolly. Turns upstage, with back to them.*] A pleasant task you have set yourself, Mr. Harker.
VAN HELSING: Ten seconds. Be ready when he collapses.
   [SEWARD *crosses to hold* DRACULA's *cape on left of* DRACULA. HARKER *holds cape on right of* DRACULA.]
HARKER: *The sun!* The stake, Professor . . . the stake! Hold him, Doctor!
SEWARD: I've got him.
   [DRACULA, *with a loud burst of mocking laughter, goes down trap on the word "sun," leaving the two men holding the empty cape. As soon as they've seen the trap back in place,* HARKER *backs down left, dropping the cape in front of the desk, then a flash goes off in front of fireplace.*]
HARKER: Up the chimney, as a bat!

According to Jarrett, Lugosi was leery of the stunt, and more than a bit perturbed that he had to skip dinner to rehearse the scene's mechanics. But

Horace Liveright and his **Dracula** *letterhead.*

he was also hungry for the role, and for the play to be a success. The trick was not without risks. While nowhere as dangerous as a catapulting star trap, the counterweighted floor platform was meant to move quickly. As Jarrett recalled, "When Dracula, in reeling, turned his back, two men below pulled the skip [trap platform] with the speed of a drop," a safety door immediately closing the opening. It is almost inconceivable that Lugosi didn't experience his share of arm, elbow, and shoulder bruises during the run of the show.

Audiences didn't care. As the appreciative reviewer for the *New York Telegram* noted, when "the Count ingeniously melted out of the hands of his captors, you might say, 'I wouldn't believe it, not even if it was Houdini.'"

Liveright modified other effects as the show continued its run. For early productions, Dracula's first-act attempt to drain Lucy saw Lugosi rise from behind the divan in some kind of werewolf disguise, no photograph of which has survived. One critic, however, facetiously compared the costume to the bearskin rug that greeted visitors to the Liveright offices. Whatever titters it caused, the looming wolf persisted for some time in the production and is mentioned in some of the press clippings from the 1928–29 national tour. But when Samuel French began to administer the stock and amateur rights in 1933, its acting edition of the script eliminated any animal transformation except for the bat. It was the beginning of an enduring trend in horror entertainment, wherein the werewolf trope would keep closer company with Dr. Jekyll and Mr. Hyde than with Count Dracula.

Liveright's third change was the late addition of Deane's coffin trick. In early performances Lugosi remained completely invisible in a deep sarcophagus when Van Helsing drove in the stake, his piteous groans being the only evidence of Dracula's destruction. But now, the audience could have the satisfaction of seeing Dracula evaporate into dust, just as he had been doing in England for the past four years. It is peculiar Liveright didn't include the impressive effect from the outset, but the delay may have been a thoroughly calculated move to guarantee additional publicity and potentially drive repeat business. The Liveright production also retained Deane's gimmick of a nurse in the lobby. Unlike in London, where the nurse freely dispensed "medicinal" brandy (sometimes causing eager near-epidemics of "nervous prostration"), in Prohibition-era New York swooning patrons were offered only "faint checks" granting admission to a future performance.

In 1897, just as *Dracula* was making its debut in London bookstalls, Aubrey Beardsley was spitting up blood.

Now, three decades later, it was Harry Clarke's turn.

The forty-year-old, Dublin-born artist would live far longer than the enfant terrible who powerfully influenced him; Clarke was himself diagnosed with tuberculosis long past the age at which Beardsley had died. By 1929 Clarke was the most prodigious and revered designer of stained glass in Ireland, and an illustrator whose fantastic interpretations of Edgar Allan Poe, the fairy tales of Hans Christian Andersen and Charles Perrault, and Goethe's *Faust* were showcased in deluxe editions that remain collectors' trophies. He inherited and enhanced Beardsley's dramatic pen-and-ink mastery of black and white space, as well as a fascination with the grotesque, the perverse, and the erotic. He kept alive the fin-de-siècle energies of Symbolism and Art Nouveau well into the age of Art Deco and German Expressionism.

And one of his dying wishes was to illustrate an edition de luxe of *Dracula*.

We can't precisely ascertain when Clarke first encountered the book. He was only eight years old in 1897, but *Dracula* was steadily in print and readily available all through his adolescence and early adulthood. Recent commentators have suggested that it was *Nosferatu* that brought him to consider the visual possibilities of *Dracula*. Although the film was not shown outside of Germany until 1925, publicity photos and artwork began appearing in art periodicals like *Bühne und Film* (*Stage and Screen*) by late 1921, and Expressionism was certainly an influence on his own art. The following year, Clarke contributed a bizarre frontispiece to a book called *Dublin of the Future* that seemed instead wedded to its medieval past.[3] "The Last Hour of the Night" depicted an androgynous, emaciated creature presiding over the destruction and decay of Dublin. The image is a kind of Irish analogy to *Nosferatu*'s presentation of Max Schreck as an Expressionist symbol of the deadened, hollowed-out soul of Germany after World War I.

Clarke may have signaled his keen interest in *Nosferatu* by including a deathly-looking lutenist—another nearly perfect image of Schreck—strumming some danse macabre in the border of a panel in his 1924 stained-glass masterpiece *The Eve of St. Agnes*. (The same window includes an especially atmospheric bedroom tableau with two women that could easily be taken as a scene from *Carmilla*.) *Nosferatu* contains several stunning visual compositions that amount to conceptual treatments for stained-glass interpretation, particularly a shot in which the vampire stares out from his house,

---

[3] See illustration in chapter 1.

clutching a window's crossbars, framed and defined by them as if by leaden partitions.

There can be no doubt Harry Clarke would have been *Dracula*'s ideal illustrator.

Whether Florence Stoker would agree would be another matter entirely. His interest in *Nosferatu* would hardly endear him to the widow. Had he known about her conversion, Catholicism might have been a better route to ingratiation. The Jesuit-educated Clarke's deeply mystical and often sinister religious imagery played to the ambivalent Protestant fascination with "Catholic magic." (Most of his church commissions were, in fact, for the Church of England and the Church of Ireland.) Morbid Catholicism, of course, was a special fixation of the Irish literary Gothic novel, beginning with *Melmoth the Wanderer* and its energies revived most notably in *Dracula*. Clarke's religious stained-glass work proved he was also a consummate technician of color; he revived and blended the fevered chromatic intensity of medieval windows with ethereal figures of martyrs, saints, and angels inspired by Pre-Raphaelitism and the curious workings of his own imagination.

Neither Charlotte nor Bram Stoker would live to see the legendary Clarke edition of Poe's *Tales of Mystery and Imagination* (1919), but it would have impressed them as it impressed everyone. Britain's leading art periodical, the *Studio*, declared Clarke Poe's quintessential illustrator. "Never before have these marvelous tales been visually interpreted with such flesh-creeping, brain-haunting illusions of horror, terror and the unspeakable," the reviewer enthusiastically observed. "In black and white, Mr. Clarke sets pictures before us that glimpse for us fresh meanings in the tales and at the same time give us artistic satisfaction." Florence may have had no use for Poe, or may never have seen Clarke's sumptuous 1925 limited edition of Goethe's *Faust*—which, considering how much of her husband's professional energies had been devoted to Irving's version, might have given her a good idea of how an edition de luxe might elevate *Dracula*'s reputation. Harry Clarke didn't illustrate penny dreadfuls, after all. *Faust* was reviewed in the journal *Artwork*, which praised Clarke's "sublunar world of phantoms" in which "the world of the psychoanalyst was made visible." The reviewer also coined an especially clever portmanteau word in reference to the sexually ambiguous visuals: "hermaphrodisiac." Clarke was likened to Aubrey Beardsley and Gustave Doré interpreting Rabelais and Chaucer, all through a Gothic lens.

Illustration by Harry Clarke for Poe's "The Fall of the House of Usher" (1925).

The *Irish Statesman,* in a 1930 assessment of what would be the artist's final exhibition, declared that Clarke "might have been incarnated from the dark side of the moon," glutting his "imagination on the worm and the wormy grave, and their sinister and spectral emanations. . . . Sometimes these creatures of Clarke's imagination seem like fabulous incubi and succubi of medieval wizardry living beyond the grave with the dark passions persisting, but with forms too frail for bodily enjoyment of any desire." No one knows the source of Clarke's special affinity for dark and otherworldly themes, though there are clues. As it did for Stoker, the shadow of illness and death came to him early in life. Pulmonary problems followed Clarke from childhood, possibly because of toxic chemical exposure from his years apprenticing in the family glassworks. The premonition of an early death may well have haunted him, and he surely suspected his tubercular fate long before it was officially diagnosed. Dark-haired and wide-eyed, he had a haunted, waif-like look. A clear anticipation of personal damnation can be read into the habit of using himself as a model, most notably for Faust (and, in a preliminary study, as Mephistopheles). He photographed his own stripped-to-the-waist body as a template for the Crucifixion and used his face as a not-so-secret signature, Michelangelo-style, in a window of the Last Judgment, his features instantly recognizable even upside down on their inverted trajectory into the pit of hell.

The sense of a limited life fueled an extraordinary creative output. Clarke's ambitious bucket list of illustration projects included Shakespeare's *Macbeth*, Sir Richard Burton's *Arabian Nights*, and, to follow his completed 1928 edition of Swinburne's poems, two final excursions into dazzling visual decadence—Baudelaire's *Les fleurs de mal* and Huysmans's *À rebours*.

Last but definitely not least was *Dracula*. In esteeming Stoker alongside geniuses like Goethe, Poe, Swinburne, Baudelaire, Huysmans, and even Wilde (he had done a striking, unpublished watercolor impression of *De Profundis* in 1913, powerfully capturing a grim, judgmental moment "from the depths"), Harry Clarke intuitively grasped essential things about *Dracula*—its affinity to fairy tales and Celtic superstition, and to the medieval danse macabre and its evocation of plague and penitence, let alone its bottomless psychosexual dimensions—that wouldn't even begin to occur to literary minds for another half century.

Clarke was an avid and sophisticated reader from an early age. So was Stoker, though as a literary stylist he was no match to the other authors who obsessed him. But as a writer who could summon unforgettable mental images from the dark side, Stoker was the equal of them all. It isn't difficult to catch visual hints of *Dracula* all through the Clarke oeuvre with its countless depictions of death, resurrection (sacred and profane), scenes of spooky bedchambers, spectral sleep, and dark passions surviving the grave. Female figures as delineated by Clarke often have the aspect of possessed sleepwalkers in states of stylized enervation. Clarke's male subjects frequently radiate demonic obsession with trademark, transfixing stares. In one's mind's eye, specific tableaux from *Dracula* are easily visualized in the style of Clarke. How would he have interpreted the Count's lizard-like descent from Castle Dracula's battlements? Or the stealthy moonlit approach of Dracula's vampire wives? Think of the wreck of the ghost-ship. The death, resurrection, and gruesome final destruction of Lucy Westenra.

And finally, the book's decadent-erotic apogee: Dracula's ménage-à-trois conquest of Jonathan and Mina Harker, with commingled blood trickling down the bedclothes like the inky lines of M. Valdemar's putrescence.

In addition to sharing early health problems, both Clarke and Bram Stoker had ambivalent feelings about God, religion, and the Christian concept of an afterlife, and wrestled with them in their work. As stated by the fantasy art historian Brigid Peppin, "Many of [Clarke's] images seem to contain bizarre perversions of religious iconography; diabolical gestures parody those traditionally ascribed to saints; flying witches and monsters with truncated or skeletal wings appear to be the antithesis of angels." In *Dracula*, Stoker also inverted Christianity, bringing a devil rather than a savior back from the grave and turning survival after death into a hellish Darwinian limbo.

The writer and the artist were made for one another. In their creative output, both Stoker and Clarke repeatedly focused on transgressed gender boundaries, with frequent expressions of androgyny and homoeroticism. In some of his renderings for *Faust*, Mephistopheles appears seductively hermaphroditic. According to Clarke's biographer Nicola Gordon Bowe, all throughout his late work "one sees monsters in a state of metamorphosis, intermingled with phalluses, buttocks, breasts and more amorphous fleshy projections." Peppin adds, "In his perverse and satanic imagery, which often had strong homosexual overtones, Clarke exceeded the Decadents of the 1890s." Indeed, one of Clarke's later, satirical drawings (unpublished even after a clumsy attempt at censoring) incorporated more rigid, writhing, or flaccid penises than all the works of Aubrey Beardsley.

By October 1929, Clarke had left Dublin under doctor's orders for an indefinite sanatorium stay in Davos, Switzerland. Treatment for tuberculosis in the 1920s was essentially pseudo-scientific, descended from the miasma theories of the nineteenth century, emphasizing clean fresh air, sunlight, and bed rest. In the pre-antibiotic era, some of the stranger treatments included weighing down patients' chests with sandbags, to force the lungs to work harder, or the removal of ribs, which supposedly would allow diseased lungs to expand. Wreaths of garlic and wolfsbane were not used—though it is interesting to note the degree to which untreatable wasting disease and beautiful, dying women were romantically fetishized in nineteenth-century literature, a recurrent motif from Poe to Puccini to *Dracula*. Bored and restless in semiquarantine, and eager to return to Dublin,

Clarke stayed involved as best he could with the ongoing work of his glass studio, while continuing to solicit new commissions. He had his London book agent, Sharmid,[4] write directly to Florence Stoker in Knightsbridge.

The combative widow was at low ebb, still recovering in a nursing home from cataract surgery, and barely able to read or write. Philippa Adams, her niece, wrote to the Society of Authors on her behalf, asking if they knew anything of Clarke or his agents, and whether the author (in this case, Florence) would retain any interest in the drawings. The society's secretary, G. Herbert Thring, replied that the agency was reputable, but making a contract with an illustrator instead of a publisher was highly unusual. "I have never heard of an arrangement made direct with an artist," he wrote. "I think, however, it would be possible for you to make an arrangement with a publisher if Mr. Harry Clarke found a publisher and was willing to negotiate for an edition de luxe." He advised her that Clarke's agents had not given her "anything like sufficient information" on how they defined an edition de luxe, how many copies they intended to print, or what they intended to pay. Thring assured her that she must be given approval over the drawings.

While trying to be helpful, he just gave a naturally mistrustful woman more cause than ever to be suspicious. The real reason Clarke wanted a direct contract was to assure that his representatives would have the finished art to offer publishers even if he died. Harry Clarke's *Dracula*, like the vampire itself, would likely be condemned to a postmortem life. To Florence Stoker, any "irregular" arrangement was simply a calculated ruse. But Clarke knew that book commissions didn't come quickly, especially in the current economy. There couldn't be a worse time for business propositions of any kind than October 1929. The London Stock Exchange had already crashed in September, and the terrifying week-long tumble of Wall Street, culminating in the "Black Tuesday" of October 29, was already brewing in New York.

Florence never agreed to the edition de luxe, which must be considered one of the great tragedies in the history of book illustration. But it is also difficult to imagine Clarke creating drawings that Florence would approve, especially given the psychosexual extremes of his later work, and his determination to please himself. He had no experience having to please

---

[4] The blended surnames of the agency's principals, Sharman and Middleton.

living authors, much less their difficult estates. At least Goethe, Poe, and Huysmans were all dead. Stoker would be tricky, given the especially cantankerous personality of his widow. In the case of *Nosferatu*, Florence evidenced no use, interest, or sympathy for the aims or importance of German Expressionism. Here, Clarke's undisputed reputation as the artistic heir of Beardsley, the prestige of his Poe and *Faust* editions, his election to the Royal Hibernian Academy—all meant nothing. Although she treasured her signed edition of Wilde's *Salome*, with the Beardsley illustrations considered so scandalous in their time, it didn't occur to her that a Clarke edition of *Dracula* might similarly elevate the fame of her husband's book. Who was Harry Clarke? She knew nothing about the comparisons to Beardsley, and at least Oscar Wilde wanted to marry her. Finally, given her incapacitated vision at the time of Clarke's approach, it is difficult to know how she could possibly approve drawings or even conceptual sketches.

The sun, rest, and diet regimen in Davos had no effect on Clarke's health. He returned to Dublin to throw himself into work, or at least to try. Clarke's agents finally did secure him a contract to illustrate *À rebours* for an American publishing house in Chicago, but by July 1930 he had to inform all concerned that it was not going to be possible for him to meet the January deadline, and he urged the publisher, Argus, to find another artist. This was done, but in the end, the crashed economy caused publication to be canceled. Desperately sick, the artist was encouraged to return to the sunny Alps from dreary Dublin. After four months he only sickened more. Wanting to end his days at home, he set off for Ireland but only got as far as the small Swiss village of Coire, where he died on January 6, 1931, and was buried.

It is usually reported that Florence Stoker sold the screen rights to *Dracula* to Universal Pictures for $40,000, which is a bit of a factoid. In reality, she split the proceeds with Deane and Balderston—Florence received $20,000, and each playwright received $10,000, minus agency commissions. Universal acquired the rights not just to the book but to the West End and Broadway scripts, as well as a briefly produced adaptation by an actor/playwright named Charles Morrell that Florence owned outright. In today's currency, the total amount paid by Universal for *Dracula* would be well over half a million dollars.

The driving force behind horror movies at Universal was Carl Laemmle Jr., who had been given the reins of the studio as a twenty-first-birthday present and scored a major success with the studio's "superproduction" *All Quiet on the Western Front* in 1930. As a teenager he had idolized Lon Chaney, and had seen him working at Universal for *The Hunchback of Notre Dame* (1923) and *The Phantom of the Opera* (1925), wearing his legendary, self-created makeups. "He loved everything macabre," according to his cousin, the actress and dancer Carla Laemmle,[5] who also observed "the Man of a Thousand Faces" acting in *Hunchback*. At least some of Carl Jr.'s morbid fixations could be traced to his legendary hypochrondria. He was a dwarfish man fearful of disease and mortality, and it's not surprising that the classic horror movies he developed had the recurrent theme of cheating death.

Under the supervision of the scenario department head, Richard Schayer, the studio developed a number of treatments and scripts by several writers, all attempting in their own ways to reconcile a problematic original novel with a proven stage adaptation. The results (including the finished film) were all clumsily handled, but there were a number of interesting moments that went unproduced. The most elaborate treatment, by the novelist Louis Bromfield, ran fifty pages and included more dialogue than is customary in a treatment. It made the most of key moments from Stoker, especially Dracula crawling down the wall of his castle, and the graphic staking of Lucy, complete with her bloodcurdling "wild cry." Both would ultimately be jettisoned, the latter if only to avoid censorship. Bromfield also included opportunities for special makeup effects, likely because Universal thought it might woo Lon Chaney—Junior Laemmle even dreamed of putting him under personal contract. It was all pretty much an adolescent fantasy about owning his favorite movie star as a pet, but nonetheless he put Universal's contract department to work on offers for Chaney to star in *Dracula* as well as a talking sequel to *The Phantom of the Opera*. The idea of Chaney playing a dual role in *Dracula*—presumably the vampire and Van Helsing—was briefly floated; the director, Tod Browning, had used Chaney in his *Dracula*-inspired *London after Midnight*

---

[5] Carl Jr. was born Julius, and Carla's birth name was Rebekah. They both changed their names in tribute to Carl Laemmle Sr. Carla, who died in June 2014 at the age of 104, was one of the longest-living links to the Universal Studios horror tradition. In *Dracula*, she had the distinction of speaking the first words of dialogue in the studio's first horror talkie: "Among the rugged peaks that frown down upon the Borgo Pass are found crumbling castles of a bygone age."

(1927), playing both a seeming vampire and the detective who unravels the costumed crime.

Had Chaney actually played the part (never a realistic proposition, for many reasons other than the most serious one: he had developed terminal lung cancer), it is a safe bet the actor would have incorporated Dracula's metamorphosing wall-crawl, much in the manner he scaled cathedral bricks in *The Hunchback of Notre Dame*. As for his makeup, Bromfield included a sidebar in his treatment: "In his unnatural unearthly manifestations the Count De Ville [the too-cute-by-half alias was actually Stoker's, from the novel] assumes the wolfish appearance of Dracula. His eyes grow dilated and his canine teeth appear to grow much longer." Gruesome details such as these grew scarcer and scarcer, and in the final shooting script by Garrett Fort and Dudley Murphy, with an unbilled assist from Browning, the last remaining script reference to fangs (during Dracula's deadly sea voyage) was just ignored.

Bela Lugosi was not the studio's first, second, or even third choice for the title role. After Chaney, the tough-guy screen actor Chester Morris and the Shakespearean stage specialist Ian Keith were seriously considered. But in the end, the cost-saving dynamic of Lugosi's stage casting was repeated, and he accepted Universal's flat offer of $500 a week for seven weeks' production. The title-role salary was one of the smaller line items in the film's $355,000 budget. It was the beginning of a career full of poor business choices for Lugosi, whose identification with Dracula was so powerful it would severely limit the future roles he was offered. Lugosi's personal Dracula curse would be one of the worst imaginable—the impossibility to ever really profit from an iconic performance that would earn others millions. Lugosi's well-publicized descent into drug addiction, with a valiant brief recovery in 1955 followed within a year by an impoverished death and theatrically fetishistic black-cape burial, only accentuated the sense of Bram Stoker's creation intruding into the real world as a life-draining hex.

"The cutting-room floor" is another perennial curse in Hollywood, and among the unseen elements and artifacts from Browning's *Dracula* are more than ten minutes of studio cuts that were never preserved in negative or positive. Fortunately, in the early days of talking pictures, before dubbing was practical, Hollywood simultaneously produced many of its films in foreign languages. The Spanish-language *Dracula*, directed by George

Melford, starring Carlos Villarias and Lupita Tovar, used the entire shoot-ing script and gives us a reliable sense of what is lost from the Browning version, including several outtakes from the English-language film. While Melford's production is usually praised as being technically superior, the English-language film is far more effective in presenting Dracula as a mesmeric presence. Where Lugosi unnerved audiences with a motionless stare, Villarias mugged and rolled his eyes. Horror aficionados continue to debate the merits of both versions of the film. While the overall pacing of the Browning version is sluggish—the director never really adapted to the demands of talkies—the Spanish film, produced on a shoestring, still conveys an endearing energy of the hey-kids-let's-put-on-a-show variety. The producer, Paul Kohner, had been Carl Laemmle Sr.'s protégé and was still smarting at the unexpected ascendancy of Carl Jr. Kohner had coveted *Dracula* as his own prestige project and had favored Conrad Veidt for the title role. He was also in love with his ingenue star, Tovar, and treated the Spanish *Dracula* as a personal showcase for her, with many artistic touches that only hint at what he could have accomplished with the main produc-tion if it hadn't been snatched away.

The onset of the Depression coincided with the preparation of *Dracula* and primed 1931 audiences for cultural rituals that might exorcise their deepest fears. *Dracula* filled the bill admirably, if unexpectedly. In the silent era, spooky dealings in Hollywood films usually had a criminal causation. But the advertising campaign for *Dracula* included a tag line that signaled the arrival of unabashedly fantastic themes in American entertainment: NO DETECTIVES! NO TRAP DOORS!

A few months after the film's New York debut, Florence Stoker attended a London screening of *Dracula* with her granddaughter, Ann, who in 1979 remembered it as a fussed-over affair (it was likely a trade screening and not a public premiere) but had no clear memories of the movie itself. Whatever Florence thought, she never made a comment for the record, and appar-ently none privately, even to her son, who could not recall whether she ever saw the film.

While *Dracula* was being filmed at Universal at the end of 1930, Horace Liveright was also in Hollywood, and making a fool of himself.

He had signed a quitclaim to any rights to the film sale, having already lost his license to produce *Dracula* onstage because of paltry royalties owed to Florence. He had already been eased out of his almost bankrupt publishing firm, brought to near-ruin by continued wild spending and imprudent investments, and it all came to a halt with the stock market crash. In the wake of the crash he had accepted a position at Paramount, ostensibly to develop films based on books in the Boni & Liveright catalog. He had sold the rights to Theodore Dreiser's *An American Tragedy* to Paramount a few years before (for $90,000, then reneged on most of the share he had promised to Liveright, throwing a cup of coffee in the publisher's face to boot), but the studio's efforts to produce the film with Sergei Eisenstein at the helm were scuttled amid allegations of the Russian director's perceived anti-Americanism. Liveright ended up spending salaried time rancorously demanding more money for Dreiser and himself, arguing that Paramount had purchased the silent film rights only and needed to pay again for a talkie.[6] When it finally did, Dreiser refused to give the publisher anything, but Liveright further insisted upon, and received, an additional $4,000 directly from the studio.

It was hardly surprising that his six-month trial contract was not extended.

Perhaps Dracula could come to his aid again. After all, each did have a terrible thirst. And to hell with Florence Stoker. He didn't need her permission to remind the world who was responsible for bringing the Count to Broadway and ultimately to Hollywood.

Only weeks before Paramount let him go, Liveright had a studio photographer take new publicity photos of him, so eerily lit there could be no doubt that this man had something masterful to do with mystery and horror. The effect was unintentionally enhanced by the cumulative ravages of smoking and alcohol clearly visible on his face. He was not yet fifty, yet looked in his sixties. He finagled his way onto the Universal lot in the San Fernando Valley and managed to stand before a large-format still camera on the curving staircase of Carfax Abbey, smiling proudly at a costumed Bela Lugosi and flanked by director Browning and screenwriter Murphy.

---

[6] Paramount ultimately did produce a talkie version of *An American Tragedy* in 1931, directed by Josef von Sternberg, but it flopped badly. Exactly twenty years later the studio remade it as *A Place in the Sun*, starring Elizabeth Taylor and Montgomery Clift, and directed by George Stevens. This time it was a tremendous hit.

Horace Liveright congratulates Bela Lugosi and Tod Browning on the set of Universal's **Dracula** *in late 1930.* (Courtesy of Ronald V. Borst / Hollywood Movie Posters)

Browning and Liveright would have had much in common to talk about, had they been so inclined. Aside from their shared interest in *Dracula*, and their mutual fondness for liquor, they both were carnivalesque showmen who knew enough about Sigmund Freud to spin serious money out of his theories. They were both self-made men who, in their own ways, would both unmake themselves by way of the bottle. The conversation would have been fascinating.

Liveright's visit to Universal City had another objective. Before he left New York, he had offended and alienated John Balderston and Hamilton Deane in a sputtering attempt to bring Deane's British production of *Frankenstein* to Broadway. The theme of the Mary Shelley story, as written by Peggy Webling and rewritten by Balderston, only exacerbated Liveright's tendency toward Promethean overreaching. Balderston's wife was alarmed

by a telegram she had received: HORACE ASKS EXTENSION OPTION BELIEVING
UNIVERSAL WILL BACK PRODUCTION BUY FILM HIMSELF PERSONALLY DIRECT-
ING. Indeed, the Laemmles had announced their intention to start devel-
oping screen properties onstage. But whatever appeal the broken-down
Liveright made to Carl Laemmle Jr. may have convinced Paramount exec-
utives that they might be better off staying clear of the Great White Way
entirely. Instead, they bought the screen rights directly from Balderston,
Deane, and Webling, avoiding any stage venture.

Liveright, who had midwifed the stage and screen careers of the two
most famous monsters of all time, returned to New York, right around
the time *Dracula* had its world premiere at the massive Roxy Theatre on
February 12, 1931. The long lines of patrons, especially impressive in the
dead of a New York winter, presaged the phenomenal box office the film
would enjoy in city after city. If Liveright saw the film, he bought his own
ticket. He was shockingly gaunt; with a shaved head and a little nose putty
he could have passed as Max Schreck in *Nosferatu*. He certainly frightened
people away. It had become unbearable to listen to his fantastic plans for
Broadway plays and new publishing ventures that everyone but Liveright
understood would never be.

He continued to live far beyond his means, maintaining a penthouse
apartment on West Fifty-eighth Street with an extraordinary view of the
Manhattan skyline. Inevitably, and not for the first time since he returned
to New York, he was evicted. Barred from removing his belongings, including his clothes and all of his treasured pictures and mementos, he told a
party of visitors to leave with as many of his autographed books—presentation volumes from writers like Hemingway, Pound, and O'Neill—as they
could successfully conceal on their persons. Afterward, with the help of an
unknown number of drinking companions, he flew into a whiskey-fueled
rage. As described by his biographer Dardis, friends who examined the
apartment two days later "found a scene of near-total destruction: all of
Horace's favorite photos of the authors he had published over the years
were lying torn to bits or trampled on the floor. Their frames had been
smashed; broken glass littered the floor. Nearly all the furniture in the
suite had been destroyed."

When he left the ruined penthouse, Liveright was wearing a blue
serge suit with cuffs so frayed he touched them up with ink and hoped
no one would notice. *Dracula* and *Frankenstein* had helped Universal stave
off bankruptcy, but power to advance Liveright's fortunes had evaporated

like a vampire in the daylight. The dark gods had abandoned him, and a decade of Faustian dissipation would finally have its due. Over the next year and a half, he would be repeatedly hospitalized, at least once for acute alcoholism, and once more for emphysema. Pneumonia was a common and dangerous outcome for both conditions. With his lungs failing and his money depleted, he was no longer able to hold court at the Algonquin, or anywhere else. Amid the sounds of the demolition by dynamite of the neighborhood that had once been home to the Boni & Liveright town house and all the speakeasies that surrounded it—room was being made for the new Rockefeller Center—Horace Liveright died shabbily in a West Fifty-first Street apartment hotel on September 25, 1933. He was forty-eight years old.

Vincent Leonard Price Jr., a twenty-four-year-old student from Yale continuing his art history studies at London's Courtauld Institute in 1935, had been born to a well-to-do St. Louis family in 1911. He had nothing in his background or interests to predict his becoming world-famous as an superstar of cinematic terror. Only four years later he would make his first onscreen appearance with Boris Karloff, in Universal's *Tower of London* (1939). But fright films didn't interest him at all in 1935, even though it was a banner year for classic chills onscreen, including such gems as James Whale's *Bride of Frankenstein*, Karl Freund's *Mad Love*, and Tod Browning's *Dracula*-inspired *Mark of the Vampire*. Therefore, it came as a complete surprise when Vincent Price was invited, one memorable afternoon, to take tea with the real-life bride of Dracula.

Price's good friend Stanley Dunn worked in British publishing and was useful at making social introductions in London's literary and artistic circles. He arranged an invitation for Price to visit Florence Stoker at Kinnerton Studios, in the company of three much older men. The first, R. B. Cunninghame Graham, was a politician, journalist, and longtime friend of Oscar Wilde, who exchanged letters with him before and after prison, and who wrote one of the most sympathetic appraisals of *De Profundis* when it was published as a book in 1905.[7] Next was Axel Munthe,

---

[7] From Cunninghame Graham's rambling, though worshipful, review: "His joy of life, and all the sufferings which to such a man those two fell years must have entailed, speak for him to us,

the Swiss psychologist and humanitarian, one of the first persons to extend hospitality to Wilde after his release from Reading Gaol, entertaining Wilde and Lord Alfred Douglas at his estate on the Isle of Capri after they had been turned away at a hotel. Also present was A. F. Tschiffley, the world-famous "long rider" who made a celebrated ten-thousand-mile trek on horseback from Buenos Aires to New York in 1925–28. Tschiffley had no personal connection to Wilde but was a close friend of both Cunninghame Graham and Munthe.

In 1989, Price recalled, in correspondence with this author, his visit to Florence's compact but nonetheless "fabulous" Knightsbridge home. "Among her treasures were portraits by Wilde, Burne-Jones, Rossetti—and all her books were signed by the great artists and literati of her lifetime." He remembered her as "quite beautiful" for her age (then seventy-six), "very petite" and "nearly blind." Overall, he found her "very dear—I felt I'd stepped into a most romantic past." In 1935 he had written to his parents in St. Louis, offering more detail: "All over the house there are the most wonderful things. . . . Oscar Wilde was one of her closest friends and gave her the only watercolor of his that he ever thought good enough to keep. And it is lovely, though more interesting than beautiful." (Florence would later tell her sister Philippa Knott, "Oscar's little water-colour creates much envy in the breasts of the Oscar cult.")

One piece of art Price did not mention was the beautiful Walter Frederick Osborne 1897 portrait of Florence that had been displayed at the Royal Academy at the height of the Wilde scandal. No living member of the Stoker family knows what happened to it, and it was not specifically mentioned in her will. It may well have been sold in the difficult last years of Bram's life, along with the Osborne portraits of Charlotte and Abraham, which similarly cannot be traced.[8] If it is true that Florence refused to be photographed after the age of forty (just about the time she sat for Osborne), there is also the possibility that a reverse Dorian Gray dynamic took hold,

---

asking us now, after his death, to pardon, and when we speak of him, to call him by his name, to make no mystery of his fall, and to regard him as a star, which looking at its own reflection in some dank marsh, fell down and smirched itself, and then became extinct ere it had time to soar aloft again."

[8] Osborne died at the age of forty-four in 1902, before reaching his full artistic potential, but nonetheless has attained the status of one of Ireland's most collectible Impressionist/Post-Impressionist painters. More than one of his canvases has commanded over $1 million at auction.

Left: When Vincent Price met Florence Stoker in 1935, he was an art student and photographer's model in London. Right: Price as Oscar Wilde in the one-man show **Diversions and Delights** *(1977).*

making it easier for her to relinquish a never-aging portrait that became less attractive to its subject as she herself aged, even if both her son and Vincent Price described her as agelessly beautiful. Writing of "Mrs. Bram" (as she was called in Victorian London and still called in 1935), Price marveled at her "spark," her "lovely sense of humor," and, best of all, the fact that "she is very fond of me and has asked me again."

Memories of the 1935 close encounter with four people who had known Wilde so intimately served the actor well in 1997 when he starred in a one-man show within a one-man show, John Gay's *Diversions and Delights*, about Wilde's grim last days in Paris, performed around the world and on Broadway. The script employs the invented device of an impoverished Oscar reduced to selling his own notoriety for morbidly curious, eager-to-pay audiences, in a shabby little lecture hall. In the first act, in the persona of his Gothic alter ego Sebastian Melmoth and all the while sipping absinthe, Price lovingly caressed vintage Wilde bon mots; in the darker second act, an undisguised Oscar recounted his fall and living damnation, drawing upon emotionally affecting passages from *De Profundis*.

Despite her promise of a return invitation, the actor never saw Florence Stoker again. Colon cancer had already taken silent hold of her. One of the insidious things about the long-gestating disease, especially in an era before routine screenings, is that when symptoms appear it is often too late for treatment. In the 1930s there was no chemotherapy, and no antibiotics to follow surgery even if surgery was attempted. Diagnosis was often a short-notice death sentence. As in mid-nineteenth-century Dublin, the most useful palliative was still opium, in the newer incarnation of morphine.

During her last months on earth Florence could not dismiss Oscar Wilde from her mind. The flame had likely been rekindled about a decade before, when Ellen Terry, very near her own end, came across an 1881 letter from Wilde in a batch of correspondence she was otherwise busy destroying. She sent the letter to Florence, accompanied by a note in her faltering hand, saying, "By rights this belongs to you." Oscar had written to his "Nellie," wishing her the best on the first-night performance of Tennyson's *The Cup*, in which Florence appeared in the chorus.

> I send you some flowers—two crowns. Will you accept one of them, whichever you think will suit you best. The other—don't think me treacherous, Nellie—but the other please give to Florrie *from yourself*. I should like to think that she was wearing something of mine that first night she comes on the stage, that anything of mine should touch her. Of course if you think—but you won't think she will suspect? How could she?

The letter, previously unknown to Florence, closed with two extraordinary lines, expressing a sentiment from the grave she was now receiving for the first time: *"She thinks I never loved her, thinks I forget. My God how could I?"*

In the last months of her life she wrote to her sister, praising the 1936 book *Aspects of Wilde* by Vincent O'Sullivan ("the best book I've read on poor O"). O'Sullivan, much like Cunninghame Graham, had known Wilde well and personally paid his travel costs for the famous postprison reunion with Bosie in Naples. Curious enough, O'Sullivan was also a writer of macabre fiction whom Wilde felt was too stuck in "the standpoint of the tomb" (an estimation quickly confirmed by even a cursory look at his truly morbid writings). A year before *Dracula*, a collection of his short fiction included

(along with a frontispiece by Aubrey Beardsley) a story of psychic vampirism entitled "Will," in which a man drains the life energy from his hated
wife through mental concentration. The dead wife returns the favor by
coming back as a stinking beetle and dragging him to her grave, reclaiming enough of her stolen vitality to restore her corpse to beauty, if not to
life. The husband is left a decayed husk in a story about the supernatural
transference of corruption that immediately brings to mind the climax
of *Dorian Gray*. Since O'Sullivan lived in London, and was much admired
by Florence, it is more than just possible he was part of the "Oscar cult"
himself.

Another Stoker family acquaintance who certainly deserved cult mem-
bership, or at least an invitation, was Hester Travers Smith, the society
spiritualist who claimed extensive postmortem conversations with Wilde.
Her *Oscar Wilde from Purgatory*, also known as *Psychic Messages from Oscar
Wilde* (1924), made quite a splash during the period when England was
still processing the cataclysmic grief brought on by World War I, and the
book's claims were given a surprising amount of credence. The *Times
Literary Supplement* gave it a special endorsement, believing that Wilde's
postmortem pronouncements would "not be out of place in any selection
of his acknowledged writings." Spiritualism had been made respectable by
such prominent friends of the Stokers as Sir Arthur Conan Doyle, and as
the daughter of Bram's Trinity College mentor Edward Dowden, Hester
had been part of the Stoker social circle for quite some time. The question is not so much whether Florence approached Hester for an ethereal
reunion with her onetime swain, but rather how she could have passed up
the opportunity.

One of the last and most intriguing things we know about Florence is
her end-of-life desire to meet Oscar Wilde's surviving son, Vyvyan Holland,
whom she had known as a boy in Chelsea. When Florence met the brother
of Oscar's intimate friend Robbie Ross, and learned he was still in touch
with Vyvyan, she begged him for a meeting. Frankly, Cyril might have been
more reachable by Ouija board than Vyvyan in person. His connection to
the Wilde name and the difficult childhood that resulted left him painfully shy and reticent, and he didn't even begin talking openly about his
father until the end of World War II. His memoir, *Son of Oscar Wilde*, did
not appear until 1954. "I wanted him to come and see me, being so fond
of his Father, but he never turned up," Florence lamented. In any case, a

meeting might have been awkward. Did she want to show him the portrait, the letters? Nobody, except perhaps her sister, knew about Wilde's Dublin letters in her lifetime, much less the broken courtship. And what did Noel Stoker, her real son, make of her sudden avid interest in Vyvyan Holland, that elusive "son" that never was? Or the fixation on Wilde himself? Was that what the Catholic pretensions were all about, all along? Some fantastic, "aesthetic" union, finally blessed by the Church of Rome? And where and what was he, Noel, in all this—some repulsive changeling child to be discarded and replaced?

' As much as Edgar Allan Poe believed "there is no more poetical topic in the world than the death of a beautiful woman," the poet who might shed a more poignant light on the widow's end is John Greenleaf Whittier in his famous observation, "Of all sad words of tongue or pen, the saddest are these: 'It might have been.'"

Noel never said anything on the record concerning his mother's death, much less her life, her anger, her regrets, or her unrealized dreams. He would have known these all by heart. When he was a boy, she made it clear he was more acceptable seen than heard, and he took her instruction literally. But however quiet he remained on the subject of his mother, Florence could not have been an easy patient, or parent, with whom to deal in her final months. People whose lives have centered around extraordinary beauty rarely accept the physical assaults and indignities of terminal illness gracefully.

Florence Stoker died on May 25, 1937, at home in Knightsbridge. Even though she had lost heavily on American investments at the beginning of the Depression, her total estate was valued at £20,000—today the equivalent of nearly $2 million.[9] In the end, owing to the fortuitous film sale and steady worldwide royalties on the book and stage play, Dracula had proved to be a guardian devil indeed.

Two days after her death, at ten in the morning (the time was recorded, but not the names of the persons in attendance), she was cremated at Golders Green—despite the Catholic Church's then-adamant opposition to the practice, which it considered to be an affront to its doctrine of

---

[9] In addition to whatever money Florence realized from the sale of the Stokers' Chelsea leasehold, a bequest of £1,000 from Thornley would also have begun earning significant interest, especially in the economic gallop of the 1920s. Nonetheless, Florence always resented the fact that Thornley had left a much larger amount to his end-of-life female companion, and not to her.

the resurrection of the body at the Last Judgment. There is no evidence Florence ever renounced her adopted faith—a canonical impossibility, the only recognized means of egress being excommunication. Once received into the Church, you belonged to the Church, and it could dispose of your soul any way it saw fit. She never lost interest in attending the fashionable services at the Brompton Oratory. And why would she? If Oscar Wilde's transgressive flirtations with Catholicism at the same time he flirted with her had been titillating at an impressionable age, how could she forget his later, fashion-conscious declaration that there was simply *no* other church in which to die?

Even when Rome loosened its objections to cremation, decades later, it remained a strict requirement that ashes at least be buried in hallowed ground. "Cremation is not and cannot be Christian burial" was the official Catholic position from the Victorian era until the 1960s. According to the London-based publication *The Month: A Catholic Magazine and Review*, "The Christian hatred of the funeral pile was a practical and intelligible protest against the teaching of paganism respecting the final destiny of the body. If such a protest was needed [by the early Church] it is needed none the less in the present day, when a modern paganism threatens to revive the vices, the ideas, the customs, the scepticism of the past and looks for its ideal to a purely Pagan civilization."

Golders Green is a secular crematorium and memorial site, its grounds unconsecrated. Nonetheless, her son scattered Florence's ashes in the garden outside the columbarium that housed his father's cremains.[10] The Stokers' beloved, longtime cook and retainer, Maria Mitchell, who had continued to look after the widow, was given a niche near her master. Florence, his wife, was not.

Burning a body and/or denying its burial in hallowed ground was also a time-honored ritual in the elimination of vampires. In the real world, it was an effective last rebuke or insult to dead persons who had been particularly difficult or unpleasant in life. Bram Stoker's stone urn had a blank panel on its reverse, customarily used for the names of the partner first

[10] One family-friendly biographer has stated, without documentation, that the scattering was at Florence's instructions. This is highly unlikely—except, perhaps, as a final declaration of independence and estrangement from her husband? None of the principals can speak, but from any perspective from which one might analyze the situation, someone resents someone in a rancorous end-of-life story of familial dysfunction.

deceased and then the spouse. Noel decided that it would be he, and not his mother, who would spend eternity with the creator of *Dracula*.

If Florence's idea of eternity included an ethereal reunion with Oscar Wilde, her disappointment was foreordained. The only biographies published in her lifetime all reported, reassuringly, that Wilde's dying wish was to be received by the Church, and that his wish was granted at the last possible moment. She didn't know that he was baptized delirious if not unconscious, or understand that the eccentric, flippant, ambivalent, and even blasphemous things he believed about the faith would disqualify him as a candidate for conversion—the idea, for instance, that heaven and hell had no existence outside the body. He could hardly be expected to greet her in the former. Much like his mother, he was, at best, a candidate for the designation of "cafeteria Catholic," had the term then existed or been in any way an official option. And it's debatable whether Florence ever was a "good" Catholic, or was merely going through the motions as a deluded gesture to the suitor who got away. At best, her soul was left to wander the eternal night in an ambiguous state of undeath; at worst, she would never be gazed upon or flattered by Oscar Wilde again.

Unknown to Florence or Noel Stoker, Universal Pictures had reduced Dracula himself to ashes just the previous year. In one of the opening scenes of *Dracula's Daughter* (1936), set in a misty clearing in an English woods, a woman in a cowled black cape held a crucifix over a body on a ceremonial pyre.

> Into the keeping of the lords of the flames of the lower pit, I consign this body, to be evermore consumed in their purging fire. Let all baleful spirits that threaten the souls of men be banished by the sprinkling of this salt. Be thou exorcised, O Dracula, and thy body long undead find destruction throughout eternity in the name of thy dark, unholy master. In the name of the all-holiest, and through this cross, be the evil spirit cast out until the end of time.

Initially, the studio did not want to dispose of Dracula, but in the end it was the only option available. Joseph Breen, head of the Motion Picture Producers and Distributors of America, the industry's self-policing censorship office, had made it clear that in the age of a reenergized Production Code (the industry guide to onscreen conduct, previously mostly winked at), the character of Dracula—an unseemly admixture of sexual predation and death—was now too objectionable and unrepentant to star in a film, though a contrite and conflicted vampire's daughter might be morally tolerable.

Despite the studio's ownership of the screen rights to the novel *Dracula*, the film *Dracula's Daughter* came to Universal by an extremely circuitous and convoluted route. In 1933, for a flat price of $5,000, Florence had sold the rights to the story "Dracula's Guest," which included an intriguing encounter with a female vampire, directly to a Hollywood producer who, as far as she knew, was independent of any studio. In fact, David O. Selznick was working for MGM and had just finished production of the star-studded *Grand Hotel*. But his name then was hardly a household word, and Florence would never live to see *Gone with the Wind*. Selznick had personally bought the rights to the story as a private citizen of Los Angeles after MGM's attorneys cautioned him that it might be legally hazardous for Metro to attempt to produce a sequel to Universal's *Dracula*.

Universal's surviving negotiation and legal files on *Dracula* have never been made public; all that has been so far accessed is the studio's correspondence with the agent for Florence Stoker, John L. Balderston, and Hamilton Deane, and Balderston's marvelously chatty reports on the negotiations. Balderston found the finished film disappointing, and after little of his material for *Return of Frankenstein* (released in 1935 as *Bride of Frankenstein*) was appreciated or used, he happily provided rival producer Selznick a treatment for *Dracula's Daughter*—a problematic concept brimming with sexual sadism.

Whether Selznick really intended to produce the film or just profitably resell his rights to Stoker's short story "Dracula's Guest" to Universal is not known, but he made good on the latter gambit. Carl Laemmle Jr. turned the project over to the director James Whale, who hoped he would be finished with horror films after *Bride of Frankenstein*. In collaboration with R. C. Sherriff, who also scripted Whale's *The Invisible Man* (1933), he helped craft a script so outrageous it would never interfere with projects he really cared about, most specifically a musical version of Edna Ferber's *Show Boat*, realized in 1936.

In his autobiography, *No Leading Lady*, Sherriff doesn't even acknowledge his substantial work on multiple drafts of the project, perhaps understanding the whole thing as a joke or delaying gambit for Whale, and not a serious script. Whale had entertained himself with an extended game of cat-and-mouse with the censors over *Bride of Frankenstein* and knew how to play them for time.

The script has been the object of much speculation but only recently has been made public. Sherriff's narrative is obviously written with Lugosi in mind (and the studio used Lugosi's image prominently in trade announcements), but it is the actor's contemporaneous, torture-minded turn as Dr. Vollin in Universal's *The Raven* (1935) rather than *Dracula* that Sherriff seems to anticipate. Although Dracula is described as being clad completely in black, as per Stoker's description, Sherriff never mentions a cape. Think of Lugosi's Roxor in *Chandu the Magician* (1932), minus the turban. The reader can almost hear Bela's familiar, purring cadences as the proposed scenes unfold.

"You have eaten my food, dear friends—you have drunk my wine and honoured a lonely man in his lonely Castle with your innocent gaiety and delicate jokes," Dracula tells his gluttonous guests, decadent aristocrats from all over Europe. "In return I've prepared for each of you a little dish gathered freshly from the fields this very morning." In reality, he has kidnapped young women from their beds. "I wouldn't like to see these delicate morsels damaged before they are eaten." The guests throw dice to pick their prizes. But the fiancé of one of the victims has smuggled himself into the castle and is seized by Dracula's men.

"There's no need for my little girl to be afraid," Dracula assures the girl, who now commands special interest. "Your lover will come to you, and you will be together again. . . . He will come to you and place his strong arm around you; you will be together again, husband and wife—and I shall adopt you as a daughter. Doesn't it thrill that fluttering little heart? Dracula's daughter!"

She is taken to a room where a male figure in Arabian robes appears. He raises a hand, and she recognizes his engagement ring. She runs to him—and pulls away a hacked-off arm. Dracula throws off his disguise. In Sherriff's description, "The girl, as if fighting a terrible nightmare, gazes round. Her lover's severed arm still hangs over her shoulder—it drops down between her back and the cushion of the couch when she moves—and the hand sticks up like a drowning soldier's from the sea." Dracula has kept his promise: "The strong arm of your lover has come to comfort you," he purrs.

Dracula's crimes prompt the outraged townsfolk to retain the services of a wizard named Talifer—a role believed to have been written with Boris Karloff in mind—who confronts Dracula and his debauchers and curses them magically down the evolutionary ladder:

> The CAMERA focuses on the terrified Baron—his bulbous eyes shrink up—his nose broadens—his fat arms shrink within their sleeves—and sitting at the table—ridiculous in the rich robes of the Baron Heydendorf—sits a great grunting hog that struggles and squeals in terror.

Others become monkeys, snakes and spiders, even a toad. But for Dracula Talifer saves a special kind of punishment—to be trapped forever between the human and animal realms as a bloodthirsty vampire.

Then, as if the already grotesque spectacle is not enough, comes the final flourish, perhaps inspired by *Great Expectations*:

> The CAMERA sweeps down the long table. A moment previously it has been lavishly set with dishes of food—fine decorations and magnificent ornaments—but as the CAMERA moves over it, everything crumbles to hideous decay. Great dust-hung cobwebs cling to the dishes—the fruit crumbles into black dirt—a boar's head falls to a whitened skull; through the cobwebs creeps the giant Spider, and upon a tattered napkin sits the great impassive toad. . . . The CAMERA moves swiftly as the Great Hall disintegrates: we see the magnificent tapestries crumble and the stately curtains that cover the windows drip into rags. The walls themselves crumble and the roof falls in with a sudden crash.

Dracula flies to the traumatized girl and, as a vampire bat, seroconverts her into eternal undeath. For the balance of the film, Sherriff cleverly inverts the original Stoker plot and characters: Dracula's blood-adopted daughter travels to London, where she invades the lives of two male friends, one of whom grows hysterical and weak under her predation, but ultimately turns against her and destroys her during a sea voyage back to Transylvania.

Dracula's backstory amounted to a third of Sherriff's script.

Unfortunately, it was also the most cinematic material, and its removal for the censors was effectively the death knell for the production. James Whale went on to his triumphant production of *Show Boat*, and a completely new version of *Dracula's Daughter* was concocted by the screenwriter Garrett Fort and involved the quasi-lesbian Countess Zaleska (her name likely inspired by Sherriff's Countess Szelinski), who burns the staked body of her father at the beginning of the film. Lambert Hillyer ultimately directed the production, and Bela Lugosi was paid for the use of a dummy in his likeness for the cremation scene.

As played by Gloria Holden, Zaleska epitomized a certain ambiguous look and demeanor (dark, soignée, with features more strikingly handsome than conventionally beautiful) associated with the lesbian literary and artistic circles of the Left Bank in the twenties and thirties—the kind of woman usually referred to as "bohemian," "unconventional," or, with characteristic euphemism, "very private." Holden bore a rather striking resemblance to Dolly Wilde, Oscar's lesbian niece, the longtime lover of Natalie Clifford Barney, an American expatriate writer in Paris whose legendary salon at 20 rue Jacob ran for sixty years and who is usually credited as the inspiration for Radclyffe Hall's *The Well of Loneliness*.

Universal's screenwriter Garrett Fort knew this territory and its personalities. He was well acquainted with the accomplished lesbian playwright but unsuccessful screenwriter Mercedes de Acosta in both New York and Hollywood.[11] (Fort was also a transplanted New York playwright.) The two writers failed together in their attempt to sell a screenplay based on the life of the Indian spiritual master Meher Baba, of whom both were devotees; the project might have had better luck if it had been conceived as a silent film, since Baba had taken a vow of silence and never spoke a word between 1925 and his death in 1969. De Acosta had a highly theatrical persona and was a record-breaking lover to female stars, her serial conquests including Greta Garbo, Marlene Dietrich, Isadora Duncan, and Eva Le Galliene, with many others rumored. As Robert A. Schanke notes in his biography *"That Furious Lesbian": The Story of Mercedes de Acosta*, "Mercedes was notorious for walking the streets of New York in mannish pants, pointed shoes trimmed with buckles, tricorn hat, and cape. Her chalk-white face, deep-set eyes,

---

[11] De Acosta's only Hollywood assignment, for MGM's *Rasputin and the Empress* (1932), went uncredited.

In **Dracula's Daughter**
(1936), the artist
Countess Zaleska (Gloria
Holden) reaches out
to a psychiatrist (Otto
Kreuger) to dispel the
morbid obsessions
reflected in her work.

Mercedes de Acosta, Greta Garbo's legendary lesbian
lover—known by detractors as "Countess Dracula"—
painted by Abram Poole, circa 1923.

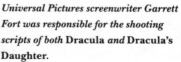

Universal Pictures screenwriter Garrett
Fort was responsible for the shooting
scripts of both **Dracula** *and* **Dracula's**
Daughter.

thin red lips, and jet black hair slicked back with brilliantine prompted Tallulah Bankhead to call her Countess Dracula."

Fort had been the first scenarist to use vampirism as a coded screen signifier of homosexuality in the original *Dracula*,[12] wherein the whole first meeting between Dracula and Renfield at the castle is charged with an air of male-male seduction, culminating in the Count's driving back the approaching female vampires to feast upon Renfield himself (on the floor, no less, crawling atop him in the act). For Fort, Stoker's line "This man is mine!" certainly struck a resonant chord. In 1931, the scene was the closest thing to a male rape ever depicted onscreen.

In a somewhat cryptic studio memo concerning *Dracula's Daughter*, Fort expressed his excitement about the daring psychological approach he was taking with the script, something he was reluctant to completely describe. This, of course, was the equation of vampirism with lesbianism, and a soft-pedaled play for social sympathy paired with the possibility of a psychiatric cure. Although the Breen Office restricted Zaleska's streetwalker-model from posing in the nude, it seems not to have noticed, adorning the wall of her London apartment, a morbidly Impressionistic canvas including a naked woman, which she shows to her psychiatrist, perhaps as a bit of a wink. Like *The Well of Loneliness*, *Dracula's Daughter* finally drew a despairing picture of gay life, but given the still-censorious climate of the 1920s and 1930s, even this was a significant step forward into cultural visibility.

Dracula's Daughter received mostly positive reviews upon its American release, but its London debut was not so welcoming. Although approved for public exhibition by the British Board of Film Censors (BBFC), the film would nonetheless be subject to restricted screenings by local governments. The *Times* reported that the Entertainment Committees of the London, Surrey, and Middlesex County Councils unanimously judged the film as "horrific" in the openly expressed hope that such a judgment would negatively "affect the takings of the cinemas showing it." Lord Tyrell, the BBFC's president, noted that the censor's "horrific" category, introduced in 1934, no longer existed, but ad hoc rulings might be additionally useful in slowing a rising tide of frightening entertainment on British shores. He specifically

---

[12] For a classic discussion of the convoluted strategies used by filmmakers to introduce gay characters and situations in early Hollywood, see Vito Russo, *The Celluloid Closet*, rev. ed. (New York: Harper & Row, 1987).

THE CURSE OF DRACULA 553

deplored "an unnecessary number of films of scenes in hospitals which were too intense in detail and unwholesome in their cumulative effect." Ironically, the hospital scene in *Dracula's Daughter*—in which the streetwalker dies of vampire-induced shock—was insisted upon by American censors as a way of sparing the girl a sex murder directly delivered by Countess Zaleska.

Since his mother was in worsening health, it is hardly surprising Noel Stoker failed to notice the appearance of *Dracula's Daughter* in London in the summer of 1936. Since David O. Selznick had bought the rights to "Dracula's Guest" outright, he was under no obligation to notify Florence about its resale to Universal, its production or nonproduction, or any other development. The following year Noel was approached by the Amalgamated Press, publishers of the popular women's story magazine *The Miracle*, with a proposal to publish an all-new serial called *Dracula's Daughter* by a minor British mystery writer, Walter Tyrer. Noel sought the advice of G. Herbert Thring, who told him there was nothing in the Selznick agreement preventing the licensing of the title for a new work of fiction. Selznick and Universal had separately contracted for motion picture rights and only motion picture rights. Thring cautioned, however, that there could be "serious difficulties" in assigning any motion picture rights to the new story that included characters or situations from *Dracula*.

Noel reached an agreement with Amalgamated Press, with the stipulation that publication be accompanied by a printed disclaimer: "This is a completely new story written especially for Miracle readers. Permission for the use of the title 'Dracula's Daughter' has been granted by the legal representative of the late Bram Stoker, author of 'Dracula.'" The publisher also requested that Tyrer be granted book publication rights as well, and Stoker gave the additional permission based on a 15 percent royalty participation in any book.

At this point the paper trail goes cold, but for some reason the agreement fizzled, and Stoker never bothered to update the Society of Authors about the reasons. Instead of *Dracula's Daughter*, Tyrer published his story in book form as *Jane the Ripper* in 1939. The most likely reason was the Stoker estate's inability to assign valuable motion picture rights. But a Jack the Ripper connection might be equally exploitable, and in the end the rather lazy writer simply took his finished manuscript (about a bloodthirsty serial killer stalking victims in a small English town), deleted every appearance of the words "Dracula's Daughter," and replaced them with "Jane the Ripper."

He made no other edits, leaving in place some giveaway references to night-time attacks and werewolfery, but the poorly written and unbelievably plotted book was not successful and never attracted motion picture interest.

In 1957, a young English journalist named Harry Ludlam had been interested in Bram Stoker and *Dracula* for half a dozen years, ever since he interviewed Bela Lugosi during a 1951 British stage tour of the Deane and Balderston play. As a boy, just before World War II, he had been so frightened by Lugosi at a Middlesex revival screening of 1932's *White Zombie* that he actually walked out of the theatre. The Lugosi he met in his dressing room at the Dudley Hippodrome was more wistful than terrifying. After complaining caustically about the deficiencies of English hotel plumbing, the man who to the entire world was Dracula incarnate told him, "I look into the mirror and I say to myself, 'Can it be that you once played Romeo?' Always it is the same. When a film company is in the red they come to me and say, 'Okay, so we make a horror film.' And so that is what we do. It is what I always do."

Lugosi's death in August 1956 had reawakened Ludlam's fascination with the world's favorite vampire, and he was soon deep into research for a possible biography of Bram Stoker. He was curious about the many references to the extremely close relationship between Stoker and Henry Irving. "A description of them as 'intimate friends' set me wondering," Ludlam wrote in 2000. "I have to remind you that this was the 1950s. Nowadays it seems to be *de rigueur* for 'biographers' to rush to comb through the still warm bed of the deceased for any evidence of sexual yo-ho-ho. I was not into that. I was working at a time many years before homosexuality 'came out' and if there was anything physical between the two men the project was off."

When he finally tracked down Noel Stoker at his accounting firm (Noel stayed in the profession for his entire working life), he was surprised that no one had ever even approached him for information about his father before. Noel worked carefully with Ludlam on the manuscript, though it was understood from the beginning that his main concern was "not to include anything of which my parents would have disapproved." In other words, exactly the things that might be of real interest to a biographer or reader. But at least Ludlam was spared even the possibility of any of that yo-ho-ho being lobbed in his direction by the straitlaced accountant. We don't know exactly what kinds of information Noel withheld, but some of it had to do with Florence. In a letter from Florence's niece Philippa Adams, it is made clear that certain facts about her were deliberately not shared, being of interest only to the family. That letter was not shared with Ludlam, who was overjoyed simply with having access to the family papers and Noel's cooperation. He would not have had a publishable biography otherwise.

The finished book, *A Biography of Dracula: The Life Story of Bram Stoker*, did not find a publisher until 1962, a year after Noel Stoker's death. While groundbreaking in its simple presentation of the outward facts of Bram's life, Ludlam's account maintained the same wall around Stoker's inner life the writer himself had erected. And so little was said about Florence by way of her son that she appeared only as a beautiful, barely glimpsed sphinx.

Throughout the 1940s and 1950s, Dracula's screen appearances were similarly sparse. The king of vampires appeared, usually as a supporting character, in only a handful of films. At the same time, the pocket-sized Armed Forces Edition of *Dracula*, made available to millions of American enlisted men and women in the late 1940s, had an incalculable effect on the book's general popularity after the war. And soon, even as Hollywood was hitching its horror wagon to atomic anxieties and Cold War jitters, filmmakers were taking another look at the original Stoker novel. A particularly intriguing project, proposed but abandoned in the late 1950s, would have featured Boris Karloff as the Count. Karloff reportedly accepted, with the proviso, "Just so long as I don't have to imitate Bela!" However, the idea was swept away in the wake of Hammer Studios' *Horror of Dracula* (1958; UK title: *Dracula*) and the immensely successful franchise starring Christopher Lee that would follow.

Lee had entered film acting following his service in World War II but did not find a niche for his talents until he was cast as the monster in Hammer Films' *Curse of Frankenstein* in 1957, a great success that led to his starring in *Horror of Dracula* the following year.[13] Lee's identification with the part would almost eclipse Lugosi's, and for sheer number of screen assignments as the Count (nine in all, as opposed to Lugosi's two) did just

---

[13] Interestingly enough, when working as a contract player for the Rank Organisation, Lee appeared as a spear carrier in Laurence Olivier's 1949 film version of *Hamlet* in the company of three other actors with important *Dracula* associations: Hamilton Deane, John Laurie (one of Deane's touring stage Draculas), and Peter Cushing, who would go on to become almost as well known as Van Helsing to Hammer audiences as Lee as the Count.

Christopher Lee and Melissa Stribling in **Horror of Dracula** *(1958).*

that. For Lee, the repeated casting was more an irritant than a curse. At the time of this writing, his more than two hundred film appearances make him one of the busiest actors in cinema history. But each of his reincarnations in the role was contentious. As the actor recalled:

> The process went like this: The telephone would ring and my agent would say, "Jimmy Carreras [president of Hammer Films] has been on the phone, they've got another Dracula for you." And I would say, "Forget it! I don't want to do another one." I'd get a call from Jimmy Carreras, in a state of hysteria. "What's all this about?!" "Jim, I don't want to do it, and I don't have to do it." "No, you have to do it!" And I said, "Why?" He replied, "Because I've already sold it to the American distributor with you playing the part. Think of all the people you know so well, that you will put out of work!" Emotional blackmail. That's the only reason I did them.

A good part of Lee's frustration with the part came from his impatience at the fact that script after script veered ever farther from Stoker. After a while he stopped complaining that Hammer was simply throwing away an interesting character given potentially very playable dialogue by the novelist, and agreed to appear in a low-budget Italian/German/Spanish coproduction, *Count Dracula* (1970), directed by Jess Franco, in which Dracula's appearance finally conformed to Stoker's description, and the Count was finally permitted to relate the proud history of the Dracula family in vanquishing the Turks.

In 1972, Shane Briant, a rising British stage actor, was surprised to be approached by Hammer with the offer of a term contract, which, tantalizingly, included the chance to play Bram Stoker in a proposed biographical feature called *Victim of His Imagination*. Two Hammer actors were well suited to play the actor Henry Irving, now widely presumed to be the inspiration for Stoker's vampire: Christopher Lee and Peter Cushing, who had, respectively, played Dracula and Van Helsing in *Horror of Dracula* (and continued to reprise the roles), would have both been splendid in the part, and a graphic depiction of Lee would appear in Hammer's trade announcement of the project. It is possible that Cushing was also initially considered for the role of Stoker before Briant, but the casting details remain maddeningly vague.

Trade advertisement for Hammer Films' unproduced Stoker biopic,
Victim of His Imagination *(1972).*

"How interesting!" Briant told this author in 2010. "I didn't think anyone knew about this proposed film. I was asked to become a Hammer contract player for two years. My agent had talks with Michael Carreras at Hammer and the idea—the incentive/lure—was that I should play the lead in a bio of Bram Stoker. The second proposed film was to be a remake of a non-Gothic classic film—I wish I could remember what it was. I was, you see, unsure at that time whether I wanted to commit to two years of horror films if they were to be run-of-the-mill horrors. I had just been nominated by the London Theatre Critics for Best Newcomer of the Year for my portrayal of the young man in *Children of the Wolf* [1969] at the Apollo in London's West End. Ultimately the lure proved too tempting and I signed for two years. But instead of the films that were proposed, I ended up making *Demons of the Mind, Straight on Till Morning* [both 1972], *Frankenstein and the Monster from Hell*, and *Captain Kronos, Vampire Hunter* [both 1974]. I never saw the Bram Stoker script, I'm afraid, and I was *very* disappointed to be doing *Demons* rather than Bram Stoker." Briant would, however, be given the chance to deliver an impressive Stoker-era performance in the title role of *The Picture of Dorian Gray* (opposite Nigel Davenport as Lord Henry) for the television producer Dan Curtis in 1973.

The *Victim* script Briant never saw (until 2010) was a detailed, twenty-nine-page treatment by Don Houghton, who had just written *Dracula A.D. 1972* and would write and produce *The Satanic Rites of Dracula* (1973) and *Legend of the 7 Golden Vampires* (1974). At the time of the *Victim* project, Houghton had only one Stoker biography to consult: Ludlam's *A Biography of Dracula*. He comes to dramatic and psychological conclusions that are not explicitly drawn by Ludlam but are certainly suggested in the book. Stoker is presented as having suffered from terrifying visions and nightmares since an early age, turning to writing horror stories to exorcise his own demons. Stoker's well-documented adoration of Walt Whitman is elaborated by Houghton into the receipt of creative advice from the American poet, namely, "that BRAM should continue writing, should unload the dark shadows, into his stories and books, thereby cleansing himself of the unknown spectre that haunts him. WHITMAN is certain that BRAM's sanity is not in jeopardy, but it could become so if he allows the nightmare to take control of his mind." Stoker responds by using "every spare moment of his already crowded tour schedule to jot down notes and thoughts for proposed stories and novels."

Shane Briant as Dorian Gray (1974).

The exercise only exhausts him; back in London, lovemaking with his wife is aborted when Florence Stoker's caressing fingers melt into hideous, writhing worms. In an aside, Houghton notes that "a perpetually returning theme, BRAM's preoccupation with hands, tortured, tormented, constantly referred to in fact and in the fantasy of his stories, must have a deep significance. . . . In almost every story written by BRAM STOKER he finds it necessary to describe the hands of his characters in great detail. It may or may not be significant. For the purpose of this treatment I have made it so." The deathbed doctor who attends Stoker engages in some strained psychoanalytic sleight-of-hand to root out the writer's primal conflict, ultimately found in repressed childhood memories of the ghastly cholera scourge that swept Ireland, and to which Stoker's family was witness. The images of death, blood, and clutching hands culminate in Stoker's mother severing the arm of a frenzied cholera victim.

The story that Henry Irving's personality inspired or informed the character of Count Dracula has now achieved such mythic status that it is surprising that Houghton makes so little of it. It is equally strange that Ludlam made no such connection whatsoever in his biography, especially considering his direct access to Stoker's son and *Dracula*'s first dramatist, Hamilton Deane. Houghton may be, in fact, the first biographical writer of any kind to have considered a direct Irving/Dracula connection, seemingly drawn from nowhere but his own instincts as a screenwriter. Irving's celebrated production of *Macbeth* is now featured prominently in most studies that explore Irving-as-Dracula, but Houghton scores a more original point as Irving's Othello, killing Desdemona in her bed, morphs into Dracula attacking a victim. Stoker's wife and mother look on hungrily in the guise of vampire wives. Ellen Terry, Irving's acting partner—his Desdemona—warns Stoker that Irving "feeds off his good nature and calm competence." In Houghton's vision, "These words seem to stick in Bram's mind. To feed off him. To suck him dry."

Later, when the real Irving lies dead on a hotel lobby floor, Dracula's death scene flashes in Stoker's brain. Houghton is ultimately less interested in Henry Irving than in cholera as an inspiration for *Dracula*, and additionally includes horrific dramatized excerpts from Stoker's short stories "The Squaw" and "The Burial of the Rats," as well as *The Lair of the White Worm*. At the end, in a fevered delirium, Stoker wrestles with Irving's demon: Did he really hate the actor? Was Irving truly responsible for his life of mental torment? At this point he fully and therapeutically surrenders to the awful cholera visions. As Stoker's own death swiftly approaches, Irving is exonerated. "BRAM is quiet, contemplative. The lines of torment are slowly soothed away. Now his life has a pattern, an ordered reason for everything that has happened. He can take leave of it now in peace. The vision of Hell and Purgatory is vanished."

It is remarkable that Hammer's unrealized film turned on a particular family incident—Charlotte's gruesome removal of a cholera victim's arm—that could have come from only one source: Daniel Farson, Bram Stoker's grandnephew by way of his grandfather Tom and his wife, Enid, who heard the tale personally from his grandmother and had never publicly repeated the account. He was saving it for a media project or book. *Victim of His Imagination* was the story's first audition, one that unfortunately did not receive a callback. Like Stoker, Farson was a writer and journalist drawn irresistibly to the arts and their outsized personalities. As a television

Stoker's great-nephew and biographer Daniel Farson.
Publicity photo by Alan Ball for **The Man Who Wrote Dracula** *(1975).*

interviewer, art critic, celebrity photographer, and raconteur, Farson was never at a loss for extraordinary, if often freely embellished, anecdotes about the literary lions, angry young artists, and glitterati of all types and persuasions who lit up the sky of postwar British culture. A reliable fixture of the painter Francis Bacon's notorious Soho drinking circle, he was also on personal terms with Somerset Maugham, Lucian Freud, Salvador Dalí, Brendan Behan, Colin Wilson, Noël Coward, and Richard Burton. Like his great-uncle Bram, he came into regular professional contact with everybody who was anybody in London.

Farson also bore an uncanny physical resemblance to Stoker, more than any of Bram's own direct descendants, from his burly frame to his gray-blue eyes to the part of his hair to the distinctive arch of his nostrils. Certain photos of him (bearded in the 1950s) reflect a likeness akin to reincarnation or resurrection. Had he ever entertained the idea of impersonating his great-uncle in a one-man show, it might have been an extraordinary experience.

Significantly, and rather like his ancestor, Farson had a problematic relationship with Oscar Wilde. As he wrote near the end of his life, "When did I realize I was homosexual? It is hardly something that occurs overnight, like measles, and I suppose it dawns on everyone differently at vastly varying ages. I felt guilty long before I knew why. Having bought a book on Oscar Wilde, I was so alarmed in case it was discovered that I hid it between the stones of the overgrown bank of the stream which ran down to the sea from our new home in Devon. I looked for that book years later, but I could never find it again."

It was not the last time he would find himself awkwardly separated from Wilde-related documents. Not long after his mother's death, Noel Stoker, knowing the young Farson was interested in autographs—and likely happy to be rid of a last reminder of Dorian Gray's unwelcome visits to his house, not to mention that irritating flame his mother carried for Wilde thirty-seven years after he was gone—gave the boy an old sack of correspondence including the letters between Wilde and Florence Balcombe at the time of their Dublin courtship.

Our understanding of the relationship between Florence and Oscar might be clearer if it weren't for Farson's later actions. Although he didn't hide the letters between the rocks of a stream, they nonetheless left his possession. "Many were disposed of, some were lost," he wrote, a bit disingenuously, in his 1975 book *The Man Who Wrote "Dracula."* Later he would be more forthcoming. To cover the bill for an ill-considered drinking binge with Francis Bacon and debts incurred for an AWOL young sailor he had taken under his wing, Farson sold all the letters between Florence and Oscar, as well as celebrity missives addressed to Stoker, to an autograph dealer in Bond Street ("I recall the glee of the woman who bought them"). He expressed relief, on more than one occasion, that many of the letters ultimately found their way to manuscript collections in libraries at Harvard and UCLA, but the "lost" correspondence includes some significant gaps. Only three letters from Oscar to Florence are known to have survived, and only one from Florence to Oscar. In the absence of telephones or anything even remotely like the Internet, their notes and letters would have been far more voluminous.[14]

Grinnell, the gruesome barkeep of Stoker's *The Primrose Path*, was never on duty at Soho's Colony Room, the afternoon drinking club favored by Farson and his art world friends, but he might as well have been, given Farson's Liveright-like dependence on alcohol and its hampering effect on his career. In *The Gilded Gutter Life of Francis Bacon* (1993), Farson recounts being "easily bribed by champagne" in Bacon's company, and how that cursed the possibility of a *Dracula*-related media coup in the early 1970s.

> One Christmas I had a crucial meeting with Alan Yentob, the Controller of BBC2, at Television Centre to discuss a script on my great-uncle Bram Stoker. I phoned from the Colony with the warning that I might be late. I was about to add that it would be safer to fix another appointment when his secretary assured me there was no problem and I should just arrive as soon as I could. Francis was at his best that afternoon, my friends were mesmerized, and when I tore myself away I found myself stuck in a taxi in a Christmas rush-hour. I burst into the BBC bar half-hysterical, three-quarters drunk and an hour late. The program on Bram Stoker has yet to be made.[15]

The veteran British journalist Robin Carmody has commented on Farson's "sense of otherness, the sense that would ultimately lead him to drown himself in drink and a kind of self-imposed underachievement and semi-exile."

Farson finally made use of his Stoker knowledge and research in *The Man Who Wrote "Dracula,"* a hurriedly assembled biography that is still of great interest because of the close involvement of Stoker descendants. Considering Farson's own personal life and experience, it comes as a

---

[14] The letters were not the only Stoker family heirlooms Farson may have disposed of for quick cash. Wilde's portrait of Florence and his landscape watercolor also ended up in a major research collection, but they were not directly deposited by the Stoker family.

[15] Farson did appear in, and receive a producer's credit for, a 1974 BBC2 documentary called *The Dracula Business*, but this is clearly not the biographical project he originally envisioned, since he still considered that film "yet to be made" as late as 1997. Perhaps, fully recognizing his own striking resemblance to Stoker, he wanted to finally appear as him, narrating and commenting on his life and work? It is a tantalizing question, but unfortunately we will never have an answer.

surprise that *The Man Who Wrote "Dracula"* makes nothing of the homoerotic aspects of Stoker's infatuation with Walt Whitman, much less his
slavish, unrequited adoration of Henry Irving, or the curious decades-long
bonding with Hall Caine. Oscar Wilde makes his obligatory entrances
and exits in connection with Florence alone. Farson knew every possibility and nuance of male-male camaraderie—and more—inside and out.
And yet his speculation on Stoker's sexuality doesn't go beyond wondering
if Bram's sexless marriage might have driven him to female prostitutes
(something on the same plane of likelihood as a romance with Genevieve
Ward). While he does cite the psychoanalyst Ernest Jones's belief that vampire superstition (and, by implication, fictional entertainment and the creators of same) yields "plain indication of most kinds of sexual perversions,"
Farson steers carefully clear of attributing any nonheterosexual tendencies
to Stoker himself.

But any different approach might have struck too close to home in the
early 1970s. Homosexual acts in private between consenting adult men had
been partially decriminalized in Great Britain by 1967, but prosecution
for less discreet behavior surged, and Farson's bad-boy proclivities did not
always fall on the safe side of the law. Robin Carmody recalled that in the
1950s Farson was "petrified" that his private life might create a Wilde-like
scandal, especially given his high visibility as a television interviewer who
frequently sided with social outsiders, including teenage rebels, interracial
couples, and even nudists. He was particularly concerned that one rabidly
Conservative parliamentary candidate, James Wentworth Day (with whom
he sparred frequently on camera) suspected his secret and might conceivably seize the media opportunity to become his personal, tormenting
Marquess of Queensberry. Wentworth Day was not at all reticent in expressing opinions that would have been perfectly at home amid the Victorian
"degeneration" debates that had informed *Dracula* and *The Island of Dr.
Moreau*. According to the sneering politician, racially mixed marriages created "mongrels" and "coffee colored imps" that no decent British woman
could ever recognize as legitimate children. Blacks were mentally inferior
and, after all, only a few generations removed from cannibalism. As for
homosexuals, there was only one solution, of course—they should all be
hanged. This final on-camera utterance was enough cause for Farson to
cancel the program about transvestism for which it had been filmed. He

was truly afraid that challenging his combative interviewee on the point could well be his own Waterloo.

Although Farson could have written a more probing and provocative book about Stoker, he did add the publicity-generating postscript about syphilis that succeeded in making the biography controversial. He called the information "tragic" and stated that "I hesitated to include this until I was convinced by revealing it, I would show Bram Stoker in a clearer light. It explains so much."

But other descendants—on both sides of the Atlantic—were scandalized. Frankly, no one in the family other than Farson had any real historical or literary interest in Stoker or *Dracula*. While it was a distinction to have a famous ancestor who wrote a famous story, many Stokers had grown up warned not to even read the "nasty" book. Now Farson's biography was adding another note of embarrassment, endlessly spit back in newspaper articles and reviews.

Farson gave the book's lead dedication to Ann Elizabeth Stoker, Bram's granddaughter, for her assistance, but she was nonetheless incensed that he had quoted her opinion that Florence Stoker was indeed a frigid woman, one who became "very antisex" after Noel's birth. Although she later denied having said such a thing, it is more likely that she was simply mortified at seeing a private family conversation on an unseemly topic actually appear in print. According to Farson, her views only reinforced the similar thoughts of his own grandmother Enid Stoker.

But it was the syphilis allegation that really gnawed. Ann wrote to the medical school of Trinity College Dublin, asking for help refuting Farson's claims, and received an encouraging preliminary reply. The fact that she saved no later correspondence suggests that the school was finally unable or unwilling to give her the opinion she wanted. A similar situation arose after the working notes for *Dracula* were acquired by the Rosenbach Museum & Library in Philadelphia and began attracting the attention of academic researchers. Ann was initially agreeable to allowing the papers to be transcribed, annotated, and published by Dr. Joseph S. Bierman, a psychoanalyst and critic, perhaps without fully understanding the implications of his already-published essay "*Dracula*, Prolonged Childhood Illness, and the Oral Triad," in which he posited that the novel reflected Stoker's sickness-fueled and infanticidal rage against his baby brothers Tom and

George, whom he longed to devour. For Stoker's granddaughter, syphilis had been one thing, and quite enough, but . . . cannibalism? It is hardly surprising that this correspondence trail also ends abruptly.[16]

Ann Stoker, born four years after her grandfather Bram's death, claimed never to have read *Dracula*. "Isn't it awful to confess?" she asked an interviewer in 1979. "I've been flicking through it to check on a few things but I've never worked up the courage to read it. You see, my father, Noel, Bram's only son, told me it was too frightening for me and that put me off for life."[17] Like her father and her grandmother Florence, she never had what Noel Stoker called "the macabre streak," and personal tragedy had further inured her to frightening stories. "I had one terrible shock in my life when my first husband was killed in the war and I have never wanted any more." She eschewed the whole Dracula industry, almost religiously. Other than accompanying Florence Stoker to the 1931 red-carpet London premiere of the Universal film, visiting the set of one of the Hammer films with Christopher Lee in the 1960s, and attending a private screening of Universal's 1979 remake (which she actually enjoyed), she had no familiarity with the dozens of other adaptations and spin-offs that had captured the world's imagination over the decades. "I never believed in cashing in on my family name, and while I am flattered in the interest in shown in me now, I still don't." Since the media rights to the novel were sold outright (the 1930 purchase contract even specified television), the family never made a penny from any *Dracula* entertainment franchise. But the royalties from the book, which ended when the copyright expired in 1962, at least allowed Ann and her husband to give a handsome public school education to their two sons.

As for Dracula aficionados and vampire obsessives—a truly sprawling lot, in and out of academia—she ruffled more than a few feathers with her tart comment, "All those Dracula Society people, running around

[16] The Rosenbach Museum & Library finally authorized the publication of *Bram Stoker's Notes for "Dracula": A Facsimile Edition*, transcribed, edited, and annotated by Robert Eighteen-Bisang and Elizabeth Miller (Jefferson, NC, and London: McFarland, 2008).

[17] Ann Stoker (1916–98) was married twice, first to Richard Arthur William Dobbs (1912–39) and later to Brian Arthur MacCaw (1920–96). In Stoker biography and commentary she is variously called Ann McCaw, Ann Dobbs, and Ann Stoker Dobbs, but she told interviewer Charles Catchpole that she preferred her maiden name, Ann Stoker, for purposes of Dracula-related publicity.

Transylvania in cloaks, playing at vampires . . . ugghh! I wouldn't touch that sort of thing with a barge pole."

Although the creator of Dracula never visited Transylvania himself, the 1970s kicked off a wave of Stoker-related tourism in Romania, all inspired by a best-selling book, *In Search of Dracula* (1972), by Boston University professors Raymond T. McNally and Radu Florescu. Without knowledge of Stoker's cursory research into Vlad "Dracula" Tepeş, contained in his notes (which they would eventually cite and incorporate into later works), McNally and Florescu mounted voluminous independent research into the historical Dracula and his gruesome exploits, including mass impalement of his enemies on wooden stakes. This detail alone was enough to "prove" a connection to vampires, especially in a media environment becoming increasingly fond of factoids and sound bites. In reality, Tepeş was never historically linked to vampire superstitions in any way.

Florescu's 2014 obituary in the *New York Times* noted that "the thesis of *In Search of Dracula* has not been universally accepted by scholars, nor did all reviewers embrace it. But for the authors, who became the toast of the television talk-show circuit, that did not matter." Given the obscurity that is the fate of most academic books, McNally and Florescu cannot be faulted for making the most of all the attention they received, and they were generally careful not to claim that the details of their own massive research, unrelated to Stoker's, was evidence that Vlad was a primary inspiration for *Dracula*. The media were more than happy to connect the dots.

The most authoritative rebuttals of the Vlad/Stoker connection have come from Elizabeth Miller, the Canadian academic and esteemed doyenne of *Dracula* studies, who has been especially rigorous in debunking the large body of half-truths, speculation presented as established fact, and completely fabricated claims that have wormed their way into every aspect of Stoker criticism and biography. (Her highly informative, clean-out-the-cobwebs book *Dracula: Sense and Nonsense* should be a required primer for anyone even considering writing about Stoker.) In a comprehensive essay, "Filing for Divorce: Count Dracula vs. Vlad Tepeş," Miller sums up her position:

> I do not dispute that in using the name "Dracula" Stoker appropriated the sobriquet of the fifteenth-century voivode. Nor do I deny that he added bits and pieces of obscure historical detail to flesh out a past for his

vampire. But I do vehemently challenge the widespread view that Stoker was knowledgeable about the historical Dracula (beyond what he read in Wilkinson) and that he based his Count on the life and character of Vlad. While it is true that the resurgence of interest in Dracula since the early 1970s is due in no small measure to the theories about such connections, the theories themselves do not withstand the test of close scrutiny.

McNally and Florescu, however, created enough awareness of Vlad the Impaler that the historical figure is now a standard part of Dracula's backstory, at least as far as filmmakers are concerned. The screenwriter Richard Matheson (also the author of *I Am Legend*, one of the most influential American vampire novels) was the first adapter to incorporate the legend of Vlad, in the 1974 television film starring Jack Palance. Matheson added the now-familiar idea that Dracula has found in Mina (or Lucy, depending on the adaptation) the reincarnation of his lost Transylvanian love. The idea was presented even more floridly at the center of Francis Ford Coppola's *Bram Stoker's Dracula* (1992), surely one of the most misleading film titles of all time. Matheson's script borrowed significantly from two earlier horror sources: John Balderston's script for 1932's *The Mummy*, in which a back-from-the grave Boris Karloff found the reincarnation of his Egyptian lover in modern Cairo; and television's 1960's Gothic soap opera *Dark Shadows*, wherein the vampire Barnabas Collins similarly stalked the image of his eighteenth-century inamorata in modern-day New England. From the 1970s onward, Dracula was cursed to wander, lovesick, throughout eternity, regardless of Bram Stoker's intentions.

Oscar Wilde is generally credited as the first public avatar of camp, the faux-flippant and ironical sensibility that would be widely embraced by gay culture in the twentieth century. An attitudinal affectation brimming with wit and wicked paradox—often aimed at personalities and pretensions in the performing arts—camp simultaneously idolizes and skewers establishment convention and outdated fashion. Christopher Isherwood was the first writer to discuss the term in his novel *The World in the Evening* (1954), making an important distinction between "low" and "high" camp. "High camp always has an underlying seriousness," Isherwood wrote. "You can't camp about something you don't take seriously. You're not making fun of it; you're making fun out of it. You're expressing what's basically serious to you in terms of fun and artifice and elegance."

It is not at all surprising that Dracula, among his many achievements, has become a sturdy target for camp representation. Of the many versions of Stoker's story, the Deane and Balderston version is the template that lends itself best to affectionate parody, be it Lugosi's accent freely appropriated by Lenny Bruce in cadences of the Borscht Belt, or the very existence of Count Chocula or Grandpa Munster. If, as Isherwood posits, Baroque art is nothing but religious camp, and classical ballet the camping up of romantic love, then Dracula vamps and camps all kinds of transcendent subjects, including life, death, and resurrection; religious doubt; and the terrifying aggression that might lurk behind a kiss.

One of the most iconic American visual artists of the 1960s and 1970s was the illustrator Edward Gorey, whose finely crosshatched drawings were exercises in deadpan camp—style for style's sake in a manner Wilde would have approved. The Gorey universe is a curiously curlicued realm of Victorian/Edwardian affectation that swirls together merriment and malevolence in equal, paradoxical measure. His macabre, rhyming compendium of childhood fatalities, *The Gashlycrumb Tinies* (1965), had gained a cult following and was, in many ways, a return to the *Slovenly Peter* phenomenon of Bram Stoker's childhood, the major difference being that *Peter* was intended to actually frighten Victorian children while *Gashlycrumb* was all about droll amusement for modern adults.

Gorey had only one previous Stoker credit—an illustration for "The Squaw" in Eric Protter's 1965 anthology *Monster Festival* —when he was approached to design a small-scale stage production of Deane and Balderston's *Dracula* for the Nantucket Stage Company in 1975. "A very good friend of mine produced it,"[18] Gorey recalled, "and in that sense he was very smart, but I thought the whole *Dracula* thing was perfect nonsense. Since I was in on it from its inception, I think I can say with authority that I don't think anybody knew what they were doing. It started out on a stage that was on one of those raised platforms in a grammar school gymnasium in Nantucket. For some reason, it caught on down there. Artistically, it was a hodgepodge to end all hodgepodges. I knew nothing about set design."

---

[18]John Wulp, who staged the Broadway production in association with producer Elizabeth Ireland McCann.

In her famous 1966 essay "Notes on Camp," Susan Sontag likened camp to a woman wearing a dress made of a million feathers; Gorey's mise-en-scène for *Dracula* was composed of a similar multitude of inky crosshatches, with an absurd number of bat motifs embedded into the scenery and even the costumes. Four years after Nantucket, a more grandiose, scaled-for-Broadway production opened at the Martin Beck Theatre, starring Frank Langella in a role he had first essayed in a more traditional production at the Berkshire Theatre Festival ten years earlier. A genuine tourist attraction, *Dracula* played nine hundred performances. Gorey was nominated for the Tony Awards for both set and costumes, and won for costumes. The artist didn't believe he deserved either, but was especially mystified that the attention-grabbing scenery was snubbed in favor of what he considered his "tacky" costumes. "The set is more menacing than a Pinter pause," wrote the critic Mel Gussow in the *New York Times Magazine*. "There are bats' wings flickering on the windows and woven into the wallpaper. Clouds assume the shape of vampires. Hedges arch their backs into running wolves. Soon our eyes begin to play tricks: We see corpses in copses, vultures in vaults, asps in apses." Gussow couldn't help but note that the thirty-foot-high flats, along with the costumes and props, were rendered completely in black and white, "except for an occasional flash of flaming red: a rose, a glass of wine, a drop of blood. And thou, Dracula, beside me in the wilderness."

If he could have gotten past the creative liberties of the Deane/Balderston adaptation, Bram Stoker's reaction to seeing his novel essentially reproduced as a large-scale version of a Victorian toy theatre would be fascinating. Dioramas of the beloved pantomimes of Stoker's childhood, with positionable characters and movable settings, were popular nineteenth-century diversions. If Stoker didn't actually have one of them as a child, he would have wanted one. As it turns out, a handsome toy theatre version of Gorey's *Dracula* is still commercially available, forty years after the initial production.

The acerbic *New York Magazine* critic John Simon had no use for camp, and had been one of the few dissenting voices on Sontag's intellectual elevation of the subject. His caustic theatre reviews were regularly protested by the theatre community for their use of phrases like "faggot nonsense" and one never-to-be-lived-down comment at a Broadway opening, quoted by *New York Daily News* columnist Liz Smith: "Homosexuals in the theatre! My God, I can't wait until AIDS gets all of them."

Simon wrote that *Dracula* was "rather like a sophomoric parody of Noël Coward," with "mugging and sashaying, quivering and quavering, and enough eyeball rolling to look like a bowling alley in miniature." He recommended that the actor playing Dr. Seward "should only act in plays with vividly colored sets; here, with Gorey's grays, he tends to disappear into the scenery." Langella, in Simon's opinion, conveyed "no suggestion of lethal force or heterosexual fascination; moreover, there is a curious kind of narcissism here (abetted by the front-and-center staging)—as if, not being able to see himself reflected in mirrors, this Dracula desperately sought his image in the audience's rapt gaze." Having dispensed with the production's alleged heterosexual flabbiness, Simon then delivered a misogynistic salvo at Ann Sachs as Lucy, "a curious ingénue indeed, looking sixty from some angles, like a boy from others, and from nowhere like an actress."[19]

A far more sympathetic critic, Dan Sullivan, writing for the *Los Angeles Times*, felt that Langella was "too much of a presence in the drawing room for men to warm to him—Langella suggests Bishop [Fulton J.] Sheen[20] at the height of his charisma—but women would be drawn in, would love to share his secrets." Sullivan accurately described the bedroom scene at the end of act 2: "He is a hawk fixing a rabbit, but before the final stroke, he raises his head and looks directly at the audience, as if daring us to do something about it. Then, he attacks."

Rex Reed, in the *New York Sunday News*, was also receptive to the production. "Mr. Langella, accomplished craftsman that he is, brings to the role of the creepy count more charm and sexiness than anyone thought possible. In the big seduction scene, he choreographs his movements like Baryshnikov dancing." The audience responded with "a crescendo of cheers, and several women have been known to pass out from sheer ecstasy.

---

[19] With his pronounced Yugoslavian accent and carefully cultivated reputation for figuratively drawing blood, Simon himself would have been excellent casting for an Eastern European vampire. When Wilfred Sheed used the word "Transylvanian" to describe the critic, Simon replied, "My accent is admittedly slightly foreign, but not . . . Draculan or Lugosian. I would say it is more like that of an American or British actor trying to sound Continental European, and, I am happy to report, has proved rather pleasing to some charming American women who have lent an ear—and more—to it."

[20] For readers of a certain age, Fulton Sheen will be remembered as a highly popular Catholic televangelist of the 1950s and '60s. Sullivan is quite correct: especially in ceremonial attire, Sheen indeed brings to mind Langella's understated Dracula, in both his soothing voice and regally hypnotic presence.

One New York porno shop has introduced Dracula fangs as the newest sensation in sex toys."

Langella was succeeded on Broadway by four other actors: David Dukes (the first, temporary replacement), Jeremy Brett, Jean LeClerc, and

Al Hirschfeld's evocative impression of Frank Langella in the 1977 Broadway revival of **Dracula.** (Copyright © The Al Hirschfeld Foundation)

Press photo of the 1978 London production of **Dracula,** *starring Terence Stamp (center), with sets and costumes by Edward Gorey.*

finally Raul Julia. Martin Landau appeared in a touring version (and later had a sweet revenge on critics who disparaged his "hammy" Bela Lugosi impersonation by winning a Best Supporting Actor Oscar for his nuanced and affecting role as Lugosi in Tim Burton's *Ed Wood* in 1994). But a 1978 London production starring Terence Stamp, then one of the most expensive plays ever mounted in the West End, flopped badly. British audiences simply couldn't relate to Gorey's preciously eccentric brand of Anglophilia, and *Dracula* was not the season's cup of tea. For Stamp, being "crucified" by the critics contributed to his decision, after assaying only one more role, to permanently leave the stage for film.

Repeating the stage-to-screen trajectory of the late 1920s, Universal Studios capitalized on the Broadway success with a new film version, directed by John Badham and released in 1979. Unlike the 1931 film, which overplayed the staginess for budgetary reasons, the new, well-financed *Dracula* bore no resemblance to the Gorey conception, except for the casting of Frank Langella. Laurence Olivier (who, by a complete—but completely appropriate—coincidence was then living with his wife Joan Plowright in one of Bram Stoker's Chelsea homes on St. Leonard's Terrace) lent considerable star power as Van Helsing. Langella's experience with Dracula's curse was not as career-killing as Lugosi's, but it definitely hampered the type of screen work he was thereafter offered, and for quite a long time. "It took the industry ten years to forget that I played Dracula," he recalled. "It took me ten minutes."

The Universal remake effectively derailed a remarkable 1978 script by the British director Ken Russell, well known for his flamboyant excursions into overheated historical and literary subjects, including *Women in Love* (1969) and *The Devils* (1971). The loss of his *Dracula* was a great shame, because Russell's unproduced adaptation stands as an object lesson in just how shrewdly, inventively, and entertainingly *Dracula* can be embellished and transformed.

Russell's conception, envisioned as a star vehicle for the musician and actor Mick Fleetwood, opens with Jonathan Harker's familiar wild ride to Castle Dracula, in which the wolves, bats, flames, and frightened peasants are all part of an elaborate welcome-wagon joke on the unsuspecting visitor. But lest the viewer think that this Dracula is a harmless prankster, things quickly turn truly weird. For instance, as Dracula's wives approach Harker for their midnight nip, Aubrey Beardsley's most erotic imagery looms over the proceedings: "The CAMERA pans over the wallpaper show-ing four men with giant erections dancing before an audience of beautiful women." Dracula laments, "Beardsley was surely one of your finest artists. It is to my everlasting regret that I never met him. So talented, and to die so young. A tragedy! I might have helped him." Jonathan: "Are you a doctor, sir?" Dracula (laughing): "I dabble a little in acupuncture, certainly; I'm also something of a patron of the arts." Later, when Dracula plays a recording of Schubert's Eighth Symphony—famously unfinished—Jonathan quips, "Pity you weren't around to help him as well. He might have finished it." "Yes," says Dracula, this time dead serious, "that is one of the great regrets of my life."

This Dracula, we learn, is a die-hard arts philanthropist, with a spe-cial appreciation for the vocal gifts of opera diva Lucy Weber—Stoker's transmogrified Lucy Westenra, this time not Mina Murray's friend but her employer. Weber is dying of leukemia, but evidently strong enough to mount a farewell tour for her morbid, mournful public. When she finally meets the Count, he offers Dracu-puncture, and she finally recog-nizes those eyes she had often seen just beyond the footlights at theatres all over Europe. Lucy's voice, in Dracula's estimation, "has more colour than Turner ever dreamed of, there is more music in your every movement than in a romance by Silbelius, more poetry in your smile than a verse by Baudelaire." And after Lucy's death, undeath, and final death, Dracula tells Mina that "some of our greatest artists are 'Nosferatu.' . . . Have you never pondered on the resemblance between Beethoven and Sibelius? And does not Rembrandt look like Picasso, just a little bit?"

The script continues to follow Stoker's general plot, with more of Russell's clever embellishments. The madman Renfield is another leukemia victim, who ill-advisedly sought a miracle cure in Transylvania. When Dracula's coffin-filled ship lands in England, it plows through a concert pier where Lucy and Mina are enjoying (what else?) Strauss's overture to *Die Fledermaus*. Beyond the usual mesmeric ministrations, Dracula's seductions involve psy-chedelic lectures on hematology. And after naked, Icarus-like demise, his two surviving wives lament, "He could not love; he could not love!"

But readers and audiences have not stopped loving Dracula, and there is no real sign that they ever will. *Dracula* changes in precisely the same way folktales do, each teller and reteller adding something to the narrative caul-dron. The age of the moving image has rekindled the communal campfire. Like human life, a novel has a certain finite duration, and ultimately must come to an end. But the pile of dust Stoker left at the end of his book is as much an affront to the modern, story-spinning mind as the prospect of spiritual annihilation was to the Victorians.

The contemporary readers of *Dracula* were participants in a vast cultural séance, seeking reassurance that science was wrong and death was not the final curtain. Stoker was not entirely successful in addressing this anxiety, perhaps because he had doubts of his own. The new afterlife he imagined was problematic, and almost as frightening as personal oblivion, ultimately offering only another kind of spiritual annihilation. Like Stoker, the adapters and transformers of *Dracula* today continue to use up-to-date technology to entrap the vampire; unlike Stoker, their aim is not to kill him but to keep him alive. As for *Dracula*'s literary reputation, perhaps it never was a "real" novel—at least the kind that was ever destined to fit comfortably into a standard English Department curriculum. It may take a village—or at least an interdisciplinary community of literary scholars, mythologists and anthropologists, film historians and other cultural archaeologists—to begin to fully comprehend the book's meaning.

July 2012: The scene is St. Ann's Church in central Dublin's Dawson Street, where the one hundredth anniversary year of Bram Stoker's death is being marked with a special memorial service, the first of its kind since the writer's funeral, taking place in the very church in which he was married in 1878. Among those attending are Stoker's greatgrandson and great- and great-great-nephews and their families, along with the participants in an academic conference just concluded at Trinity College Dublin, "Bram Stoker: Life and Work," along with members of the curious public.

Overleaf: The changing face of Count Dracula. 1922: Max Schreck in Nosferatu. *1931: Bela Lugosi in* Dracula. *1931: Carlos Villarias in Universal's simultaneously produced Spanish-language version. 1943: Lon Chaney Jr. in* Son of Dracula. *1944: John Carradine in* House of Frankenstein. *1953: Atif Kaptan in* Drakula Istanbul'da. (Courtesy of Ronald V. Borst / Hollywood Movie Posters) *1958: Christopher Lee in* Horror of Dracula. *1970: Christopher Lee in* Count Dracula. *1972: William Marshall in* Blacula. *1974: Jack Palance in* Dracula. *1977: Louis Jourdan in* Count Dracula. *1979: Frank Langella in* Dracula. *1979: Klaus Kinski in* Nosferatu the Vampyre. *1992: Gary Oldman in* Bram Stoker's Dracula. *1994: Leslie Nielsen in* Dracula: Dead and Loving It. *2002: Zhang Wei-Qiang in* Dracula: Pages from a Virgin's Diary. *2013: Jonathan Rhys Meyers in the NBC television series* Dracula. *2014: Luke Evans in* Dracula Untold.

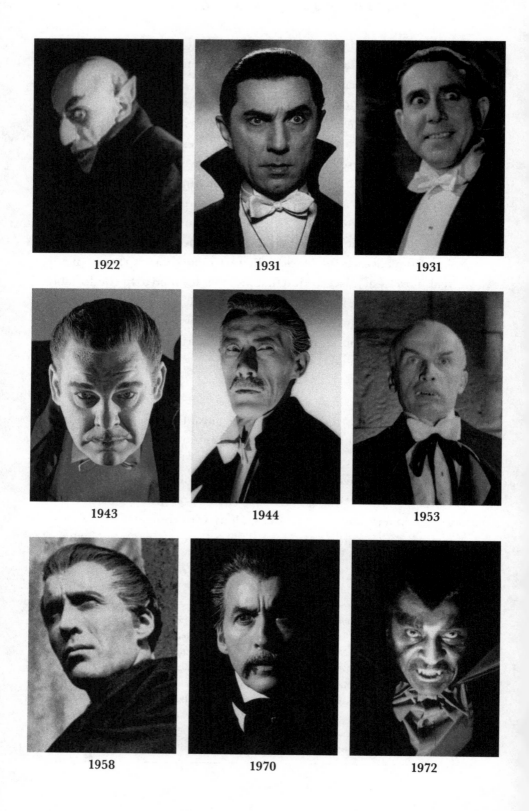

1922   1931   1931

1943   1944   1953

1958   1970   1972

1974   1977   1979

1979   1992   1994

2002   2013   2014

What would Bram Stoker himself make of our strange new world, where marriage now includes same-sex marriage, and Olympic athletes, far more accomplished than Bram in his youth, have the freedom to change their sex if they choose? In a way, there are two couples being recognized today, one of which is decidedly unconventional, at least for Stoker's time.

The service nominally commemorates the wedding of Bram Stoker to Florence Balcombe, but the bride is mentioned only in passing. The real wedding celebrated is the coming together, in 1897, of two men on the dedication page of *Dracula*, with the printed inscription to MY DEAR FRIEND HOMMY-BEG, amended in hand: "To Hall Caine, from his loving friend, Bram Stoker."

Other than the perfunctory dedication "To My Wife" in *Miss Betty*—arguably his weakest work of fiction—no written appreciation of Florence by Bram has ever been discovered. Just as there is no marker for her grave—for no grave exists—there is no substantive mention of her in any of his letters, papers, or journals. In the end, like so many other Victorian women, Florence Stoker is a wraithlike, bodiless ideal, a hovering offstage presence despite her central, embattled role in securing *Dracula*'s afterlife in the twentieth and twenty-first centuries.

The vicar of St. Ann's brings the yellow book with its stamp of lurid red lettering to the front of the church, where it is displayed in the chancel next to a newly commissioned bust of Stoker. *Dracula* is surely the only object of diabolical veneration ever given ceremonial acknowledgment in an Anglican house of worship. Beneath the morning light of a striking stained-glass window personifying Faith, Hope, and Charity, an object representing every inverse value is given an ironic recognition, if not quite a benediction. A murmur passes among the assembled as the vicar informs them that the current estimated auction value of the book—the crown jewel of a private Dublin library dedicated to Stoker—is one-quarter of a million dollars. Although the information is given with a smile and a twinkling glance, the religious invocation of money conjoined to malevolence is, nonetheless, a remarkably paradoxical experience. Paradoxes are something the alleged ghost of Oscar Wilde defined for a spirit medium as "thoughts that do not go to church on Sunday."

This Sunday, however, is the exception that proves the epigram.

Dracula was never reviewed by Wilde—he fled England just as it was being published—but given his predilection for witty deconstruction of the hypocrisies and anxieties and obsessions of Victorian culture, his thoughts might well have resulted in some provocative quips.

Stoker himself was no quipster. The deadly serious boy in the breeching portrait, already transfixed by a world of famine and plague, is about to make his life's journey through a tumultuous, transitional century fed and driven by paradoxes of mind, matter, and metaphysics, the riddles of sex and gender, the war between conformity and transgression, the ascendancy of science, and the death of God. *Dracula* represents a powerful dream-struggle between humankind's darkest fears and its most transcendent aspirations, wedded uneasily and forever in the fevered pantomime theatre of Bram Stoker's mind—a perfect marriage of heaven and hell.

ACKNOWLEDGMENTS

Primary research for this book was made possible by the Long Room Hub of the Trinity College Dublin Library, which named me a Visiting Research Fellow for the Michaelmas Term, 2010. For their enthusiastic support, assistance, great conversation, and hospitality during several trips to Ireland, including a three-month residency, I thank the following faculty, staff, and students at TCD: Meg Black, Jennifer Edmond, Tiffany Hearsey, Darryl Jones, Jarlath Killeen, Elizabeth McCarthy, Orla McCarthy, Jason McElligot, Eva Mühlhause, Bernice Murphy, Sorcha Ní Fhlainn, Clemens Ruthner, Diane Sadler, and Simon Williams. I am especially grateful to Professor Jones and Dr. Murphy for inviting me to conduct a very successful graduate seminar based on my book *The Monster Show*, and to Dr. Ruthner and Dr. Killeen for asking me to participate in their respective 2012 conferences, "Vampire (&) Science" and "Bram Stoker: Life and Work." I was privileged to have met and/or reconnected with an impressive roster of conferees, including Jürgen Barkhoff, Roy Foster, Christopher Frayling, William Hughes, Brendan Kelly, Shaun McCann, Elizabeth Miller, Christina Morin, Paul Murray, Hannah Priest, Christian Reiter, and Carol Senf.

Also in Dublin, the collector John Moore gave me unfettered access to what must be the most extensive private Stoker library on the planet, and kind permission to reproduce dozens of rare images and documents, many appearing in print for the first time.

Two individuals went beyond the call of duty in research assistance. Brian J. Showers provided invaluable support in Dublin long after my return to California, tirelessly accessing microforms at the National Library of Ireland, and other materials that were simply not available in the United States. His efforts led to the discovery of Stoker's first published piece of supernatural fiction, "Saved by a Ghost," previously unknown. Brian is also responsible for a striking new set of author photos, taken at Dublin's Mount Jerome Cemetery, an appropriately atmospheric family burial site for the Stoker, Wilde, and Le Fanu families.

John Edgar Browning, a leading light in American Stoker studies, was a constant friend and cheerleader, who freely shared valuable research, as well as his knowledge and expertise in the brave new realm of digitized historical newspapers and documents. Without his keen interest and support, *Something in the Blood* would be a much-diminished effort.

Research institutions consulted included the Boston Public Library, British

Library Department of Manuscripts, Burbank Public Library, Fales Manuscript Library at New York University, Folger Shakespeare Library, Glendale Public Library, Los Angeles Public Library, Manx National Heritage and Museum, National Library of Ireland, New York Public Library (especially the Library for the Performing Arts at Lincoln Center), Occidental College Library, Pasadena Public Library, all divisions of the Trinity College Dublin Library, and UCLA Libraries, especially the Young Research Library and the William Andrews Clark Memorial Library. Among librarians and archivists, I must first thank Wendy Thirkettle and Paul Wetherall at Manx National Heritage. With the aid of tireless volunteers, Ms. Thirkettle generously began sifting through hitherto uncataloged papers and correspondence of Hall Caine months before my arrival on the Isle of Man, resulting in some wonderful discoveries. At the Fales Library, director Marvin J. Taylor graciously accommodated a short-notice request to access Stoker's rarely studied manuscripts for *The Lair of the White Worm* and *Under the Sunset*. The entire staff of the Trinity College Dublin Department of Manuscripts was helpful on a nearly daily basis for eleven weeks as I immersed myself in TCD's treasure trove of Stoker family papers.

I am privileged to be among a handful of scholars permitted to study Stoker's hand-emended typescript for *Dracula*, presently owned by Microsoft cofounder Paul Allen. I am most grateful for this opportunity, and thank Mr. Allen, the library staff of Vulcan, Inc., and Leslie S. Klinger, editor of *The New Annotated Dracula*, for making an introduction, and for his ongoing interest in my work.

Since Horace Liveright was more responsible than any other individual for bringing *Dracula* to the New York stage, and ultimately to the attention of Hollywood, it is only appropriate that this book appears under the Liveright imprimatur. I thank my agent Malaga Baldi for introducing me to editor Will Menaker; his enthusiasm for the project and many perceptive and intelligent suggestions helped shape a longer and more satisfying book than I originally imagined. Thanks also to Liveright's editor in chief, Bob Weil, for greenlighting the project, and, for their efforts and expertise at publicity, Peter Miller, Cordelia Calvert, and Phil Marino. Rodrigo Corral created a jacket design that would be the envy of any author. India Cooper proved that copyeditors are truly the unheralded heroines and heroes of publishing. I am much indebted to Steve Fisher at the Agency for the Performing Arts, Beverly Hills, for all his advice and efforts in handling dramatic media rights.

During TCD's Stoker conference I was privileged to be invited on a private tour of Dublin's now sadly shuttered Bram Stoker Dracula Museum, in the company of three direct Stoker descendants: Bram's great-great nephew Dacre Stoker and great-grandsons Robin MacCaw and Noel Dobbs, as well as Noel's wife, Susan Dobbs. Thanks to all for some delightful and informative conversation in the city of Bram Stoker's birth. Dacre Stoker and his wife, Jenne, also provided valuable genealogical data.

I am grateful to Bob Madison and Russell Frost for a week of hospitality in New York City and for decades of friendship. For ongoing encouragement, feedback, and interest in the project, and for generally indulging and abetting my severe Dracula habit in a multitude of ways over many years: Dave Alexander, Jay Blotcher, Christopher Bram, Keith Clark, Mark Dery, Robert Eighteen-Bisang, my dedicatee Peter Gölz (who first gave me the chance to teach a course based on my own books at the University of Victoria in 2005); Lokke Heiss, Mike Hill, Hilary Hinzmann, Del and Sue Howison, J. V. Johnson, Leslie S. Klinger, the late Carla Laemmle, Bryan Moore, Scott Martin, William G. Obbagy, Terry and Anita Pace, Mark Redfield, Elias Savada, Jeffrey Schwarz, Carol Senf, Mona Simpson, Jim Steinmeyer, Brinke Stevens, Anthony Taylor, Johanne Tournier, and Jeanne Youngson. I owe Steve Robin a particularly warm acknowledgment, simply for convincing me to take on such a daunting project as *Something in the Blood* in the first place.

For photo research, image scanning, and permissions, I thank Ron and Margaret Borst, Mark Dawidziak, Paul S. McAlduff, Steve Prince, Katharine Kay Marshall at the Al Hirschfeld Foundation, Eleanor Novick at Lebrecht Art and Music, and Joanna Ling at the Cecil Beaton Archive at Sotheby's. John Eastwood kindly provided an unpublished photograph of his ancestor Edmund Blake, the first actor to play the role of Dracula on the legitimate stage.

Biography is a cumulative endeavor, and this project could never have been realized without the work of four previous authors: the late Harry Ludlam, the late Daniel Farson, Barbara Belford, and Paul Murray. Special thanks go to Mr. Murray for personally and generously answering questions on several puzzling research matters. Beyond biographies, the books of Stoker scholars Nina Auerbach, John Edgar Browning, Christopher Frayling, David Glover, William Hughes, Leslie S. Klinger, Clive Leatherdale, and Elizabeth Miller have been particularly useful and inspiring.

On a very personal note, I thank my parents, Lois and John Skal, and my brother, James Skal, all three of whom did not live to see this project come to fruition, as well as my sister, Sandra Skal-Gerlock, my sister-in-law, Mona Skal, and their families, who survive to celebrate. Lastly, I give my deepest love and thanks to Bob Postawko, who, more than anyone else on earth, makes all of my books possible.

NOTES

For complete publication data on all works cited, see Bibliography.
"Stoker" in notes refers to Bram Stoker only.

Abbreviations

BEL   Barbara Belford, *Bram Stoker: A Biography of the Author of "Dracula"*
BLDM   British Library Department of Manuscripts
DEM   *Dublin Evening Mail* (National Library of Ireland microform)
DOR   Oscar Wilde, *The Picture of Dorian Gray: A Norton Critical Edition*, ed. Gillespie
DRA   Bram Stoker, *Dracula: A Norton Critical Edition*, ed. Auerbach and Skal
ELL   Richard Ellman, *Oscar Wilde*
FAR   Daniel Farson, *The Man Who Wrote "Dracula"*
GUE   Bram Stoker, *"Dracula's Guest" and Other Weird Stories*, ed. Hebblethwaite
HAR   Frank Harris, *Oscar Wilde*
IRV   Laurence Irving, *Henry Irving: The Actor and His World*
LET   Oscar Wilde, *Complete Letters*
LUD   Harry Ludlam, *A Biography of Dracula: The Life Story of Bram Stoker*
LWW   Bram Stoker, *The Lair of the White Worm*, ed. Hebbelthwaite
MUR   Paul Murray, *From the Shadow of Dracula*
REM-1   Bram Stoker, *Personal Reminiscences of Henry Irving*, vol. 1
REM-2   Bram Stoker, *Personal Reminiscences of Henry Irving*, vol. 2
SFP   Stoker Family Papers
SHA   *The Norton Shakespeare*, ed. Greenblatt, Cohen, Howard, and Maus
SHE   Robert Harborough Sherard, *The Life of Oscar Wilde*
TCD   Trinity College Dublin Department of Manuscripts
WHI   Walt Whitman, *The Complete Poems*, ed. Francis Murphy
WIL   Oscar Wilde, *Complete Works*

Introduction: Bram Stoker, the Final Curtain?
xiii   **"What manner of man is this?":** *DRA*, p. 39.

1. The Child That Went with the Fairies
1   **"Monster! Give me my child":** *DRA*, p. 48.
1   **"In my babyhood":** *REM-1*, p. 31.

1 **"long illnesses"**: Noel Stoker, "BRAM STOKER by His Son, Noel Thornley Stoker," undated typewritten manuscript circa November 8, 1947. SFP, TCD.

4 **"I have attended funerals"**: Richard Ardille (letter), "Prevention of Diseases in Dublin," *DEM*, October 8, 1847.

10 **"In Ballinrobe"**: Quoted in Toíbín and Ferriter, *Irish Famine*, pp. 40–41.

12 **"amid cushions on the grass"**: *REM-1* (holograph manuscript, ca. 1905–6). Folger Shakespeare Library, Washington, DC. Deleted passage from chap. 2.

12 **completely landfilled**: A thoroughly fascinating account of Dublin's nineteenth-century expansion and growing pains can be found in Barry's lavishly illustrated *Victorian Dublin Revealed*. For an account of the Clontarf waterfront, see p. 70.

12 **"blood-letting is a remedy"**: Clutterbuck, "Lectures on Bloodletting," p. 9.

13 **siphoning vacuum**: An ingenious, Dracula-like use of this device figures in the plot resolution of Tod Browning's 1935 film *Mark of the Vampire*.

13 **"a filthy leech"**: *DRA*, p. 53.

17 **"a mingled repulsion"**: Foster, *Paddy and Mr. Punch*, p. 220.

17 **"In the days of my early youth"**: Mrs. C. M. B. (Thornley) Stoker, "Experience of the Cholera in Ireland" (typewritten manuscript, May 6, 1873; Caen, France), p. 1. TCD.

18 **"*It was in Ireland*"**: Ibid., p. 2.

18 **"They dug a pit"**: Ibid.

18 **"One house would be"**: Ibid.

19 **"no one moved a yard"**: Ibid., p. 8.

19 **Irish whiskey**: Quinn, *Father Mathew's Crusade*, p. 45.

19 **"The nurses died"**: "Experience of the Cholera," p. 3.

19 **"*burn the cholera people*"**: Ibid., p. 11.

20 **"on one of the last"**: FAR, p. 15.

20 **"A man, his face yellow"**: Don Houghton, unproduced screenplay treatment for *Victim of His Imagination* (January 1972), p. 28. Manuscript courtesy of Wayne Kinsey.

20 **"the final terrible"**: Ibid., p. 29.

20 **"this scourge of mankind"**: *DEM*, November 6, 1847.

22 **"The fever spreads"**: Gerald Keegan, "The Summer of Sorrow," in Sellar, *Gleaner Tales*, pp. 341–458.

26 **"We defer it, my dear"**: Sterne, *Tristram Shandy*, pp. 362–63.

26 **"a neurotic woman"**: Melville, *Mother of Oscar*, p. 79.

27 **"for of course, the fairies"**: Wilson, *Victorian Doctor*, p. 324.

28 **"a certain resentment"**: Stoker, *The Man*, p.17.

28 **"a handsome, strong minded woman"**: Leatherdale, *Dracula: The Novel and the Legend*, p. 57.

29 **"was not a fanciful"**: FAR, p. 13.

29 **"didn't care a tuppence"**: MUR, p. 14.

29 **"matrimonial speculation"**: Charlotte M. B. Stoker, "On Female Emigration from Workhouses" (printer's proof of pamphlet; Dublin, 1864), p. 9. TCD.

29 **"is a perfect blank"**: Charlotte M. B. Stoker, "On the Necessity of a State Provision . . . ," *Journal of the Statistical and Social Inquiry Society of Ireland* (December 1863), p. 456.SFP, TCD.

29 **"no idea of a God"**: Ibid.

30 **"They are to be found"**: Yeats, *Fairy and Folk Tales of Ireland*, p. 7.

31 **"mythopoetic faculty"**: Lady Wilde, *Legends, Charms*, p. 7.

33 **"They were yet young"**: Cruikshank, *Fairy-Book*, pp. 211–12. In this reprint compilation of his famous temperance-tract revisions of classic fairy tales (*The Cruikshank Fairy Library*, 1853–54), the writer and caricaturist follows his own sanitized version of Perrault with an afterword to parents, and takes Charles Dickens to task for championing the stories in their original, unexpurgated form: "I would like to ask if this *peculiarity* of the young Ogres—'*Biting little children on purpose to suck their blood*,' is any part of the 'many such good things' to 'have been first nourished in a child's heart.'"

33 **"Oh! yes, my dears"**: Hoffman, *Struwwelpeter*, p. 62.

36 **From 1855 to 1864:** Levey and O'Rorke, *Annals*, pp. 69–71.

36 **"Going to its first pantomime"**: Stoker, "Theatre Royal—The Pantomime. Juvenile Nights" (unsigned review of *Fee Faw Fum*), *DEM*, January 10, 1872.

37 **"strange effects upon my imagination"**: Graves, *To Return to All That*, p. 13.

38 **"I was an imaginative"**: Ibid., p. 11.

38 **"'Are we to have nothing'"**: *DRA*, p. 43.

39 **"geographic insularity"**: Jones, *Essays*, p. 401.

39 **commercial laudanum preparations:** Wohl, *Endangered Lives*, pp. 34–35.

40 **infanticidal "baby farms":** See Jordan, *Victorian Childhood*, pp. 90–92 for a detailed discussion.

41 **"I was stared at"**: De Quincey, *Confessions*, pp. 118–19.

41 **"shrank up into little old men"**: Ibid.

41 **Le Fanu's wistful story:** Le Fanu, "The Child That Went with the Fairies," in Bannatyne, *A Halloween Reader*, pp. 105–12.

2. Mesmeric Influences

45 **"He wanted to meet"**: Joyce, *Portrait of the Artist*, p. 65.

45 **daunting entrance examination:** All information on Trinity College's entrance requirements, regulations, and courses of study at the time of Bram Stoker's matriculation is drawn from *Dublin University Calendar for the Year 1865*. TCD.

46 **only teacher:** On October 12, 1871, at the age of twenty-three, Stoker made an employment application to the census office, writing of his primary education, "Was at only one school. Reverend Woods' now in 15 Rutland Square E. Dublin." SFP, TCD.

48 **"already a bit of a scribbler"**: LUD, p. 13.

49 **"Rules for Domestic Happiness"**: Undated manuscript by Charlotte Stoker, reprinted in Stoker, *Four Romances*, pp. 37–39.

51 **"He is one and several"**: Simon, *Victor Cousin*, p. 49.

52 **"Sensualism was the reigning doctrine"**: Cousin, *Elements of Psychology*, p. 66.

52 **literary sensationalism:** See Daly, *Sensation and Modernity*, for an extended discussion.

54 **"He lay like a corse"**: Liddell, *"Wizard" . . . and Other Poems*, p. 46.

55 **defensive introductory note:** Le Fanu, *Uncle Silas*, "A Preliminary Word," pp. 3–4.

55 **would specifically recommend the book:** Undated correspondence circa 1960 from Noel Stoker to Harry Ludlam regarding Ludlam's then book-in-progress, *A Biography of Dracula*. TCD.

55 **"a face like marble"**: Le Fanu, *Uncle Silas*, pp. 200, 205.

56 **"At an early age"**: Le Fanu, *Seventy Years of Irish Life*, p. 2.

56 **"I have made a lady"**: Ibid., p. 282.

56 **"As I rapidly made the mesmeric passes"**: Poe, *Essays and Reviews*, p. 842.

57 **"MAGIC PHANTASMAGORIA"**: *DEM*, advertisement, January 17, 1874.

59 **"At school I was"**: Stoker, *Mystery of the Sea*, p. 8.

59 **"my big body and athletic power"**: Ibid.

60 **"That the Novels of the Nineteenth Century"**: Trinity College Historical Society, "Debates for the Season 1871–72." TCD.

61 **"an autodidaktos"**: Stanford and McDowell, *Mahaffy*, p. 113.

61 **"A most distinguished Dublin 'grinder'"**: Cullinan, "Trinity College, Dublin," p. 437.

62 **"I represented in my own person"**: *REM-1*, p. 32.

62 **"He was an excellent "**: "Society in Dublin," unsourced, undated newspaper column, Percy Fitzgerald Scrapbooks, Garrick Club, London, quoted in *MUR*, p. 52.

62 **holiday offerings at the Theatre Royal**: "List of Pantomimes from 1820," in Levey and O'Rorke, *Annals*, pp. 69–71.

63 **"What I saw, to my amazement"**: *REM-1*, p. 3.

63 **"could only be possible"**: Ibid., p. 4.

64 **"I say without any hesitation"**: Hall Caine, "Bram Stoker: The Story of a Great Friendship," *Daily Telegraph*, April 24, 1912.

65 **"Are you going to keep making"**: *IRV*, p. 200.

66 **"There was not a word"**: *REM-1*, p. 11.

66 **"*Two Roses* has created"**: *IRV*, p. 177.

67 **"Dublin's Invisible Prince"**: So called by Alfred Perceval Graves, "A Memoir of Sheridan Le Fanu," in Showers et al., *Reflections*, p. 24.

67 **"When the floodgates of Comment are opened"**: *REM-1*, p. 11.

68 **"From my beginning the work"**: *REM-1*, p. 13.

68 **"In a spectacular sense"**: Stoker, unsigned review of *Amy Robsart*, *DEM*, November 22, 1871.

68 **"The story may be engaging"**: Stoker, "Theatre Royal—The Pantomime—Scenery" (unsigned review of *Fee Faw Fum*), *DEM*, January 2, 1872.

69 **"To look at the legions of sparkling eyes"**: Stoker, "Theatre Royal—The Pantomime. Juvenile Nights" (unsigned review of *Fee Faw Fum*), *DEM*, January 10, 1872.

71 **single 1882 letter**: To Mrs. Billington from Eliza Sarah Stoker, London, concerning her acting career, illness, and financial circumstances. SFP, TCD, Ms. 11076/15/15. In *MUR*, addressee is given as "Mr. Billington." Either way, the surname is indeed used by Stoker in *Dracula*.

72 **Eliza Sarah Stoker's difficult life**: *MUR*, p. 57.

72 **"Old maids are great at pantomimes"**: Stoker, "Theatre Royal—The Pantomime. Juvenile Nights" (unsigned review of *Fee Faw Fum*), *DEM*, January 10, 1872.

72 **"One sad drawback"**: Stoker, "Gaiety Theatre—Italian Operas" (unsigned review of Gounod's *Faust*), *DEM*, September 1, 1873.

73 **"Sometimes after an hour of apathy"**: Le Fanu, *In a Glass Darkly*, p. 264.

74 **"may be thankful to be spared"**: Review of *Carmilla* quoted in Showers et al., *Reflections*, pp. 249–50.

75 **"I can never forget his livid face"**: Quoted in Fawkes, *Dion Boucicault*, p. 74.

76 **"a ballet of great cleverness"**: Stoker, review of *The Vampire* (comic ballet), *DEM*, December 27, 1872.

77 **accused him of rape**: See Melville, *Mother of Oscar*, pp. 95–116, for one of the most detailed accounts of the accusation and trial.

77 **"had a family in every farmhouse":** G. B. Shaw, "My Memories of Oscar Wilde," HAR, p. 330.

77 **they died horribly:** See Melville, *Mother of Oscar*, pp. 128–29.

78 **"Why are Sir William's fingernails black?"** I have been unable to find a definitive version of this quote; mine is its own variant of endless slight variations given in ELL, HAR, and many other biographies.

78 **"a society for the suppression of Virtue":** Quoted in Friedman, *Wilde in America*, p. 24.

78 **"Portraits of her husband, sons":** Schenkar, *Truly Wilde, p.* 55.

79 **"a walking family mausoleum":** Melville, *Mother of Oscar*, p. 124.

79 **"She must have had two crinolines":** Schenkar, *Truly Wilde*, p. 55.

79 **"too thick for any ordinary light":** HAR, p. 17.

79 **"hide the decline of her beauty":** Julian, *Oscar Wilde*, p. 32.

79 **"Her clinging to youth":** SHE, p. 73.

80 **"You know there is a disease":** G. B. Shaw, "My Memories of Oscar Wilde," HAR, p. 334.

80 **ape-slur "pithecoid":** HAR, p. 17.

82 **"he did not say 'goodbye'":** Ibid., p. 21.

82 **dismissed as "barbarian":** Ibid., p. 27.

82 **"I'll prove it to you":** O'Sullivan, *Aspects of Wilde*, pp. 171–72.

83 **"I once knew a little boy":** Stoker, *Lost Journal*, p. 66.

3. Songs of Calamus, Songs of Sappho

85 **"Let shadows be furnished with genitals!":** WHI, 606. This poem, which appeared in the original 1856 edition of *Leaves of Grass* but was omitted from later editions, is included in the *Complete Poems* under the title "Respondez!"

85 **Dublin relocations:** *MUR*; see chapters 2 and 4. Three previous biographers took it for granted that the Stokers remained in Clontarf for most of Bram's life in Dublin, and mistakenly assumed that Florence Balcombe was a childhood acquaintance. Murray was the first to document the family's frequent moves.

86 **"And if the body does not":** WHI, p. 128.

87 **"nothing in common":** Anonymous, "The Poetry of the Future," *Temple Bar* 27 (October 1869), p. 327.

87 **"For days we all talked":** REM-2, p. 94.

88 **"The bitter-minded critics of the time":** Ibid., p. 93.

88 **"unfortunately, there were passages":** Ibid.

88 **"A mass of stupid filth":** Rufus W. Griswold, untitled review, *Criterion*, November 10, 1855, p. 24.

89 **"I mind how once we lay":** WHI, p. 67.

89 **"From these excerpts":** REM-2, p. 94.

89 **"These yearnings why are they?":** WHI, p. 183.

89 **"For an athlete is enamored of me":** Ibid., p. 164.

90 **term and concept of "heterosexuality":** See Blank, *Straight*, for an especially good discussion.

90 **"Little by little we got recruits":** REM-2, p. 95.

90 **"recalls the features which Vandyke":** Hinkson, *Student Life*, p. 42.

91 **"If there be any class of subjects":** "The Poetry of Democracy: Walt Whitman," in Dowden, *Studies in Literature*, p. 502.

92 **"Dowden was a married man":** REM-2, p. 98.

92 **"If you are the man"**: The complete texts of Stoker's 1871 and 1875 letters, with Whitman's commentary, appear in Traubel, *With Walt Whitman*, vol. 4, pp. 151–54.

98 **"Will men ever believe"**: Stoker, *Lost Journal*, p. 134.

98 **"I felt as tho'"**: Ibid., p. 143.

99 **pioneering German activists**: For a comprehensive overview of German activism, see Beachy, *Gay Berlin*, especially chapter 1, "The German Invention of Homosexuality," and chapter 3, "The First Homosexual Rights Movement and the Struggle to Shape Society."

100 **"The universe of intimate friendship"**: Katz, *Love Letters*, p. 6.

100 **Victorian euphemisms**: See Robb, *Strangers*, especially pp. 149–50.

101 **"Sad and plaintive is the song"**: Stoker, "The Crystal Cup," *Shades of Dracula*, p. 27.

101 **"And then the brush was given"**: Poe, *Essays and Reviews*, pp. 483–44.

102 **"Oratory is not in itself a sufficient object"**: Stoker, "The Necessity for Political Honesty," in *A Glimpse of America*, p. 33.

102 **"He could at best move"**: *REM-2*, p. 99.

103 **"has evinced a strong partiality"**: Stoker, unsigned review of *Kissi-Kissi*, *DEM*, December 1, 1873.

103 **"So ends my dream"**: Stoker, *Lost Journal*, pp. 29–30.

105 **"a frightful monster"**: Stoker (unsigned column), *Irish Echo*, November 25, 1873.

106 **"worked up one of those sensational sermons"**: Stoker, "Exciting Scene in St. James Church" (unsigned column), *Irish Echo*, November 7, 1873.

106 **another mordantly funny item**: Stoker, "Pinching an Actress" (unsigned column), *Irish Echo*, December 11, 1873.

107 **"Do any of you believe in ghosts?"**: Stoker, "Saved by a Ghost" (unsigned short story), *Irish Echo*, December 26, 1873; reprinted in *The Green Book: Writings on Irish Gothic, Supernatural and Fantastic Literature* (Autumn 2015), pp. 3–13.

109 **"A sad tale's best for winter"**: *SHA*, *Winter's Tale*, act 2, scene 1, line 27, p. 2905.

109 **"that speak of spirits and ghosts"**: Marlowe, *Jew of Malta*, act 2, scene 1, p. 23.

109 **"whenever five or six English-speaking people"**: Jerome, *Told after Supper*, pp. 15–16.

110 **"little short of perfection"**: Stoker, unsigned review of *La Sonnambula*, *DEM*, September 3, 1878.

111 **"mystic yet picturesque"**: Stoker, unsigned review of *Roberto il diavolo*. *DEM*, October 9, 1877.

112 **"the end seat O.P."**: *REM-2*, p. 167.

113 **"cordial and appreciative"**: Stoker, unsigned review of *Lucrezia Borgia*, *DEM*, November 18, 1873.

113 **"Mem. will be a great actress"**: *REM-2*, p. 169.

113 **"It is a daring thing"**: Stoker, "Theatre Royal. Miss Genevieve Ward. *Medea*" (unsigned review), *Irish Echo*, November 25, 1873.

113 **"From first to last"**: Ibid.

114 **"And then there began a close friendship"**: *REM-2*, p. 169.

114 **"not human"**: Gustavson, *Genevieve Ward*, p. 12.

115 **"had all the vices of a full grown man"**: Ibid., p. 69.

115 **"personal power with both men and women"**: Ibid.

115 **"is entirely a matter of chance"**: Austen, *Pride and Prejudice*, p. 21.

116 **"I consider it a funeral":** Gustavson, *Genevieve Ward*, p. 66.

116 **"None but genius of the highest class":** Stoker, unsigned review of *Medea*, *DEM*, undated, quoted in Gustavson, *Genevieve Ward*, pp. 124–25.

117 **"She was a grand woman":** Ward and Whiteing, *Both Sides of the Curtain*, p. 104.

117 **"strange similarity":** Ibid., p. 77.

119 **"bottled orations" . . . "to come":** Ibid, p. 274.

120 **"He died last night":** Stoker, "The Burial of the Rats," *GUE*, p. 117.

120 **"Other cities resemble all the birds":** ibid., P. 94.

120 **Stoker wrote to his father:** Mur, p. 58.

121 **he jotted a note** Stoker, *Lost Journal*, p. 66.

121 **"hardened to rejection":** Stoker, *Primrose Path*, "Series Editor's Note," p. 13.

121 **"The general belief that Reggie's mother was a":** Hart-Davis, *Max Beerbohm's Letters to Reggie Turner*, pp. 11–12.

122 **"Moth-like he had buzzed":** Stoker, *Primrose Path*, p. 39.

122 **"When the bar-keeper turned round":** Ibid., p. 52.

122 **"primrose path":** *SHA, Hamlet*, act 1, scene 3, line 50, p. 1708.

124 **using vomit to lubricate:** Stoker, *Lost Journal*, pp. 199–200.

124 **"a veritable tragedy of family resemblance":** Schenkar, *Truly Wilde*, p. 57.

124 **described him in his later London days:** Ibid.

125 **"America needs a leisure class":** Ibid., p. 59.

125 **"not only disgusting":** Cruikshank, *Fairy-Book*, p. 210.

126 **"the use of strong drink":** Ibid., p. 195.

126 **"'With all deference to your Majesty'":** Ibid., pp. 195–96.

127 **"of sorts":** Ward and Whiteing, *Both Sides of the Curtain*, p. 73.

127 **"was immediately surrounded":** Ward and Whiteing, *Both Sides of the Curtain*, p. 73.

127 **"He had proposed":** Ibid., 74.

127 **"His nature was a most affectionate one":** Stoker, "Recollections," p. 145.

128 **"It was on this holiday":** Stoker, "Recollections of the Late W. G. Wills" [1891], *Forgotten Writings*, p. 146.

129 **"drink thy veins as wine":** Swinburne, "Anactoria," *Collected Poems*, p. 67.

129 **"a braggart in manners of vice":** Hyde, *Oscar Wilde*, p. 168.

131 **"We were in full rehearsal":** *REM-2*, deleted material in holograph manuscript, Folger Shakespeare Library, Washington, DC.

131 **"in great distress":** Ibid.

131 **"Live, Sappho! Live! Live!":** Ibid.

132 **"the play is one of great force":** Stoker, "Gaiety Theatre—Miss Genevieve Ward" (unsigned announcement of *Sappho*), *DEM*, June 7, 1875.

132 **"the soul of Sappho is no empty name":** Stoker, "Miss Genevieve Ward as Sappho" (unsigned review), *DEM*, June 9, 1875.

133 **"If males find intercourse":** Quoted by Elizabeth D. Harvey, "Ventriloquizing Sappho, or the Lesbian Muse," in Greene, *Re-Reading Sappho*, p. 91.

134 **"the peculiar delight and excitement":** Mahaffy, *Social Life in Greece*, p. 305.

134 **"imagine a modern Irishman":** Ibid., p. 306.

134 **"The Darwinians say":** Ibid., p. 307.

134 **"a great proportion":** Ibid., p. 308.

134 **public urinals:** Lacey, *Terrible Queer Creatures*, p. 139.

134 **male brothel:** Ibid., p. 141.

135 **"a whiff of the 'musical'":** Ibid., p. 152.

135 **"Yes, but not in any offensive sense":** Stanford and McDowell, *Mahaffy*, p. 128.

135 **"Oh, no, we don't":** Ibid.

135 **"I can't conceive":** Fadiman, *Bartlett's Book*, p. 367.

135 **"As to the epithet *unnatural*":** Mahaffy, *Social Life in Greece*, p. 308.

136 **"In place of the offending pages":** Stanford and McDowell, *Mahaffy*, p. 157.

136 **"to make a proper pagan":** Pearson, *Life of Oscar Wilde*, p. 38.

136 **"We no longer speak of Mr. Oscar Wilde":** Stanford and McDowell, *Mahaffy*, p. 87.

136 **"Spoke—I think well":** *REM-2*, p. 96.

136 **"My dear Mr. Whitman":** Traubel, *With Walt Whitman*, vol. 4, pp. 181–85.

138 **"my letters were only of the usual pattern":** *REM-2*, p. 97.

138 **"My dear young man":** Ibid.

4. Engagements and Commitments

141 **"Women are pictures":** *WIL*, p. 460.

141 **"Wilde noticed women's faces":** Belford, *Oscar Wilde*, p. 55.

142 **"in scenes of passionate invective":** Stoker, "Theatre Royal—*Leah*" (unsigned review), *DEM*, October 22, 1872.

142 **"wrinkled as though"** . . . **"Greeks and Japanese":** *DRA*, p. 188.

142 **"the savage glitter of the eye":** Stoker, "Madame Ristori in 'Medea'" (unsigned review), *DEM*, August 7, 1873.

142 **"almost beyond belief":** Stoker, "Theatre Royal—Madame Ristori" (unsigned review), *DEM*, August 9, 1873.

142 **"She is best in those scenes":** Stoker, "Theatre Royal—*Leah*" (unsigned review), *DEM*, October 22, 1872.

144 **"I know your present income":** Undated letter to Stoker from Abraham Stoker, quoted in LUD, p. 39.

144 **"He never gets into debt":** Quoted in White, *Parents of Oscar Wilde*, p. 238.

144 **"An outsider has no chance":** Undated letter from Abraham Stoker to Stoker. SFP, TCD.

144 **"She is a Protestant":** Stoker, *Lost Journal*, 146.

144 **"Strange scenes, dark, secret, and cruel":** Lady Wilde, *Legends*, p. 326.

145 **"I am sure you will not think":** Quoted in MUR, p. 51.

145 **"latest move on the family chessboard":** Stoker, *Lost Journal*, p. 105.

146 *Go to the moon—you selfish dreamer!*: Williams, *Plays, 1937–1955*, p. 464.

146 **"immortal longings":** SHA, *Antony and Cleopatra*, act 5, scene 2, lines 271–72, p. 2719.

147 **"half English and half Irish":** Wyndham, *Speranza*, p. 70.

148 **"In walking, he plants one foot":** Anonymous, *Fashionable Tragedian.*, p. 7.

148 **Midlands or North Country accent:** See ibid., pp. 7–9 for examples of Irving's pronunciation; also IRV, p. 298.

149 **"farceur's tricks":** *IRV*, pp. 309–10.

149 **wax cylinder recording:** The *Richard III* wax recording can be heard at youtube.com/watch?v=7Z4gXiNKR4s. For information on other possible recordings of Irving's voice, see "The Voice of Henry Irving" at the Irving Society: theirvingsociety.Org.Uk/the-voice-of-henry-irving/.

149 **"naturally harsh voice":** Anonymous, *Tragedian*, p. 7.

149 **"His intensity hypnotized me":** Wilson, *Edwardian Theatre*, p. 48.

149 **"Apart from his fatal mannerisms":** Anonymous, *Tragedian*, p. 9.

150 **"There are those":** Ibid., p. 14.

150 **"It was all very tiresome":** *IRV*, p. 293.

150 **"a hard fight"**: *REM-1*, p. 19.

150 **"Mr. Irving's very appearance"**: Stoker, "Mr. Irving's Hamlet" (unsigned review), *DEM*, November 28, 1876.

151 **"It is the strangest love story on record"**: Dowden, *Tragedy of Hamlet*, p. xxviii.

152 **description of a new family maid as "very pretty"**: Stoker, *Lost Journal*, p. 140.

152 **" 'Tis now the very witching time of night"**: *SHA*, *Hamlet*, act 3, scene 2, line 358, p. 1745.

153 **"The great, deep, underlying ideal"**: Stoker, "Mr. Irving's Hamlet. Second Notice" (unsigned review), *DEM*, December 2, 1876.

153 **"the defiant cock's feather"**: Brereton, *Life of Irving*, vol. 2, p. 92.

153 **"lingering methodism"**: Ibid.

153 **"Toward the end of 1864"**: *IRV*, p. 119.

155 **Venoma the Spiteful Fairy**: Ibid., p. 86.

155 **"An actor *never* forgets a hiss!"**: *REM-1*, p. 18.

156 **"would peep over the bannisters"**: Millward, *Myself and Others*, pp. 31–32.

156 **"weird and thrilling"**: Saintsbury and Palmer, *We Saw Him Act*, p. 82.

157 **" 'Twas in the prime of summer-time"**: Hood, "The Dream of Eugene Aram," *Works*, vol. 1, pp. 283–300.

158 **"That I knew the story"**: All Stoker quotes on Irving's recitation of "The Dream" are taken from *REM-1*, pp. 28–33.

159 **"I can only say"**: Stoker, original holograph manuscript of *REM-1*, chapter 3, Folger Shakespeare Library.

161 *This man belongs to me I want him*: Stoker, *Notes*, p. 17.

161 **"His worst is his being incapable of caring"**: Quoted in Morgan, *Dramatic Critic*, p. 226.

161 **"The effect of his recitation upon Stoker"**: *IRV*, p. 279.

162 **"Anything more splendid"**: Stoker, "Mr Irving and *The Bells*" (unsigned review), *DEM*, December 4, 1876.

162 **"princely; it is noble"**: Stoker, "Mr Irving as Charles I" (unsigned review), *DEM*, December 6, 1876.

162 **"They had come prepared"**: *REM-1*, p. 40.

163 **"Hats and handkerchiefs were waved"**: Stoker, "University Night for Mr Irving" (unsigned column), *DEM*, December 11, 1876.

163 **"Choir Boy"**: McKenna, *Secret Life of Oscar Wilde*, p. 7.

164 **"only mentally spoons the boy"**: ELL, p. 62.

165 **"*exquisitely pretty girl*"**: LET, p. 29.

166 **"George Francis Miles"**: Croft-Cooke, *Unreported Life*, p. 40.

167 **"Women were half of the question of love"**: McKenna, *Secret Life of Oscar Wilde*, p. 10.

169 **"The fuming censers"**: *WIL*, p. 106.

169 **"a pleasant cheery fellow"**: Quoted in McKenna, *Secret Life of Oscar Wilde*, p. 12.

169 **"And now upon thy walls"**: *WIL*, p. 730.

169 **"It was so very good of you"**: Undated letter from Florence Balcombe to Oscar Wilde (summer 1877), William Andrews Clark Library, Los Angeles.

170 **folktale-like story**: Yeats, *Autobiography*, p. 120.

170 **flirted with other Dublin girls**: See McKenna, *Secret Life of Oscar Wilde*, p. 9.

170 **"It was at Oxford"**: ELL, p. 92.

171 **"His death [in 1900]"**: Ransome, *Oscar Wilde*, p. 199.

171 **"knew himself to be syphilitic"**: Sherard, May 1937 letter to Arthur Symons, quoted in Hayden, *Pox*, p. 207.

171 **"The main physical effect of mercury"**: ELL, p. 92.
171 **caustic wash of nitric acid:** Wynbrandt, *Excruciating History*, p. 49.
172 **"Whatever your first purpose"**: ELL, pp. 93–94.
172 **"The word 'syphilis' was taboo"**: Hayden, *Pox*, p. 70.
173 **various accounts:** For discussions of the Oxford prostitute see Hyde, quoting Harris, *Trials of Oscar Wilde*, p. 56; and ELL, p. 92. R. F. Foster, in *Lord Randolph Churchill: A Political Life*, convincingly affirms Churchill's syphilis but rejects the prostitute claims.
173 **"Wasted Days"**: WIL, p. 732.
174 **"pricked ears, two rows of yellow teeth"**: Huysmans, *Against the Grain*, p. 92.
176 **"Many Demons and Divinities"**: Quoted in Andersen, *Picasso's Brothel*, p. 147.
177 **Irving made him a personal introduction:** REM-1, pp. 44–47.
178 **"We were quite alone"**: Ibid., p. 53.
178 **"London in view!"**: Ibid., p. 54.
178 **"I closed my eyes in a languorous ecstasy"**: DRA, p. 43.
179 **"could not speak, he could not walk"**: Terry, *Story of My Life*, p. 81.
180 **"Why can't they let a girl marry three men"**: DRA, p. 60.
180 **likened to a bulldog:** Manvell, *Ellen Terry*, p. 99.
180 **"definite" commitment:** Holroyd, *Strange Eventful History*, p. 115.
181 **"one of the dullest and most uninteresting performances"**: Unsigned Times (London) review of Vanderdecken, June 10, 1878.
181 **"In his face is the ghastly pallor"**: Stoker, Dublin review of *Vanderdecken*, quoted in *REM-1*, p. 56.
182 **"A more cleverly-managed"**: Unsigned *Times* (London) review of *Vanderdecken*, June 10, 1878.
182 **"The play proved less buoyant"**: IRV, p. 309.
183 **oft-repeated story:** LUD, p. 114. Apparently the first publication of this anecdote, given to Ludlam by Stoker's son, Noel. Did Irving really call the reading of *Dracula* "dreadful"? "He probably did," said Noel, "and it probably was."
183 **"You are quite wrong"**: Bingham, *Henry Irving*, p. 270.
183 **"I spent hours with Irving"**: REM-1, p. 57.
183 **"mysterious-looking house"**: Hatton, "Sir Henry Irving," p. 16.
184 **"over so many miles of land and sea"**: LET, p. 67.
185 **"one of his stage tricks"**: IRV, p. 310.
186 **"great friends"**: REM-1, p. 60.
186 **"an intensive period of probation"**: irv, p. 309.
187 **"received a telegram"**: rem-1, p. 60.
187 **rather quaintly, as "spinster":** 1878 Certificate of Marriage for Abraham Stoker and Florence Balcombe. SFP, TCD.
188 **"Though you have not thought it worth while"**: LET, p. 71.
188 **"Whatever difference of opinion"**: Unsigned review (presumably by Stoker) of *The Tempest*, DEM, November 26, 1878.

5. Londoners

191 **"I long to go through the crowded streets"**: DRA, p. 26.
191 **London was filthy:** See Jackson, *Dirty Old London*, for a comprehensive overview of urban dirt in the Victorian era.
192 **"the fog in London assumes all sorts of colors"**: Quoted in Corton, *London Fog*, p. 185.
192 **"child's play compared with the next two weeks"**: REM-1, p. 62.

193 **The Lyceum property:** See Wilson, *Lyceum*, for a complete history of the theatre's numerous incarnations.

193 **Stoker occupied a work alcove:** *IRV*, p. 322.

194 **"I don't know what to do":** Lady Wilde, undated letter to Oscar Wilde (early 1899), quoted in Melville, *Mother of Oscar*, p. 154.

195 **"faded splendor was more striking":** White, *Parents of Oscar Wilde*, p. 248.

195 **"desperate affairs":** HAR, p. 330.

196 **"To Helen formerly of Troy":** ELL, p. 143.

196 **"epigrams are always better than argument":** Lady Wilde, *Social Studies*, p. 70.

196 **"a kindly, handsome fellow":** Edwin Ward, *Recollections*, p. 108.

196 **demonstration of "thought reading":** Friedman, *Wilde in America*, p. 45.

197 **truly spooky personal end:** For a good précis of Irving's career and macabre death, see "The Strange Life and Death of Washington Irving Bishop," themagicdetective.com/2011/03/strange-life-death-of-washington-irving.html.

198 **"If a man leads an evil life":** ELL, p. 147.

198 **"the old-fashioned cleric became alarmed":** Ward, *Recollections*, pp. 110–11.

199 **"If you try to look at it":** WIL, p. 92.

199 **Frank Miles had syphilis:** McKenna, *Secret Life of Oscar Wilde*, p. 52. The author attests to Miles's disease, but not Wilde's, suggesting that only the fear of syphilis drove him to seek a "marriage cure" for his sexual proclivities.

200 **"Tell George I have given up his idea":** ELL, p. 149.

201 **"The more I think of it":** Joseph Robinson, Dublin, letters on the birth of Stoker's son, January 1880. SFP, TCD.

202 **"I must lose not a moment":** Ibid.

202 **"You did not answer my letter":** Ibid.

202 **"My family, speaking of her":** FAR, p. 213.

203 **listed her occupation as "artist":** Stoker entry, London census for 1881. Digital facsimile courtesy of John Edgar Browning.

205 **paying bills in gold sovereigns:** Harry Ludlam, unpublished notes of interview with Robert George Hillburn, East Sheen, October 1957, for *A Biography of Dracula*. SFP, TCD.

205 **"To attain the necessary degree of secrecy":** Noel Stoker, "BRAM STOKER by His Son, Noel Thornley Stoker," undated typewritten manuscript circa November 8, 1947. SFP, TCD.

205 **a full-throated roar:** Ibid.

207 **"somewhat out of keeping":** *DEM* review of *Under the Sunset*, November 16, 1881, quoted in "Some Opinions of the Press" (publisher's promotional flyer), Fales Library, New York University.

207 **"It is whispered that Death":** Stoker, *Under the Sunset*, p. 11.

209 **"Pass not the Portal of the Sunset Land!":** Ibid., p. 104.

210 **"a charming book":** *Punch* review of *Under the Sunset*, December 3, 1881, quoted in "Some Opinions of the Press" (publisher's promotional flyer), Fales Library, New York University.

210 **"If, as in the":** Unsigned *Morning Post* review of *Under the Sunset*, December 1, 1881.

212 **"Under the pleasant stories":** Unsigned *Norfolk News* review of *Under the Sunset*, November 26, 1881.

212 **"is upon the same ground as Nathaniel Hawthorne":** Unsigned *Spectator* review of *Under the Sunset*, November 12, 1881.

212 **a vanity project:** MUR, p. 151.

213 **"The plight of the hospital's sick children":** John Moore, Dublin, in correspondence with the author, January 2015.

213 **"a book as kind, and genial":** Unsigned *Dublin Freeman's Journal* review of *Under the Sunset*, November 12, 1881.

213 **"a red-bearded giant":** Noel Stoker, "BRAM STOKER by His Son, Noel Thornley Stoker," undated typewritten manuscript circa November 8, 1947. SFP, TCD.

214 **impromptu swimming lesson:** FAR, p. 215.

215 **wet nurse "starved" him:** MUR, p. 111.

215 **A FILIAL REPROOF:** *Punch*, September 11, 1886.

217 **"Oscar Wilde, the long-haired":** Friedman, *Wilde in America*, p. 208.

218 **"I don't see why such mocking things":** "Wilde and Whitman: The Aesthetic Singer Visits the Good Gray Poet," *Philadelphia Press*, January 19, 1882.

218 **"the grandest man I have ever seen":** ELL, p. 170.

218 **"In free conversation with intimate friends":** Harrison Reeves, *Mercure de France*, June 1, 1913, quoted in McKenna, *Secret Life of Oscar Wilde, p.* 32.

218 **"after embracing, greeting each other":** Ibid.

219 **"The Opera House was draped in crimson silk":** *REM-1*, pp. 159–60.

220 **"We had amongst others":** Ibid, p. 169.

221 **"He bears the body":** Ibid, pp. 96–98.

223 **"are wanting in the imagination of tragedy":** Richards, *Sir Henry Irving: A Victorian Actor*, p. 56.

223 **"intrepid swimmer":** Noel Stoker, "BRAM STOKER by His Son, Noel Thornley Stoker," undated typewritten manuscript circa November 8, 1947. SFP, TCD.

224 **"the recollection of a clammy corpse":** Ibid.

225 **"icebergs, blocks, stone":** *IRV*, p. 424.

226 **"old man of leonine appearance":** *REM-2*, pp. 92–93.

227 **"Be it remembered":** Ibid., p. 100.

227 **"all that I had ever dreamed of":** Ibid.

229 **unafraid to disagree:** *IRV*, pp. 362–63.

229 **"Hypnotism was at that time":** Millward, *Myself and Others*, pp. 99–100.

230 **"His house, 328 Mickle Street":** *REM-2*, pp. 102–3.

230 **Whitman's account of the assassination:** Ibid., p. 104.

230 **"Well, well; what a broth of a boy":** Ibid., p. 105.

231 **"agreed that it was a great pity":** Ibid., p. 106.

232 **"I want you to read it all to me":** Whitman's comments on Stoker appear in Traubel, *With Walt Whitman*, vol. 4, pp. 179–185.

233 **"Shortly after I came in":** *REM-2*, p. 111.

234 **Constance's pregnancies disgusted him:** HAR, pp. 284–85.

235 **"The Harlot's House":** *WIL*, p. 789.

236 **"I hope you will like them":** Hart-Davis, *More Letters of Oscar Wilde*, p. 75. The editor notes that the copy of *The Happy Prince* inscribed to Florence sold for $8,500 at Christie's, New York, in 1984.

236 **"whole forepart of the boat was underwater":** BEL, pp. 195–96.

236 **His decision was reported in the press:** MUR, p. 114.

237 **"I feel somewhat like a guilty man":** Stoker, letter to J. B. Pond, August 13, 1887. Fales Library, New York University.

6. Pantomimes from Hell

239 **"'Tis the eye of childhood":** *SHA*, *Macbeth*, act 2, scene 2, lines 52–53, p. 2594.

239 **severed head:** One candidate for the spectral woman is Madame Marie

Tussaud, who, according to legend, was forced by the leaders of the Terror to make death masks from guillotined heads. Tussaud's first London exhibition in 1802 was located at the later site of the Lyceum. It has also been suggested that the head belonged to one Henry Courtenay, an earlier owner of the underlying land, sentenced to beheading by Oliver Cromwell during the English Civil War. The original source of this story has proved impossible to trace, but it appears repeatedly in surveys of theatrical ghost lore. See, for example, Douglas McPherson, "Theatrical Haunts: The Ghosts of the West End," *The Stage* (website) October 29, 2010, thestage.co.uk/features/2010/theatrical-haunts-the-ghosts-of-the-west-end; and "The Real Ghosts of London's Theatres," December 11, 2012, hubpages.com/religion-philosophy/Real-Ghosts-in-London-Theatres.

240 **clueless Chinese ambassador:** *REM-1*, pp. 78–79.
240 **Goethe's introduction:** Goethe first saw the puppet version of *Faust*, descended from Marlowe, between 1753 and 1758 ("Johann Wolfgang von Goethe: A Chronology," in *Faust: A Norton Critical Edition*, p. 731). Bantam Classics translator Peter Salm cites Goethe's comment in his autobiography, *Poetry and Truth*: "The important puppet-fable [of Faust] continued to echo and buzz many-toned within me" (p. x).
241 **"Irving's intuition as a showman":** *IRV*, p. 470.
242 **"When Irving was about":** *REM-1*, pp. 178–79.
242 **wanted to give Irving a knighthood:** Holroyd, *Strange Eventful History*, p. 259.
242 **"And then the spikes did their work":** Stoker, "The Squaw," *GUE*, p. 49.
244 **"a spectacle sufficiently ghastly":** Mead, "In a Munich Deadhouse," pp. 460–61.
244 **"Sees old man on bier":** Stoker, *Notes*, p. 35.
244 **"and he thought now the man of the Munich Dead House":** Stoker (Klinger), *New Annotated "Dracula,"* p. 264.
244 **"had dealings with the Evil One":** *DRA*, p. 212.
244 **"school supposed to exist":** Emily Gerard, "Transylvanian Superstitions" [1882], excerpted in Miller, *Bram Stoker's "Dracula,"* p. 184.
245 **"Even then at that awful moment":** Stoker (Klinger), *New Annotated "Dracula,"* p. 390.
245 **"Sooth, this man is an enemy":** Wills, *Faust*, p. 39.
246 **"By what pretence":** Ibid., p. 42.
247 **"never cared much for Henry's Mephistopheles":** Terry, *Story of My Life*, p. 264.
247 **"Henry looked to grow":** Ibid.
247 **"See here this skull":** Wills, *Faust*, p. 4.
247 **"The lord of the frogs":** Goethe, *Faust* (Anster trans.), p. 84.
248 **"Dost thou not wish you had a broomstick":** Ibid., p. 54.
249 **"I began to have certain grave doubts":** *REM-1*, pp. 146–47.
251 **"Gone was the debonair, cheery, holiday companion":** Holroyd, *Strange Eventful History*, p. 172.
251 **"Many of the effects were experimental":** *REM-1*, p. 176.
251 **"This effect was arranged by Colonel Gouraud":** Ibid.
252 **"Altogether the effects of light and flame":** Ibid., pp. 176–77.
252 **"steam and mist are elements":** Ibid., p. 177.
253 **"was performed in London":** Ibid., p. 175.
253 **"It wouldn't matter":** Henry James, "The Acting in Mr. Irving's 'Faust'" (unsigned review), *Saturday Review*, December 1887, pp. 312–13.
257 **"That idiot Stoker wrote a speech":** *IRV*, pp. 452–53.

258 **"One night early in the run"**: *REM-1*, p. 183.

259 **"Mr. Irving's 'Faust'"**: "Irving's 'Faust'" (unsigned review), *New York Times*, November 8, 1887.

260 **"In New York the business"**: *REM-1*, p. 184.

262 **"there is for an outsider"**: Ibid., p. 140.

262 **"So like were the knives"**: Stoker, "The Dualitists," pp. 23–24.

264 **"'Macbeth' occupies a peculiar position amongst plays"**: Stoker, "Theatre Royal—*Macbeth*" (unsigned review), *DEM*, October 20, 1873.

265 **"It was supposed to be vast"**: *REM-1*, p. 23.

267 **"his dagger soliloquy"**: Stoker, "Theatre Royal—*Macbeth*" (unsigned review), *DEM*, October 20, 1873.

267 **"a famished wolf"**: Terry, *Story of My Life*, p. 329.

269 **"would give the appearance"**: Alice Comyns Carr, quoted in Holroyd, *Strange Eventful History*, p. 200.

269 **"The whole thing is Rossetti"**: Terry, *Story of My Life*, p. 333.

269 **"Lady Macbeth seems to be an economical housekeeper"**: Quoted in Holland, *Shakespeare, Memory, and Performance*, p. 151.

270 **"The street that on a wet"**: Oscar Wilde, quoted in Holroyd, *Strange Eventful History*, p. 200.

7. The Isle of Men

273 **"Heaven save me from this fiend"**: Caine's *Drink* is long out of print and virtually impossible to find in libraries, but the full text has been made available online by Manx National Heritage. All quotations in this chapter are taken from this unpaginated transcription: isle-of-man.com/manxnotebook/fulltext/hcdr1906/index.htm.

273 **"Delighted to see you tonight"**: Allen, *Hall Caine*, pp. 64–65.

274 **"She believed in every kind of supernatural"**: Caine, *My Story*, p. 10.

275 **"To see Stoker in his element"**: Wyndham, *Nineteen Hundreds*, pp. 118–19.

276 **"So mediocre is Mr. Caine's book"**: Oscar Wilde, "Coleridge's Life," *Essays*, pp. 372–74.

276 **"Mr. Hall Caine, it is true"**: *WIL*, p. 973.

277 **"lavish heavy wealth of coppery golden hair"**: Rossetti, *His Family Letters*, vol. 1, p. 171.

277 **"sunny ripples" of hair**: *DRA*, p. 146.

279 **"You see, my dear Hall Caine"**: Stoker, letter to Hall Caine (damaged, date missing, circa 1890). Hall Caine Papers, Manx National Heritage.

280 **"the conversation tended towards weird subjects"**: *REM-2*, p. 122.

280 **"During many years I spent time"**: Caine, *My Story*, p. 349.

280 **engaged Florence Stoker**: The typescript of *Mahomet*, personally examined by the author among Caine's papers at Manx National Heritage, has the line "Translated by Mrs. Bram Stoker" written in pencil on the title page. The entire script seems to have been typed on the same, uniquely charactered machine as Stoker's one typed letter to Caine, suggesting it was transcribed by the same typewriting service. Both the script and the letter are undated but contemporaneous, circa 1890.

280 **"Now in the dim twilight"**: *REM-2*, pp. 119–20.

281 **"I spent months on 'Mohammed'"**: Caine, *My Story*, p. 343.

281 **"In spite of the utmost sincerity"**: Ibid., p. 349.

282 **Irving himself had passed up the chance**: *REM-2*, p. 137. According to Stoker,

Irving paid handsomely for an unproduced stage adaptation of *Jekyll and Hyde* by O. Booth and J. Dixon but never performed in it. Mansfield did not use this adaptation, and neither did Irving's son Laurence. There is no record of the Booth/Dixon version actually being performed anywhere.

282 **one impressionable theatregoer:** The original October 5, 1988, letter accusing Mansfield is archived at the British Library and can be examined online: bl.uk/collection-items/anonymous-letter-to-city-of-london-police-about-jack-the-ripper.

283 **"There is but little scope":** *Times* (London), August 6, 1988.

283 **"the same way as children are":** "A Thirst for Blood," *East End Advertiser*, October 6, 1888.

284 **Return-addressed "From hell":** Eddleston, *Jack the Ripper*, pp. 160–61.

285 **American quack doctor, Francis Tumblety:** For the basic facts of Tumblety's life and career, the author has relied primarily on Evans and Gainey, *Jack the Ripper*, as well as Riordan's *Prince of Quacks*. In addition to the Manx National Heritage letters from Tumblety to Caine personally transcribed by the author, revealing correspondence appears in Storey's *Dracula Secrets*, pp. 112–28. See also Allen, *Hall Caine*, pp. 37–42.

285 **"a dirty, awkward, ignorant":** Evans and Gainey, *Jack the Ripper*, p. 190.

285 **According to Colonel C. A. Dunham:** Ibid., pp. 194–96.

287 **"He had a seeming mania":** Ibid., p. 212.

287 **"Your letter just received";** Francis Tumblety, letter to hall caine, april 2, 1875. Hall caine papers, manx national heritage library.

288 **"Don't trifle with my patience":** Tumblety to Caine, August 6, 1875. Ibid.

289 **"Dear boy wire at once":** Tumblety to Caine, April 1875, Allen, *Hall Caine*, p. 39.

289 **"Come here tomorrow evening":** Undated telegram, ibid.

291 **"The chinamen are as nasty as Locust":** Tumblety to Caine, March 31, 1876. Hall Caine Papers, Manx National Heritage Library.

291 **"Travel for Tumblety was not a source of amusement":** Evans and Gainey, *Jack the Ripper*, p. 260.

295 **"Unclean! unclean!":** *DRA*, p. 259.

295 **"a place of popular entertainment":** Caine, *Drink* (see first note to this chapter).

295 **"It was still an hour earlier":** Ibid.

295 **"Dr. La Mothe," he asks:** Ibid.

298 **"the great hypnotizer":** Ibid.; see Appendix.

298 **leading advocate was Dr. John D. Quackenbos:** Katz, *Gay American History*, pp. 220–22.

299 **"psychical hermaphrodites":** Krafft-Ebing's coinage, quoted by Schfrenck-Notzig in *Therapeutic Suggestion*, in which he personally uses the term "psycho-hermaphrodite." See Schrenck-Notzig's extended and illuminating discussion in chapter 12, "Histories Illustrating Suggestion Therapeutics in Perversions of the Sexual Instinct," pp. 210–305.

299 **"portrayed 'unnatural lust' ":** Katz, *Gay American History*, p. 222.

299 **"In one case of complete effemination":** Schrenck-Notzig, Therapeutic Suggestion, p. 208.

299 **"I'm an unspeakable of the Oscar Wilde sort":** Forster, *Maurice*, p. 159.

300 **"These hypnotic cures sometimes lasted several years":** Robb, *Strangers*, pp. 75–76.

300 **"was conducting a series of torrid love affairs"**: Allen, *Hall Caine*, p. 292.

302 **"To Bram Stoker"**: Caine, *Cap'n Davy's Honeymoon*, unpaginated dedication.

303 *Old Count interferes*: Stoker, *Notes*, p. 17.

8. A Land Beyond the Forest

305 **"You go into the woods"**: Stephen Sondheim and James Lapine, *Into the Woods* (original Broadway cast recording, Sony Music Entertainment, 1986).

305 **"a too-generous helping of dressed crab"**: LUD, p. 99.

305 **"an undigested bit of beef"**: Dickens, *Bleak House*, p. 76.

307 **"Then the convulsion of the bog"**: Stoker, *The Snake's Pass*, p. 302.

308 **A certain "Count_____"**: Stoker, *Notes*, p. 17.

308 **"is told to visit Castle"**: Ibid.

308 **"This man belongs to me I want him"**: Ibid.

309 **"the visitors"**: Ibid., p. 39.

309 **the word "man"**: Stoker, unpublished typescript for *The Un-Dead* [*Dracula*], p. 60. Private collection.

309 **"Back, back to your own place!"**: DRA, p. 52.

309 **"the last I saw of Count Dracula"**: Ibid.

309 **"derives from Dracula's hovering interest"**: Christopher Craft, "Kiss Me with Those Red Lips: Gender and Inversion in Bram Stoker's *Dracula*" [1984], excerpted in *DRA*, p. 446.

309 **"I shuddered as I bent over"**: DRA, p. 53.

310 **"unconscious cerebration"**: Ibid., p. 69.

310 **Ulrichs's short story:** There does not seem to be an English version of "Manor" currently in print, but an online translation by Michael Lombardi-Nash can be read at angelfire.com/fl3/uraniamanuscripts/manor7.html.

310 **"Vampire stories are generally located in Styria"**: Stenbock, "A True Story of a Vampire," in Skal, *Vampires: Encounters with the Undead*, p. 171.

310 **"one of those extraordinary Slav creatures"**: Ibid.

311 **"it touches both on mystery and fact"**: Stoker quoted by Jane Stoddard, "A Chat with the Author of *Dracula*" [1897], in Miller, *Bram Stoker's "Dracula,"* p. 276.

312 **"hands are broad"**: Baring-Gould, *Book of Were-Wolves*, p. 108.

314 **"Basil Hallward is what I think I am"**: ELL, p. 319.

314 **"Why is your friendship so fatal"**: DOR, p. 126.

315 **"the leprosies of sin"**: Ibid., pp. 131–32.

315 **"withered, wrinkled, and loathsome of visage"**: Ibid., p. 184.

315 **"It is a tale spawned from the leprous literature"**: Ibid., "Reviews and Reactions," p. 362.

315 **"had monopolized the attention of Londoners"**: Ibid., p. 347.

319 **encountered the name "Dracula"**: Wilkinson, *Account of the Principalities*, p. 19.

319 **extraordinarily sadistic method:** McNally and Florescu's *In Search of Dracula* was the first book to chronicle Vlad's atrocities for modern readers.

321 **all-too-obvious "Count Wampyr"**: Stoker, *Notes*, pp. 26–27.

321 **"in one manuscript this very Dracula"**: DRA, p. 212.

321 **early page of notes:** Stoker, *Notes*, pp. 26–27.

322 **"looked like a dead man"**: REM-2, p. 166.

322 **sleeping in a coffin:** See Dijkstra, *Idols of Perversity*, pp. 45–46. Among many other sources, see especially Skinner, *Madame Sarah*, and Gold and Fizdale's *Divine Sarah*.

324 **"Abominable, disgusting, bestial, fetid"**: William Archer, "Ghosts and Gibberings," *Pall Mall Gazette*, April 8, 1891.

324 **"softening of the brain"**: Ibsen, *"Ghosts" and Other Plays*, p. 98.

324 **"ninety-seven percent of the people"**: Archer, "Ghosts and Gibberings."

324 **"open drain"**: Ibid.

324 **"muck-ferreting dogs"**: Ibid.

325 **"My dear Bram—my wife is not very well"**: *LET*, p. 394.

327 **"The audience"**: McKenna, *Secret Life of Oscar Wilde*, p. 171.

328 **"We're all in the gutter"**: *WIL*, p. 417.

328 **"daintily gloved"**: McKenna, *Secret Life of Oscar Wilde*, p. 170.

328 **"Ladies and gentlemen," he said:** Ibid.

328 **"marvelous evening wrap"**: Hyde, *Oscar Wilde*, p. 172.

329 **"Stoker was a very inept writer"**: Letter from H. P. Lovecraft to Robert Barlow, December 10, 1932, Lovecraft Collection, John Hay Library, Brown University, quoted in Stoker (McNally and Florescu), *Essential "Dracula,"* p. 24.

329 **"Mrs. Miniter saw Dracula in manuscript"**: Lovecraft, *Selected Letters, 1911– 1924*, p. 255.

329 **"Have you read"**: Quoted in Steinmeyer, *Who Was Dracula?*, p. 129.

330 **"Notwithstanding her saturation"**: H. P. Lovecraft, "Mrs. Miniter—Estimates and Recollections," in Miniter, *Dead Houses*, p. 56.

331 **"Its Editorials are pungent"**: *Boston Home Journal*, house advertisement, January 1894. Boston Public Library microform.

331 **"She is not a great actress"**: *Boston Home Journal*, unsigned profile of Ellen Terry, undated clipping, early January 1894. Boston Public Library microform.

331 **"Mr. Irving"**: *Boston Evening Transcript*, unsigned appraisal of Henry Irving's engagement, undated clipping, January 2, 1894. Boston Public Library microform.

332 **"In representing, or attempting"**: *Boston Home Journal*, review of *The Merchant of Venice*, undated clipping, January 20, 1894. Boston Public Library microform.

332 **"a Hebrew of rather"**: *DRA*, p. 302.

334 **"tramps, and other excretions"**: Stoker, *A Glimpse of America*, p. 15.

335 **"Who said anything about dramatic criticism"**: "The Week at the Theatres," *New York Times*, March 4, 1894.

336 **"Undead" was an existing word:** See Tupper, *Tropes and Figures in Anglo Saxon Prose*, p. 55.

337 **"the leader and financier of an international elitist conspiracy"**: Hans Cornell de Roos. *"Makt Myrkranna*: Mother of All *Dracula* Modifications?" *Letter from Castle Dracula (Newsletter of the Transylvanian Society of Dracula)*, February 2014, pp. 3–21.

337 **"Iceland and the Isle of Man are so closely linked"**: Stoker, 1895 introduction to reprint of Hall Caine's *The Bondman* [1890], in Showers, *To My Dear Friend Hommy-Beg*, p. 25.

340 **"born criminals"**: Lombroso, *Criminal Man*, p. 161 and passim. Lombroso began using the term in the third edition of his book (1884).

341 **"When under any kind of noxious influences"**: Nordau, *Degeneration*, p. 16.

341 **"Ghost stories are very popular"**: Ibid., pp. 13–14.

342 **"Where, if not from the Impressionists"**: Wilde, "The Decay of Lying," quoted in ibid., p. 321.

342 **"He asserts that painters"**: Nordau, *Degeneration*, p. 322.

342 **"His mouth covered"**: Atherton, *Adventures of a Novelist*, p. 184.

343 **"The face was clean-shaven"**: Wyndham, *Nineteen Hundreds*, p. 62.

343 **"He is like a very bad copy"**: Alice Kipling, Letter to Rudyard Kipling, March 18, 1882, quoted in Taylor, *Victorian Sisters*, pp. 136–37.

344 **"A creature manifestly between"**: "The Missing Link," *Punch*, October 18, 1862, p. 165.

344 **"I am haunted by"**: Kingsley, *His Letters and Memories*, p. 308.

344 **he supported home rule**: See Glover, *Vampires, Mummies, and Liberals*, for the best examination of Stoker's political leanings and influences.

345 **"all the men who wore them"**: Hichens, *Green Carnation*, p. 17.

345 **"allusions, thinly veiled"**: Ibid., p. xxv.

345 **long-simmering syphilis**: The most recent book to examine syphilis as a probable cause of Queensberry's mental derangement is Linda Stratmann's *Marquess of Queensberry: Wilde's Nemesis*.

345 **was having an affair with his eldest son**: See McKenna, *Secret Life of Oscar Wilde*, pp. 313–22 for a full account of Queensberry's obsession with the relationship between his son and Lord Rosebery.

346 **"For Oscar Wilde posing Somdomite"**: Queenberry's famously misspelled message is partially indecipherable, and has been alternatively interpreted as "posing somdomite," "posing as a somdomite," and "ponce and somdomite."

346 **called Queensberry "an incubus"**: Hyde, *Trials of Oscar Wilde*, p. 78.

346 **"Blindly I staggered"**: Wilde, *"De Profundis" and Other Prison Writings*, p. 53.

346 **"immoral and obscene work"**: Holland, *Real Trial of Oscar Wilde*, p. 39.

347 **"Each man sees his own sin"**: *LET*, p. 439.

347 **"I see little of him"**: For the complete account of her visit with Lady Wilde, see Atherton, *Adventures of a Novelist*, pp. 182–84.

347 **"a terrifying and severe old lady"**: Holland, *Son of Oscar Wilde*, p. 24.

349 **a "splendid score"**: Wilde, *"De Profundis" and Other Prison Writings*, p. 79.

350 **"malformation of the parts of generation"**: Murray, *Bosie*, pp. 66–67.

351 **"Willie, give me shelter"**: ELL, p. 467.

351 **"His successful brother"**: Yeats, *Autobiographies*, p. 227.

351 **"If you stay"**: ELL, p. 468.

351 **"the worst case I have ever tried"**: HAR, p. 175.

352 **"One half-expected to see"**: Olson, *Confessions of Aubrey Beardsley*, p. 236.

354 **"It haunts men"**: Allen, *Hall Caine*, p. 292.

354 **"the graceless and pitiful downfall"**: Wells, *Collected Works*, p. ix.

354 **"A fool there was"**: Rudyard Kipling, "The Vampire" [1897], from a 1902 souvenir postcard of the Burne-Jones painting with poem. Author's collection.

354 **"it was not until I had read Mr. Stoker's book"**: "Books and Bookmen," *Weekly Sun*, June 6, 1897.

355 **"Your most kind promise"**: Philip Burne-Jones to Stoker, June 16, 1897, reproduced in Miller, *Bram Stoker's "Dracula,"* p. 93.

355 **"Bram, my friend"**: Willie Wilde to Stoker, July 16, 1897, quoted in BEL, pp. 245–46.

356 **the prime minister had qualms**: Holroyd, *Strange Eventful History*, p. 259.

357 **"an ever-widening circle of semi-demons"**: DRA, pp. 53–54.

357 **"the center of a hideous circle of corruption"**: HAR, p. 186.

357 **"abounds in overwrought protestations of friendship"**: Auerbach, *Our Vampires, Ourselves*, p. 81.

357 **"a new monster of its own clinical making"**: DRA, p. xi. See also Talia Schaffer,

"'A Wilde Desire Took Me': The Homoerotic History of *Dracula*" [1994], excerpted in *DRA*, pp. 470–82.

358 **"who'd ever heard of a sub-text?":** Fay Weldon, "Bram Stoker: Hello, Thank You, and Goodbye," *Bram Stoker's "Dracula" Omnibus*, p. viii.

358 **"The novel is deeply":** Killeen, *Gothic Literature*, pp. 84–85.

359 **"There is a matter which I want to ask you about":** Stoker to Caine, June 3, 1896. Hall Caine Papers, Manx National Heritage.

360 **"Your letter is like yourself":** Stoker to Caine, June 6, 1896. Ibid.

360 **"very testy":** Ludlam, *My Quest for Bram Stoker*, p. 26.

361 **"striding out on long walks":** LUD, p. 95.

361 **"used to read his stories":** Florence Stoker, introduction to a 1926 serialization of *Dracula* in the *Argosy* (London), reprinted in Miller, *Bram Stoker's "Dracula,"* p. 284.

362 **"As we looked there came":** *DRA*, p. 235.

362 **"Stoker told me":** Schoolfield, *Baedecker of Decadence*, p. 218.

362 **Hoar reportedly met Stoker:** Stoker, *Shades of Dracula*, pp. 134–35.

363 **received no advance:** Miller, *Bram Stoker's "Dracula."* Stoker's holograph contract with Constable is reproduced on pp. 246–47.

365 **"I was thinking, if you would not object":** Stoker to Caine, March 2, 1897. Hall Caine Papers, Manx National Heritage.

365 **"Well, this is a pretty nice state":** Stoker, *Dracula; or, The Un-Dead*, p. 1.

367 **"The Thing in the coffin writhed":** *DRA*, p. 192.

367 **"With his left hand":** Ibid., p. 247.

367 **"See Dracula holding Mrs. Harker's face":** Stoker, *Dracula; or, The Un-Dead*, p. 143.

367 **"He pulled open his shirt":** *DRA*, p. 252.

369 **"In seeking a parallel":** Unsigned *Daily Mail* review, June 1, 1897.

369 **"Since Wilkie Collins left us":** "DRACULA by Bram Stoker," unsigned *Bookman* review, August 1897, p. 129.

369 **"Stories and novels appear":** Unsigned *Athenaeum* review, June 26, 1897.

370 **"Dear Sir—let me thank":** MUR, p. 47.

370 **a three-day stay at Slains Castle:** BEL, p. 234.

370 **"had some curious vicissitudes":** Stoker's copyright efforts on behalf of *Dracula* are discussed in the unsigned *Bookman* piece "Frankenstein," June 12, 1912, pp. 342–48.

371 **first known illustration for the book:** Special thanks to Paul S. McAlduff for sharing this rare image.

376 **"Upon an age of materialism":** *Brooklyn Daily Eagle* review of *Dracula*, January 15, 1900. Reprinted in Browning, *Bram Stoker's "Dracula": The Critical Feast*, pp. 105–9.

376 **"The Insanity of the Horrible":** Unsigned *Wave* review of *Dracula*, December 9, 1899, pp. 101–3.

377 **"entering a twilight borderland":** Maurice Richardson, "The Psychoanalysis of Ghost Stories"[1959], excerpted as "The Psychoanalysis of Count Dracula" in Frayling, *Vampyres*, pp. 418–22.

377 **"He wrote his book as":** Henry C. Dickens, quoted in Ludlam, *My Quest for Bram Stoker*, p. 60.

377 **"He knew he had written":** Frederick Donaghey, review of Deane and Balderston's *Dracula*, *Chicago Daily Tribune*, April 3, 1929.

9. Undead Oscar

379 **"For he who lives more lives than one":** *WIL*, p. 853.

379 **"Now God be thanked":** Stoker, *Dracula; or, The Un-Dead*, p. 193.

381 **given a reading by the famous palmist:** ELL, p. 382.

381 **"I see a very brilliant":** O'Sullivan, *Aspects of Wilde*, p. 27.

382 **"The shriek of the wretched female":** Maturin, *Melmoth the Wanderer*, p. 236.

383 **"hard labour, hard fare, and a hard bed":** ELL, p. 506.

383 **"seems almost to have for its aim":** Wilde, *"De Profundis" and Other Prison Writings*, p. 204.

384 **"What is it about the macabre":** Scott Martin, *Children of the Night*, a chamber musical produced at the Beverly Hills Playhouse, October 2009. Script courtesy of Mr. Martin.

384 **"create all the effects of inebriation":** Wilde's quip, included in many collections of his epigrams, comes from a secondhand source and never appears in the writer's published work. It is frequently adapted with slight variations—"drunkenness" for "inebriation," for example.

385 **"I cannot bear being alone":** Letter from Oscar Wilde to Robbie Ross, quoted in Belford, *Oscar Wilde*, p. 295.

385 **"I will never outlive the century":** Quoted in Wilde, *The Picture of Dorian Gray: An Uncensored, Annotated Edition*, p. 4.

385 **"Around twenty-five percent of Victorian men":** Quoted in Hayden, *Pox*, p. 221.

386 **creeping spinal paralysis:** Ibid., pp. 213–14.

386 **"And you know that you made me ill":** Ibid., 214.

386 **"My dear Oscar, you were":** HAR, p. 349.

386 **"After 5:30 in the morning":** HAR, p. 351.

387 **"He had scarcely breathed":** Ibid, p. 316.

387 **"The Morgue yawns for me":** ELL, p. 580.

388 **"After examining the body":** HAR, p. 353.

388 **"When preparing the body for the grave":** HAR, p. 316.

389 **"And all the while the burning lime":** *WIL*, p. 855.

389 **"like an old fat prostitute":** HAR, p. 305.

390 **"rumour afloat so sensational":** George Sylvester Viereck, "Is Oscar Wilde Living or Dead?," letter to the *Critic*, July 1905, pp. 86–88.

392 **Who on earth was this George Sylvester Viereck person:** Viereck is the subject of two full-length biographies, Elmer Gertz's *Odyssey of a Barbarian* and Neil M. Johnson's *George Sylvester Viereck: German-American Propagandist*, as well as his own memoir, *My Flesh and Blood: A Lyric Autobiography with Indiscreet Annotations*.

393 **"his amourous tastes were dubious":** Gertz, *Odyssey of a Barbarian*, p. 34.

393 **"too rabid admiration for Wilde":** Ibid.

393 **"There is no such thing":** Ibid., p. 226.

393 **"a word invented by good people":** "Phrases and Philosophies for the Use of the Young," *WIL*, p. 1205.

393 **"Wilde is splendid":** Gertz, *Odyssey of a Barbarian*, p. 37.

394 **"one who had clasped the hand of god":** Ibid., p. 38.

394 **he could be recognized by his fur coat:** Murray, *Bosie*, p. 129.

394 **boyish and lesbian-leaning:** Ibid, p. 124.

394 **"I have met many charming people here":** Ibid., pp. 130–31.

395 **his connection to "objectionable persons":** Gertz, *Odyssey of a Barbarian*, p. 35.

395 **"Bosie with fangs":** Unsigned *Evening Standard* review of *Brides of Dracula*, July 7, 1960.

395 **American epic of the undead:** Owen Wister's uncompleted vampire novel is a subject worthy of further research. The present author has consulted Wister's papers at the Library of Congress and found no manuscripts or correspondence, but the writer's plans for a vampire epic were widely reported in newspapers. See, for example, an untitled item in the *Terre Haute Daily Tribune*, February 8, 1903, in which Wister tells an interviewer, "Would you believe that within the sound of the locomotives' whistle on the New York, New Haven and Hartford railroad there are people, many people, who firmly believe in real old fashioned vampires? It should make a good novel."

397 **"It will come again, in a month":** Viereck, *House of the Vampire*, pp. 15–17.

398 **"absorbing from life the elements":** Ibid, p. 23.

398 **"You've heard of":** Saint-Amour, *Copywrights*, p. 137.

399 **"Except in the final scene":** Unsigned *New York Times* review of *House of the Vampire*, October 5, 1907.

399 **"The difficulty with Mr. Viereck's treatment":** Unsigned *Nation* review of *House of the Vampire*, October 3, 1907.

399 **"creatures who had once been women":** Viereck, *House of the Vampire*, p. 38.

399 **"But what on earth could you find":** Ibid., p. 122.

399 **"He stood up at full length":** Ibid., p. 183.

402 **"inextricably associated with the saddest":** "The Theatres Last Night: An Oscar Wilde Play Revived at the Empire," *New York Times*, April 15, 1902.

402 **"a clean shaven Svengali":** Review of *The Vampire*, unsourced 1909 newspaper clipping, Billy Rose Theatre Collection, New York Library for the Performing Arts at Lincoln Center.

402 **"I am really sorry the charge is not true":** Saint-Amour, *Copywrights*, p. 140.

403 **"Without ever mentioning the word 'copyright'":** Ibid.

405 **"homosexuality clung to them":** Auerbach, *Our Vampires, Ourselves*, p. 102.

405 **wondrous child named Hester Dowden:** Basic facts of Hester's life have been gleaned primarily from Bentley's *Far Horizon*.

406 **"crew of disorderly persons, often of the fair sex":** Dowden, "The Interpretation of Literature," *Transcripts and Studies*, p. 241.

406 **"The great quad of Trinity College":** Bentley, *Far Horizon*, pp. 19–20.

407 **One of her "great friends":** Ibid., p. 166.

407 **refused W. B. Yeats's plea:** ELL, p. 466.

409 **"one of the relatively few means":** Sword, *Ghostwriting Modernism*, p. 13.

409 **"an intellectual lady who acted as writing medium":** Sherard, *Real Oscar Wilde*, pp. 214–15.

410 **"Wherever Dolly went":** Schenkar, *Truly Wilde*, p. 224.

411 **Radclyffe Hall:** For a full examination of Hall's adventures in spiritualism, see the chapter "The Eternal Triangle" in Souhami, *Trials of Radclyffe Hall*, pp. 89–99.

412 **"Being dead is the most boring experience in life":** Travers Smith, *Oscar Wilde from Purgatory*, p. 7.

412 **"I am doing what is little better than":** Ibid., p. 9.

414 **"the dimming of the senses":** Ibid., p. 13.

414 **"I almost forget":** Ibid., p.16.

414 **"Men are ever interested":** Ibid., p.18.

414 **"Charity begins at home":** Lazar, *Ghost Epigrams of Oscar Wilde*, p. 20.

415 **"The women of my time were beautiful"**: Travers Smith, *Oscar Wilde from Purgatory*, p. 12.

415 **"sensations were so varied"**: Ibid., p. 21.

415 **"crawl into your mind like a sick worm"**: Ibid., p 15.

415 **"It is a singular matter"**: Ibid., p. 18.

416 **"six impossible things before breakfast"**: Carroll, *Through the Looking-Glass*, p. 93.

416 **a barely disguised Hester Dowden**: Yeats, "The Words upon the Window Pane" [1934], *Selected Poems and Four Plays*, pp. 158–71.

417 **"I have been deeply moved"**: Ibid., p. 170.

418 **campaign against her father**: Kahan, *Shakespiritualism*, pp. 77–79.

418 **"Bill Shakespere had a lot to do"**: Ibid., p. 81.

419 **"To his horror"**: HAR, p. 317.

419 **The postmortem shrinking of skin**: See Barber, *Vampires, Burial, and Death*, for a comprehensive examination of how normal processes of decomposition can create misleading appearances.

419 **"At once Ross sent the son away"**: HAR, p. 317.

419 **"doubtless invented as a perquisite for someone"**: Holland, *Son of Oscar Wilde*, p. 196.

419 **"This was the last straw"**: Ibid, p. 197.

421 **"an atom of that power"**: Travers Smith, *Oscar Wilde from Purgatory*, p. 32.

10. Mortal Coils

423 **"The whole place"**: *LWW*, p. 364.

424 **"a former super"**: Millward, *My Life among Others*, p. 232.

425 **"Just as I reached the pass door"**: Ibid., p. 230.

425 **Born Richard Archer in Dundee**: For a detailed biographical and criminal précis, see King, *Undiscovered Dundee*, pp. 153–63.

426 **"I was told afterwards"**: Millward, *My Life among Others*, p. 232.

427 **"They will find some excuse"**: *IRV*, p. 602.

427 **"When he was placed in the dock"**: Ibid.

427 **"Irving was Christ"**: Aria, *My Sentimental Self*, p. 108.

428 **costumed apparition**: McPherson, "Theatrical Haunts" (cited in second note to chapter 6 above).

429 **"At ten minutes past five"**: *REM-2*, p. 297.

429 **"The fire was so fierce"**: Ibid., p. 302.

429 **"But the cost price"**: Ibid., p. 301.

430 **"To My Mother, in her loneliness"**: Stoker, *The Watter's Mou'*, unpaginated dedication page.

430 **"My dear it is splendid"**: Charlotte Stoker to Stoker, LUD, pp. 108–9.

430 **"I have not been well"**: LUD, p. 123.

431 **"illiterate maid"**: MUR, p. 16.

431 **with no further elaboration**: BEL, p. 289.

431 **"'Euthanasia' is an excellent"**: DRA, p. 291.

431 **"If this change should come"**: Ibid.

432 **"With characteristic fortitude"**: Terry, *Story of My Life*, p. 360.

432 **"when we were on tour"**: Ibid.

432 **"I think there must be something"**: *REM-2*, p. 327.

432 **"At first, of course"**: Ibid., p. 329.

432 **"There he lay looking"**: DRA, p. 53.

433 **"a very considerable sum of money"**: *REM-2*, p. 327.

433 **"At the turn of the century"**: *IRV*, p. 637.

433 **"Both plays were out of joint"**: *REM-2*, p. 343.

434 **"Bram Stoker told me"**: Frederick Donaghey, review of Deane and Balderston's *Dracula, Chicago Daily Tribune*, April 3, 1929.

435 **"The story is not saturated"**: *New York Tribune* review of *Mystery of the Sea*, June 21, 1902.

435 **"Marjory, my wife, the end is close!"**: Stoker, *Mystery of the Sea*, p. 299.

436 **"may be of some interest to the cranks"**: "Novels and Stories," *Glasgow Herald* review of *Mystery of the Sea*, July 31, 1902; reprinted in Senf, *Bram Stoker's Other Gothics*, p. 21.

436 **"Through it all beams the breezy"**: *Punch* review of *Mystery of the Sea*, August 20, 1902; reprinted in ibid., pp. 22–23.

436 **"His nose was aquiline"**: Lewis, *The Monk*, p. 18.

436 **"His face was strong and merciless"**: Stoker, "The Judge's House," *GUE*, p. 32.

436 in broad daylight, just **"beaky"**: *DRA*, p. 155.

436 **"great-eyed, aquiline-featured, gaunt old woman"**: Stoker, *Mystery of the Sea*, p. 9.

436 **"his high aquiline nose and black eagle eyes"**: Ibid., p. 269.

437 owned by Stoker: Stoker, *The Jewel of Seven Stars*, introduction by Hebblethwaite, pp. xvii–xviii.

438 **"is composed of mummies three thousand years old"**: Twain, *The Innocents Abroad*, vol. 2, p. 429.

438 **"this book is not a shilling shocker"**: "Reviews," *Reader Magazine* (New York), no. 3, 1904; reprinted in Senf, *Bram Stoker's Other Gothics*, pp. 29–30.

439 **"British attitudes towards Egypt"**: Stoker, *The Jewel of Seven Stars*, introduction by Hebblethwaite, pp. xvii–xviii.

440 **"Strange indeed was the appearance"**: Gautier, *Romance of a Mummy*, p. 301.

440 **"We all stood awed"**: Stoker, *The Jewel of Seven Stars*, p. 235.

441 **"This was a certain shrinkage"**: *REM-2*, p. 335.

441 **"clergyman's sore throat"**: Ibid., p. 336.

441 **"month by month and year by year"**: Ibid., p. 337.

442 **"Day or night; in stillness; in travel"**: Ibid., p. 338.

442 **"He made throughout years a great fortune"**: Ibid., p. 339.

442 **"The great stars are sacred monsters"**: Paglia, "The Star as Sacred Monster," *Vamps and Tramps*, p. 366.

443 religious crisis: Florence Stoker's 1904 conversion is recorded in the 1910 edition of Burnand, *Catholic Who's Who and Year-Book*.

444 **"had become so alarmingly ill"**: *REM-2*, p.347.

445 **"It is imperatively necessary that"**: Ibid., p. 349.

445 **"He had become adept at concealing"**: Ibid., p. 352.

445 **"A kindly continent to me"**: Aria, *My Sentimental Self*, p. 142.

445 **"At the right hand of Power"**: Tennyson, *Becket*, p. 186.

446 **"At the close last night"**: "Sir Henry Irving Is Dead," *Bradford Daily Telegraph*, October 14, 1905.

446 **"I stood up to go"**: *REM-2*. See pp. 352–61 for Stoker's full account of Irving's death and arrangements made at Bradford.

450 **"No one could deny Stoker's signal devotion"**: Martin-Harvey, *Autobiography*, pp. 64–65.

451 **"There will be nothing of the sort":** Aria, *My Sentimental Self*, p. 105.

451 **snapped up the performance rights:** Holland, *Son of Oscar Wilde*, p. 270.

454 **Ellen Terry expressed her regret:** MUR, p. 236.

454 **"The chair was marked in pencil":** Millward, *Myself and Others*, p. 274.

454 **Armitage Robinson's eye doctor:** *IRV*, p. 672.

455 **family did not want the fact publicized:** "Irving's Body Cremated," *New York Times*, October 18, 1905.

455 **"an illiterate mutilator":** MUR, p. 236.

455 **"implacable Irish hatred":** Ibid.

456 **"Now that the excitement of Sir Henry":** Holroyd, *Strange Eventful History*, p. 149.

456 **According to the English correspondent:** "Sir Henry Irving's Funeral," *France Times*, November 2, 1905.

457 **"Surely such a pall was never before seen":** REM-2, p. 362.

458 **"As from the steps of the Sanctuary":** Ibid., p. 365.

458 **"It was like a miracle":** *DRA*, p. 325.

458 **interviewed the ghost of Dame Ellen Terry:** Bentley, *Far Horizon*, p. 168.

458 **they filled a room:** Noel Stoker's correspondence with author Harry Ludlam for *A Biography of Dracula*. TCD.

459 **"Almost everyone criticizes it":** *New York Times* review of *REM*, October 20, 1906.

459 **"Oh, Harold!":** Stoker, *The Man*, p. 42.

460 **"Stoker, for many years":** "Doings Theatrical," *San Francisco Chronicle Sunday Supplement*, April 1, 1906.

460 **"a painful illness that dragged on for weeks":** LUD, p. 134.

462 **"I hate being interviewed":** "Mr. Winston Churchill Talks of His Hopes, His Works, and His Ideals to Bram Stoker," *Daily Chronicle*, January 15, 1908, reprinted in Stoker, *Glimpse of America*, p. 121.

463 **"each individual must have a preponderance":** Stoker, *Lady Athlyne*, p. 82.

463 **"Something was wrong":** Stoker, "A Star Trap," *Snowbound*, p. 140.

464 **"At last night's meeting":** "Prurient Novel Is Condemned," *Los Angeles Times*, October 20, 1907.

465 **"perpetually combatting human weakness":** Stoker, "The Censorship of Fiction," *Nineteenth Century & After*, September 1908, reprinted in *Glimpse of America*, pp. 154–61.

466 **"There, outside on the balcony":** Stoker, *Lady of the Shroud*, pp. 96–97.

467 **"It was all like a dream":** Ibid., p. 104.

467 **"Within, pillowed on soft cushions":** Ibid., p. 130.

468 **"an age when self-seeking women":** Ibid., p. 319.

469 **"My Dear Bram," he wrote:** Letter from Hall Caine to Stoker, March 11, 1910, in Dalby, *To My Dear Hommy-Beg*, p. 42.

469 **"a most villainous place":** Cobbett, *Rural Rides*, p. 251.

469 **"the narrow streets of Deal":** Dickens, *Bleak House*, p. 495.

469 **alternative to the free medical care:** For a complete overview of the evolution of these facilities in Victorian times, see Burdett's *Cottage Hospitals*.

470 **"May I not help a little":** Letter from Hall Caine to Stoker, March 11, 1910, in Dalby, *To My Dear Hommy-Beg*, p. 42.

470 **"Indeed I have taken your permission":** Ibid.

470 **"I can stand now":** BEL, p. 115.

470 "Poor old Bram is no worse": MUR, p. 266.

471 dinner party that became notorious: Gogarty, *As I Was Going Down Sackville Street*, p. 292.

471 Belford notes: BEL, p. 244.

471 "my poor wife" as "dead to me": *DRA*, p. 158.

471 "Not much for a living wage": BEL, p. 315.

471 "It is harder on poor Florence": Ibid.

472 "For some years she flourished": Stoker, *Famous Impostors*, p. 239.

472 "His clean shaven face": Ibid., p. 275.

472 dismiss the Bisley Boy as "tommyrot": "Some Famous Impostors: Mr. Bram Stoker Includes among Them the 'Man' Known as Queen Elizabeth," *New York Times*, February 26, 1911.

473 "Mr. Stoker is not indulging": Ibid.

473 "The subject of Imposture": Stoker, holograph manuscript preface (preliminary draft) to *Famous Impostors*. SFP, TCD.

474 "The histories of famous cases of imposture": Stoker, *Famous Impostors*, p. v.

475 a few shillings per sitting: MUR, p. 249.

475 "I wrote you only yesterday with a petition": Anne Ritchie, letter to Arthur Llewelyn Roberts, Committee of the Royal Literary Fund, February 20, 1911. BLDM.

475 Stoker wrote personally: Stoker, letter to the Royal Literary Fund, February 25, 1911. BLDM.

476 "I have enjoyed the privilege": W. S. Gilbert, letter of support to the Committee of the Royal Literary Fund, February 25, 1911. BDLM.

476 "This is not a mere formal backing": Henry F. Strickland, letter of support to the Committee of the Royal Literary Fund, February 24, 1911. BDLM.

477 "I am looking forward to going": Florence Stoker, note to unknown addressee, March 9, 1911, reproduced online at bramstokerestate.com.

477 "The aquiline features which marked them": LWW, p. 166.

477 "glowed with a red fiery light": Ibid., p. 217.

478 "negroid of the lowest type": Ibid., p. 178.

480 "Her dress alone was sufficient": Ibid., p. 175.

481 "Hitherto the mongoose": Ibid., pp. 200–201.

481 "In the uncertain, tremulous light": Ibid., p. 211.

481 "In both of these legends": "Just Published. New Novel by the Author of *Dracula*," *Occult Review*, Special Number, January 1912; reprinted in Senf, *Bram Stoker's Other Gothics*, pp. 39–40.

482 "I don't really know what a Gorgon is like": WIL, p. 335.

483 "sharper than a serpent's tooth": SHA, *King Lear* (conflated text), act 1, scene 4, line 265, p. 2510.

483 "There's hell, there's darkness": Ibid., act 4, scene 5, line 124, p. 2551.

483 "The open well-hole": LWW, p. 266–67.

483 "looked as if a sea of blood": Ibid., p. 364.

484 "some mountainous mass of flesh": Ibid.

484 "After a few minutes": Ibid., p. 368.

485 "At last the explosive power": Ibid., pp. 364–65.

485 "Mr. Bram Stoker has a genius": "Current Literature," *Daily Telegraph*, November 22, 1911; reprinted in Senf, *Bram Stoker's Other Gothics*, pp. 37–38.

485 "In attempting to exceed the supernatural horrors": *Times Literary Supplement* review of *The Lair of the White Worm*, November 16, 1911, p. 466.

486 **"Since coming to St. Moritz"**: Hall Caine, letter to Stoker, January 31, 1912, in Dalby, *To My Dear Friend Hommy-Beg*, p. 44.

488 **"My dear friend"**: Florence Stoker, undated 1912 letter to Hall Caine. Hall Caine Papers, Manx National Heritage.

488 **"Of the devotion of his wife"**: Hall Caine, "Bram Stoker: The Story of a Great Friendship," *Daily Telegraph*, April 24, 1912.

488 **"the master of a particularly lurid"**: "Obituary. Mr. Bram Stoker," *Times* (London), April 22, 1912.

489 **"Bram Stoker is to be buried today"**: Hall Caine, "Bram Stoker: The Story of a Great Friendship," *Daily Telegraph*, April 24, 1912.

490 **"English forsooth!"**: "Bram Stoker, Irishman," *Boston Pilot*, undated 1913 clipping, reprinted in Stoker, *Forgotten Writings*, pp. 217–18.

491 **"Bram died of tertiary syphilis"**: FAR, p. 233.

491 **cause of death:** Stoker death certificate, filed April 22, 1912, county of London, subdistrict of Belgrave. SFP, TCD.

491 **"Tabes, tabes dorsalis, or locomotor ataxia"**: Lambkin, *Syphilis*, p. 96.

491 **"nephritis is of the chronic interstitial variety"**: Ibid., p. 81.

492 **"the characteristic gait of ataxia"**: Ibid., pp. 100–101.

492 **"the Arylarsonates"**: Ibid., p. 172.

492 **"As a cause of aneurysm syphilis stands pre-eminent"**: Ibid., p. 89.

492 **"one patient may become hopelessly ataxic"**: Ibid., p. 102.

493 **"His wife's frigidity drove him to other women"**: FAR, p. 234.

493 **"Among the treasures"**: "Bram Stoker's Valuable Library to Be Sold," unsourced, undated 1913 American newspaper clipping, reprinted in Stoker, *Forgotten Writings*, pp. 243–44.

494 **"I made £400 on the 'Bram Stoker Library'"**: MUR, p. 271.

494 **"Two persons have hitherto watched the coming storm"**: Stoker, *The Russian Professor*, undated manuscript fragment. John Moore Library, Dublin.

494 **"Richard Power, the journalist"**: Ibid.

496 **"Although he was always drawn to women"**: Lawrence, *Women in Love*, Appendix II (deleted prologue), p. 501.

496 **"To be spiritual, he must have a Hermoine"**: Ibid., p. 500.

496 **"Aren't I enough for you"**: Ibid., p. 487.

11. The Curse of Dracula

499 **"painters cannot paint him"**: Stoker, *Notes*, p. 21.

501 **publisher's initial offer of publication:** Publishing contract and correspondence for *GUE*, December 1913. SFP, TCD.

502 **"A few months before the lamented death"**: Stoker, *GUE*, Appendix I, p. 371.

503 **According to Noel Stoker:** Noel Stoker, undated letter fragment to Harry Ludlam, July 24, 1957. SFP, TCD.

504 **"honourable understanding"**: Publishing contract and correspondence for *GUE*, December 1913. SFP, TCD.

504 **"She was teased mercilessly"**: Charles Catchpole, "The Last of the Dracula Family—And She Daren't Even Read the Book!" *Daily Mail*, August 13, 1979.

507 **"Suffering and grief have shaken men's hearts"**: Albin Grau, "Vampires," *Bühne und Film* 21 (1921), reprinted in Bouvier and Leutrat, *Nosferatu*, pp. 17–20. Translated from German by Jean-Charles Margotton. Translated from French by the author.

508 **"an inoffensive young man":** Gide, *Journals*, entry for February 27, 1928, pp. 7–8.

509 **Galeen's script:** The *Nosferatu* screenplay appears only in the British edition of Lotte Eisner's *Murnau*, but is worth any researcher's time to track down.

510 **involved in motion picture negotiations:** Florence Stoker to the Society of American Dramatists and Composers, October 12, 1925. BLDM.

511 **"I have been alive for a thousand years":** Rhodes, *"Drakula halála*: The Screen's First Dracula,"*, p. 37.

512 **retain as much of the original dialogue as possible:** Ludlam, *My Quest for Bram Stoker*, p. 38.

512 **"lived and breathed and looked theatre":** Ibid., pp. 39–40.

513 **"his cloak spread out around him like great wings":** Deane and Balderston, *Dracula*, p. 3.

513 **appeared in several silent films:** I am indebted to John Eastwood for information on his ancestor Edmund Blake, as well as the accompanying, previously unpublished photograph of the actor.

514 **"I was simply coining money":** LUD, p. 156.

514 **The actress Vera Raven recalled:** Vera Raven, letter to Harry Ludlam, April 24, 1960. SFP, TCD.

514 **"signs" of a baby being born:** Noel Stoker, letter to Harry Ludlam, July 24, 1957. SFP, TCD.

516 **"Just a moment, Ladies and Gentlemen!":** Deane and Balderston, *Dracula*, p. 150.

516 **"appallingly pompous":** Unsourced clipping, London newspaper review of *Dracula*, February 20, 1927.

516 **"ill-fitting mask":** Raymond Huntley, letter to the *London Evening Standard*, February 19, 1927.

517 **"The late Mr. Bram Stoker's":** *Punch* review of *Dracula*, February 23, 1927, p. 218.

517 **"There is very little of Bram Stoker in it":** *Times* (London) review of *Dracula*, February 15, 1927.

518 **"Liveright's critics considered a book publisher's involvement":** Dardis, *Firebrand*, p. xiv.

520 **"a Jewish Edgar Allan Poe":** Ibid., p. 291.

520 **"they had cast everybody but the Count":** John L. Balderston Jr., on-camera interview for this author's DVD documentary *The Road to Dracula* (Universal Studios Home Video, 1999).

520 **turned down Liveright's offer:** Raymond Huntley, interview with the author, November 1989, London.

521 **"youthful indiscreton":** Ibid.

523 **"I thank you for reminding me of the time":** Deane and Balderston, *Dracula*, p. 147.

524 **"When Dracula, in reeling":** Jarrett and Steinmeyer, *Complete Jarrett*, p. 163.

525 **forty-year-old, Dublin-born artist:** The outline of Clarke's life and career is drawn from Bowe, *Harry Clarke: The Life and Work*.

526 **edition de luxe:** Florence Stoker to British Society of Authors correspondence, 1929, various letters, passim. BLDM.

526 **depicted an androgynous, emaciated creature:** Reproduced as a text illustration in chapter 1.

527 **"Never before have these marvelous tales"**: Bowe, *Harry Clarke: His Graphic Art*, p. 18.

527 **"sublunar world of phantoms"**: Bowe, *Harry Clarke: The Life and Work*, p. 257.

528 **"Might have been incarnated from the dark"**: Bowe, *Harry Clarke: His Graphic Art*, p. 99.

530 **"Many of [Clark's] images seem"**: Bowe, *Harry Clarke: The Life and Work*, p. 257.

530 **"one sees monsters in a state"**: Bowe, *Harry Clarke: His Graphic Work*, p. 145.

531 **"I have never heard of"**: G. Herbert Thring, Society of Authors, to P. N. Adams, October 8, 1929, BLDM.

533 **"He loved everything macabre"**: Carla Laemmle, narration for this author's DVD documentary *The Road to Dracula* (Universal Studios Home Video, 1999).

533 **The most elaborate treatment:** Bromfield's full treatment is included in Riley, *MagicImage Filmbooks Presents "Dracula,"* pp. 42–54.

534 **"In his unnatural unearthly manifestations"**: Ibid., p. 49.

535 **NO DETECTIVES! NO TRAP DOORS!:** Unsourced 1931 Vancouver, BC, newspaper advertisement for *Dracula*. Author's collection.

535 **a fussed-over affair:** "Dracula Gets Promotion," unsourced 1979 newspaper clipping. SFP, TCD.

538 **HORACE ASKS EXTENSION OPTION:** Skal, *Monster Show*, p. 109.

538 **"found a scene of near-total destruction"**: Dardis, *Firebrand*, pp. 348–49.

538 **so frayed he touched them up with ink:** Ibid., p. 345.

539 **good friend Stanley Dunn:** Price, *Vincent Price*, p. 66.

539 **company of three much older men:** Vincent Price, correspondence with the author, October 1989.

540 **"fabulous" Knightsbridge home:** Ibid.

540 **"Oscar's little water-colour"**: BEL, p. 325.

541 **"she is very fond of me"**: Price, *Vincent Price*, p. 66.

542 **"By rights this belongs to you"**: FAR, p. 61.

542 **"*She thinks I never loved her*"**: Oscar Wilde to Ellen Terry, January 3, 1881, *LET*, p. 107.

542 **"the best book I've read on poor O"**: BEL, p. 325.

542 **"the standpoint of the tomb"**: *LET*, p. 1191.

542 **collection of his short fiction:** O'Sullivan's story collection *The Green Window* was published in 1899.

543 **"I wanted him to come and see me"**: BEL, p. 325.

544 **"there is no more poetical topic"**: Edgar Allan Poe, "The Philosophy of Composition" [1846], *Essays and Reviews*, p. 19.

545 **"The Christian hatred of the funeral pile"**: "Is Cremation Christian Burial?," *The Month: A Catholic Magazine and Review*, June 1885, p. 13.

546 **"Into the keeping of the lords of the flames"**: *Dracula's Daughter* (1936), directed by Lambert Hillyer. Universal Studios Home Video DVD. Dialogue transcription by the author.

547 **marvelously chatty reports:** Balderston's letters are quoted extensively in this author's *Hollywood Gothic*.

548 **"You have eaten my food, dear friends"**: Sherriff, screenplay for *Dracula's Daughter*, reprinted in Riley, *James Whale's "Dracula's Daughter,"* pp. 41–42.

548 **"There's no need for my little girl to be afraid"**: Ibid., p. 47.

548 **"The girl, as if fighting"**: Ibid., 49.

549 **"The CAMERA focuses on the terrified Baron"**: Ibid., p. 62.

549 **"The CAMERA sweeps"**: Ibid., pp. 65–66.

550 **"Mercedes was notorious":** Schanke, *"That Furious Lesbian,"* p. 1.

552 **cultural visibility:** See this author's *Monster Show,* pp. 195–200, for a detailed account of Universal's censorship struggle over *Dracula's Daughter.*

552 **judged the film as "horrific":** *"Dracula's Daughter* Ban," *Times* (London), July 11, 1936.

553 **"an unnecessary number of films":** "Classified as 'Horrific,' " *Times* (London), July 21, 1936.

553 **proposal to publish an all-new serial:** Correspondence between Noel Stoker, the Incorporated Society of Authors, and Amalgamated Press, September 1937 to January 1938. BLDM.

554 **ever since he interviewed Bela Lugosi:** Ludlam, *My Quest for Bram Stoker,* p. 1.

554 **"I look into the mirror":** Ibid., p. 3.

554 **"I have to remind you":** Ibid., p. 15.

554 **"not to include anything":** Ibid.

555 **pocket-sized Armed Forces Edition:** For a complete overview of the Armed Services Editions program and its cultural impact, see Manning, *When Books Went to War.*

555 **"Just so long as I don't have to imitate Bela!":** Producer Richard Gordon, in conversation with the author, 1999.

556 **"The process went like this":** Christopher Lee, interviewed in Landis, *Monsters in the Movies,* p. 45.

558 **"How interesting!":** Shane Briant, correspondence with author, October 8, 2009.

558 **"that BRAM should continue writing":** Don Houghton, screenplay treatment for *Victim of His Imagination,* January 1972, p. 9.

559 **"a perpetually returning theme":** Ibid., p. 15.

560 **"These words seem to stick":** Ibid.

560 **"BRAM is quiet, contemplative":** Ibid., p. 29.

562 **"When did I realize I was homosexual?":** Farson, *Never a Normal Man,* p. 86.

562 **"Many were disposed of":** FAR, p. 40.

562 **"I recall the glee":** Farson, *Never a Normal Man,* p. 154.

563 **"easily bribed by champagne":** Farson, *Gilded Gutter Life of Francis Bacon,* p. 212.

563 **"One Christmas I had a crucial meeting":** Ibid., p. 212.

563 **"sense of otherness":** Robin Carmody, "Daniel Farson" (Transdiffusion Broadcasting System website feature article), October 1, 2006, transdiffusion. org/2006/10/01/daniel_farson.

564 **"plain indication of most kinds of sexual perversions":** Jones, *On the Nightmare,* p. 98.

564 **Farson was "petrified":** Robin Carmody, "Daniel Farson" (Transdiffusion Broadcasting System website feature article, October 1, 2006, transdiffusion. org/2006/10/01/daniel_farson.

564 **"mongrels" and "coffee coloured imps":** Farson's interview with Wentworth Day is included in the 1958 television documentary "People in Trouble: Mixed Marriages," available at youtube.com/watch?v=ybqLRF1zFUI.

565 **"I hesitated to include this":** FAR, p. 234.

565 **became "very antisex":** Ibid., pp. 213–14.

565 **wrote to the medical school:** Letter from Trinity College Dublin medical school to Ann Stoker Dobbs. SFP, TCD.

565 **Ann was initially agreeable:** Correspondence between Ann Stoker Dobbs and the Rosenbach Library and Museum. SFP, TCD.

566 **"Isn't it awful to confess?":** Charles Catchpole, "The Last of the Dracula Family—And She Daren't Even Read the Book!" *Daily Mail*, August 13, 1979.

566 **"the macabre streak":** Noel Stoker, undated letter to Harry Ludlam, SFP, TCD.

566 **"I had one terrible shock":** Charles Catchpole, "The Last of the Dracula Family—And She Daren't Even Read the Book!" *Daily Mail*, August 13, 1979.

566 **"I never believed in cashing in on my family name":** Ibid.

566 **"All those Dracula Society people":** Ibid.

567 **"the thesis of *In Search of Dracula*":** Margalit Fox, "Radu R. Florescu, Scholar Who Linked Dracula and Vlad the Impaler, Dies at 88," *New York Times*, May 27, 2014.

567 **"I do not dispute":** Elizabeth Miller, "Count Dracula and Vlad Tepeş: Filing for Divorce," in Miller, *Dracula: The Shade and the Shadow*, p. 175.

568 **"High camp always has an underlying seriousness":** Isherwood, *World in the Evening*, p. 110.

569 **"A very good friend of mine produced it":** Quotes by Edward Gorey on *Dracula* are taken from a documentary by Christopher Seufert titled "Edward Gorey Dracula Animation," excerpted on YouTube: youtube.com/watch?v=6myUHZl-wcWs&feature=youtu.be.

570 **"The set is more menacing":** Mel Gussow, "Gorey Goes Batty," p. 42.

570 **"faggot nonsense":** See Christopher Bram, *Eminent Outlaws*, pp. 224 and 346, for an examination of Simon's incendiary comments, and variant versions of them reported in the New York media.

570 **"Homosexuals in the theatre!":** Ibid.

571 **"rather like a sophomoric parody of Noël Coward":** John Simon, "Dingbat," *New York Magazine*, November 7, 1977, p. 75.

571 **"too much of a presence in the drawing room":** Dan Sullivan, syndicated *Los Angeles Times* theatre review of *Dracula* in the *Louisville Courier Journal and Times*, December 11, 1977.

571 **"Mr. Langella, accomplished craftsmen":** Rex Reed, "Cult of the Count," *New York Sunday News*, October 30, 1977.

571 **pronounced Yugoslavian accent:** John Simon, "The Critic, Public and Private," December 11, 2011, uncensoredjohnsimon.blogspot.com.

573 **"crucified":** Lauren Wissot, "Talking Legends with Terence Stamp," filmmakermagazine.com, February 8, 2013.

573 **"It took the industry ten years":** James Abbott, "Frank Langella at the Cornell Club," November 14, 2011, thejadesphinx.blogspot.com/search/label/Frank Langella.

574 **"The CAMERA pans over the wallpaper":** Ken Russell, unproduced screenplay of *Dracula* (1977). Author's collection. All quotations are from the same source.

578 **"thoughts that do not go to church on Sunday":** Lazar, *Ghost Epigrams*, p. 25.

BIBLIOGRAPHY

Following are printed books, essays, and journal and magazine articles directly quoted or referenced in *Something in the Blood,* as well as selected works that have significantly influenced the author's perspective on Bram Stoker and *Dracula* and are recommended for further reading. Manuscript collections, private libraries, daily newspaper articles and reviews, individual essays included in anthologies listed below, anonymous works, online sources, and ephemera can be found in the endnotes.

Allen, Vivien. *Hall Caine: Portrait of a Victorian Romancer.* Sheffield: Sheffield Academic Press, 1997.

American Psychiatric Association. *Diagnostic and Statistical Manual of Mental Disorders.* 3rd ed. Washington, DC: American Psychiatric Association, 1980.

Amor, Anne Clark. *Mrs. Oscar Wilde: A Woman of Some Importance.* London: Sidgwick & Jackson, 1983.

Andersen, Wayne. *Picasso's Brothel.* New York: Other Press, 2001.

Anonymous. *The Fashionable Tragedian: A Criticism* (Edinburgh: Thomas Gray, 1877).

Archer, William. *Henry Irving.* London: Field and Turner, 1883.

Aria, Mrs. [Eliza Davis]. *My Sentimental Self.* London: Chapman & Hall, 1922.

Atherton, Gertrude. *Adventures of a Novelist.* New York: Horace Liveright, 1932.

Auerbach, Nina. *Ellen Terry: Player in Her Time.* New York: W. W. Norton, 1987.

———. *Our Vampires, Ourselves.* Chicago: University of Chicago Press, 1997.

Austen, Jane. *Pride and Prejudice* [1813]. New York: Charles Scribner's Sons, 1918.

Bannatyne, Lesley Pratt. *A Halloween Reader.* Gretna, LA: Pelican Publishing, 2004.

Barber, Paul. *Vampires, Burial, and Death: Folklore and Reality.* 2nd ed. New Haven, CT: Yale University Press, 2010.

Baring-Gould, Sabine. *The Book of Were-Wolves.* London: Smith, Elder, 1865.

Barry, Michael. *Victorian Dublin Revealed.* Dublin: Andalus Press, 2011.

Belford, Barbara. *Bram Stoker: A Biography of the Author of "Dracula."* New York: Alfred A. Knopf, 1997.

———. *Oscar Wilde: A Certain Genius.* New York: Random House, 2000.

Beachy, Robert. *Gay Berlin: Birthplace of a Modern Identity.* New York: Alfred A. Knopf, 2014.

Bentley, Edmund. *Far Horizon: A Biography of Hester Dowden, Medium and Psychic Investigator.* London: Rider, 1951.

Bingham, Madeleine. *Henry Irving: The Greatest Victorian Actor.* New York: Stein & Day, 1978.

Blank, Hanne. *Straight: The Surprisingly Short History of Heterosexuality.* Boston: Beacon Press, 2012.

Bouvier, M., and J.-L. Leutrat. *Nosferatu.* Paris: Cahiers du Cinema/Gallimard, 1981.

Bowe, Nicola Gordon. *Harry Clarke: His Graphic Art.* Mountrath, Ireland: Dolmen Press, 1983.

———. *Harry Clarke: The Life and Work.* Dublin: History Press Ireland, 2012.

Braddon, Mary Elizabeth. *Lady Audley's Secret* [1861–62]. Edited by David Skilton. Oxford: Oxford University Press, 2008.

Bram, Christopher. *Eminent Outlaws: The Gay Writers Who Changed America.* New York: Twelve, 2012.

Brasol, Boris. *Oscar Wilde: The Man, the Artist, the Martyr.* New York: Charles Scribner's Sons, 1938.

Brereton, Austin. *The Life of Henry Irving,* vol. 2. London: Longmans, Green, 1908.

Brown, Terence. *Ireland's Literature: Selected Essays.* Totowa, NJ: Barnes & Noble Books, 1988.

Browning, John Edgar. *Bram Stoker's "Dracula": The Critical Feast.* Berkeley: Apocryphile Press, 2011.

Burdett, Henry C. *Cottage Hospitals: General, Fever, and Convalescent: Their Progress, Management and Work.* London: J. & A. Churchill, 1880.

Burnand, F. C., ed. *The Catholic Who's Who and Year-Book.* London: Burns & Oates, 1910.

Cahill, Thomas. *How the Irish Saved Civilization.* New York: Nan A. Talese/Doubleday, 1995.

Caine, Hall. *Cap'n Davy's Honeymoon.* London: William Heinemann, 1892.

———. *Drink: A Love Story on a Great Question.* London: George Newnes, 1906.

Caine, Hall. *My Story.* London: Heinemann, 1908.

Carroll, Lewis. *Through the Looking-Glass and What Alice Found There* [1871]. New York and London: Harper & Brothers, 1902.

Cline, Sally. *Radclyffe Hall: A Man Called John.* Woodstock, Eng., and New York: Overlook Press, 1998.

Clutterbuck, Henry, M.D. "Lectures on Bloodletting." *London Medical Gazette* 28 (1838).

Cobbett, William. *Rural Rides.* London: A. Cobbett, 1853.

Cohen, William A. *Embodied: Victorian Literature and the Senses.* Minneapolis: University of Minnesota Press, 2008.

Corton, Christine. *London Fog: The Biography.* Cambridge, MA: Belknap Press of Harvard University Press, 2015.

Cousin, Victor. *Elements of Psychology.* Translated by Caleb S. Henry. 4th ed. New York: Ivison & Phinney, 1856.

Craft, Christopher. "Kiss Me with Those Red Lips: Gender and Inversion in Bram Stoker's *Dracula.*" *Representations* 8 (Fall 1984): 107–33.

Craigshead, W. Edward, and Charles B. Nemeroff, eds. *Corsini Encyclopedia of Psychology and Behavioral Science,* vol. 1. New York: Wiley, 2000.

Crawford, Gary William, Jim Rockwell, and Brian J. Showers, eds. *Reflections in a Glass Darkly: Essays on J. Sheridan Le Fanu*. New York: Hippocampus Press, 2011.

Croft-Cooke, Rupert. *Bosie*. New York: Bobbs-Merrill, 1963.

———. *The Unreported Life of Oscar Wilde*. London: W. H. Allen, 1972.

Croker, T. Crofton. *Irish Fairy Legends* [1882]. Mineola, NY: Dover Books, 2008.

Cruikshank, George. *The Cruikshank Fairy-Book* [1853–54]. New York: G. P. Putnam, 1911.

Cullen, Fintan, and R. F. Foster. *Conquering England: Ireland in Victorian London*. London: National Portrait Gallery, 2005.

Cullinan, Max. "Trinity College, Dublin." *Fortnightly Review*, October 1, 1870, 429–41.

Dalby, Richard, ed. *To My Dear Friend Hommy-Beg: The Great Friendship of Bram Stoker and Hall Caine*. Dublin: Swan River Press, 2011.

Daly, Frederic [L. F. Austin]. *Henry Irving in England and America 1838–84*. London: T. Fisher Undin, 1884.

Daly, Gay. *Pre-Raphaelites in Love*. Boston: Ticknor & Fields, 1989.

Daly, Nicholas. *Sensation and Modernity in the 1860s*. Cambridge: Cambridge University Press, 2009.

Dardis, Tom. *Firebrand: The Life of Horace Liveright*. New York: Random House, 1995.

De Quincey, Thomas. *Confessions of an English Opium Eater* [1821–22]. Boston: Ticknor & Fields, 1868.

Deane, Hamilton, and John L. Balderston. *Dracula: The Ultimate Illustrated Edition of the World-Famous Vampire Play*. Edited by David J. Skal. New York: St. Martin's Press, 1993.

Dickens, Charles. *Bleak House* [1852–53]. London: Chapman & Hall, 1892.

Dijkstra, Bram. *Idols of Perversity: Images of Evil in Fin-de -Siècle Culture*. New York and Oxford: Oxford University Press, 1986.

Dowden, Edward. *Shakespere: A Critical Study of His Mind and Art*. 2nd ed. London: Henry S. King, 1876.

———. *Studies in Literature, 1789–1877*. London: Kegan, Paul, Trench, Trübner, 1892.

———, ed. *The Tragedy of Hamlet*. The Arden Shakespeare. London: Methuen, 1899.

———. *Transcripts and Studies*. London: Kegan Paul, Trench, 1888.

Dublin University Calendar for the Year 1865. Dublin: Hodges, Smith, 1865.

Eddleston, John J. *Jack the Ripper: An Encyclopedia*. Santa Barbara, CA: ABC-CLIO, 2001.

Eighteen-Bisang, Robert and J. Gordon Melton. *"Dracula": A Century of Editions, Adaptations and Translations*. Santa Barbara, CA: Transylvanian Society of Dracula, 1998.

Eisner, Lotte. *Murnau*. London: Seeker & Warburg, 1973.

Ellis, Havelock. *Studies in the Psychology of Sex*, vol. 2, *Sexual Inversion*. Philadelphia: F. A. Davis, 1915.

Ellis, Peter Berresford. *Eyewitness to Irish History*. Hoboken, NJ: John Wiley & Sons, 2004.

Ellman, Richard. *Oscar Wilde*. New York: Alfred A. Knopf, 1988.

Evans, Stewart P. and Paul Gainey. *Jack the Ripper: First American Serial Killer*. New York, Tokyo, and London: Kodansha International, 1995.

Fadiman, Clifton and André Bernard, eds. *Bartlett's Book of Anecdotes*. Boston: Little, Brown, 2000.

Farson, Daniel. *The Gilded Gutter Life of Francis Bacon*. New York: Pantheon, 1994.

———. *The Man Who Wrote "Dracula."* New York: St. Martin's Press, 1975.

———. *Never a Normal Man: An Autobiography*. London: HarperCollins, 1997.

Fawkes, Richard. *Dion Boucicault: A Biography*. London: Quartet Books, 1979.

Florescu, Radu R., and Raymond McNally. *Dracula: Prince of Many Faces*. Boston: Back Bay Books, 1989.

Forster, E. M. *Maurice* [1971]. New York: W. W. Norton, 1989.

Foster, R. F. *Lord Randolph Churchill: A Political Life*. Oxford and New York: Oxford University Press, 1981.

———. *Modern Ireland, 1600-1972*. London: Penguin Books, 1989.

———. *Paddy and Mr. Punch: Connections in Irish and English History*. London: Allen Lane/Penguin Press, 1993.

Frayling, Christopher. *Vampyres: Lord Byron to Count Dracula*. London: Faber & Faber, 1991.

Friedman, David M. *Wilde in America*. New York: W. W. Norton, 2014.

Gautier, Théophile. *The Romance of a Mummy*. Vol 5 of *The Works of Théophile Gautier*. Translated and edited by F. C. de Sumichrast. Cambridge, MA: Jenson Society/University Press/John Wilson and Son, 1906.

Gerard, Emily de Laszowska. "Transylvanian Superstitions." *Nineteenth Century*, July–December 1885. Reprinted in Miller, *Bram Stoker's "Dracula": A Documentary Journey*.

Gertz, Elmer. *Odyssey of a Barbarian: The Biography of George Sylvester Viereck*. Buffalo, New York: Prometheus Books, 1978.

Gide, André. *The Journals of André Gide*. Translated by Justin O'Brien. New York: Alfred A. Knopf, 1949.

Gilmer, Walker. *Horace Liveright: Publisher of the Twenties*. New York: David Lewis, 1970.

Glover, David. *Vampires, Mummies, and Liberals: Bram Stoker and the Politics of Popular Fiction*. Durham, NC, and London: Duke University Press, 1996.

Goethe, Johann Wolfgang von, *Faust* [Part 1, 1808]. Edited by Peter Salm. New York: Bantam Classics, 2007.

———. *Faust*. Translated by John Anster. Mineola, NY: Calla Editions, 2013.

———. *Faust: A Norton Critical Edition*. Translated by Walter Arndt. Edited by Cyrus Hamlin. 2nd ed. New York and London: W. W. Norton, 2001.

Gogarty, Oliver St. John. *As I Was Going Down Sackville Street*. London: Rich & Cowan, 1937.

Gold, Arthur, and Robert Fizdale. *The Divine Sarah: A Life of Sarah Bernhardt*. New York: Alfred A. Knopf, 1991.

Goodman, Ruth. *How to Be a Victorian*. New York: Liveright, 2014.

Graves, Alfred Perceval. *To Return to All That: An Autobiography*. London: Jonathan Cape, 1930.

Greene, Ellen, ed. *Re-Reading Sappho: Reception and Transmission*. Berkeley: University of California Press, 1996.

Gussow, Mel. "Gorey Goes Batty," *New York Times Magazine*, October 16, 1977, p. 41.

Gustavson, Zadel Barnes. *Genevieve Ward: A Biographical Sketch from Original Material Derived from Her Family and Friends*. Boston: James R. Osgood, 1882.

Hall, Radclyffe. *The Well of Loneliness* [1928]. London: Wordsworth Editions, 2014.

Harris, Frank. *Oscar Wilde* [1916]. New York: Dorset Press, 1989.

Hart-Davis, Rupert, ed. *Max Beerbohm's Letters to Reggie Turner*. Philadelphia: J. P. Lippincott, 1973.

Harvey, Sir George Martin. *The Autobiography of Sir George Martin Harvey*. London: Sampson Low, Marston, 1933.

Hatton, Joseph. "Sir Henry Irving: His Romantic Career on and off the Stage." *Grand Magazine*, December 1905.

Hayden, Deborah. *Pox: Genius, Madness, and the Mysteries of Syphilis*. New York: Basic Books, 2003.

Hendershot, Cyndy. *The Animal Within: Masculinity and the Gothic*. Ann Arbor: University of Michigan Press, 1998.

Hichens, Robert. *The Green Carnation* [1894]. Edited by Stanley Weintraub. Lincoln: University of Nebraska Press, 1970.

Hinkson, H[enry] A[lbert]. *Student Life in Trinity College, Dublin*. Dublin: J. Charles & Son, 1892.

Hoffman, Heinrich. *Struwwelpeter* [1854]. Venice, CA: Feral House, 1999, subtitled *Fearful Stories and Vile Pictures to Instruct Good Little Folks*.

Holland, Merlin. *The Real Trial of Oscar Wilde*. New York: Fourth Estate, 2003.

———. *The Wilde Album*. New York: Henry Holt, 1997.

Holland, Merlin, and Rupert Hart-Davis, eds. *The Complete Letters of Oscar Wilde*. New York: Henry Holt, 2000.

Holland, Peter. *Shakespeare, Memory, and Performance*. Cambridge: Cambridge University Press, 2006.

Holland, Vyvyan. *Son of Oscar Wilde*. Rev. ed., 1988. New York: Carroll & Graf, 1999.

Holroyd, Michael. *A Strange Eventful History: The Dramatic Lives of Ellen Terry, Henry Irving, and Their Remarkable Families*. New York: Picador, 2008.

Hood, Thomas. *The Poetical Works*, vol. 1. Boston: Little, Brown, 1857.

Houghton, Walter E. *The Victorian Frame of Mind, 1830–1870*. New Haven, CT: Yale University Press, 1957.

Houston, Gail Hurley. *From Dickens to Dracula: Gothic, Economics, and Victorian Fiction*. Cambridge: Cambridge University Press, 2007.

Hughes, William. *Beyond Dracula: Bram Stoker's Fiction and Its Cultural Context*. New York: Palgrave Macmillan, 2000.

Hurley, Kelly. *The Gothic Body: Sexuality, Materialism, and Degeneration at the Fin de Siècle*. Cambridge: Cambridge University Press, 1996.

Huysmans, J. K. *Against the Grain* [*A rebours*, 1884]. Introduction by Havelock Ellis. Mineola, NY: Dover Publications, 1969.

Hyde, H. Montgomery. *Oscar Wilde: A Biography*. London: Methuen, 1951.

———, ed. *The Three Trials of Oscar Wilde*. New York: University Books, 1956.

———. *The Trials of Oscar Wilde*. Mineola, NY: Dover Publications, 1964.

Ibsen, Henrik. *"Ghosts" and Other Plays*. Translated by Peter Watts. London: Penguin Classics, 1964.

Irving, Laurence. *Henry Irving: The Actor and His World* [1951]. London: Columbus Books, 1989.

Isherwood, Christopher. *The World in the Evening* [1954]. New York: Farrar, Straus & Giroux, 1988.

Jackson, Lee. *Dirty Old London: The Victorian Fight against Filth*. New Haven, CT: Yale University Press, 2014.

James, M. R. *Collected Ghost Stories*. Edited by Darryl Jones. Oxford: Oxford University Press, 2011.

Jarrett, Guy E., and Jim Steinmeyer. *The Complete Jarrett*. Burbank, CA: Hahne, 2001.

Jerome, Jerome K. *Told after Supper*. London: Leadenhall Press, 1891.

Johnson, Neil M. *George Sylvester Viereck: German-American Propagandist*. Urbana: University of Illinois Press, 1972.

Jones, Ernest. *Essays in Applied Psycho-Analysis*. London and Vienna: International Psycho-Analytical Press, 1923.

———. *On the Nightmare* [1931]. New York: Liveright, 1951.

Jordan, Thomas. *Victorian Childhood: Themes and Variations.* Albany: State University of New York Press, 1987.

Joyce, James. *A Portrait of the Artist as a Young Man* [1916]. New York: Viking Press, 1956.

Julian, Philippe. *Oscar Wilde.* Translated by Violet Wyndham. New York: Viking Press, 1969.

Kahan, Jeffrey. *Shakespiritualism: Shakespeare and the Occult, 1850–1950.* New York: Palgrave Macmillan, 2013.

Kaplan, Justin. *Walt Whitman: A Life.* New York: Bantam Books, 1982.

Katz, Jonathan [Ned]. *Gay American History.* New York: Avon Books, 1976.

———. *Love Letters: Sex Between Men Before Homosexuality.* Chicago: University of Chicago Press, 2001.

Kiberd, Declan. "Irish Literature and Irish History." In *The Oxford Illustrated History of Ireland,* edited by R. F. Foster. Oxford and New York: Oxford University Press, 1989.

Killeen, Jarlath, ed. *Bram Stoker: Centenary Essays.* Dublin: Four Courts Press, 2014.

———. *Gothic Literature, 1825–1914.* Cardiff: University of Wales Press, 2009.

King, Brian. *Undiscovered Dundee.* Edinburgh: Black and White Publishing, 2011.

Kingsley, Charles. *His Letters and Memories of His Life. Edited by His Wife.* New York: Charles Scribner's Sons, 1885.

Knox, Melissa. *Oscar Wilde: A Long and Lovely Suicide.* New Haven, CT: Yale University Press, 1994.

Krieg, Joann P. *Whitman and the Irish.* Iowa City: University of Iowa Press, 2000.

Lacey, Brian. *Terrible Queer Creatures: Homosexuality in Irish History.* Dublin: Wordwell, 2008.

Lawrence, D. H. *The First "Women in Love."* Edited by John Worthen and Linden Vasey. Cambridge: Cambridge University Press, 2002.

———. *Women in Love.* Edited by David Farmer, John Worthen, and Lindeth Vasey. Cambridge: Cambridge University Press, 1987.

Lambkin, F. J. *Syphilis: Its Diagnosis and Treatment.* London: Bailliere, Tindall & Cox, 1910.

Landis, John. *Monsters in the Movies: 100 Years of Cinematic Nightmares.* London: Dorling Kindersley, 2011.

Lazar. *The Ghost Epigrams of Oscar Wilde.* New York: Covici-Friede, 1928.

Leahey, Thomas Hardy, and Grace Evans Leahey. *Psychology's Occult Doubles: Psychology and the Problem of Pseudoscience.* Chicago: Nelson Hall, 1984.

Leatherdale, Clive. *Dracula: The Novel and the Legend.* Rev ed. Brighton, East Sussex: Desert Island Books, 1993.

———. *The Origins of Dracula.* London: William Kimber, 1987.

Le Fanu, J. Sheridan. *In a Glass Darkly* [1872]. Edited by Robert Tracey. Oxford: Oxford University Press, 1993.

———. *Uncle Silas* [1864]. Edited by Victor Sage. London: Penguin Classics, 2000.

Le Fanu, William Richard. *Seventy Years of Irish Life: Being Anecdotes and Reminiscences.* London: Edward Arnold, 1893.

Lewis, Matthew. *The Monk* [1796]. Edited by Howard Anderson. Introduction and notes by Emma McEvoy. Oxford: Oxford University Press, 2008.

Levey, R[ichard] M[ichael], and J. O'Rorke, *Annals of the Theatre Royal, Dublin.* Dublin: Joseph Dollard, 1880.

Liddell, Henry. *"The Wizard of the North," "The Vampire Bride," and Other Poems.* Edinburgh and London: William Blackwood & T. Cadell, 1833.

Lombroso, Cesare. *Criminal Man* [in five editions, 1876–97]. Edited by Mary Gibson and Nicole Hahn Rafter. Durham, NC, and London: Duke University Press, 2006.

Lombroso, Cesare, and Guglielmo Ferrero. *Criminal Woman, the Prostitute, and the Normal Woman* [1893], Nicole Hahn Rafter and Mary Gibson, trans. Durham, N.C. and London: Duke University Press, 2004.

Lovecraft, H. P. *Selected Letters, 1911–1924.* Sauk City, WI: Arkham House, 1964.

Ludlam, Harry. *A Biography of Dracula: The Life Story of Bram Stoker.* London: Fireside Press/W. Foulsham, 1962.

———. *My Quest for Bram Stoker.* New York: Dracula Press, 2000.

Manvell, Roger. *Ellen Terry: The Life of One of the Greatest Actresses and Women of Her Time.* New York: G. P. Putnam's Sons, 1968.

Marlowe, Christopher. *The Jew of Malta* [c. 1590]. Edited by Stephen J. Lynch. Indianapolis, IN, and Cambridge: Hackett, 2009.

McCaffrey, Carmel, and Leo Eaton. *In Search of Ancient Ireland: The Origins of the Irish from Neolithic Times to the Coming of the English.* Chicago: New Amsterdam Books, 2002.

McCormack, W. J. *Sheridan Le Fanu.* Oxford: Clarendon Press, 1980.

McDowell, R. B., and D. A. Webb. *Trinity College Dublin, 1592–1952: An Academic History.* Cambridge: Cambridge University Press, 1982.

McKenna, Neil. *The Secret Life of Oscar Wilde.* New York: Basic Books, 2005.

McNally, Raymond T., and Radu Florescu. *In Search of Dracula.* Greenwich, CT: New York Graphic Society, 1972.

McNamara, Patrick. *Nightmares: The Science and Solution of Those Frightening Visions During Sleep.* Westport, CT: Praeger, 2008.

Mahaffy, John Pentland. *Social Life in Greece from Homer to Menander.* London: Macmillan, 1874.

Magnusson, Magnus. *Landlord or Tenant? A View of Irish History.* London, Sydney, and Toronto: The Bodley Head, 1978.

Manning, Molly Guptill. *When Books Went to War.* New York: Houghton Mifflin Harcourt, 2014.

Martin-Harvey, Sir John. *The Autobiography of Sir John Martin-Harvey.* London: Sampson Low, Marston, 1933.

Maturin, Charles Robert. *Melmoth the Wanderer* [1820]. Edited by Victor Sage. London: Penguin Classics, 2000.

Mavromatis, Andreas. *Hypnogogia.* London and New York: Routledge & Kegan Paul, 1991.

Mead, Leon. "In a Munich Deadhouse." *Frank Leslie's Popular Monthly,* April 1892, pp. 459–62.

Melville, Joy. *Mother of Oscar: The Life of Jane Francesca Wilde.* London: John Murray, 1994.

Menzer, Paul. *Anecdotal Shakespeare: A New Performance History.* London and New York: Bloomsbury, 2015.

Merrill, Lisa. *When Romeo Was a Woman: Charlotte Cushman and Her Circle of Female Spectators.* Ann Arbor: University of Michigan Press, 1999.

Miller, Elizabeth, ed. *Bram Stoker's "Dracula": A Documentary Journey.* New York: Pegasus, 2009.

———. *Dracula: Sense and Nonsense.* Westcliff-on-Sea, Essex: Desert Island Books, 2000.

————, ed. *Dracula: The Shade and the Shadow.* Westcliff-on-Sea, Essex: Desert Island Books, 1998.

————. *Reflections on Dracula: Ten Essays.* White Rock, BC: Transylvania Press, 1997.

Millward, Jessie, in collaboration with J. B. Booth. *Myself and Others.* London: Hutchinson, 1923.

Miniter, Edith. *"Dead Houses" and Other Works.* Edited by Kenneth W. Faig Jr. and Sean Donnelly. New York: Hippocampus Press, 2008.

Morgan, Charles. *Dramatic Critic: Selected Reviews (1922–1939).* London: Oberon Press, 2013.

Moyle, Franny. *Constance: The Tragic and Scandalous Life of Mrs. Oscar Wilde.* New York: Pegasus Books, 2012.

Murray, Douglas. *Bosie: The Man, the Poet, the Lover of Oscar Wilde.* New York: Hyperion, 2000.

Murray, Paul. *From the Shadow of Dracula: A Life of Bram Stoker.* London: Jonathan Cape, 2004.

Nordau, Max. *Degeneration.* New York: D. Appleton, 1895.

Ó Gráda, Cormac. *Black '47 and Beyond: The Great Irish Famine.* Princeton: Princeton University Press, 1999.

O'Sullivan, Vincent. *Aspects of Wilde.* New York: Henry Holt, 1936.

Olson, Donald S. *The Confessions of Aubrey Beardsley.* London: Bantam Press, 1993.

Paglia, Camille. *Vamps and Tramps: New Essays.* New York: Vintage Books, 1994.

Pearson, Hesketh. *The Life of Oscar Wilde.* London: Methuen, 1951.

Pick, Daniel. *Faces of Degeneration: A European Disorder, c. 1848–c. 1919.* Cambridge: Cambridge University Press, 1989.

Poe, Edgar Allan. *Essays and Reviews.* Edited by G. R. Thompson. New York: Library of America, 1984.

Quinn, John F. *Father Mathew's Crusade.* Amherst: University of Massachusetts Press, 2002.

Radcliffe, Ann. *The Italian* [1797]. Edited by Frederick Garber. Oxford: Oxford University Press, 1981.

Ransome, Arthur. *Oscar Wilde: A Critical Study.* New York: Mitchell Kimberley, 1912.

Reese, James. *The Dracula Dossier.* New York: William Morrow, 2008.

Reynolds, David S. *Walt Whitman's America: A Cultural Biography.* New York: Vintage Books, 1996.

Rhodes, Gary D. "Drakula halála: The Screen's First Dracula." *Horror Studies* 1, no.1 (January 2010): 25–31.

Richards, Jeffrey. *Sir Henry Irving: A Victorian Actor and His World.* London and New York: Hambledon & London, 2005.

————. *Sir Henry Irving: Theatre, Culture and Society.* Keele, Staffordshire: Keele University Press, 1994.

Richardson, Maurice. "The Psychoanalysis of Ghost Stories." *Twentieth Century,* December 1959.

Riley, Philip J., ed. *MagicImage Filmbooks Presents "Dracula."* Atlantic City, NJ: MagicImage Filmbooks, 1990.

Riordan, Timothy B. *Prince of Quacks: The Notorious Life of Dr. Francis Tumblety, Charlatan and Jack the Ripper Suspect.* Jefferson, NC, and London: McFarland, 2009.

Robb, Graham. *Strangers: Homosexual Love in the Nineteenth Century.* New York and London: W. W. Norton, 2003.

Roos, Hans Corneel de. "Makt Myrkranna: Mother of All *Dracula* Modifications?"

Letter from Castle Dracula: Official News Bulletin of the Transylvanian Society of Dracula, February 2014.

Rossetti, Dante Gabriel. *His Family Letters*, vol. 1. London: Ellis & Elvey, 1895.

Rowell, George. *Theatre in the Age of Irving*. Oxford: Basil Blackwell, 1981.

——, ed. *Victorian Dramatic Criticism*. London: Methuen, 1971.

Ryan, Philip B. *The Lost Theatres of Dublin*. Westbury: Badger Books, 1998.

Saint-Amour, Paul K. *The Copywrights*. Ithaca, NY, and London: Cornell University Press, 2003.

Saintsbury, H. A., and Cecil Palmer, eds. *We Saw Him Act: A Symposium on the Art of Sir Henry Irving*. New York and London: Benjamin Blom, 1939.

Schanke, Robert A. *"That Furious Lesbian": The Story of Mercedes de Acosta*. Carbondale: Southern Illinois University Press, 2003.

Schenkar, Joan. *Truly Wilde: The Unsettling Story of Dolly Wilde, Oscar's Unusual Niece.* New York: Basic Books, 2000.

Schmidgall, Gary. *The Stranger Wilde: Interpreting Oscar*. New York: Dutton, 1994.

——. *Walt Whitman: A Gay Life*. New York: Dutton, 1997.

Schoenbaum, S. *Shakespeare's Lives*. Oxford: Oxford University Press, 1991.

Schoolfield, George C. *A Baedeker of Decadence: Charting a Literary Fashion, 1884–1927*. New Haven, CT: Yale University Press, 2003.

Schrenck-Notzig, Dr. A[lbert] Von. *Therapeutic Suggestion in Psychopathia Sexualis (Pathological Manifestations of the Sexual Sense), with Especial Reference to Contrary Sexual Instinct.* Philadelphia: F. A. Davis, 1895.

Sebba, Anne. *Jennie Churchill: Winston's American Mother*. London: John Murray, 2007.

Sellar, Robert. *Gleaner Tales* [1895]. London: Forgotten Books, 2015.

Senf, Carol A. *Bram Stoker's Other Gothics: Contemporary Reviews*. Dublin: Swan River Press, 2010.

Shakespeare, William. *The Norton Shakespeare*. Edited by Stephen Greenblatt, Walter Cohen, Jean E. Howard, and Katharine Eisaman Maus. 2nd ed. New York: W. W. Norton, 2008.

——. *The Tragedy of Hamlet*. Edited by Edward Dowden. The Arden Shakespeare. London: Methuen, 1899.

Sherard, Robert H. *The Life of Oscar Wilde*. New York: Brentano's, 1911.

——. *Oscar Wilde: The Story of an Unhappy Friendship*. London: Greening, 1905.

——. *The Real Oscar Wilde*. London: T. Werner Laurie, 1916.

Sherriff, R. C. *Dracula's Daughter*. Preliminary screenplay for Universal Pictures, September 1935. In *James Whale's "Dracula's Daughter,"* edited by Phillip J. Riley. Albany, GA: BearManor Media, 2009.

——. *No Leading Lady*. London: Victor Gollancz, 1968.

Simon, John. "Dingbat." *New York Magazine*, November 7, 1977, 75.

Simon, Jules. *Victor Cousin*. Translated by Melville B. Anderson and Edward Playfair Anderson. Chicago: A. C. McClurg, 1888.

Skal, David J., *Hollywood Gothic: The Tangled Web of Dracula from Novel to Stage to Screen.* 1990; rev. ed. New York: Faber & Faber, 2004.

——. *The Monster Show: A Cultural History of Horror*. New York: W. W. Norton, 1993.

——. *Screams of Reason: Mad Science and Modern Culture*. New York and London: W. W. Norton, 1997.

——, ed. *Vampires: Encounters with the Undead*. New York: Black Dog and Leventhal, 2001.

Skinner, Cornelia Otis. *Madame Sarah*. New York: Houghton Mifflin, 1966.

Souhami, Diana. *The Trials of Radclyffe Hall*. New York: Doubleday, 1999.

Stanford, W. B., and R. B. McDowell. *Mahaffy: A Biography of an Anglo-Irishman.* London: Routledge & Kegan Paul, 1971.

Steinmeyer, Jim. *Who Was Dracula? Bram Stoker's Trail of Blood.* New York: Jeremy P. Tarcher/Penguin, 2013.

Sterne, Lawrence. *The Life and Opinions of Tristram Shandy, Gentleman* [1759–67]. London: George Routledge & Sons, 1893.

Stoker, Bram. *A Bram Stoker Omnibus.* Edited by Richard Dalby. London: W. Foulsham Books, 1986.

———. *Bram Stoker's "Dracula" Omnibus.* Introduction by Fay Weldon. New York: Book Sales, 1994.

———. *Bram Stoker's Notes for "Dracula": A Facsimile Edition.* Edited by Robert Eighteen-Bisang and Elizabeth Miller. Jefferson, NC, and London: McFarland, 2008.

———. *Dracula: A Norton Critical Edition.* Edited by Nina Auerbach and David J. Skal. New York and London: W. W. Norton, 1997.

———. *Dracula; or, The Un-dead* [1897]. Edited by Sylvia Starshine. Nottingham, Eng.: Pumpkin Books, 1997.

———. *"Dracula's Guest" and Other Weird Stories* [1914]. Edited by Kate Hebblethwaite. London: Penguin Books, 2008.

———. *"The Dualitists; or, The Death Doom of the Double Born." Theatre Annual* (London: Carson and Comderford, 1887), 23–24.

———. *The Essential "Dracula."* Edited by Raymond T. McNally and Radu Florescu. New York: Mayflower Books, 1979.

———. *Famous Impostors.* New York: Sturgis and Walton, 1910.

———. *Four Romances by Mr. Bram Stoker.* Edited by Paul Murray. Dublin: Swan River Press, 2010.

———. *"A Glimpse of America"* [1885]. In *"A Glimpse of America" and Other Lectures, Interviews and Essays.* Edited by Clive Leatherdale. Southend-on-Sea, Essex: Desert Island Books, 2002.

———. *Jewel of the Seven Stars* [1903]. Edited by Kate Hebblethwaite. London: Penguin Classics, 2008.

———. *Lady Athlyne.* New York: Paul R. Reynolds, 1908.

———. *The Lady of the Shroud.* London: William Heinemann, 1909.

———. *The Lair of the White Worm* [1911]. In *"Dracula's Guest" and Other Weird Stories,* edited by Kathe Hebblethwaite. New York: Penguin Classics, 2006.

———. *The Lost Journal of Bram Stoker.* Edited by Elizabeth Miller and Dacre Stoker. London: Robson Press, 2012.

———. *The Man* [1905]. London: Bibliolis, 2010.

———. *Miss Betty.* London: C. Arthur Pearson, 1898.

———. *The Mystery of the Sea.* London: William Heinemann, 1902.

———. *The New Annotated "Dracula."* Edited by Leslie S. Klinger. New York: W. W. Norton, 2008.

———. *Personal Reminiscences of Henry Irving,* 2 vols. New York: Macmillan, 1906.

———. *The Primrose Path* [1875]. Edited by Clive Leatherdale. Introduction by Richard Dalby. Westcliff-on-Sea, Essex: Desert Island Books, 1999.

———. *Shades of Dracula: Bram Stoker's Uncollected Stories.* Edited by Peter Haining. Berkeley, CA: Apocryphile Press, 2006.

———. *The Shoulder of Shasta.* London: Archibald Constable, 1895.

———. *The Snake's Pass* [1891]. Chicago: Valancourt Books, 2006.

———. *Snowbound: The Record of a Theatrical Touring Party* [1908]. Edited by Bruce Wightman. Westcliff-on-Sea, Essex: Desert Island Books, 2000.

————. *Under the Sunset* [1884]. Doylestown, PA: Wildside Press, n.d.

————. *The Unknown Writings of Bram Stoker*. Edited by John Edgar Browning. New York: Palgrave Macmillan, 2012.

————. *The Watter's Mou'*. London: Archibald Constable, 1895.

Storey, Gladys. *Dickens and Daughter* [1939]. New York: Haskell House, 1971.

Storey, Neil R. *The Dracula Secrets: Jack the Ripper and the Darkest Sources of Bram Stoker*. Stroud, UK: History Press, 2012.

Stratmann, Linda. *The Marquess of Queensberry: Wilde's Nemesis*. New Haven, CT: Yale University Press, 2013.

Swinburne, Algernon. *Selected Lyrical Poems*. New York and London: Harper & Brothers, 1906.

Sword, Helen. *Ghostwriting Modernism*. Ithaca, NY, and London: Cornell University Press, 2002.

Tatar, Maria, ed. *The Classic Fairy Tales: A Norton Critical Edition*. New York and London: W. W. Norton, 1999.

Taylor, Ina. *Victorian Sisters: The Remarkable MacDonald Women and the Great Men They Inspired*. Bethesda, MD: Adler & Adler, 1987.

Tennyson, Alfred, Lord. *Becket*. New York: Dodd, Mead, 1894.

Terry, Ellen. *The Story of My Life: Recollections and Reflections*. New York: McClure, 1908.

Tóibín, Colm, and Diarmaid Ferrier. *The Irish Famine: A Documentary*. London: Profile Books, 2004.

Travers Smith, Hester. *Oscar Wilde from Purgatory* [1924]. Whitefish, MT: Kessinger Publishing, 2011.

Traubel, Horace. *With Walt Whitman in Camden*, vol. 4. Philadelphia: University of Pennsylvania Press, 1953.

Tupper, James Waddell. *Tropes and Figures in Anglo-Saxon Prose*. Baltimore: John Murphy, 1897.

Twain, Mark. *The Innocents Abroad; or, The New Pilgrim's Progress* [1869, 2 vols.]. New York: Harper & Brothers, 1911.

Viereck, George Sylvester. *The House of the Vampire*. New York: Moffat, Yard, 1907.

————. *My Flesh and Blood: A Lyric Autobiography with Indiscreet Annotations*. New York: Horace Liveright, 1931.

Ward, Edwin. *Recollections of a Savage*. New York: Frederick A. Stokes, 1923.

Ward, Genevieve, and Richard Whiteing. *Both Sides of the Curtain*. London and New York: Cassell, 1918.

Wells, H. G. *Collected Works*, vol. 2. London: T. Fisher Unwin, 1924.

White, Terence de Vere. *The Parents of Oscar Wilde*. London: T. V. Boardman, 1949.

Whitman, Walt. *Complete Poems*. Edited by Francis Murphy. New York: Penguin, 1986.

Wikoff, Henry. *Memoir of Ginevra Guerrabella* [Genevieve Ward]. New York: T. J. Crown, 1863.

Wilde, Lady [Jane]. *Legends, Charms and Superstitions of Ireland* [1887]. Mineola, NY: Dover Publications, 2006.

————. *Social Studies*. London: Ward and Downey, 1893.

Wilde, Oscar. *Complete Letters*. Edited by Merlin Holland and Rupert Hart-Davis. New York: Henry Holt, 2000.

————. *Complete Works*. New York: Barnes & Noble Books, 1994.

————. *"De Profundis" and Other Prison Writings*. Edited by Colm Tóibín. London: Penguin Classics, 2013.

————. *The Essays of Oscar Wilde*. New York: Cosmopolitan Book Corporation, 1916.

————. *More Letters of Oscar Wilde*. Edited by Rupert Hart-Davis. New York: Vanguard Press, 1985.

————. *The Picture of Dorian Gray: A Norton Critical Edition*. Edited by Michael Patrick Gillespie. 2nd ed. New York: W. W. Norton, 2007.

————. *The Picture of Dorian Gray: An Annotated, Uncensored Edition*. Edited by Nicholas Frankel. Cambridge, MA, and London: Belknap Press of Harvard University Press, 2011.

Wilkinson, William. *An Account of the Principalities of Wallachia and Moldavia*. London: Longman, Hurst, Rees, Orme & Brown, 1820.

Williams, Tennessee. *Tennessee Williams: Plays, 1937–1955*. New York: Library of America, 2000.

Wills, Freeman. *W. G. Wills, Dramatist and Painter*. London: Longman, 1898.

Wills, W. G. *Faust, in a Prologue and Five Acts, Adapted and Arranged for the Lyceum Theatre from the First Part of Goethe's Tragedy*. London, 1886.

Wilson, A. E. *The Lyceum*. London: Dennis Yates, 1952.

Wilson, T. G. *Victorian Doctor*. London: Methuen, 1942.

Wohl, Anthony S. *Endangered Lives: Public Health in Victorian Britain*. Cambridge, MA: Harvard University Press, 1983.

Woodham-Smith, Cecil. *The Great Hunger*. New York: Harper & Row, 1962.

Wynbrandt, James. *The Excruciating History of Dentistry: Toothsome Tales and Oral Oddities from Babylon to Braces*. New York: St. Martin's Griffin, 1998.

Wyndham, Horace. *The Nineteen Hundreds*. New York: Thomas Seltzer, 1923.

————. *Speranza: A Biography of Lady Wilde*. London: T. V. Boardman, 1951.

Wynne, Catherine. *Bram Stoker, Dracula, and the Victorian Gothic Stage*. London: Palgrave Macmillan, 2013.

Yeats, W. B. *Autobiographies*. London: Macmillan, 1955.

————, ed. *Fairy and Folk Tales of Ireland* [1888/1892]. New York: Touchstone/Simon & Schuster, 1998.

————. *Selected Poems and Four Plays*. New York: Scribner, 1996.

Zimmerman, Bonnie, ed. *Lesbian Histories and Cultures: An Encyclopedia*. New York: Garland Publishing, 2000.

INDEX

Page numbers in *italics* refer to illustrations.

Erté, 411
Essays in Applied Psycho-Analysis (Jones), 39
Essential Dracula, The (McNally and Florescu), 338
Étretat, France, 127
Euclid, 50
Eugene Aram (Wills), 241
Euripides, 46, 48
Evans, Luke, *575*
Evans, Stewart, 291
Evelina Hospital for Sick Children, 213, *213*
Eve of St. Agnes, The (Clarke), 526

"Fabien dei Franchi" (Wilde), 327
"Facts in the Case of M. Valdemar, The" (Poe), 56–57, *58*, 296–97, 387
Faerie Queen, The (Spenser), 37–38
Fairlight Lawn cottages (Deal, England), 469
Fairy Library (*The Cruikshank Fairy-Book*) (Cruikshank), 125
"Fall of the House of Usher, The" (Poe), 121, 308, 362n, 369, 485, *528*
"Famine Year, The" (Jane Wilde), 22
Famous Fantastic Mysteries, *279*
Famous Impostors (Stoker), 28, 50, 470, 471–74, 476
Farley, Ralph Milne, *see* Hoar, Roger Sherman
Farson, Daniel, 19–20, 29, 202–3, 215, 491, 492–93, 560–65, *561*
Fashionable Tragedian, The (pamphlet), 148, 149–50
Faust (Goethe), 123, 240–42, 247, 250n, *252*, 254, 255, 405, 423, 526, 527, 529, 530, 532, 597n
Faust (Gounod opera), 72–73, 112, 122, 153, 241, 245, 259, 513
Faust (Wills adaptation), xiv, xv, 153, 229, 231, *239*, 240, 241–42, *243*, 245–56, *248*, *250*, *257*, 258–62, 281, 317, 429, 434
Ferber, Edna, 547
"Fidgety Philip" (Hoffmann), 33, 40
Fielding, Ernest (char.), 397–98, 399, 400, 401
Fiends, Ghosts and Sprites (J. N. Radcliffe), 55

"Filing for Divorce: Count Dracula vs. Vlad Tepeş" (Miller), 567–68
Finnegans Wake (Joyce), xi
Fitzgerald, Percy, 180
Fitzgerald, William, 206–7, *206, 208, 209, 210*
Fjallkonan, 340
Fleetwood, Mick, 573
Fleurs de mal, Les (Baudelaire), 176
Florescu, Radu, 329, 338, 567, 568, 600n
Flotsam (film), 513
Flying Dutchman, The (opera), 180
Flynn, Edward, 86
Fool There Was, A (Brown), 404
Forbes-Robertson, Norman, 451, 454, 457
Ford, Ford Madox (Ford Madox Hueffer), 488
Ford's Theatre, 117
Forestier, Amédée, *261*
Forster, E. M., 299
Fort, Garrett, 534, 550, *551*, 552
Fortnightly Club, 132, 136, 137
Fortnightly Review, 61, 258, 323–24
Foster, R. F., 17
Frampton, George James, 451, 452
France, 13, 18, 56, 86, 120, 143, 145, 147, 236, 237, *274*, 291, 350, 351, 384, 430, 452n, 494
France Times, 456, 458
Franco, Jess, 556
Frankenstein (film), 446n
Frankenstein (Shelley), 41, 53, 369, 430, 537
Frankenstein (Webling and Balderston; stage adaptation), 537–39
Frankenstein and the Monster from Hell (film), 558
French, Samuel, 525
Freud, Lucian, 561
Freud, Sigmund, 24–25, 35, 39, 262, 350, 392, 518, 519, 537
Freund, Karl, 539
Fritz, Idle (char.), 33
Frohman, Charles, 445
Funeral March (Chopin), 456
Furniss, Harry, 80–81, *80, 81*, 275

Gaiety Theatre (Dublin), 68, 76, 102, 104, 131, 132, 164
Gaiety Theatre (London), 121n
Gainey, Paul, 291

ABOUT THE AUTHOR

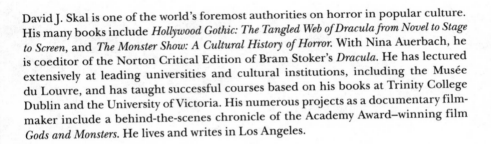

David J. Skal is one of the world's foremost authorities on horror in popular culture. His many books include *Hollywood Gothic: The Tangled Web of Dracula from Novel to Stage to Screen*, and *The Monster Show: A Cultural History of Horror*. With Nina Auerbach, he is coeditor of the Norton Critical Edition of Bram Stoker's *Dracula*. He has lectured extensively at leading universities and cultural institutions, including the Musée du Louvre, and has taught successful courses based on his books at Trinity College Dublin and the University of Victoria. His numerous projects as a documentary filmmaker include a behind-the-scenes chronicle of the Academy Award–winning film *Gods and Monsters*. He lives and writes in Los Angeles.